Classic Essays in Early Rabbinic Culture and History

This volume brings together a set of classic essays on early rabbinic history and culture, seven of which have been translated into English especially for this publication. The studies are presented in three sections according to theme: (1) sources, methods and meaning; (2) tradition and self-invention; and (3) Rabbinic contexts. The first section contains essays that made a pioneering contribution to the identification of sources for the historical and cultural study of the rabbinic period, articulated methodologies for the study of rabbinic history and culture, or addressed historical topics that continue to engage scholars to the present day. The second section contains pioneering contributions to our understanding of the culture of the sages whose sources we deploy for the purposes of historical reconstruction, contributions which grappled with the riddle and rhythm of the rabbis' emergence to authority, or pierced the veil of their self-presentation. The essays in the third section made contributions of fundamental importance to our understanding of the broader cultural contexts of rabbinic sources, identified patterns of rabbinic participation in prevailing cultural systems, or sought to define with greater precision the social location of the rabbinic class within Jewish society of late antiquity. The volume is introduced by a new essay from the editor, summarizing the field and contextualizing the reprinted papers.

Christine Hayes is Robert F. and Patricia R. Weis Professor of Religious Studies in Classical Judaica, Yale University, USA, and author of several books in biblical and rabbinic studies, including *Gentile Impurities and Jewish Identities* (2002) and *What's Divine about Divine Law? Early Perspectives* (2015).

Edited by Christine Hayes

Classic Essays in Early Rabbinic Culture and History

Routledge
Taylor & Francis Group
LONDON AND NEW YORK

First published 2018
by Routledge
2 Park Square, Milton Park, Abingdon, Oxon OX14 4RN

and by Routledge
711 Third Avenue, New York, NY 10017

Routledge is an imprint of the Taylor & Francis Group, an informa business

© 2018 selection and editorial matter, Christine Hayes; individual chapters, the contributors

The right of Christine Hayes to be identified as the author of the editorial material, and of the authors for their individual chapters, has been asserted in accordance with sections 77 and 78 of the Copyright, Designs and Patents Act 1988.

All rights reserved. No part of this book may be reprinted or reproduced or utilised in any form or by any electronic, mechanical, or other means, now known or hereafter invented, including photocopying and recording, or in any information storage or retrieval system, without permission in writing from the publishers.

Trademark notice: Product or corporate names may be trademarks or registered trademarks, and are used only for identification and explanation without intent to infringe.

British Library Cataloguing in Publication Data
A catalogue record for this book is available from the British Library

Library of Congress Cataloging in Publication Data
A catalog record for this title has been requested

ISBN: 978-1-4094-2505-2 (hbk)
ISBN: 978-1-315-12190-1 (ebk)

Typeset in Times New Roman
by Servis Filmsetting Ltd, Stockport, Cheshire

Printed in the United Kingdom
by Henry Ling Limited

CONTENTS

Acknowledgements   ix
Introduction   1

Part I. Rabbinic History – Sources, Methods and Meaning

1. Leopold Zunz, "Etwas über die rabbinische Litteratur" in 1818 (republished in *Gesammelte Schriften*, 1875–76), pp. 1–31. *Translated by James Redfield*   27

2. Heinrich Graetz (1817–1891), "Hagadische Elemente bei den Kirchenvatern" in *Monatsschrift fur geschichte und Wissenschaft des Judentums*, Vol. 3, No. 8 (1854), pp. 311–19. *Translated by James Redfield*   43

3. Victor Aptowitzer, "Observations on the Criminal Law of the Jews" in *Jewish Quarterly Review*, Vol. 15 (1924), pp. 55–118   51

4. Adolf Büchler, "The Levitical Impurity of the Gentile in Palestine before the Year 70" in *Jewish Quarterly Review*, New Series, Vol. 17 (1926), pp. 1–81   115

5. Gedalyahu Alon, "Those appointed for Money" in *Zion* 12 (1947) 101–35; translated and reprinted in *Jews, Judaism and the Classical World* by Israel Abrahams (Jerusalem: Magnes Press, 1977), pp. 374–435   197

Part II. Rabbinic Culture – Tradition and Self-Invention

6. Israel Levy, "L'Origine Davidique de Hillel" in *REJ*, Vol. 31 (1895), pp. 202–211. *Translated by Erin Brust*   249

CONTENTS

7. Wilhelm Bacher, "Das altjüdische Schulwesen" in *Jahrbuch für Jüdische Geschichte und Literatur*, Vol. 6 (1903), pp. 48–81. Translated by Eva Kiesele ... 259

8. E.E. Urbach, "The *Derashah* as the Basis for the Halakhah and the Problem of the *Soferim*" in *Tarbiz*, Vol. 27 (1958), pp. 168–82 (Hebrew). Translated by Christine Hayes ... *281*

9. David Zvi Hoffman, pp. 1–12 of "*Le-Heqer Midreshei ha-Tanna'im*" in *Mesilot le-Torat ha-Tanna'im* (Tel Aviv: M. Drisner, 1928). Translation by A. S. Rabinowitz of "*Zur Einleitung in die halachischen Midraschim*," (Berlin, 1888). Translated by James Redfield ... 303

10. Solomon Zeitlin, "The Pharisees: A Historical Study" in *The Jewish Quarterly Review*, New Series, Vol. 52, No. 2 (Oct., 1961), pp. 97–129 ... 315

Part III. Rabbinic Contexts

11. Saul Lieberman, "The Martyrs of Caesarea" in *Annuaire de L'Institut de Philologie et D'Histoire Orientales et Slaves*, Vol. 7 (1944), pp. 395–446 ... 351

12. David Daube (1909–1999), "Rabbinic Methods of Interpretation and Hellenistic Rhetoric" in *Hebrew Union College Annual*, Vol. 22 (1949), pp. 239–264 ... 393

13. Elias Bickerman, "La chaîne de la tradition pharisienne" in *Revue biblique*, Vol. 59, No. 14 (1952), pp. 44–54; later in English in *Studies in Jewish and Christian History II* (1980), pp. 256–269 ... 419

14. Morton Smith (1915–1991), "Palestinian Judaism in the First Century" in M. Davis (ed.), *Israel, Its Role in Civilization* (1956), pp. 67–81 ... 435

15. Erwin R. Goodenough (1893–1965), "The Rabbis and Jewish Art in the Greco-Roman Period" in *Hebrew Union College Annual*, Vol. 32 (1961), pp. 269–279 ... 447

16. Morton Smith (1915–1991), "Goodenough's Jewish Symbols in Retrospect" in *JBL*, Vol. 86 (1967), pp. 53–68 ... 459

CONTENTS

17. Henry Fischel, "Story and History: Observations on Greco-Roman Rhetoric and Pharisaism" in *American Oriental Society*, Middle West Branch, Semi-Centennial Volume (1969), pp. 59–88 — 475

18. Alexander Kohut, "Die talmudisch-midraschische Adamssage in ihrer Ruckbeziehung auf die persische Yima und Meshiasage" in **Zeitschrift der Deutschen Morgenländischen Gesellschaft** (1871), pp. 59–94. *Translated by Eva Kiesele* — 505

Index — 541

ACKNOWLEDGEMENTS

In preparing this volume I benefited from the research and translation skills of a number of individuals. I extend my sincere thanks to my doctoral students Sara Ronis and Yoni Pomeranz who provided critically important assistance in researching and locating the works included in this volume. I am also extremely grateful to Erin Brust for translating the article by Levy from the original French, James Redfield for translating the articles by Graetz, Hoffman and Zunz from the original German, and Eva Kiesele for translating the articles by Bacher and Kohut from the original German. The high quality of these translations is its own tribute to these young scholars. Finally, I would like to thank Prods Oktor Skjaervø for his expert assistance with the Kohut article and Kenneth Stow for both his guiding vision and his patience in what turned out to be a longer than expected period of gestation for this project.

INTRODUCTION

Christine Hayes

When I undertook to edit a volume entitled *Classic Essays in Early Rabbinic Culture and History*, I did not anticipate the challenge I would face. A classic essay is one that has a recognizable value or high quality over time, but the scholarly study of the rabbinic period has undergone more than one sea change since the early days of *Wissenschaft des Judentums*. The discovery of new textual sources, the increased availability of critical editions, the stunning contributions of archaeology, the development and refinement of historical-critical methodologies, the rejection of both historical positivism and historical idealism, the embrace of comparative approaches, and the integration of methods and theories from across the humanities have utterly transformed the scholarly study of the rabbinic period. In light of these seismic shifts one may be forgiven for wondering whether it is even possible for works of a certain age to be perceived by modern scholars as possessing high quality or recognizable value. Fortunately, in the course of preparing this volume, I have come to the conclusion that even a somewhat outdated work can possess both high quality and recognizable value.

In selecting these essays I adopted five criteria. First, I confined myself to scholars who are no longer living and to essays and articles published for the first time before 1970. I considered this to be a completely non-negotiable criterion. Second, I gave preference to items that are less readily available either because they are out-of-print and have not been widely reproduced or digitized or because they have not been translated into English until now. This was, however, a somewhat negotiable criterion; on occasion, an essay readily available online or in other anthologies cried out to be included. Third, I did not include essays devoted entirely to the philological and textual study of rabbinic literature, though it is clear that reliable scholarly research in rabbinic history and culture depends upon those who labor in the fields of lower criticism, higher criticism and in the publication of critical editions. Fourth, I favored stand-alone studies rather than book chapters or excerpts from monographs. Fifth, I chose essays that I consider to be pioneering – either because they inspired scholars to do something they hadn't done before or because they enabled scholars to do things in a different way. In the Introduction, I detail the specific reasons for my choices and highlight the enduring legacy of each essay. Where possible, I point to subsequent scholarship that has followed the trail blazed by the essay.

This is, inevitably, a subjective and perhaps even idiosyncratic list. While some of the essays included here would likely appear in any scholar's list of "Classic Essays in Early Rabbinic Culture and History," others would not. These essays are here because they have generated an intellectual energy and ongoing scholarly conversation that I have found to be stimulating and of enduring significance. It is entirely possible, and indeed likely, that another editor's intellectual passions would dictate a substantially different list.

The essays in this volume are divided into three parts. Part I contains essays that made a pioneering contribution to the identification of sources for the historical and cultural study of the rabbinic period, articulated methodologies for the study of rabbinic history and culture, or addressed historical topics that continue to engage scholars to the present day. Part II contains essays that made a pioneering contribution to our understanding of the culture of the sages whose sources we deploy for the purposes of historical reconstruction, grappled with the riddle and rhythm of the rabbis' emergence to authority, or pierced the veil of their self-presentation. Part III contains essays that made pioneering contributions to our understanding of the broader cultural contexts of rabbinic sources, identified patterns of rabbinic participation in prevailing cultural systems, or sought to define with greater precision the social location of the rabbinic class within Jewish society of late antiquity.

A. Rabbinic History – Sources and Methods

In 1818, Leopold Zunz (1794–1886) launched a new era in the history of Jewish scholarship with an essay entitled "**Etwas über die rabbinische Litteratur.**" As Ismar Schorsch notes: "The unmistakable thrust of the essay was toward transferring the study of Hebrew literature from the synagogue to the university, the only proper forum for pursuing the history of mankind."[1] The essay established Zunz as the founder of the modern "Science of Judaism" or *Wissenschaft des Judentums*, whose practitioners advocated the application of historical-critical methods to the study of Judaism and the integration of Jewish studies into the humanities. To make the case for the recognition of Judaism and its literature in university research and teaching, Zunz argued that Jews had made important contributions to all areas of Western civilization, contributions that should be included in its history. To achieve a full integration of the study of ancient Judaism into the study of ancient history in general and Roman history in particular, Zunz and the other members of the *Wissenschaft* movement believed they "had to show

---

1 Ismar Schorsch, "Ideology and History in the Age of Emancipation" in Heinrich Graetz, *The Structure of Jewish History and Other Essays*, trans. and ed. Ismar Schorsch (New York: JTSA, 1975), 6.

classicists that their own source material had historical value and justified historical consideration."[2] In his pioneering essay, Zunz surveyed the great expanse of post-biblical Hebrew literature, some of it previously unknown, in order to demonstrate that Jewish literary activity was rich and deep, that it was not confined to law but embraced all areas of human endeavor. The essay was the first attempt to document all branches of Hebrew literature and to outline the vision of the *Wissenschaft* movement.

In 1819, Zunz joined with Edward Gans and Moses Moser to found the "Verein für Kultur und Wissenschaft der Juden" (Society for Jewish Culture and Science) which promoted the scientific study of Jewish history, literature and science as a means to securing an equal place for Jews in European society. Zunz edited the sole issue of the *Zeitschrift für die Wissenschaft des Judentums* published by the society (1922), and when the society disbanded a few years later, Zunz continued its work alone as the unofficial leader of a generation of scholars dedicated to *Wissenschaft des Judentums*. In 1832, he published what is considered one of the most important Jewish books of the 19th century, his *Gottesdienstliche Vorträge der Juden* ("The Worship Sermons of the Jews, Historically Developed"). A methodological model for the study of Jewish literature, the work analyzed the development of Jewish homiletical literature from classical rabbinic *midrash*, the Haggadah and the prayer-book up to the modern-day sermon. Zunz's explorations and expositions of Jewish literature and history continued in *Zur Geschichte und Literatur* ("On History and Literature," 1845), which repeated many of the themes of his 1818 essay: the scope of Jewish literature was expansive and included all post-biblical Hebrew writing; Jewish literature and general literature have mutually influenced one another; the study of the former should be an integral part of the latter; and the exclusion of Jewish studies from the university is an outrage that must end.

Although originally sympathetic with the goals of the Reformers, Zunz became increasingly frustrated with their selective approach to the Jewish past. Denigrating the religious orientation of Jewish literature as parochial, the Reformers saw no value in the scientific study of rabbinic writings and exegesis. Such parochial works could not constitute a national literature. In the 1940s, Zunz broke openly with this view and articulated an alternative program of *Wissenschaft* that was comprehensive in its vision of Jewish history and literature. Although a distaste for Talmud is evident in some of his writings, his major works[3] drew upon hundreds of manuscripts and thousands of liturgical works to present the historical development of liturgical poetry and synagogue customs, in an effort to counter the vision of *Wissenschaft* promoted by Geiger and other Reform figures.

---

2 Catherine Hezser, "Samuel Krauss' Contribution to the Study of Ancient Judaism, Christianity, and Graeco-Roman Culture within the Context of *Wissenschaft* Scholarship," *Modern Judaism* 33:3 (2013), 1–31, p. 12.

3 Zunz's major works are *Synagogale Poesie des Mittelalters* (1855), *Die Ritus des Synagogalen Gottesdienstes Geschichtlich Entwickelt* (1859), and *Literaturgeschichte der Synagogalen Poesie* (1865).

INTRODUCTION

One of the goals of the *Wissenschaft des Judentums* movement was to demonstrate the Jewish contribution to the development of European civilization, a goal well served by identifying Jewish materials in non-Jewish literature. The 19th century saw an increased interest in the effort to uncover evidence of Jewish traditions in the writings of the church fathers. Scholars of patristics were not in general well suited to this task; it took scholars with both yeshiva training and a Western classical university education to undertake the comparative study of these two bodies of literature.[4] One of the pioneers in the effort was Heinrich Graetz (1817–1891).[5]

Graetz is best known for his comprehensive eleven-volume *History of the Jews* (1853 to 1876). While the historian Salo Baron criticized the work for its "lachrymose conception of Jewish history," it was hailed more than a century later as "the best single introduction to the totality of Jewish history."[6] In contrast to the attention paid to this magisterial work, many of Graetz's other works (he translated and wrote commentaries on biblical books as well as analyses of rabbinic texts) have been overlooked and are no longer available. And yet, his articles investigating aggadic elements in the writings of the church fathers – a topic of continuing scholarly interest – inspired a flurry of research.

In 1854 Graetz published "**Hagadische Elemente bei den Kirchenvatern**," the first of two articles (the second was published in 1855) investigating midrashic elements and parallels in the writings of Justin Martyr, Origen, Ephrem Cyrus and Jerome, in order to show the influence of rabbinic thought on patristic literature. Judith Baskin notes the many dissertations, articles and books between 1863 and 1900 that followed Graetz's lead, including: D. Gerson on Ephrem (1868), A.H. Goldfahn on Justin Martyr (1873), C. Siegfried on Jerome (1883–84), M. Rahmer on Jerome and Pseudo-Jerome (various studies from 1861 to 1903), S. Funk on Aphrahates (1891) and two important articles by S. Krauss in 1893–94.[7]

Krauss's articles, which focused on Justin, Clement of Alexandria, Origen, Eusebius, Aphrahates, Ephrem and Jerome, emphasized the importance of patristic writings not only for a better understanding of the rabbinic sources and the polemical context in which the latter were produced, but also for evidence of early Christian representations of Jews and Judaism. The 19th century search for rabbinic parallels in patristic texts culminated in the studies of Louis Ginzberg between 1899 and 1935.[8] His findings were included in his classic multi-volume

---

4 Harold Revelson, "Ontological Torah: An Instrument of Religious and Social Discourse," Ph.D. dissertation, University of Texas at Austin, 2005, p. 1.
5 Judith Baskin, "Rabbinic-Patristic Exegetical Contacts in Late Antiquity: A Bibliographical Reappraisal" in *Approaches to Ancient Judaism*, Vol. 5, ed. William S. Green, Brown Judaic Studies 32 (Atlanta, GA: Scholars Press, 1985), 53–80, p. 54.
6 Schorsch, "Ideology and History," 1.
7 For bibliographic details of these works see Baskin, "Rabbinic-Patristic Exegetical Contacts," 75–80.
8 Ibid., 55.

work *The Legends of the Jews* (1909) which contains many references to the church fathers. In the mid-20th century, E.E. Urbach insisted on the importance of patristic literature and its polemical practices for a full understanding and explanation of certain rabbinic interpretations and sayings.[9] More recently, Oded Irshai, Paula Fredriksen, and Hillel Newman have continued to make important advances in the study of the treatment of the Jews in patristic literature;[10] Marc Hirshman has inquired into the literary polemics and borrowing between these two literatures;[11] Judith Baskin has compared Jewish and Christian exegetical methodologies and interpretive traditions;[12] and Daniel Boyarin has explored the relation of Judaism and Christianity, arguing that the separation of the two was the work of rabbis and church fathers of the 4th century C.E.[13] Connections between the literature of Eastern Christianity and the Babylonian Talmud have been identified by Isaiah Gafni, Naomi Koltun-Fromm, Shlomo Naeh, Adam Becker, Michal Bar-Asher Siegal and others.[14] Nevertheless, debate continues over the contacts between rabbinic and patristic figures (and Christians generally), their

---

9   E.E. Urbach, "*Derashot Ḥazal 'al nevi'e 'umot ha'olam ve-al parashat bil'am le'or ha-vikuah hayehudi-notsri*," *Tarbiz* 25 (1956), 271–89. For a detailed survey of scholarship in this field through 1985, including studies of individual church fathers, see Baskin, op. cit., 57–71.
10 See for example, Oded Irshai and Paula Fredriksen, "Christian Anti-Judaism: Polemics and Policies – From the Second to the Seventh Centuries" in *The Cambridge History of Judaism*, Vol. 4, ed. S. Katz (Cambridge: Cambridge University Press, 2006), 977–1034; also, Oded Irshai, "Jews and Judaism in Early Christian Historiography: The Case of Eusebius of Caesarea (preliminary observations)" in *Jewish Life in Byzantium: Dialectics of Minority and Majority Cultures*, ed. Robert Bonfil, Oded Irshai, Guy G. Stroumsa and Rina Talgam (Leiden: Brill, 2011), 799–828. See also, Hillel Newman, "Jerome and the Jews," Ph.D. dissertation, Hebrew University, 1997.
11 Marc Hirshman, "Polemic Literary Units in the Classical Midrashim and Justin Martyr's Dialogue with Trypho," *Jewish Quarterly Review* 83 (1993), 369–84 and *A Rivalry of Genius: Jewish and Christian Biblical Interpretation in Late Antiquity*, trans. Batya Stein (Albany, NY: State University of New York Press, 1996).
12 Judith Baskin, *Pharaoh's Counsellors* (Chico, CA: Scholars Press, 1983).
13 Daniel Boyarin, *Dying for God: Martyrdom and the Making of Christianity and Judaism* (Berkeley, CA: UC Press, 1999) and *Border Lines: The Partition of Judaeo-Christianity* (Divinations; Philadelphia: University of Pennsylvania, 2004).
14 For representative examples, see Isaiah Gafni, "Nestorian Literature as a Source for the History of the Babylonian Yeshivot," (Hebrew) *Tarbiz* 51 (1982), 567–76; Naomi Koltun-Fromm, *Hermeneutics of Holiness: Ancient Jewish and Christian Notions of Sexuality and Religious Community* (Oxford: Oxford University Press, 2010), 129–238 and *Jewish-Christian Conversation in Fourth-Century Persian Mesopotamia: A Reconstructed Conversation* (Piscataway, NJ: Gorgias Press, 2011); Shlomo Naeh, "Freedom and Celibacy: A Talmudic Variation on Tales of Temptation and Fall in Genesis and its Syrian Background" in *The Book of Genesis in Jewish and Oriental Christian Interpretation*, ed. Judith Frishman and Lucas Van Rompay (Lovanii: Peeters, 1997), 73–89; Adam Becker, "The Comparative Study of 'Scholasticism' in Late Antique Mesopotamia: Rabbis and East Syrians," *AJS Review* 34 (2010), 91–113; and Michal Bar-Asher Siegal, *Early Christian Monastic Literature and the Babylonian Talmud* (Cambridge: Cambridge University Press, 2013); and Aaron Butts and Simcha Gross, *Jews and Syriac Christians: Interaction and Identity* (forthcoming).

mutual influence or interaction, and proper methods for the identification of both parallels and polemics.

A leading scholar of the early 20th century *Wissenschaft*, Avigdor (Victor) Aptowitzer (1871–1942) investigated a wide array of subjects in Jewish history and literature. While his most famous scholarly work is his 1913–35 annotated edition of the *Sefer Ravyah* (R. Eliezer b. Joel ha-Levi, a scholar of medieval Ashkenaz), he also produced a four-volume work on biblical citations in Talmudic-midrashic literature that deviate from the Masoretic text (*Das Schriftwort in Der Rabbinischen Literatur*, 1906–1915), and dealt extensively with *aggadah* (in *Kain und Abel in der Agada* [1922] and *Parteipolitik der Hasmonäerzeit im rabbinischen und pseudoepighaphischen Schrifttum* [1927]). In his work on *aggadah*, he developed criteria for distinguishing folk legends from legends produced by rabbinic academies, and compared the content and literary form of *aggadah* with non-rabbinic works such as the Apocrypha and patristic literature.

Aptowitzer was one of the first scholars to recognize the close and mutually illuminating relationship between *halakhah* and *aggadah*. His 1924 article **"Observations on the Criminal law of the Jews"** drew on both halakhic and aggadic texts in an attempt to produce an intellectual history of rabbinic criminal law.[15] His attention to the relationship of *halakhah* and *aggadah* and to the larger intellectual universe of the rabbis foreshadowed the rise of law and narrative studies in rabbinics scholarship beginning in the latter part of the 20th century with the work of American and Israeli scholars, including Jeffrey Rubenstein, Steven Fraade, Suzanne Last Stone, Yair Lorberbaum, Moshe Simon-Shoshan, Yonatan Feintuch, Beth Berkowitz, Chaya Halberstam, and Barry Wimpfheimer.[16]

---

15 For a contemporary example of this approach, see Beth Berkowitz, *Execution and Invention: Death Penalty Discourse in Early Rabbinic and Christian Cultures* (New York: Oxford University Press, 2006), 53.

16 See Jeffrey Rubenstein, *Talmudic Stories: Narrative Art, Composition, and Culture* (Baltimore, MD: Johns Hopkins University Press, 2003); Steven Fraade, "Nomos and Narrative before Nomos and Narrative," *Yale Journal of Law and the Humanities* 17 (2005), 81–96 and Fraade, "Ancient Jewish Law and Narrative in Comparative Perspective: The Damascus Document and the Mishnah," *Diné Israel: Studies in Halakhah and Jewish Law* 24 (2007), 65–99; Suzanne Last Stone, "Rabbinic Legal Magic: A New Look at Honi's Circle as the Construction of Law's Space," *Yale Journal of Law and the Humanities* 17:1 (2005), 97–123, and Stone, "On the Interplay of Rules, Cases, and Concepts in Rabbinic Legal Literature: Another Look at the Aggadot on Honi the Circle-Drawer," *Diné Israel* 24 (2007); Yair Lorberbaun, *Image of God: Halakha and Aggadah* [Hebrew] (Tel Aviv and Jerusalem: Schocken, 2004); Moshe Simon-Shoshan, *Stories of the Law: Narrative Discourse and the Construction of Authority in the Mishnah* (New York: Oxford University Press, 2013); Yonatan Feintuch, "Uncovering Covert Links between Halakha and Aggada in the Babylonian Talmud – The Talmudic Discussion of the Yom Kippur Afflictions in bYoma," *AJS Review* 40 (2016), 17–32; Beth Berkowitz, *Defining Jewish Difference: From Antiquity to the Present* (New York: Cambridge University Press, 2012), and Berkowitz, "Reclaiming Halakhah: On the Recent Works of Aharon Shemesh," *AJS Review* 35:1 (2011), 125–36; Chaya Halberstam, "The Art of Biblical Law," *Prooftexts* 27:2 (2007) and Halberstam, "Encircling the Law: The Legal Boundaries of Rabbinic Judaism," *Jewish Studies Quarterly*

These scholars, influenced directly or indirectly by jurisprudential approaches informed by literary theory (in particular Ronald Dworkin's theory of law as interpretation and Robert Cover's emphasis on the role of narrative in transforming law from a system of social control to a system of meaning), highlight the many ways in which law and narrative interact and overlap in the larger complex of rabbinic thought. In resisting the isolation of *halakhah* and *aggadah* as distinct discourses they return to a path pioneered by Victor Aptowitzer nearly a century ago.[17] At the same time, they forged new pathways in the study of rabbinic legal culture in the light of legal theory.[18]

Adolf Büchler (1867–1939) was a historian of the social, economic and religious life of Jews in Palestine in the centuries immediately preceding and following the rise of Christianity. Büchler is noted for his insistence on the basic credibility and reliability of rabbinic texts as historical sources, despite a widespread scholarly bias in favor of contemporaneous Greek and Roman sources. The debate over the suitability of rabbinic sources for the task of historical reconstruction continues to occupy scholars to the present day.[19]

In his wide-ranging researches, Büchler mined Second Temple and Talmudic materials, arriving at conclusions that significantly altered the presentation of Judaism in the first few centuries of the Common Era. Some of his most innovative studies concern ethical and religious concepts, particularly around matters of purity, sin, and atonement. Büchler was one of two early scholars to take seriously the notion of sin as a defiling force.[20] Despite certain flaws (such as the failure to consider New Testament evidence and an assumption of continuity between the biblical and rabbinic periods) Büchler's basic distinction, refined and

---

(2009); and Barry Wimpfheimer, *Narrating the Law: A Poetics of Talmudic Legal Stories* (Philadelphia, PA: University of Pennsylvania Press, 2011).

17 For the impact of Robert Cover's work on the study of rabbinic culture, see the essays in the *Yale Journal of Law and the Humanities* 17:1 (2005) and Suzanne Last Stone's Preface to the Proceedings of a conference on "The Relationship between Halakhah and Aggada" held at the Harvard Law School in May 2005 and published in *Diné Israel* 24 (2007), English section.

18 For some examples of the integration of legal theory in the study of classical rabbinic law and legal culture, see Devorah Steinmetz, *Punishment and Freedom: The Rabbinic Construction of Criminal Law* (Philadelphia, PA: University of Pennsylvania Press, 2008); Tzvi Novick, *What is Good and What God Demands* (Leiden: Brill, 2010); Christine Hayes, *What's Divine about Divine Law? Early Perspectives* (Princeton, NJ: Princeton University Press, 2015); and David Flatto, *Justice Unbound: Separation of Powers in the Early Jewish Imagination* (Cambridge, MA: Harvard University Press, forthcoming).

19 In this regard, see Richard Kalmin, *Sages, Stories, Authors and Editors in Rabbinic Babylonia* (Atlanta, GA: Scholars Press, 1994); also Christine Hayes, *Between the Babylonian and Palestinian Talmuds* (New York: Oxford University Press, 1997), pp. 3–31.

20 In 1905, David Zvi Hoffmann distinguished two kinds of impurity in biblical sources – an impurity that stands in opposition to holiness and an impurity that stands in opposition to (ritual) purity. In *Studies in Sin and Atonement in Rabbinic Literature of the First Century* (1928), Büchler focused on the defiling force of sin as a source of impurity distinct from what he termed levitical impurity.

supplemented, has been revived to great advantage in recent studies of impurity in ancient Jewish culture.[21]

Büchler also addressed the social consequences of ritual impurity in two major works. The first, a monograph length study entitled *Der Galiläische 'am-Ha'areṣ Des Zweiten Jahrhunderts* (1906), demonstrated that purity concerns did not prevent social interaction among Jewish groups. In recent years, younger scholars such as Yair Furstenberg and Mira Balberg have applied new methodological tools and theoretical frameworks to the study of purity and impurity and their social and ideological consequences in rabbinic texts.[22] The second, an essay entitled **"The Levitical Impurity of the Gentile in Palestine before the Year 70"** appeared in 1926 and was an important corrective to the views advanced by many 19th-century scholars of ancient Judaism such as Emil Schürer. Schürer claimed that Gentiles were considered by biblical Israelites and Pharisaic rabbis in late antiquity to communicate a ritual impurity because they did not observe the biblical laws of ritual purity. This impurity was believed to be the basis for a strict and burdensome policy of separation. In his essay, Büchler argued that the ritual impurity of Gentiles was the de novo creation of first-century rabbis prior to the Roman–Jewish war of 66 C.E. and that this statutory and non-intrinsic ritual impurity was a response to specific historical circumstances. While the essay contains errors and methodological flaws, the basic thesis, that the ritual impurity of Gentiles was not an ancient legal tradition traceable to biblical times, was a major contribution. In the 1950s, Gedalyahu Alon would criticize Büchler's thesis and posit an ancient tradition of *inherent* ritual impurity arising from the Gentile *qua* Gentile. The evidence for such a view is slim, however, as noted in the recent studies of Klawans and Hayes.[23] Nevertheless, some recent Israeli scholarship has returned to Alon's notion of an ancient Gentile impurity in ancient Judaism.[24] The legacy of Adolf Büchler lives on in this continuing debate.

---

21 See especially, Jonathan Klawans, *Impurity and Sin in Ancient Judaism* (New York: Oxford University Press, 2004). The pioneering contributions of Hoffmann and Büchler are discussed in Klawans's Introduction. See also Christine Hayes, *Gentile Impurities and Jewish Identities: Intermarriage and Conversion from the Bible to the Talmud* (New York: Oxford University Press, 2002); and Vered Noam, *From Qumran to the Rabbinic Revolution: Conceptions of Impurity* (Hebrew) (Jerusalem: Yad BenZvi Press, 2010).

22 See Yair Furstenberg, "Eating in the State of Purity in the Tannaitic Period: Tractate Tohorot in its Historical and Cultural Contexts," (Hebrew), Ph.D. dissertation, Hebrew University, 2010; Mira Balberg, *Purity, Body and Self in Early Rabbinic Literature* (Berkeley, CA: University of California Press, 2014).

23 Jonathan Klawans, "Notions of Gentile Impurity in Ancient Judaism," *AJS Review* 20:2 (1995), 285–312 and Hayes, *Gentile Impurities*.

24 Vered Noam, "Another Look at the Rabbinic Conception of Gentiles from the Perspective of Impurity Laws," in *Judaea-Palaestina, Babylon and Rome: Jews in Antiquity*, ed. Benjamin Isaac and Yuval Shahar, TSAJ 147 (Tübingen: Mohr Siebeck, 2012), 89–110 and Noam, *From Qumran to the Rabbinic Revolution: Conception of Impurity* (Jerusalem: Yad Ben Zvi Press, 2010) [Hebrew]. For the rabbinic construction of the gentile as *"Goy"* see Ishay Rosen-Zvi and Adi Ophir, *"Goy:* Toward a Genealogy," *Dine Yisrael* 28 (2011), 69–112.

The early *Wissenschaft* scholars led by Zunz fought to demonstrate the historical value of Jewish source materials. Scholars such as Aptowitzer and Büchler heeded the call and utilized aggadic and midrashic materials as well as the history of *halakhah* to reconstruct the social, economic, political and ideational history of ancient Judaism. Little changed in the next generation: Saul Lieberman, Gedalyahu Alon and E.E. Urbach all sought to reconstruct ancient Jewish history from "historical kernels" extracted from a wide range of Talmudic sources.

Gedalyahu Alon (1901–1950) was one of 20th century's foremost historians of the Talmudic period who also utilized rabbinic sources in his reconstruction of the social, political, and economic world of Jewish Palestine. He regarded the Jews as a single nation, united and resistant to external cultural influences.[25] Alon's nationalist orientation is also evident in his assertion that Jewish political life and official institutions did not end with the destruction in 70 C.E., but continued under the leadership of sages and Patriarchs until the Muslim conquest in the 7th century. The assumption of a post-destruction Jewish nation united under the rule of sages and Patriarchs and impervious to outside influence may be seen in Alon's 1947 essay "**Those Appointed for Money**."

In the essay, Alon responded to Hirsch Zvi Chajes's 1899 article "Les juges juifs en Palestine de l'an 70 à l'an 500" (*REJ*) which argued that there were no formal rabbinic courts after the destruction. According to Chajes, individual rabbis authorized by the Roman government made judgments but, with the exception of some of the Patriarchs, rabbis in Palestine in the Talmudic period lacked civil authority. Against this view, Alon read rabbinic sources as providing evidence for a tri-partite judicial system consisting of (a) communal judiciaries independent of the Patriarch and Sanhedrin and ruling according to local custom and equity, (b) rabbinic courts run by ordained sages and authorized by the Patriarch and Sanhedrin to rule according to rabbinic law, and (c) a system of arbitration. According to Alon, the rabbis were antagonistic towards the communal courts and in time were able to limit the scope of their authority. Alon's thesis exerted a strong influence on some subsequent scholarship, but has recently been challenged by the work of Martin Goodman and Seth Schwartz.[26]

The debate between Chajes and Alon is symptomatic of a larger debate over the place of the rabbis in Palestinian Jewish society in the first four centuries of the Common Era. A significant contribution to that debate, in addition to the works mentioned above, is Catherine Hezser's 1997 book, *The Social Structure of the Rabbinic Movement in Roman Palestine*,[27] which shows that for most

---

25 Seth Schwartz, "Historiography on the Jews in the 'Talmudic Period': 70–640 CE" in *The Oxford Handbook of Jewish Studies*, ed. Martin Goodman (Oxford: Oxford University Press, 2002) 79–114, p. 85.
26 Martin Goodman, *State and Society in Roman Galilee: 132–212* (Portland, OR: Vallentine Mitchell, 2000); and Seth Schwartz, *Imperialism and Jewish Society: 200 BCE to 640 CE* (Princeton, NJ: Princeton University Press, 2004).
27 Texts and Studies in Ancient Judaism; v.66 (Tübingen: Mohr Siebeck).

of this period the Palestinian rabbis were not an institutionalized class but a loosely agglomerated group. The assertion of a more central role for the rabbis in Palestinian Jewish society in the early centuries C.E. may be seen in the papers delivered at a recent symposium entitled "In the Wake of the Destruction: Was Rabbinic Judaism Normative?"[28] while other recent scholarship brings archaeological and other evidence to bear on the question of the place of the rabbis in post-destruction Jewish society.[29]

The pioneers of the historical and cultural study of the rabbinic period concerned themselves primarily with the rabbinic estate, or that of ancient Jews writ large, with little interest in the experience or representation of women or the application of theories of gender. In the last forty years, the task of historical and cultural reconstruction of the rabbinic period initiated by these scholars has embraced a broader vision as demonstrated by investigations of women's history by such scholars as Tal Ilan, Cynthia Baker and Miriam Peskowitz;[30] analyses of rabbinic discourses of gender, gender roles, and sexuality by such scholars as Daniel Boyarin, Charlotte Fonrobert;[31] and studies of women and the *halakhah* by Judith Hauptman, Gail Labovitz and Elizabeth Alexander.[32]

B. Rabbinic Culture – Tradition and Self-Invention

The scientific study of Judaism was predicated on the adoption of a critical approach to traditional Jewish sources. One of the most remarkable early instances of a "hermeneutic of suspicion" in rabbinic scholarship may be seen in Israel Levy's 1895 essay "**L'Origine Davidique de Hillel**." Levy (1856–1939) was a French scholar of Jewish history and literature who made important contributions to the fields of *aggadah, midrash*, Talmud, Jewish folk-lore, Jewish-Christian controversies and the history of French Jewry. In his essay on the claim

---

28 The proceedings were published in *Jewish Identities in Antiquity: Studies in Memory of Menahem Stern*, ed. Lee I. Levine and Daniel R. Schwartz (Tübingen: Mohr Siebeck, 2009), 163–266.
29 See for example, many of the papers included in *Yavne Revisited: The Historical Rabbis and the Rabbis of History*, ed. Peter J. Tomson and Joshua Schwartz (Leiden: Brill, 2018).
30 See for example, Tal Ilan, *Mine and Yours are Hers: Retrieving Women's History from Rabbinic Literature* (Leiden, New York and Cologne: Brill, 1997); Cynthia Baker, *Rebuilding the House of Israel: Architectures of Gender in Jewish Antiquity* (Stanford, CA: Stanford University Press, 2002); and Miriam Peskowitz, *Spinning Fantasies: Rabbis, Gender and History* (Berkeley, CA: University of California Press, 1997).
31 See for example, Daniel Boyarin, *Carnal Israel: Reading Sex in Talmudic Culture* (Berkeley, CA: University of California Press, 1993); Charlotte Fonrobert, *Menstrual Purity: Rabbinic and Christian Reconstructions of Biblical Gender* (Stanford, CA: Stanford University Press, 2002).
32 See for example, Judith Hauptman, *Rereading the Rabbis: A Woman's Voice* (Boulder, CO: Westview Press, 1998); Gail Labovitz, *Marriage and Metaphor: Constructions of Gender in Rabbinic Literature* (Lanham, MD: Lexington Books, 2009); and Elizabeth Alexander, *Between Man and Woman: Reading for Gender in Early Rabbinic Law and Exegesis* (New York: Cambridge University Press, 2013).

of Davidic descent for the house of Hillel, Levy approached the relevant sources with a healthy dose of skepticism. Noting that the claim of Davidic origin is not attributed to any Gamalielian Patriarch or his colleagues prior to Judah ha-Nasi at the end of the 2nd century, Levy concluded that the idea is a fabrication datable to the time of that Patriarch. Levy speculated on the reasons for the invention of this genealogy and suggested R. Judah's need to counter the claim to authority of his contemporary, R. Ḥiyya, whose relation to the Exilarch conferred upon him a connection with the house of David. In a continuation of the article published in *REJ* 33 (1896), Levy rejected the argument that Hillel and his descendants hid their Davidic ancestry from the Roman authorities.

Levy's essay may be seen as an important precedent for subsequent work on the patriarchate, the exilarchate, and models of leadership in rabbinic culture, including a monograph by David Goodblatt and studies by Shaye J.D. Cohen, Martin Goodman, Lee Levine, and Seth Schwartz among others.[33] Moreover, his hermeneutic of suspicion in debunking one aspect of the rabbinic "myth of origins," presaged more contemporary scholarly approaches that focus on the invention of rabbinic identity and authority.[34]

Increasingly scholars turned their attention to the rabbinic class itself – who were these individuals? What do their texts reveal about the rabbis themselves and about the culture of learning with which they were so closely identified? How

---

33 David Goodblatt, *The Monarchic Principle: Studies in Jewish Self-Government in Antiquity*, Texte und Studien zum Antiken Judentum 38 (Tübingen: J.C.B. Mohr, 1994). See also, Shaye J.D. Cohen, "Patriarchs and Scholarchs," *PAAJR* 48 (1981), 57–85, and *The Three Crowns: Structures of Communal Politics in Early Rabbinic Jewry* (Cambridge: Cambridge University Press, 1990), 179–212; Daniel. R. Schwartz, "Josephus on the Jewish Constitutions and Community," *Scripta Classica Israelica* 7 (1983–1984), 30–52; Martin Goodman, *State and Society*, op. cit., 111–18; Martin Jacobs, *Die Institution des jüdischen Patriarchen* (Tübingen: Mohr Siebeck 1995), 342–52; Lee Levine, "The Status of the Patriarch in the Third and Fourth Centuries: Sources and Methodology," *JJS* 47 (1996), 1–32; Ephrat Habas (Rubin), "Rabban Gamaliel of Yavneh and his Sons: The Patriarchate before and after the Bar Kokhva Revolt," *JJS* 50 (1999), 21–37; Seth Schwartz, "The Patriarchs and the Diaspora," *JJS* 50 (1999), 208–22; and most recently, David Flatto's *Justice Unbound: Hebraic Jurists and the Early Separation of Law from Power* (Cambridge, MA: Harvard University Press, forthcoming).

34 See for example, Daniel Boyarin, *Border Lines*, on the invention of rabbinic heresiology; also, Beth A. Berkowitz, *Execution and Invention*; Ishay Rosen-Zvi and Orr Scharf, *The Mishnaic Sotah Ritual: Temple, Gender and Midrash*, Supplements to the Journal for the Study of Judaism (Leiden: Brill, 2012); Moshe Simon-Shoshan, *Stories of the Law*; and Naftali Cohn, *The Memory of the Temple and the Making of the Rabbis* (Philadelphia, PA: University of Pennsylvania Press, 2012). For the role of gender as well as the control of bodily states in the invention of rabbinic authority, see Charlotte Fonrobert, "When Women Walk in the Way of their Fathers: On Gendering the Rabbinic Claim for Authority," *Journal of the History of Sexuality* 10 (2001), 398–416; Fonrobert, "Blood and Law: Uterine Fluids and Rabbinic Maps of Identity" in *Blood and the Boundaries of Jewish and Christian Identities in Late Antiquity*, Henoch Theme-Issue 30:2 (2008), 243–66, ed. Ra'anan S. Boustan and Annette Yoshiko Reed; and Mira Balberg, "Rabbinic Authority, Medical Rhetoric, and Body Hermeneutics in Mishnah Nega'im," *AJS Review* 35:2 (2011), 323–46.

were they connected with groups known to have existed in the pre-rabbinic period and how did they gain authority?

The astonishingly prolific Wilhelm Bacher (Ludwig Blau's bibliography lists 48 books and nearly 700 articles), helped to shed light on some of these questions. A master of Hebrew, Aramaic, Arabic and Persian, Bacher is best known as a pioneer in the scientific study of the *aggadah* and *midrash*, and his major works include *Die Agada der Babylonischen Amoräer* (1878); *Die Agada der Tannaiten* (2 vols., 1884–90); *Die Agada der Palaestinischen Amoräer* (3 vols., 1892–99; repr. 1965); *Die Prooemien der Alten juedischen Homilie* (1913); *Rabbanan, Beitrag zur Geschichte der anonymen Agada* (1914); and *Tradition und Tradenten in den Schulen Palaestinas und Babyloniens* (1914).

Tradition und Tradenten examined the vocabulary and the transmission processes of the attributed traditions in the Talmud, and reflected Bacher's scholarly interest in rabbinic learning and Jewish education more broadly. These interests were already apparent in Bacher's 1903 essay "**Das altjüdische Schulwesen.**" This essay surveyed late biblical and rabbinic sources in order to reconstruct the origins, institutions and methods of Jewish education in the Second Temple and Talmudic periods. Bacher located the origins of Jewish primary education in the Hasmonean period, rather than the 1st century C.E. and argued for the wide dissemination of scriptural knowledge among the Jews of antiquity. Sections of the essay dealt with techniques of teaching and learning, discipline, the organization of schools and the school day, the use of private tutors, and teachers' salaries.

While some of its conclusions and methodological assumptions are flawed, Bacher's essay drew scholarly attention to basic and enduring aspects of rabbinic and ancient Jewish culture: the cultivation and transmission of learning. In her 1931 book on Jewish education in the Talmudic period, Towa Perlow cited Bacher's work approvingly before developing her own detailed account of the historical growth of elementary Jewish education based on rabbinic and non-rabbinic materials.[35] Catherine Hezser has traced the conjunction of Greco-Roman educational practices and specifically Jewish alternatives.[36] Most recently, Marc Hirshman has explored the ideals and practices of Jewish learning that developed under rabbinic leadership in the first centuries C.E.[37] In an Appendix,[38] Hirshman reviews the major contributions to the study of Jewish education in the rabbinic period, including work by Shmuel Safrai, David Goodblatt, Isaiah Gafni, and

---

35 Towa Perlow, *L'éducation et l'enseignment chez les Juifs a l'époque talmudique* (Paris: Leroux, 1931).
36 Catherine Hezser, "Private and Public Education" in *The Oxford Handbook of Jewish Daily Life*, ed. Catherine Hezser (Oxford: Oxford University Press, 2010), 465–81.
37 Marc Hirshman, *Stabilization of Rabbinic Culture, 100 C.E. – 350 C.E.: Texts on Education and Their Late Antique Context* (New York: Oxford University Press, 2012).
38 "A Survey of Secondary Literature on Education and Literacy in Rabbinic Literature" in Hirschman, *Stabilization*, 121–6.

Haim Shapira,[39] and volumes of collected essays.[40] In recent years, scholarship on rabbinic learning has benefited from the insights of orality studies, a focus on questions of literacy, and a fuller integration of recent work on Greco-Roman *paideia*, as seen in the important studies of Martin Jaffee, Yaakov Elman, Yaakov Sussman, and especially Catherine Hezser.[41]

In their quest to uncover the origins of rabbinic Judaism and *halakhah*, scholars have turned their attention to the two primary modalities of rabbinic learning and what those modalities might tell us about the status of Torah and tradition in Second Temple Judaism and about the emergence of a rabbinic class. Those two modalities are *midrash halakhah* (learning arising from the interpretation of Scripture) and the form adopted in the Mishnah and Tosefta (free-standing legal teachings not explicitly derived from interpretation of Scripture). In 1958, Ephraim Elimelekh Urbach (1912–1991) published "**The Derashah as the Basis for the Halakhah and the Problem of the Soferim**," which surveyed and critiqued prevailing theories of the interpretation of Scripture by Second Temple period scribes and the relationship of the scribes' legal interpretation to that of the rabbinic sages.

Urbach is best known for his monumental work *The Sages: Their Concepts and Beliefs* (Hebrew edition, 1969)[42] and *The Halakhah: Its Sources and Development* (1986) which employ a philological-historical method to examine rabbinic thought and *halakhah* with attention to their institutional and cultural context. In his 1958 article included here, Urbach concurred with those who traced midrashic activity to the early Second Temple period. However, he took issue with those who assumed that later rabbinic *midrash* was a relatively untroubled continuation of Second Temple legal interpretation and that this basic continuity paved the way for the post-destruction emergence to authority of the rabbis. Urbach drew a distinction between early *halakhah* emerging from the institutions of government and the

---

39 See Shmuel Safrai, "Education and the Study of Torah" in S. Safrai and M. Stern (eds.), *Compendia Rerum Iudaicarum ad Novum Testamentum: The Jewish People in the First Century* (Philadelphia, PA: Fortress Press, 1974), 945–70; David Goodblatt, *Rabbinic Instruction in Sasanian Babylonia* (Leiden: Brill, 1975); Isaiah Gafni, *The Jews of Babylonia in the Talmudic Era: A Social and Cultural History* [in Hebrew] (Jerusalem: Merkaz Zalman Shazar, 1990), 177–236; and Haim Shapira, "*Beit ha-Midrash* (The House of Study) During the Late Second Temple Period and the Age of the Mishnah: Institutional and Ideological Aspects," (Hebrew), Ph.D. dissertation, Hebrew University, 2002.

40 H.Z. Dimitrovsky, ed., *Exploring the Talmud* (New York: Ktav, 1976), and M. Aberbach, ed., *Jewish Education in the Period of the Mishna and the Talmud* (Jerusalem, 1982).

41 See Martin Jaffee, *Torah in the Mouth: Writing and Oral Tradition in Palestinian Judaism 200 BCE–400 CE* (Oxford: Oxford University Press, 2001); Yaakov Elman, *Transmitting Jewish Traditions: Orality, Textuality, and Cultural Diffusion* (New York: Yale University Press, 2000); Yaakov Sussman, "Torah Shebe'al Peh" in *Mehqerei Talmud III: Talmudic Studies Dedicated to the Memory of Professor Ephraim E. Urbach*, ed. Y. Sussman and D. Rosenthal (Jerusalem: Magnes Press, 2005), 209–384; and Catherine Hezser, *Jewish Literacy in Roman Palestine* (Tübingen: Mohr Siebeck, 2001).

42 Jerusalem: Magnes Press, 1975.

judiciary of the time (the free-standing decrees and enactments of the High Priest, the elders and sages, the courts and Sanhedrin) and the work of scribes who were engaged in preserving, transcribing and expounding the biblical text. He likened the scribes to the Greek grammarians who expounded the works of Homer in 3rd century B.C.E. Alexandria. According to Urbach, the idea of textual exegesis as a source of law developed only gradually and was still a point of debate in the first century C.E. as may be seen by Hillel's appeal to both textual legal *midrash* and the authority of tradition in his discussion with the sons of Bathrya. After the destruction, midrashic techniques for determining the law became increasingly important and eventually the entire Oral Torah was subordinated to the scriptural text by exegetical processes. Urbach argued that the controversy between the Pharisees and the Sadducees lay not in their rival exegeses, as widely supposed, but in their different approaches to the oral tradition and its relation to Scripture. Several of the issues addressed in this essay – the origins of *midrash*, the relation of *midrash* and mishnah, the rival approaches of the Pharisees and the Sadducees, and Second Temple biblical interpretation and its relation to rabbinic interpretative practices – continue to exercise scholars to this day.[43]

Interest in the origins of *halakhah* drew scholars to study the primary texts of *midrash halakhah*, which contain rabbinic interpretations of the (primarily) legal portions of the Pentateuch. Late 19th- and early 20th-century scholars, such as Israel Levy, Solomon Schechter, H. S. Horovitz, and David Hoffman, labored to produce critical editions of the major Halakhic Midrashim and to reconstruct lost works from medieval citations and manuscript fragments. In the opening pages

---

[43] On the origins of *midrash*, see Paul Mandel, "The Origins of Midrash in the Second Temple Period" in *Current Trends in the Study of Midrash*, ed. Carol Bakhos (Leiden: Brill, 2006) and Mandel, "Legal Midrash Between Hillel and Rabbi Akiva: Did 70 Make a Difference?" in *Was 70 CE a Watershed in Jewish History?: On Jews and Judaism before and after the Destruction of the Second Temple*, ed. Daniel R. Schwartz and Zeev Weiss with Ruth A. Clements (Leiden: Brill 2012). On the relation of *midrash* and *mishnah*, see David Weiss Halivni, "*Midrash, Mishnah, and Gemara: The Jewish Predilection for Justified Law* (Cambridge, MA: Harvard University Press, 1986). On the rival approaches of the Pharisees and the Sadducees, see Aharon Shemesh, "The Laws of Incest in the Dead Sea Scrolls and the History of Halakhah" in *Halakhah in Light of Epigraphy*, JAJSup 3 (Göttingen: Vandenhoeck & Ruprecht, 2011), 81–99. On biblical interpretation in the Second Temple period, see Michael Fishbane, "The Role of Scribes in the Transmission of Biblical Literature" in *Biblical Interpretation in Ancient Israel* (New York: Oxford, 1985), 24–37 and "From Scribalism to Rabbinism: Perspectives on the Emergence of Classical Judaism" in *The Sage in Israel and the Ancient Near East*, ed. J.G. Gammie and L.G. Perdue (Winona Lake, IN: Eisenbrauns, 1990); and Adiel Schremer, "'[T]he[y] Did Not Read in the Sealed Book': Qumran Halakhic Revolution and the Emergence of Torah Study in Second Temple Judaism'" in *Historical Perspectives From the Hasmoneans to Bar Kokhba in Light of the Dead Sea Scrolls*, ed. D.M. Goodblatt, A. Pinnick, and D.R. Schwartz (Leiden: Brill, 2001). On the relation of Second Temple and rabbinic biblical interpretation, see James Kugel, *Traditions of the Bible: A Guide to the Bible As it Was at the Start of the Common Era* (Cambridge, MA: Harvard University Press, 1998); Yonah Fraenkel, *Darkei ha-Aggadah veha-Midrash* (Givatayim: Yad la-Talmud, 1990) and *Midrash veAggadah* (Tel Aviv: Open University, 1997).

of *Zur Einleitung in die halachischen Midraschim* (only a portion of which is translated for the present volume) published in 1888, David Hoffman proposed a division of the works of Halakhic Midrashim into two groups, or schools, based on differences in exegetical terminology, the names of the sages, exegetical method, and correspondences between anonymous teachings in the midrashim and attributed teachings in parallel texts. According to Hoffmann, a complete *midrash* on the books of Exodus through Deuteronomy was produced by the school of R. Akiva (the Mekhilta deRabbi Shimon bar Yohai, the Sifra, Sifre Zuta and Sifre Deuteronomy) and another by the school of R. Yishmael (the Mekhilta deRabbi Yishmael, fragments of a commentary on Leviticus incorporated in the Sifra, Sifre Numbers and a Mekhilta to Deuteronomy, or Midrash Tannaim). Hoffman was instrumental in reconstructing some of these lost midrashim on the basis of citations in later works. The labor of reconstruction has occupied many scholars to the present day. Most recently, a project spearheaded by Michal Bar-Asher Siegal, Moshe Koppel and Avi Shmidman offers a reconstruction of the early Mekhilta to Deuteronomy from the later Midrash HaGadol using both philological and computational tools.

No serious scholar of the Halakhic Midrashim can avoid reckoning with Hoffmann's two schools thesis. Y.N. Epstein accepted and sharpened Hoffmann's basic distinction by defining the unique character of each school;[44] Hanoch Albeck objected that differences existed not in substance or method but in terminology only and were therefore a product of late-stage redaction rather than two distinct schools in tannaitic times;[45] and Finkelstein argued for an original core common to the schools of R. Akiva and R. Yishmael.[46] Yet, despite qualifications and criticisms, Hoffman's basic division has had remarkable staying power. Menahem Kahana concludes from his extensive research on these texts that the difference between the schools in substance, exegetical terms, and names, is expressed in the halakhic sections but is hardly visible in the aggadic sections.[47] Recently, Azzan Yadin has argued that the R. Akiva/R. Yishmael distinction should not be understood as a claim of historical authorship but as shorthand for a set of distinct and recognizable interpretive practices, assumptions and terms that appear in the halakhic sections of these works.[48] Yadin's research has illuminated two distinct

---

[44] Y.N. Epstein, *Introduction to Tannaitic Literature* (Hebrew) (Jerusalem, 1948).

[45] Hanokh Albeck, *Untersuchungen über die halakischen Midraschim* (Berlin, 1927).

[46] Louis Finkelstein, "The Sources of the Tannaitic Midrashim," i *JQR* n.s. 31 (1940–1941), 211–43.

[47] Menahem Kahana, "The Halakhic Midrashim" in *Literature of the Sages*, Part 2, *CRINT* (Amsterdam: Royal Van Gorcum and Fortress Press, 2006) and Kahana, *The Two Mekhiltot on the Amalek Portion: The Originality of the Version of the Mekhilta d'Rabbi Ishmael with Respect to the Mekhilta of Rabbi Shim'on ben Yohay* (Jerusalem: Magnes Press, 1999) [Hebrew].

[48] Azzan Yadin, *Scripture as Logos: Rabbi Ishmael and the Origins of Midrash* (Philadelphia, PA: University of Pennsylvania Press, 2004) and "Resistance to Midrash? Midrash and Halakhah in the Halakhic Midrashim" in Bakhos, ed., *Current Trends*, 35–58.

interpretive ideologies in tannaitic literature regarding the relationship of *midrash* to extra-scriptural *halakhah*.

As continuing research uncovered the rich complexity of Jewish society in late antique Palestine, the origins of various Jewish groups and their evolving inter-relationships increasingly occupied scholarly attention. Of particular interest was the question of the origin and character of the Second Temple Pharisees and their relation to the rabbinic sages. In 1936, Solomon Zeitlin (d. 1976) published *Ha-Tsadoqim veha-Perushim: Pereq behitpathut ha-Halakhah* (Horeb, III:5–6, 56–89) describing the halakhic, social and religious differences between the Pharisees and the Sadducees as expressed in Talmudic literature. He returned to the question of the Pharisees in 1961 with an essay entitled "**The Pharisees: A Historical Study**" (*JQR* 52:2, pp. 97–129).

The Pharisees received unsympathetic treatment at the hands of Christian scholars due to their negative portrayal in the gospels and in patristic literature. Indeed, the very term Pharisee was synonymous with "hypocrite" and the idea that Pharisees might have been religiously sincere or devout was inconceivable. In his essay tracing the origins, beliefs and practices of the Pharisees, Zeitlin considered the various hypotheses for the rise of the name "Pharisee." He argued that in the absence of rabbinic evidence for hostility between Pharisees and persons lax in the observance of tithing laws and purity practices (the *am ha'aretz*, or ordinary Jew) or between Pharisees and Essenes, the name "Pharisee" must not have been adopted in order to signal a desire to be separate (*perush*) from other groups. According to Zeitlin, the term "Pharisee" was a derisive nickname bestowed upon the Pharisees by their opponents, the Sadducees, because in the view of the latter the Pharisees had separated themselves from God and Torah. This explains why the sages, though the successors of the Pharisees, did not apply the name to themselves in their voluminous literature. Zeitlin dated the emergence of the Pharisees to the period of the Restoration and described the controversy between Pharisees and Sadducees as centering on such issues as the divine origin and authority of the Oral Torah, the modification of the law, and attitudes to proselytes.

The questions addressed in Zeitlin's study, have been the subject of ongoing debate. Specifically, scholars have continued to investigate the reasons for the formation of sects in the Second Temple period; to attempt to account for the divergent evidence of Josephus and rabbinic sources regarding the issues dividing the sects; to ascertain the fate of the sects after the destruction; and to determine the relationship of the rabbinic sages not only to the Pharisees but to other Second Temple period groups.[49]

---

49 See for example, Albert Baumgarten, "The Name of the Pharisees," *JBL* 102:3 (1983), 411–28; Baumgarten, *The Flourishing of Jewish Sects in the Maccabean Era: An Interpretation*, Journal for the Study of Judaism in the Persian, Hellenistic and Roman Period, Supplement Series, Volume 55 (Leiden: Brill, 1997); and Baumgarten, *Second Temple Sectarianism: A Social and Religious Historical Essay* (Jerusalem: Ministry of Defense, 2001). See also Shaye Cohen "The Significance of Yavneh: Pharisees, Rabbis, and the End of Jewish Sectarianism," *Hebrew Union College Annual*

C. Rabbinic Contexts

The Judaism of the rabbinic period developed within the context of Greco-Roman and Byzantine civilization in the West and the Parthian and Sassanian Persian empires in the East. Few would deny that these host cultures influenced the course of Jewish history and the development of Jewish culture in the rabbinic period, but there has been little consensus on the nature and extent of this influence.

The question of Hellenization and the Jews in the Greco-Roman West has been debated for more than a century.[50] In the late 19th and early 20th centuries, many studies highlighted the evidence for Hellenistic contacts with and influences on Jews and Judaism.[51] The Talmudic scholar Saul Lieberman (1898–1983), was known for his path-breaking textual studies of the Palestinian Talmud (*Al Ha-Yerushalmi*, 1929; *Ha-Yerushalmi ki-Feshuto*, 1934; *Talmudah shel Qesarin*, 1931) and the Tosefta (*Tosefet Rishonim*, 1937–39; *Tashlum Tosefta*, 1937; and *Tosefta Ki-Feshuta*, 1955 to 1967). Nevertheless, his extensive knowledge of Classical Greek language and literature, patristic literature and Roman history combined with his deep knowledge of rabbinic texts to shed light on the life, institutions, literary output, textual practices and ideas of Jewish Palestine in the period of the Talmuds. The collection of articles published in *Greek in Jewish Palestine* (1942) and *Hellenism in Jewish Palestine* (1950), illustrate the influence of Greco-Roman culture on the rabbis. In the words of Seth Schwartz, "[h]is main legacy was in contributing to a form of scholarship on ancient Judaism according to which the Jews did not react to the destruction with resistance and self enclosure but with creative engagement with the majority culture."[52]

In the early 1940s, Lieberman published an important essay entitled "**The Martyrs of Caesarea**." He used the essay to argue that Talmudic literature is a valuable source for historical information *about the events of its own time*, and to urge rabbinic scholars to draw upon a broader knowledge of the languages and cultures of late antiquity in order to derive maximum advantage from their sources. In demonstration of these desiderata, Lieberman painted a portrait of the relations among Jews, Christians, Samaritans and pagans in Roman Galilee on the basis of a close reading of both Talmudic texts and Eusebius' *De Martyribus*

---

55 (1984), 27–53 and the response of Daniel Boyarin, "A Tale of Two Synods: Nicaea, Yavneh, and Rabbinic Ecclesiology," *Exemplaria* 12 (2000), 21–62. More recently, see Shaye Cohen, *From the Maccabees to the Mishnah* (Louisville, KY: Westminster John Knox Press, 2006) and Jonathan Klawans, *Josephus and the Theologies of Ancient Judaism* (New York: Oxford University Press, 2012).

50 A detailed survey of the scholars in this debate may be found in the first chapter of Lee I. Levines's *Judaism and Hellenism in Antiquity: Conflict or Confluence* (Seattle, WA: University of Washington Press, 1998: 3–32). Our discussion will center on the scholars whose essays are included in this volume, beginning with Saul Lieberman (1898–1983).

51 An important early contribution was Samuel Krauss's *Griechische und Lateinische Lehnwörter im Talmud, Midrasch, und Targum* (Berlin, 1898–1899).

52 Seth Schwartz, "Historiography," p. 98.

Palaestinae, as well as linguistic analysis of Greek, Latin, and Aramaic terms. Lieberman responded to criticisms of the article in 1946[53] and published a greatly reworked version as "*Redifat Dat Yisrael*" (Hebrew) in the Salo Wittmayer Baron Jubilee Volume.[54] Despite some well-deserved criticisms, the original 1944 essay, reproduced here, challenged historians of the Talmudic period to utilize the riches of classical culture and a wide range of comparative tools in their study of rabbinic texts.

In his 1949, article "**Rabbinic Methods of Interpretation and Hellenistic Rhetoric**" David Daube argued for the indebtedness of Talmudic jurisprudence to Hellenistic rhetoric. Daube (1909–1999) was a legal scholar who made highly original and inter-disciplinary contributions to the fields of biblical law and literature, Greek and Latin literature, Roman law, New Testament and Talmudic law. In this essay, Daube focused on the figure of Hillel, his theory of the relation between statute, tradition, and interpretation, and his seven norms of legal interpretation. According to Daube, in both theory and practice, Hillel's norms of interpretation betray the influence of the rhetorical teachings of the age and find parallels in non-Jewish argumentation (especially Stoic writers and Cicero). This essay was followed four years later by "Alexandrian Methods of Interpretation and the Rabbis" (in Festschrift Hans Lewald [Basel, 1953]) in which Daube argued that the rabbinic mode of interpretation known as *seres* originated in both substance and name in Alexandria, and the rabbinic term *hekhre'a* derived from a particular Hellenistic treatment of Greek syntax.

The article drew a response from Saul Lieberman. In 1950, Lieberman published *Hellenism in Jewish Palestine: Studies in the Literary Transmission, Beliefs, and Manners of Palestine in the 1st Century BCE-IV Century CE* and included a chapter entitled "Rabbinic Interpretation of Scripture" in which he acknowledged some of the parallels highlighted by Daube, but argued against Daube's claim of overt borrowing. According to Lieberman, it is only the terminology that is on occasion borrowed by the rabbis. The methods of interpretation employed by the rabbis show no definitive sign of Greek influence and are likely rooted in long-standing interpretative practices. The Hebrew terminology for these methods is often a translation of equivalent Greek terms; Greek influence may be broad, but it is not deep.

Daniel Patte outlines the positions of Daube and Lieberman in *Early Jewish Hermeneutic in Palestine* (Missoula, MT: Scholars Press, 1975), 113–15, and the debate over these two positions continues to the present day.[55] In the 1980s and 1990s, Daube's position was endorsed by William Horbury and Philip Alexander[56]

---

53 Saul Liebermn, "The Martyrs of Caesarea," *JQR* 36 (1945–1946), 239–53.
54 Saul Lieberman, ed. (Jerusalem: American Academy for Jewish Research, 1975).
55 See further the discussion in Michael L. Chernick, *Hermeneutical Studies in Talmudic and Midrashic Literature* (Lod: Haberman Institute, 1984).
56 Philip Alexander, "'Quid Athenis et Hierosolymis? Rabbinic Midrash and Hermeneutics in the Graeco-Roman World" in *A Tribute to Geza Vermes: Essays on Jewish and Christian Literature*

while Stephen J. Lieberman sided with Saul Lieberman and asserted the Ancient Near Eastern roots of rabbinic interpretive techniques.[57] More recently, Richard Hidary has argued for a deep rabbinic familiarity with, and adaptation of, Hellenistic interpretative, rhetorical and forensic practices,[58] and Maren Niehoff has examined Alexandrian Jewish Bible exegesis in the light of the textual and interpretative practices of Homeric scholarship.[59]

The issue of Hellenization featured prominently in the work of another scholar active in the middle of the 20th century. Elias Bickerman (1897–1981) was a historian of the Second Temple period whose research provided new insights on the Maccabees, the Pharisees and Jewish attitudes towards Gentiles. One of Bickerman's major contributions was to highlight the extent to which Palestinian Judaism was Hellenized. As Shaye J.D. Cohen has noted in regard to both *The God of the Maccabees* (Berlin, 1937) and *From Ezra to the Last of the Maccabees* (New York, 1962), Bickerman was "the first to show that the Maccabees were *not* 'anti-Hellenistic,' but were prepared to draw upon the riches of Hellenistic culture so long as Judaism would be enriched, not threatened, by the process." Not only did Bickerman demonstrate "the Maccabean willingness to incorporate the ways of the Greeks," he "advanced the same thesis for the rabbis of the Talmud."[60] His 1952 essay "**La chaîne de la tradition pharisienne**," on the chain of tradition found in Mishnah Avot 1, exemplified this claim. Bickerman began with the observation that the chain of rabbinic tradition set forth in Mishnah Avot 1 (stretching from Moses through the prophets, the men of the Great Assembly, the 'pairs' and finally the rabbis and the Hillelide Patriarchs) is highly unusual and in need of explanation. He argued that the "chain of tradition" form was adapted from succession lists composed in Greek philosophical academies. The purpose of this form was to bolster the authority of the rabbis as the sole interpreters of Torah at the expense of the priests: the chain replaced the priestly model of inherited authority with a paideic model of master–disciple transmission characteristic of the rabbinic class. Employing a hermeneutic of suspicion to pierce the rhetoric of insularity and even hostility to Greek culture, Bickerman showed

---

and History, ed. Philip R. Davies and Richard T. White, Journal for the Study of the Old Testament, Supplement Series 100 (Sheffield: JSOT, 1990), 101–24.

57 Stephen Lieberman, "A Mesopotamian Background for the So-Called '*Aggadic* Measures' of Biblical Hermeneutics?" *HUCA* 58 (1987), 157–225.

58 Richard Hidary, "Classical Rhetorical Arrangement and Reasoning in the Talmud: The Case of Yerushalmi Berakhot 1:1," AJS Review 34:1 (2010), 33–64. Also, Hidary, "The Agonistic Bavli: Greco-Roman Rhetoric in Sasanian Persia" in *Shoshannat Yaakov: Jewish and Iranian Studies in Honor of Yaakov Elman*, ed. Shai Secunda and Steven Fine (Leiden: Brill, 2012) and *Rabbis and Classical Rhetoric: Sophistic Education and Oratory in the Talmud and Midrash* (Cambridge: Cambridge University Press, 2017).

59 Maren Niehoff, *Jewish Exegesis and Homeric Scholarship in Alexandria* (Cambridge and New York: Cambridge University Press, 2011).

60 Shaye J.D. Cohen, "Elias J. Bickerman: An Appreciation," *Jewish Book Annual* 40 (1982–1983), 162–5.

"that ancient Judaism was part of the ancient world and had to be interpreted in the light of the host culture."[61]

The 1950s and 1960s saw further contributions to the question of Hellenization and the Jews. In 1956, Morton Smith published **"Palestinian Judaism in the First Century,"**[62] a brief but compelling exposition of the Hellenization of Palestinian Judaism. Smith was a scholar of ancient history whose interests spanned biblical Israel, ancient Judaism, Greco-Roman religion, New Testament and early Christianity. In this essay, Smith declared that first-century Palestine was "profoundly Hellenized and that the Hellenization extended even to the basic structure of much Rabbinic thought" (71). How then, he asked, are the rabbis who appear in rabbinic writings to be situated within the wider context of Palestinian Judaism? What part did they play in the history of the period? Smith went on to argue that the rabbis (whom he identifies with the Pharisees) were neither unopposed nor united, as Jewish society contained a number of sects. Moreover, "[t]he average Palestinian Jew of the first century was probably the *'am ha'areṣ*, any member of the class which made up the "people of the land," a biblical phrase probably used to mean *hoi polloi* (73)." These "ordinary Jews" were not without religion but they did not follow Pharisaic rules. The apparent dominance of the Pharisees is the result of their representation in rabbinic sources and in the writings of Josephus. Applying a hermeneutic of suspicion to these texts, Smith argued that the role of the Pharisees prior to the destruction had been exaggerated. Smith concluded the essay by reiterating his basic thesis: Palestinian Judaism in the first century emerged from a long period of thoroughgoing Hellenization. If there was an "orthodox" Judaism then it was not Pharisaism but the religion of the average "people of the land" (although, in truth, Smith has little use for such terms as "orthodox" or "normative"). A significant study advancing claims similar to Smith's was Martin Hengel's *Judaism and Hellenism* (German edition, 1969; English edition, 1974). Like Smith, Hengel argued that Jews and Judaism encountered significant Hellenistic influence in the third century B.C.E., an influence that permeated all strata of Jewish society. In recent times, Hayim Lapin has argued that the small rabbinic movement is best understood as a product of the provincial context of Roman Palestine rather than a natural development of Jewish national practices. He describes the rabbinic movement as "an association of religious experts claiming ancestral knowledge, employing a rhetoric of self-representation with affinities to Greco-Roman associations and especially to philosophical schools, and capable of using wider cultural motifs to their own ends."[63]

---

61 Ibid., 165.
62 In *Israel, Its Role in Civilization*, ed. M. Davis (New York: JTSA, 1956), 67–81.
63 Hayim Lapin, "The Origins and Development of the Rabbinic Movement in the Land of Israel" in *The Cambridge History of Judaism*, ed. Steven T. Katz (1st edn, Cambridge: Cambridge University Press, 2006) vol. 4, p. 225. These ideas find full development and exposition in Lapin's recent book *Rabbis as Romans: The Rabbinic Movement in Palestine, 100–400 C.E.* (New York: Oxford University Press, 2012).

Morton Smith's claim that Palestinian Judaism was thoroughly Hellenized went hand-in-hand with his skepticism about the scope of Pharisaic-rabbinic influence. These ideas were also held by Erwin R. Goodenough, though the latter scholar approached the issue from an entirely different direction.

In the 1920s, Goodenough became convinced that the Hellenistic elements of early Christianity derived from an already Hellenized Judaism. He located this Hellenized Judaism in the artistic record uncovered by archaeology. Since rabbinic Judaism objected to figural art, it stood to reason that such figural art as existed held the key to understanding a non-rabbinic (or Hellenized) Judaism. Goodenough's portrait of Hellenized Judaism, a counterpoint to George Foot Moore's portrait of rabbinic Judaism, was thus based on an impressive assemblage of previously neglected and often misunderstood archaeological material. In his monumental and multi-volume *Jewish Symbols in the Greco-Roman Period* (New York: Pantheon Books, 1953–64), Goodenough explained the symbols in ancient Jewish art in light of both universal psychology (drawing on Jungian psychology) and the symbolism common to Hellenistic religions of antiquity. Properly understood, he argued, these symbols point to the existence of a mystical Judaism like that evident in the writings of Philo. The first three volumes of *Jewish Symbols* (1953) provoked a storm of protest from those who objected both to Goodenough's interpretation of the artwork and his claim that since the rabbis would have been violently opposed to figural art, its existence means they must have lacked the authority to control or prevent its production and use. According to Urbach, the rabbis would have had no objection to purely decorative uses of figurative art and its existence does not signal their marginality.[64]

In 1961, Goodenough responded to his detractors in an article entitled "**The Rabbis and Jewish Art in the Greco-Roman Period.**" In this article, he forcefully reasserted his notion of a mystical Hellenized Judaism attested in the writings of Philo, before defending his interpretation of Jewish art in the Greco-Roman period. The symbols in this artwork, he argued, cannot be dismissed as purely decorative. Their presence attests to a mystical religiosity that rejected rabbinic Judaism, and forces a reconsideration of the authority of the rabbis in this period.

Morton Smith was sympathetic to certain aspects of Goodenough's work, which he considered important and revolutionary, but he was critical of other aspects. In his 1967 essay, "**Goodenough's Jewish Symbols in Retrospect**," Smith took issue with Goodenough's portrait of a mystical Hellenistic Judaism that stood in dichotomous opposition to rabbinic Judaism. Certainly, the material assembled by Goodenough pointed to a Jewish religiosity different from that of the rabbis – a topic taken up by scholars of Jewish mysticism, such as Peter Schäfer and some

---

64 E.E. Urbach, "The Rabbinical Laws of Idolatry in the Second and Third Centuries in the Light of Archaeological and Historical Facts," *Israel Exploration Journal* 9:3 (1959), 149–65 and 9:4 (1959), 229–45.

of his students,[65] and Jewish magic, such as Gideon Bohak[66] – but it was not at all clear to Smith that hostility existed between the rabbis and the Jewish producers and consumers of figural art.

Despite its errors and binary assumptions, the work of Goodenough has had a profound and lasting influence, particularly as mediated by Morton Smith, many of whose students – Jacob Neusner, Lee Levine, Shaye J.D. Cohen and Seth Schwartz – have accepted Goodenough's skepticism about the scope of rabbinic Judaism in late antique Palestine.[67] As Steven Fine writes "Goodenough's unique contribution to scholarship is found in the paradigm shift that his counter history generated. *Jewish Symbols* sparked two generations of scholars to actively seek out alternate voices in the extant sources, both archaeological and literary. This in itself is a major contribution."[68]

Two years after Morton Smith's review of Goodenough's *Jewish Symbols*, Henry Fischel (1913– 2008), following in the footsteps of David Daube, published an article that posited connections between rabbinic *midrash* and the larger Greco-Roman world. In "**Story and History: Observations on Greco-Roman rhetoric and Pharisaism**" (1969), Fischel noted similarities between rabbinic stories about sages (particularly the stories about Hillel the Elder) and Greco-Roman stories about *sophoi* (sages). This type of story, known as a *chreia* (in Greek) or *chria* (in Latin), depicts an encounter in which the sage's wit and/or wisdom are revealed. The stories have the same function in both literatures – to elevate the founder-sage about whom the story is told. According to Fischel, this parallel constituted evidence of the Hellenization of the Pharisees, who resembled Hellenistic sages as a class and functioned as an elite scholarly bureaucracy. At the same time, the Pharisees adapted the *chreia* to their own purposes – to celebrate their own heroes and spread Torah. While some scholars denied the similarity highlighted by Fischel, Catherine Hezser has supported Fischel's basic

---

65 See for example, Peter Schäfer, *The Origins of Jewish Mysticism* (Tübingen: Mohr Siebeck, 2009).
66 Gideon Bohak, *Ancient Jewish Magic: A History* (Cambridge: Cambridge University Press, 2008).
67 To varying degrees, these scholars assume a rabbinic marginality and are skeptical of the rabbis' self-presentation. These ideas became the cornerstone of Jacob Neusner's work. In the 1970s, Neusner began to insist upon a high degree of skepticism regarding the utility of rabbinic sources for the purposes of historical reconstruction, preferring an emphasis on form-criticism and tradition-criticism in the analysis of rabbinic texts. Neusner's skepticism has challenged subsequent scholars to prove rather than assume the suitability of historical approaches to rabbinic literature. In this connection, see the work of Richard Kalmin, *Sages, Stories*, and Christine Hayes, *Between the Babylonian*. On the social location of the rabbis see S.J.D. Cohen, "The Place of the Rabbi in Jewish Society of the Second Century" in *The Galilee in Late Antiquity*, ed. Lee I. Levine (New York and Jerusalem; JTS, 1992) 157–73; Lee I. Levine, *The Rabbinic Class of Roman Palestine in Late Antiquity* (Jerusalem and New York: Yad Izhak Ben-Zvi and JTS, 1989) 98–195; and Levine, "The Sages and the Synagogue in Late Antiquity: The Evidence of the Galilee" in Lee Levine, *Galilee in Late Antiquity*, op. cit., 201–33. For a more recent discussion, see Catherine Hezser, *The Social Structure of the Rabbinic Movement in Roman Palestine* (Tübingen: Mohr Siebeck, 1997), 214–24.
68 Steven Fine, *Art and Judaism in the Greco-Roman World: Toward a New Jewish Archaeology* (Cambridge: Cambridge University Press, 2005), 45.

conclusions and pointed to additional literary forms that appear in both rabbinic and philosophical texts.[69]

Scholars arguing for the Hellenization of Jews and other provincials in the Greco-Roman period have continually encountered resistance to the idea of "influence": Alon was critical of Lieberman; Urbach, Baumgarten, and Blidstein dismissed Goodenough's work; Louis Feldman, Moshe David Herr, and Saul Tcherikover objected to Hengel's claims. Some of these scholars doubted Hellenization altogether while others argued over its extent and reach, leading proponents of the Hellenization thesis to avoid the term "influence" when describing the collocations and interactions of Jews, Greeks and others in late antiquity.[70]

The scientific study of Judaism called for the investigation of rabbinic literature as the product of a historical time and place. Palestinian rabbinic literature benefited from the classical training of the early practitioners of Wissenschaft and a concentrated focus on the Greco-Roman environment of Roman provincial Palestine. The Babylonian Talmud fared less well. Few scholars were equipped to explore the cultural, religious and linguistic milieu of Sasanian Iran. Nevertheless, some took up the study of Persian, Sassanian history and Iranian religion. A pioneer in this area was Alexander Kohut, whose *Arukh ha-Shalem* (1878–1892) updated the *Arukh* of Nathan b. Yehiel of Rome and provided numerous Persian loanwords and etymologies. In 1871, Kohut published "**Die talmudisch-midraschische Adamssage in ihrer Ruckbeziehung auf die persische Yima und Meshiasage,**" one in a series of articles exploring the relationship between Judaism and Zoroastrianism and broaching the (then sensitive) question of Zoroastrian influence.

Shai Secunda provides a brief survey of the subsequent generations of scholars who continued to research the content, nature and extent of Iranian and rabbinic intersections, including the historical work, *Die Juden in Babylonien, 200–500* of Salomen Funk.[71] A new era in the study of the Babylonian Talmud in its Sasanian context was ushered in by Yaakov Elman whose many articles explore the impact of Persian culture on every level of Babylonian Jewish culture.[72] Today, Elman's students and others, equipped with the requisite linguistic and textual skills, are shedding new light on the world of the Babylonian Talmud.[73] The school

---

69 Catherine Hezser, "Interfaces between Rabbinic Literature and Graeco-Roman Philosophy" in *The Talmud Yerushalmi in its Graeco-Roman Context*, vol. 2, ed. Peter Schäfer and Catherine Hezser (Tubingen: Mohr Siebeck, 2000), 161–88.
70 See Michael Satlow's very important and influential (!) "Beyond Influence: Toward a New Historiographic Paradigm" in *Jewish Literatures and Cultures: Context and Intertext*, ed. Anita Norich and Yaron Z. Eliav (Providence, RI: Brown University Press, 2008), 37–53.
71 Shai Secunda, *The Iranian Talmud: Reading the Bavli in its Sasanian Context* (Philadelphia, PA: University of Pennsylvania, 2013), 10–14. Readers are referred to this survey for further bibliography.
72 See the many works cited in Secunda, op. cit., 153n38.
73 See for example, Shai Secunda, *The Iranian Talmud*; Geoffrey Hermann, *Prince without a Kingdom: The Exilarch in the Sasanian Era* (Tübingen: Mohr Siebeck, 2012); Yishai Kiel,

of Irano-Talmudica has not been without its critics. While some criticism has been dismissive,[74] other criticism has been constructive, encouraging a fuller investigation of the Sasanian context so as to include not merely Zoroastrian sources (which present a host of methodological problems) but Syriac Christian, Manichaean, and other sources (including Hellenistic materials imported from the West) that are known to have circulated in the Sasanid East. In this category, we may point to the scholarship of Yishai Kiel, Richard Kalmin, Yakir Paz, Sara Ronis, Aaron Butts and Simcha Gross.[75]

* * *

This volume owes its final shape to many individuals. I would like to thank my students Yoni Pomeranz and Sara Ronis for their invaluable research assistance. I would never have arrived at this particular selection of essays without their detective work. I would also like to thank James Redfield, Eva Kiesele and Erin Brust for their excellent translation work, Elisa Ronzheimer for casting a trained eye over the translations from German, and Travis Tzadeh for assistance with the Arabic in the Kohut article. I am indebted to Prods Oktor Skjærvø for his erudite revisions and comments to the Kohut essay. This essay has been more thoroughly updated and annotated than the others in light of the current rebirth of interest in Irano-Talmudica. Needless to say, bringing the Kohut article into the 21st century would never have been possible without the vast linguistic and textual expertise of Professor Skjærvø.

"Cognizance of Sin and Penalty in the Babylonian Talmud and Pahlavi Literature: A Comparative Analysis," *Oqimta* 1 (2013), 1–49, and Kiel, "The Systematization of Penitence in Zoroastrianism in Light of Rabbinic and Islamic Literature," *Bulletin of the Asia Institute* 22 (2008) [2012], 119–35; Jason Mokhtarian, *Rabbis, Sorcerers, Kings and Priests: The Culture of the Talmud in Ancient Iran* (Oakland, CA: University of California Press, 2015); Jeffrey Rubenstein is also producing work in this vein. See for example, his article "King Herod in Ardashir's Court: The Rabbinic Story of Herod (B. Bava Batra 3b–4a) in light of Persian Sources," *AJS Review* 38 (2014) 2:249–74.

74 See Robert Brody, "Irano-Talmudica: The New Parallelomania?" *Jewish Studies Quarterly* 106:2 (2016), 209–32.

75 Yishai Kiel, *Sexuality in the Babylonian Talmud: Christian and Sasanian Contexts in Late Antiquity* (Cambridge: Cambridge University Press, 2016); Richard Kalmin, "The Bavli, the Roman East, and Mesopotamian Christianity," *Jewish Studies Quarterly* 106:2 (2016), 242–7 and Kalmin, *Migrating Tales: The Talmud's Narratives and Their Historical Contexts* (Oakland, CA: University of California Press, 2014); Sara Ronis, "'Do Not Go Out Alone at Night': Law and Demonic Discourse in the Babylonian Talmud," Ph.D. Dissertation, Yale University, 2015; Simcha Gross, "Irano-Talmudica and Beyond: Next Steps in the Contextualization of the Babylonian Talmud," *Jewish Studies Quarterly* 106:2 (2016), 248–55, and Gross, "Empire and Neighbors: Babylonian Jewish Persecution in its Imperial and Local Contexts," Ph.D. Dissertation, Yale University, 2016.

Part I

Rabbinic History – Sources, Methods and Meaning

REMARKS ON RABBINIC LITERATURE, FOLLOWED BY A NOTICE ON AN OLD, PREVIOUSLY UNPUBLISHED HEBREW WORK*

Leopold Zunz (Berlin 1818, Mauerer Booksellers)

Translated by James Redfield

Foreword

"Anyone can praise," says Nushirvan, "but it is a good deal harder to criticize in a well-reasoned and humble manner."[1] As there is more at stake in my text than my self-esteem, and more in science than both together, I entreat the thoughtful expert to tell me in his review what has gone wrong with the essay at hand – mine, that is, as I do acknowledge it to be.

In this foreword, I speak of myself in the singular, and in the little work itself, in the plural – not in order to satisfy the nigglers from both camps, but because I believe it is only in documents, travelogues and memoirs, checks, prolegomena, objections, blurbs, receipts, counter-critiques, hotel bills, etc., that the writer comes through *as a person*. He uses I with good humor, yet still manages to go beyond himself; when expounding doctrine, he opts for the humble "we," thereby casting his lot with the whole battalion of officers who take to the field of battle for the sake of voiceless science.

Finally, I must beg forgiveness from the reader of this text for all its typographical errors. The author's coincidental displacement caused them to travel from the

---

* This translation of the main text and most footnotes was completed by James Redfield and reviewed by Elisa Ronzheimer, with translation of additional footnotes by Christine Hayes. The footnotes contain allusions to many secondary works, not all of which are easily identified or available. Some have been omitted, while full bibliographic information for others has been added by Christine Hayes. Some footnotes have been abbreviated while others deemed more decorative than substantive have been omitted altogether. Comments and corrections are also set in square brackets and the author identified by initials: JR = James Redfield and CH = Christine Hayes.

1 "Anecdoten zu Nushirvan's Leben," in A.G. Meissner, *Erzählungen*, Vienna, 1813, II:77.

attached corrections into the text itself; any good reader will fix them ahead of time, and not shirk this task.²

Bielefeld, May 1818.

> Primum hoc statuo esse virtutis conciliare animos hominum.
> [I set it down as the peculiar function of virtue to win the hearts of men.]
> (Cicero, *De Officiis* 2, 17)

Aside from the interest that age and content grant, the formidable remains of the ancient Hebrews' golden age owe their greatest importance to chance. Thanks to the revolutions which arose in the midst of the Jewish people and had their greatest impact on them, no less than on the rest of the globe, even the detritus which remained under the banner of the Hebrew canon was upheld as the foundations of the Christian states; from then on, the relentless progress of the sciences did its part to make even these few books into a haven for intellectual industry, one which is all the more astonishing than the Greeks' inasmuch as it has culled its riches from the flimsiest materials.

The Hebrew nation's later products, however, never attained such adulation. After plummeting from its political and intellectual heights, this nation seemed to have gradually lost its potency, contenting itself with the more or less adequate exegesis of a bygone era's writings. Yet as, little by little, the shadows of barbarism shrank from the benighted globe where the Jews were everywhere, of course the light also fell upon Jews everywhere. Thus a new, foreign education joined with the ancient Hebrews' remains and these, across many centuries and minds, were assembled into the literature that we call "rabbinic."³

With the Reformation, a necessary byproduct of the efflorescence of classical education, began a lively study of the biblical books; they were seized upon by a, we might say, restless curiosity to paw through the Orient, whereby rabbinic wisdom was beset for a century with a fervor that has suddenly faded and may never return, now that the fatherland's richer and more admirable products have begun to possess and exhilarate men's spirits. Yet rabbinic literature too began to sink in tandem with the rise of European literature as Jews became more closely connected with the latter. What was common property just a half-century ago has bequeathed only its language in the form of an accessible intellectual costume for ideas; ideas that stand only to pave the way for a time when rabbinic literature will have expired altogether.

Yet precisely because in our times we see the Jews – speaking, for the moment, only of the German Jews – so earnestly prizing German language and German

---

2 In this printing, the typographical errors were corrected in the text itself; therefore, the attached list is now superfluous.

3 This designates only texts whose authors or content are rabbinic; and in fact, "Rabbi", to which everyone accords courtesy, means a good deal less than "Doctor." So why not "neo-Hebraic" or "Jewish" literature?

education, and thereby – perhaps often without intending or realizing it – bearing witness to the burial of neo-Hebraic literature, science butts in and demands an itemized account. Now that no new publications of any import may crop up to interrupt our overview, and we have a more substantial funding apparatus at our disposal than the scholars of the 16th and 17th centuries, and an increase in cultivation leads one to expect a more illuminating treatment, and Hebrew books are not as hard to acquire as they might be in, say, 1919 ... now, we believe, it is our duty to exposit our science in high style; and an even more pressing duty this is, as it seems that it can address at least a few paragraphs of the complex question of the fate of the Jews. After all, the external influences of national law and religion are not in themselves sufficient to obtain a satisfactory harmony if one does not know the nature of the instrument and has not learned how to play it. To know the Jews of today theoretically or juridically, theologically or economically is to know them in but one dimension. As for the mind, it can only be penetrated by established ideas, by knowledge of mores and of the will. Every heedless so-called improvement will be avenged by a misdirected outcome; over-hasty innovations bestow a higher value upon old and – more insidious still – upon outdated ones. If we are, then, to glean and to assort what is useful of the old, hazardous of the outdated, and desirable of the new, we must prudently approach the study of the people and its history – political as well as moral. This precisely uncovers the great drawback that the matter of the Jews has been dealt with just like their literature: both have been overwhelmed by a fervor that has charged them with either too little or too much.

We have not veered from the literature of this people into its civic existence in order to disentangle a knot to which more adroit fingers should apply themselves. Having sketched their mutual interactions in a few lines, let us now return to literature and direct our attention to its origins, its content, its relation to older and contemporary sisters, its timely potential and its particularities. Here and there, we do find little lamps for that purpose, but the oil in them is not always enough, or good enough; our eyes strain for sunlight. How can it be, one might ask, that in a time when a tremendous panorama casts its bright rays over all the sciences, all the deeds of mankind, a time when the most remote corner of the earth is well-trodden, the least-known languages are studied, and not a thing is disdained that can serve the edifice of wisdom – how can it be that only our science lags behind? What holds us back from knowing the content of rabbinic literature in its entirety, understanding it properly, explaining it felicitously, adjudging it correctly,[4] and keeping it all in view with ease?

As only diverse, numerous, and sound preparations can take us to this height, the question again becomes the lack thereof. In our answer, we are therefore

---

4 We have no fear of being misunderstood: here, the entire literature of the Jews, to its fullest extent, is proposed as an *object of research*, without being concerned about whether its total contents should or can also be a *norm for our own judgment*.

obliged to specify what we mean by such literary preparations, and to prove that these are truly lacking. Once we have tried to explain this phenomenon, it will turn out that based on a deficit of such proportions, clarity about our immediate object – not to mention its achievement – is unthinkable.

We call literary works "preparations" which extend, either partially over an entire science, or entirely over a part of it. The latter includes any single properly researched item – any scientific question that is, if not completely answered, at least exposited for a future answerer with full acuity; any noteworthy discovery put to the test of what is already known; even just one difficult passage that is critically illuminated. So-called *editiones principes*, as soon as they offer more than replication of the manuscript, as well as good translations, proper handbooks, biographies, and the like, can rightly claim to be called literary preparations.

Yet we must accord a still higher place to works that encompass a whole science, enrich it with new discoveries, or reshape it with new perspectives, bringing this hundred- or thousand-year-old literature beyond its bounds and leaving behind tracks from its gigantic strides that are wide enough for a hundred more to follow. This includes expositions of philosophical systems, histories of particular doctrines and parallels, literary corpora, etc.

Praiseworthy and useful as these individual efforts are, however, they will never rise to the real challenge if the laborer misses the forest for the tree that he has chopped down to refashion and then, self-satisfied with his finished product, rested, the better to admire the beautification that nature has acquired under his hands. One who recognizes a nation's literature as the way to access a comprehensive understanding of its cultural progress over the course of time – just as, at each moment, its being is formed by the given and that which is added to it, i.e. by the inner and the outer – as fate, climate, mores, religion, and chance meet in an amicable or inimical embrace – and as the present is a necessary consequence of all foregoing phenomena – he, truly, approaches the temple of this pantheon with reverence, and has himself meekly led into the vestibule, that someday he may be among those who deserve to enjoy the sublime view from atop the pediment.[5]

Only he will be so deserving who has taken upon himself the pain of this ascent, and even he cannot give a satisfactory account of the whole until he has considered each part with a craftsman's trained eye. From this elevated perspective, our science metamorphoses into many branches of the sciences, each of which merits attention in all its parts, lest the whole be disfigured by substantial errors. Now, if we examine this unquantifiable stuff a bit more closely, so as to investigate, classify, and reform it under the aegis of critique, we perceive that a threefold critique is just as helpful for our own work, specifically, by helping us

---

5 [Though he uses polytheistic and Greek architectural vocabulary here, Zunz is also alluding to the rabbinic image of the "vestibule" (*prozdor*, itself a Greek loanword), as in Mishnah tractate Avot 4:16: "Rabbi Jacob says: This world is like a vestibule before the world to come: make yourself ready in the vestibule (*prozdor*) so that you may enter the banquet-hall (*traqlin*)" (JR).]

to recognize and to judge any given thought (whatever is imparted), as well as our own understanding thereof. With this in mind, we therefore divide critique, theoretically speaking, into three parts: the doctrinal, including ideas; the grammatical, including language; and the historical, which comprises the accumulated past of these ideas, from the moment when they were imparted until the present moment when they enter our understanding.

Let us now proceed to the literary products of the Jewish people and ask, first and foremost: what *are* their contents? Here we intend to give the reader an overview of the very best in this scientific table of contents, adding along the way whatever we can by way of comment, though we would rather hear these comments conveyed by our betters than surrender them to the all-too-usual lust for superficial criticism.

Let us begin straight away with theology: it must be freely admitted that the Jews never constructed their theological system in a clear and comprehensive manner, but certain admirable fragments speak plainly enough of it – more plainly than does Bartolocci,[6] who has kneaded together an *elenchus de Rabbinorum blasphemiis*[7] from myths and fairytales. Aside from a few valuable writings about the more ancient mythology of the Jews, we lag far behind on that score – which is all the more striking, as it is closely connected to Christian dogmatics, if Röder[8] is to be believed. In the domain of religion, one has sinned in such a thorough, willful, and orderly way! There is nothing in the world that has ever been written about with greater defamation, bias and injustice than the Jewish religion, and here, the art of inciting hatred has been brought to its peak. No distinction has been drawn between *mores*, liturgy, and religious principles; thus, one condemnable thing has brought ill repute upon ten innocent ones. Especially at the moment, any history of the synagogue ritual[9] based on the sources would be a desirable undertaking, albeit a difficult one.

Let us now leave the tributary of the Church and lower our anchor in that of the State; we now find ourselves in the area of legislation and jurisprudence where a certain amount of proper work by Jews is available for our scientific analysis. The fact that constitutional writings were composed in conditions of oppression is enough to make them interesting. It would hardly be a fruitless investigation,

---

6 This fellow is exceedingly harsh, e.g. [several examples are provided – CH].
7 Jacob Basnage, *History of the Jews*, vol. III, p. 9 says something similar but much more beautiful.
8 Johann Ulrich Roeder, *Archäologie der Kirchendogmen*, 1812, contains a treasury of materials that should, at least, be considered. See Pico Della Mirandola in his *Apologia*, p. 123.
9 Here, we believe that one should consider and distinguish the following: 1) The spirit of the liturgy; its position in the ceremonial law; its influence upon disposition and character; 2) The form and content of the liturgical forms; statements of Jewish authors on the subject; 3) The type of service; views of non-Jewish authors. If the treatment of this subject – which should be classified and evaluated separately in each country and period – falls into the right hands, it will indeed be a felicitous development to have a pragmatic contribution towards drawing distinctions between past mistakes, frustrated improvements, and the struggle for modifications (a struggle which has indeed already begun).

then, to ask how the identity of the *poskim*[10] was formed, and why authority is attributed to certain names[11] in the *responsis Rabbinorum*.[12] It would be of even greater interest to systematically compare the whole doctrine of the *culpa*, as it is so perspicaciously expounded in the three talmudic *Bavot*, with Roman law.[13] A Hebraic juridical vocabulary in comparison with its Roman and Hellenistic equivalents would also be rewarding. Only after conducting many such arduous studies can one portray the gradual change in Jewish law and its incessant dissolution within European law.

Ethics may be viewed primarily as a source of both religious and juridical principles, and it is high time to organize, in a substantive way,[14] the great writings about it in the Talmud and later sages,[15] but also to clarify whatever may contradict or seem to contradict it, when this originates from established authors;[16] these discoveries could have spared Eisenmenger the trouble of providing his own. What seems to us no less important are the science or, rather, the capacity of which humanity consists, including moral principles, the conventions of human associations, rules of so-called "practical wisdom," as taught by certain Jewish sages – though all this can only be acquired through one's upbringing in close conjunction with the sciences if the teacher's hand has been primed by a felicitous predisposition. One may read a good deal about this in the tractates Sotah – Soferim – Shabbat – Avot – Derekh-Eretz, etc., as well as in *Chobat halebaboth*, and *Mivḥar Ha-peninim*, and there is much to read about in others.[17]

Now that we have taken a look at Man, we may also investigate him as a denizen of the earth, contemplating his planet; a natural scientist, an astronomer

---

10 "Decisors"; from פסק: *seco, decido*.
11 In the Talmud, sometimes the majority accords with the House of Hillel and sometimes with the individual teachers (e.g. R. Meir and R. Akiva). All the remnants of the differences between the Houses of Shammai and Hillel, and their members, ought to be put in order.
12 In the Talmud as well, the well-known *halakah ke-ploni* should be given a historical foundation.
13 Such comparative works as do exist for Mosaic law are lacking for later law, and we have only cited the first and best example by way of introduction. There might also be some interesting parallels between the two legal sensibilities, e.g., on disinheriting heirs; on a building where another's property has been stolen.
14 The moral instinct is alive in every human being and man remains man in all his variations. Hence even the newest ethical literature refers to the oldest, purely Mosaic one, and arranging the aphorisms of the Old Testament according to their cardinal virtues seems to us a feasible enterprise even for a beginner.
15 Maimonides – Bechai the elder – Nachmanides – Jacob (known as Tam) – Albo – Shem Tov – Joseph the commentator and translator of Aristotelian ethics – Elijah de Vidas – Menasseh ben Israel – Mendelssohn etc. – not to neglect some precious kernels in the little-read book *Zohar*.
16 One should not only seek to know the life and circumstances of the people, but also the authority that the author may have had over it in his own context. When have there *not* been bad authors and bad events that carried on no effect? Hence, an intimate acquaintance with Jewish literature and *mores* is crucial if one is to write of Jewish morality.
17 One might also add an Arabic work on *mores*, completed by Gabirol in Saragossa in 1116.

who measures the heavens, a geographer who travels the seas. If we focus on the common denominator of all three, mathematics, we seem to need a thorough dictionary for a significant number of Jewish writings, as each has its own idiom.[18] No less welcome would be a presentation of their older traces in the Talmud[19] and their most recent history.[20] The Jews' treatment of astronomy would yield an even greater harvest, which should be preceded by an etymological investigation of the oldest terms and an arrangement of fragments from roughly 80 works[21] before proceeding with the real literature (which begins around 1100). It seems to us that one must also link astronomy with chronology, even if one prefers to leave astrology out of the picture. One noteworthy example among others has been pointed out by Azariah de Rossi from the *Zohar*, in a passage treated more extensively in our note below.[22] True, travelogues and geographical works are less numerous and of less interest; but one may still extract topographical information[23] and linguistic resources[24] from these works.

Nobody has made use of the store of expertise about nature that lies hidden in the Talmud[25] and can also be found in later works exclusively devoted to this subject. Secular rabbinic literature provides no *hierobotanica, hierozoica, physicas or medicas saeras*, though it would have been just not to constantly rail against superstition without having also heeded its opponent: physics. Alongside physics is medicine, based on an understanding of nature, of Man (i.e. psychology, anthropology and physiology) as well as on a skillful application of such understanding. But we still know of no example in which a learned doctor took the trouble to explain to us the schools, discoveries, biographies and writings of much older[26] Jewish doctors, and Imbonati's[27] index of translators refers to merely three medical works.

---

18 That said, there are some interesting parallels, e.g. Cylinder (אצטונות פלוש – חוג גשמי), etc., in the *Diction. hebr. Math. et philos.* of Joannes Pastritius.
19 E.g. b. Erubin 13b, 56b, 57a – m. Kilayim 5:5 etc.
20 For example, it is certainly of historical interest that in 1794, Eliakim ben Abraham, in London (following Green) dared to refute Newton in *Milḥamot haShem*.
21 Even the Chaldean paraphrases have left remains, as have the *Maḥzor* and other unnamed works, in *Halakhot Gedolot, Zohar, Bahir, She'elot ve-teshuvot*, etc.
22 [Here Zunz includes a two-page-long note on an astronomical tradition in the *Zohar* (JR).]
23 Moses Tibbon calls his hometown (Granada) *"rimmon."*
24 According to Josephus Assemani (*Bibliotheca Orientalis*, I, 174), Tagrit (Gk. *marytyopolis*) is called the same in Hebrew, מדינת שהדים. The Syriac translation of Matthew 5:25 renders Gk. *Decapolis* as עשרת מדינתא.
25 E.g. in tractate Kilayim, 53 plant-species are named. In Alfas I, 117a insects in clothing are distinguished from those in fruit [examples are provided (CH)]. There is zootomy in tractate Ḥullin.
26 On the orders of the Caliph Merwan, a Jew named Masseriawaih translated Aaron's medical works already in the 17th century (*Bibliotheca Hebræa*, 4 vols, Hamburg, 1715-33), IV, p. 903.
27 C.I. Imbonati (*Biblioteca magna rabbinica: de scriptoribus, & scriptis hebraicis, ordine alphabetico hebraicè, & latinè digestis*, 1675–1693, pp. 51–21) gives a list of 130 Christian translators; of these, however, only 70 have translated talmudic or rabbinic works, and the number of translated texts declines in direct proportion to the passage of years after Christ.

Only one step separates the understanding of nature from its use. Yet scholars have seldom found it worth their trouble to train themselves in the technical arts and trade; nor have dukes commanded any excavations in Syria and Babylonia. As a result, many passages of the Mishnah – especially in the sixth order – remain insufficiently explained. To this must be added industry and trade; it would be a significant piece of work, with still more significant consequences, to bring to light their oldest history in comparison to the views of the most highly esteemed authors. In the printed currency system, if we are not mistaken about this unfamiliar subject, one may also find some things that Jews are responsible for creating. Yet we possess not only writings about the use of material goods, but also about their decoration and their art – too many, it seems, for the critique to which they have been subjected, but too few for us to describe their inner and outer qualities without falling back on our own reconnaissance. Except for poetry, which we will discuss later, architecture may be the only art to have received a certain attention.[28] But we do not recall finding any allusion to Hebrew writing about letterpress printing among the Jews. Why have masterpieces of calligraphy[29] never been collected? Works on music[30] are largely still unprinted. The chapter on inventions is still scant, though it may be enriched by the liberal era and more free employment that we now enjoy.

Finally, we alight upon the universal life of the nation, where it remains to distinguish between the transient and the enduring, that is, between history and mere antiquarianism. But whence is to be furnished a non-partisan Paolo Sarpi [an Italian historian, d. 1623 (CH)] for Jewish history? Hebrew writings – already largely worn out in any case – are just as inadequate for a comprehensive account of the fate of the Jews in all countries where they have sojourned as the most praiseworthy works of more recent scholars like Basnage, Holdberg, Prideaux, etc. Insights may be recovered from the most marginal works; just as the people is dispersed, so is its history. Furthermore, our understanding is now roughly a century behind the times; the material piles up as the hands to work it grow fewer. It would certainly help the erstwhile collector if annals were produced, like those of Gans and Prussia, along with well-edited community records. The same can be said for antiquities, where (aside from isolated studies) no major works exist that deserve to be compared with research on the ancient Hebrew[31] period. One must slowly and diligently creep back from more recent times toward more remote

---

28 E.g. the tractate Middot of Eliezer ben Jacob.
29 A connoisseur could even collect a good bit of painting and embroidery, at least in modern times.
30 Why have the melodies of Jewish liturgy been so widely diffused? Abraham b. Ḥiyya (1100); Judah Moscato's *Nefutzot Yehudah* (Venice 1588, 4 cols); Abraham Portaleone's *Shiltei HaGibburim* (Mantua 1612) and others speak about music. Illuminating works are only from the early authorities – such as Andreas Sennert, Joel Löwe, J.N. Forkel, Guilio Bartolocci (vol. 4, p. 127) and Introductions to the Old Testament.
31 The clothing of the ancient Hebrews is the only exception; Schröder, Salmasius (see W.M.L. de Wette's *Lehrbuch der hebräisch-jüdischen Archäologie*, 1814, p. 160), Bänäus, A. de

ones, one must demonstrate and penetrate, in the whole array of countries[32] and in each significant epoch, the grounds for the transformation that this people's inner life has borne.[33]

Turning now to the lever for grasping and fixing this immense mass, we find language, which, scorning casual attention, withholds from us all its greatest treasures, and mocks our attempts to wrest Pythian oracles out of thin air with theorems about the distinctive characteristics of a widely diffused, universally marginalized people. For language is the first consort who, debasing herself, guides us onto the path toward science – and the last to whom we strain to return. Only she can tear the veil from the past. Only she can prepare our sensibilities to meet the future; so the researcher must also tolerate her willfulness, and what has been produced over centuries can only be refined over centuries.

Let us begin with the origins of all verbal form, with poetry; while the more ancient[34] still lacks some explication, the more recent lacks any.[35] Certain essential questions have hardly been raised, such as whether or not Jews in earlier[36] times wrote drama, what poetic products were generated during the first millennium of the Christian era, when our *piyyutim* (liturgical poems) were composed, what Chaldean poetry is all about, and so forth. Matters are even worse when it comes to rhetoric or, rather, the art of style. The less common Hebrew writings are on this subject, the more diligently should one derive its rules by abstraction, especially as Hebrew style began to achieve a purer and more beautiful form about a century ago. One might conscript many individual studies to this empty field on, e.g., the widely misunderstood nature of hyperbole,[37] the talmudic *remez*,[38]

Rossi (pp. 148–158), Bartholimi, Braun and especially Hartmann, have produced masterful investigations.

32 Compare, here, the Chinese, Abyssinian, German, Romanian, Polish, and other Jews, of whom much remains in the dark.
33 Exilarchs, Geonim, Rabbis, and Consistors have introduced changes in the church, as have governments in the constitution, authors in mentalities, exemplary individuals in *mores*.
34 Not only its internals but also its externals. See Azariah de Rossi, chap. 60.
35 There is so much of quality available here [a list of works is provided (CH)] that it would be worthwhile to develop a metrics of the modern period. Jacob Romano has written a Hebrew prosody in which he establishes 1248 types of poem (Buxt, *Bibl.*, p. 169). Where is it? [Zunz refers to other works that have not yet been collected (CH)].
36 Except for a dozen pieces from the last century wherein M.C. Luzzato, *La-Yesharim Tehillah* (Amsterdam, 1743; Berlin 1780 and 1799), shines like a star of the first magnitude, we are not aware of anything.
37 It is not always exaggeration but has quite varied sources, perhaps even a stronger imaginative color, for, as Simonis says (following Schüssler): *Hebraei natura aliis gentibus sunt ferventiores*. For examples of hyperbole in anecdotes, see t. Pesaḥim 118b; in ecstatic portraiture, see *Zohar* III, 205, 12. Sleepers were often awakened by it, as can be seen from Song Rabbah 1, 15. Compare also Shlomo b. Adret to b. Berakhot 54a.
38 On the other hand, this also holds for *asmakhta*; ignorance of this has also caused errors, e.g., in the *Die Alterthümer des Israelitischen Volks* (by A. Rücker, Berlin, 1817) p. 80, it is not the subject (see t. Sanhedrin 43a) but the prooftext (Prov 31:6) that is incorrect and incomprehensible.

later philosophical style,[39] the difference between prose poetry and poetic prose,[40] the literature of the comic,[41] etc. In grammar, the work is doubled! We must recover the neglected[42] history of Jewish grammarians from more recent times, and establish a system for the structure of neo-Hebraic language. This, however, must be preceded by a scholarly study of the Chaldean language;[43] only then might we lay claim to a basic history of the Hebrew language[44] and, only then, to philosophical parallels[45] between ancient and later Hebrew. But even for this, there are not enough tools: we lack a lexicon like Forcellini's, which can only come together from the coordinated labors of many who produce indices, and especially concordances, about individual works. No proof is needed that the old Hebrew dictionaries are useless for lexicology so long as they abide in their isolation, stuck in libraries. Synonymy is in an even worse state, as it has incorporated hardly anything from Jewish authors, and even less from the ancient Hebrew language, while etymology woefully proclaims that most of our rabbinicists neglect Oriental languages just as Orientalists neglect Hebrew.

And so we have finally gained an overview of the numerous written resources that can be understood with much that is useful, judicious, and even great in the works of scholars, yet to which much – indeed, very much – might be added. One might, for instance, round out diplomatics,[46] and execute a chronology of facsimiles according to authenticated colophons in order to further classify undated

---

39 The Tibbonites are the prime exemplars of this. Compare ibn Ezra's philosophical writings with later ones. We might also compare the principles of the translators and their history; True, it is not marked in any of our Hebrew libraries that Joseph Kimḥi translated the book *Hovot ha-levavot*, but this is well-founded.

40 E.g., Levita's *Pirkei Shira* and much later rhyming speech. Through this sort of exercise at spoiling taste, one lost the feel for poetry altogether, and the Psalms have been more often commented upon than understood. If this were the place, one might also contribute a good deal of verbal gestures, wordplay, acrostics, lipography, and other techniques that have, by the way, utility for deciphering names and dates, understanding accents, etc.

41 [Examples from modern pieces (JR).]

42 Why was the judicious Gesenius so reticent about Jews' philological efforts over the last centuries in his *Introduction*? We will name here only: the restorer of grammatical studies among the Jews, Salomon Hanau; further Wessely, Satnaw, Joel Löwe, Pappenheim, Sal. Dubno, Heydenheim, Cohen, Bensew.

43 The various periods of the Chaldean language have barely been covered.

44 The sources begin with the Mishnah, where we first see distinctions between new and old language. Gesenius has already conceded two periods of the ancient language.

45 Including pronunciation and orthography. T. Bava Metsia 5:1 חטיי; from b. Shab. 55b, אל תקרא יצועי אלא יצועיי, we see that one still did not vocalize; see also b. Avodah Zarah 29: היאך אתה קורא כי טובים דודיך או דודייך.

46 [The study of certain formal features of historical documents; only etymologically related to "diplomacy." Zunz's note here reads, in part: "The cursive script, developed in Germany, is still unknown to most rabbinicists, let alone most Jews; should we not immediately oblige our women to write codices, as did the nuns of the middle ages? A certain Estellina, who wrote the *Beḥinat-Olam* in the library of Turin puts the men to shame" (JR).]

manuscripts. If one were to add to this a history of the manuscripts,[47] and the still pending annals of Hebrew typography, only expedient catalogs of collections of privately and publicly held books, such as the Dibdin catalog created by the Spencer Library, are still lacking in order to achieve the much-needed comprehensive organization of Hebrew literature, so as to proceed more vigorously towards critical analysis[48] of what is (and, especially, of what used to be) available.

To comprehend this dearth of literature, we must first deal with those who would like to blame us for disparaging what emerged in – as Schickard said – the "rabbinic abyss." We ourselves explain such finger-pointing and head-wagging at the eminently praiseworthy and useful works of our predecessors and contemporaries as a token of prime ignorance, or, to put it more mildly, a lack of understanding. Our intervention is only to point out certain gaps as we strive to reawaken a field that once bloomed, albeit in a somewhat misdirected way, more than it does today, when it is left to itself by everyone. Our science is not only burdened by the common infelicity of human imperfection, as all others are; here, highly particular ills may be exposed, which are at the root of, and may help to explain, this or that defect or decline.

Indifference toward rabbinic literature is twofold. It is directed, either toward scholarship in general – in which case it cannot be helped – or toward rabbinic scholarship in particular, perhaps in the view that it is useless, that it contains nothing so formidable, that it may spoil one's taste, that one cannot make much of it, that it is godless,[49] or that it will never have a favorable reception. Usually, this sort of neutral indifference degenerates into open contempt, and it is not an unfamiliar sight for scholars to take up arms against our science. If only they had always done so against our science rather than against its practitioners! Yet worse than any indifference, more egregious than this contempt, is the partisanship with which one has often taken to this field; not in love, but in hate. Anything that even seemed superficially to bear witness against Jews and Judaism was a welcome find; scholars have plucked half-understood florid phrases from the four corners of the earth in order to prod their opponents into the stocks, and for

---

47 It does not seem to precede the 12th century. Autograph mss. are very rare. We would appreciate an index of well-known scribes, correctors, and vocalizers, and the orthography of those who have left behind writings should be established. It is no indifferent matter to know the fate of a codex, if any bibliographer or other scholar wants to indicate precisely when, where, by whom, and in what tangible form the manuscript before him was created.

48 Everyone knows, for instance, that the more recent editions of the Talmud have been censored, that is, mutilated. Rashi clarifies the existence of historical data on variants, see b. Shabbat 119a, s.v. אותביה בסיינה, where he introduces two different readings according to Levi and Isaac ben Judah. One should also edit the now rare *Sefer ha-shorashim* by the *Radak*, according, however, to the Florence ms. which was written in 1446, and is thus 45 years older than the oldest edition of 1491, which can be found in the Oppenh. Library (Wolf, III, 194).

49 Such accusations have also been levied against Hebrew literature in general [examples are provided (CH)].

roughly the past hundred years, there is not a single example of a Doctor collecting beautiful and good Hebrew writings in order to present the Jews' more lovable side.[50]

Thanks be to You, God of the Universe,[51] that those days are over! Pens plain and bold are now spreading true enlightenment to the people, and greater rulers lend to the pens their dignity and power.

This foreign fanaticism has been accompanied by an indigenous one, and familiarity with the subject matter has not infrequently bred carelessness, hastening the downfall of the most judicious works,[52] and robbing otherwise sound minds of the ability to impartially and clear-sightedly scrutinize their material. Even where there was goodwill, classical education was often lacking, just as, conversely, many scholars sinned by not making themselves at home in the Hebrew mind[53] and learning to empathize with the author.

Yet if, today, many Jews are lost to the field of rabbinic literature, this is due to ignorance pure and simple, produced by the ever-shrinking instruction in Hebrew language. In part, it is caused by poor prospects of future advancement, a smoother path toward other sciences, and the very admirable access to arts and crafts, farming and military service; in part, it is also due to a coolness toward religion in general, especially toward the ancestors' literature, the delusion that one may discredit oneself through the occupation with it, and a lovable modern shallowness (of which we shall speak a bit later on).

That said, there is some substantive basis to it, in the form of obstacles which drive even deft Hebraists to other, more pleasant, occupations, e.g. the rarity of codices, the not-always-great promise of bread and material progress, the beleaguered trade in Jewish books, the general example, and the accumulation of the field, which prevents almost anyone from getting by with just Hebrew. Conversely, however, it is not an unusual error that scholars are born from a few glances into German books, aided and abetted by the recent writing-frenzy – creating the kind of person who is a dilly dallying centrist, pursuing his field with no fervor at all or going after it with inadequate preparation for Hebrew

---

50 Even Fr. Becker shirked this; what he calls honorable courage and love of the fatherland for Samaritans, Spartans, Carthaginians, Peruvians, and Germans, becomes ignoble arrogance and desperation for the Jews.
51 *Dii ultro nobis viam salutis ostendunt, nostrae nobis sunt inter nos irae discordiaeque plaeandae*, Cic. de Har. resp. fin.
52 Once, for instance, a mad rabbi had the only manuscript of M.C. Luzzato's judicious psalms burned, in his zeal for the Davidic ones. Baptized Jews very often tried to insinuate themselves by means of fanatical persecution; consider, e.g., the text by Friedrich (formerly Samuel) Brentzius' with the dreadful title: *The Stripped Skin of the Jews*. [Zunz then lists other known works that are missing (CH).]
53 To see things properly at all, one must be completely at home in the language, and violations thereof instill no great confidence in even a great scholar [Zunz provides an example from Bernard de Montfaucon's *Diarium Italicum*, 1702, and J.F. Hirt's *Orientalische und Exegetische Bibliothek*, 1772–76 (CH)].

writings – the sort of person who harms science and proliferates stuff uselessly. One sins against interpretation, criticism, and above all against method; another passes cursorily over his topic, without due ceremony, with just as little regard for science and for the reader as for truth and comprehensiveness; a third makes it even easier for himself by setting to work with what he seeks already at hand and is then pleased with himself to have found it;[54] a fourth, finally, balks at the trouble of putting his nose to the grindstone where his predecessors have not prepared it for him. So the aphorisms of the fathers are confirmed: *One mistake always produces another!*[55]

Given such phenomena, it is self-evident why we have no satisfactory Hebrew literature and will not soon have any, for even armed with the requisite facilities, knowledge, and tools, we will always produce new ideas and new material as we rework ideas; so it is that bibliography, the study of reception,[56] and history are not produced by science alone, but also by history itself. The same holds for previously discovered materials that we integrate into science in an objective form, though they were originally the subjective version of an inherited idea. Thus the distinctive art whereby we make science our own transforms itself into new raw materials both for us and for the world to come.

And above all these realms of science, above the vast preserve of human endeavor, philosophy reigns in its supreme majesty – invisible everywhere, yet devoting itself with impregnable self-sufficiency to all human understanding. This is why we did not want to regard her only as a specialized science or the epitome of Jewish wisdom,[57] for she is also the highest historical understanding of how this wisdom has progressed over centuries, being treated and mistreated in the course of its inscription by Jews and non-Jews. Indeed, she is the most beatific guide when we take it upon ourselves to recognize the people's intellectual greatness and to pass on this recognition. Thus does each historical fact

---

54 From all ancient Hebrew writings, for example, one may adduce more and more substantial witnesses *for* than *against* the claim that Jews hold the ritual bath in high regard. One may also easily find prooftexts for nonsense; what matters, however, is what has been received and perceived, and what corresponds to the whole picture.

55 [The reference is to m. Avot 4:2: "Ben Azzai says: 'Be as hasty toward a light commandment as toward a weighty one, and flee from sin, for one commandment leads to another and one transgression leads to another, for the reward of a commandment is a commandment and the reward of a transgression is a transgression." Zunz's description of the four types of bad scholar also roughly corresponds to the Passover Haggadah's four children: the 'wise' (relatively speaking), the wicked, the simple, and the one who does not how to ask (JR).]

56 The much-discussed *Masora*, the oldest critical study of textual reception, has never been investigated historically and universally or properly explained. [Zunz comments on a few examples (CH).]

57 Philosophy never became a distinct discipline among Jews. Traditional and scholastic wisdom were amalgamated, and brighter minds soon assured that the talmudic canon has no authority in scientific matters, no more than Joshua's miracle has any in astronomy (as Maimonides says quite explicitly in his *Guide*, 3:14). Further, older philosophical works have a strong ethical and religious element and were also composed in Arabic; such originals should be used.

that industriousness discovers, acumen deciphers, philosophy utilizes, or taste assigns to its appropriate place become a contribution to the most dignified aim of all research: the understanding of man. Yet only this higher viewpoint befits science, which survives, sublime, above all earthly minutiae, lands and nations; only science can ever guide us to a true history of Jewish philosophy,[58] where the succession of thinkers' ideas must be parsed, understood,[59] and pursued according to the stringent commandments of history in tandem with the comprehensive general formation of the globe.[60]

These pleasant ascents into the kingdom of hope may not be put off by any subaltern philosopher with his question of their *utility*. We have nothing to say to whomever does not perceive science in its dignified whole throughout all its highest interconnections with each detail as an integral part of its spiritual creation. We would much rather address ourselves to those of subtler feeling, the people's nobility, who know that man must never pause in his upward motion, who have an eye less to what has been done than to what is yet undone. Some fields, covered in weeds,[61] are still to be planted, with the promise of a ripe harvest under better care; some noxious kernels are still sown and steal the health and vitality of their hardier neighbors; some rich harvests are still pounded down by the hail of impetuousness, meanness, pseudo-wisdom; some ripened fruit still lies scattered underfoot or downtrodden by arrogance.

Let us conclude our overview of the universal with a notice on a single unprinted and heretofore almost unknown Hebrew work that we are now studying with the support of Herr Dr. Phil. C.S. Günsburg and inclined to edit at the earliest opportunity, namely, the *Sefer haMa'alot* (*liber graduum*) of R. Shem Tov ben Yosef ibn Falaquera, a famous Spanish rabbi of the 13th century. Partly thanks to the author's polished reflections, it unfolds the various stages of humankind and the formation of its intellect in a pure, heavily stressed, yet fluid style. The very manner of analysis betrays a fine, well-read and educated thinker who is sometimes more reticent with his keener opinions. But there are also alternative

---

58 Authors have been made into representatives of the whole people, while neither periods nor countries were distinguished. J.F. Buddens provides only one introduction (*Einleitung in die Moral-Theologie*) and this is scarcely enough.
59 The sect of the Boethusians remains inadequately clarified. The little book, *Yeṣira*, is neither so clever nor so daft as the partisans would have it – most who have engaged with Kabbalah were tripped up by it. The Messiah who appears in the more recent religious books of the Jews, who ought to bring salvation and happiness to the whole world, is the embodied dogma of the desires of any articulate human being, and has squashed the former Jewish Messiah (who still hovers around only as a dim outline).
60 E.g. the influence of Arabic philosophy, of grammatical and astronomical fields, of scholasticism, of ideas of tolerance, etc.
61 By which is meant the talmudic quibblers who have no clue about the study of Hebrew literature. Staged duels of wits, so-called *pilpul*, first emerged in the 16th century, and already had many distinguished opponents at that time. We enthusiastically endorse the attenuation of such Talmudism and of vulgo-rabbinism.

sources of information[62] as to Shem Tov's eminence, of which a good deal will be provided in our prologomena to his book.

As we have not yet managed, however, despite a few inquiries,[63] to find any other text by our author than the codex of the aforementioned *Sefer haMa'alot* that is in our hands, or even another manuscript of this work, we will present a double edition. A Latin[64] edition will contain the text of our codex, printed in the finest detail, combined with prolegomena, notes, and the manuscript facsimile; another, smaller Hebrew edition, on the other hand, will include just a text for ease of comprehension, though we would like to avoid what one of the greatest men has called *levius et quasi desultorium emendationis genus*.[65] Perhaps a future editor shall thus meet with more favorable circumstances.

In keeping with the stringency that we have commended for scientific analysis in general, no less have we sought, in our particular case, to resurrect for ourselves a challenge that may be met by such a work: to present not only the theoretical bones of critique but, even more, its full beautiful form where nothing remains unaccounted for, even if it is still in its wrappings. Yet, far removed from its completion, we desire only that this effort of ours will marshal followers who will be more worthy of the object and nearer to the goal. For all this was done not only to wrest from oblivion a scientific product, dignified by age, distinguished by its authorship, stimulating by its contents, more easily consigned to ruin by its peculiarity; our painstaking business was sweetened by more pleasant hopes! The hope that the Jewish nation's drive towards fundamental, fertile analysis of its most exemplary works, with their panorama in constant view, might be more powerfully awakened – the hope that a clarification of what rabbinic literature has produced may help to banish the general prejudice levied against it.[66] Truly, as we burst so boldly into the midst of the literary world, we can be justified in the eyes of the competent and charitable reader not by our talent but by our fiery will to strive for the good and the beautiful. To that end, we would very much welcome a sensible critique of this argument, lest we be obliged to consider it unremarkable simply because it remained unremarked.

---

62 Specifically, the esteem in which Shem Tov's text was held by Pico della Mirandola, Jac. Gaffarelli, Joh. Buxtorf and Jac. Romanus.
63 Not only was a formal request made to the major libraries (e.g. Göttingen, Leiden, Berlin, Copenhagen, Rome, Wolfenbüttel, etc.), a call for such a work was also placed in the classified ads.
64 Our selection of this language will be justified more explicitly in the work itself.
65 Friedrich August Wolf, *Prolegomena ad Homerum* (1795), p. IV; because only a codex has critical value.
66 Cursing and debasing befits the Roman statesman against an enemy people (see Cicero) but not the Christian preacher against tolerated fellow-citizens (see J. Fr. Röhr, *Palästina, od. hist. geogr. Beschreibung des jüdischen Landes zur Zeit Jesu*, 1816, 180). The painstaking Friedrich Rühs also condemns them generally and severely (*Handbuch der Geschichte des Mittelalters*, Berlin 1816, 150.).

AGGADIC ELEMENTS IN THE CHURCH FATHERS*

Heinrich Graetz

Translated by James Redfield

The origin, formation, crystallization and collection of the *aggadah* are almost as obscure today as they were before Zunz's *Gottesdienstliche Vorträge* had been written. A great number of questions that naturally present themselves when we engage with the *aggadah* are still waiting to be resolved. Is everything that we conceive of as "*aggadah*" in the wider sense simply the free appropriation and application of the Bible's didactic content? Does tradition have no part in the *aggadah*, as it indisputably does in the *halakhah*? Yet if it has no part, how did it come about that aggadic phenomena are found in such diverse literary spheres? Through what delicate spiral vessels has the aggadic fluid percolated, meandering along such broad branches to just where it is least expected? It is well known that the *disjecta membra* of the *aggadah* are scattered throughout Jewish-Alexandrian literature: in the Septuagint, in Artapan, in the Jewish Sibylline Oracles, in Philo, Josephus, and even in some New Testament writings and Pseudepigrapha. But it is impossible to discuss the historical stabilization of the diverse parts of the *aggadah* until we have achieved a clear and comprehensive overview of aggadic elements in the Jewish-Greek literary sphere. By means of such parallels, the conclusion is likely to present itself that certain aggadic dicta we would be inclined to call *new*—according to the superficial appearance of their setting or tradents—are, rather, indisputably ancient. It is not my concern here to arrange the aggadic elements contained in pre-talmudic literature, as we can expect this from our esteemed editor [Zechariah Frankel] who has already begun to resolve this problem in his *Vorstudien zu der Septuaginta* [Leipzig, 1841] and in his work, *Ueber den Einfluss der palästinischen Exegese auf die alexandrinische Hermeneutik* [Leipzig, 1851]. Rather, the goal of the present analysis is to compare the aggadic elements in the

---

* This translation was completed by James Redfield and reviewed by Elisa Ronzheimer. Because the author's presentation of sources is often paraphrastic, translations of primary sources, as well as fuller bibliographic information for secondary sources, have been added in square brackets (usually footnotes) by Christine Hayes. Comments and corrections are also set in square brackets and the author identified by initials: JR = James Redfield and CH = Christine Hayes.

literature of the Church Fathers with their parallels in our midrashic works and to pursue the ramification and the dissemination of the *aggadah*. The aggadic elements of the Church Fathers are related to those of the Jewish-Greek literature in the sense that the former are indisputably dependent upon talmudic authorities, whereas for the latter, it is still *prima facie* unclear which can lay claim to greater originality. The Church Fathers themselves make it plain that they have received "Hebrew traditions" (as they call the *aggadah*) through the medium of contemporary Jewish "teachers." But even where the source is suppressed, as in Ephrem Cyrus, comparison allows us to determine that it belongs to the Jewish sphere. In this study I am not proposing a merely superficial juxtaposition of aggadic parallels in *midrashim* and Church Fathers; rather, I want to establish the point that we ought to be very cautious in judging the youth or age of aggadic dicta. We will very often encounter dicta that at first glance one might want to consider subjective fancies of a younger authority but which in fact are already found in a more pronounced form in earlier Church Fathers. For the reader to be properly oriented, then, I hold that it is essential to always pay close attention to chronology in order to be able to stipulate the first appearance of a dictum.

Aggadic elements are found in Justin Martyr (fl. c. 150), Clement of Alexandria (200) and Origen (240), but especially in Ephrem Cyrus (350) and Jerome (400). Hence these Church Fathers belong to the tannaitic and amoraic periods. Almost no *aggadah* is found in [the work of] the rest of the Greek and Latin Church Fathers, and the Syrians, other than Ephrem Cyrus, because they were not in direct contact with Jews; we are aware of only disconnected fragments. I begin with a parallel from Justin.

1) We read in the *midrash* by third-century *aggadists* (Genesis Rabbah 8) of a controversy over the plural [verb form] that Genesis uses for God's creation of man [suggesting] a sort of consultation between God and other entities; should we see in this the idiosyncratic views of the tradents? ויאמר אלקים נעשה אדם במי נמלך.[1] R. Joshua explains in the name of R. Levi (a disciple of R. Yoḥanan): God took counsel with heaven and earth, as a lord takes counsel with his advisers: ר' יהושע בשם ר' לוי אמר במלאכת שמים וארץ נמלך משל למלך שהיה לו סנקתדרון וכו'.[2] R. Ammi interprets this as follows: God sought his own counsel: ר' אמי אמר בלבו נמלך, and according to R. Ḥanina I, God took counsel with the angels: ר' חנינא לא אמר כן אלא בשעה שבא לבראת את אדם הראשון נמלך במלאכי השרת.[3] But we learn from Justin that these views were already *au courant* in Jewish circles over a century earlier. Inasmuch as this Church Father wants to prove the duality of Father and Son from this use of the plural, he rejects the Jews' views that God has taken

---

1 ["And God said, 'Let us make man' – with whom did he consult?"]
2 ["R. Joshua said in the name of R. Levi: he consulted with the works of heaven and earth like a king who had advisors."]
3 ["R. Ḥanina did not say thus but rather when the time came to create the first human, he consulted the ministering angels."]

counsel with himself, with the earth and the elements or with the angels. καὶ ὅπως μὴ ἀλλάσσοντες τοὺς προλελεγμένους λόγους ἐκεῖνα λέγητε, ἃ οἱ διδάσκαλοι ὑμῶν λέγουσιν: ἢ ὅτι πρὸς ἑαυτὸν ἔλεγεν ὁ θεός: ποιήσωμεν, ὁποῖον καὶ ἡμεῖς μέλλοντες τὶ ποιεῖν πολλάκις πρὸς ἑαυτοὺς λέγομεν: ποιήσωμεν: ἢ ὅτι πρὸς τὰ στοιχεῖα, τουτέστι τὴν γῆν καὶ τὰ ἄλλα ὁμοίως, ἐξ ὧν νοῦμεν τὸν ἄνθρωτον γενονέναι, θεος εἰρηκέναι: ποιήσωμεν. — ἢ ὅτι ἀγγέλοις ἔλεγεν (*Dialogue with Trypho* 62).[4] One must therefore concede that this aggadic interpretation was not invented by R. Yoḥanan's disciples; rather, they acquired it from tradition and each of them appropriated one of the various explanations.

2) The *aggadah*, which only appears in a rough outline, to the effect that the three men whom Abraham hospitably invited into his home were angels, each with a different mission—Michael to bring glad tidings to Sarah, Raphael to heal Abraham and Gabriel to destroy Sodom: מיכאל שבא לבשר את שרה רפאל שבא לרפא את אברהם גבריאל אזל למהפכיה לסדום (b. Bava Metsia 86b)—is alluded to by Justin as one whose basic contours were popular in his time. Οἱ τρεῖς ἐκεῖνοι, οὓς ἄνδρας ὁ λόγος ὀνομάξει, ἄγγελοι ἦσαν δύο μὲν αὐτῶν τεμφθέντες ἐπὶ τὴν Σοδόμων ἀ πώλειαν, εἷς δὲ εὐαγγελιξόμενος τῇ Σάρρᾳ (*Dialogue with Trypho* 5b).[5] Trypho, who is ostensibly Justin's opponent, brings forward this explanation in order to reject the Christological interpretation of this biblical passage, namely, that these three are an allusion to the trinity.

3) An aggadic parallel from Clement of Alexandria is especially interesting as it proves the existence of Seder Olam Rabbah [SOR] at his time. In accordance with the dating given by this chronological work, and in contradiction with himself, this Church Father counts 410 years between the Jews' return from the Babylonian Exile and the destruction of the Temple under Vespasian:

πάλιν τε αὖ ἀπὸ τῆς ἑβδομήκοντα ἔτους αἰχμαλωσίας καὶ τῆς τοῦ λάου εἰς πάτρῳ ἂν γῆν ἀποκαταρτάσεος, εἰς τὴν αἰχμαλωσίαν τὴν ἐπὶ Οὐεσπασιανοῦ ἔτη συνάγεται τετρακοσία δέκα

(*Stromata* I. 21)[6]

It is well known that R. Yosi gives the duration of the Second Temple as 420 years (SOR, end; b. Yoma 9a), and this calculation is based on the whole chronological

---

4 ["And that you may not change the [force of the] words just quoted, and repeat what your teachers assert—either that God said to Himself, 'Let Us make,' just as when we are about to do something, we often say to ourselves, 'Let us make'; or that God spoke to the elements, i.e., the earth and other similar substances of which we believe man was formed, 'Let Us make' ... or that he spoke to the angels ..."]

5 ["Then those three whom the Scripture calls men, were angels; two of them were sent to destroy Sodom, and one to announce the joyful tidings to Sarah."] [This passage is found in chapter 56 (CEH).]

6 ["Then, from the seventy years' captivity, and the restoration of the people into their own land to the captivity in the time of Vespasian, is four hundred and ten years."]

system of Seder Olam. This system allots only 34 years for the existence of the Persian empire after the rebuilding of the Temple under Darius: מלכות פרס בפני הבית ל״ד שנים ["The kingdom of Persia during the Temple time was 34 years"] and limits the overall duration of the Mede-Persian empire to just 52 years: כל מלכי מדי ופרס חמשים ושתים שנה ["all the kings of Media and Persia—52 years"] (SOR chap. 30, beginning) such that, of these, 34 fall after the building of the Temple and 18 beforehand: ג׳ של כורש וי״ד של אחשורוש ושתים של דריוש ובשנת שתים לדריוש נבנה הבית ["3 of Cyrus, 14 of Ahashverosh, 2 of Darius and in the second year of Darius the Temple was built"] (SOR chap. 29). R. Yosi or Seder Olam adds this first 34 years of the Persian empire to the remainder, that is, to the 180 years of Persian rule (מלכות יון ק״פ),[7] 103 years of the Hasmonean dynasty (מלכות בית חשמונאי ק״ג),[8] and 103 years of the Herodians (מלכות הורדוס ק״ג), thereby bringing the sum to 420 years. Clement could have derived the above sum of 410 years for the existence of the Temple only from this source, as Josephus reckons its duration at over 600 years and, according to Clement's own calculations, a much higher number should result, given that he himself calculates the duration of the Persian monarchy at 235 years (*Stromata, loc. cit.*)—200 years more, that is, than does Seder Olam. Clement must have borrowed this calculation from a Jewish source or, specifically, from the chronology of Seder Olam. Yet his figure of 410 years since the return from Babylonia until the fall of the Jewish state is inexact in any case, for, as we have seen, if the Jewish traditional chronology were to count 420 years (assuming δεκα is not a copyist's error), these 410 or 420 years should not be counted beginning with the return from exile but with the rebuilding of the Temple, and this, as noted above, adds up to a discrepancy of 18 years.

4) An aggadic parallel that appears in Origen will confirm the initial observation that *aggadot* transmitted by younger *aggadists* have much older origins. An old tradition recounts that the prophet Isaiah was killed by the King Manasseh or, specifically, sawn to pieces; this is communicated by an old apocryphal tradition

---

7 [This appears to be an error; the Hebrew reads: "The reign of Greece, 180 years" not Persia (CEH).]

8 The beginning of the Hasmonean dynasty, for which the chronology of Seder Olam is not negligible, seems to be assigned by this chronicle only to the first year of John Hyrcanus's reign (136 of the pre-Christian era) rather than under Simon. Two details support this: 1) If we convert the 180 of the Greek, 103 of the Hasmonean, and 103 of the Herodian eras to 386 years of the Christian era, then the beginning of the former falls in the year 316 B.C.E., when Ptolemy I captured Palestine for Egypt, after which the end of the following 180 falls in 136 B.C.E.; 2) Seder Olam Zutta, which I believe I have proven in my history (vol. IV, p. 537) has Seder Olam Rabba as a source, comprises 103 years of the Hasmoneans beginning with Hyrcanus: Hyrcanus 37, Yannai 27, Aristobulus 13, Antigonus 26 = 103 years. Seder Olam seems to consider Hyrcanus to be the first Hasmonean king, whom the historical fragment (b Qiddushin 64a) also calls ["king"] מלך. Oddly enough, Josephus and his source—the Arabic book of the Maccabees (chap. XXII; in the London Polyglot vol. IV), departing from Josephus—also claim that Hyrcanus was the first to occupy the king's throne. Seder Olam may have given a forced reading to the expression מלכות בית חשמונאי ["the kingdom of the Hasmonean dynasty"] and thereby have it exclude Simon and Jonathan who were both High Priests.

of the Church Fathers and in the Megillat Yuḥasin that was discovered by Simon b. Azzai in Jerusalem: Ἐσαῖαου πεπρίσται ["Isaiah was sawn asunder"] (Justin Martyr *Dialogue with Trypho* 273 [chap. 120]. Origen to Matt. XXIII, *Letter to Africanus*; *Homily* I on Isaiah) מנשה הרג את ישעיהו specifically explained as ונסרוהו ["they sawed it" (i.e., the tree hiding Isaiah)] (b. Yevamot 49b). The Epistle to the Hebrews (11:37) seems to allude to Isaiah's death with the word ἐπίσθησαν ["they are sawn"]. Yet the great antiquity of this apparently young *aggadah* is shown, not by this reference, but by the way in which Origen recounts the death. When one reads from the fourth-century C.E. amora Rava that Manasseh had Isaiah executed as a false prophet because his prophetic statements stood in contradiction to the laws, one is inclined at first to attribute it to the idiosyncratic fancy or rabbinic lens of Rava. But here, Origen teaches us that this reference, too, is quite old. Let us compare the almost verbatim parallels: אמר רבא · מדין דייניה וקטליה אמר ליה משה רבך אמר כי לא יראני האדם וחי ואת אמרת וראאה את ה' יושב (b. Yevamot 49b).[9] And Origen: *Cur non dicamus in praesenti traditionem quandam Judaeorum verisimilem quidem nec tamen veram, et solutionem ejus quare non inveniamus? Ajunt ideo Esaiam esse sectum a populo quasi legem praevicantem et extra scripturas annunciantem. Scriptura enim dicit: Nemo videbit faciem meam et vivet. Iste vero ait: vidi Dominum Sabaoth. Moyses, ajunt, non vidit, et tu vidisti? Et propter hoc eum secuerunt et condamnaverunt eum ac impium* (*Homily on Isaiah*). The sole discrepancy between the talmudic and patristic versions of this *aggadah* is that, for the former, it was King Manasseh who ended Isaiah's life, whereas for the latter, it was the people. But one is by no means justified in concluding that the *aggadah* varied [the tradition]; it seems much more likely that the tradition acquired this tendentious bent of pinning the crime on the people in Christian circles, so that one more example of a prophet's murder could be imputed to the Jewish people. Hence it is a commonplace among the Church Fathers that Isaiah was sawn to pieces by the people: Ἐσαιὰν πεπρίσθαι ὑπὸ τοῦ λαοῦ ["Isaiah was sawn asunder by the people"] (Tertullian in *Antidote for the Scorpion's Sting*, chap. 8), and in the polemical disputations between Christians and Jews the latter are directly accused of murdering Isaiah: τὸν Εσαιὰν ἐπρίσατε (Gregentius, *Dialogue with Herbanus the Jew*, p. 19). For our purposes, it is quite sufficient that the *aggadah* transmitted by Rava was in any event already in circulation a century earlier and was considered ancient.

5) Furthermore, in the time of Origen, the *aggadah* that sought to explain the absence of the phrase "and God saw that it was good" after the second day of creation was already disseminated: Καὶ ἐν τῇ γενέσσει δε τὸ: "εἶδεν ὁ θεὸς ὅτι κάλον" ἐπὶ τῷ γενέσθαι στερέωμα, παρ᾽ Ἑβραίοις οὐχ εὑρίσκεται, καὶ πρόβλημα δὲ ἐστι παρ᾽ αὐτοῖς οὐ τὸ τυχὸν τοῦτο (*Letter to Africanus* 4.16).[10] Origen did not

---

9 ["Rava said: He [Manasseh] brought him to trial and then slew him. He said to him: Your teacher Moses said, '*For men shall not see Me and live*' (Ex 33:20) and you [Isaiah] said, '*I saw the Lord sitting on a throne, high and lifted up*' (Isa 6:1).]

10 ["Again, in Genesis, the words, 'God saw that it was good,' when the firmament was made, are

consider the aggadic explanation itself worth transmitting, but Jerome knew it, and it corresponds in part to the one preserved in the midrashic source. למה אין כתיב בשני כי טוב? ר' יוחנן תני לה בשם ר' יוסי בר חלפתא שבו נבראת גיהנם ר' חנינא אמר שבו נבראת מחלוקת (Genesis Rabbah 4:6).[11] Precisely the latter sensible explanation—that the second day could not receive the divine seal of approval due to its meaning of division and schism [a reference to the dividing of the waters on the second day of creation (CEH)]—probably reached Jerome from a Jewish source, though he does not expressly cite it. *Denique in Genesi, cum in primo die dictum sit et in tertio et in quarto et in sexto post consumationem operum singulorum: "et vidit Deus quia bonum est" in secundo, juxta hebraicum et Aquilam et Symmachum et Theodotionem non habet. Neque enim poterat secundus dies qui numerum facit qui ab unione dividit, quod bonus esset dei sententia comprobari* (*Comment on Haggai* I, beginning).

6) Finally, Origen knows from Jewish lips the *aggadah* that seeks to conceal the injustice of Noah's curse falling upon Canaan, the grandson, when it was Ham who had seen his father [Noah] naked. In reality it is not Ham but Canaan who committed the crime. In the *midrash* (Genesis Rabbah 36:7), this explanation in defense of divine justice is asserted by R. Neḥemiah: ר' חם ראה וכנען נתקלל?! אתמהא! נחמיה אמר כנען ראה והגיד לחם.[12] This aggadic tradition is communicated by Origen in the name of a Jew who taught him many things: ἔφερε δε ὁ Ἑβραῖος καὶ παράδοσιν τοιαύτην ἐπενεγκὼν ἀπόδειξιν τῇ παραδόσει. ὡς ἄρα ὁ χαναὰν πρότερος εἶδε τὴν αἰσχύνην τοῦ πάππου ἀνήγγειλεν αὐτοῦ τῳ πατρὶ μόνῳ καταμωκώμενος ὥσπερ τοῦ γέροντος (*Selections on Genesis* 9.18).

The Syrian Church Father Ephrem has woven aggadic materials into his homiletical commentary to the Old Testament writings more copiously than these three Greek Church Fathers. Although at the time, northern Mesopotamia, that is, the region of Edessa which vied with Antioch, Alexandria and Rome for preeminence in Christianity and scholarship, had few Jewish communities and no talmudic study-houses, the ancient Jewish colony Nisibis where Ephrem was also born and taught for many years must have yet retained enough Jewish knowledge to provide material for the receptive Church Fathers, even after its study-house was eclipsed by the Babylonian Jewish schools. The influence of Jewish traditions on Ephrem's biblical exegesis is indisputable. Professor C.V. Lengerke has clearly recognized this influence in his work on the hermeneutics of this Church Father (C. von Lengerke, *De Ephraemi Syri Arte Hermeneutica Liber*, [8 volumes; Region, 1831]) but has insufficiently appreciated and still less

---

not found in the Hebrew, and there is no small dispute among them about this"; trans. Roberts-Donaldson.]

11 ["Why is 'that it was good' not written in connection with the second day? R. Yoḥanan taught in the name of R. Yosi bar Ḥalafta that Gehinnom was created on it (i.e., the second day) ... R. Ḥanina said that schism was created on it" (Genesis Rabbah 4:6).]

12 ["Ham sinned and Canaan was cursed!? ... R. Neḥemiah said, 'Canaan saw [Noah's nakedness] and reported it to Ham.']

corroborated its specifics. He presents this thesis: *Atque ex his, qual modo dixi, et si universe Ephraemi interpretation habitué et colorem consideraveris, jam verisimillimum esse debet: Ephraemum maximam suae rerum scientia et eruditionis partem in Judaeorum consuetudine sibi comperasse* (p. 17). *Multas enim habet (Ephraemus) ex Judaeorum commentis fictas sententias et narratiunculas, quae ad illud genus propius accidunt, quod Judaei* אגדות *appelare solent* (p. 20). But of the examples that von Lengerke provides as proof, not a single one is really striking or decisive, while others are positively vacuous. Anyone with even a slight familiarity with aggadic literature will discover aggadic traces introduced into it by Ephrem, whether it be that the seventh age of man is favored by God, or that Isaiah's gift for prophecy was interrupted for a long period of time. Von Lengerke considers these and other similar accretions, which have mostly passed through apocryphal channels, to be Jewish *aggadah*, in order to then curse Jewish superstition brutally[13] (p. 21–30). He also fails to provide evidence that Ephrem meant Jewish exegetes when using the phrase אנשין מן or אנשין אמרו or אית דאמרין ספרא, אנשין מן מפשקנא. This evidence could only be found by conducting a deeper comparison of Ephrem's exegesis and the *aggadah*. In the extensive commentary of Ephrem, I have not once encountered a single place where this Syrian Church Father names a Jew in his explanation of a verse, as if it shames the "Harp of the Holy Spirit" (as he is called in all effusive wonder) to admit having borrowed something from the circumcised teachers of lies (as he calls the Jews). A lone parallel proves irrefutably that Ephrem drew from a Jewish source and therefore knew the aggadic exegesis.

7) The real transgression of the Aaronides Nadab and Abihu, for which they received instantaneous death right in the middle of their priestly service, is extensively explored by Ephrem, who, in the process, rejects certain views which formulate this transgression differently. "They were punished," he remarks, "not because the sacred flame was extinguished (due to their contribution to it), as some claim, nor because they were drunk, as others claim, but due to diverse causes, as Scripture suggests. First, because they added strange fire to the fire that fell from heaven; second, because they circumvented Moses and Aaron in offering spices without instructions from either; third, because they disrupted the proper order of their service by bringing spices at the wrong moment (into the Holy of Holies), and fourth because they entered the Holy of Holies, where even their father Aaron could only come once a year." I cite the entire passage in the original: לא דין דנורא דעכת איך דאנשין אמרין — — אפלא תוב בחמרא רוין הוו איך דאחרינא אמרו — אלא מטול סגיאתא איך דכתבא רמז חדא מן מטול דאעלו נורא נוכריתא על נורא דנחתא דתרתין דאשטו למושא ולאהרון ואעלו בסמא כד מנהון מפסנותא לא קבלו דתלת דבלבלו שוריא ותשמשתהון ואעלו בסמא דלא בעדנהון וארבע דעלו לגו מן אפי תרעא לאתרא דחדא בשנתא אעל

---

13 [Graetz's use of the rare *weidlich* ("brutally") may allude to the beginning of Luther's infamous 1514 work "On the Jews and their Lies" (JR).]

הוא לה אהרון אבוהון (*Ephrami Syri opera* edit. Benedictine I. 240).[14] The parallels to this exposition in Talmud and Midrashim will immediately occur to any expert in *aggadah*, where all of these causes are proposed by one authority or another. Moreover, even the fourfold enumeration of the transgressions is asserted in the *aggadah*. The view rejected by Ephrem that both of the Aaronides were punished due to drunkenness is advanced by R. Simon: ר׳ שמעון אומר שתויי יין נכנסו למקדש (בדנ והיבאו) (*Torat Kohanim ad loc.*)[15] This conclusion is deduced from the fact that immediately after the chapter on the death of these Aaronides, the prohibition of wine for officiating priests is specified. R. Akiva presents the explanation that they were punished because they circumvented their superiors: ר׳ עקיבא אומר לא הכניסוה אלא מן הכריים א״כ למה נאמר אשר לא צוה אותם לא נמלכו במשה רבן.[16] R. Ishmael gives the explanation that the punishment was effected due to the ill-timed sacrifice: ר׳ ישמעאל אומר יכול אש זרה ממש תלמוד לומר אשר לא צוה אותם הכניסוה בלא עטה.[17] Finally, the explanation that it was because of forbidden entry into the Holy of Holies is transmitted in the name of R. Yirmiyah b. Eliezer, who, like Ephrem, enumerates four offenses: בר קפרא בשם ר׳ ירמיה בן אלעזר בשביל ארבע דברים מתו על הקריבה ועל ההקרבה ועל אש זרה ועל שלא נטלו עצה בשביל ד׳ דברים מתו[18] ר׳ מני אמר (cf. *Yalqut* Leviticus § 524, where all of these views are laid out). It cannot be coincidental that Ephrem so closely corresponds to the Jewish *aggadah* in enumeration and in content; rather, we must concede that he took them from Jewish *aggadists*. Ephrem's dependence upon the Jewish exegesis of his time should, then, be considered proven, and we must also concede the priority of the Jews with regards to the other parallels between his hermeneutics and the *aggadah*.

14 [*Sancti Patris Nostri Ephraem Syri Opera Omnia quae existant Graece, Syriace, Latine*, edited by P. Mobarak (Benedictus) and S.E. Assemani in 6 volumes (Rome: 1732–46).]
15 ["R. Simon says, 'They entered the sanctuary drunk with wine.'"]
16 ["R. Akiva says, 'They brought it from the piles. If so, why does it say, '*which He had not commanded them*' (Lev 10:1)? Because they did not consult with Moses their master.'"]
17 ["R. Ishmael says, 'Perhaps it means an actual alien fire; [no, because] Scripture says, '*which He had not commanded them*' (Lev 10:1), meaning that they brought it in at the wrong time."]
18 ["Bar Qappara in the name of R. Yirmiyah b. Eliezer: they died on account of four things – because they made an offering, because of the offering, because of the alien fire and because they didn't accept advice. R. Mani says: they died on account of four things."]

OBSERVATIONS ON THE CRIMINAL LAW OF THE JEWS

By V. Aptowitzer

Israelitisch-Theologische Lehranstalt, Vienna.

I

HAGGADIC BACKGROUND OF CRIMINAL LAWS
Criminal Laws as Basis of Haggadic Sayings

Some theories, decisions, and even fundamental principles of criminal law rest on haggadic views and can only be explained through them. Likewise we find numerous haggadic sayings which can only be understood through that branch of the Halakah which deals with criminal law. Furthermore, there are a number of haggadahs and criminal statutes which, it is true, are independent of one another, yet stand in close relation insofar as they rest on one and the same principle. In a word: there is a close connection between Halakah and Haggadah. This I purpose to prove with reference to one section of criminal law, viz. the decisions concerning the death penalty.

1. The basis for the following deductions rests on a haggadic controversy on Gen. 4.8, which in itself needs an explanation. Hence I must deal with this haggadah first and at greater length. Then from the explanation arrived at the haggadic-halakic connections will be easily recognized. The passage reads as follows: "And he slew him. With what did he slay him? R. Simon says: he slew him with a *cane*, for we find: 'a child through my *boil*' (4.23), something that causes a *boil*. And the Rabbis say: he slew him with a *stone*, for we find: 'for a man I have

slain through my *wound'*, something that produces a *wound*". [1]

The difficulty in this midrashic passage is evident at a glance. 1. How can we ascertain from the quoted words of Lamech the kind of murderous instrument which Cain employed in slaying his brother? 2. By what right do the representatives of both views each one urge a fragment of a sentence in his favor, without the least concern about the other fragment speaking in favor of the opposite view?

The first query is answered by Einhorn pointing to Gen. r. XXIII, 4, where Lamech's words are interpreted in such a manner as to refer to the murder of Abel by Cain. However, through this interpretation the difficulty raised in the second question becomes even greater. If Gen. 4.23b contains an allusion to the murder of Abel by Cain, then just as איש and ילד refer to Abel [2] so also לפצעי and לחברתי must refer to the manner of Abel's death, whence it necessarily follows that Abel was killed through wounds *and* boils. How then is it possible for R. Simon and the Rabbis to assume in their controversy that

---

[1] Gen. r., XXII, 8: ויהרגנהו במה הרגו? רבי שמעון אמר בקנה הרגו, שנאמר וילד לחברתי, דבר שעושה חבורה; רבנן אמרי באבן הרגו, שנאמר כי איש הרגתי לפצעי, דבר שהוא עושה פצעים. So in ed. Theodor, p. 214. Other editions have רשב"נ. As to the meaning of חבורה opinions differ, some considering it a boil with blood congestion but no bleeding, while others construe it as a bleeding wound. Comp. Rashi on Gen. 4.23; Ex.21.25; Is.1.6, and Sanh. 37b; Ibn Ezra on Ex. 21.25; Kimḥi on Is. 1.6 and his Dictionary s. v. חבר end. In talmudic literature חבורה signifies sometimes "boil" and sometimes "bleeding wound". Comp. Tosefta Ket.I,1; Shab. 106a, 107b; Ket. 5b–6b; Baba ḳamma 34b, 86a, 98a; Sanh. 84b; Ḥul. 45b; p. Ber. II, 65a; Shab. II, 25a. Comp. especially p. Sanh. I, 1. It is important that in opposition to the Palestinian Talmud the Mekilta of R. Simeon, p, 126, contains the following: עד שיצא טפת דם או עד שיצרר הדם. However, there is no doubt that חבורה by the side of or in opposition to פצע can signify only "boil". Comp. p. Baba ḳamma VIII, 1: אם בשפצעו והוציא דמו כבר כתיב פצע. תחת פצע ומה תלמוד לומר חבורה אלא, שאם כואו בשפוד על כף ידו וצבת על כף רגלו וצבת. Comp. also Lurya on Gen. r., Kimḥi on Gen. 4.23. The opinion of the Rabbis on this matter is lacking in Bacher, *Rabanan die Gelehrten der Tradition*, Budapest, 1914.

[2] As R. Johanan interprets: "a man" in bodily strength, "a child" in years איש לעובדים וילד לשנים. In this interpretation, and only in this, is contained the allusion to the murder of Abel in that midrashic passage, urged by Einhorn and after him by Theodor.—As to this interpretation itself, it is much older than R. Johanan, it is presupposed already by Philo and Josephus, as I expect to prove in one of the coming numbers of the *REJ*.

haggadic interpretation from which one must infer that both assertions are erroneous?

Our controversialists therefore cannot see in the words of Lamech an allusion to the slaying of Abel by Cain. If nevertheless they conclude from his words what kind of weapon Cain employed, this can be explained only in the following manner.

Both R. Simon and the Rabbis render לפצעי "through[3] my wound", i. e. through a wound which I dealt him, and לחברתי "through my boil", i. e. through a boil with which I afflicted him. It follows therefore from Gen. 4.23b that a איש, a grown-up person, may be killed through a wound, a weak child, however, may die merely through a boil caused by the blow of a stick. In a mature and strongly constituted man death is brought about by hemorrhage, while in the frail and tender child the mere stoppage of blood circulation caused by a boil is sufficient to bring about death.[4] Now there are in the Haggadah two different views as to the age of Abel. According to one view Abel was a grown-up man when he died,[5] but according to another view he was no more than fifty or seventy days old.[6] R. Simon is of the latter view, hence he maintains that Abel could have been killed as well through a boil, which may be caused also by hitting with a cane, while the Rabbis follow the former view, letting Abel die at a mature age, when he could be killed only through a wound dealt him by Cain with a stone.

But we would do an injustice to R. Simon were we to be satisfied with this explanation, since by it his opinion

---

[3] Comp. Rashi Gen. 4.23: על ידי חבורתי. The Peshitta renders בצולפתי "through my wounds" (לפִצְעִי) and בשוקפי "through my blows" (לחבורתי). Smith, *Theasurus Syriacus*, II, 4295, incorrectly *ad vibicem meam*.

[4] Comp. Kimḥi *ad loc.*: ופצע שהוא מכה שהוציאה דם, זכר לאיש שלא ימות בחבורה ברוב, וחבורה היא מכה שאינה מוציאה דם, ולפיכך זכר חבורה לילד שימות בחבורה פעמים.

[5] Tanḥuma בראשית 9: Abel was killed at the age of 40 years.

[6] Gen. r. XXII, 4. Detailed information about these stories will be found elsewhere.

53

loses its intrinsic value and justification. A child, it is true, can be killed through a boil, but even more so through a wound. A boil may be caused by hitting with a stick, but also by hitting with a stone. But R. Simon, as his words prove, maintains positively that the murderous instrument was a cane and that death was brought about through a boil. We must therefore look for another confirmation of this assertion. This results from the answer to the question: how had Cain died?

The Haggadah answers this question in two different ways. According to R. Simon ben Lakish, Cain perished in the flood;[7] another legend makes him die at the hands of Lamech, who shoots an arrow at him.[8]

Following the view of Simon ben Lakish, Cain found his death through drowning. This kind of death corresponds, according to the Baraita handed down by R. Ḥiyya, to capital punishment by strangulation (חנק).[9] Now it is easy to see that death through a boil is a kind of *ḥeneḳ*: there the prevention of the passage of air, here stoppage of blood circulation. But the *talio* requires that the murderer lose his life in the same manner in which he deprived his neighbor of his life,[10] and hence we may also reverse the reasoning and draw from the death of the murderer a conclusion concerning the kind of death of the victim. If then Cain perished in the flood, i. e. suffered the capital punishment *ḥeneḳ*, so he must have killed Abel through some such kind of death resembling *ḥeneḳ*. On the other hand, if Cain died through Lamech's arrow, i. e. loss of blood, he must have brought about Abel's death through loss of blood. R. Simon follows the first view, hence in his opinion Abel must have died through a stoppage of blood, therefore the murder weapon must have been a

[7] Gen. r. XXII, 12.
[8] Tanḥuma בראשית 11. Elsewhere I treat of these stories in greater detail.
[9] Comp. further below, No. III.
[10] Comp. further below, No. II.

cane. The Rabbis, on the other hand, accept the Lamech legend, hence Abel must have died from hemorrhage, and therefore the instrument of murder must have been a stone.

From our deductions so far we obtain the following combinations:

(a) Abel dies as a child—is killed by a blow from a cane—Cain finds his death in the flood.

(b) Abel dies as an adult—is killed by a stone—Cain is slain by Lamech's arrow.[11]

Now we really come to our theme. From the diversity of views concerning Cain's death the following halakic views and principles find their explanation:

(a) The punishment which the Noahide undergoes for the transgression of the so-called Noahide commandments is, according to one view, death through decapitation (סייף),[12] but according to another view, emanating from the school of Menashe, death by strangulation (חנק).[13] The first view is substantiated by the fact that in the only biblical passage, wherein the Noahide is threatened with death, also the kind of death—his blood shall be shed—is indicated at the same time.[14] The second view, however, has no plausible support, while the literal sense of the biblical text is against it. The latter difficulty is removed in the Talmud through the explanation that the school of Menashe interprets *"in* the man[15] shall his blood be shed", and a killing in the man is only possible through strangulation. But what caused the school of Menashe to lean to such a violent interpretation? Because this school refuses to accept the Lamech story and lets Cain perish

---

[11] Comp. in addition Aptowitzer, *Freie Jüdische Lehrerstimme*, VI (Vienna 1917), Nos. 1 and 2.

[12] Sanh. 57b and Rashi s v. בא על, Sanh. 71b and Rashi s. v. ונשתנית; p. Kid. I, 58c; Mishne Torah, Melakim IX, 14; Kesef Mishne ad loc. inexactly "a baraita".

[13] Sanh. as above; p. Kid. as above; Gen. r. XXXIV, 14.

[14] Gen. 9.6.—In a similar way proof is adduced for capital punishment generally for the violation of the Noahide commandments except murder. Comp. Sanh. 57a: גלי רחמנא בחדא.

[15] Comp. further below, No. V.

in the flood, therefore the first capital punishment inflicted by God on man—the flood—was death by strangulation (חנק). The first view, however, is based on the Lamech story, hence the first capital punishment inflicted by God on the Noahides was death through the sword (סייף). As a matter of fact we notice that R. Simon, who—as we have seen above—lets Cain perish in the flood, really takes his stand with the school of Menashe.[16]

(b) This explains the difference in the deduction of capital punishment by the sword (סייף) for murder in both Mekiltas.[17] The Mekilta of R. Ishmael, after a long discussion, points to Gen. 9.6: "Whoso sheddeth blood, his blood shall be shed." The Mekilta of R. Simeon, on the other hand, points to the death sentence on the bondman (Ex. 21.20), where the expression "he shall be avenged" with reference to Lev. 26.25 must signify death by the sword. That the proof of R. Ishmael is more simple and evident and, indeed, suggests itself spontaneously, could not have escaped R. Simeon; if nevertheless he does not accept it and suggests another derivation, there must have been an important reason for it. This reason is revealed through the following circumstances: R. Ishmael, as we learn from other sources, decrees capital punishment on the Noahide also for murder of the *nasciturus*; he reads Gen. 9.6: "Whoso sheddeth the blood of man found in the man"—i. e. the child in the mother's womb—his blood shall be shed.[18] The opponents of R. Ishmael, who do not inflict death even on the Noahide for murder of the *nasciturus*, read with the school of Menashe: "Whoso sheddeth man's blood, in the man shall his blood be shed"—he shall be strangled.[19] It is now clear that in accordance with this reading murder in general must be punished either

---

[16] Sanh. 71b: רבי שמעון סבר לה כתנא דבי מנשה.
[17] Comp. further below, No. IV.
[18] Comp. further below, No. V.
[19] Sanh. 57b. Comp. further below, No. V.

by strangulation, or else by death through the sword derived from another passage of the Bible.[20] Now we know that R. Simeon adheres to the view of the school of Menashe, hence he had to derive capital punishment through the sword from Ex. 21.20, while R. Ishmael, the opponent of the school of Menashe, was in a position to offer a simple and unsophisticated proof.

(c) In this way is likewise to be explained the well-known halakic principle enunciated by R. Jonathan: Wherever the Torah decrees capital punishment without qualification, death by strangulation is meant.[21] This sentence is the more inconceivable since the Torah ignores altogether capital punishment by strangulation.[22] Rabbi substantiates this sentence as follows: The Torah commands death penalty by man's hands and in the Torah occurs also death through the agency of Heaven; just as death through the agency of Heaven does not call forth any outward signs, so also death by man's hands should not occasion any outward signs.[23] But on the basis of this analogy it could as well be maintained that the unqualified death penalty of the Torah is death through burning, since also this death, in the form in which it is prescribed in

---

[20] So indeed *Ḥinnuk*, Commandment 471. That this might be a mistake of the copyist, as is assumed by Minḥat Ḥinnuk *ad loc.*, is impossible in view of the whole deduction. Friedmann, in his comment on Mekilta 80a, note 10, thinks that the author of the Ḥinnuk was misled by a faulty text of the Mekilta. But even this is not sufficient, since in view of the express statement in the Mishnah Sanh. 76b the consideration of a contrary Baraita is inadmissible. The statement of the Ḥinnuk appears even more puzzling, since also in a primary source, in the Mishne Torah, the killing of the murderer by the sword is emphasized 3 times; comp. Rozeaḥ I, 1 and Sanh. XIV, 1 and XV, 12.

[21] כל מיתה האמורה בתורה סתם אינה אלא חנק. Mekilta Mishpaṭim V on Ex. 21.15 and 16. Mekilta of R. Simeon, pp. 126, 127. Sifre Deut. 155, 178, 273. Sifra Ḳedoshim, Chapter VIII, 8. Sanh. 52c, 84b, 89a, 89b; p. Sanh. VII, 4.

[22] חנק לית משכח ליה אמרת כל מיתה האמורה בתורה סתם אין אתה רשאי להחמיר עליה אלא בחנק להקל עליה ותלו אותה. P. Sanh. VII, 1 and 4, 24b: Ḥenek is not found in the Torah. B. Sanh. 53a, above: How do we know that there is at all a death penalty ḥenek? ממאי דאיכא חנק בעולם? The Gaon Rab Zemaḥ replies to the people of Kairwan: ואין בתורה מיתת חנק, וחכמים דרשוה ואמרו כל מיתה האמורה בתורה סתם אינה אלא חנק. Comp. Epstein, *Eldad ha-Dani*, p. 7, n. 13.

[23] Sanh. 52b ר׳ אומר נאמר מיתה בידי שמים ונאמר מיתה בידי אדם מה מיתה האמורה בידי שמים מיתה שאין בו רושם אף מיתה האמורה בידי אדם מיתה שאין בה רושם.

the Mishnah,[24] is executed without any visible change in the body. This question is already proposed in the Talmud. But the answer—death through burning to which the adulterous daughter of a priest is condemned constitutes an exception and proves that any other adultery is punished by strangulation[25]—covers only the case of adultery, and not all the other crimes for which the Mishnah lays down the death penalty through strangulation.[26] But if we refuse to follow the Lamech story, then there remains as the first capital punishment decreed and inflicted by Heaven, the flood [27]—therefore *henek*, which is meant wherever the Torah does not qualify the death penalty. In fact the following combinations are established in the Talmud:

(a) R. Simeon, who considers the punishment through strangulation as graver than death by the sword (A),

---

[24] Sanh. 52a.
[25] ואימא שריפה, מדאמר רחמנא בת כהן בשריפה מכלל דהא לא בת שריפה היא.
[26] Sanh. 84b. Comp. *ibid.* 84a, 87a, 89a.
[27] This is what Rabbi means in the sentence "the Torah contains death through Heaven" etc. Death through drowning does not bring about any visible changes in the body.

In the same way also Rashi *ad loc.* and *Semag*, Prohibition No. 103, construe the well-known penalty "death through Heaven" in the case before us. Aruk s. v. רשם explains against the current meaning of the expression that what is meant is natural death. Now there is a previous opinion that the penalty of death through Heaven consists in the abbreviation of the normal duration of life (comp. Rashi Shab. 25a *s. v.* ונכרת, Tosafot *ibid. s. v.* כרת and Yebamot 2a *s. v.* אשה; see also Mo'ed ḳaṭan 28a and Tosafot *ibid. s. v.* מח; Semaḥot III, 8 and p. Bikkurim II, 1; in opposition R. Ḥananel, Solomon ben ha-Yathom and Rabbinowicz to Mo'ed ḳaṭan quoted above and נחלת יעקב on Semaḥot), but we find "death through Heaven" in cases where the penalty consisted in an unnatural death; comp. further below No. 2. Hence "death through Heaven" can only mean a penalty imposed and executed by Heaven, and, to be sure, the first penalty of this kind.

With regard, however, to the natural death, the cause for the entrance of death is, in the opinion of the Haggadah, the poisoning through the gall drop which falls from the sword of the angel of death into the mouth of the dying person. Comp. 'Arakin 7a: בשעת פטירתו. טיפה של מלאך המות. This is based on the Baraita 'Abodah Zarah 20b: של חולה עומד מעל מראשותיו חרבו שלופה בידו וטיפה של מרה תלויה בו כיון שחולה רואה אותו מזדעזע ופותח פיו חורקה לתוך פיו וממנה מת. Comp. Jellinek, *Beth ha-Midrash*, I, 150. This corresponds to the capital punishment שריפה. To infer from Ber. 8a and Mo'ed ḳaṭan 29a that suffocation is the cause of death in the case of a natural decease—as is done by Büchler in the *Monatsschrift* for 1906, p. 685—there is not sufficient reason, since in these passages only the pains at the parting of the soul from the body are set forth; that the soul slips out through the alimentary canal is not mentioned there. Comp. in addition Lev. r. IV, 1; Tanḥuma מקץ 10 (ed. Buber 15); Koh. r. to 6.7 and especially Midrash Psalms, ed. Buber, IX, 6, p. 102.

must therefore lean to the standpoint of the school of Menashe, that the death penalty of the Noahides is חנק (B).[28]

(b) R. Jonathan, who lays down the unqualified death penalty of the Torah as חנק (C), must be of the same opinion as R. Simeon, that חנק is graver than death by the sword (A)[29].

Therefore: A = B, C = A; C = B.

R. Jonathan must likewise stand with the school of Menashe.

2. We read in the Mishnah: "He who suppresses his prophecy (1)—by not proclaiming it—and he who neglects the command of a prophet (2) and the prophet who transgresses his own prophecy, (3) are condemned to death by Heaven".[30] This is explained in the Tosefta:[31] "He who suppresses his prophecy—as, for instance, Jonah the son of Amittai; he who neglects a prophecy—as, for instance, the companion of Micah; he who transgresses his own prophecy—as, e. g., Iddo." Likewise Sifre.[32] In the Talmud[33] this explanation is supplemented by references to the respective passages in the Bible: the companion of

---

[28] Sanh. 71b: אלא לרבי שמעון דאמר חנק חמור מאי איכא למימר סבר לה כתנא דבי מנשה דאמר כל מיתה האמורה לבני נח אינה אלא חנק.

[29] Sanh. 53a above.

As a matter of fact we find that R. Simeon adopts the same standpoint as R. Jonathan: the unqualified death penalty in the Torah is חנק. Sanh. 89b below: נביא שהדיח בסקילה רבי שמעון אומר בחנק...ור"ש, מיתה כתיבה ביה וכל מיתה האמורה בתורה סתם אינה אלא חנק. This is in accord with the circumstance that in the Sifre, which following the well-known canon Sanh. 86a reproduces the opinions of R. Simeon, only the opinion of R. Jonathan is quoted, and to be sure anonymously. Comp. Sifre Deut. 155, 178, 273. Even according to the most radical modern criticism of the above-mentioned canon (comp. Lewy, *Ein Wort über die Mechilta des R. Simon*, p. 34, and Horowitz, *Einleitung zu Sifre d'Be-Rab*, Leipzig 1917, pp. V-VI) Sifre Deut. from the section ראה belongs to R. Simeon.

[30] Sanh. XI, 5; הכובש את נבואתו והמותר על דברי נביא ונביא שעבר על דברי עצמו מיתה בידי שמים.

[31] Sanh. XIV, 15.

[32] Sifre Deut. 177.

[33] Sanh. 89a f.; p. *ibid*. XI, 7 30 b f.

Micah—I Kings 20.35-37[34]—is killed by a lion; Iddo—I Kings 13.8-24[35]—is likewise killed by a lion.[36] But as to Jonah, there is no evidence adduced from the Bible, since there is not the least trace in the Bible leading to the belief that Jonah had died an unnatural death. And yet this is presupposed by all the halakic sources, and hence by the entire halakic tradition. How is that?

An answer is furnished by the Haggadah:

(a) "The son of the widow from Sarepta,[37] namely Jonah the son of Amittai,[38] was perfectly just . He was purged in the depth of the sea and through his being swallowed by the fishes; but he did not die, for God spoke to the fish that he should spit Jonah out on dry land (Jonah 2.11). He came alive to paradise".[39]

Therefore: Jonah who refuses to proclaim the prophecy imparted to him by God is thrown into the sea as a punishment for his refusal. However, because he is just, i. e., as emphasized in the Haggadah elsewhere, because his refusal was the result of his intense love for Israel,[40] he

---

[34–35] In the biblical text the names of the prophets are not mentioned, but tradition identifies them with Iddo and Micah. Comp. also Seder 'Olam r. ch. 20 and Sanh. 104a. Josephus too knows the names of the prophets as voiced by tradition: Ἰάδων and Μιχαίας, comp. *Antiquities*, VIII 8,5 and VIII 14, 5 (ed. Niese II 226 § 231, 260 § 389ff).—Some texts of *Antiquities* X 4,4 (Niese II 345 § 62) exhibit Ἀχία in place of Ἰάδων, but the correct texts lack the name altogether. Comp. in addition Seder 'Olam r., ed. Ratner, 43a, notes 29 and 34.

[36] It follows from this that "death through Heaven" in the parlance of Rabbi in Sanh. 52b and elsewhere can only signify death decreed by Heaven as a penalty, and not the natural death, as explained in the 'Aruk. Comp. above, note 27.

[37] I Kings 17.9.

[38] That Jonah was the son of the woman of Zarepta is stated also in Pirke R. Eliezer, ch. 33. It is presupposed in p. Suk. VI 55a and Gen. r. XCVIII 11.

[39] Midr. Psalms, ed. Buber, 26 7: אבל בן הצרפת[ית] האלמנה והוא יונה בן אמתי היה צדיק גמור ונצרף בבליעת דגים ובמצולות ימים ולא מת, אלא ויאמר ה' לדג ויקא את יונה אל היבשה ונכנס בחייו בכבודו לגן עדן. That Jonah entered into paradise alive does not occur elsewhere. The haggadah enumerates now 9, now 13 persons, who entered paradise alive, but Jonah is not included among them. Comp. Derek Erez zutta, ch. I end; Kallah rabbati, ch. 3 end; *Beth ha-Midrash*, II, 100; פרקי רבינו הקדוש, ed. Grünhut (*Sefer ha-Likkutim*, III), p. 83; Alphabet of Ben Sira, ed. Steinschneider, 28a; Bereshit rabbati MS. Prague (Jellinek, *Beth ha-Midrash*. VI, p. XII; Epstein, *Beiträge zur jüdischen Altertumskunde*, p. 111, n.4).

[40] Mekilta, introduction; p. Sanh. XI 5 30b; Tanhuma ויקרא 8, צ end; Pirke R. Eliezer ch. 10; comp. R. Hai's responsum in קהלת שלמה No. 4 and Abraham bar Ḥiyya, *Hegion ha-Nefesh*,

paid for his punishment with terror of death, without actually dying. This conception is presupposed by the halakic sources as well-known, therefore they consider the brief allusion to Jonah sufficient.

(b) In this light the saying of R. Jonathan becomes evident: "Jonah fled with the intention to drown himself in the sea".[41] If this were meant only as evidence that Jonah wanted to sacrifice himself for Israel, there would seem to be no particular reason why just the sea should be chosen for that purpose. But Jonah who refused to proclaim a prophecy imparted to him by God wanted to undergo the punishment of drowning which has been decreed for this kind of sin.

(c) Now we are able to understand also the following remarkable haggadah: "Moses hesitates to undertake the mission. God persuades him, Moses raises objections, God disproves these objections, Moses interposes new ones. At last God says: From the legal standpoint thou hast deserved to be drowned at once, but I am the Merciful".[42] Moses who wants to be freed from his mission is a כובש נבואתו, whose punishment is drowning.

Now drowning corresponds to the punishment of strangulation (חנק).[43] This explains the following haggadahs:

(d) When David ordered the Shithin to be dug the Tehom ascended and threatened to drown the world. Then David spoke: "Whoever here knows that it is permitted to write God's name on a sherd and throw it into the waters and does not say it, will be strangled." Therefore Ahithophel died by strangling himself.[44]

[41] Mekilta, introduction: לא הלך יונה אלא לאבד עצמו בים. In Yalkut Jonah 550 and Yalkut ha-Makiri Jonah, p. 7, R. Nathan is the author of the sentence.
[42] Mekilta of R. Simeon, ed. Hoffmann, p. 3: מן הדין היית ראוי לשטיפה מיד אבל מה אעשה בעל רחמים אני. Comp. Midrash ha-gadol, ed. Hoffmann, p. 34, and Ozar Midrashim, ed. Wertheimer, I, 60.
[43] Comp. further, below, No. III.
[44] Suk. 53b, Mak. 11b: אכר דוד כל דידע למימר ואינו אומר יחנק בגרונו. Another version of this legend is found in p. Sanh. X 29a. Concerning the writings comp Feuchtwang in the Monatsschrift for 1910, p. 503 f.—Ahithophel's death II Sam. 17.23.

(e) When David wanted to transfer the ark of the covenant from the house of Abinadab to Jerusalem he forgot the precept of the Torah (Num. 7.9) that the ark of the covenant should be carried on the shoulders, and let it be placed on a wagon. The priests who accompanied the holy ark were thrown into the air and fell to the ground and they were again thrown on high and fell back again. Then David spoke: "He who knows the cause of the phenomenon and the means to appease the ark and does not say it, will be strangled later on." Ahithophel who knew it but—out of offended pride—did not say it ended his life through suicide, strangling himself.[45]

He who in urgent cases keeps his knowledge to himself and does not impart it to others is a כובש נבואתו and as such is punished by strangulation (חנק). "Ahithophel hanged himself because he kept the halakic decision back in his throat and refused to impart it to the world at large."[46]

3. R. Akiba imparted to his pupil R. Simeon, among other things, the following rule: "If thou wishest to be strangled, then hang thyself on a big tree."[47] What is the sense of this obscure passage? R. Hananel explains: "If thou hast something to ask in ritual affairs, then ask a great scholar and follow his decision."[48] R. Samuel ben Meir explains: "If thou wishest that people pay attention to thy words, then be instructed by a teacher and quote his lessons in his name." However, apart from the fact that these precepts are altogether too evident and very little wit is hidden in them, the expression "be strangled" remains obscure.[49]

---

[45] Comp. אמר דוד כל מאן דידע למיקמה ולא מקימה יהא סופיה מית חנקא P. as above Num. r, XII, 20. Another version in Seder Eliyyahu r. ch. 31 (ed. Friedmann, p. 157). Comp. Num. r. XXI, 12.

[46] Seder Eliyyahu as quoted above שכשם שתפס אחיתופל הגילוני הלכה בגרונו ולא אמרה לרבים לפיכך מת בחניקה אחת מארבע מיתות שנמסרו לבית דין.

[47] אם בקשת ליחנק התלה באילן גדול. Pes. 112a; Beth ha-Midrash, ed. Jellinek II, 98; פרקא דרבינו הקדוש, ed. Schönblum, 13b, No. 2.

[48] Commentary ad loc. Anonymous in 'Aruk s. v. חנק.

[49] Lewy, Neuhebr. Wörterbuch, I, 65a, s. v. אילן, offers the following explanation:

Rashi interprets as follows: "If thou wishest that thy words find approval with people, then tell them in the name of an acknowledged authority". The question involved then is pseudepigraphy. R. Akiba says: If under certain circumstances thou art compelled, in order to give weight to thy words, to proclaim them in the name of others, then call upon an eminent scholar, an acknowledged authority.

If this interpretation is correct, then it is eminently fitting that this rule be followed immediately by another to this effect: "If thou instructest thy son, instruct him from a correct copy." If one studies from an incorrect text one gets used to quote in the name of the author of the book sayings and expressions which do not belong to him; and unconsciously one becomes guilty of pseudepigraphy.[50]

However, Rashi's exposition is in fact the only correct one, because it alone explains the figure of speech "be strangled". For indeed the pseudepigraph does the same

"hang thyself to a big tree, in order to appear imposing even during the destruction." This is indeed a literal construction of the sentence! And did R. Akiba really recommend the grand pose? Schuhl, *Sentences et proverbes du Talmud*, p. 73, rejects the old explanations, because they do not explain the expression "if thou wishest to strangle thyself", and offers then an explanation of his own: "Si tu crains que, par tes propres forces, tu ne puisses pas parvenir, et que tu tiennes à réussir par tes relations, tâche au moins de fréquenter des hommes éminents: ne t'étrangle pas à un petit arbre, n'aneantis pas ton initiative et ta personalité pour te laisser subjuguer par un esprit ordinaire; mais attache-toi à un maître distingué ou à un protecteur qui jouit d'une grande consideration " Also Bacher, *Agada der Tannaiten*, I¹, 279, n. 3, accepts this explanation. But why should one's own incapacity and leaning on others be expressed by "wishing to hang oneself"? The sentence of Publilius Syrus, however, *rel strangulari pulchero de ligno juvat*—is a parallel to R. Akiba's expression only insofar as the literal sense goes. Its meaning is probably the same which Lewy attributes to R. Akiba's sentence. This meaning hinges on *strangulari*, but R. Akiba says: "if thou *wishest* to hang thyself". At any rate Schuhl should not seek support in the phrase of Publilius. Rashi's explanations, however, is supported by the Responsa of the Gaonim, ed. Ginzberg, *Geonica*, II, p. 31.

[50] In the responsum by R. Paltoi in חמדה גנוזה, No. 102, we read as follows: "If someone is convinced that an expression corresponds to the Halakah, but the people refuse to accept it from him, then he may say it in the name of his teacher, in order that it should be accepted; but if he is not fully convinced of the agreement of the expression with the Halakah, he must not ascribe it to his teacher." אם מכיר באותה שמועה שהיא כהלכה ואין מקבלין אותה ממנו אומרה משום רבו כדי שיקבלו ממנו, ואם אין ברור לו שהלכה היא אל יתלה ברבו. The responsum is an explanation of the saying of R. Eliezer, Ber. 27b, above: האומר דבר שלא שמע מפי רבו. Comp. also R. Jonah on Berakot. Tractate Kallah end: וכל האומר דבר בשם חכם שלא אמרו גורם לשכינה שתסתלק מישראל. Comp., however, 'Erubin 51a. This place is probably the source of the Gaon.

as the false prophet "who proclaims what was not imparted to him".[51] But the false prophet, according to the Halakah, receives the punishment of strangulation (חנק).[52] Therefore pseudepigraphy is called figuratively "be strangled" החנק, i. e. a deed which brings with it the punishment חנק.

It is not known whether R. Simeon ben Yohai ever made use of this precept imparted to him; but it is known that people employed this rule with reference to him, using him as "a big tree" on which to hang many a thing.

4. In criminal law, as also in civil law and in other fields of Halakah, there are effective in various questions two opposite views with reference to the child in the mother's womb. According to one view the child in the mother's womb is a part of the mother and has no independent existence; while the other view tends to assume an independent existence for such a child. These views are closely connected with the question as to the point of time when the embryo is endowed with a soul. The first view lets the soul enter the body only at the moment of the child's exit from the mother's womb; but according to the second view the connection between soul and body begins even in the mother's womb.[53] From this clash of ideas in the Halakah are elucidated the following haggadic controversies and sententious observations, whereby the connection between Haggadah and Halakah is clearly shown through the fact that the difference of opinions in the Haggadah is a consequence of the difference of opinions in the Halakah, which every one of the controversialists, from his halakic standpoint, cannot explain in any other way. This is shown especially clearly in the following haggadah, the only place in talmudic literature in which the two physiologic-psychological views are mentioned expressly.

[51] Sanh. XI, 5: נביא השקר המתנבא מה שלא שמע ומה שלא נאמר לו.
[52] Sanh. 89a.
[53] This theme is treated extensively in No. V. Hence I limit myself here to the statement of the results of that investigation.

(a) "Antoninus asked our teacher: from what time on does the soul dwell in man, before his exit from his mother's womb or after his exit from his mother's womb? Rabbi answered: Not before his exit from his mother's womb. Thereupon Antoninus answered: Not so, for if thou lettest flesh lie three days without salt[54] it is spoiled; but the connection with the soul takes place already during the impregnation. Rabbi then adopted the view of his royal friend."[55] But Rabbi figures otherwise as

[54] The soul as salt of the body in the popular proverb Niddah 31a. Comp. Rashi s. v. פוך and Toroth ha-Nefesh, ed. Broyde, p. 57f.

[55] Gen. r. XXXIV, 10: ועוד שאלו מאימתי נשמה נתנת באדם אמר לו משיצא ממעי אמו. אמר לו שים בשר בלא מלח שלשה ימים הלא יסריח, אלא משנפקד. והודה לו רבינו. In b. Sanh. 91b the question of Antoninus is put as follows: נשמה מאימתי נתנת באדם משעת פקידה או משעת יצירה, from the moment of conception or from the moment of formation? and Rabbi's answer is: from the moment of formation, משעת יצירה. This constitutes a transmutation of the legend and an accommodation to the point of view of the editors of the Babli, which corresponds to that of Philo, as we shall see further below in No. V.—To the place in Babli comp. Toroth ha-Nefesh 57a f. Interesting is the author's view concerning the person of Antoninus: He was a Syrian scholar who inherited the genuine science of Solomon through tradition. Then he communicates also the view of "some expositor" that Antoninus was a Roman emperor. But with reference to Rabbi's difference of opinion, there is nothing noticeable about it either in Rabbi's halakah or in his haggadah. A slight trace of it might perhaps be found in the narrative Yoma 82b: "Rabbi advised to whisper into the ear of a pregnant woman, who demands food on the Day of Atonement: To-day is the Day of Atonement. As the woman let herself be appeased by this admonition, Rabbi applied to it the biblical verse: 'Before I formed thee in the belly I knew thee' (Jer.1.5). The fruit of this pregnancy was R. Johanan". But the text is not altogether reliable. MS. Munich and the Iṭṭur read R. Ḥanina, as in the second narrative. Comp. Rabbinowicz. But what Rabbinowicz asserts in favor of the reading of the editions is not sound. 1.R. Johanan was also a pupil of R. Ḥanina, comp. Frankel, Introductio, 87a. In Gen. r. IV, 2, R. Johanan says: יפה למדני רבי חנינא. 2. It is not a halakic decision that is involved here, and in urgent cases we cannot be so exact as to the question of competence. Moreover, we must consider also the following circumstance. In the Mishnah Yoma VIII, 5, it is set down that a pregnant woman who demands food should be given to eat until she is appeased. Now if Rabbi had ascribed to the means of admonition any effect whatever, he would have recommended its employment in the Mishnah and would not have permitted without further hesitation to interrupt the fasting. For this reason the reading רבי, although followed also by R. Ḥananel and Alfasi, cannot be original. חנינה must have dropped out. In p. Yoma VIII, 4 45a below, it is R. Tarphon who recommends the means of admonition, and, to be sure, exactly as in the Bible once with success and another time without success. Rabbi's change of opinion, if it is historical, must therefore have been brought about towards the last years of his life, so that he found no opportunity in his capacity as teacher to give expression to his new view. But perhaps the assertion is not too farfetched that the statement that Rabbi became converted to the view of Antoninus is merely a presupposition and a reflection of the fact that the view fathered by Antoninus became the dominant view in the period succeeding Rabbi's death; comp. further below, No. V end. But this is in contradiction with the Halakah transmitted by Rabbi in the Mishnah, which rests on the standpoint that the child in the mother's womb is only a part of the mother (comp. further below, No.V), a view which is represented

exponent of the halakic view that the child in the mother's womb is a part of the mother,[56] and he advocated this view also in his own sphere of activity.

(b) R. Jose the Galilean says: When Israel came out of the sea and saw himself saved while his pursuers lay dead there below on the shore of the sea, he intoned a song of praise. The child lay in the mother's lap, the suckling sucked at the mother's breast; but as they beheld the Shekinah the child (עולל) stretched its neck, the suckling let the breast slip from its mouth, all of them spoke: "This is my God, and I will glorify Him" (Ex. 15,2). R. Meir used to say: Whence do we know that even the children in the mother's womb took part in the singing? We read: "Bless ye God in full assemblies, even the Lord, ye that are from the fountain of Israel" (Ps. 68.27)[57].

by Rabbi personally both in the Halakah and the Haggadah. Hence it was presupposed that Rabbi himself must have become converted to the new view, so that also the new view has for itself the authority of Rabbi, and at any rate does not conflict with it. —But it is interesting in that narrative that the child which reacted in the desired sense to the exhortation was R. Johanan. It is R. Johanan who in the Halakah emphasizes sharply the standpoint that the mother and the child in her womb are two bodies. Comp. further below, No. V, introduction end, and § 7. In this sense could be conceived his interpretation Gen. r. LXIII, 6 to Gen. 25.22: "The children struggled together within her womb. They ran one against another, each wanted to kill the other". But it is not meant here that they did this in the mother's womb, but that the struggling was a symbol for the later hostile relations between Esau and Jacob (Rome and Israel). Likewise Simeon ben Lakish, who in the struggling of the children wants to find a hint to the subsequent religious wars. Against these interpretations Berekyah maintains in the name of Levi: Do not believe that the struggle began only after their birth, but already in the mother's womb Esau clenched his fist against Jacob.—On the subject of "whispering into the ear of a pregnant woman" comp. Lucian I, 41-44; Tertullian, *De anima*, ch. 26 end (Opera, ed. Leopold, IV, 206). Tertullian interprets likewise Jer. 1.5 as in the Babli. Comp. in addition Löw, *Lebensalter*, p. 379, n. 141. It is a remarkable oversight in Löw when he maintains that according to the Babli "*the Biblical verses* were whispered into the ear of the pregnant woman".

[56] Giṭṭin 23b: מאי טעמא דרבי קסבר עובר ירך אמו. Comp. n. 125.
[57] Tosefta Soṭah VI, 4; Baraita Soṭah 30b; p. Soṭah V, 6 20c above. R. Meir's interpretation is found also in Mekilta to Ex. 15.1 and Tanḥuma בשלח § 11. In the Palestinian Talmud this interpretation is quoted in the name of R. Gamaliel, ר"ג. Unless this is simply a misscript of ר"מ, it agrees with the point of view of R. Gamaliel in the Halakah that the child in the mother's womb is a being in itself. Comp. further below, No. V.

On this haggadah comp. Wisdom of Solomon 10,21: "For Wisdom opened the mouth of the dumb, and made the tongues of babes eloquent." Comp. Bacher, *Agada der Tannaiten*, I¹, 364, n. 2. With reference to R. Meir's interpretation there is still the following to be said: In Midrash Psalms 8 § 3 it is told that during the revelation on Sinai the children in the mother's womb had taken the pledge upon themselves that

R. Jose of Galilee follows in the Halakah the view of Rabbi that the child in the mother's womb is but a part of the mother;[58] therefore he does not admit the unborn children to participation in the song. R. Meir, on the other hand, considers in the Halakah the child in the mother's womb as an independent existence,[59] therefore he lets it here participate in the singing.

(c) Both R. Jose and Rabbi refer Ps. 8.3 "Out of the mouth of babes and sucklings hast thou founded strength" to the song intoned during the passage of the sea, in which also children took part. But they differ as to the meaning of עוללים. R. Jose says: These are the children in the mother's womb, as we read in Job 3.16: "like עוללים that never saw light". Rabbi says: These are children that are outside—who walk on the street, as we read in Jer. 9.20: "to cut off עולל from the street" and in Lam. 4.4: "עוללים ask bread."[60] Since both views find clear

Israel will observe the Torah. But the connection in which this haggadah occurs is a deduction by R. Meir in Cant. r. to 1.4, where, however, children are the subject of discussion. Comp. also Tanḥuma ויש § 2.

[58] Kid. 69b, Tem. 25b. Comp. Mishne Torah, 'Abadim VII, 5, and commentaries ad. loc.

[59] Ḥul. IV, 4-5, Babli 72b f. Comp. Geiger, קבוצת מאמרים, ed Poznanski, I, 117f. Comp. Löw, Lebensalter, p. 65 and 379, n. 130. Herefrom is explained R. Meir's difficult standpoint in the controversy Yebamot 36b, 42a, Soṭah 26a. Comp. Mishne Torah נירושין II, 25, and commentaries ad. loc.

[60] Mekilta to Ex. 15.1 (ed. Friedmann 35a-b) and thence in Tanḥuma בשלח §11 end and Mid. Ps. 8 § 5. At first sight we see the name רבי יוסי הגלילי, but already Löw, Ben Chananya, IX, 698, n. 57, made the remark "that the reading in Mekilta, Shira I, is incorrect", without, however, suggesting any emendation. Also Bacher, Agada der Tannaiten, I¹, 364, n.2, notes that with respect to the Baraita in both Talmudim (comp. above, n. 57) this text cannot be original. But when Bacher thinks he must assume "that by a mistake what belongs to R. Judah I רבי was ascribed to Jose, while it was transmitted under the former's name that עולל means older children"—then this is in the first place an assumption of too great an insecurity of tradition, and secondly with regard to Rabbi also essentially not to the point, as we have seen above. And Bacher himself communicates later Rabbi's view according to the Mekilta. Comp. Agada der Tannaiten, II, 482. After all it is much more simple to strike out הגלילי. As a matter of fact we find רבי יוסי both times in Yalkut Ps. § 440 in the citation from Midr. Ps. Also in the old editions of Midr. Ps. הגלילי is missing, but there we find in both cases only ר"י. The older correction, which in the interpretation of R. Jose of Galilee reads: שיצאין ממעי אמן for שבמעי אמן, is impossible in view of the evidence from Job 3.16. In Yalkut ha-Makiri Ps. § 8 the Mekilta text reads עוללים שבמעי אמן.—In Midr. Ps. we find in Rabbi's interpretation יונקים אלו שבמעי אמן, which is naturally absurd, and should be as in the Mekilta שעל שדי אמן. But Buber maintains with all seriousness that the Mekilta should be corrected after Midr. Ps.! This might indeed be styled putting things upside down.

support in the Bible, the controversy cannot be settled on philological-exegetical lines. But it is a difference of principle: R. Jose, in halakic matters, considers the child in the mother's womb as a person possessing rights, and qualified to inherit,[61] therefore he endows it with spiritual life. But Rabbi, who maintains that the child in the mother's womb has no soul and independent life, cannot accept as valid that children in the mother's womb participated in the singing.

(d) R. Jose of Galilee and R. Akiba vary as to the exact wording of the call to grace. R. Jose of Galilee deduces his opinion from Ps. 68.27, while R. Akiba points to the house of prayer, where the call is always couched as follows: Praise ye God, to whom praise is due.[62] To this the Talmud propounds the usual question: How does R. Akiba explain the proof offered by his opponent? Answer: He interprets it in the same wise as R. Meir, that even the children in the mother's womb took part in the singing during the passage of the sea.[63]

This corresponds to the standpoint of R. Akiba in the Halakah that the child in the mother's womb is an independent being.[64] R. Jose of Galilee, however, in

[61] Yebamot VII, 4; Babli 67a; Yerushalmi 8b. Comp. Baba batra 143b.
[62] Berakot VII, 3.
[63] Berakot 50a.
[64] R. Akiba teaches that the dead child in the womb of the living mother constitutes a pollution like a corpse. Sifre Num. 127. Ḥul. 72a: עובר במעי אשה טמא. Thus R. Akiba considers the dead child in the mother's womb as a dead person. In the Talmud R. Akiba's opinion is derived from Num. 19.13, which is interpreted thus: "Whosoever toucheth the dead in the body of a man—which dead is found in the body of a man—the child in the mother's womb". It is the same interpretation which is employed by R. Ishmael in Gen. 9.6 in order to prove the death penalty of the Noahide for the murder of an embryo: "Whoso sheddeth man's blood in the man, his blood shall be shed". Comp. above, I, 1b, and further below, No. V. But it need hardly be stated that R. Ishmael and R. Akiba had not arrived at their doctrines through this forcible interpretation defying the natural meaning of the words. They could only employ this unnatural interpretation for the sole purpose of countering their opponents, who in their turn make use of the biblical text, by verifying their doctrines, which are founded on firm views and principles, also in an exegetical way. To R. Akiba in our case this verification was particularly required, as it is stated in Num. 19.16: "And whosoever toucheth in open field one murdered or dead", from which, literally constructed, it follows that the embryo enclosed in the mother's womb does not constitute a pollution: "in open field" means to exclude the child in the mother's womb.

consequence of his halakic standpoint, must decline R. Meir's interpretation, which he does quite clearly in the face of its originator, as we have seen.[65]

(e) Before the child leaves the mother's womb an oath is administered to it in the following way: "Become righteous and not wicked! And even if the whole world tells thee thou art just, thou shalt be a sinner in thy eyes.

R. Ishmael, who imposes a death penalty on the Noahide for the killing of an embryo considers indeed the child in the mother's womb as a "man" in the man, but in spite of this he refuses to admit its ability to defile as a corpse, because the Torah prescribes this (גזרת הכתוב). R. Ishmael, the rational exegete, sacrifices his view to the plain literal sense of a biblical passage; while R. Akiba interprets this passage in such a way that it does not contradict his view. The basic view of R. Ishmael, however, finds expression also here: "Whoever toucheth in open field one murdered or *dead* excepting the child in the mother's womb", thus the dead child in the mother's womb is one *dead*, an independent corpse, just as the living child in the mother's womb is an independent "man".

This difference of opinion between R. Ishmael and R. Akiba, with regard to the ability of the embryo to defile as a corpse, is therefore not fundamental but purely exegetical, the theoretical principle being the same. Should this need further confirmation, the following might be cited. The controversy betwen R. Meir and R. Jose in the Mishnah Ahiloth VII, 4 and Tosefta VIII end, according to the current conception, rests mainly on the difference of opinion between R. Ishmael and R. Akiba; comp. Maimonides and R. Simson, *ad loc.*, and Mishne Torah טומאת מת XXV, 7—in contradiction to Ra'bed, *ibid*. But we know that both R. Meir and R. Jose adhere to the standpoint that the child in the mother's womb is independent, And R. Meir who elaborates this principle very thoroughly, adheres in the question of the Levitic impurity of the embryo to the standpoint of R. Ishmael!—Therefore Gronemann, *Die Jonathansche Pentateuchübersetzung*, p. 122, n. 1, misses the point when he thinks that the controversy in question between R. Ishmael and R. Akiba rests on the difference of view concerning the independence of the embryo. This would seem to imply that R. Akiba considers the child in the mother's womb as something independent, while R. Ishmael looks upon it as a part of the mother. At the same time he remarks immediately after "that in R. Ishmael's statement, that the Noahide is punished with death also for the killing of an embryo, one may find expressed the independence of the embryo."

R. Simson to Ahiloth *loc. cit.* thinks that in the controversy between R. Ishmael and R. Akiba it must be presupposed that it was נפתח הקבר which is considered as birth—otherwise, however, the child in the mother's womb is indeed only a part of the mother and cannot effect the impurity of a corpse. This construction is adopted also by R. Asher *ad loc.* Tosafot Ḥul. under the caption מירה are not satisfied with נפתח הקבר and propose the condition that the child stretch out its hand. This view is adopted by R. Meir of Rothenburg *ad loc.* In the sources, however (comp. also Sifre zutta to 19,13 and 16, ed. Horowitz, Leipzig 1919, pp. 306, 310, and Jon. in V. 16), there is not the slightest indication of such conditions. As a matter of fact R. Solomon ben Aderet knows nothing of all this and answers the question of the Tosafot in a different way. Moreover, we should note the following: Sifre zutta accepts the view of R. Ishmael that the dead embryo does not defile. Now Horowitz in his introduction has made it appear probable that this Midrash is derived from the school of R. Eliezer ben Jacob. But R. Eliezer ben Jacob adheres to the standpoint that the child in the mother's womb is an independent being. Comp. further below, No. V.

[65] If the Talmud says that R. Jose of Galilee finds R. Meir's interpretation in the expression ממקור, it is to be understood that R. Jose would derive this interpretation from ממקור, if he should own it. Comp. also יפה עינים *ad loc.*

Know that God is pure, His servants are pure, and the soul that He has given thee is pure. If thou wilt preserve it in purity, well and good; if not, thou shalt be deprived of it". The school of R. Ishmael propounds hereby the following simile: A priest transmits the heave-offering to an *'am ha-arez* and says to him: "If thou wilt preserve it in purity, well and good; but if not, I shall burn it in thy presence".[66]

This corresponds to the standpoint of R. Ishmael in the Halakah, that the child in the mother's womb is an independent being, a "man", whose killing is punished by death.[67]

(f) The halakah that the benedictions at the wedding-meal must be pronounced only in the presence of ten persons is derived by Rab Nahman from Ruth 4.2.[68] R. Abahu, on the other hand, derives it from Ps. 68.27.[69] This difference of opinion with respect to the deduction of one and the same halakah is explained thus in the Talmud: Rab Nahman employs Ps. 68.27 for the interpretation of R. Meir, while R. Abahu thinks that the verse cannot be interpreted that way.[70]

Here the halakic correspondence is given only for Rab Nahman. His point of view is that the child in the mother's womb is a person possessing rights, certainly to the extent even of acquiring gifts under certain conditions.[71] R. Abahu's standpoint in the Halakah is not known. He may also consider the child in the mother's womb as an independent being and yet not refer the verse in Psalms

---

[66] Nid. 30b: אינו יוצא משם עד שמשביעין אותו ... אם אתה משמרה בטהרה מוטב ואם לא הריני נוטלה ממך תנא דבי רבי ישמעאל משל לכהן. The picture of the burning of the heave-offering for the death corresponds at once to the haggadic conception that the natural death enters through the burning of the inner organs. Comp. above.

[67] Comp. above, note 64.

[68] Ket. 7b; p. Ket. I, 25a; Midr. Ps. 92 §7; Pirke R. Eliezer ch. 19.

[69] Comp. hereon Tosafot s. v. במקהלות and p. Ber. VII, 3.1. Comp. Norzi on Ps. 68.27.

[70] Ket. *l. c.*: אם כן לימא קרא מבטן מאי ממקור על עסקי מקור.

[71] Baba batra 141b, 142a, comp. Tosafot 141b s. v. איתיביה.

to the song of the children. What is sure according to our principle is this, that he who as haggadist ascribes spiritual life to the child in the mother's womb cannot consider it in the Halakah as a part of the mother.

(g) On a par with Rab Nahman also R. Eleazar ben Pedath considers the child in the mother's womb as a person possessing rights and capable of inheriting and acquiring gifts.[72] Therefore R. Eleazar says: "The hypocrite is cursed even by the children in the mother's womb."[73] Hence R. Eleazar accepts the haggadah according to which the child is exhorted and administered an oath before leaving the mother's womb, and he adduces a proof for it from the Bible.[74]

(h) It is told of R. Hanina that he recommended that pregnant women who wanted something to eat on the Day of Atonement have it whispered in their ear: To-day is the day of Atonement. Accordingly he ascribes to the child in the mother's womb spiritual life and power of thinking, which corresponds to his standpoint in the Halakah that the Noahide is punished with death for murder of the *nasciturus*.[75]

II

THE TALIO IN TERRESTRIAL AND CELESTIAL JURISDICTION

The foundation of the deductions in I, 1 is based on the idea that according to the requirements of *talio* the murderer must lose his life in the same way in which he deprived his neighbor of his life. This will now be proved. We read in the Book of Jubilees 4.31: "His house fell on him and he died in the midst of his house, and he was killed by its stones, for with a stone he had killed

---

[72] Cp. Yeb. IV. 1 5c; abbreviated in Baba Batra IX, 1 16a. It is the standpoint of R. Johanan, Baba batra 142b.
[73] Soṭah 41b.
[74] Niddah 31a above.
[75] Comp. notes 55 and 142.

Abel, and by a stone was he killed in righteous judgment. For this reason it was ordained on the heavenly tables: 'With the instrument with which a man killeth his neighbour with the same shall he be killed; after the manner that he wounded him, in like manner shall they deal with him.' "[76] This constitutes the Samaritan and Sadducean standpoint,[77] which the Pharisees combated with the help of exegesis. Thus we read in a Baraita transmitted by R. Johanan: "The murderer shall be slain (Num. 35.30). Wherewith shall he be slain? We might think that if he had killed with a sword, he too shall perish by a sword, but if he had killed with a stick, he too shall perish by a stick, therefore it says" etc.[78] That Philo adheres to the standpoint of the Sadducees, as Büchler[79] maintains, is not sure.[80] There is no support for the conception of Josephus = Philo, Büchler, *loc. cit.*, since the passage adduced by Büchler

[76] In the Armenian Code of Laws 155 it is said with regard to the murderer through arson: "and he must, in case he is involved in that guilt, be condemned to the same fire". *Ibid.* 133: "If someone strangles or kills a child in the act of prostitution or for the sake of some other infamous act, the law ordains that...he shall die exactly the same death as that child". Comp. Aptowitzer, *Beiträge zur mosaischen Rezeption im armenischen Recht*, p. 41.

An allusion to the legend contained in the Book of Jubilees is found perhaps in the folowing sentence: נתחייב אדם סקילה ביתו נופל עליו או חיה נזרתו, Sifre zutta, ed. Horowitz, Leipzig 1917, p. 354. In all other texts of the Baraita of R. Ḥiyya—comp. further below note—we find instead: נופל מן הגג.

[77] From these circles the Book of Jubilees is derived. Comp. the literature in the introduction to Kautzsch's translation of the book, *Apokryphen und Pseudepigraphen des alten Testamentes*, II.

[78] p. Sanh. VII, 3 24b: אמר ר' יוחנן ותני כן ירצח [את] הרוצח במה ירצח? יכול אם הרגו בסייף, יהרגנו בסייף, במקל יהרגנו במקל נאמר כאן נקימה וכו'.

[79] *Monatsschrift* for 1906, p. 678, n. 1.

[80] Comp. Ritter, *Philo und die Halacha*, p. 22, n. 1. And even if Büchler were right, there would still be no justification to conclude from Philo's remarks that the view of the Sadducees had practical application. Further on—comp. No. V—we shall come across an example illustrating that Philo, out of ignorance and faulty reflection, quotes Egyptian-Greek legal practices as biblical laws. This may be the case here too. As a matter of fact we find that the "mirroring penalties"—and it is such of which Philo treats—played an important part in the penal code of the Egyptians. Comp. Diodorus Siculus, I, ch. 18. Comp. also Günther, *Idee der Wiedervergeltung*, p. 30, n. 26–29, and Weissman, *Talion und öffentliche Strafe im Mosaischen Recht*, p. 24. It is also possible that Philo, likewise out of faulty reflection, had transferred the thought of the mirroring of the penalty from heavenly to earthly jurisdiction.

By mirroring penalties we understand such kinds of punishment as call forth a memory of the actions and moments during the commission of the crime. Comp. Brunner, *Zeitschrift der Savignystiftung*, XI, Germanic division, p. 235; Brunner, *Deutsche Rechtsgeschichte*, III, 139, n. 9; Weissman, *Talion und öffentliche Strafe im Mosaischen Recht*, p. 22, 3.

deals only with bodily wounds. It is to be accepted with great probability that at the time of Philo the standpoint of the Sadducees had long been overcome and the old practice of indemnity in case of wounds and uniform punishment for murder had been rehabilitated.

The compensation in case of bodily wounds and the uniformity of capital punishment for murder, both are derived from one and the same motive: because the extent of the pain suffered during the wounding and dying cannot be estimated exactly and it is to be feared that the injurer and the murderer might suffer a greater pain than that suffered by the injured and murdered. However, these scruples are in question only in terrestrial jurisdiction; as to divine justice, it can effect the *talio* exactly. For this reason also the offences which are punished with death through Heaven are not subject to the *conditiones sine quibus non* by which a temporal court is guided in its decree of capital punishment.[81] As a matter of fact we see that in rabbinic literature, which does not consider the *talio* valid for temporal jurisdiction, the idea of divine retaliation "measure for measure" occurs very frequently. Thus we read in the Mishnah, Sotah 8b: "With the same measure, with which man measures, he is measured by God".[82] At greater length Tosefta Sotah III, 1, where R. Meir deduces from Is. 27.3 and Eccles. 7.27 that measure for measure extends even to very small measures.[83] Comp. Sotah 8b; Sanh. 100a; p. Sotah I, 7, 17a top, and Midrash on Ps. 81 § 20. The theme is discussed also in Tosefta Sotah III–IV; Mekilta (ed. Friedmann) 7b, 25a, 26a, 28b,

---

[81] Comp. Aptowitzer, *Monatsschrift* for 1916, p. 430f. Comp. Rashi in Sanh. 40b below: והאי קרא גבי כרת כתיב ואם אינו ענין לחיוב כרת, דהאי דין שמים הוא ולא בעי התראה, דקמי שמיא גליא אם שוגג הוא או מזיד.

[82] במדה שאדם מודד מודדין לו.

[83] היה ר' מאיר אומר מנין שבמדה שאדם מודד מודדין לו שנאמר בסאסאה בשלחה תריבנה וגו' אין לי אלא שמדד בסאה מנין לרבות תרקב חצי תרקב ת"ל כי כל סאון סואן ברעש אין לי אלא דבר שבמדה מנין שאפילו פרוטות קטנות מצטרפין לחשבון גדול ת"ל אחת לאחת למצוא חשבון.

32b[84], 35a, 38b, 59a; Mekilta of R. Simeon, pp. 40, 42, 47, 53, 58, 62, 88; Sifre Num. 43, Deut. 18, 106; Sifre zutta (ed. Horwitz), p. 236; b. Shab. 105b, Meg. 12b, Baba meṣ. 86b, Sanh. 90a under מדה כנגד מדה, *ibid.* 94a-b, 108a-b; p. Sotah II, 3, 33b; Gen. r. IX, 11 and XLVIII, 10, l. 8; Pesikta d'Rab Kahana 81b-83a; Lev. r. XXXIV, 8; Midrash Deut. r. MS. Munich in Buber's ליקוטים, p. 23, No. 23; Cant. r. to 1.9; Eccles. r. on 11. 1; Tanhuma בראשית 12, וירא 4 (ed. Buber 5), וארא 14, בשלח 6, 12; Pesikta rabbati ch. 14, 37a, 44a; Seder Eliyyahu r. ch. 8 p. 40 ff, ch. 12 p. 50f., 111; Midrash on Ps. 17 4, 18 14, 22 1; Ex. r. I, 9; IV, 10; X, 3; XI, 3; XVI, 5; Num. r. IX, 18; XIV, 2. Comp. also Midrash haggadol (ed. Hoffmann) pp. 62, 63, 67; also Sanh. 108 a-b; Pes. r. 165b; Seder Eliyyahu r. ch. 3 p. 14.

Wisdom of Solomon 11.15–17 and 20: "In requital of the foolish imaginings of their unrighteousness, by which they were led astray, they worshipped senseless reptiles and wretched vermin, Thou having sent upon them for vengeance a multitude of senseless animals in order that they might know that by what things a man sinneth, by these he is punished. For Thine all-powerful hand, that created the world out of formless matter, lacked not the means to send upon them a multitude of bears or fierce lions...And without these they might have fallen by a single breath, being pursued by justice, and scattered abroad by the breath of Thy power. But all things by measure and number and weight didst Thou order".[85] Matthew

[84] שבמדה שחשבו מצרים לאבד את ישראל בה אני דנן, הם חשבו לאבד את בני במים איני נפרע מהם אלא במים.

[85] ἀντὶ δὲ λογισμῶν ἀσυνέτων ἀδικίας αὐτῶν, ἐν οἷς πλανηθέντες ἐθρήσκευον ἄλογα ἑρπετὰ καὶ κνώδαλα εὐτελῆ, ἐπαπέστειλας αὐτοῖς πλῆθος ἀλόγων ζῴων εἰς ἐκδίκησιν, ἵνα γνῶσιν ὅτι δι' ὧν τις ἁμαρτάνει, διὰ τούτων κολάζεται. οὐ γὰρ ἠπόρει ἡ παντοδύναμός σου χεὶρ καὶ κτίσασα τὸν κόσμον ἐξ ἀμόρφου ὕλης ἐπιπέμψαι αὐτοῖς πλῆθος ἄρκων ἢ θρασεῖς λέοντας. καὶ χωρὶς δὲ τούτων ἑνὶ πνεύματι πεσεῖν ἐδύνατο ὑπὸ τῆς δίκης διοχθέντες καὶ λικμηθέντες ὑπὸ πνεύματος δυνάμεως σου. ἀλλὰ πάντα μέτρῳ καὶ ἀριθμῷ καὶ σταθμῷ διέταξας.

7.2: "For with what judgment ye judge, ye shall be judged; and with what measure ye mete, it shall be measured to you again".[86]

III

The Punishment for Adultery in Jewish Law and in the Code of Hammurabi

The Mishnah lays down death by strangulation (חנק) for adultery.[87] And from the canon of the Baraita of R. Hiyya we know that death through drowning corresponds to death through strangulation: "He who commits a sin punishable by strangulation drowns in the river or dies through suffocation".[88] Accordingly the law of the Mishnah corresponds to the analogous law in the Code of Hammurabi. For among the death penalties in the Code of Hammurabi death through drowning occurs five times, and in four cases out of five the crime is adultery.[89]

<small>Weissman, *Talion und öffentliche Strafe im Mosaischen Recht*, p. 24, finds in this passage some support for the Egyptian provenance of the Wisdom of Solomon, since in Egyptian law the "mirroring penalties" were of great importance; comp. above, note 80. But we have seen that the mirroring of the penalty in the case of divine retaliation is a fundamental thought of Palestinian Judaism. The agreement of the passage in Wisdom with the sentence במדה שאדם מודד מודדין לו is pointed out also by Weinstein, *Zur Genesis der Agada*, II, 18, but he knows this sentence only from Sanh. 100a.

To the expression ἐξ ἀμόρφου ὕλης in v. 18 comp. I. Cohn, *Guttmann-Festschrift*, pp. 22–29, and in connection therewith Aptowitzer, *Freie Jüdische Lehrerstimme* for 1915, p. 100a, n. 1.

[86] Μὴ κρίνετε, ἵνα μὴ κριθῆτε. ἐν ᾧ γὰρ κρίματι κρίνετε κριθήσεσθε, καὶ ἐν ᾧ μέτρῳ μετρεῖτε μετρηθήσεται ὑμῖν.

[87] Sanh. X, 1.

[88] Other correspondences are: Stoning = plunging from the roof or being torn by wild animals; burning = plunging into a conflagration or being bitten by a snake; decapitation = being condemned by a pagan court or being attacked by robbers. שנתחייב סקילה או נופל מן הגג או חיה דורסתו מי שנתחייב שריפה או נופל בדליקה או נחש מכישו מי שנתחייב הריגה או נמסר למלכות או לסטין באין עליו מי שנתחייב חנק או טובע בנהר או מת בסרונכי. Ket. 30b, Soṭah 8b, Sanh. 37b. Comp. Sifre zutta, ed. Horowits, Leipzig 1927, p. 354; Agadat Bereshit, ch. 1, ed. Buber p. 2; Num. r. XIV, 7.

[89] §§129, 133, 143, 155. D. H. Müller, *Die Gesetze Hammurabis*, pp. 34, 35, 39, 42. §129: "If a man's wife is caught cohabiting with another man, they are (both) bound and thrown into the water". Karl Emil Franzos relates in his *Halbasien* of a popular song current in Ukraine, the burden of which is that a young adulteress is lured by her husband's relatives to a bridge and thence she is thrown into the water. Perhaps there is here a trace of the old penalty for adultery, which was the same to the forefathers of the Ukrainians as in Hammurabi and in Jewish law. For another similar agreement see Aptowitzer, *Freie Jüdische Lehrerstimme*, IV (1915), Nos. 1 and 2, article 4.</small>

Thus the statute of the received halakah reaches back into gray antiquity, indeed goes back to primitive Semitic tradition.

In later times, in the days of Ezekiel and Jeremiah, we find in Babylonia and Assyria two other death penalties for adultery: stoning[90] or burning.[91] This explains the account in the story of Susanna according to the Septuagint version. For we read there, after the two elders, who had accused Susanna of adultery, had been convicted of false testimony, as follows: "And they dealt with them according as the Law prescribes, doing to them just as they maliciously intended against their sister. So when they had gagged them, they led them out and hurled them into a chasm; then the angel of the Lord cast fire in the midst of them."[92] The narrator combined both kinds of death customary in the Babylonian courts, stoning and burning, which were perhaps inflicted on the adulteress also among the Jews, when they were in possession of their own criminal jurisdiction.[93]

The Sadducees, supported by the wording in Ezekiel, punished adultery by stoning.[94] But they were not aware that in Ezekiel the punishment is meted out to

[90] Ez. 16.38–41; 23.45–48. Comp. Dillmann, *Die Genesis*, p. 401, in Gen. 38.19–29; Delitzsch, *Neuer Kommentar über die Genesis*, p. 450; but especially Büchler, *Monatsschrift* for 1906, p. 546ff.

[91] Jer. 29.22–23: "May God make thee like Zedekiah and Ahab whom the king of Babel hath burned in fire. Because they had done shameful deeds in Israel and committed adultery with the wives of their neighbours". אשר קלם מלך בבל באש יען אשר עשו נבלה בישראל וינאפו את נשי רעיהם. Comp. hereon Sanh. 93a, Pesikta ed. Buber 164b f., Tanḥuma ויקרא 6 (ed. Buber 10), Pirke R. Eliezer ch. 33.

[92] Verses 62–63. In the version of Theodotion: "and dealt with them after the evil which they had brought again upon their neighbour, acting in accordance with the law of Moses, and killed them".

[93] Comp. especially the addition in a Syriac version as recorded by Charles, *Apocrypha*, II, 338. Comp. also Büchler in the *Monatsschrift* for 1906, p. 670.

[94] Comp. John 8. 4–5, and Büchler *l. c.* If in that passage it is the Pharisees who maintain that according to the law of Moses the adulteress is to be stoned, this is to be explained from the circumstance that the inventor of this narrative simply and, as it were, mechanically puts forth his usual opponents. Of course it is not impossible that we have here not a reminiscence of a practical exercise of the law, which in the days of the author of this narrative had long come into desuetude among the Jews in cases of crimes involving death, but only a utilization of the close of the Susanna narrative.

Jerusalem by the Assyrians and Babylonians, who judge in accordance with Assyrian-Babylonian law, as it is said expressly 23.23-24: The Babylonians and all the Chaldeans, Pekod and Shoa and Koa, and all the Assyrains with them...and I will commit the judgment unto them, and they shall judge thee according to their judgments". The Pharisees recognized this and stuck to the old legal usage, punishing adultery with strangulation (חנק).

The Haggadah, however, has retained reminiscences from the time when jurisdiction lay in the hands of the Sadducees and adultery was punished by stoning.

(1) Ben Azzai says: He who hates his wife is a shedder of blood. For there comes a time when he produces false witnesses and hands his wife over to be stoned.[95]

(2) The apocryphal story of R. Meir and the wife of his host: The same thing happened to R. Meir and the wife of his host that Gen. 19.33-35 tells of Lot and his daughter. When he became aware of it he was seized by a great despair. He went forthwith to the head of the academy and told him his misfortune, with the remark: "I will submit to everything, be it that you order me to be killed or to be devoured by wild beasts." The head of the academy postponed the decision to the next day. The following day he said to R Meir: "We have investigated your case and resolved to cast you before the wild beasts, namely the lions". He then ordered R. Meir to be led into the woods and be left there bound. At midnight a lion came, sniffed at R. Meir and went away. On the third night at last a lion came, roared at R. Meir and tore away one of his ribs. With that his guilt was atoned.[96]

---

[95] Derek Erez zutta ch. 11: בן עזאי אומר השונא את אשתו הרי זה משופכי דמים. So שנאמר ושם לה עלילות דברים, סוף שהוא שוכר עדים ומקדימה לסקילה (Deut.22.14). manuscripts in Epstein's *Beiträge zur jüdischen Altertumskunde*, p. 115. Comp. Aptowitzer in Büchler, *Monatsschrift* for 1906, p. 760, n. 3. So also Maḥzor Vitry, p. 734. In the editions לסקילה was changed to לבית הסקילה, that is the general designation for the place of execution, as it seems to appear from Sanh. VI, 1-VII, 3.

[96] The narrative is found in the Midrash of the Ten Commandments (Jellinek's

But we know that to be torn by wild animals is equivalent to the punishment of death through stoning.[97]

IV

THE EXEGETICAL FOUNDATION OF THE PUNISHMENT OF DECAPITATION FOR MURDER

THE punishment of the murderer is death through the sword (הרג).[98] On this point there is universal agreement. But opinions differ as to the exegetical proofs brought to bear on this law. According to the canon that the unqualified death penalty in the Bible is death through strangulation,[99] the murderer whose punishment is not indicated in the Torah should suffer the death penalty of חנק. The ancient law, however, has—always or after the removal of *talio* in capital punishment[100]—punished murder with decapitation. For this a biblical source was sought. Now there are in rabbinic writings two different deductions. The Mekilta of R. Ishmael points to Gen. 9.6: "Whoso sheddeth man's blood, by man shall his blood be shed".[101] The Mekilta of R. Simeon, on the other hand, points to the smiting of the bondman (Ex. 21.20), where the expression "he shall be revenged" with reference to Lev. 26.25 must mean death through the sword.[102] In the

---

Bet ha-Midrash, I. 81–83; *Botte Midrashot*, ed. Wertheimer, II, 26–28), which probably dates from the tenth century; comp. Zunz, *Gottesdienstliche Vorträge*², p. 151. In the *Seder ha-Dorot s. v.* ר' מאיר (ed. Zitomir 1867), p. 110c ff., from a "small book" by which the author as a rule means the חיבור יפה מהישועה by R. Nissim ben Jacob of Kairuwan, comp. Harkavy in *Steinschneider-Festschrift*, p. 11; but here the narrative reads quite differently, comp. ed. Amsterdam, 28a–b.

[97] Comp. above n. 88.
[98] Sanh. IX, I. Comp. Büchler in *Monatsschrift* for 1906, p. 601ff.
[99] Comp. above I.
[100] Comp. above II
[101] Mekilta on Ex. 21.12, ed. Friedmann 80a.
[102] Ed. Hoffmann, p. 125: מות יומת אין אנו יודעין במה תהא מיתתו של זה, הרי הוא אומר נקם ינקם ונאמר להלן הבאתי עליכם חרב נוקמת נקם הברית, מה נקימה האמורה להלן בסייף אף נקימה האמורה כאן בסייף. So also p. Sanh. VII, 1 and the baraita transmitted by R. Johanan, *ibid.* VII, 3 24b: אמר רבי יוחנן ותני כן ירצח הרוצח במה ירצח יכול אם הרגו בסייף יהרגנו בסייף במקל יהרגנו במקל, נאמר כאן נקימה ונאמר להלן והבאתי עליכם חרב נקמת נקם ברית, מה נקימה שנאמר להלן בחרב אף נקימה שנאמר כאן מיתה בחרב. Comp. Mishne Torah, Rozeah, I, 1. The source of Maimonides is not—as Schwarz, *Der Mischneh Torah*, p. 214, No. 139, thinks—Mekilta Mishpatim 6, since the Mekilta is

same way also a Baraita in the Babylonian Talmud,[103] where the following discussion is involved.

Question: Now it is true that we find proof for the case that a bondman is killed; but whence do we know that also the killing of a freeman is punished by the sword?

Answer: Is it not a necessary corollary? If the killing of a bondman is punished by the sword, how should the killing of a freeman be punished only by strangulation?

Question: This conclusion is justified only if we take the standpoint that the decree of strangulation is lesser than that of decapitation; but how about the opinion of others who consider strangulation as a much severer punishment?

Result: In accordance with this opinion the corollary, indeed, falls away, and we must look for another proof to support the punishment of the murderer with death through the sword.[104] Now the opinion that strangulation is a severer punishment than decaptitation has R. Simeon as its main supporter,[105] and accordingly, in keeping with the consequence drawn in the Babylonian Talmud from this opinion, the deduction of the punishment of decapitation for murder in the Mekilta of R. Simeon should not be attributed to him. But in reality the result arrived at through the discussion in the Babyl. Talmud is a necessary consequence only when the קל וחמר syllogism is employed; if, however, plain analogy is used, as it happens in the Mekilta, then the discussion falls away and with it its result. The conclusion reads: Murder in the case of a freeman (A) is punished by death (P), murder in the case

altogether ignorant of this deduction. Another foundation Mishne Torah, Sanh. XIV,1; comp. Leḥem Mishne *ad loc.* Or השמועה = מפי משה; מפי.

[103] Sanh. 52b: דתניא נקם ינקם נקימה זו איני יודע מה היא, כשהוא אומר והבאתי עליכם חרב נוקמת נקם ברית הוי אומר נקימה זו חרב. Comp. Mekilta 83b and Mekilta of R. Simeon, p. 129.

[104] אשכחן דקטל עבדא בן חורין מנא לן? ולאו קל וחומר הוא, קטל בסייף בן חורין בחנק? הניחא למאן דאמר חנק קל, אלא למאן דאמר חנק חמור מאי איכא למימר? נפקא ליה מדתניא.

[105] Sanh. VII, 1. Babli 49b, Yerushalmi 24b.

of a bondman (B) is likewise punished by death; in the latter case the punishment is decapitation (S), therefore also in the former case the punishment is decapitation:

$$A \text{ is } P$$
$$B \text{ " } P$$
$$PB = S$$
$$\overline{}$$
$$PA = S$$

As a matter of fact we find this analogy in the Mekilta of R. Simeon: "It is a syllogism by analogy. One is liable to death for murder of a bondman and one is liable to death for murder of a freeman; just as murder of a freeman is only punishable with death when the stroke was fatal, so also murder of a bondman is punishable with death only when the stroke was fatal".[106]

A similar case of analogy by R. Simeon is found in Mekilta to Ex. 21.20.[107] For the death penalty by the sword for murder this analogy finds also strong support in the fact that the death penalty for both murder of the

---

[106] p. 129: ודין הוא חייב בעבד וחייב בבן חורין, מה בן חורין עד שיהא במכה כדי להמית אף בעבד עד שיהא במכה כדי להמית.

[107] Ed. Friedmann 84a: רבי שמעון בן יוחאי אומר למה נאמר עד שלא יאמר יש לי בדין הואיל ושורו במיתה על עבדו ועל אמתו ושור אחר במיתה על עבדו ועל אמתו הוא במיתה על עבדו ועל אמתו ואחר במיתה על עבדו ועל אמתו אם למדת שלא חלק בין שורו לשור אחר במיתה על עבדו ועל אמתו לא נחלק בינו לבין אחר במיתה על עבדו ועל אמתו ת"ל לא יוקם כי כספו הוא מגיד הכתוב שאף על פי שלא חלק בין שורו לשור אחר במיתה על עבדו ועל אמתו נחלוק בינו לבין אחר במיתה על עבדו ועל אמתו. This deduction is preceded by the following sentence: לא יוקם כי כספו הוא וזהו שהיה רבי ישמעאל אומר בכנעני הכתוב מדבר. It refers to R. Ishmael's remark on verse 20, 83b above. Hereto Ginzberg remarks in *Festschrift zu Israel Lewy's 70. Geburtstag*, p. 433: "Of the two Derashot of the Mekilta on כי כספו MS. 128 knows only one, and, to be sure, that one which is there ascribed to R. Ishmael but is quoted in the MS. in the name of R. Simeon. In view of the fact that R. Ishmael's views are very seldom taken cognizance of in the MS., and, furthermore, that in the MS this Derash is opposed by R. Judah, the colleague of R. Simeon, it would appear that in the Mekilta the names ר' ישמעאל and ר' שמעון had interchanged, and we should read: זהו שהיה ר' שמעון אומר בכנעני הכתוב מדבר רבי ישמעאל אומר למה וכו'. Likewise l. c. 83b רי"ש should be emended to ר"ש. But with this the difficulty is not sidetracked. For the view which in the Mekilta of R. Simeon is quoted in the name of R. Judah, belongs in the Mekilta to R. Eliezer. Moreover, the texts of the Mekiltas are confirmed by weighty witnesses: We-Hizhir ed. Freimann, I, 134f., 138; Lekaḥ Ṭob on verse 20; Yalkut, II, §§334, 335. The text of the Mekilta is therefore irreproachable. If we want to retain both texts, we must think of different traditions, which is favored also by a linguistic difference, or else we must declare the text of the Midrash ha-gadol to be faulty; in this case we have four witnesses against a single one.

freeman and murder of the bondman is decreed in one and the same sentence—Ex. 21.12.[108] Now if the Torah qualifies the punishment in the case of murder of a bondman, this qualification serves also for the case of murder of a freeman. It is the eighth Middah of R. Ishmael.[109]

An express application of this Middah by R. Simeon is found in the Mishnah, Temurah I, 6.[110]

V

THE STATUS OF THE EMBRYO IN CRIMINAL LAW

IN the juridico-criminal treatment of the killing of a child in the mother's womb, the *nasciturus*, Jewish law advances two opposite views. One view considers the killing of the *nasciturus* as murder and punishes it with death, another view pronounces the killer of the *nasciturus* free.

The severer tendency finds its earliest attestation in the Septuagint.[111] It is followed by Philo,[112] the Didache[113] Samaritans,[114] and Karaites.[115] The milder conception

[108] Comp. Mekilta on Ex. 21.20, 83a: עבדו ושפחתו בכלל מכה איש ומת.
[109] דבר שהיה בכלל ויצא מן הכלל ללמד לא ללמד על עצמו יצא אלא ללמד על הכלל כלו יצא. Comp. Schwarz, *Die hermeneutische Induction*, p. 175, and Schwarz, *Die hermeneutische Quantitätsrelation*, p. 195f.
[110] Comp. also Mekilta of R. Simeon, p. 130: חבורה בכלל היתה ויצאת ללמד, ולא ללמד על עצמה אלא ללמד על הכלל.
[111] It translates Ex. 21.22–23 as follows: If two men wrestle with one another and hit a woman that has [a child] in her womb, and the child comes forth while it is not formed yet, the penalty shall be a money penalty...But if it was formed, then thou shalt give a life for a life. Ἐὰν δὲ μάχωνται δύο ἄνδρες καὶ πατάξωσιν γυναῖκα ἐν γαστρὶ ἔχουσαν, καὶ ἐξέλθῃ τὸ παιδίον αὐτῆς μὴ ἐξεικονισμένον ἐπιζήμιον ζημιωθήσεται καθότι ἂν ἐπιβάλῃ ὁ ἀνὴρ τῆς γυναικός, δώσει μετὰ ἀξιώματος. ἐὰν δὲ ἐξεικονισμένον ἦν δώσει ψυχὴν ἀντὶ ψυχῆς. Comp. Frankel, *Ueber den Einfluss*, p. 80.
[112] Comp. further below.
[113] Didache 2.1–2: "Now the second command of the teaching: Thou shalt not kill...Thou shalt not murder the child in the mother's womb nor kill the newly born". This extension of the biblical command is directed against the immoral practice, current among the Greeks, of seed diversion and exposure of the newly born. The first six chapters of the Didache are a special treatise by a Jew "intended for proselytes, based on the Decalogue and an attenuation of its commandments". Comp. Drews in Hennecke, *Neutestamentliche Apokryphen*, p. 185.
[114] Comp. Geiger, *Urschrift*, p. 439; *Hebräische Aufsätze*, ed. Poznanski, I, 119.
[115] Kirkisani (Poznanski in *Kaufmann-Gedenkschrift*, p. 186 above, p. 177). Hadassi, *Eshkol ha-Kofer*, alphabet 270, p. 103b, alphabet 275 p. 104b; Mibḥar and Keter Torah on Ex. 21.22–23; Gan 'Eden 177d. Comp. Geiger *l. c.* pp. 438, 116, 119; Löw, *Lebensalter*, p. 44, 373, note 6. The Karaites lay no stress on the difference between

is transmitted and accepted in rabbinic sources [116] and has its first unequivocal witness in Josephus. [117]

a formed and unformed embryo; but this differentiation among them must be tacitly presumed, since in another connection they expressly emphasize and explicitly confirm that the undeveloped foetus cannot be considered as a man. Comp. Hadassi, *Eshkol ha-Kofer*, alphabet 308, 114b; Gan 'Eden 114b. This was overlooked by Löw, *Ben Chananja*, IX, 692.

[116] Mekilta on Ex. *l. c.*: אסון "death stroke" refers only to the woman. For the killing of the embryo, however, in case the woman is not killed, only an indemnity is paid. Mekilta, ed. Hoffmann, p. 129; Jonathan *ad loc.*, also Onkelos *ad loc.*; Sanh. 74a, 79a. Comp. Mishnah Baba Ḳamma V, 4; Tosefta IX, 20; Babli 42b, 49a. Comp. Mishnah Niddah 44a above.

In accord with the Halakah is the translation of the Vulgate: *sed ipsa vixerit... si autem mors eius fuerit subsecuta.* The Peshitta renders אסון by כאארסא—as Gen. 42.4, 38 and 44.29—meaning "accident". Comp. Smith, *Thesaurus Syriacus*, II, col. 3753. There is therefore no support whatever to the assumption of Holzinger, in his commentary on Ex., p. 86, that the Peshita agrees perhaps with the Septuagint.

Remarkable is the translation of this passage in Ephraim Syrus. He renders verse 22 in the sense of the Halakah, but verse 23 in accordance with the Septuagint. Explanation of Ex. ch. 21 (*Sämmtliche Werke der Kirchenväter*, Kempten 1842, XXVII, 329f.): "If two men quarrel and hit a pregnant woman and her life is not in danger, then, because the fruit was not yet wholly formed and provided with all the limbs, he shall pay an indemnity. But if the fruit of the womb was formed, he shall give a life for a life."

Even more striking is the rendition of the Exodus passage in Mechitar Gosh, *Armenisches Rechtsbuch*, col. Karst, I, 131: Statute concerning the case that men quarrel and a pregnant woman is killed (Polish-Armenian Code, ch. 25: *De eo qui contentione commissa percusserit mulierem praegnantem*): "And if two men fight with one another and hit a pregnant woman, so that her fruit departs when it is still formless, then he shall be held subject to half compensation of the damages as high as the husband of the woman fixes it, and shall pay it before the referees. But if the fruit is already formed, he shall give life for life". Thus in the superscription verse 23 is reproduced in the sense of the Halakah, while the exact provision corresponds to the Septuagint. Comp. also D. H. Müller, *Semitica*, II, 8.

This amalgamation of the two opposite constructions can only be explained by the assumption that in the sources, from which Ephraem and Mechitar drew their statement these two interpretations were mentioned one beside the other, and in the process of translation they became confused. Ephraim's source was probably the oral information of a Jewish scholar, while Gosh could also draw from one of the biblical-talmudical compendia which he used. Concerning the latter comp. Aptowitzer, *WZKM.*, XXI, 256f. From this it would result that at the time of Ephraim in the fourth century and at the time of the composition of the above-mentioned compendia—perhaps likewise the fourth or fifth century, comp. Aptowitzer *l. c.*, p. 261f.—the construction of the Septuagint and of Philo was known also among the representatives of the rabbinic tradition and found some adherents among them.

The "half compensation of the damage" in Gosh, which has no analogy in either the Halakah or in the Septuagint, comp. Müller *l. c*, n. 4, comes probably from an analogy of words, instituted by Gosh but more probably by his source, in accordance with the ordinance Ex. 21.35, where the act requiring a reparation of half the damage is expressed by the word נגף, as in the passage before us; therefore in the case of נגיפה only half the damage is repaired. But that in verse 35 verb and punishment hang together is evident from the fact that immediately after in verse 36 at the rendering of compensation to the full amount the animal is designated as נגח and not as נגף. Also in the ordinance Ex. 21.28–32 נגח is used. This difference in the use of נגח and נגף has been observed in rabbinic interpretation; hence it has to stress expressly and verify by way of exegesis that in practice נגיחה and נגיפה are of equal value. Comp. Mekilta on both passages, ed. Friedmann, 85b f., 88a; ed. Hoffmann, pp. 131, 135.

[117] *Antiquitiess*, IV, 8, 33 (*Opera*, ed. Niese, I, 280, 278): "He that kicks a

If it were possible to judge with certainty from the antiquity and lateness of the sources as to the antiquity and lateness of the views contained in them,[118] then we might be justified in speaking in this case of an older and

woman with child, so that the woman miscarry, let him pay a fine in money, as the judges shall determine, as having diminished the multitude by the destruction of what was in her womb; and let money also be given the woman's husband by him that kicked her". ὁ γυναῖκα λακτίσας ἔγκυον, ἂν μὴ ἐξαμβλώσῃ ἡ γυνὴ ζημιούσθω χρήμασιν ὑπὸ τῶν δικαστῶν ὡς παρὰ τὸ διαφθαρὲν ἐν τῇ γαστρὶ μειώσας τὸ πλῆθος, διδόσθω δὲ καὶ τῷ ἀνδρὶ τῆς γυναικὸς παρ' αὐτοῦ χρήματα.

In opposition to this we find in another passage of Josephus, Contra Apionem, II, 24 (Opera, ed. Niese, V, 83, 202): "The law enjoins us to bring up all our offspring, and forbids women to cause abortion of what is begotten, or to destroy it afterward. If any woman appears to have so done, she will be a murderer of her child, by destroying a living creature and diminishing human kind". τέκνα τρέφειν ἅπαντα προσέταξεν, καὶ γυναιξὶν ἀπεῖπεν μήτ' ἀμβλοῦν τὸ σπαρὲν μήτε διαφθείρειν ἀλλὰ ἢν φανείη τεκνοκτόνος ἂν εἴη ψυχὴν ἀφανίζουσα καὶ τὸ γένος ἐλαττοῦσα. And it is remarkable that until now—as far as I know—no one has pointed out the contradiction between these two passages of Josephus, although they formed a subject of frequent discussion. Comp. Geiger, *Urschrift*, p. 36f.; Frankel, *Monatsschrift*, I, 132; Zipser, *Josephus Flavius Schrift gegen Apion*, p. 164f; Löw, *Lebensalter*, pp. 44, 70; Weiss, *Zur Geschichte der jüdischen Tradition*, II, 23, n.1; Ritter, *Philo und die Halacha*, p. 36; Olitzki, *Josephus und die Halacha*, p. 21; Weyl, *Die jüdischen Strafgesetze bei Flavius Josephus*, pp. 50–52, 57f. But it is most remarkable that Löw and Weyl, who deal with both passages and construe the latter in such a way—as also Frankel and Zipser—as to imply legal prosecution and punishment, did not note the gross contradiction between the two statements.

Now with regard to the latter passage in itself, Zipser thinks that Josephus made this statement for his Greek readers, for apologetic purposes. Similarly Weyl, who for the prohibition of the purposeless killing of the embryo points very well to the Mishnah Ahilot VII, 6—which was done previously by Weiss—but designates the treatment of abortion like death as an intentional exaggeration. Now it is true and should be admitted that Josephus for apologetic purposes often quotes the Jewish laws incorrectly, comp. especially Olitzki, *l. c.*, p. 27ff., but in our case such an assumption would do him injustice. The passage in *Contra Apionem* has been misunderstood. In no wise does it refer to a condemnation through the temporal court. Josephus only says that the destruction of the fruit is considered a great crime, as murder of an already born child. The matter under consideration is only moral valuation, but not legal punishment. That Josephus means only this and nothing else is evident from the difference of expression here and in the passage immediately preceding. There we read: "To have to do with another man's wife is a wicked thing, which, if any one ventures upon, death is inevitably his punishment". ταύτῃ συνεῖναι δεῖ τὸν γήμαντα μόνῃ, τὸ δὲ τὴν ἄλλου πειρᾶν ἀνόσιον. εἰ δέ τις τοῦτο πράξειεν, οὐδεμία θανάτου παραίτησις. But here: "If any woman appear to have so done, she will be a murderer of her child", τεκνοκτόνος ἂν εἴη. In the first case a law is reproduced, hence the language of the lawgiver, in the second case a moral valuation is involved, hence the language of the moralist, which recalls vividly the rabbinic כאילו in such teachings. Comp. for instance Yebamot 63b below: כל יהודי שאינו עוסק בפריה ורביה כאילו שופך דמים

But if this is the right sense of the passage in Josephus, then there is a clear parallel to it in the following baraita: "Whoever has sexual intercourse with his wife on the ninetieth day of her pregnancy, is, as it were, a shedder of blood". המשמש מטתו ליום תשעים כאילו שופך דמים. Niddah 37a. Thus injury of the embryo=shedding of blood, as in Josephus. Comp. also Yebamot 12b and 42a. Comp. Responsa Ḥawwot Yair, No.3.

[118] Which, however, is not a safe conclusion. Comp. hereon Aptowitzer, *Festschrift Adolf Schwarz*, Wien 1917, p. 124f.

younger tendency, of an older and younger law, as is done by Geiger[119] with headstrong conviction in face of the time interval between the Septuagint and Josephus.

Nowadays, however, we are in the position to recognize that the two legal views—as far as their validity in Jewish law is concerned—are, with reference to their age, to be judged in an entirely opposite direction. The apparently late law proves to be old and primitive, and the apparently old law appears to be comparatively late. The conception that the killing of the unborn child is not to be treated as murder or death blow was indeed current practice already at the time of Hammurabi—2000 years before the common era, hence more than seventeen centuries before the origin of the Greek version of the Septuagint. Hammurabi §209-210: "If a man strike a man's daughter and bring about a miscarriage, he shall pay ten shekels of silver for her miscarriage.—If that woman die, they shall put his daughter to death".[120]

This is exactly the same case as in Ex. 21.22-23. Thus the rabbinic conception of the passage proves to be the only correct one and in agreement with the primitive tradition which reaches as far as the Pentateuch and beyond it to Abraham—in fact to the origin of Israel and to primitive Semitic tradition, while the view expressed in the Septuagint must be designated as a later tendency, which in addition is not genuinely Jewish but must have originated in Alexandria under Egyptian-Greek influence. But I go even further and maintain that the translation of the passage in question found in our Septuagint is not original but represents one of the numerous later transformations

---

[119] *Urschrift*, p. 436ff.; *Nachgelassene Schriften*, III, 263; *Hebräische Aufsätze*, ed. Poznanski, pp. 116ff.

[120] D. H. Müller, *Die Gesetze Hammurabis*, p. 57. As to the last point comp. Müller, p. 152, and I. Horowitz, *Judaica. Festschrift zu Herman Cohens 70. Geburtstag*, p. 627ff.

of the original Palestinian [121] text of the Septuagint—though, it must be admitted, one of the oldest transformations, since it existed already at the time of Philo.

Accordingly we are not justified in speaking of an older and later law, i. e. of a development and transformation within the genuine Jewish law, but of a Palestinian and an Alexandrian point of view.

The theoretical foundation of both these tendencies, their physiological motivation, is found in Philo. Philo writes:

"But if any one have a contest with a woman who is pregnant,[122] and strike her a blow on her belly, and she miscarry, if the child which was conceived within her is still unfashioned and unformed, he shall be punished by a fine, both for the assault which he committed and also because he has prevented nature, which was fashioning and preparing that most excellent of all creatures, a human being, from bringing him into existence. But if the child which was conceived has assumed a distinct shape in all its parts, having received all its proper connective and distinctive qualities, he shall die; for such a creature as that is a man, whom he has slain while still in the workshop of nature, which had not thought it as yet a proper time to produce him to the light, but had kept him like a statue lying in a sculptor's workshop, requiring nothing more than to be released and sent out into the world".[123]

---

[121] Concerning the Palestinian origin of the Septuagint comp. Aptowitzer, *Ha-Kedem*, II, 117ff.

[122] The Bible speaks of a strife between two men. But even Josephus apparently speaks of a strife between a man and a woman, as Ritter, *Philo und die Halacha*, p. 36, n. 3, correctly remarks in accordance with the letter of the text. The objections of Olitzki, *Flavius Josephus und die Halacha*, p. 21, n.25, and Weyl, *Die jüdischen Strafgesetze bei Flavius Josephus*, p. 57, n. 1, to Ritter's remark are not right. According to their conception Josephus would have had to say: "But if a woman with child" ἂν δὲ γυναῖκα, but ὁ γυναῖκα can only be the beginning of a new case. It is, however, striking that Ritter has not emphasized this deviation from the biblical text which is indubitable in Philo.

[123] *De Special. legibus*, II,§ 19 end (ed. Mangey, II, 315f.; ed. Cohn, V, 180f.): ἐὰν δὲ συμπλακείς γυναικί τις ἐγκύῳ πληγὴν ἐμφορήσῃ κατὰ τὴν γαστέρα, ἡ δὲ ἀμβλώσῃ, ἐὰν μὲν ἄπλαστον καὶ ἀδιατύπωτον τὸ ἀμβλωθὲν τύχῃ, ζη-

This yields for the Palestinian view the following supposition: the child not yet born, even if it is fashioned and formed, is not a being in itself, but a part of the mother's womb.[124]

In addition to this conclusion by contrast there is also a conclusion by agreement. In the received talmudic law the child not yet born cannot be considered a legal person, it is deprived of any rights.[125] Likewise in Roman law. Now just as in Roman law the legal unfitness of the unborn child arises from the view that the embryo is but a part of the mother's womb—*foetus pars ventris*[126]—so talmudic law must likewise be based on this standpoint. Similar decisions presuppose similar motivations. In fact we find already in the Talmud a civil law decision affecting an unborn child explained by this standpoint: The child in the mother's womb is but a part of its mother.[127] The same is true with reference to statutes in the prescriptions concerning Levitic impurity[128]—and in the law of matrimony.[129]

μιούστω, καὶ διὰ τὴν ὕβριν καὶ ὅτι ἐμποδὼν ἐγένετο τῇ φύσῃ ζωογονῆσαι τὸ κάλλιστον τεχνιτευούσῃ καὶ δημιουργούσῃ ζῷον, ἄνθρωπον. εἰ δὲ ἤδη μεμορφωμένον, ἀπάντων μελῶν τὰς οἰκείους τάξεις καὶ ποιότητας ἀπειληφότων, θνήσκετω, τὸ γὰρ τοιοῦτον ἄνθρωπός ἐστιν, ὃν ἐν τῷ τῆς φύσεως ἐργαστηρίῳ διεχρήσατο μήπω καιρὸν εἶναι νομιζούσης εἰς φῶς προαγαγεῖν, ἔοικὸς ἀνδριάντι ἐν πλαστικῇ κατακειμένῳ, πλέον οὐδὲν ἢ τὴν ἔξω παραπομπὴν καὶ ἄνεσιν ἐπιζητοῦντι.

[124] עובר ירך אמו. Comp. Geiger, *Hebr. Aufsätze*, ed. Poznanski, p. 117f.
[125] Niddah V, 2. Comp. Babli *ibid.* 45a, Baba batra 142a.
[126] *Partus mulieris portio sive viscerum.* L 1, §1 D. Savigny, *System des heutigen römischen Rechtes* II, IV. Beilage; Windscheid, *Pandekten* I §52; Brassloff, *Zeitschrift der Savignystiftung*, XXVI, 169–194; Wenger, *Das Recht der Griechen und Römer*, p. 186 (in the series *Die Kultur der Gegenwart*, ed. Hinneberg, vol. II). Therefore among the Romans the killing of the fruit of the womb was not a punishable act. Comp. Rein, *Römisches Criminalrecht*, p. 445f.; Mommsen, *Römisches Strafrecht*, p. 636f.
[127] Giṭṭin 23b, p. Ḳid. I, 3 9a: עובר ירך אמו עשו אותו כאחד מאבריה. Comp. Temurah 25a below.
[128] Nazir 51a: עובר במעי אשה הרי גלגלים או לא כיון דאמר מר עובר ירך אמו הילכך נפש הוא ולא הוו נלגלים וכו'.
[129] Yebamot 78a.—Löw, *Ben Chananja*, IX, 698, n. 53, remarks: "according to Dr. F.'s view עובר ירך אמו is connected with the Stoic and the opposite proposition with the Platonic doctrine of the foetus. But the dispute over this occurs in the Talmud only with reference to animals (Ḥullin 58a and the parallel passages) and slaves (Giṭṭin 23b), never with reference to free men (comp. Yebamot 62a), although the opportunity for it would have offered itself quite frequently. The same mistake is committed by Dr. Mayer, *Die Rechte der Israeliten, Griechen und Römer*, 121, n. 45.

On this physiological point of view, which is valid for animals as well as for men, rest numerous doctrines and statutes in the field of sacrifice—and food laws,[130] damages caused by animals [131] and buying and selling.[132]

This is the point of view of the received Halakah. But the view that the child not yet born is a being in itself penetrated also to Palestine and won over some Jewish scholars to its side. On this view rest those opinions of individual teachers which ascribe to the unborn child a certain amount of legal fitness.[133] On this view rest also a number of precepts in the laws and statutes concerning sacrifices and food.[134] Here it is indeed R. Johanan who un-

While the Tosafists discuss the doctrine in question, they include in their discussion the statutes concerning the human foetus without, however applying to it the principle itself (Sanh. 80b, caption אלא). In Yebamot 78a the ע״א is not to be taken in its exact sense". This view is repeated briefly in *Lebensalter*, p. 380, n. 150: "עובר ירך אמו is used in the Talmud itself only with reference to animals and slaves, but never with reference to free people". Apparently he had overlooked the passage in Nazir, above n. 128. But even without this it is inconceivable how a scholar of the rank of Löw can think seriously that the free are governed by other physiological laws than the slaves even were we willing to admit such a difference in our question between animal and man. With reference, however, to the passage in Yebamot 78a Löw's assertion is unfounded. Comp. also Tosafot *ibid. s. v.* בעלמא and *s. v.* אלא.

[130] Ḥullin 58a, 79b, Temurah 30b. Comp. also further below note 134.
[131] Baba Ḳamma 47a: פרה שהזיקה גובה מולדה מאי טעמא גופה היא.
[132] Baba Ḳamma 78b. Comp. Sanh. 80b.
[133] Comp. above I,
[134] Ḥullin 58a, 74b; Temurah 10b, 11a, 19a, 25b, 30b. Comp. Menaḥot 81a and Tos. *s. v.* דילמא. In these passages, as well as in those quoted above, notes 130–132, the principles עובר ירך אמו and עובר לאו ירך אמו are expressly emphasized in the Talmud itself. But there is also a great number of statutes in various domains of the Halakah which can be explained only from these points of view, without its being mentioned in the Talmud. The treatment of these halakahs is reserved for a special article. In some controversies concerning the food laws Geiger had already recognized this conflict of principles, comp. his *Hebr. Aufsätze*, ed. Poznanski, p. 118f. Geiger's deductions, it is true, are in great need of correction (comp. Pineles, דרכה של תורה, p. 190ff. and Ginzberg's remarks in Geiger's articles, p. 398–401), but his explanation of the controversy in Ḥullin IV, 5, and Babli *ibid*. 74b (p. 118) is absolutely true, and even Ginzberg does not object to it in principle (p. 399 f). But the attempt made by some to misinterpret the natural sense of this controversy, to put things upside down, and to construe inconceivable concepts, must fail when confronted with common sense. Like Geiger also R. J. Z. Jolles explains the controversy in question in his מלוא הרועים, *s. v.* The difference between the Rabbis and the Karaites with regard to שליל is explained in this sense already by R. Meshullam ben Kalonymos. Comp. his polemic against the Karaites, refutation 9 (ed. Freimann in *Judaica, Festschrift zu Hermann Cohens 70. Geburtstage*, p. 577f.). Comp. in addition R. Simson and R. Asher in Parah II, 1. Philo, *De virtute*, 18 (M., II, 398), does not speak against it, because he differentiates between a developed and an undeveloped embryo and hence must explain the respective law also with reference to the undeveloped embryo. Comp. further below, note 139.

mistakably defends this view, as emphasized time and again in the Talmud; the same R. Johanan who ascribes to the unborn child a rather large amount of personal right.[135]

However, what interests us here is criminal law only: the treatment of the killing of the *nasciturus* and the question closely connected with it as to the consideration of the life of the unborn child or its non-consideration in favor of other important interests. Hence I want to confine myself to the discussion of a few decisions pertaining thereto, insofar as from them may be observed the efficacy of both physiological views involved in this question.

1. According to the Halakah the killing of a man is treated as murder or death blow only when the person killed was (1) born (2) capable of living.[136] The condition of fitness to live is derived from Ex. 21.12: "Whoso killeth a man shall be killed". The concept "man" (איש) implies necessarily the quality of being capable to live. The Torah has thus, through the use of the term "man", circumscribed the term "man" employed with reference to another provision about killing (Lev.24.17).

Thus the deduction. It is now pertinent to ask: Why have the teachers omitted to derive from the same passage in Exodus also the condition of birth, since the term "man" includes the characteristic "be born" as surely as the characteristic "fit to live"? Indeed, it is one of the most common principles of halakic exegesis that the term "man" excludes the minor, on which ground it is compelled also to reject in the Leviticus passage, with the help of the term "man", the negation of the death blow in the case of killing a minor as implied in the Exodus passage. Thus

---

[135] Comp. above note 55 end and further below, No. 7.

[136] Birth—the passages above n. 125. Ability to live—Mishnah Sanh. IX, 2: Tosefta XII, 5; Mekilta Mishpatim IV 80a, VIII 84a; Mekilta of R. Simeon, p. 125 above; Sifra Emor Perek XX hal. 1; Sanh. 84b; Niddah 44b. Hence capital punishment is withheld also from him who kills someone who in consequence of an injury or sickness had forfeited his ability to live. Sanh. 78a.

"man" presupposes birth. Why is this not emphasized in the deduction?

To this it might be answered: Just because it is not necessary with regard to the principle mentioned. Well and good. But whence does the Halakah know to employ the circumscription furnished by איש and the amplification contained in אדם in such a manner as it does, coming in conflict with its other principle that איש excludes the minor? Rather should it, in conformity with that principle, exclude the minor and include the one fit to live. And further: The Torah, says the exegesis, invalidates in this case, through the term "man", the customary meaning of איש always supported by the Halakah, and makes no difference between adults and minors. However, the Torah does not indicate any age limit. Whence does the Halakah know to designate the moment of birth as the limit? Perhaps Philo is right when he derives the non-difference of age just from the provision concerning the death blow to the embryo? He remarks: "But when the children are brought forth and are separated from that which is produced with them, and are set free and placed by themselves...so that then, beyond all question, he who slays an infant commits homicide, and the law shows its indignation at such an action; not being guided by the age but by the species of the creature in whom its ordinances are violated".[137] These questions urge us therefore to the only possible answer: The condition of "being born" cannot be found by the Halakah in the exegetical way;[138] but it really does not need it,

[137] *De Special. Legibus*, III, 20 (M. II, 319; Cohn-Wendland, V, 183): τὰ δὲ ἀποκυηθέντα τῆς τε συμφυΐας ἀπέζευκται καὶ διυφειμένα καθ᾿ αὑτὰ ζῷα γέγονεν οὐδενὸς ἐπιδεᾶ τῶν ὅσα συμπληρωτικὰ τῆς ἀνθρωπίνης φύσεώς ἐστιν, ὥστε ἀνενδοιάστως ἀνδροφόνον εἶναι τὸν βρέφος ἀναιροῦντα, τοῦ νόμου μὴ ἐπὶ ταῖς ἡλικίαις ἀλλ᾿ ἐπὶ τῷ γένει παρασπονδουμένῳ δυσχεραίνοντος.

[138] But the Halakah likewise cannot derive the condition of birth from the condition of the ability to live, since it adheres to the standpoint that the ability to live can be presupposed or established before the birth, as is evident especially from the statement treated in 2. Comp. further below, note 139. Thus the Halakah considers

because this condition follows immediately from the physiological ideas of the halakists, that the child in the mother's womb, even when already formed, is not a being itself but a part of the mother's womb. Therefore the slaying of a child not yet born can be treated only as an injury to the body of the mother. This birth is the age limit designed by nature, when the child receives the right to full protection of its life. On this is based the following provision.

2. "In the case of a difficult birth, where the mother is in danger, the child in the mother's womb may be cut to pieces and drawn forth member by member, for her life is prior to its life. But if the greater part of the child's body or its head had come forth, then it should not be touched, for one must not remove one life in favor of another life".[139]

Therefore only at the moment of birth does the child become a life, a being, a person. The choice is offered between two equal, independent beings, of whom only

---

birth as a condition *per se* and not as a proof for the ability to live. Only in consonance with the view that the ability to live can be presupposed only when the child is alive 30 days after the birth, can the birth be considered as a supposition for the establishment of the ability to live. Comp. on this point further below. According to this view from איש=able to live follows indirectly also the condition of birth. In this sense we are to understand Mekilta of R. Simeon, p. 129 below, where the embryo is excluded from איש: מכה איש פרט לולדות.

[139] Ahiloth VII, 6: האשה שהיא מקשה לילד מחתכין את הולד במעיה ומוציאין אותו אברים אברים מפני שחייה קודמין לחייו יצא רובו אין נוגעין בו שאין דחין נפש מפני נפש. Tosefta Yebamot IX end and Sanh. 72b: יצא ראשו; p. Shab. XIV, 4 14d below and 'Abodah Zarah II, 2 40d below: יצא רובו; p. Sanh. VIII end: ראשו או רובו *i. e.* ראשו ורובו.—Rashi Sanh. *l. c.* explains: as long as the child has not left the mother's womb it is not life, לאו נפש הוא. A difficulty is presented by Mishne Torah, Rozeah I, 9, to which comp. Responsa Ḥawwot Yair, No. 31, question 2 (ed. pr. 37b). The first case of our Mishnah in Tosefta Giṭṭin III (ed. Zuckermandel IV end).—Tertullian, *De anima*, ch. 25 (*Opera*, ed. Leopold, IV, 204): *Atquin et in ipsa adhuc utero infans trucidatur necessaria crudelitate, quum in exitu obliquatus denegat partum; matricida ni moriturus*. In the second case it is presupposed that the child is capable of living, otherwise the life of the mother would not be jeopardized in its favor, since the killing of those incapable of living goes without punishment. Comp. above, note 136. It follows from this that the child's ability to live can be presupposed also before the birth either on the basis of experience, that most children are capable of living, or through actual confirmation of the time of pregnancy. For the development, which otherwise serves as a token of full carriage, cannot come here into consideration, since of the signs of development—the growth of hair and nails—one is lacking, according to whether ראשו or רובו comes out first. More details further below.

one can be saved. The decision does not belong to man. Before the birth, however, the child is not a being in itself, not an independent existence; it stands before the attainment of independent life which its mother had attained long ago. Hence it is self-evident that the life of the child must yield to the life of the mother. The word "prior" in the first case must not therefore be understood in the sense of "more valuable", "more important", since after all the greater value of the mother's life was not lessened in the least by the child's attempt at birth.

3. "In case a woman who is pregnant is condemned to death, the execution is not deferred until she bears. But if she is already sitting on the chair of delivery then one waits until she bears".[140]

The Gemara explains: In the first case the child is a part of the mother's body;[141] in the second case, where the child had separated itself, it is a separate body.[142] Thus exactly like Philo. But against this explanation there arise serious considerations. Through it there occurs an irreparable gap between this mishnic statute and another commonly valid halakic principle, resulting from the following consideration. With every pregnant woman it is to be feared that during the execution the child may be severed from the bearing mother. Yet the execution is not delayed. Thus with regard to a simple prohibition[143] an act is ordained which may lead to the annihilation of a human life. But the Halakah teaches that the desecra-

---

[140] 'Arakin I, 6; Tosefta I, 4.

[141] 'Arakin 7a גופה הוא. Comp. R. Solomon ben Adret in Ḥullin 58a, R. Nissim in Ḥullin III, No. 774. Comp. Tos. Sanh. 80b s. v. עובר end. Comp. Frankel, Monatsschrift for 1859, p. 439f.

[142] כיון דעקר גופא אחרינא הוא. Geiger, Hebr. Aufsätze, ed. Poznanski, p. 120, explains so of his own accord, without any reference to the Talmud. Also Ginzberg, in Geiger l. c., p. 401, who rejects Geiger's explanation, fails to analyse the explanation of the Gemara.

[143] To postpone the execution of the verdict, עינוי הדין. Comp. Tos. 'Arakin, l. c., s. v. ישבה, and Mishne Torah, Sanh. XII, 4. Comp. Sanh. XI, 4; Tosefta VXI, 7; Sifre Deut. 91; Sanh. 35; p. Sanh. IV, 4 22b. Comp. in addition Mo'ëd ḳaṭan 14b and Pseudo-Rashi s. v. מענה (= Rashi 'Arakin) and Tos. s. v. נמצאת.

tion of the Sabbath, which is otherwise punished by death or *Karet*, is commanded, if through it a human life may be saved.[144] Is not the contradiction between these two laws irreconcilable? This contradiction appears even more glaring when we contrast the following two statutes of R. Samuel:

(a) When a pregnant woman is executed, she receives a beating on her womb, in order to bring about first the death of the child, so that she should not be put to shame through a possible miscarriage.[145]

(b) If on the Sabbath a woman sits on the chair of delivery and dies before the confinement, then, even in a manner involving the desecration of the Sabbath, a knife should be brought, her womb cut open, and the child removed.[146]

This difficulty requires the assumption that the originator of the explanation in the Gemara explains the mishnic statute from his own standpoint,[147] which, however, cannot be the standpoint of the Mishnah. In fact we see that R. Johanan, who considers the formed embryo as a being in itself,[148] finds no reasonable basis for the mishnic statute in question, and is compelled to designate it as a provision defying any logical examination.

However, also this forced deduction from the particle גם—Deut.22.22[149]—fails to satisfy us. At the utmost it is just sufficient to justify the statute formally and in practice; but the difficulty is not removed through it, only deferred. Now there is a conflict between a biblical prescription and a halakic principle, which on its side

---

[144] ספק נפשות דוחה את השבת, Yoma VII, 6, 7; Tosefta Shab. XVI (XV) end; Yoma 84b, 'Arakin 7b above.

[145-146] 'Arakin 7a.

[147] Comp. above, note 129.

[148] Comp. above, note 134.

[149] Comp. Jonathan *ad loc.* and Baraita of the 32 norms, No. 1. The examples in this baraita are of later origin. Comp. Aptowitzer, *Festschrift Adolf Schwarz zum 70 Geburtsjahr*, p. 122, 132, n. 1.

wants to and must be biblical likewise. But if not, why does the Halakah cling just in the one case to the word גם? And also this: If our provision had its source in the verse of the Torah quoted by R. Johanan it would be valid without exception, since the biblical passage does not indicate any exceptions; but whence does the Mishnah know to prescribe the delay in the second case? We also see that in the Sifre[150] the word גם is employed for another deduction.

The same queries apply also to another exegetical confirmation of our statute, which is found in Sifre Zutta: One might think that if the murderer is a pregnant woman the execution is deferred until she bears, therefore it says: 'Surely the murderer shall be put to death' (Num.35.21). Now one might think that if the woman is in the third month of her pregnancy the execution is not deferred, but when she is the ninth month of her pregnancy the execution must be deferred, therefore it says: Surely the murderer shall be put to death".[151] Here an additional difficulty is the fact that the biblical verse does not state when the killing of the murderer is to take place, and it is only a logical requirement to have the punishment executed immediately after the deed, while logical consideration may admit exceptions from other motives—as it, indeed, happens in the second case of the Mishnah, without doing violence to the exact wording of the Torah. But Sifre Zutta, which—as we shall see later and as is already evident from the hypothetical difference between the third and the ninth month of pregnancy, i. e. the beginning of perceptibility and full carriage—puts itself on the standpoint that the child in the mother's womb is a being in itself, cannot explain the statute logically, hence it is in search

[150] Deut. §241.
[151] Sifre zutta, ed. Horowitz, Leipzig 1917, p. 334: יכול אם היתה אשה עוברה יאריכו לה עד שתלד ת"ל מות יומת המכה, יכול אם היתה בת שלשה חדשים לא יאריכו לה עד שתלד אבל אם היתה בת תשעה חדשים יאריכו לה עד שתלד ת"ל, מות יומת.

of forced exegetical explanation, since it will not combat it on the basis that it is an old tradition. The same holds true of R. Johanan.[152]

The mishnic statute, however, can be explained only in the following manner: The child in the mother's womb, even when it is already formed and separated, is not a being in itself, has no independent life, is only a part of its mother; hence one does not have to take any consideration of it when it gets into conflict with another important interest. In the second case, however, where the child is about to reach independence of life, where it is already preparing to become a being in itself, a man, nothing should be done to disturb it; in such a case no hindrance shall be placed in the way of nature immediately before the accomplishment of its end. The execution of the delinquent woman must be delayed. In the first place the opposite interest is injured only very slightly through it; in the second place, when the execution consists of stoning, it is to be feared that the child might be born during the execution and stoned together with its mother, as it is stated in the Tosefta, especially since the mere coming out of the head is already considered a full birth.

The opposite interest, however, is the state of soul of the mother about to be executed, the endeavor to spare her the pangs of death. Now in the second case the birth of the child is to be expected any moment, it is a question there of minutes, at the utmost of hours. So much can be sacrificed from the interest of the mother in favor of the child. But contrariwise the entrance of the birth is uncertain even with regard to the time; it can be effected at the earliest in days, but perhaps not before weeks or even months. Shall the mother be exposed during all

[152] R. Johanan has a saying: "Every rule which is not clear should be supported by numerous proofs from the Holy Scripture". כל מילא דלא מחוורא מסמכין לה מן אתרין סגין, p. Ber. II, 3 4c; 'Erubin X, 1 26a.

this time to the agonies of death awaiting her, shall she suffer the most dreadful tortures of soul, in the assumption that from one part of her body there will develop a child capable of living? Here to the interest of a full-grown person there is opposed the interest of an embryo, a young organism more or less advanced in developnent; here consideration for the mother must be preferred.

Politics, it is true, would demand the opposite, for it subordinates the welfare of the individual to the interest of the state; ethics, however, protects the individual in the first place. Politics knows subjects of state: taxpayers and soldiers; ethics knows but men. To politics men are members of the state, wheels of a machine; to ethics the state is a union of men. To politics the condemned mother is a part of a machine rendered useless, but her expected child is a freshly wrought screw; the former is cast to the heap of old iron, the latter is guarded carefully. To ethics, however, the condemned mother is still a woman having claim to forbearance. Hence the politically motivated law of the Egyptians, Greeks, and Romans, refused to admit the execution of a pregnant woman;[153] while the ethically motivated law of the Jews prescribes it.

That this is the case, however, is best evident from the Egyptians, Greeks, and Romans. They did not allow a pregnant woman to be executed, but the exposure and even the direct and well-planned killing of children not altogether fit for military duty was a prevailing custom with them.[154] Certainly, the weakly children are valueless to the state, even a burden, while the pregnant de-

---

[153] Diodorus, I, 77; Plutarch, *De sera num. vind.*, 7; Ael. Var., *Historia*, V. 18.—Clemens Alex., *Stromata*, II, 18, ed. Pott., p. 478. Digestae 48, 19, 3: *Praegnantis mulieris consumendae damnatae poena differtur quoad pariat.*

[154] Comp. Philo, *De special. legibus*, 20 (M. II, 319); *Vita Mosis*, §3. Comp. Wendland, *Philo und die Kynisch-Stoische Diatribe*, p. 37f.; Heinemann, *Schriften aer jüdisch-hellenistischen Literatur*, II, 217, n. 3; Weiss, *Zur Geschichte der jüdischen Tradition*, p. 23. Also Aristotle demands that the legislature prescribe the exposure of weakly children, *Polit.*, VII, 16. Comp. Zeller, *Philosophie*[3], II 2, 731.

linquent woman may bring to the world a strong soldier or a robust soldier's wife; that is what must be considered. But the mother? She is consecrated to death and lost to the state; the state has no more interest in her and hence none for her. The state is not at all concerned about the agony of her soul, for the state must not be sentimental, and all she has to do is to quietly carry to completion the future citizen; and even if he should prove to be inferior and defective—which is always possible under the state of soul in which the mother finds herself—still he can be exposed or killed at any time. Through the delay of the execution there is a potential gain and no loss to the state, while to ethics there is a sure loss, mitigated only by a doubly doubtful gain. Therefore Jewish law spared the mother, who even after her condemnation has not ceased to be a woman who must be spared torments of soul and mortification.[155]

This clear state of affairs was overlooked by all those who saw cruelty in our mishnic statute and in face of it felt ashamed of the contrary provision of Roman law, partly endeavoring to palliate it apologetically and partly using it as a weapon in party strife.[156]

From the difference between the ethical and political motivation of the law may be explained also another important difference between the Jewish and Greek law. It is the compass of the right of asylum. Jewish law limits the right of asylum to the man who kills without intention,[157] while Greek law makes no difference between unintentional and intentional killing, leaving the temples

[155] This difference between ethics and politics is articulated also in other questions. Thus the Jewish law imposes a sentence of death for adultery and incest, while Plato considers that state most perfect in which community of wives and children rules, *Repub.*, IV, 410f. Comp. Sparta!

[156] Comp. Meyer, *Die Rechte der Israeliten* etc., p. 10; Löw, *Lebensalter*, p. 59–61; Ginzberg's glosses in Geiger's Hebrew essays, ed. Poznanski, p. 400.

[157] Num. 35. 9–25; Jos. 20. 1–6.

of the gods open even to a man who kills with intention.[158] Extremely humane and advanced indeed. But already in Euripides we hear complaints to the effect that the asylums are of benefit to both the righteous and unrighteous.[159] Also modern scholars are in search of an explanation for the limitlessness of the Greek right of asylum. Mommsen thinks the lack of difference in the granting of the right of asylum was not part of the original Greek law, but a misuse brought about by the perpetual legal insecurity of the Greek states.[160] Against this it is justly maintained that the legal insecurity could only have preserved the wide extension of the right of asylum, but could not have brought it about.[161] However, the unlimited extension of the Greek right of asylum is explained from the political basis of Greek law. From the standpoint of political law the punishment of the murderer is a state necessity: the individual who is dangerous to the state and the community must be made harmless. But the criminal, through his flight to an asylum, withdrew from the community and the state, so that neither of them is threatened henceforth with any danger from him; in fact he has rendered himself harmless. Therefore the state has no cause any longer to insist on the punishment of the murderer. Not so in ethical law, to which the punishment of the murderer is an ethical command, a moral duty: injustice must be atoned for, land and people should not be burdened with blood-guilt; hence it commands to lead the murderer away from the altar to the seat of judgment.[162] "He who destroys a man's life, destroys the whole world at the same time, and he who preserves a man's life, preserves

---

[158] Comp. Stengel, *Pauly-Wissowas Realencyclopädie der klassischen Altertumswissenschaft*, article Asylon; Mommsen, *Römisches Strafrecht*, p. 458f.

[159] *Ion* 1315. Comp. Stengel l. c.

[160] Mommsen, *Römisches Strafrecht*, p. 458.

[161] Comp. Weissmann, *Talion und öffentliche Strafe im mosaischen Rechte*, p. 72, n. 4 (reprint from the *Festschrift für Adolf Wach*, Leipzig 1913).

[162] Num. 35.33–34; Ex. 12.14. Comp. I Kings 2.28–31.

the whole world at the same time. For the whole world had been created because of every single man".[163]

The creation of the world for every single man! This is the fundamental thought of Jewish ethics, the basis of Jewish law.

But we must return for a moment to our mishnic statute. Just as the basic decree of Jewish law with reference to the killing of the child not yet born goes back to primitive Semitic tradition, so also our special mishnic decree ascends as far as the patriarchal period. "And it came to pass about three months after, that it was told Judah, saying: 'Tamar thy daughter-in-law hath played the harlot; and, moreover, behold, she is with child by harlotry'. And Judah said: 'Bring her forth, and let her be burnt'." (Gen. 38.24).[164]

In Alexandria, however, where in the basic question the old tradition was supplanted by Egyptian-Greek influence, our special case had to be judged necessarily in the sense of the new conception. Hence Philo maintains indeed that the Mosaic law forbids the execution of a pregnant woman. Philo discusses the law in Lev. 22.28 and remarks: "For it is the most impious of all customs, to slay both offspring and mother at one time and on one

---

[163] Sanh. IV, 5; Aboth R. Nathan, recension I, ch. 31; recension II, ch. 36 45a.
Now it is hardly necessary to emphasize that this differentiation does not mean that the political law aims only at the protection of the state and the ethical law only at that of the individual. This is by no means the case. Both laws, the one based on politics as well as the one based on ethics, aim and strive to protect the individual and the community, the man and the state; the difference consists only in the succession, in the relation of the individual to the state with reference to cause and effect, aim and means. The political law arrives from the protection of the state to the protection of the individual, since without men there is no state, for men are necessary to the preservation of the state, the state is primary, man is secondary; the protection of the state is the cause and aim, while that of man is consequence and means. Man begins, as it were, with the state. The ethical law, on the other hand, traverses the opposite road, starting from the protection of the individual and arriving to the protection of the community, from man to the state. The state is protected because it serves the individual, man is primary, the aim, while the state is secondary, the means.

[164] It is remarkable that none of the scholars who deal with this Mishnah—comp. above, notes 141, 142, 156—has thought of this biblical narration, and Löw expects from "historical investigation" the proof that the rule of the Mishnah is of Persian origin!

day. And it appears to me that some lawgivers, having started from this point, have also promulgated the law about condemned women, with commands that pregnant women, if they have committed any offence worthy of death, shall nevertheless not be executed until they have brought forth in order that the creature in their womb may not be slain with them when they are put to death. But these men have established these enactments with reference to human beings, but this lawgiver of ours, going beyond them all, extends his humanity even to brute beasts".[165]

The indirect, casual, and timid form of his assertion proves his uncertainty about it, since he cannot point to a biblical passage nor an experience or tradition in support of this assertion. He only pre-supposes, what is certainly correct in itself, that the Torah which in the Septuagint exclusively used by Philo considers a death blow administered to a formed embryo as murder, cannot permit the execution of a pregnant woman. We are dealing here therefore only with exegesis and reflection, not with tradition and experience. But the supposition is logically irrefutable.

4. A repetition of our mishnic statute is found in the halakic provision that the woman suspected of adultery must drink the curse-bringing water even if she is pregnant.[166] If the woman is guilty and the water exerts its deadly effect, then also the child in her womb is destroyed; and

[165] De *virtute*, 18 (M. II, 398f.; Cohn-Wendland, V. 308f.): πάντων γὰρ ἀνοσιώτατον ἐνὶ καιρῷ καὶ ἡμέρᾳ μιᾷ ἔγγονον ὁμοῦ καὶ μητέρα κτείνειν. ἐνθένδε μοι δοκοῦσιν ὁρμηθέντες ἔνιοι τῶν νομοθετῶν τὸν ἐπὶ ταῖς κατακρίτοις γυναιξὶν ἐισηγήσασται νόμον, ὃς κελεύει τὰς ἐγκύους, ἐὰν ἄξια θανάτου δράσωσιν, φυλάττεσθαι μέχρις ἂν ἀποτέκωσιν, ἵνα μὴ ἀναιρουμένων συναπόληται τὰ κατὰ γαστρός. ἀλλ' οὗτοι μὲν ἐπ' ἀνθρώπων ταῦτα ἔγνωσαν. ὁ δὲ καὶ προσυπερβάλλων ἔτι ἄχρι καὶ τῶν ἀλόγων ζῴων τὸ ἐπιεικὲς ἀπέτεινεν.

[166] Soṭah IV, 4; Tosefta V, 3; Babli 26a. Comp. Rashi s. v. שמתה; Mishne Torah, Soṭah II, 7, and משנה למלך ad loc. The objections of Tosafot, s. v. מעוברת, to Rashi are done away with through our explanation. Since it is a court decision that is involved, the motive עינוי הדין is effective.

yet the drinking is not postponed. The reasons for the admissibility and necessity of non-postponement are the same as in the case of execution. If the woman is guilty, then the decision of the judge that she must drink the water is a decree of death. And here too it is a court procedure that is involved, an unusually solemn court procedure: filing of the complaint and investigation by the authorized local court, arrival at a decision and condemnation by the great Beth-Din in Jerusalem consisting of 71 members.[167]

In this case, however, the decision of the Halakah did not remain without opposition. For we gather from Sifre Zutta that R. Gamaliel held the opinion that a Sotah who is pregnant does not drink the water of proof. R. Gamaliel bases his opinion on the sentence "then she shall conceive seed" (Num.5.28), in consideration of which the woman who had already conceived seed is excluded.[168] But this deduction is extremely difficult. For either this sentence contains a reward or promise of hereafter—as is emphasized alike by Palestinian exegesis and Philo[169]—in which case it has no reference whatever to the exemption of

[167] Soṭah I, 3–4. As to the deduction for the great Beth Din comp. Babli 7b. Whether the passage in the Midrash ha-gadol in Num. 5.30 belongs to the Sifre zutta—as is presupposed by Königsberger, Sifre zutta, p. 17a, and after him Büchler, *Das Synhedrion*, p. 50—or is derived from the Talmud Babli—as is assumed by Horowitz in his edition of the Sifre, p. 239—it is difficult to decide.

The decision of the Mishnah is found also in Philo, *De special. legibus*, II, §10. M. II, 308. Comp. Ritter, *Philo und die Halacha*, p. 83. Comp. also Heinemann, *Schriften der jüdisch-hellenistischen Literatur*, II, 199, n.2.

[168] Sifre zutta, ed. Horowitz, Leipzig 1917, p. 237: רבן גמליאל אומר ונקתה ונזרעה זרע פרט לזרועה לומר אין עוברה שותה.

[169] Tosefta Soṭah II, 3; Sifre Num. §19; Sifre zutta, p. 237f.; Berakot 31b; Soṭah 28a; p. Soṭah III, 3 18d; Num. r. XIX, 25; Philo *l. c.*, p. 310. Heinemann *l. c.*, p. 201, 62: "She may expect then either a reward for her immaculate behavior or the heaviest penalty for her licentiousness. For if she is slandered, she may hope for product of the womb and blessing of children and can banish from her mind the worries and thoughts about unproductiveness and barrenness". Comp. Josephus, *Antiquities*, II, 11,6 (ed. Niese. I, 212, 272): "Now if she has been indicted unjustly, then she becomes pregnant and carries to the very end" ἡ δ' εἰ μὲν ἀδίκως ἐνεκλήθη ἐγκύμων τε γίνεται καὶ τελεσφορεῖται κατὰ τὴν γαστέρα. To the "blessing of children" in Philo corresponds in the Palestinian sources היתה יולדת לשתי שנים יולדת בכך שנה יולדת אחד תלד שנים שנים. Ritter, *l. c.*, n. 1, is mistaken. Comp. also Olitzki, *Flavius Josephus und die Halachah*, p. 23, n. 28.

a pregnant woman; or it contains also a condition for the previous period, when she has not yet conceived seed, then all the women who ever gave birth to children would have to be excluded, and the biblical law would be valid only for sterile women, since only in the case of sterile women does the gift of children after the test signify an evident sign of reward, while in the case of women who had children before the act of bearing after the test is nothing extraordinary, as the carrying of a child in her womb is something of a daily occurrence to a pregnant woman. But what justification is there to split the thought and to refuse to follow it straight to its very end? This difficulty which R. Gamaliel could not overlook suggests the supposition that R. Gamaliel's opinion was not derived first from this deduction, that the deduction serves only as a formal justification for his point of view which differs from tradition, but this view itself goes back to an opinion held by R. Gamaliel. This opinion can be no other than that the child in the mother's womb is a being in itself which may lay claim to forbearance to itself. Indeed we see that the Karaites, who adopt this point of view (comp. note 113), do not let the pregnant Sotah drink the proof-bringing water.[170] Consequently, according to whether we are dealing here with R. Gamaliel I or II, we may have here the oldest or one of the oldest traces of Alexandrian points of view in Palestine.

If this be true, then also the place where this opinion of R. Gamaliel is found gains importance. For then it is perhaps no mere accident that this opinion occurs in no other source than the Sifre Zutta. There are important reasons for the assumption that the Sifre Zutta is derived from the school of R. Eliezer ben Jacob,[171]

[170] Comp. *Gan 'Eden* 156d below; *Keter Torah* to Num. 8a: וההרה דנו חכמים שלא ישקה כי לא נהרוג נפש בלי מרת התורה; Adderet Eliyyahu 166b below.

[171] Comp. Sifre Num., ed. Horowitz, Leipzig 1917, introduction, p. XVIIf.

of whom we shall soon be convinced that he shares the view of the Alexandrians. We learn this from the following comment on Ex. 21.22.

5. "And hurt a woman that is *pregnant*". Wherefore is it said? Since we find "and her fruit depart", then we know that we are dealing here with a pregnant woman, to what purpose then serves "that is pregnant"? For we might believe that if he struck the woman on her head or on one of her other limbs, he is guilty, therefore it is said "that is pregnant", which means that he is guilty only if he strikes her at the place where her child is found.[172]

This means therefore that the punishment of killing an embryo depends on the condition that the stroke is delivered against the mother's womb, hence directly against the child. This requirement can only be understood from the point of view that the child in the mother's womb is a being in itself. With this supposition in mind the stroke must be delivered directly against the mother's womb, for in the case of a blow on any other part of her body we are left without warrant that the child was killed by the blow; the death of the child might be an accident which certainly coincides with the blow but does not follow from it as a cause. What follows a thing is not always that which follows because of a thing. But if the child is a part of the mother, then, in keeping with our notion of cause and effect, the death of the child subsequent to the stroke on the mother's head is as much a result of the stroke as a head-ache appearing immediately after a wounding of the hand is the result of that wounding; here *post hoc* is also *propter hoc*. Such is logic. But such also are the facts. For on the one hand Philo emphasizes "and deals her a blow against her womb" and on the other

---

[172] Mekilta Mishpatim VIII 84a: וננפו אשה הרה למה נאמר לפי שנאמר ויצאו ילדיה הא למדנו שהיא הרה ומה תלמוד לומר הרה שאם הכה על ראשה או על אחת מאיבריה שומע אני יהא חייב תלמוד לומר הרה מגיד שאינו חייב עד שיכה במקום עובדה. Palest. Baba ḳamma V, 6 5a above, Babyl. Baba ḳamma 49a: לעולם אינו חייב עד שיכה כנגד בית ההריון.

hand the Mishnah ignores this forcing of the phrase: "If someone wants to strike another, but the blow misses its aim and hits a pregnant woman, so her fruit departs, then he pays the value of the child".[173] It concerns therefore only the hitting of the woman in general. Hence also Maimonides did not codify the requirement in question, though it is transmitted in the Mekilta and in the two Talmudim and in the Babylonian Talmud it is even attributed to R. Simeon ben Gamaliel. Apparently Maimonides realized that this requirement could not be made to harmonize with the standpoint of the received Halakah, that the child in the mother's womb is part of its mother.

But who is the Palestinian teacher who proposes this requirement? In the Mekilta it is Abba Jose ben Ḥanin in the name of R. Eliezer, in the Palestianian Talmud it is Abba Jose ben Ḥanin, in the Babylonian Talmud it is R. Eliezer ben Jacob. Now the Mekilta and the Babylonian Talmud agree that Abba Jose is only the transmitter and not the originator of this interpretation, hence the text in the Palestinian Talmud is abbreviated and cannot be considered in the question before us. There remains the decision between the Mekilta and the Babylonian Talmud. But R. Eliezer, i. e. R. Eliezer ben Hyrkanos, cannot be the author of the deduction in the Mekilta, for his standpoint is that the child in the mother's womb is a part of the mother[174]; consequently the only correct reading is that of the Babylonian Talmud: R. Eliezer ben Jacob. In the Mekilta the words "ben Jacob" had been omitted, similarly the entire name of the author in the Palestinian Talmud and the name of the transmitter in the Babylonian Talmud.—Rejection or acceptance of our requirement is connected with the following controversy

---

[173] Baba ḳamma V, 7: אדם שהיה מתכוין לחבירו והכה את האשה ויצאו ילדיה משלם דמי ולדות. Comp. Mishne Torah, Hobel IV, 2 and 6.

[174] Hullin 58a, Temurah 25b et al.

which likewise finds its explanation only from the attitude we take in the main question: Is the embryo a part of the mother or a being in itself?

6. How do we determine the value of the child killed in miscarriage through a blow? We estimate the value of the mother before and after the miscarriage, the difference between the two values constituting the indemnity to be offered. Thus the anonymous view in the Mishnah, to which R. Simeon ben Gamaliel objects as follows: "Is it really so? Is it not true that the woman has greater value after bearing? Hence we must estimate the value of the child" [175]

The first mode of valuation is exactly the same employed in ordinary wounds of the body: "How do we determine the compensation? If he blinded an eye, cut off a hand, fractured a foot, we consider the wounded person as a slave intended for sale and we estimate his value before and after the wounding".[176] Now since the child in the mother's womb is nothing more than another part of its mother's body, it stands to reason that in the case of a miscarriage caused by a blow inflicted on the mother there is likewise nothing more than an ordinary wounding of the mother's body. Hence the valuation is the same as in the case of other woundings, where not the wounded member but the wounded person is appraised. But R. Simeon ben Gamaliel considers the embryo as an independent being, hence it must be appraised by itself. Only in this way is the controversy to be understood. For after all the question whether the value of the woman after the act of bearing is greater or smaller than before cannot be the subject of a learned controversy, the slave traders

[175] Baba kamma V, 4: כיצד משלם דמי ולדות שמין את האישה כמה היא יפה עד שלא ילדה וכמה היא יפה משילדה. אמר רשב״נ א״כ משהאשה יולדת משבחת, אלא שמין את הולדות כמה הן יפין.

[176] Baba kamma VIII, 1: בנזק כיצד. סימא את עינו קטע את ידו שיבר את רגלו רואין אותו כאילו הוא עבד נמכר בשוק ושמין כמה היה יפה וכמה הוא יפה.

and slave brokers being more competent to decide it. The difference of opinion with reference to this question can therefore hinge only on the consideration as to which of the circumstances, which are equally possible in the valuation, are more probable: the increase in value on account of the disappearance of dangers attendant upon pregnancy and child-birth or the decrease in value owing to the diminution in the size of the body. But then the question arises again: Since both moments are equally existent, what causes the one to consider the one moment so decisive and the other to lend superiority to the other moment? If, however, the anonymous view in the Mishnah considers the embryo as a part of the mother's body, then the mother is the one damaged, and her compensation can only be fixed in the same manner as in other cases of damage. It is true that here too there is a gain, but only the visible damage can be paramount and not the invisible gain. And when R. Simeon ben Gamaliel considers the embryo as a being in itself, then the embryo is the one damage, and the visible damage to it must be estimated; the size of the mother's body cannot come here into consideration, for it was not her body that was hurt; what may be considered in the valuation of the mother is her invisible gain, since she suffered no damage whatever.

In accordance with this the anonymous view of the Mishnah will reject the requirement of R. Eliezer ben Jacob and of Philo, treated above in No. 5, that the blow must be inflicted against the woman's womb if the action is to be punishable, while R. Simeon ben Gamaliel will approve of it. This deduction, gained by us through logical necessity—similar views give rise to similar norms—is arrived at in the Babylonian Talmud for reasons of exegetical economy,[177] which, however, does not in itself

[177] Baba ḳamma 49a.

make it absolutely necessary that R. Simeon ben Gamaliel, who cannot employ the word הרה "pregnant" in the sense of his opponents, must construe it exactly in the sense of R. Eliezer ben Jacob, since still another meaning is possible, as may be seen in the sources.[178] But already the editor of the Mishnah presupposed this connection. This is evident from the place which he gave to this controversy. Its natural place would be in the eighth section dealing with the fixing of compensation and other acts relating to bodily wounds, while in its present place, in the fifth section, it stands quite isolated. However, because it is connected in principle with the above-mentioned decision, therefore it was added to it. But that only this inner, principle-involving connection and not the merely external moment of the mention of the decision was responsible for it, is evident from the fact that the fixing of compensation for the embryo is mentioned also in VIII, 2, and, to be sure, directly and in proper connection, in organic combination with similar decisions, while here it is recorded only incidentally, because of a remote association. It would certainly be quite unnatural to leave unmentioned the closer substantiation of a decision there where the decision appears in its natural place, while mentioning it there where the decision itself is quoted only incidentally. But from the phrase in VIII, 2 "the man makes amends for the embryo" the conditions under which the duty of compensation arises are not recognizable, while from the wording in V, 4 it appears that the blow must not be aimed against the womb. Why this? Because the child is a part of the mother. But on this view rests also the mode of valuation, which is now communicated here in organic connection.

7. In the compulsory releasing of a female slave, when

[178] Comp. note 172, Tosefta Baba ḳamma IX, 10. Mekilta of R. Simeon, p. 129.

her master knocks out one of her eyes or one of her teeth (Ex. 21.26–27), the child found in her womb does not attain freedom.[179] This decision is sensible and legitimate only if the child in the mother's womb is considered as a being in itself. On this point there can be no doubt. As a matter of fact the originator of this decision is R. Johanan, of whom we know that also in other matters he takes this view.[180]

8. Thus we have come to know Palestinian teachers who share the view of the Alexandrians that the child in the mother's womb is a being in itself. Now what was the position of these teachers in the question of the killing of the unborn child? Did they follow the Alexandrians to their last conclusion, considering the killing of the child in the mother's womb as murder?

This question should be negatived with certainty. It may be presupposed without hesitation that in practice no Pharisaic council of judges would have been bold enough to make a decision in conflict with tradition and practice, especially where a human life was the stake in the play of opinions, and this even aside from the endeavor of the Pharisees to make decrees of death altogether impossible or at least extremely rare.[181] The question therefore can only be discussed in its theoretical aspect. And even here opposition to tradition and the view of the majority

[179] Palest. Baba kamma V, 6 5a: כיני מתניתין עוברין אין יוצאין בשן ועין של אמן. Previously, however, R. Johanan appears as the originator of the sentence. No doubt a baraita transmitted by R. Johanan is here involved.
[180] Comp. above note 134.
[181] This aim permeates the entire Halakah dealing with criminal jurisdiction. Already the requirement of a warning התראה with its minute and detailed provisions is apt to make a death sentence impossible. Assuming that all the other conditions are fulfilled—which in practice is hardly imaginable—the forewarned must still say expressly: I do it, although I know that I become guilty of death therefor! Tosefta Sanh. XI, 4; Sanh. 40b, 72b. And do not the impossbible conditions, of which the stoning of the refractory son is made dependent (Sanh. VIII, Tosefta XI, 6), show distinctly that the Pharisees aimed at making this case impossible? As a matter of fact they say themselves that בן סורר ומורה did not exist and will not exist. Tosefta Sanh. l. c.; Sanh. 71a. Comp. also the sayings of R. Eleazar ben Azariah, R. Tarphon, and R. Akiba in Makkot I, 10 7a.

is not really necessary. For even if the child in the mother's womb is a being in itself, thereby only one of the two conditions is given which, in consonance with the Halakah, must be fulfilled if a killing is to be qualified as a murder punishable by law; even if the independent existence of the embryo is granted, still its ability to live is not yet assured. For this reason the Palestinian teacher, who considers the child in the mother's womb as a being in itself, must nevertheless absolve the killer of an unborn child from capital punishment.[182] As to him who considers the child in the mother's womb as a part of the mother, he must be aware that in the killing of an unborn child murder is absent for the consideration that the condition of independent existence is lacking; ability to live may then be granted or not.

However, the expectation of the ability to live is granted if the child is carried the full time—7 or 9 months. But since this cannot be determined by computation for the purpose of the court,[183] therefore the following symp-

[182] This vitiates Geiger's hypothesis that the older Halakah, which considers the embryo as a being in itself, punished the killing of a child in the mother's womb with death. *Urschrift*, p. 436f.; *Nachgelassene Schriften*, III, 263f.; *Hebr. Aufsätze*, ed. Poznanski, p. 116f. This instance against Geiger has already been pointed out by Pineles, תורה של דכה p. 191, in another form. Other instances in Löw, *Ben Chananja* IX, 698, n. 56. But the objections of Gronemann, *Die Jonathansche Pentateuchübersetzung*, p. 122, n. 1, and Ginzberg in Poznanski, *l. c.*, p. 398, against Geiger, are unimportant. Ginzberg states: "A one-day pupil knows that in the entire talmudic literature (בכל התלמוד) the expressions בן שמנה, בן שבעה etc., designate only the child born after 8 or 7 months of pregnancy, and not the child in the mother's womb". But a two-day pupil knows that the expressions in question are used also of a child in the mother's womb. Comp. Mishnah Ḥullin 74a-b; Tosefta *ibid*. IV, 5-8; Sifra שמיני Par. II end; Ḥullin 74a, 75a-b, 92b.

[183] Comp. R. Ḥananel on Shab. 136b; R. ABN 67a; Rashi Shab. 136a above *s.v.* לא נצרכה; *Mahzor Vitry*, p. 245; *Sefer ha-Orah*, p. 225f., No. 147; *Or Zarua* II, No. 428; Meir ben Baruk *Hil. Semahot*, No. 95; *Hag. Maimoniot* אבל, I, 7, No. 4. But Niddah 30b proves that even lock and bar do not afford sure safety. The court, however, cannot take into consideration the certainty of the man, even if it were absolute, since it is the testimony of a single witness, who in addition is himself a party in the lawsuit.— Also Rashi Niddah 44b *s. v.*כמאן the certainty of full carriage refers to all cases in the Mishnah, which was overlooked by Tos. Yom Tob on Niddah V, 3, and R. H. Chajes in his glosses on Niddah 44b. Comp. also Mishne Torah, Rozeaḥ I, 6 (אבל I, 7 and יבום I, 5) and Tosafot 'Arakin 2a *s.v.* לאתויי.

Some commentators think that for the presupposition of the ability to live the principle רוב is decisive. Comp. *Maggid Mishne* and לח״ם on יבום I, 5; comp. also

toms have been set down: (1) Development of the limbs as far as the growth of hair and nails,[184] (2) living at least 30 days after the birth.[185] Now on this the opinions of the teachers vary, some being satisfied with the first symptom, while others advance the second as the only valid one. The Palestinian teachers, who consider the embryo as a being in itself and yet will and must construe the passage Ex. 21.22 in the traditional sense, will necessarily reject the development as a proof of the ability to live and retain only the second proof. Indeed we see that R. Simeon ben Gamaliel, who holds the child in the mother's womb a being in itself, requires the thirty days existence after the birth as a proof of the ability to live. Rabbi, however, who considers the child in the mother's womb as a part of the mother, may see in the full development of the limbs a proof of full carriage and ability to live.

9. The condition of the ability to live, as was seen above, is derived from the expression איש, which the Torah employs in the first passage dealing with killing, while the expression employed in the second passage, אדם, also includes those able to live.[186] Now in the prohibition to murder addressed to the Noahides in Gen. 9.6 the Torah employs exclusively the word אדם, whence the condition of the ability to live is not required of the Noahide, and

Rashi Shab. 136a *s.v.* נפל, and M. b. Baruk *l. c.*, No. 95 beginning. But on the contrary according to Tosafot Niddah 44b *s. v.* דקים there is no רוב here. Comp. however, above note 139.

[184] Yebamot 80b from Tosefta Shab. XVI, 4. In both texts the representative of this view is Rabbi, so also R. Hananel Shab. 136b from Tosefta. In Tosefta ed. Zuckermandel R. Jose by mistake.

[185] R. Simeon ben Gamaliel, Tosefta and Babli *l. c.*, and in many other places. Comp. hereon Tosafot Yebamot *l. c., s. v.* כיון, Shab. 136a *s. v.* מימה, and Niddah 44b *s.v.* דקים.

[186] Ability to live is no characteristic of the concept אדם. Comp. Mekilta on Ex. 21.12-13, 80a and 84a; Mekilta of R. Simeon, p. 125; Sifra אמור Perek 20 beginning and Sanh. 84b; Sifre Num. 124 on Num. 19.11 and 13. Comp. Tosefta Shab. XVI,1; Nazir 50a and Hullin 89b. Comp. in addition Mekilta 81b and Mekilta of R. Simeon, p. 127.—Jonathan on Num. 19.11 and 13 goes back to Sifre, which escaped R. H. Chajes אמרי בינה 8b and Gronemann, *Die Jonathansche Pentateuchübersetzung*, p. 121. In Jonathan one should read תמנא instead of תשע.

therefore the Noahide receives capital punishment for the killing of an unborn child. This is what R. Ishmael teaches.[187] He considers the child in the mother's womb an independent being, a man.[188] The opponents of R. Ishmael, however, take the view that the child in the mother's womb is only a part of its mother, not yet a man; hence they teach that even the Noahide is not given capital punishment for the killing of an embryo.

R. Ishmael's view is substantiated in the Talmud by the statement that he reads Gen. 9.6 thus: "Whoso sheddeth man's blood in man, his blood shall be shed". So also the Septuagint in some correct codices: ὁ ἐκχέων αἷμα ἀνθρώπου ἐν τῷ ἀνθρώπῳ τὸ αἷμα αὐτοῦ χεθήσεται. The Septuagint, however, as was seen above, treats the killing of an unborn child as murder.

But while the Septuagint and Philo differentiate between the developed and fully carried child and the still undeveloped embryo, R. Ishmael speaks in general of the embryo, which admits a two-fold construction: 1. R. Ishmael holds it self-evident that only the developed embryo is a man; therefore he does not have to emphasize the difference between the developed and the undeveloped

[187] Sanh. 57b. The same R. Hanina in Gen. r. XXXIV, 14, ed. Theodor, p. 325. Löw, *Lebensalter*, p. 70, thinks: "But it was not unknown to the Jewish scholars of the second century that among the Romans the mother of the child, who destroys its life before birth, as well as the stranger, who co-operates herein, were menaced by criminal penalties. They endeavor therefore to find support for it in the laws of the Noahides". As if R. Ishmael had supposed that the Romans consider themselves as Noahides and deduct their laws from Gen. 9.6! This might be a good joke, if the fact were not that the Roman laws under consideration had no existence yet in the days of R. Ishmael. The first traces of a law against abortion, *abortio partus*, showed themselves not earlier than 200 under the emperors Septimus Severus and Antoninus. Comp. Rein, *Römisches Criminalrecht*, p. 447; Mommsen, *Römisches Strafrecht*, p. 637. Comp. Weyl, *Die jüdischen Strafgesetze bei Flavius Josephus*, p. 52 note. Noteworthy is the opinion of Weiss, *Zur Geschichte der jüdische Tradition*, II, 23, that R. Ishmael's rule is directed against the abortion which is current among the Romans. But the connection of the passage teaches that its aim is neither an exegetical proof for, nor a refutation against, the Romans, but an interpretation of the Noahide law important to the Jewish court. Comp. especially the literal wording in Gen. r. and Mishne Torah Melakim X, 11.

[188] Comp. above note 134. In R. Hanina likewise this motive becomes evident. Comp. above, No. IV.

embryo. 2. R. Ishamel considers even the still undeveloped embryo as a man; therefore he cannot make the difference and must deal out capital punishment to the Noahide even for the killing of the still undeveloped embryo. The latter construction is more correct. We should not assume that R. Ishmael, in so important a question and at a time when his teaching was still novel, would rely on something as self-evident and fail to emphasize the condition for the development of the embryo if he had required it.[189] Moreover, also the other Palestinian teachers, who consider the child in the mother's womb as a being in itself, do not differentiate between developed and undeveloped.

10. Now it follows from the above that these Palestinian teachers had not borrowed their view from the Alexandrians, but derived it from a purely Greek source,[190] in the same manner as their opponents who consider the child in the mother's womb as a part of the mother without difference whether it is not yet developed or already developed. For the teaching of the Septuagint and Philo is nothing else but a compromise between two opposite views of Greek schools of philosophy, the Stoa and the Academy. Plato maintains, "The child in the mother's womb is a living being, for it moves about in the womb and draws nourishment to itself".[191] The Stoics, on the other hand, teach that "the child in the mother's womb is a part of the womb, no living being", and they weaken Plato's proof by this exposition: The child in the womb is nourished physically like a plant; but when it is born and it receives the soul from the air, then it becomes a

[189] Comp. R. I. Z. Jolles, glosses to Sanh. 57b; Geiger, *Urschrift*, p. 437; *Nachgelassene Schriften*, III, 263; *Hebr. Aufsätze*, ed. Poznanski, p. 116. Comp. also above note 134.

[190] Frankel, *Monatsschrift* for 1859, p. 400, was first to call attention to the agreement between the talmudic controversy עובר ירך אמו or לאו ירך אמו and the views of the Greek philosophers concerning the nature of the embryo. For Löw's counter-argument comp. above, note 129.

[191] Plutarch, *De placitis philosophorum*, V. 15: Πλάτων, ζῷον τὸ ἔμβρυον καὶ γὰρ κινεῖσθαι ἐν γαστερὶ καὶ τρέφεσθαι. Comp. Frankel *l. c.*

living being. Hence the soul is called ψυχή, from ψύξις "cooling".[192] It is to this that Philo refers in his remark: "For even admitting that the fruit of the womb continually growing after the manner of the plant and considered as a part of the pregnant animal ... is protected".[193] The controversy against the Stoics is led by the Church Fathers: "The soul is not air received through the mouth, for the soul originates much earlier than when it can receive air."[194]

Thus the question whether the child in the mother's womb is a being in itself or a part of the mother coincides with the question as to when the soul enters into the fruit of the womb. This connection we have learned to know also from rabbinic literature, when Rabbi, who considers the child in the mother's womb as a part of the mother, maintains expressly that the entrance of the soul takes place only at the moment of birth, while the teachers who hold that the embryo is a being in itself ascribe to it even

[192] Plutarch *l. c.*: οἱ Στοϊκοί, μέρος εἶναι αὐτὸ τῆς γαστρὸς οὐ ζῷον. Comp. Frankel, *l. c.*, and Löw, *Ben Chananja*, IX, 691f.—Plutarch, *De Stoicorum repugn.*, ch. 41, Op. 1052f.: τὸ φοβερὸς ἐν τῇ γαστρὶ φύσει τρέφεσται νομίξει καθάπερ φυτόν. ὅταν δὲ τεχθῇ, ψυχόμενον ὑπὸ τοῦ ἀέρος καὶ στομούμενον τὸ πνεῦμα μεταβάλλειν καὶ γίνεσθαι ζῷον ὅθεν οὐκ ἀπὸ τρόπον τὴν ψυχὴν ὠνομάσθα παρὰ τὴν ψῦξιν. Ibid., p. 1053; γίνεσθαι μὲν γάρ φησι τὴν ψυχὴν ὅταν τὸ βρέφον ἀποτεχθῇ, καθάπερ στομώσει τῇ περιψύξει τοῦ πνεύματος μεταβαλόντος. Comp. Armin, *Stoicorum veterum fragm.* II, 220, 222, No. 796f., 806. Comp. Ebstein, *Die Medizin im Neuen Testamente*, p. 148, n. 1. Comp. Tertullian, *De anima*, ch. 25, above note 139. Tertullian credits also Plato with the view that the soul is joined to the body at the first breathing after birth. *L. c.*, p. 203: *Ceterum semen ex concubitu muliebribus locis sequestratum motuque naturali vegetatum compinguescere in solam substantiam carnis, eam editam, et de uteri fornace fumantem et calore solutam, ut ferrum ignitum et ibidem frigidae immersum, ita aeris rigore percussam et vim animalem rapere et vocalem sonum reddere. Hoc Stoici cum Aenesidemo, et ipse interdum Plato, quum dicit perinde animam extraneam alias et extorrem uteri prima aspiratione nascentis infantis adduci, sicut exspiratione novissima educi.* Further ch. 26, p. 206: *Et si ipse animam de prima spiratione potabat Platonica more aut de aeris rigore carpebat Stoica forma.* Comp. Phaed., p. 76.

[193] *De virtute*, 18, quoted above, note 165. The remark refers to the law mentioned by Philo previously that pregnant animals are excluded from the altar. Comp. Ritter, *Philo und die Halacha*, p. 109f. Now since this law concerns all pregnant animals, also those that find themselves at the beginning of pregnancy, Philo is compelled to prove the sparing of the embryo at this stage through the expectation of the future birth. This remark of his is therefore not in contradiction to his view in *De special. leg.*, which we have learned to know before. Comp. also above, note 135

[194] Tertullian, *De anima*, ch. 25–27; Lactantius, *De opific. Dei*, ch. 17. Comp. Ebstein, *Die Medizin im Neuen Testament*, p. 148, n. 1.

spiritual life.[195] But R. Johanan, who maintains that the child is not a part of the mother,[196] teaches that the

[195] Comp. above.
Other haggadic statements bearing on this view:

(a) R. Judah: In his exit from his mother's womb Esau cut Rebeccah's matrix in pieces so that she could not bear any more. Pes. ed. Buber 23a; Tanḥuma ed. Buber כי תצא § 4; Pers. ch. 12 48a; comp. *Midr. ha-gadol*, ed. Schechter, p. 340f. Comp. on all this Aptowitzer, *Freie jüdische Lehrerstimme*, V, Nos. 1, 2, 5.

(b) Levi: Already in the mother's womb Esau stretched his fist against Jacob. Gen. r. LXIII, 6; both Tanh. כי תצא, 4. Comp. Pes. ed. Buber 23b, n. 47. Comp. also Rab's and Levi's sayings in Midr. Ps. 8, 5; Soṭah 31a above in the name of R. Tanḥum.

(c) As Rebeccah passed along prayer-houses and schools Jacob pressed himself to come out from the mother's womb; when she passed near houses of heathen worship Esau forced himself to come out from the mother's womb. Gen. r. LXIII. Comp. similar interpretations in Jonathan on Gen. 25.22; Midrash Abkir in Yal. Gen. 110 (Buber's ליקוטים, p. 6, No. 17); Seder Eliyahuy zutta, ch. 19 (ed. Friedmann, נספחים, p. 16f.); Rashi on Gen. 25.22 and Zohar *ibid.* I, 137b.
On the contrary, the sayings of R. Johanan and Simeon ben Lakish, Gen.r.LXIII beginning, do not belong here. What is meant is that the wrestling of the children was a foreboding for the future (Rome and Israel), as is proved by the subsequent objection of Levi שלא תאמר עד שלא יצא.

Löw, *Ben Chananja*, IX, 692, below, maintains: "R. Simeon ben Yoḥai lets king David sing thanksgiving-songs already in the mother's womb". The same is repeated in *Lebensalter*, p. 65. He points out R. Simeon's statement in Berakot 10a, Lev. r. IV 7, and Midr. Ps. 103 3. But this conception of the statement in question is not correct, It is true that it corresponds to the wording שדר בחמשה עולמות, but already Rashi explains that David composed at a later date psalms corresponding to the five worlds, i. e. stages of man's life. In this way the passage was understood also by the author of תורות הנפש, p. 89f.: ואמרו גם כן על דוד שאמר ברכי נפשי את ה' ארבעה פעמים כמספר החדושים אשר נתחדשו בו בראשית יצירתו, ועל כל אחד מהם אמר ברכי כנגד חמשה עולמות שאדם רואה נפשי...ואחר זה אמר ברכי נפש פעם חמישית[ן]. Similarly in Lev. r. and in Midr. Ps. ראה דוד חמשה עולמות. The author of the statement is probably R. Johanan, as in Midr. Ps. and Lev. r. even in the Munich MS. and in *Torot ha-Nefesh* the words משום רשב"י are wanting. Comp., however, Yal. ha-Makiri, Ps. 103, 1. As to the literature in Lev. r. comp. Bacher, *Ag. d. Tan.*³, p. 132, n. 4.

The question when the soul joins the body is dicussed extensively in *Torot ha-Nefesh*, p. 50–59, with the result that a part of the soul joins the seed already at the time of conception, while the complete soul comes after at the time of birth. According to Joseph Ibn Saddiḳ, '*Olam Ḳaṭan*, ed. Horowitz, p. 27, l. 31f., the animal soul joins the body after the development of the form of the limbs, i. e.—as quoted p. 26, l. 6f.—on the fortieth day of pregnancy in case of a male embryo and on the sixtieth in case of a female embryo. It is therefore an error when Horowitz, *Die Psychologie bei den jüdischen Religionsphilosophen*, III, 183, notes that according to Ibn Saddiḳ the connection does not take place before the child leaves the mother's womb. (The time of the development in Ibn Saddiḳ does not agree with either the statements of the Rabbis or the views of the Greeks. Comp. Niddah 30a f. and Preuss, *Schwangerschaft, Geburt und Wochenbett nach Bibel und Talmud*, p. 21. Reprint from *Zeitschrift für Geburtshilfe und Gynäekologie*, LIII, Part 3).

In *Torot ha-Nefesh*, p. 53, is quoted the otherwise unknown custom, that during the birth of a child some of those present say: "Praised be He who grants life" or "Praised be He who animates the dead", while others answer: "Life and peace!" This custom is based on the view of the Stoics that the product does not receive life before the moment of birth. Comp. Aptowitzer, *Wiener Morgenzeitung* of Aug. 28. 1920, p. 7, n. III.

[196] Comp. above. note 134.

soul is united to the drop of seed.[197] "The question *de animatione foetus*", remarks Preuss,[198] "had a practical significance to the legislators, who looked upon the animated fruit as upon a man and therefore intended to punish the repulsion of fruit like murder, to the physicians insofar as the partisans of the Stoic doctrine *partem ventris non animal foetus* certainly decided very easily in favor of the dismemberment of the living child. In the talmudic law it has no importance whatever." However, we have just seen that this question as to the point of time when the animation of the fruit enters has its significance in talmudic law as well.

---

[197] "Forthwith God makes a sign to the angel, who is in charge of the spirits, and says to him: Bring me that spirit. At once he comes before the Holy One, praised be He, and bows down before Him. Then the Holy One, praised be He, says to him: Betake thyself into this drop...Immediately God brings him against his will into the drop, and the angel goes back and brings the spirit in the drop back again into the womb of the mother". The passage occurs in the description of the formation of the embryo in Tanḥuma מקדי 3; *Bet ha-Midrash*, I, 153. Similarly R. Simlai, Niddah 30b, comp. with *Bet ha-Midrash* I, 79. As to the Platonic elements in the description of R. Simlai comp. Mendelssohn, *Gesammelte Schriften*, II, 10; Freudenthal, *Hellenistische Studien*, II, 72; Löw, *Ben Chananja*, IX, 693; Schulz, *Dokumente der Gnosis*, p. 8ff., where are found also parallels from Egyptian-Greek and Germanic myths and tales. That the soul is joined to the seed drop is the doctrine of Aristotle, *Gen. an.*, II, 3. Comp. Zeller, *Die Philosophie der Griechen* [3], II 2, 483.

[198] *Schwangerschaft, Geburt und Wochenbett*, p. 19. Comp. also Theodor to Gen. r. XXXIV, 10, p. 321.

THE LEVITICAL IMPURITY OF THE GENTILE IN PALESTINE BEFORE THE YEAR 70

By A. Büchler, Jews' College, London

In his statement about the deliberate and consistent separation of the Jew from the Gentile by the religious authorities of the first century, Professor Schürer[1] asserts: "Die Trennung wurde noch verschärft durch die Anschauung, dass der Heide, weil er die Reinheitsgesetze nicht beobachtet, unrein sei; daher aller Verkehr mit ihm verunreinige... Wenn es in der Apostelgeschichte heisst, dass ein Jude nicht mit einem Heiden verkehren dürfe, 10, 28, so ist dies zwar nicht dahin misszuverstehen, als ob der Verkehr schlechthin verboten gewesen wäre; wohl aber ist damit gesagt, dass jeder solche Verkehr eine Verunreinigung bewirkte." It is hardly accidental that the great scholar who in his work never made a statement, ever so unimportant, about the life and the history of the Greeks or the Romans, without supporting it by numerous references, in this instance of Jewish-Palestinian life failed to adduce one single proof from Philo, Josephus, or the rabbinic literature. Yet he points out himself[2] that not less than twelve tractates of the Mishnah deal with the levitical purity and impurity! And he should have added that just as many tractates of the Tosefta, and a great number of Baraitas scattered over the two Talmuds and the halakic Midrash-works are devoted to the same subjects. Consequently, it was his duty to cite from that literature some evidence for his definite assertion. It is true, in the course

---
[1] *Geschichte*, II, 4th edition, p. 91; cf. III, 183.
[2] *l. c.* p. 561.

of the paragraph he refers to Weber's well-known book, *System der altsynagogalen palästinischen Theologie aus Targum, Midrasch und Talmud dargestellt*.[3] But it is most instructive that even Weber did not quote one single rabbinic statement as bearing on that point, and, as far as I can see, did not even assert such levitical impurity of the Gentile at all. And so Professor Schürer's only evidence is the passage in Acts which he qualifies considerably, and into which he reads a reason of his own for the assumed impurity. He and other Christian scholars also refer to the view of the Hillelites in Pesaḥim 8, 8, without even attempting to explain the facts implied by that Mishnah, and without inquiring into the actual validity of the rule of the Hillelites.

In spite of Professor Schürer's dogmatic assertions, and his misrepresentation of other views, it must be stated at the outset, and will, I hope, be proved by the following investigation, that, as far as my knowledge of the available information goes, such levitical impurity was not attributed to the Gentile in Jerusalem in Temple times, that the intercourse between Jew and Gentile was neither wholly prevented nor even restricted thereby, that the non-observance by the Gentile of the rules of the levitical purity had nothing to do with any actual levitical impurity of his, and that, at best, its defiling effect was the same as that of the same degree of levitical impurity of the Jew, or even less, as it affected exclusively the priest on duty, the Temple, the Jew specially purified for the sacrifice, and the sacrificial meal,—nobody and nothing beyond. In the law of the Pentateuch the Gentile was not subject to the various defilements enumerated in Lev. 15, nor to that by a corpse, so fully discussed in Num. 19. But the rabbinic authorities of the last century of the Temple gradually

[3] p. 91 ff.

extended one kind of levitical impurity to non-Jews, that of the menstruous Jewish woman to the Gentile woman. The Gentile as such was even then not regarded as impure, but only as defiled by his wife. It was only about the year 65 that the two schools of the Hillelites and the Shammaites declared the Gentile himself affected by a grave levitical impurity, not because he was as a Gentile considered impure, but as a precautionary measure against Roman sodomy, as is expressly stated in the Talmud. To trace the development of the levitical impurity of the Gentile woman and man is the main object of this essay. Owing to its special difficulty and the complex historical problems connected therewith, the relevant rabbinic material has not been studied even by Jewish rabbinical scholars generally. Therefore, a collection of the rabbinic data on the levitical character of the Gentile, and an objective interpretation of them, and a discussion of the various problems of the levitical impurity concerned will be attempted here. Early statements about the actual observance of any law of the levitical purity are scanty; and the progressive legislation itself, as well as the binding force of those rules for certain individuals or certain sections of the Palestinian Jews are matters of doubt and of dispute. Therefore, scholars interested in the religious life and thought of Palestinian Jewry in the first century should combine their forces, to establish, without preconceived ideas, the facts about the actual extent of the observance of the levitical purity in Temple times, the levitical character of the Gentile, the authors and the dates of the various rules, the avowed or assumed objects of the several legislators, and the effect of their laws on the private and the public life of the Palestinian Jewish community.

1. *The levitical impurity of the Sadducee women.*

A Baraita reports the actual observance by Sadducee women of a certain Pharisee levitical rule. Its reference to the Sadducees attracted the attention of several scholars; but the legal antecedents of the rule in question, and their bearing on the history of the levitical law have, to my knowledge, not been analyzed. The report states:[4] "When once a Sadducee was speaking to a high priest in the market, and a stream of spittle issued from the mouth of the Sadducee and fell upon the clothes of the high priest, his face turned pale. He went to see his wife (or the wife of the Sadducee) who told him: Though they are the wives of Sadducees, they are afraid of the Pharisees, and show their blood to the scholars. According to R. José, they told him: We know them very well, and know that they show their blood to the scholars, except one woman who lived in our district and who, as she showed not her blood to the scholars, died." At the time when that incident occurred, the opinion of the Pharisees on the practice of the religious law was followed by the people generally, and not only in the service of the Temple, in prayers and sacrifices;[5] it was accepted by the Sadducees in their official capacity, as otherwise the multitude would not have borne them.[6] So, when, in the service on the Day of Atonement, one of the several ephemeral high priests deliberately brought the incense into the Holy of Holies according to the interpretation of Lev. 16, 12. 13 by the Sadducees, his father remarked to him:[7] 'Though we are Sadducees, we fear the Pharisees.'

[4] Niddah 33b; Tos. 5, 3: תנו רבנן מעשה בצדוקי אחד שספר עם כהן גדול בשוק ונתזה צנורה מפיו ונפלה לכהן גדול על בגדיו והוריקו פניו של כהן גדול וקדם אצל אשתו. אמרה לו אף על פי שנשי צדוקים הן מתיראות מן הפרושים ומראות דם לחכמים. אמר רבי יוסי בקיאין אנו בהן יותר מן הכל והם מראות דם לחכמים חוץ מאשה אחת שהיתה בשכונתינו שלא הראת דם לחכמים ומתה החלוץ. Cf. Geiger in 5, 1860, 29; 6, 1861, 29; *Jüd. ZS* 1; 1862, 51; Leszynsky, *Die Sadduzäer* 73 ff.
[5] Josephus, *Antiquit.* 18, 1, 3, 15.
[6] *Antiquit.* 18, 1, 17.
[7] b. *Yoma* 19b; Tos. 1, 8.

In the same way, the wives of the Sadducees followed the practice of the Pharisee women,[8] and submitted doubtful and irregular cases of their monthly purification to the Pharisee scholars. The high priest himself in the above report considered the Pharisee interpretation of the law about the woman's purification to be authoritative; and as he was not sure whether the wife of the Sadducee in front of him followed the Pharisee rule in her purification, and whether, in the contrary case, she had not defiled her husband, he was anxious about it. For, in referring to conditions obtaining before the year 70, the Mishnah states:[9] "When Sadducee women walk in the ways of their fathers, they are (levitically impure) like Samaritan women; when, however, they turn away, and walk in the ways of Israelites, they are like Jewesses. R. José says: They are ever like Jewesses, unless they turn away, and walk in the ways of their fathers." As to the levitical state of the Samaritan women, the Mishnah declares:[10] "They are from

[8] *Kohel. rab.* 4, 17; 2 ARN 41, 57b.
[9] Niddah 4, 2; Baraita 33b: בנות צדוקין בזמן שנהגו ללכת בדרכי אבותיהן הרי הן ככותיות, פרשו ללכת בדרכי ישראל הרי הן כישראליות, רבי יוסי אומר לעולם כישראליות עד שיפרשו ללכת בדרכי אבותיהן.
[10] Niddah 4, 1: בנות כותים נדות מעריסתן והכותים מטמאין משכב תחתון כעליון מפני שהן בועלי נדות. In Shabb. 16b bottom, R. Naḥman asserts that that rule was passed by the two schools of the Shammaites and the Hillelites as one of the eighteen decrees, that is, in the year 65-66, see below p. 39. Little is known of the levitical position assigned by the religious authorities in Jerusalem to the Samaritans before the year 70. *Antiquit.* 18, 2, 2, 30 reports how in the early morning of Nisan 14th in the days of the governor Coponius (6-9 c. E.), some Samaritans came secretly to Jerusalem, and scattered human bones in the cloisters of the Temple Mount. On account of that, all were excluded henceforth from the Temple, against the custom observed before on such occasions. Accordingly, there was no objection to the admission of the Samaritans to the Temple on any levitical ground before that incident; while their deliberate defilement of the Temple in Jerusalem by human bones clearly showed not only their utter disregard of the purity of that Temple, but also their determination to defile it by the gravest of all levitical impurities. Would it not have been natural, if the religious authorities of Jerusalem had, on account of that, declared the Samaritans permanently defiled by a corpse, and, therefore, to be kept away strictly from the Temple Mount? Perhaps that was their argument for the exclusion of the Samaritans and for the stricter guarding of the Temple. As we shall see p. 16, the Hillelites attributed to the Gentiles such defilement by a corpse; and it is not improbable that the Samaritan action in the Temple suggested to those scholars that idea. If there is any ground for that assumption, it would follow that the attribution of the impurity of the menstruous Jewess to the Gentile woman was preceded by the same attribution to the Samaritan woman; but there is no direct evidence available.

their cradles regarded as being permanently in the state of menstruous women, and their husbands, owing to their intercourse with their wives, are permanently defiled." Consequently, if the high priest found that the wife of the Sadducee did not regularly observe the Pharisee rule of the monthly purification, she was, in his opinion, permanently in the state of the levitical impurity of a menstruous woman. And as she lived with her husband, she communicated her grave and permanent defilement to him, Lev. 15, 24, and consequently, his levitical impurity would, similarly, be constant.

But, as the Sadducee woman herself only defiled others in the several ways enumerated in Lev. 15, 19-24, and these do not include the communication of her impurity by her spittle, her husband should not, by the impurity acquired from his wife, have defiled the high priest by his spittle. The only person levitically impure whose spittle defiles according to the Pentateuch, and this only for the rest of the day, is the man with an issue, Lev. 15, 8. From the above incident of the high priest, however, it is evident that at the time of the occurrence, at some date before the year 70, in Jerusalem, the spittle of the heedless Sadducee husband of a Sadducee woman who, in her monthly purification, followed the Sadducee view, was regarded by the high priest and the Pharisee teachers as levitically defiling. And as the only source of the Sadducee's impurity was his wife, it naturally follows that the Pharisee authorities had declared the spittle of the menstruous woman herself levitically impure and defiling. The exact date before the year 70 of that extension of the levitical defilement in question is nowhere indicated, though another incident, to be discussed presently, will suggest the means for fixing it approximately. But it may be pointed out already at this early stage of the inquiry that the great anxiety of the high priest about his probable defilement, and his immediate action to ascertain the facts, suggest that the incident occurred immediately before or on the Day of Atonement, or on one of the festivals of pilgrimage on all of which the high priest had to take an active part in the sacrificial service of the Temple.[11] It was most probably on the eve of the Day of Atonement; for on that festival he had to enter the Holy of Holies, and only in the case of a levitical defilement could another priest of high standing act as his substitute. It should also be noted that in the incident the point of the defilement arose in connection with the high priest. Whether it would have been raised at all, if the spittle of the Sadducee had fallen on the clothes of one not a priest, and whether it would have been of any consequence for anything else but the Temple, is not suggested by the report.

2. *The levitical impurity of the Gentile woman.*

In a Baraita it is recorded:[12] "It is reported of Ishmael son of Kamḥith that he once came out (of the Temple), and when he conversed with an Arab in the street, a stream of spittle issued from the mouth of the latter and fell upon the clothes of the high priest; and (on account of that) his brother Yeshebab went in and ministered in his stead. So their mother saw two of her sons as high priests on one day. Again, it is reported of Ishmael son of Kamḥith that he once came out, and when he conversed with a lord in the street, a stream of spittle issued from the mouth of the latter and fell upon the clothes of the high priest; and his brother

---

[11] *Antiquit.* 15, 11, 4, 408 the festivals, 18, 4, 3, 94 the three festivals and the Day of Atonement; in *Wars* 5, 5, 7, 230 sabbaths, new moons, festivals, or a general assembly. The last list does not seem to reflect facts, but to be based on Ezek. 46, 1-11.

[12] *Yoma* 47a: אמרו עליו על ישמעאל בן קמחית פעם אחת יצא וסיפר דברים עם ערבי אחד בשוק וניתזה צינורה מפיו על בנדיו ונכנס ישבב אחיו ושמש תחתיו וראתה אמן שני כהנים גדולים ביום אחד. ושוב אמרו על ישמעאל בן קמחית פעם אחת יצא וסיפר עם אדון אחד בשוק וניתזה צינורה מפיו על בנדיו ונכנס יוסף אחיו ושמש תחתיו וראתה אמן שני כהנים גדולים ביום אחד.

Joseph went in and ministered in his stead. So their mother saw two of her sons as high priests on one day."[13] As Graetz has shown, the high priest concerned here was Simeon, a son of Kamithos, *Antiquit.* 18, 2, 2, 35, who was appointed by Valerius Gratus in the year 17-18,[14] and the hegemon was probably Valerius Gratus himself. Now, it is stated in the above report that the spittle of the Gentile hegemon defiled the clothes of the high priest, and that the high priest himself was thereby disqualified from participating in the sacrificial service on the Day of Atonement. As neither the Pentateuch nor any other book of the Bible knows anything of the defiling nature of the Gentile's spittle, we are confronted here by a post-biblical extension of the law in Lev. 15, 8, which refers to the defiling force of the spittle of the Israelite who has an issue. It is an exact parallel to the account of the defilement of a highpriest by the spittle of a Sadducee; and the exact identity of all points suggests that, in both instances, the source of the defiling person's levitical impurity was the same, namely his wife, who also in the third case, in the defiling state of the

---

[13] The two accounts seem to refer to the same incident, as Simeon Kamithos probably held his office only during one Day of Atonement. The redactor of the Talmud, or his source, had two parallel reports before him which differed in the name of the high priest's temporary substitute, and that is why both were included. The parallel account in Tos. Yoma 4, 20 gives only the first incident; the high priest in the ordinary editions is Simeon, as Rabbinovicz also notes from some texts of the Talmud, in Zuckermandel, Ishmael the stranger is המלך ערבי; ARN 35, 53a has Ishmael and הגמון, as also Rabbinovicz has for אדון. On the other hand, in Jer. Yoma I, 38d 8 it is related of Simeon שיצא לדבר עם המלך ערב יום הכפורים וניתזה צינורה של רוק מפיו על בנדיו וטימאתו ונכנס יהודה אחיו that he went out to speak to the king on the eve of the Day of Atonement, and a stream of spittle fell from the mouth of the latter upon the high priest's clothes and defiled him, and his brother Judah went in and ministered in his stead. In the parallel in Jer. Megil. I 72a 58 שיצא עם מלך ערבי יום הכפורים he went out with an Arabian king; in Jer. Horay. III 47d 14 שיצא לטייל עם המלך ערב יום הכפורים עם חשיכה with a king on the eve of the Day of Atonement before nightfall. The Palestinian Midrash works borrowed their account of the incident from the Palestinian Talmud, and all of them have המלך הערבי and no day, Lev. r. 20, 11; Pesikt. 174a; Tanḥuma אחרי, B. 9; Num. r. 2, 26. Graetz, *Geschichte* III, 4th edition, note 19 § 2 thinks that the original report had ערב יום הכפורים, and that ערבי is a corruption of ערב dittographed. Buber on Pesikt. 174a accepts ערבי as the original, and declares ערב יום הכפורים a late, mistaken emendation. Schwarz in MGWJ 64, 1920, 41 decides, on the basis of ARN and Rashi, for יום הכפורים without ערב.

[14] Schürer, *Geschichte* II, 271.

Samaritan, communicated her own levitical impurity to her husband. But there is one great difficulty in the case of the Gentile woman. The Samaritan and the Sadducee women in accordance with Lev. 15, 19-24 observed the law of the monthly purification very strictly;[14a] but as they did not follow the Pharisee interpretation of the rules about the symptoms of their impurity, the Pharisee scholars declared them to be permanently in the levitical state of menstruous women. But the attribution of such levitical impurity to Gentile women, and, by communication, to their Gentile husbands, contradicts the fundamental principle underlying the laws of levitical purity and impurity, that those rules only apply to Israelites to whom they were exclusively addressed, but not to Gentiles. In order to substantiate the assumed parallelism in the case of the Gentile woman, it is necessary to ascertain whether the law of the menstruous Jewess was actually extended to apply to the Gentile woman, what the motive of such an extension was, who was responsible for it, how long before the incident with the high priest Simeon Kamithos in the year 17/18 it was introduced, and to what extent the impurity actually applied.

A Mishnah states:[15] "The Shammaites declared the blood of the Gentile woman not defiling, the Hillelites declared it defiling to the same degree as her spittle and her urine." It is not the levitical impurity of the person of the Gentile woman that formed the subject of the dispute between the two schools, but that of her blood alone, and the Hillelites compare its defiling force with that of her other secretions, her spittle and her urine. The biblical law knows nothing of the impurity of the three secretions in connection with

[14a] *Niddah* 4, 1; *Baraita* 33a bottom; Leszynsky, *Die Sadduzäer* 73 ff., above p. 5, note 10.
[15] 'Eduy. 5, 1; Niddah 4, 3: דם נכרית ודם טהרה של מצורעת בית שמאי מטהרין ובית הלל אומרים כרוקה וכמימי רגליה.

Gentiles, and not even with Israelites; therefore their occurrence must first be established elsewhere. As mentioned before, only the secretions of the Israelite with an issue are expressly stated in the Pentateuch as defiling, his spittle in Lev. 15, 8 and his issue in 15, 2. As his urine as well as his semen are, naturally, affected by his morbid issue, it was almost obvious that the biblical defilement of the issue was extended, probably at an early date, to his urine and his semen. So we find his four secretions brought under the same rule[16] in several Mishnahs of the first quarter of the second century, which are, undoubtedly, based on materials going back to the first half of the first century. But these deal with the secretions of the male only. The corresponding law about the similar disease of the Israelitish woman is not so fully stated in Lev. 15, 25-27, and all reference even to her spittle is absent. But it is only natural that all the forms of the levitical impurity of the man with an issue were, so far as they would physically apply, extended to the woman. So the wife communicates her defilement to her husband,[17] and her blood defiles just as the semen of the man with an issue. Now the morbid state of the woman with an issue in Lev. 15, 25 is merely an aggravation of the menstruous condition, as the law referring to the former expressly enjoins: 'All the days of

[16] Zabim 5, 7; Tos. 5, 2-4, cf. Niddah 55b bottom: הנוגע בזובו של זב ובדוקו בשכבת זרעו במימי רגליו ובדם הנדה מטמא שנים ופוסל אחד.
Makhshir. 6, 6: אלו מטמאין ומכשירין זובו של זב ורוקו ושכבת זרעו ומימי רגליו למעלה מהן זובו של זב ורוקו ושכבת. Kelim 1, 3: ורביעית מן הזב ודם הנדה. Baraita Nazir 66a, Tos. Zabim 5, 2: זרעו ומימי רגליו ודם הנדה שהן מטמאין במגע ובמשא רבי אליעזר אומר שכבת זרעו של זב אינו מטמא במשא, רבי יהושע אומר מטמא במשא. Makhshir. 6, 6: רבי אליעזר אומר שכבת. לפי שאי אפשר לה בלא צחצוחי זיבה. זרעו אינה מכשרת רבי אלעזר בן עזריה אומר דם הנדה אינו מכשיר.
In the last two passages the degree of the defilement of his semen is discussed by two teachers who taught between the years 90 and 120; their dispute may represent the last stage in the development of the relevant law, so that the points on which those teachers agreed were of an earlier date. In fact, already the two schools discussed one form of the impurity of the successive symptoms of the recurring issues even before the decisive stage that determined the disease, Tos. Zabim I, 1-3. The same schools dealt with the relations of husband and wife affected with an issue in Shabb. 1, 3, and the report of R. Simeon b. Eleazar in Tos. Shabb. 1, 14. 15; b, 13a; Jer. I 3b73-3c4.

[17] Kelim 1, 4: למעלה מן הזב זבה שהיא מטמאה את בועלה.

the issue of her uncleanness she shall be as in the days of her impurity'; so that the degree of the levitical impurity of the blood of the two women would be the same.

And the same is the degree of the impurity of the woman after childbirth, as Lev. 12, 2 says of her: 'as in the days of the impurity of her sickness shall she be unclean.' From the identical terms, נדת דותה here and in Lev. 15, 33, and נדה and זוב in Lev. 15, 25 and 19, it would certainly follow for the three women that the degree of the defiling force of their blood was the same. So we actually find[18] that, along with the four secretions of the man with an issue, the blood of the menstruous woman is stated as defiling, and[19] that it defiles, whether liquid or dry. Similarly, of the blood of the woman after childbirth[20] R. Eliezer said: 'It is one of the cases in which the Shammaites are lenient and the Hillelites strict; the Shammaites hold that the blood of the woman after childbirth, so long as she did not immerse, defiles when liquid, but not when dry; the Hillelites hold that it defiles not only when liquid, but also when dry.' In the parallel statement in the Mishnah[20a] the terms for the same impurity of the same woman are characteristically different; for the Shammaites say that the blood of the woman after childbirth, so long as she did not immerse, defiles as her spittle and her urine does, the Hillelites say that it defiles not only when liquid, but also when dry. It should be noted that at the time when that dispute between the two schools took place, the levitical impurity of both, the spittle and the urine of the woman after childbirth, was settled, but not yet that of her blood. This

[18] Kelim 1, 3; Zabim 5, 7; Tos. 5, 24; Niddah 54b bottom; Makhshir. 6, 6.
[19] Niddah 7, 1.
[20] Tos. Niddah 5, 5; Tos. 'Eduy. 2, 8: דם היולדת שלא טבלה מטמא לח ואין מטמא יבש דברי רבי מאיר, ורבי יהודה מטמא לח ויבש. (5) רבי אליעזר אומר מקולי בית שמאי ומחומרי בית הלל בית שמאי אומרים מטמא לח ואין מטמא יבש ובית הלל אומרים מטמא לח ויבש.
[20a] Niddah 4, 3: דם היולדת שלא טבלה בית שמאי אומרים כרוקה וכמימי רגליה ובית הלל אומרים מטמא לח ויבש.

distinction would indicate that the levitical impurity of her blood was not so obvious as in the cases of the menstruous woman and of that with an issue, as the woman after childbirth in this instance had already observed the time of her purification, as prescribed in Lev. 12, 2, but had not immersed yet. That is why the Shammaites held that her blood only defiled when liquid, just like her spittle and her urine. At the same time, it follows from the two different terms used by the Shammaites for the same thing that, at the time of that dispute, the impurity of spittle and urine which, unlike her blood in Lev. 12, 7. 4. 4, are not mentioned in Lev. 12, had already been extended from the menstruous woman and the woman with an issue to the woman after childbirth.

The two schools also differ, as we have seen, about the degree of the levitical impurity of the Gentile woman; the Shammaites represent the lenient view also in this instance, and declare her blood as not defiling at all, while the Hillelites hold that it defiles to the same extent as her spittle and her urine. It is clear, not only from the reference to her blood, that they are dealing with the Gentile menstruous woman, but also from the place assigned to the statement in the Mishnah immediately after the declaration that the Samaritan women are unconditionally, and the Sadducee women in a certain case, regarded as being permanently in the levitical impurity of menstruous women. The Gentile woman is in this respect different from those two and also from the Jewess, as her blood is, according to the Shammaites, not defiling at all; and that seems to imply that even she herself, while actually in the menstruous state, is not regarded as defiling. Consequently, this view of the Shammaites seems to exclude the Gentile woman from coming under the law in Lev. 15, 19-24, and they seem to have taken the words דבר אל בני ישראל in Lev. 15, 2, in the heading of the various laws, literally, and the latter as applying to Jews and Jewesses only. That was, in fact, the opinion concerning the part of the chapter, which refers to the man with an issue, in the anonymous Baraita:[21] "Israelites defile by their issue, but not Gentiles," which in the same terms, might have been enunciated by the Shammaites. Nor did the stricter view of the Hillelites ascribe to the blood of the Gentile woman the degree of the levitical impurity of the blood of the Jewess. For the blood of the latter, at least in the uncontested Mishnah,[22] defiles in a liquid as well as in a dry condition, whereas that of the Gentile woman defiles only when liquid, just like her spittle and her urine. According to the Shammaites, it is levitically on the same level as the blood of the woman after childbirth who had observed her time of purification, but did not immerse.

On the other hand, it must be admitted that the Shammaites did not state expressly that the Gentile menstruous woman was not levitically impure at all; and the stricter view of the opposing Hillelites might even suggest that the levitical purity of her blood need not necessarily imply the levitical purity of the woman herself. For how could the Hillelites have declared her blood defiling, if it had not first been admitted by both schools that she herself was a source of levitical impurity? She might, then, in her menstruous state, have been regarded even by the Shammaites as defiling. Also the term מטהרין used by the Shammaites might be understood to mean: they declare her blood, but not also her person, not-defiling. Again, the Hillelites presuppose in their statement that the defiling force of the Gentile menstruous woman's spittle and urine

---

[21] Shabb. 83a; Niddah 34a, cf. Sifra Lev. 15, 2, 74d; Tos. Zabim 2, 1: תניא דברו אל בני ישראל ואמרתם אליהם איש איש כי יהיה זב, בני ישראל מטמאין בזיבה ואין נכרים מטמאין בזיבה.

[22] Niddah 7, 1: דם הנדה ובשר המת מטמאין לחין ומטמאין יבשין.

was established; and it is not improbable that the Shammaites did not dispute that part at all. Again, from the instances in which the spittle and the urine of the man with an issue, and of the woman who, after her childbirth, had completed her time of purification, but did not immerse, defile, it is evident that the source of the two defiling secretions is the levitically impure state of the persons themselves. So the Hillelites certainly, and the Shammaites very probably, regarded the Gentile menstruous woman as defiling to a certain degree, sufficient to impart some levitical impurity to her spittle and her urine. This is in full agreement with the incident in which the high priest Simeon Kamithos in the year 17/18 was defiled by the spittle of a Gentile. For, like the Jewess, and the Sadducee and the Samaritan women, by the law in Lev. 15, 19-24, so the Gentile woman, by a special decree, was during her menstruous state regarded as defiling. As she did not observe the rules of purification, nor cleansed herself of her monthly defilement, she was declared to be permanently in the state of a menstruous woman, just like, for other reasons, the Samaritan and some Sadducee women. And just as the Samaritan and the Sadducee husbands, so the Gentile himself was not, as Schürer decreed, considered to be levitically impure as a Gentile; no statement of any kind about him is to be found in the rabbinic literature of the date of the two schools that would attribute to him personally a levitical impurity. But, exactly as in the cases of the Samaritan and the Sadducee, so the Gentile's defilement was communicated to him by his levitically impure wife; and as, according to the Hillelites, her spittle defiled, so did now his spittle defile the high priest.

But who was the author of the extension of the law in Lev. 15, 19-20, which was addressed to the Israelites only, to the Gentile woman? Considering that the levitical institutions introduced by José b. Joezer of Ṣeredah and José b. Johanan of Jerusalem, by Simeon b. Shetaḥ, and by Hillel and Shammai are all recorded in a Baraita,[23] and do not include the extension of the levitical impurity to the Gentile menstruous woman, it might be inferred that it was decreed either after Hillel and Shammai, or before José b. Joezer, who was put to death under the high priest Alkimos[24] about the year 162 B. C. E. In fact, a Palestinian reports states[25] that a council of Hashmonai decreed that a Jew who has carnal intercourse with a Gentile woman transgresses the law prohibiting intercourse with a menstruous woman, etc. The heaping up of four transgressions committed by the one act was intended to deter sinners from continuing the prevalent sin; so that the decree originated at a time when carnal intercourse with Gentile women was prevalent. This would point to the time of the Hellenists, and to conditions reflected also in Sirach, though otherwise nothing is known of that evil immediately before the Maccabean rising. Still, in the absence of other information, there is neither an occasion for, nor a possibility of, questioning the authenticity of the definite report or the date of the decree which, for a clear purpose, declared the Gentile woman to be permanently in the levitical state of a menstruous woman. But it is possible that, when those conditions changed after the victories of the Maccabees, the decree lapsed, and had, for reasons suggested by the presence of many Gentiles in Jerusalem at a later date, to be renewed some time before the year 17/18.[26]

[23] Shabb. 14b, 15a bottom; Jer. I 3d, 43-47.
[24] Gen. r. 65, 22; I Macc. 7, 16-25; *Antiquit.* 12, 10, 2-3; Schürer, *Geschichte* I, 217.
[25] 'Abod. Zar. 36b; Synh. 82a: כי אתא רב דימי אמר בית דין של חשמונאי גזרו ישראל הבא על הנכרית חייב משום נדה שפחה גויה ואשת איש, כי אתא רבין אמר משום נדה שפחה גויה זונה.
[26] This date would imply that when a Gentile, woman or man, adopted Judaism she or he required the purifying immersion of the proselyte, at the latest, since the year 17/18, and not only since the Eighteen prohibitions were passed by the two schools in the year 65 or 66, as suggested by Dr. Zeitlin in JQR 14, 1923, 131 ff.

3. *The levitical impurity of the Gentile.*

The Gentile's own levitical impurity forms the subject of a dispute between the two schools in the Mishnah:[27] "A Gentile who becomes a proselyte on Nisan 14th may, after his immersion, in the opinion of the Shammaites, partake of his Paschal lamb in the evening; the Hillelites say that he who separates from the foreskin is like him who separates from a grave."[28] In the view of the Shammaites the levitical impurity of the Gentile was not grave, as, after the immersion, it disappeared completely the same evening, and did not even necessitate the washing of his garment.[29] This relative leniency of the Shammaites in the case of the Gentile, which was also evident in their treatment of the Gentile woman, may have been due either to their consideration of the great duty of every Israelite and proselyte to eat, if only possible, of the Paschal lamb on the proper date; or to their definite view that the Gentile's general levitical impurity was of a slight degree, and that for its removal there were required neither several days of purification nor any longer interval between his circumcision and the sacrificial meal. On the other hand, the Hillelites who were stricter about the defilement of the Gentile woman, compare the impurity attaching to the Gentile, and now removed by his circumcision, with the grave defilement of the tomb, which requires a purification extending over seven days, Num. 19, 16-19. But the statement of the Hillelites in the Mishnah does not suggest why they compared the levitical impurity of the Gentile with that of a grave, and whether, in their opinion, the defilement by a grave applied to the Gentile at all. R. Johanan,

---

[27] Pesah. 8, 8; 'Eduy. 5, 2: גר שנתגייר בערב פסח בית שמאי אומרים טובל ואוכל את פסחו לערב, ובית הלל אומרים הפורש מן הערלה כפורש מן הקבר.

[28] See also in the Baraita Pesah. 92a R. Simeon b. Eleazar, in Tos. 7, 13 R. Jose b. R. Jehudah, in the editions of Tos. R. Eleazar b. R. Sadok or Jacob, who expressly states that the dispute of the two schools referred to a Gentile, and not to a Jew.

[29] Compare e. g. Lev. 15, 5. 6. 7. 8. 10. 11 with Lev. 22, 4b-7.

the Amora of the third century, explained their strict rule as a precaution against a possible mistake of the proselyte a year later in the case of an actual defilement by a corpse.[30] But the plain words of the Hillelites do not suggest any such consideration of a possible contingency, but convey the impression that the impurity of a grave had something to do with that of the Gentile. Undoubtedly, the unnamed teacher [31] in the Palestinian Talmud understood it in that sense, when he traced the divergent views of the two schools to their different interpretations of Num. 31, 19:[32] "What is the reason of the Shammaites? Because it says: 'Ye and your captives,' which means: just as ye were defiled only after ye had entered into the covenant, so your captives are defiled only after entering into the covenant. What is the reason of the Hillelites? Because it says: 'Ye and your captives,' which means: Just as ye require sprinkling with the purifying ashes on the third and the seventh day, Num. 19, 19, so also your captives.'" The Shammaites, according to this explanation and against the plain sense of Num. 31, 19, held that a Gentile cannot be defiled by a corpse; the Hillelites, on the other hand, in accordance with the plain meaning of the verse, were of the opinion that a Gentile can be defiled by a corpse, and has to be purified in the same way as an Israelite, by the purifying ashes.[33]

[30] Pesah. 92a.
[31] From Sifre Zuta, Num. 19, 10, 133: אמר רבי אליעזר [בן יעקב] בני ישראל מקבלין הזאה ואין הנכרים מקבלין הזאה, אמר לו רבי מאיר והלא כבר נאמר תתחטאו אתם ושביכם, אמר לו בוודאי אמרת אלא שהנחת דבר אחד ואין אנו צריכין לו, אתם ושביכם מה אתם בני ברית אף השבויה כשתבוא לברית ותטמא מקבלת הזאה.
It is evident that R. Meir represents the same view as assigned by the anonymous teacher to the Shammaites, and R. Eliezer b. Jacob holds the opinion attributed to the Hillelites. The two teachers taught in Galilee between the years 140 and 160.
[32] Jer. Pesah. VIII 36b 37: מה טעמון דבית שמאי, אתם ושביכם מה אתם לא נטמאתם עד שנכנסתם לברית אף שביכם לא נטמאו עד שנכנסו לברית. מה טעמון דבית הלל, מה אתם טעונין הזייה בשלישי ובשביעי אף שביכם טעונין הזייה בשלישי ובשביעי. In Sifre Zuta, Num. 31, 19 and 19, 10, Horovitz, p. 177 and 133: אתם ושביכם, מה אתם בני ברית מקבלין הזאה אף שבויה כשתבוא לברית ותטמא מקבלת הזאה; Sifre Num. 31, 19, 60a: אתם ושביכם, מה אתם בני ברית אף שביכם בני ברית.
[33] Schwarz, *Die Erleichterungen der Schammaiten*, 88 ff., suggests a different biblical basis for the controversy of the two schools.

For this inquiry it is most instructive to find that both schools agree that the Midianites were not levitically impure as Gentiles, and did not require any special purification as Gentiles. Both schools trace the levitical impurity of the Midianites and the need of their purification exclusively to their contact with those slain in the battle against the Israelites, as it is expressly stated in Num. 31, 19: 'And encamp ye without the camp seven days; whosoever hath killed any person, and whosoever hath touched any slain, purify yourselves on the third day and on the seventh day, ye and your captives.' But whose corpses were those that had defiled Israelites and Midianites? According to Num. 31, 49 not one Israelite fell in the battle, so that all the slain were Midianites; did, then, the corpses of the Gentiles defile levitically the Israelite and the Gentile? The words in the verse: 'whosoever hath killed any person,' leaves no doubt about it; but did the members of the Shammaite school admit that the corpse of the Gentile defiled for a week the Jew and the Gentile? While the unnamed opponent of R. Simeon b. Yoḥai in the Baraita[34] accepted Num. 31, 19 without qualification, R. Simeon b. Yoḥai declared, against the clear meaning of the words in that passage,[35] that the corpse of the Gentile does not defile when carried, as it only defiles altogether by a rabbinic decree. Again, he declared that the graves of the Gentiles do not defile a person under the same roof,[36] that is, their corpses do not defile like those of Jews. His contemporary, R. Simeon b. Gamaliel II, held that the dwellings of the Gentiles defile,[37] the reason being the assumed presence of the corpse of a Gentile buried in the ground

[34] Yebam. 61a top.
[35] Tos. Niddah 9, 14; Mishnah 10, 4; b. 69b: וכן היה רבי שמעון אומר נכרי שמת טהור מלטמא במשא שאין טומאתו אלא מדברי סופרים.
[36] Yebam. 61a top: תניא וכן היה רבי שמעון בן יוחאי אומר קברי נכרים אין מטמאין באהל; cf. Nazir 61b.
[37] Ohal. 18, 9; see Tosafot Yebam. 61a s. v. טמנע and the contrary decision of Maimonides, ה' טומאת מת I, 13 and the commentaries.

of the house. This view was held a generation earlier by R. Eliezer b. Hyrkanos;[38] as he merely defined a secondary point of the rule, it would suggest that the rule itself was in existence before the year 70.[38a] As it represents the extension of a levitical impurity to the Gentile, which places him on the same level as the Jew, it very probably originated with the Hillelites who, as was shown, connected the levitical impurity of the Gentile with that of a grave. Thereby they revived the biblical law applied to the Midianites which, as appears from the attitude of the Shammaites and from other evidence to be adduced presently, had not been applied to the Gentiles living in Judea before the time of the two schools.

But what did the Hillelites mean by their declaration that he who separates from the foreskin is like him who separates from a grave? Did they hold that every Gentile should be considered as having come in contact with a corpse or as having walked over graves, and is 'like one who separates from a grave' to be taken literally and as pointing to actual defilement? There is otherwise no evidence for such an assumption in the Gentile. Only the statement of the Mishnah:[39] "The first terrace within the wall of the Temple Mount is more holy than the space immediately within the wall of the Temple Mount, for the Gentile, and the Jew defiled by a corpse must not enter there," suggests by the juxtaposition of these two persons a common kind and degree of levitical impurity in them.[40] The view of the Hillelites was opposed by the Shammaites, and not only in

---

[38] Tos. Ahil. 18, 7: וכמה ישהא בתוכו ויהא צריך בדיקה, העיד אבא יודן איש צידן משום רבי אליעזר ארבעים יום אף על פי שאין עמו אשה, והלכה כדבריו.

[38a] In Ohal. 18, 8 already the two schools differ on a detail of that rule.

[39] Kelim. 1, 8: החיל מקודש ממנו שאין נכרי וטמא מת נכנסים לשם, Sifre Zuta, Num. 5, 2, p. 4: החיל מקודש מהר הבית שנכרים וטמאי מתים נכנסין בהר הבית ואין נכנסין לחיל.

[40]Cf. RS who remarks: The impurity decreed to be in the Gentile is only that of one defiled by a corpse. In Tos. Kelim 1, I, 8 it says: The space within the wall of the Temple Mount may be entered by a person defiled by a corpse, and even a corpse may be brought in there.

an academic dispute, but also in a practical case. "R. Eliezer b. Jacob[41] stated that there were soldiers, (and) guards of צירין in Jerusalem who immersed, and ate of their Passover sacrifice in the evening." איסרטיוטות invariably designates soldiers, often officers, of the foreign power ruling over Palestine, mostly of the Romans, rarely of the Syrians;[42] so that the report undoubtedy refers to Gentiles, and not, as the context in the Palestinian Talmud appears to suggest, to Jews. The employment of those soldiers as guards of צירין is obscure, as the word usually denotes hinges.[43] The incident is quoted as bearing out the view of the Shammaites against the Hillelites; and it is even probable that the controversy between them arose in connection with the occurrence itself. It is important to note that, on that occasion, the opinion of the Shammaites prevailed, and so the question whether the Gentile was affected with the grave levitical impurity imparted by a corpse or any other similar defilement, was negatived. It is, therefore, a mistake, when Schürer and other scholars refer to the opinion of the Hillelites as evidence for their assertion that the Gentile was considered by the rabbinic authorities levitically unclean. Unfortunately, the date of the incident and of the practical decision is not indicated; it would have enabled us to see how long the religious authorities refused to recognize the assumed levitical impurity of the Gentile in Judea in practice altogether, or treated it, even in the case of a sacrificial meal demanding full levitical purification, as being of a slight degree. And let it be noted, the question of such impurity of the Gentile was not raised

[41] Jer. Pesah. VIII 36b.60: ותני כן רבי אליעזר בן יעקב אומר איסרטיוטות היו אצטרדיות ושומרי; Tos. 7, 13. שומרי צירין בירושלים וטבלו ואכלו פסחיהן לערב צירין היו בירושלים שהיו טובלין ואוכלין את פסחיהן לערב.

[42] In Baraita Sukkah 56b and parallels.

[43] As on the pilgrimage festivals Roman guards were placed on the colonnades encompassing the Temple Mount, Josephus, *Wars*, 5, 5, 8, 244; *Antiquit.*, 20, 5, 3, 106; *Wars*, 2, 12, I, 224; *Antiquit.* 20, 8, II, 192, it is possible that the word describes those.

in connection with the private and social intercourse between the Jew and the Gentile, but only in relation to a sacrificial meal.

4. *The Gentile in Jerusalem during the festival of pilgrimage.*

When, over five centuries before the Hillelites, Isaiah 52, 1: "Awake, awake, put on thy strength, O Zion; put on thy beautiful garments, O Jerusalem, the holy city; for henceforth there shall no more come into thee the uncircumcised and the unclean," put next to each other the uncircumcised and the unclean, he laid the stress on the holy character of Jerusalem from which he excluded the Gentile. In his image, the city is sanctified for the presence of God and for one of the feasts of pilgrimage, and every Jew present on that occasion is clothed in his festive garments.[44] The general state of sanctification would be disturbed, if a non-purified person, even a Jew, entered the city and went among the specially purified people, and even more so, if the intruder were a Gentile who not only had not purified himself, but was not a member of the covenant, and was therefore in the impurity of the idolater. Similar in idea is Is. 35, 8: "And a highway shall be there, and a way, and it shall be called the way of holiness; the unclean shall not pass over it; and it shall be for those." Also here the contrast is between the *holy* way and the non-hallowed Gentile. Instead of the uncircumcised and the unclean, Joel, 4, 17 has: "So shall ye know that I am the Lord your God, dwelling in Zion My holy mountain; then shall Jerusalem be holy, and there shall no stranger pass through her any more." First he emphasizes the presence of God in the city and its holiness through His presence, then the exclusion of the armies of enemies. That the prophet

[44] Cf. Psalms of Solomon 11,8: Put on, O Jerusalem, the garments of thy glory: make ready thine holy apparel, בגדי קדשך, for God hath spoken comfortably unto Israel world without end.

borrowed for such descriptions mainly the condition of the pilgrimage festivals and God's dwelling in Jerusalem is also evident from Nah. 2, 1: "Behold upon the mountains the feet of him that bringeth good tidings, that announceth peace! Keep thy feasts, O Judah, perform thy vows, for the wicked one shall no more pass through thee; he is utterly cut off." Here the enemy is called בליעל, which suggests that his impurity in Isaiah might have been determined in the first instance by his sins against God and Israel. In describing the celebration of the feast of Tabernacles in the Messianic future, Zechar. 14, 21 says: "Yea, every pot in Jerusalem and in Judah shall be holy unto the Lord of hosts; and all they that sacrifice shall come and take of them, and seethe therein; and in that day there shall be no more a trafficker in the house of the Lord of hosts." In spite of the various considerations advanced by the commentators, the parallel passages quoted above point in the כנעני to a Phoenician or other Gentile trader who will be out of place amid the general sanctification of everybody and everything. And the same idea prevails in the messianic picture in Psalms of Solomon 17, 28-30: The holy people, sanctified by God, will be gathered together by God, "They will all be the sons of their God, and He shall divide them upon the land according to their tribes. (31) And the sojourner and the stranger shall dwell with them no more. (33) And He shall purge Jerusalem and make it holy, even as it was in the days of old."[45]

In full ageement with the position of the Gentile in the sanctified Jerusalem in the prophets is a report of Josephus.[46] When Herod was governor of Galilee under Hyrkanos II, he once καθ' ἑορτήν, during a religious festival, turned, at the head of armed men, to march into Jerusalem. On

---

[45] Cf. also Sibyl. V, 264: No longer will the impure foot of the Greek rave in thy land.
[46] *Wars*, 1, 11, 6, 229; *Antiquit.* 14, 11, 5, 285.

learning of his intentions, Hyrkanos, the high priest, sent him a message, ἐκώλυε τοὺς ἀλλοφύλους εἰσαγαγεῖν ἐφ' ἁγνεύοντας τοὺς ἐπιχωρίους, to prevent him from bringing in the Gentiles to the natives who were purified. Ἁγνεύω denotes the levitical purity required for visiting the Temple:[47] "Into the inner forecourt (of Solomon's Temple) τοῦ λαοῦ πάντες ὃι διαφέροντες ἁγνείᾳ καὶ παρατηρήσει τῶν νομίμων εἰσῄεσαν, all persons entered who were distinguished by purification and by the observance of our laws (=Jews)." And of the forecourt of Herod's Temple Josephus states:[48] "Through the great eastern gate we enter ἁγνοὶ μετὰ γυναικῶν, purified with our wives." Similarly, all the persons who had gathered in Jerusalem for the pilgrimage festival, when Herod approached to enter the capital, were purified for visiting the Temple, for bringing sacrifices, and for partaking of sacrificial meals. If now Gentile soldiers entered the city, they would defile the Jews in their special purity.[49] On the other hand, Josephus says of those who, in the days of Cestius, in the year 66, took part in the Passover sacrifice in Jerusalem:[50] "There were two million and seven hundred thousand men καθαρῶν ἁπάντων καὶ ἁγίων; for lepers, persons having an issue, women during their monthly purification, and persons defiled in other ways must not take part in this sacrifice, nor Gentiles who might come to worship." Josephus does not suggest any levitical impurity in the Gentile, as he even allows him to come to Jerusalem to worship; but as the

[47] *Antiquit.* 8, 3, 9, 96.
[48] *Antiquit.* 15, 11, 5, 418, cf. *Contra Ap.* II, 8; *Antiquit.* 3, 5, 1, 78; 1, 21, 2, 341. 342; 3, 11, 1, 258.
[49] It was the same with the Essenes who permanently lived in a high degree of levitical purity. Josephus, *Antiquit.* 18, 1, 5, 19, states of them: To the Temple they send ἀναθήματα, but they offer no sacrifices because of the superiority of their ἁγνειῶν, purifications (or atonements), which they all observed. And in *Wars* 2, 8, 10, 150 Josephus says: The younger members (of their order) are so much inferior to the elder ones (in the sanctifications) that when the latter are touched by the former, they wash as though ἀλλοφύλῳ συμφυρέντες, they had been defiled by a Gentile.
[50] *Wars* 6, 9, 3, 425; Graetz *Geschichte* III, note 28; cf. *Genes.* 35, 2 with *Antiquit.* 1, 21, 2, 341. 342. Cf. *Wars* 5, 3, 1, 100.

Gentile does not observe our laws, and is not in the state of purity required, he cannot participate in the sacrifice.[51] And that seems to be the plain reason why the Jews in John 18, 28 "went not into the judgment hall, lest they should be defiled; but that they might eat the Passover." In accordance with the requirements explicitly stated by Josephus, all the Jews who intended to participate in the sacrificial meal of the Passover purified themselves for that occasion by an immersion, or, if they had been defiled by a corpse, by a week's purification, as prescribed in Num. 19. As they were now in the required state of levitical purity, they must not mix with Gentiles who, by their touch, might defile them, and deprive them of their purity; therefore, they must not enter the residence of the governor where the Roman soldiers, just like those of Herod, would crowd round them.

But that this levitical impurity would have stood in the way of commercial and social contact between the Jew and Gentile in Jerusalem, even during the days of pilgrimage, is nowhere suggested. There were Gentile traders offering their wares, pots and other vessels, during the Feast of Tabernacles in Jerusalem, even on the Temple Mount, Zechar. 14, 21. A Baraita[52] relates that, when once the Jews came on pilgrimage to Jerusalem, and there was not sufficient water for drinking, Nakdimon b. Goryon went to a lord and borrowed from him twelve cisterns of water, and undertook to return the same amount of water in kind by a certain date, or, failing that, to pay twelve talents of silver. When, by the date fixed, rain had failed, and Nakdimon was unable to return the water, an exchange of messages followed, and, in the course of that day, the two men met twice. The lord concerned was a Gentile, and lived in

[51] Exod. 12, 43-49; cf. the visit of the Syrian Gentile of Nisibis to Jerusalem and his participation in the Passover sacrifice in Pesah. 3b.
[52] Ta'an. 19b ff.

Jerusalem; perhaps he was the commander of the Roman cohort in the Antonia, or the governor of Judea who, during the festivals of pilgrimage, used to stay in Jerusalem. Nakdimon was one of the wealthy councillors of the capital in the last years of Jerusalem, an observant Jew, and a follower of R. Johanan b. Zakkai. Though the incident occurred during the pilgrimage festival, when he, with the other inhabitants of Jerusalem, was preparing and purifying himself for a visit to the Temple, he negotiated personally with the Roman lord, and, as far as the report goes, the assumed levitical impurity of the Gentile seems to have been no obstacle. A Gentile asked R. Johanan b. Zakkai a question about the strange ways in which the red heifer was burned and its ashes were used for purification.[53] The details singled out by the questioner show that he had not derived his knowledge of the procedure from Num. 19, but had watched the burning of a red heifer in Jerusalem. R. Johanan b. Zakkai was a priest,[54] and still he conversed freely with the Gentile. Once[55] some scholars of Jerusalem went to Ashkelon to buy of a Gentile councillor of the city, by name Dama b. Nethina, precious stones for the Ephod of the high priest, and had to negotiate with him; in the following year they purchased of him a red heifer for the Temple. Two other instances of the purchase of a red heifer are reported[56] which clearly prove the unhampered commercial associations between Jews and non-Jews before the year 70.

Several of the many disputes between the Shammaites and the Hillelites deal with the daily relations of Jews with non-Jews. In one report the Shammaites say:[57] On the

[53] Pesikt. 40a ff. and parallels given by Buber.
[54] See Aptowitzer in MGWJ 52, 1908, 744 ff.; Weiss, *Geschichte* I, 188.
[55] Kiddush. 31a; Jer. I 61b 5.
[56] Sifre Zuta Num. 19, 2, p. 124 Horovitz. In Tos. Parah 2, 1, to refute the view of R. Eliezer who prohibited such purchase, a colleague referred him to an actual instance of such a transaction; see also Pesikt. rab. 14, 56a; 'Abod. Zar. 23a.
[57] Baraita Shabb. 18b; Jer. I 4a 57.

Friday we must not sell to the Gentile anything, nor lend him an article, nor lend him money, nor give him a present, unless he can reach his home with the goods before the Sabbath begins; the Hillelites permit it, if he can reach a house near the city wall in time. Again, the Shammaites say:[58] We must not sell on the Friday to the Gentile, nor assist him in loading his beast, nor lift the load upon him, unless he is able to reach a place before the Sabbath; the Hillelites permit it. (8) We must not give hides to the Gentile tanner, nor clothes to the Gentile launderer, unless they can finish the work before the Sabbath, when it is still day-time; the Hillelites permit it, if they can finish the work by sunset on the Friday. (9) R. Simeon b. Gamaliel said: My father's household used to hand over to the Gentile launderer white clothes three days before the Sabbath. A Baraita states:[59] We must not send letters through the Gentile on Friday or on Thursday; the Shammaites prohibit it even on Wednesday, but the Hillelites permit it. It is reported of R. José the priest, or R. José the Ḥasid, that no letter of his was ever found in the hand of a Gentile. Another Baraita records:[60] The Shammaites say: We must not sell leavened food to the Gentile, nor give him leavened

---

[58] Shabb. 1, 7. 8. 9.
[59] Jer. Shabb. I 4a 68; Tos. 13, 13; b. 19a.
[60] The form of the report deserves some attention. Tos. Pesah. 1, 7 reads: בראשונה היו אומרים אין מוכרין חמץ לנכרי ואין נותנין לו במתנה אלא כדי שיאכלנו עד שלא תגיע שעת הביעור, עד שבא רבי עקיבא ולימד שמוכרין ונותנין במתנה אף בשעת הביעור. אמר רבי יוסי אלו דברי בית שמאי ובית הלל, הכריע רבי עקיבא לסייע דברי בית הלל. The stricter prohibition of the Shammaites was followed until R. Akiba modified it in favor of the Hillelites' view. Even if R. Jose had not stated explicitly that the older usage was that of the Shammaites, the mere fact that R. Akiba reversed it would have been sufficient to suggest it. For he was the great and consistent protagonist of the Hillelites against the Shammaites who were followed by several members of the school in Jamnia, R. Gamaliel II, R. Tarfon, R. Dosa b. Harkinas, R. Eleazar b. 'Azariah, R. Eliezer, and others. Another instance is Ma'aser sheni 5, 8: בראשונה אמר רבי יהודה היו שולחין אצל בעלי בתים שבמדינה מהרו והתקינו את פירותיכם עד שלא תגיע שעת הביעור עד שבא רבי עקיבא ולימד שכל הפירות שלא באו לעונת המעשרות פטורין מן הביעור .פותחין בימים טובים ובשבתות, בראשונה היו :and Nedar. 9, 6 אומרים אותן הימים מותרין ושאר כל הימים אסורין עד שבא רבי עקיבא ולימד שהנדר שהותר מקצתו הותר כולו. It would seem that also in the last two cases the old practice followed the view of the Shammaites. In fact, the principle underlying the last dispute is discussed by the two schools in Nedar. 3, 2. About Tos. Moed Kat. 2, 10, cf. Tos. Shabb. 12, 13, and Halevy, דורות הראשונים Ic, 138b; 284a.

food as a present, unless we know that it will be consumed before the removal of leavened food is due; the Hillelites hold that, so long as we may ourselves eat it, we may sell it. Those controversies were not purely academic discussions carried on in the school, but were intended to regulate the actual life in Jerusalem and the whole country during the first decades of the first century, as also the practical illustration of their actual application conclusively proves. All these controversies convincingly show that the assumed levitical impurity of the Gentile trader, tanner, launderer, letter-carrier, or dealer did not prevent, nor even reduce, the usual business dealings between him and the Jew; and even the work of the Gentile launderer or tanner, both of whom handled the materials entrusted to their skill in a way that the communication of their assumed levitical impurity could not possibly be avoided, was invited without any hesitation, and regularly. And if the account in the Tosefta,[61] contradicted by the Baraita,[62] is correct, trade with Gentiles was carried on between the years 40 and 50 even in wine; for R. Gamaliel I stated that, if the skin bottles belonging to the Gentiles were filled with wine belonging to the Jew, the wine was permitted for drinking.

Even priests, several times in the course of the year, paid visits to the commander of the Roman garrison in the Antonia. On two occasions Josephus reports that the official robe of the high priest was, for a considerable number of years, kept by the Roman military authorities in the Antonia, and how it was handed to the treasurers of the Temple before the festivals on which the high priest officiated. Josephus states:[63] "Formerly the robe was kept under the seals of the high priest and of the treasurers (of the Temple), and one day before the festival, the treasurers

[61] Tos. 'Abod. Zar. 4, 9.
[62] b. Abod. Zar. 32a, see below.
[63] *Antiquit.* 15, 11, 4, 408.

went up to the Roman φρούραρχος, and, after the inspection of their own seals, took away the robe. Later again, immediately after the festival had passed, they brought it to the same place, and, having shown the φρούραρχος the identical seals, they deposited it." Instead of one day before the festival mentioned here, Josephus reports in another passage:[64] "Seven days before the festival, the robe was handed to them by the φρούραρχος, and, having been purified, ἁγνισθείσῃ, it was used by the high priest." For our inquiry it is important to state the fact that the robe was taken over by the Roman authorities after the deposition of Archelaus in the year 6, and remained under their control till Vitellius released it in the year 36, and handed it over to the priests.[65] In the course of the 30 years, the treasurers of the Temple apparently did not mind entering the Roman fortress, though, as may safely be assumed, it hardly differed in its heathen character and its heathen equipment from the residence of the Roman governor in Herod's palace in Jerusalem. Of entering the latter on Nisan 14th, John 18, 28 remarks: "And they themselves (the Jews) went not into the judgment hall, lest they should be defiled; but that they might eat the Passover;" that is, it is supposed to have defiled those who entered it, and disqualified them from participating in the Paschal meal. If the priestly treasurers of the Temple entered the Antonia *one* day before the festival, say, on Nisan 14th, and brought the robe to the Temple, their defilement by the Antonia and by the Gentile commandant of the fortress cannot have been grave, as they were permitted to enter the Temple buildings at once, and to partake of the Paschal sacrificial meal in the evening of the same day. The defilement contracted by the noble priests as well as that attaching to the robe was evidently removed by an immersion before night-

[64] *Antiquit.* 18, 4, 3, 94.
[65] *Antiquit.* 18, 4, 3; 20, 1, 2; Schürer, *Geschichte* I, 483.

fall.[66] Consequently, it could not have been due to the assumed presence of a corpse buried in the ground of the Antonia, as, in that case, the purification would have extended over seven days, as the Hillelites required the proselyte to undergo, though the assumed defilement was only of a rabbinic character.[67]

The contradictory statements of Josephus about the number of days before the festival, when the robe was called for by the chief representatives of the Temple, undoubtedly demands an explanation; and this might be suggested. For the Day of Atonement on which the high priest had to offer the most holy sacrifices, and to enter the Holy of Holies, his robe was submitted to a purification extending over seven days, as the possibility of its defilement by a corpse was considered for the sake of the most holy day. So we find it stated in the Mishnah[68] in the description of the preparations for the Day of Atonement and for the burning of the red heifer that the high priest himself was isolated a week before, and purified with the ashes of purification. For the other festivals he and his robe were purified for only one day, as the sacrifices at which he officiated were all offered on the external altar, and even the special sin-offering of the festival was of the usual character of sanctity. This suggestion is supported by the fact that in Antiquit. 15, 11, 4, where only one day before the festival is mentioned for the bringing of the robe, festivals are given in general, while in 18, 4, 3, where he refers to seven days, Josephus first states generally: before a festival, and then adds the three festivals and the great

[66] The immersion of the robe was probably executed in the same way as that of the defiled curtain of the Holy of Holies in Shekal. 8, 4: פרוכת שנטמאת בוולד הטומאה מטבילין אותה בפנים ומכניסין אותה מיד, ואת שנטמאה באב הטומאה מטבילין אותה בחוץ ושוטחין אותה בחיל, ואם היתה חדשה שוטחין אותה על גג האיצטבא כדי שיראו העם את מלאכתה שהיא נאה.

[67] Chwolson, Das letzte Passamahl, 55 ff.

[68] Parah 3, 1; Baraita Yoma 8a stated by R. Haninah, the vice high priest; Tos. Parah 3, 1; Jer. Yoma I 38a 55.

fast day. But just this last detailed enumeration of the various occasions is decidedly against the explanation suggested. Another solution may be this. As we have seen, the view of a grave defilement by a corpse attributed by the Hillelites to the Gentile was not only opposed by the Shammaites, but, in connection with a practical incident, even defeated. So long as the view of the Shammaites prevailed, the impurity ascribed to the Gentile was of a weak nature, and, as they expressly stated, the immersion on the same day removed it, and the proselyte was permitted to eat of the Paschal meal the same evening. In the days of Josephus, however, and the period reflected by the statement of Ḥaninah, the vice high priest, in Parah 3, 1, either the view of the Hillelites was authoritative, or, as the extreme precautions taken in connection with the burning of the red heifer and the sprinkling with the ashes show, corpses were assumed to lie buried in the soil of Jerusalem,[69] and that is why the high priest and his robe were purified for seven days. And, again, we find that the defilement of the robe by the Romans was only considered in its relation to the Temple and its sacrifices; but, so far, no instance has been found in which the Gentile's levitical impurity would have affected a layman.

The same applies to the contact of the Jews of Jerusalem with the Roman governor, and to their visits to his temporary residence in Herod's palace.[70] The leaders of the city negotiated with him, as it appears, without any consideration of his levitical impurity. When Vitellius, the legate of Syria, came to Jerusalem twice, once during the Passover, and the other time during a festival not named, the Jews received him with great honor. He then deposed the high priest Kaiaphas, and appointed in his place Jonathan,

---

[69] קבר התהום in Tos. Parah 3, 2.

[70] Pilate stayed there, Philo, Legatio ad Caium, 38 = M II 589; Schürer, Geschichte I, 458, 33; and Florus, Josephus, Wars, 2, 14, 8, 301; 2, 15, 5, 328.

the son of Ananos, in the year 36-37.[71] Soon after that, he deposed the latter, and appointed his brother Theophilos high priest.[72] It is obvious that these noble priests must have appeared before the Roman legate in his official residence, to be informed of their deposition or appointment, and, no doubt, he stated to them his reasons why they lost or received their dignity. The same procedure must have been observed toward the four high priests deposed or appointed by Valerius Gratus in the years 15-26, Ishmael son of Fiabi,[73] Eleazar son of Ananos,[74] Simeon son of Kamithos, and Joseph Kaiaphas[75] and also the high priest Ananos son of Sethi appointed by Quirinus the year 6 in the place of Joazar in who had quarreled with the people.[76] It was while staying the first time during Passover in Jerusalem, and in the course of the three days of another festival which he spent there the second time, that Vitellius appointed the high priests. If they officiated at the sacrificial service during the festivals, they could only have purified themselves by the usual immersion, and not by the ashes of the red heifer for which a full week was required. Consequently, the impurity contracted in the governor's residence could not have been due to the assumed presence of a corpse buried in the ground of the building, but only was of some slight degree.

5. *The visits of Gentiles to the Temple.*

More difficult are the problems raised by the report of Marcus Agrippa's stay in Jerusalem. He came to Judea in the days of King Herod, and visited the capital where the population received him with processions and acclamations.

[71] *Antiquit.* 18, 4, 3, 90. 95.
[72] *Antiquit.* 18, 5, 3, 122. 123.
[73] *Antiquit.* 18, 2, 2, 34.
[74] *Antiquit.* 18, 2, 2, 34.
[75] 18, 2, 2, 35.
[76] 18, 2, 1. 2.

He sacrificed to God one hundred oxen, and feasted the people in vast numbers.[77] The letter of King Agrippa I to the Emperor Caligula[78] gives a more detailed account of Marcus Agrippa's visit to Jerusalem. "And when he beheld the Temple and the decorations of the priests, and the piety of the people, he marvelled. . . . Therefore, every day that he remained in the city, by reason of his friendship for Herod, he went to the sacred place, being delighted with the sight of the building and of the sacrifices and all the ceremonies connected with the worship of God, and the regularity which was observed, and the dignity and honor paid to the high priest, and his grandeur when arrayed in his sacred vestments and when about to begin the sacrifices. After he had adorned the Temple with all the offerings in his power to contribute, and had conferred many benefits on the inhabitants, . . . $\grave{\epsilon}\pi\iota\beta\alpha\acute{\iota}\nu o\nu\tau os\ \tau o\tilde{\upsilon}\ \chi\epsilon\iota\mu\tilde{\omega}\nu os$ he departed."[79] The difficulty here is, how Herod could have brought the Gentile into the part of the forecourt of the Temple whence Agrippa could watch the piety of the people, the priests and the high priest in their vestments, the sacrifices, and the ceremonies. Could Herod, to please the great Roman, have ignored the established rule, and silenced the religious feelings of the Jews who strongly objected to the presence of a Gentile in the parts of the Temple prohibited for him? Or could a point be stretched in an exceptional case of this kind? Or did Marcus Agrippa not go beyond the limit set at all, but watched the Temple service from the Antonia, just as Aristeas did?[80] As already mentioned, Vitellius came with Herod, the tetrarch, and his friends to Jerusalem, to bring a sacrifice to God on the

[77] *Antiquit.* 16, 2, 1, 14.
[78] Philo, *Legatio ad Caium* 37 = M 589 ff.
[79] In the year 15 B. C. E., Schürer, *Geschichte* I 370. The season of the year mentioned would suggest that the stay coincided with the feast of Tabernacles, when he could have seen, in the ordinary course, the high priest officiating.
[80] Letter of Aristeas, ed. Wendland 100, Thackeray 100.

impending festival of the Jews;[81] what is meant by that? Did he enter the inner forecourt, as only a specially purified Jew could? There are several earlier instances of sacrifices by Gentile kings. Ptolemy I, son of Lagos, came to Jerusalem on a Sabbath as if he intended to bring sacrifices,[82] and was, on account of that, received without fear and suspicion.[83] Ptolemy III Euergetes visited Jerusalem, and offered there, according to our laws, many sacrifices to God, and gave gifts worthy of his victory.[84] Of Alexander the Great Josephus[85] records: "Then he went into the Temple, brought sacrifices to God according to the high priest's direction, and magnificently treated both the high priest and the priests." It is true, the whole report of Alexander's visit to Jerusalem is considered by scholars to be pure fiction, just like that of Aristeas. But even so, the reference to the sacrifice must have been justified by the author's own knowledge of the actual conditions in Jerusalem in his own time, unless he freely invented even such sacrifices of the famous king in order to extol the high recognition of the Temple in Jerusalem. But, in view of the sacrifices offered by Marcus Agrippa, and, fifty years later,

[81] *Antiquit.* 18, 5, 3, 122.
[82] *Antiquit.* 12, 1, 1, 4.
[83] In I Macc. 7, 33 it is reported: "After this went Nikanor up to Mount Zion, and there came out of the sanctuary, τὰ ἅγια, certain of the priests and certain of the elders of the people to salute him peaceably, and to show him the burnt sacrifice that was offered for the king. (34) But he mocked them, and laughed at them, and defiled them, and spake proudly. (36) Then the priests entered in, and stood before the altar and the Temple, weeping, and saying. . . ." As Grimm, 115, rightly points out, εἰσῆλθον in v. 36, and ἐξῆλθον in v. 33 clearly show that Nikanor did not enter the forecourt, but was met outside on the Temple Mount, as also Rawlinson admits. As the elders of the people were with the priests,—and nothing suggests that also they were priests and not laymen,—they cannot have come out of the ναός where no layman was permitted to enter; they came out with the officiating priests from the inner forecourt, that of the Israelites, if it already existed at the time. In II Macc. 14, 31 the parallel report reads: "He came into the great and holy Temple, and commanded the priests that were offering their usual sacrifices, to deliver him the man Judas." The words referring to the Temple are too vague to be pressed. How did the Gentile Nikanor defile the priests? From his knowledge of the incidents with the two high priests' defilement by spittle in the Talmud, Josippon of the tenth century adds: by spitting upon them.
[84] *Contra Ap.* II, 548.
[85] *Antiquit.* 11, 8, 5, 336. Cf. Genes. rab. 61, 7.

by Vitellius in the year 36, at a date not very far from Josephus's observations in Jerusalem, the assumption of a pure invention in the report of Alexander on the point of the sacrifice is not probable.[86]

Antiochos III is reported[87] to have decreed on his conquest of Jerusalem in the year 198 B. C. E. "that no stranger was allowed to enter within the περίβολος of the Temple, which is forbidden also to the Jews, εἰ μὴ οἷς ἁγνισθεῖσιν ἐστὶν ἔθιμον κατὰ τὸν πάτριον νόμον, except to those who, according to their own law, have the right to enter after purifying themselves." If the decree is genuine and not a Jewish-Hellenistic free composition, the second Temple had a fenced forecourt which, up to the prohibition of Antiochos III, was entered by non-Jews either lawfully or against the existing religious rule. According to I Macc. 9, 54 Alkimos began to pull down the wall τῆς αὐλῆς τῶν ἁγίων τῆς ἐσωτέρας, of the inner court of the sanctuary, and destroyed the work of the prophets. It seems to be identical with the περίβολος of Antiochos III which marked the boundary for the Gentile,[88] and existed, as I Macc. remarks, since the days of the prophets, meaning Haggai and Zechariah who were contemporaries of the building of the second Temple. If it was Alkimos' intention to remove the boundary set to the Gentiles, no non-Jew was permitted before his action to enter the walled court; and, as the wall pulled down was, no doubt, restored by the Maccabean rulers, as it had existed, when Nikanor went up to the Temple,[89] no Gentile could have entered the fenced space to bring sacrifices. With this should also be compared a peculiar statement of Josephus:[90] "Once some

---

[86] See also the sacrifice of Antiochos Eupator in II Macc. 13, 23, of Heliodoros in II Macc. 3, 35, and of Ptolemaios Philopator in III Macc. 1, 9.
[87] *Antiquit.* 12, 3, 4, 145, cf. II Macc. 3, 35.
[88] See Schürer, *Geschichte* I, 225, 6; Halevy, דורות הראשונים Ie, 117b.
[89] I Macc. 7, 33 ff., see above p. 33, n. 83.
[90] *Antiquit.* 3, 15, 3, 318 ff.

persons came who lived beyond Euphrates, and had journeyed, through many dangers and at great expenses, for four months in honor of our Temple; and yet when they had offered their sacrifices, they could not partake of their own sacrificial meals, because Moses had forbidden it to them, as they did not agree with us in customs and usages (=they were not Jews). Some of them left without having sacrificed at all, and others after leaving their sacrifices half-performed, and many of them had not even obtained permission to enter into the Temple. They preferred submission to the laws of Moses to an action in accordance with their own inclinations." The geography and the distance suggest that Josephus referred to the visit to Jerusalem of Queen Helena, of her son Monobazos of Adiabene, and of their, no doubt, numerous suite. The season of the year in which they arrived is not stated anywhere, though we find them celebrating the feast of Tabernacles,[91] and it is also stated [92] that Monobazos made the handles of all the vessels used at the service of the Temple on the Day of Atonement of gold; this indicates that he had watched the service on that occasion. If it might be assumed that, with many other pilgrims from the East, they were in time for the offering of the Passover sacrifice in which the whole royal family had wished to participate, what would have been the attitude of the religious authorities to the admission to that sacrifice of the queen, the king, their family, and their retinue?

It is the only private sacrifice with the details of which the Pentateuch as well as the rabbis dealt more fully. Exod. 12, 43 has: "This is the ordinance of the Passover: there shall no alien eat thereof; (44) but every man's servant that is bought for money, when thou hast circumcised him, then shall he eat thereof. (48) And when a stranger shall

[91] Tos. Sukkah 1, 1; b. 2a; Jer. I 51d 24.
[92] Yoma 3, 10.

sojourn with thee, and will keep the Passover to the Lord, let all his males be circumcised, and then let him come near and keep it; and he shall be as one who is born in the land; but no uncircumcised person shall eat thereof." Those of Helena's household who were not admitted to the part of the Temple where every Jew brought his sacrifice, the inner forecourt, were evidently uncircumcised Gentiles who, as Josephus tells us,[93] must not share in any such sacrifice. Some of the following, however, succeeded in entering the inner forecourt, and were only questioned about their religious fitness after they had brought there their lamb, and had it slaughtered. On being found to be uncircumcised Gentiles, or perhaps unpurified proselytes, they had to abandon their sacrifice half-performed, or, if its blood had already been offered up, they were not admitted to the sacrificial meal in the evening. It is true, they need not have gone all personally to the Temple, as any Jew might, on their behalf, have brought the lamb there; but as strangers and proselytes who had, the first time, come to Jerusalem, all of them were probably most anxious to see the Temple and to attend to their own sacrifices. Again, the queen seems to have consulted, on her Nazirite vows[94] and on the law of the booth of Tabernacles, the Hillelites only,[95] and if they advised her on the question as to how long a proselyte had to be purified after his circumcision, some of her followers had first to be purified for a full week before their admission to the sacrifice. If the above interpretation of Josephus' statement is correct, the religious authorities about the year 50 allowed no Gentile to enter the inner forecourt of the Temple, which seems also to have been the rule a century earlier, when Nikanor, in the days of Judas Maccabaeus, went up to the Temple Mount. Consequently,

[93] *Wars* 6, 9, 3, 427; οὐδὲ τοῖς ἀλλοφύλοις, ὅσοι κατὰ θρησκείαν παρῆσαν.
[94] Nazir 3, 6; see Brüll, *Jahrbücher* I, 1874, 75; Lewy, *Abba Saul*, 1876, 14, 24.
[95] Tos. Sukkah 1, 1; b. 2b; Jer. I 51d 24.

the sacrifices offered by Vitellius in the year 36, and by Marcus Agrippa in the year 15 B. C. E., if brought by them into the inner forecourt, were an irregularity allowed or tolerated only under the stress of exceptional circumstances. It seems more probable that they were only permitted to bring the offerings to one of the gates, most probably the eastern, of the inner forecourt, whence they were able to watch the whole of the sacrificial service conducted by the high priest and the priests. But even in that case it is evident that, if any levitical impurity was ascribed to the Gentile, it was, even in the year 36, not sufficiently grave to prevent him from proceeding to the very gate of the inner forecourt. This is all the more characteristic as in the year 17 a Roman hegemon was able to defile by his spittle the high priest Simeon Kamithos, which definitely proves that, as was shown above, a certain degree of levitical impurity attached to every Gentile in the opinion of the contemporary religious authorities. And the case of Vitellius, if it was no exception, further proves that, between the years 17 and 36, the attribution of such defilement to the Gentile had made no progress.

According to Josephus[96] and the Mishnah[97] a low balustrade erected a few cubits within the wall of the Temple Mount marked the boundary to which the Gentile was permitted to go. But the sources are not in agreement on all the deatils of the pertinent rules. In Josephus[98] the whole city of Jerusalem was prohibited to persons who had an issue, to lepers, and the Temple to menstruous women; but in the definite regulations in the rabbinic sources,[99] male and female persons afflicted with gonorrhœa, men-

[96] *Antiquit.* 15, 11, 5, 417; *Wars* 5, 5, 2, 193; 6, 2, 4, 124-126; *Contra Apion.* II, 8, 103; Schürer, *Geschichte* II, 329, 56.
[97] Midd. 2, 3; Kelim 1, 8.
[98] *Wars* 5, 5, 6, 227.
[99] Kelim 1, 8; Tos. 1, I, 8; Sifre Zuta Num. 5, 2, p. 4; see Olitzki, *Flavius Josephus und die Halacha* I, 28.

struous women, and women after childbirth were only forbidden to enter the Temple Mount. On the other hand, it is explicitly stated[100] that Gentiles were admitted not only into Jerusalem, but to worship, that is, to the Temple Mount. And a Baraita states[101] that R. Gamaliel I, or his son R. Simeon b. Gamaliel I, in walking on the Temple Mount, or on the stairs leading up to it, saw a beautiful Gentile woman, and spoke the blessing over her beauty. Even if the later date of the incident be correct, the Gentile woman was not excluded from the city, nor even from the Temple Mount, though she was regarded as being permanently in the levitical state of the menstruous woman. Again, we are not informed definitely whether Herod, when rebuilding the Temple, erected the balustrade, and set up the tablets forbidding the Gentile to go beyond that boundary, or whether it owed its origin to a later date. If Philo's reference to the point might be taken literally, it would appear that in the year 39–40 that partition had not existed yet. For he says in connection with the proposed erection of Caligula's statue in the Temple of Jerusalem:[102] "And the greatest proof of this is that death is inexorably pronounced against all those who enter into the inner circuits, εἰς τοὺς ἐντὸς περιβόλους,—for they admit all men from every country εἰς τοὺς ἐξωτέρω." He uses the plural in referring to both, the inner and the outer partitions, and presupposes that there were at least two courts into which the Gentiles were permitted to enter, which corresponds to the statements about the Temple before Herod's time. The exclusion of the Gentile from the second forecourt would, accordingly, have been instituted later.[103]

---

[100] *Wars* 6, 9, 3, 426.
[101] Jer. 'Abod. Zar. I 40a 73; b. 20a, see Rabbinovicz.
[102] *Legatio ad Caium* 31, 212 = M II 577.
[103] Cf. J.Q.R. 10, 1898, 697–706.

6. *The Gentile's grave levitical impurity.*

A much stricter degree of levitical impurity was ascribed to the Gentile shortly before the destruction of the Temple. For a Baraita[104] reports that, at a meeting of the two schools at which the Shammaites had the majority, eighteen prohibitions were decreed. Among the things prohibited in the first instance were certain articles of food of the Gentiles, bread, cheese and oil, which alone form the discussion following in the same connection;[105] then their daughters, their semen, and their urine were added. As all the scholars who dealt with the difficult matter more fully and critically[106] admit, the report of the Baraita is well informed and trustworthy in all its details. Several of the items in its list are of special interest for the inquiry about the Gentile's levitical impurity. First, though a secretion of the same class, and found, as was shown above, along with the other secretions mentioned here, the spittle of the Gentile is not included among the things which the assembly of scholars declared as defiling, because it had been accepted as such by the authorities fifty years earlier, and the rule had been observed before by the priests when on duty in the Temple. Next, the inclusion of the Gentile's urine here is difficult, as the Hillelites referred to its defiling force along with that of spittle in a Gentile menstruous woman as to an accepted fact. The suggestion that when the statement of the Hillelites was made, it was only the Gentile menstruous woman whose secretions were held to be defiling, while among the eighteen decrees also the male Gentile's urine was

---

[104] Jer. Shabb. I 3c 37: תני שמונה עשר דבר גזרו ובשמונה עשר הושוו ובשמונה עשר נחלקו, ואלו הן שגזרו על פיתן של גוים ועל גבינתן ועל שמנן ועל בנותיהן ועל שכבת זרען ועל מימי רגליהן ועל הלכות בעל קרי ועל הלכות ארץ העמים. See Halevy, דורות הראשונים Ic, 298ff; 300ff.

[105] Jer. Shabb. I 3d.

[106] Graetz, *Geschichte* III, note 26; Derenbourg, *Essai sur l'histoire* 272ff; Lerner in Magazin WJ. 9, 1882, 117ff.; Zeitlin in REJ 68, 1914, 22ff.

declared levitically impure, is of little force, as "Gentiles" in the report in connection with the foods and other items undoubtedly refers to both sexes. Similarly, another suggestion that formerly only the urine of the Gentile woman had been considered, and that the later assembly merely re-affirmed the earlier decision, is hardly convincing in the absence of any reference to the impurity of the Gentile's spittle decreed fifty years before. Nor is the assumption more satisfactory that the urine was erroneously added to the statement of the Hillelites in consequence of the fact that, in several other Mishnahs about the man with an issue and the menstruous woman, spittle is invariably followed by urine. The reason for declaring the Gentile's semen defiling can only be sought in the Israelite whose semen is levitically impure, in the man with an issue; and it would suggest that, on this point, the assembly of the two schools placed the Gentile on a level with the Israelite with an issue. In fact, a Baraita[107] states that it was decreed that the Gentiles should be like men with an issue in all respects.

That the same assembly was responsible for the last mentioned decree is stated in the explanation of the eighteen decrees by an Amora of the end of the third century, R. Yisḥaḳ, which refers to a slightly different wording of the original list in the Baraita. He said[108] that, in order to prevent sodomy between a Jewish and a Gentile youth, the scholars decreed that the Gentile defile to the same extent as a man who has an issue. In support of that they

---

[107] Niddah 34a; Sifra Lev. 15, 2, 74d, cf. RS on Zabim 2, 1: אבל גזרו עליהן שיהו כזבין לכל דבריהן.

[108] Shabb. 17b: אמר רב אחא בר אדא אמר רבי יצחק גזרו על פתן משום שמנן ועל שמנן משום יינן ועל יינן משום בנותיהן ועל בנותיהן משום דבר אחר ועל דבר אחר משום דבר אחר. מאי דבר אחר, אמר רב נחמן בר יצחק גזרו על תינוק נכרי שמטמא בזיבה שלא יהא תינוק ישראל רגיל אצלו במשכב זכור. In the parallel passage in 'Abod. Zar. 36b the last statement reads first: אמר רב נחמן בר יצחק בנותיהן מה היא, גזרו על בנותיהן נדות מעריסתן, their women were declared to be like menstruous women from their cradles; and later that their men be like men affected with gonorrhoea.

prohibited immoral relations[109] with Gentile women, then all associations with Gentile women, then the Gentile's urine, then his oil, and lastly his bread. Rab held that the object of those decrees was to prevent idolatry. It should be noted that in these prohibitions the degree of the levitical impurity is not the same in the two sexes of the Gentiles. The old declaration that the Gentile woman is permanently in the levitical state of a menstruous woman was, just as in the days of the Hasmonaeans, deemed sufficient for restraining the Jew from having sexual relations with her. On the other hand, the levitical impurity of the Gentile was not due to himself or to any physical changes of his body, but was merely communicated to him by his wife; on account of that, and as he defiled priests only, it might have appeared to be of no consequence for the ordinary man, and was, therefore, of no deterring force. Consequently, the highest possible levitical impurity had to be ascribed to him in order to be effective.[110] As the authors of this strict decree were the Shammaites and Hillelites of the year 65–66, the dispute of the two schools[111] in which the **Shammaites** declared the blood of the Gentile menstruous woman not defiling, undoubtedly took place before the eighteen decrees were passed at the

---

[109] The first דבר אחר cannot mean idolatry, as this is never designated by the two words, and their position here between the Gentile women and sodomy precludes that meaning.

[110] In Jer. זבים are not mentioned at all in connection with the eighteen decrees, but instead their semen and urine, which are the defiling secretions of the man with an issue. Against these Jer. Shabb. I 3d 37 raises a serious objection: Has not R. Joḥanan said that the Gentile's semen is not defiling, why then is it included among the eighteen decrees? Because semen is invariably accompanied by urine which is in itself defiling. The same is already stated in Baraita Niddah 34a ff; Tos. Mikv. 6, 7, cf. Mishnah 8, 4: תא שמע נמצאת אומר שיכבת זרעו של ישראל טמאה בכל מקום ואפילו במעי נכרית ושל נכרי טהורה בכל מקום ואפילו במעי ישראלית חוץ ממי רגלים שבה. Lerner in Magazin WJ, 9, 1882, 118, note, rightly points out that accordingly the order in the list of the eighteen decrees should have been the reverse: ועל מימי רגליהן ועל שכבת זרען, as the defiling force of semen was only derived from that of urine. But, in reality, the two were taken over bodily from the rules about the man with an issue, when the Gentile was declared to be like him. But the difficulty is that even in the rules about the man with an issue semen is not of the same degree of impurity as his urine, Tos. Zabim 3, 3; 5, 2; Nazir 66a.

[111] Niddah 4, 3.

suggestion of the Shammaites. For it is hardly conceivable that the Gentile woman should have been considered less defiling when she was in the actual state of impurity than when the condition of levitical impurity was merely ascribed to her.[112]

In connection with the spittle of the Gentile, reference must be made to a controversy of two teachers of the middle of the second century about the levitical state of the streets of Jerusalem before the year 70.[113] "R. Meir said that all spittle found in Jerusalem was levitically pure, except such as was found in the upper market. R. José said that, throughout the year, spittle found in the center of the street was impure, on its sides pure; during the festivals of pilgrimage, spittle found in the center of the street was pure, on its sides impure, because the impure minority of the people withdrew to the sides of the street."[114] As R. José only had Jews in view, and only

[112] It is difficult to understand that the redactor of the Mishnah should have embodied a dispute recording an early opinion of the two schools which was superseded by their later decree. In explanation of this difficulty it cannot be assumed that the reason was, because the strict view was abolished after the destruction of the Temple. For a Baraita in Shabb. 127b reports that R. Joshua b. Ḥananiah who, unlike R. Eliezer, criticised the severity of the eighteen decrees, Jer. Shabb. I 3c 30, immersed after visiting a matrona, because, as his disciples correctly surmised, spittle had issued from her mouth and fallen upon his clothes. In the parallel account in 2 ARN 19, 21a ff. the visit took place in Ashkelon, and the defilement is described thus: ושמא כשמשיחה עמך נחזה צנורה מפיה עליך ואמרת ארד ואהיה כמותם טהור. This occurred before 135, so that the old decree was then still in force. Nor was it abolished by the next generation of the teachers in Usha, which immediately preceded that of the redactor of the Mishnah; for it is presupposed as being in vogue in statements of R. Meir and R. Jehudah in Tohar. 5, 8; Tos. 6, 10. Perhaps the strictness of the decree was not extended to the Gentile woman who was actually menstruous, as her impure state was sufficient to prevent sexual relations.

[113] Shekal. 8, 1: כל הרוקין הנמצאים בירושלים טהורין חוץ משל שוק העליון דברי רבי מאיר, רבי יוסי אומר בשאר כל ימות השנה שבאמצע טמאין שבצדדין טהורין ובשעת הרגל שבאמצע טהורין שבצדדין טמאין מפני שהן מועטין מסתלקין לצדדין. Cf. the Baraita Jer. VIII 51a 51.

[114] Interesting is a statement in the Letter of Aristeas 106 (Thackeray, 24): "And there are stairs towards the thoroughfares . . . . Some persons take their way above, others underneath, this distinction of travelling being on account of those who are undergoing purification, so that they may touch nothing improper." G. A. Smith, *Jerusalem*, II, 441, note 1, misunderstood the precaution here, when he says: "But this seems to be due to some confusion, because a person desirous of avoiding unholy contact could as little effect his purpose on the higher as in the lower thoroughfares, and the higher were the further from the Temple." During the festivals of pilgrimage, there might have been a regulation of traffic issued by the religious

distinguished between pure and impure Jews and their status at the various seasons of the year, his statement does not bear on the problem of the Gentile's levitical impurity.[115] R. Meir, on the other hand, presupposes the presence of Gentiles in the upper market of Jerusalem, and his statement is illustrated by R. Joshua b. Levi who pointed out that the Roman camp, castra, was there.[116] From Josephus we learn that a Roman cohort was stationed in the Antonia throughout the year,[117] and whenever the governor came to Jerusalem and resided in Herod's palace, there always were Roman soldiers about in the city, and not invariably on a peaceful errand. So Florus, one day, seated himself in front of the palace on his judgment seat,[118] and the high priests, the heads, and the leading citizens came and stood up before the judgment seat. Florus shouted to his troops[119] to plunder the so-called upper market, and to strike down all who would come their way. This order of their commander was very welcome to the soldiers, as they were eager for spoil, and they pillaged not only the part of the city assigned to them, but rushed into any house, and murdered the inhabitants. When once Pilate stayed in Jerusalem in the royal palace,[120] and the excited people surrounded his judgment seat and shouted, he secretly distributed soldiers in civilian clothes among the multitude. In addition, there were a considerable number of soldiers in the governor's residence in the royal palace,[121] and near this was

authorities, and the persons who were purifying themselves might well have been ordered to walk in the higher thoroughfares. According to R. Jose's statement, the traffic in all the streets of Jerusalem was regulated by one rule.

[115] The distinction between the festivals and ordinary days for the levitical law occurs again in Hagig. 3, 6. 7; Jer. III 19d 3; Tos. 3, 34; b. 26a.

[116] Jer. Shekal. VIII 15a 27.

[117] *Wars* 5, 5, 8, 244; Schürer, *Geschichte* I, 464.

[118] *Wars*, 2, 14, 8, 301.

[119] 2, 14, 9, 305.

[120] 2, 9, 4, 175 ff.

[121] 2, 15, 5, 328.

a camp, distinct from the Antonia,[122] containing another group of soldiers.[123] As all of them were moving round the royal palace in the upper market, it is clear why, according to R. Meir's information, the upper market was taken to be visited by Gentiles, and spittle noticed there was considered to be levitically impure.[124]

And it was in no way different under King Herod who had in his palace a host of Gentiles in his service. Not only his secretary, Nikolaos of Damaskus, and his brother Ptolemaios, but also the rhetor Irenaios,[125] Eurykles of Sparta, his guest,[126] his friends Andromachos and Gemellus managed his affairs at embassies and consultations, and taught his sons.[127] Demetrios, the son of the former, was a friend of Herod's son Alexander. Herod's bodyguard Korinthos had grown up in the palace, and was fully trusted;[128] two other bodyguards were Jucundus and

---

[122] 2, 15, 5, 329; 2, 17, 8, 439.

[123] In addition, Jerusalem was open to strangers for worship, *Wars* 4, 4, 4, 275. In *Antiquit.* 11, 4, 3, 86 Zerubbabel and Joshua are said to have answered the Samaritans who wished to assist in the building of the Temple, that they could not grant them such permission, but the Samaritans would be allowed to worship, and in that respect only, if they so wished, would they have the same right as all who would come to the Temple to worship God. See the rendering of I Kings. 8, 41. 42 in *Antiquit.* 8, 4, 3, 116, and Bertholet, *Die Stellung des Israeliten*, 314.

[124] It is true, R. Meir's statement is contradicted in Jer. Shekal. VIII 51a 49: אמר רבי אבהו בשם רבי יוסי בן חנינה לא גזרו על הרוקים בירושלים, R. Jose b. Ḥaninah said that they decreed not concerning spittle in Jerusalem. Though that teacher lived in the middle of the third century, his opposing statement is too definite to be ignored. On the other hand, R. Jose's report, if taken literally, is contradicted by the record, just as definite, of R. Meir who taught a century before the former. In fact, the parallel statement in Pesaḥ. 19b reads: איתמר רבי אלעזר ורבי יוסי בירבי חנינא חד אמר לא גזרו על ספק הרוקין שבירושלים וחד אמר לא גזרו על ספק הכלים שבירושלים. R. Jose b. R. Ḥaninah said that no fear was entertained as to the impure origin of the spittle noticed in Jerusalem. Rashi makes its meaning clear: לא גזרו לומר שמא של זב או של נדה הוא, they did not assume that the spittle might be of a person with an issue or of a menstruous woman: in Jer.: of a Gentile. It means that only spittle of definitely Gentile origin was declared impure, but it was not assumed that spittle of uncertain origin was that of a Gentile. R. Meir, on the other hand, reported that it was assumed that spittle noticed in the neighborhood of the royal palace where the Roman soldiers moved about, that is, in the upper market, was of Gentiles, and therefore regarded as levitically impure.

[125] *Antiquit.* 17, 9, 4, 225 ff.; 9, 5, 228; *Wars* 2, 2, 3, 21.

[126] *Wars*, 1, 26, 1-4.

[127] *Antiquit.* 16, 8, 3, 242.

[128] *Antiquit.* 17, 3, 2, 55; *Wars* 1, 29, 3, 576.

Tyrannus,[129] his eunuch Bagoas, his page Carus,[130] and his scribe Diophantos.[131] Herod had five hundred slaves and freedmen;[132] there were, besides, the male and female attendants and servants of his sons and their wives, altogether hundreds of Gentile men and women in the royal palace and its various buildings, who moved about in the upper market. In addition, the mercenaries, brought together from various parts of Europe and Asia, and stationed in the Antonia and the royal palace,[133] represented a strong non-Jewish element. It would, then, be possible that the law on which the defilement of the high priest Simeon b. Kamithos by a hegemon in the year 17-18 was based, and which was hardly of a recent date, but the result of a gradual development, was originally instituted under Herod or his successor Archelaos. In support of that date could be adduced the consideration that the first stage of that levitical rule was the extension of the biblical law about the impurity of the menstruous Jewess to the Gentile woman. But such application of the law could only have been suggested by the presence of a number of Gentile women in Jerusalem. The Roman soldiers, however, who were stationed in the capital, as far as is known, did not bring their wives with them; nor does Josephus ever refer to the presence of women in the Roman governor's temporary residence in Herod's palace, as all the officials of the Roman administration of Judaea lived in Caesarea. Unless the levitical rule owed its origin to one single incident, it would appear almost impossible that it arose after the year 6 when, after Archelaos's deposition, the Romans took over the administration of

---

[129] *Antiquit.* 16, 10, 3, 314; in *Wars* 1, 26, 3, 527 they are royal cavalry officers.
[130] *Antiquit.* 17, 2, 4, 44.
[131] *Antiquit.* 16, 10, 4, 319; *Wars* 1, 26, 3, 529.
[132] *Wars* 1, 33, 9, 673; *Antiquit.* 17, 8, 3, 198. 199; see Bertholet, *Die Stellung des Israeliten* 247 ff.
[133] *Antiquit.* 17, 8, 3, 198 ff; *Wars* 1, 33, 9, 672ff.; cf. Antiquit. 15, 8, 1, 268ff.

Judea. On the other hand, the presence of so great a number of Gentile women in the king's palace and its other buildings under Herod and Archelaos (37 B. C. E. to 6 C. E.) would account for the institution of the rule by the Hillelites satisfactorily; the levitical purity of the Temple and of the officiating priests had to be protected.

7. *The Gentile's touch and the food of the Jew.*

In reviewing all the data about the levitical impurity ascribed to the Gentile by the rabbis in the course of the last seventy years before the destruction of the Temple, we find that originally it was not to the male Gentile that such defilement was attributed, but to the Gentile menstruous woman whom the Hillelites placed in that respect on a level with the menstruous Jewess. As, however, the Gentile woman did not purify herself, she was declared to be permanently in the state of a menstruous woman, just as the Samaritan and some of the Sadducee women who did not observe in their monthly purification the Pharisee rules. And just as the Samaritan and Sadducee women permanently communicated their levitical impurity to their husbands, so was the Gentile defiled by his Gentile wife; so that now the levitical impurity which applied in Lev. 15 and in the rabbinic law to Jews only was extended to the Gentile, though not to the same degree. This was decreed about the year 1. Though the degree of the Gentile's impurity was nominally grave, it affected only the high priest and the priests on duty in the Temple, whom the Gentile's spittle, just as the Sadducee's, disqualified for the day from doing service. This impurity did not prevent the admission of Marcus Agrippa in the year 15 B. C. E., and of Vitellius in the year 36 C. E., to the gate of the inner forecourt of the Temple to bring sacrifices to God. Between the years 20 and 60, the Hillelites extended to the Gentile the levitical defilement by a corpse, and demanded that the proselyte should undergo the purification by the ashes of the red heifer for a full week; but they did not carry their point in face of the opposition of the Shammaites who would not extend that defilement to the Gentile and whose view was applied in practice. Even at that stage, the Gentile's impurity only affected the Temple and the sacrificial meal, but nobody and nothing outside of them. Shortly before the destruction of the Temple, about the year 65-66, the Shammaites and the Hillelites declared the Gentile to be levitically as impure as the Jew who had an issue, and the Gentile woman to be regarded as menstruous from her childhood, in order to prevent Jews from having immoral relations with Gentiles. But there was, owing to the outbreak of war, no time left for those decrees to be applied in practice in Jerusalem, and no record of any incident to illustrate their application has been preserved.

In the presence of these facts it is all the more strange that Professor L. Ginzberg says:[134] "Nun kann zwar darüber kein Zweifel herrschen, dass zur Zeit, als das rabbinische Judentum auf der Beobachtung der Reinheitsgesetze bestand, dieses jetzt nur von den Falaschas beobachtete Gesetz, (das von einem Nichtjuden Berührte als unrein zu erklären), allgemein als undisputierte Halachah galt."[135] This statement of the great rabbinic scholar and historian is, in all its parts, a riddle to me, since, to my knowledge, it cannot be proved from the rabbinic sources. The same applies to the statement of Dr. H. P. Chajes[136] that Judith, while in the camp of Holofernes, bathed every day,[137] because the touch of the Gentiles defiled her. It is true,

[134] MGWJ 56, 1912, 434, and in his *Eine unbekannte jüdische Sekte* I, 88.
[135] Sifra to 15, 2; Tos. Zabim 2, 1; Niddah 34a; cf. also Joh. 18, 28 and Act. 10, 28.
[136] Harkavy's *Festschrift*, Hebrew section, 109.
[137] Judith 12, 7 ff.

Maimonides codified this about the Gentiles:[138] "They all defile as a man does who has an issue, in all respects, a man and vessels by touch, and a man by carrying him, only their defilement is not biblical, but rabbinic." But Maimonides merely codified the decree passed by the two schools in the year 65-66, which was unknown before that date, and could not, therefore, have been observed by any ever so strict Jew in Jerusalem. And is there any, even the slightest, indication in the rabbinic literature that the touch of a Gentile caused a defilement and that such defilement was taken into account by the strictest Jew, not an Essene, in Temple times?[139] Long after the destruction of the Temple, but certainly not before the year 138, in the second and the third centuries, when that decree of the two schools was actually and consistently translated into practice, what do we find? As far as I can see, it is only R. Meir, R. Jehudah and R. Simeon who regard the Gentile in Galilee as defiling to the same extent as a man who has an issue, inasmuch as his spittle and urine are stated to be defiling.[140] So the anonymous

---

[138] 10: 2, ה' מטמאי משכב ומושב וכולן מטמאין אדם וכלים במגע ומטמאין אדם במשא כוב לכל דבר אלא שהטומאה מדבריהן.

[139] Epiphanius, *Haeres.* IX, 3 states that the Samaritans purify themselves, on returning from abroad, from the defilement, and when they touch a stranger or a Gentile, they bathe in their clothes. Hilgenfeld, *Judentum und Judenchristentum*, 65, rightly remarks that it could not have been invented, but must rest on observation or on an earlier source. Epiphanius, *Haeres.* XXX, 2, characterizes the practice of the Ebionites to avoid contact with non-Jews as a Samaritan trait. The *Itinerarium Antonini*, chapter 8, ed. Geyer, p. 164, reports that when they passed through some towns and villages of the Samaritans, the latter purified with fire the way where the Christians and the Jews had walked. See Wreschner, *Samaritanische Traditionen*, p. xvi; *Revue Sémitique* 16, 1908, 419. cf. Horowitz, ברייתא דמסכת נדה; Naḥmani on Lev. 12, 4.

[140] Tos. Tohar. 5, 2: מי רגלים של גוי (שנתערבו) הולכין אחר הרוב, רבי יהודה 5, 4: אומר רביעית בסאתים טמא יתיר לכן טהור קליפי פולין וקליפי תורמוסין שפסטן הגוי המסיטן טמא ושבשוקים הולכין אחר הרוב, רבי יהודה בן בתירה אומר על ודאי מגען ברשות היחיד שורפין. As the preceding two parallel rules about the man with an issue show, the Gentile removed the peel with his mouth, and when now the Jew moves the peel, he is defiled, as the Gentile's spittle had come in contact with it. If peels are found in the road and it is uncertain who threw them there, we go by the majority of the passers-by. R. Jehudah (b. Bethera is rightly struck out by Elijah Wilna) bases it on the principle enunciated in Tohar. 4, 5: על ששה ספיקות שורפין את התרומה ואפילו ברשות הרבים.

THE LEVITICAL IMPURITY OF THE GENTILE—BÜCHLER 49

Mishnah[141] deals with the Gentile woman as permanently menstruous whose spittle defiles in the same way and to the same extent as that of the Samaritan woman; the parallel Baraita[142] names expressly R. Meir as the author, and his colleagues, R. Jehudah and R. Simeon b. Yoḥai, as representing different views. In another Baraita[143] the Gentile is mentioned together with the menstruous woman, his impurity is as grave as that of a man who has an issue, his spittle and the pressure of his body defile, and if the priestly heave-offering comes in contact with his spittle, it has to be burnt. The same is laid down by another Mishnah:[144] "If Jewish thieves entered a house, only the place of their feet is defiled therein, and they defile food, drink and open earthenware vessels, while beds and sitting accommodations and tightly closed earthenware vessels remain undefiled; but if there is with the thieves a Gentile or a woman, everything is defiled." Here again the Gentile is in juxtaposition with the menstruous Jewess:[145] if a Gentile is among the thieves, the defilement is grave, as he is like a man with an issue in all respects. And this could have served as Maimonides's source for his rules of the Gentile's defiling force, as he followed the Halakhahs scattered in the rabbinic literature as one undivided whole, without any consideration of date and development.

The teachers of the middle of the second century in Galilee ascribed to the Gentile also the other kind of the

---

[141] Tohar. 5, 8: שוטה אחת בעיר או נכרית או כותית כל הרוקין שבעיר טמאין.
[142] Tos. Tohar. 6, 10: שוטה אחת בעיר כל הרוקין שבעיר טמאין דברי רבי מאיר רבי יהודה אומר אם היתה רגילה ליכנס במבוי אחד... ורבי שמעון אומר כל המבואות בחזקת טומאה.
[143] Tos. Tohar. 6, 11: הנדחק בריחיים שהגוי בתוכן שהנדה בתוכה בגדיו טמאין מדרס רקק ודרס על רוקו שורפין את התרומה על בגדיו הולכין אחר הרוב....
[144] Tohar. 7, 6: הגנבים שנכנסו לתוך הבית אין טמא אלא מקום רגלי הגנבים, ומה הן מטמאין, האוכלין והמשקין וכלי החרס הפתוחים, אבל המשכבות והמושבות וכלי חרס המוקפין צמיד פתיל טהורים, ואם יש עמהם נכרי או אשה הכל טמא. Cf. also Tohar. 7, 5; Tos. 8, 5.
[145] Or with a Gentile woman, as Maimuni explains it.

grave levitical impurity attributed to him by the Hillelites, but opposed by the Shammaites, and not accepted in the practice of Temple times, the defilement by a corpse. So the anonymous Tosefta[146] says: "Vessels bought from Gentile artisans, or vessels handed over to Jewish artisans who are 'Am-haAreṣ are defiled on account of the artisans' pressure by their bodies, and on account of their being defiled by a corpse." The consistent application in Galilee of the principle of the Hillelites about the Gentile's levitical defilement is, as far as I can see, not the direct continuance of the same practice in Judea, taught and observed by the teachers of R. Meir, R. Jehudah and R. Simeon; for no trace of either such rules about the Gentile, or of such or a similar observance is to be found in the schools of Lydda and Jamnia. The incident of R. Joshua b. Ḥananiah's visit to the house of a matrona, referred to above,[147] after which he immersed, is in several respects very instructive for the problem before us. The teacher asked his disciples what they had thought of him, when they saw him taking a levitical immersion. As they had accompanied him on his way to the Gentile matrona, had seen how he entered, and, again, how he left her house, they should have accounted for his purification by his visit to the room of the Gentile lady who, according to one of the eighteen decrees, was regarded as a woman with an issue,[148] and defiled every vessel and every sitting accommodation in the room. As that obvious explanation did not occur to them, and was not suggested by the master, it follows conclusively that the levitical impurity of the Gentile woman was not of the kind mentioned,

---

[146] Tos. Tohar. 8, 9: הלוקח כלים מאומני גוים והמוסר כלים לאומני עם הארץ טמאין מדרס וטמאין טמא מת. RS on Tohar. 7, 7 and the ordinary editions of the Tosefta read instead of the Jew the Gentile; and this is correct, as a special paragraph, the next one, is devoted to the 'Am-haAreṣ.

[147] Shabb. 1, 9; b. 19a; Tos. 1, 22; Jer. I 4b 6; see above n. 112.

[148] Maimonides, מטמאי משכב ומושב 2, 10: וחכמים גזרו על הנכרים שיטמאו כובים לכל דבריהם זכרים ונקבות; this is based, as Karo notes, on Nidd. 34a.

but, as the report in the Talmud expressly states, that of the menstruous woman. Her immediate touch or her spittle defiled; and as the teacher immersed on leaving her house, his defilement only lasted till the evening of the day of the occurrence. This clearly proves that the rabbis, even after the destruction of the Temple, took account of the levitical impurity of the Gentile woman; but did they beware, in the same way, of the graver defilement of the male Gentile? Ordinary business was, certainly, not hampered by it, as the report of an incident in Lydda testifies:[149] "R. Simeon Shezuri stated: Once untithed produce was accidentally mixed with my produce, and, when I asked R. Tarfon what I could do, he said to me: Go, and buy some produce from a Gentile (in the market), and use it for giving the tithe of the untithed produce. Moreover, R. Simeon b. Gamaliel II, the president of the school of which R. Meir, R. Jehudah and R. Simeon were also members, reports that in his father's household linen and clothes were regularly given to a Gentile launderer to be washed;[150] and it would be strange to assume that R. Gamaliel II's household should have forgotten that after the decree of the two schools, the Gentile defiled the linen and the clothes as gravely as a man who has an issue. And this would be all the more unintelligible, since R. Gamaliel II observed a higher degree of levitical purity in connection with his food.[151] Evidently, the impurity of the Gentile was then not considered to be of that grave nature and degree. When, on a festival, a Gentile brought fish to R. Gamaliel II, the latter said that they were permitted for food on the same day, though they might have been caught on the

---

[149] Jer. Dammai V 24d 69; Tos. 5, 22; b. Menaḥ. 31a. The Gentile is only mentioned in Jer: Cf. Tos. 'Abod. Zar. 4, 11.
[150] Shabb. 127b; 2 ARN 19, 21a; see above p. 26.
[151] Tos. Hagig. 3, 2: רבן גמליאל היה אוכל על טהרת חולין כל ימיו; some scholars think that R. Gamaliel I of Jerusalem was meant here.

festival; but he would not accept them.[152] No consideration of the Gentile's personal levitical impurity or of his vessels' levitical condition is mentioned in the report, which would not have been ignored even in the case of live fish, had the Gentile's defilement been regarded as grave even for R. Gamaliel only. But it is possible that from the destruction of the Temple on it affected mainly, or exclusively, the priestly heave-offering which had to be protected from every levitical defilement. For even in Galilee where the Gentile's impurity was treated as grave, it was, in the first instance, the priestly heave-offering that constituted a test, as the Mishnah[153] quoted above expressly states. R. Simeon b. Eleazar, a Galilean teacher of the second half of the second century, says of the slaves who refuse to be circumcised[154] that they must not be kept in Palestine at all, as they might cause the loss of levitically pure foods. They defile the priest's heave-offering, as they are Gentiles affected with the grave impurity of a man with an issue in all respects. The spittle of slaves bought from the Gentiles and the pressure of their bodies,[155] or those of the sons of bondwomen who were circumcised, but did not immerse, defile even in the street; according to others they do not defile. Though their levitical impurity is declared to be actual, it appears that they only defile the priest's heave-offering.

But the strongest proof of the extent to which the impurity of the Gentile was meant to be observed is the actual conduct of the rabbis who defined that defilement. R. Meir was one of those teachers who strictly insisted on the observance of the levitical purity in connection with the daily food. He says:[156] "He who lives perma-

---

[152] Besah 3, 2.
[153] Tohar. 4, 5.
[154] Yebam. 48b bottom: אין משהין אותו בארץ ישראל מפני הפסד טהרות.
[155] Baraita 'Abod. Zar. 57a; Tos. 3, 11.
[156] Baraita Shekal. III 47c 73: תאנא בשם רבי מאיר כל מי שקבוע בארץ ישראל ומדבר לשון הקדש ואוכל פירותיו בטהרה וקורא קריאת שמע בבקר ובערב

nently in the land of Israel, speaks the holy language, eats his food in levitical purity, and reads the Sh'ma' in the morning and in the evening, may be assured of his share in the world-to-come." But he himself not only associated with the Gentile philosopher Oinomaos of Gadara,[157] but also visited him in his house several times.[158] But the house of a Gentile was gravely defiled by his presence, and every couch and sitting accommodation was levitically impure! How could R. Meir, if, in his opinion, such defilement was communicated to every Jew, enter the Gentile's room? But he did an even more strange thing; he tells a scholar how a Gentile of his town arranged a banquet, and invited all the elders of it, and him, R. Meir, among them, and how sumptuous the meal was.[159] Even if R. Meir ate nothing, or only some fruit, at that table, how did he sit in the company of the Gentiles, and touch any food which was defiled by the handling of the Gentile attendants? A statement of R. Meir's colleague, R. Simeon b. Yoḥai, suggests that some Jews in Galilee entertained Gentiles in their houses; for, in an illustration of Israel's acceptance of God and of the golden calf, he says:[160] "This is similar to the case of a Jew who received the scholars and their disciples, and all blessed him for that; but when he also received Gentiles, people said that it was his way to receive anybody". And R. Simeon b. Eleazar who objected to the presence of uncircumcised slaves in Palestine for the sake of the levitical purity of the priestly heave-offering, says[161] that King Hezekiah

יהא מבושר שבן העולם הבא הוא. Cf. Tos. Dammai 2, 2, and Bacher, *Agada der Tannaiten* II 24, 2.

[157] Gen. r. 65, 20; Threni rab. Prooem. No. 2; Bacher, *Agada der Tannaiten* II, 31 ff.

[158] Ruth r. 1, 8: When the mother of Oinomaos of Gadara died, R. Meir went to comfort him, and found the family mourning; after a time, when his father died, R. Meir went to comfort him, but found the family engaged in their work. Cf. Jer. Dammai IV 24a 7; b. Gittin 61a.

[159] Pesikt. 59b; Pesikt. rab. 16, 82b; Bacher, *Agada der Tannaiten* II, 32, 2.

[160] Sifre Deut. 1, 1, 1, 64b.

[161] Baraita Synh. 104a.

prepared the Babylonian captivity for his descendants by entertaining at his table Gentiles, II Kings 20, 12-19. The rabbi, evidently, deprecated the custom of his own day as did R. Simeon b. Yoḥai, and so did only a few years later Ḥizkiah, the son of R. Ḥiyya, who explicitly said:[162] "He who invites a Gentile to his house and attends on him, brings exile upon his children." R. Simeon B. Eleazar saw idolatry in the acceptance of an invitation to the banquet of a Gentile by the Jew abroad, even if he ate his own food and was attended by his own servant;[163] but neither he nor R. Meir, his teacher, nor R. Simeon B. Yoḥai referred to the grave levitical impurity emanating from the Gentile at the meal, nor to the defilement of the food by his touch. All this admits of only one explanation: neither the ordinary Jew, nor even the scholar who guarded his food from every levitical defilement, regarded the Gentile's grave impurity as defiling him personally or his food; that impurity did not prevent the visit of the Jew to the house of the Gentile, nor the acceptance of an invitation to the table of the Gentile, nor the participation of the Gentile in a meal of the Jew.[164]

As to the levitical impurity of the food of the Jew touched by the Gentile, R. Ḥiyya b. Abba, when visiting Gebalene, found there Jewish women who were with child by Gentiles who were circumcised, but had not immersed, and Jews who drank the wine mixed by non-Jews, and Jews who ate lupine boiled by Gentiles. On learning these facts, R. Johanan said: Go and declare their children

[162] Synh. 104a.
[163] Tos. 'Abod. Zar. 4, 6; b. 'Abod. Zar. 8a; ARN 26, 41b. Cf. Derekh ereṣ Zuta III: תחלת טומאות פתח לעבודה זרה.
[164] Even of the Samaritans who, on account of the non-observance of the Pharisee rules of the monthly purification by their wives, were declared levitically defiling, Niddah 4, 1 says: ואין חייבין עליהן על ביאת מקדש ואין שורפין עליהן את התרומה מפני שטומאתן ספק; if a Jew put on the clothes of a Samaritan man or woman and therein entered the Temple he would not be guilty; nor would the heave-offering of the priest, if touched by the Samaritan, be burnt, because the impurity of the Samaritan is doubtful.

mamzers, their wine idolatrous libation wine, and their lupine prohibited for food as cooked by Gentiles.[165] Nothing is said about the assumed impurity of their food, though it was handled by those Gentiles throughout its preparation; evidently, not even at the time when the Gentile was considered affected with the grave levitical impurity of the man with an issue, did his touch and handling defile ordinary food, but only the priestly heave-offering. R. Johanan once illustrated the private relations between Jews and Gentiles by this instance.[166] A Jew and a Gentile are living in the same yard; when the Jew puts his pot upon the fire and the Gentile touches it, the pot is not impure; but when the Gentile puts his pot on and the Jew touches it, the Gentile says that it is defiled, and breaks it. The contrast shows unmistakably that the Gentile's touch of the vessel conveyed no levitical impurity to it. R. Haninah said to R. Simeon b. Lakish:[167] "When in Tyre, did you not see how a Jew and a Gentile put their pots upon one hearth, and no fear was entertained by the scholars?" Though the prohibited food of the Gentile was so close to the permitted food of the Jew, the scholars did not apprehend that the Gentile might put some of his into the pot of the Jew. Even more serious is the case in the parallel report[168] where R. Haninah, in answer to a question of R. Yishak b. Nahman, said: "Did you ever, when in Tyre, see how a Jew and a Gentile were partners in a pot of food, and no fear was entertained that the Gentile might have stirred the pot?" The action of the Gentile is regarded as cooking which makes the food prohibited for the Jew. "R. Johanan said:[169] Of an animal whose hair was singed off by the Gentile the Jew may eat even

[165] Abod. Zar. 59a; in Jer. 'Abod. Zar II 42a 3 he found those conditions in Tyre.
[166] Esther rab. V, 3 on 2, 3.
[167] 'Abod. Zar. 11b ff.
[168] Jer. 'Abod. Zar. I 39d 22.
[169] 'Abod. Zar. 38a.

of the top of its ear; Samuel said: If the Jew put the meat upon the coals, and the Gentile comes and turns it, it is permitted for eating. R. Johanan said: Food half done is permitted, though cooked by the Gentile. R. Johanan said: Whether the Gentile puts the meat on the fire and the Jew turns it, or vice versa, it is permitted; it is only prohibited as food boiled by the Gentile, if the beginning and the finishing is done by him. Again,[170] R. Johanan said: When the Jew and the Gentile are partners and share in a pot, the Jew may put it on the fire, and the Gentile may stir it." All these statements show that in the second and the third quarters of the third century in Galilee the handling of the food and the vessel of the Jew by the Gentile did not impart any levitical impurity to them. Before that time, a Baraita in 'AZ 38a permitted the same handling by the non-Jew:[171] "The Jew may put the meat upon the coals, and the Gentile may come and turn it until the Jew returns from the synagogue or the school, and the Jew need not apprehend anything; the Jewess may put the pot of food upon the hearth, and the Gentile woman may come and stir the food until the Jewess returns from the baths or the synagogue, and she need not apprehend anything." How would that be permitted, if the Gentile's impurity which was that of the man with an issue and affected all vessels and foods, was really transmitted to the pot and the meat of every Jew? Other discussions follow in the same context, about salted fish and roasted eggs, between Ḥizkiah and R. Johanan, and Ḥizkiah and bar Kappara on the one hand and R. Johanan on the other, and about vegetables and fruits; the only consideration is the Gentile's share in the cooking of the

---

[170] Jer. 'Abod. Zar. II 42a 23.

[171] תניא נמי הכי מניח ישראל בשר על גבי נחלים ובא נכרי ומהפך בו עד שיבא ישראל מבית הכנסת או מבית המדרש ואינו חושש. שופתת אשה קדירה על גבי כירה ובאת נכריה ומגיסה עד שתבא מבית המרחץ או מבית הכנסת ואינה חוששת.

food, and the date is the first quarter of the third century. And all this evidence, covering the time from 140 to 250 in Galilee, cogently proves that, while the Gentile's grave levitical defilement is not only affirmed by the teachers, but even generalized and raised, it had no force whatever to defile even by direct touch the strictest teacher or his food. And, undoubtedly, the strongest proof is the Baraita:[172] "Bread which the Gentile baked, but not in the presence of the Jew, and cheese which the Gentile curdled, but not in the presence of the Jew, is prohibited. Bread which the Jew baked, though the Gentile had kneaded the dough, and cheese which the Jew curdled, though the Gentile had prepared it, is permitted." In kneading the dough the Gentile communicates to it all the levitical impurity that might attach to his body; and as explicitly no objection is raised to his immediate contact with the dough and no levitical effect is attributed to it, there can be no doubt that the Gentile's grave defilement did not act on the Jew's ordinary food.[173]

8. *The levitical impurity of the Gentile's wine.*

The defiling touch of the Gentile, however, and his levitical impurity are specially noted in the Halakah in the wine handled by him, in the first instance in wine used for idolatrous libations. The Mishnah[174] contains a list of eighteen articles, mostly of food, and among them wine, which belong to the Gentile and are, on that account, prohibited to the Jew.[175] Various considerations lead to

[172] פת שאפאה גוי שלא במעמד ישראל וגבינה שהעמידה גוי שלא במעמד ישראל אסורה. פת שאפאה ישראל אף על פי שהגוי לשה וגבינה שהעמידה ישראל אף על פי שהגוי עובדה הרי זו מותרת. Tos. 'Abod. Zar, 4, 11.

[173] All the arguments advanced by Dr. Katzenelson in MGWJ 43, 1899, 196 ff. do not impair the force of the foregoing evidence.

[174] 'Abod. Zar. 2, 3. 4. 6.

[175] Derenbourg in MGWJ 30, 1881, 172 declared these to be identical with the eighteen things prohibited by the assembly of the Shammaites and the Hillelites about the year 65-66.

the conclusion that the list is R. Meir's. First, in 2, 4, which contains three disputes about various points, his name is mentioned three times.[176] In the context the Mishnah itself informs us that, a generation before R. Meir, his teachers, R. Ishmael and R. Joshua b. Ḥananiah, held without any qualification that the prohibition of the Gentile's cheese referred to its eating only, but did not include its other uses, as e. g. trading in it; and as those teachers mentioned no exception to the rule, the singling out of the Bithynian cheese belongs to the time of R. Meir. And it is most instructive that it was R. Jehudah b. Ilai who quoted the discussion between R. Ishmael and R. Joshua about the reason that had actuated the authorities in prohibiting the cheese of the Gentiles; so that the teacher who, in opposition to R. Meir, declared even the Bithynian cheese permitted for other uses was, as in a great number of other instances, R. Jehudah. R. Ishmael's reference to those who originally forbade the eating of the Gentile's cheese pointed to the authors of the eighteen prohibitions which, according to two reports, also included, among other articles of food, cheese.[177] As the author of the Mishnah himself who, as will be shown, was R. Meir, admits[178] that several of the articles in his list are only prohibited for eating, it is clear that the authors of the eighteen decrees only forbade the eating, but no other uses, of all the articles of food included by them. It was

---

[176] a.) נודות הנכרים וקנקניהן ויין של ישראל כנוס בהן אסורין ואיסורן איסור הנאה דברי רבי מאיר וחכמים אומרים אין איסורן איסור הנאה.
b.) החרצנים והזגים של נכרים אסורין ואיסורן איסור הנאה דברי רבי מאיר וחכמים אומרים לחין אסורין יבשין מותרין.
c.) המורייס וגבינות בית אונייקי של נכרים אסורין ואיסורן איסור הנאה דברי רבי מאיר וחכמים אומרים אין איסורן איסור הנאה.

[177] Jer. Shabb. I 3c 38: ואלו הן שגזרו, על פיתן של גוים ועל גבינתן ועל שמנן ועל בנותיהן, and in a statement cited by R. Meir's colleague R. Simeon b. Yoḥai in Jer. Shabb. I 3c 51: בו ביום גזרו על פתן ועל גבינתן ועל יינן ועל חומצן ועל צידן ועל מוריים.... In the Latinus Judith 10, 5, Judith, when she went to Holofernes' camp, took with her wine, oil, bread and cheese. See Chajes in Harkavy's *Festschrift*, Hebrew section, 110, who suggests that that book was written in the Maccabean period.

[178] 'Abod. Zar. 2, 6.

only R. Meir who extended the prohibition to other uses, but was opposed by his colleagues. This interpretation is also supported by the fact that the patriarch R. Jehudah II and his council permitted the Gentile's bread and oil altogether; for they could not have done so without meeting strong opposition, if the two articles of food had been prohibited not only for eating, but also for all other uses. On the other hand, the Mishnahs 2, 3. 6 give, unlike 2, 4, only the strict view about three articles, and only about one of them the opposing view of R. Simeon b. Gamaliel II;[179] he permits a hide which was pierced, while the animal was alive, if the cut is round, but prohibits it, when the cut is oblong. As the eating of the hide could hardly have been considered by the teachers, especially for Jews, the prohibition could only have referred to other uses; but, in any case, it is evident that the author of the strict view was a colleague of R. Simeon b. Gamaliel II, probably R. Meir. This is definitely borne out by the inclusion in the same list of Hadrianic pottery; for a Baraita[180] explicitly states that the prohibition was by R. Meir, the permission by the scholars, meaning R. Jehudah. The lenient view was supported by other scholars, but was ultimately rejected by R. Jehudah I and his colleagues, when they resolved to incorporate in the Mishnah the strict view only.[181] As to the author of the strict view

[179] 2, 3: אלו דברים של נכרים אסורין ואיסורן איסור הנאה, היין, והחומץ של נכרים שהיה מתחלתו יין, וחרס הדרייני ועורות לבובין, רבן שמעון בן גמליאל אומר בזמן שהקרע שלו עגול אסור משוך מותר.
[180] Jer. 'Abod. Zar. II 41b 25: תני חרס אדרייני אסור ואיסורו איסור הנייה. Jer. 'Orlah III, 63a 14. דברי רבי מאיר וחכמים אומרים אין איסורו איסור הנייה
[181] Tos. 'Abod. Zar. 4, 8 states: הכבשין והשלקות של גוים שדרכן לתת בהן יין וחומץ וחרס הדרייני אסורין איסור הנאה. זיתים השלחין הנסכרין על פתחי מרחצאות אסורין באכילה ומותרין בהנאה ורבי יוסי אוסרן בהנאה מפני שוולפין עליהן חומץ כדי שיהו חולצין את גרעיניהן. Here an anonymous teacher prohibits all uses of the articles permitted in 'Abod. Zar. 2, 6 for use, and R. Jose forbids the use of peeled olives. Was R. Meir the author of the anonymous list which prohibits for all uses foods preserved by pressing or boiling, and did the redactor of Mishnah 2, 6 ignore R. Meir's view on those foods in favor of another opinion, perhaps that of R. Simeon b. Yoḥai with whose list of the eighteen prohibitions the several species of foods agree in detail in 2, 6?

about the Gentile's wine and vinegar, there is no direct evidence that it was R. Meir; but the explicit statement about the Hadrianic pottery, and the opposition of R. Simeon b. Gamaliel II about the pierced hide make R. Meir's authorship of the whole list very probable.[182] But in the complete prohibition of the Gentile's wine he was anticipated by R. Jehudah b. Bethera who gave expression to the same strict view a generation before R. Meir.[183] And the same was the case with the Gentile's skin-bottles and jugs used for wine, which were forbidden, at the latest, about the year 120 C. E. For a Baraita states:[184] "The wine of the Jew in the Gentile's barrels or his skin-bottles is prohibited for drinking, but permitted for other uses; Simeon b. Goda gave evidence before R. Gamaliel's son that R. Gamaliel had drunk such wine in 'Akko, but the teachers did not accept his view." Another Baraita states: "The wine of the Jew in the Gentile's skin-bottles is prohibited for drinking, but permitted for other uses; Simeon b. Gode'a gave evidence before R. Gamaliel's son that R. Gamaliel had drunk such wine in 'Akko, and the teachers accepted his view."[185] The statement that R. Gamaliel drank such wine in 'Akko points to Gamaliel II who once stayed in that town.[186] In its first, anonymous part, the Baraita represents the view held in the Mishnah by R. Meir's opponents, the scholars, meaning R. Jehudah b. Ilai, who prohibited only the drinking of such wine,

---

[182] In the Tos. quoted in note 181, R. Meir's colleague, R. Jose, holds that the Gentile's vinegar is prohibited for all uses; against that R. Simeon b. Yoḥai might have quoted the list of the eighteen prohibitions to show that they referred to eating only, and to no other uses.

[183] 'Abod. Zar. 30b ff.: סתם יינם אסור בהנאה, see below n. 188.

[184] 'Abod. Zar. 32a: מיתיבי הדרדורין והרוקבאות של נכרים ויין של ישראל כנוס בהן אסור בשתייה ומותר בהנאה. העיד שמעון בן נודא לפני בנו של רבן גמליאל על רבן גמליאל ששתה ממנו בעכו ולא הודו לו... ורמינהו יין הבא ברוקבאות של נכרים אסור בשתייה ומותר בהנאה, העיד שמעון בן נודע לפני בנו של רבן גמליאל על רבן גמליאל ששתה ממנו בעכו והודו לו.

[185] Different is the account in Tos. 'Abod. Zar. 4, 9: שאמר משום רבן גמליאל הזקן שמותר בשתייה.

[186] 'Abod. Zar. 3, 4.

while R. Gamaliel went so far as to permit it altogether. Though, evidently, no teacher in the school of Usha accepted that lenient view, as, when reported to them by Simeon b. Goda, it appeared, according to one report, unacceptable, the account is sufficient to prove that R. Gamaliel knew nothing of a prohibition in which all uses of the Gentile's wine were included. In fact, the eighteen decrees did not include the wine vessels of the Gentiles, and their prohibition, naturally of use only, seems to have been mentioned first by R. Joshua b. Kaposai;[186a] but even he does not say whether the wine of the Jew, if poured into the Gentile's vessel, would be forbidden.[187]

But the strictest view ever expressed about the character of the Gentile's wine is that of R. Jehudah b. Bethera:[188] "R. Assi in the name of R. Johanan in the name of R. Jehudah b. Bethera said: The wine offered as a libation to an idol is prohibited for all uses, and the volume of an olive of it defiles as gravely as a dead insect; the ordinary wine of the Gentile is prohibited for all uses, and the volume of a quarter of a Log of it defiles with the defile-

---

[186]a Tos. 'Abod. Zar. 4, 10: נודות של גוים רבן שמעון בן גמליאל אומר משום רבי יהושע בן קפוסאי אין עושין אותן אלא שטיחין לבהמה. He lived before 120 in Judea, where he is found in the company of R. Gamaliel II and Akylas in Ashkelon, Tos. Mikv. 6, 3. In 'Abod. Zar. 32a he prohibits to make covers for an ass from the skin-bottles of the Gentiles.

[187] To the time before 135 refers Jer. 'Abod. Zar. II 41b 58; b. 34a: R. Abba said: When R. Akiba was in Zifrin, he was asked how the jugs of the Gentiles could be made usable for the Jews. In his answer he started from the rule that unpitched vessels of the Gentiles were permitted for use; he means, naturally, not new, but used vessels, as he was asked about such, so that the gradual peeling off of the pitch by wear, as his argument seems to suggest, would remove the traces of the Gentile's prohibited wine. In any case, generally it was prohibited to use the Gentile's wine vessels. On his return to Judea, his colleagues told him that his remedy would be of no avail, as the pitch would not prevent the infiltration of the prohibited wine into the walls of the vessel. So, also the scholars of Judea before 135 held the view that the wine vessels of the Gentile must not be used by the Jew; but what they thought of the wine of the Jew which was put into the Gentile's used wine vessel is not stated.

[188] 'Abod. Zar. 30b ff.: אמר רבי אסי אמר רבי יוחנן משום רבי יהודה בן בתירא שלשה יינות הן, יין נסך אסור בהנאה ומטמא טומאה חמורה בכזית, סתם יינם אסור בהנאה ומטמא טומאת משקין ברביעית, הפקיד יינו אצל נכרי אסור בשתייה ומותר בהנאה. Jer. II, 41b 7: שראה גוי שלש יינות הן, אתא רבי אבהו בשם רבי יוחנן מנסכו ודאי דעבודה זרה מטמא טומאה חמורה כשרץ, סתם יינו של גוי אסור ואינו מטמא, הפקידו אצלו בחותם אחד אסור בשתיה ומותר בהנאה.

ment of liquids."[189] The character of the idolatrous libation also engaged the same teacher's attention in another question:[190] "If the Gentile offered the wine of the Jew as a libation, but not before an idol, the wine is prohibited; R. Jehudah b. Baba and R. Jehudah b. Bethera declare it permitted on two grounds, first, because wine can only be made a libation before an idol, and secondly, because the Jew can say to the Gentile: It is not in your power to make my wine prohibited for me against my will." Both teachers voice the lenient view, because the libation is not effective. On the other hand, the defiling nature ascribed by R. Jehudah b. Bethera to the ordinary wine of the Gentile has, to my knowledge, no parallel in the rabbinic law before the year 70.[191] Of course, everything connected with idolatry was explicitly prohibited for use already in Deut. 7, 25. 26; 13, 16-18, and the rabbis were in full agreement about that prohibition. So R. Akiba said:[192] "Flesh that is on the way to the idol is permitted,

[189] In Jer. the name of the author of the statement was, by mistake, left out, and the ordinary wine does not defile at all, and the wine deposited by the Jew with the Gentile was closed with one seal; but compare Tos. Zabim 5, 8.

[190] Baraita 'Abod. Zar. 59b: תניא נכרי שניסך יינו של ישראל שלא בפני עבודה זרה אסור ורבי יהודה בן בבא ורבי יהודה בן בתירא מתירין משום שני דברים, אחד שאין מנסכין יין אלא בפני עבודה זרה ואחד שאומר לו לא כל הימנך שתאסר ייני לאונסי. That is why Tos. Zabim. 5, 8: יין שראה את הגוי שהוא מנסכו אם יש בו כזית מטמאין טומאה חמורה ואם לאו אין מטמאין אלא טומאת משקין. שאר יינו של גוי אף על פי שאסור משום יין נסך אין טמא אלא טומאת משקה בלבד, which is R. Jehudah b. Bethera's statement about the Gentile's wine, lays special stress on the condition that the Jew saw how the Gentile offered his wine as a libation to his god; and Jer. has the same.

[191] Only ARN 8, 19a bottom; 2 ARN 19, 21a top, and כלאים in Tos. Kil'ay. 2, 16 seem to offer strange parallels: ישראל שקיים כלאים בתוך שדהו אין הכהנים נכנסים לתוך שדהו אלא רואין אותה כציון בית הקברות, into the field of a Jew where two kinds of seed are tolerated by the owner, the priests must not enter, but have to treat it as the mark of a burial ground. It is true, David Pardo, against the clear meaning of the wording, explains לתוכה to refer to the threshing floor from which the priests are about to take their heave-offering: they should not go there, as they would appear to support sinners. Another commentator deletes הכהנים as not suitable in the context; see Schwarz, Tosefta זרעים, p. 81b, note 60, whose interpretation is open to question. Another instance is the levitical defilement of the hands by the פגול ונותר in Pesaḥ. 10, 9, and flesh purchased in Jerusalem for the equivalent of the second tithe, Tos. Ma'aser sheni 1, 9; Tos. Nidd. 9, 18.

[192] 'Abod. Zar. 2, 3; Tos. Ḥullin 2, 20: בשר הנכנס לעבודה זרה מותר והיוצא אסור מפני שהוא כזבחי מתים דברי רבי עקיבא.

but that which comes out from it is forbidden, because it is like the sacrifices of the dead, Ps. 106,28." And also his master and colleague, R. Joshua b. Ḥananiah, as well as R. Ishmael shared that view, as is evident from R. Jehudah b. Ilai's account of their discussion about the reason of the prohibition of the Gentile's cheese.[193] "When once on the way, R. Ishmael asked R. Joshua, why the authorities had forbidden the Gentiles' cheese, and R. Joshua replied: Because it is curdled with the maw of animals not slaughtered; R. Ishmael retorted: The maw of the burnt-offering was more strictly forbidden than that of the animal not properly slaughtered, and still a priest who could stand it was permitted to suck it raw? R. Joshua then said: Because cheese is curdled with the maw of calves offered to idols; but R. Ishmael rejoined: Why then have they not forbidden the Gentiles' cheese for all uses, and not merely for eating?" But in no part of the Bible has a defiling force been ascribed even to the idol itself, nor to anything offered to it as a sacrifice; and yet, R. Jehudah b. Bethera's view was, to some extent, shared by several contemporary rabbis.

9. *The levitical impurity of idols and idolatrous sacrifices after the year 70.*

First, R. Akiba defines the degree of the defilement of the idol itself,[194] and proves that it defiles by being carried; and his object might have been to discourage some Jews from carrying in their pockets idolatrous figures, acquired perhaps for their trade in fine metals, or as works of art. He ascribes the same impurity to the building materials

---

[193] 'Abod. Zar. 2, 5, see above p. 58.
[194] Shabb. 9, 1: אמר רבי עקיבא מנין לעבודה זרה שמטמאה במשא כנדה שנאמר, תזרם כמו דוה צא תאמר לו מה נדה מטמאה במשא אף עבודה זרה מטמאה במשא.

of the idol's temple,[195] and another to the vessels and the furniture used in the worship of the idol.[196] Both teachers presuppose in their dispute that idols defile, and only differ about the degree of the impurity ascribed to them. R. Akiba's opponent was undoubtedly R. Jehudah b. Bethera; for in his view by which he opposed that of R. Akiba, he attributes the same degree of defilement to the idols, and in the same words as in his other statement, to the idolatrous libation wine. In addition, he holds unusually strict views about the defiling force of the sacrifices offered to the idols, of which wine was one,[197] as he infers from Psalm 106, 28 where idols are designated as dead beings, that the offerings brought to them are defiling to the same extent as a corpse, defiling everybody and everything that are with them under one roof, and for a whole week.[198] On that declaration is based the rule[198a]

[195] 'Abod. Zar. 3, 6: אבניו עציו ועפרו מטמאין כשרץ שנאמר שקץ תשקצנו, רבי עקיבא אומר כנדה שנאמר תזרם כמו דוה, מה נדה מטמאה במשא אף עבודה זרה מטמאה במשא.

[196] Shabb. 83a Baraita: מתיבי עבודה זרה כשרץ ומטמשיה כשרץ, רבי עקיבא Tos. Zabim. 5, 6: עבודה זרה כשרץ. אומר עבודה זרה כנדה ומטמשיה כשרץ ומטמשיה כשרץ שנאמר שקץ תשקצנו, רבי עקיבא אומר כנדה שנאמר תזרם כמו דוה תאמר לו מה נדה מטמאה במשא אף עבודה זרה מטמאה במשא. צא. In Jer. 'Abod. Zar. III 43a 44 the biblical basis is different: כתיב תועבה בנידה וכתיב תועבה בשרצים וכתיב תועבה בעבודה זרה, בנידה כתיב כי כל אשר יעשה מכל התועבות, בשרצים לא תאכל כל תועבה, בעבודה זרה ולא תביא תועבה אל ביתך, אבל איני יודע לאיזה דבר הוקשה, רבי עקיבה אומר לתועבה הנידה הוקשה מה הנידה מטמאה במשא אף עבודה זרה מטמאה במשא ורבנן אמרי לתועבה שבשרצים הוקשה מה השרץ מטמא בהיסט אף עבודה זרה מטמאה בהיסט... Maimonides in ה' 6, 1 אבות הטומאה says that the levitical impurity of the idol is a post-biblical institution, but is indicated in Gen. 35, 2; cf. Halevy, דורות הראשונים Ic, 454b, and Rashi on Gen. 35, 2, and against it Targum Jonathan, ibn Ezra and Naḥmani. Cf. also Midr. Tanna'im Deut. 12, 3, p. 60: מטמא כשרץ שנאמר שקץ תשקצנו, רבי עקיבא אומר כנדה שנאמר תזרם כמו דוה וגו' מטמא באהל שנאמר ויצמדו לבעל פעור וגו'.

[197] Baraita 'Abod. Zar. 32b: תניא רבי יהודה בן בתירא אומר מנין לתקרובת עבודה זרה שמטמאה באהל שנאמר ויצמדו לבעל פעור ויאכלו זבחי מתים מה מת מטמא באהל אף תקרובת עבודה זרה מטמאה באהל. In the parallel in Jer. III 43a 54 the name of the author of the statement has by mistake been left out after the name of the tradent, R. Johanan, in the statement about the idolatrous wine libation. Cf. Wars 2, 14, 5, 289.

[198] It was, on religious grounds, forbidden to enter a heathen temple; so R. Tarfon says in Baraita Shabb. 116a; Tos. 13, 5; Jer. XVI 15c 54: He who flees from a murderer or a serpent should rather flee into a temple of idolatry than into the house of a Gnostic, Min.

[198a] Tos. 'Abod. Zar. 6, 3; Tos. Zabim 5, 7 (cf. Tos. 'Abod. Zar. 6, 2; Jer. III 43a 58): המכנים ראשו ורובו לבית עבודה זרה טמא, כלי חרס שהכניס אוירו לבית עבודה זרה טמא, הספסלין והקתדראות שהכניס רובן לבית עבודה זרה טמאין.

that if a Jew enters with his head and only the greater part of his body into an idolatrous temple, he is defiled; and it is undoubtedly remarkable that such defilement is contracted by the mere fact of stepping into the building.[199] "If the Jew devotes his house to idolatry, the whole house defiles by being entered, and he who is standing in it is as if he were standing in an idolatrous temple; if the house of the Jew is close to the idol, the whole house defiles by being entered, etc." The technical terms as well as the extraordinary strictness of the law were taken over from the special rules laid down in Lev. 14, 46 about the house infected with leprosy and the house of the leper.[200] Consequently, the idol itself is given the same degree of defiling force as the leprosy of the house and the leper, and, as will presently be shown, the corpse.

In dealing with the Asherah, the Mishnah[201] enjoins: "The Jew must not sit in the shadow cast by that tree, but if he did sit there, he is not impure; he must not pass under that tree, and if he did pass, he is impure." No reason is given, though from the preceding statements about the defiling force of idols it would follow that either the tree itself was worshipped and was, consequently,

[199] Tos. 'Abod. Zar. 6, 2: המיחד ביתו לעבודה זרה כולו טמא בביאה והעומד בתוכו כאלו עומד בתוך עבודה זרה... הסמוך ביתו לעבודה זרה כולו טמא בביאה, סככו לו הן אין כולו טמא בביאה... בנאוהו הן אין כולו טמא בביאה...
[200] Kelim 1, 4: למעלה מן הובה מצורע שהוא מטמא בביאה... חמור מכולם המכניס ראשו ורובו; Tos. Nega'im 7, 7; הטת שהוא מטמא באהל שאין כולם מטמאין לבית המנוגע טמא, כלי חרס שהכניס אוירו לבית המנוגע טמא, הספסלין והקתדראות שהכניס רובן לבית המנוגע טמאים is verbally identical with Tos. Zabim 5, 7; Tos. 'Abod. Zar. 6, 3. A strange application of an even stricter law to the leprous house is enunciated by R. Meir in Tos. Nega'im 7, 13: ובית המנוגע כאוהל המת דברי רבי מאיר, the house defiles in the same way as the tent containing a corpse (the Tos. corresponds to Mishnah Neg. 13, 12 where, however, that statement of R. Meir is missing). Is this the source of the similar defiling force of the heathen temple? On the Baraita Pesaḥ. 93a; Tos. 8, 1 (הפסח) תנו רבנן אלו שעושין את השני הזבין וחזבות המצורעין והמצורעות ונדות ובועלי נדות והיולדות השוגגין והאנוסין והמזידין וטמא ושהיה בדרך רחוקה. Jer. Pesaḥ. IX 36c 57, cf. Jer. Shabb. IX 11d 14, has: טומאת עבודה זרה עשו אותה כטמא זיבה וטמא צרעת: if a person has been defiled through an idol, he is not admitted to the Paschal meal, but has to bring the sacrifice a month later just like the leper. Cf. R. Alexander's Haggadah in Threni rab. Prooem. 21.
[201] 'Abod. Zar. 3, 8.

an idol, or an idol was placed under its branches, in which case the same rule applied to it as to a heathen temple. R. José the Galilean said[202] that God revealed himself to Moses in a thorn-bush, because that bush was pure, as the natives did not worship it as an idol. It would indicate that R. José knew in his native country, Galilee, or in Judea where he had attended the schools of Lydda, first as a disciple, and later as a teacher, before 135 C. E., many an instance of the worship of holy trees.[203] R. Simeon b. Yoḥai, the Galilean, of the middle of the second century, did not recognize any idolatrous tree as Asherah, unless it was worshipped itself, while his opponent made it dependent on the presence of an idol under the tree. There was in Sidon a tree which was worshipped; when a heap (of stones) was noticed under the tree and it was examined at R. Simeon's suggestion, a figure was found in it, and he declared that the tree was permitted, as evidently not the tree, but the figure was worshipped.[204] An anonymous Baraita states[205] that he who goes under the Asherah is like him who enters the temple of an idol. The foliage forms over the figure worshipped a roof, so that he is defiled by the idol in exactly the same way as if there were under the tree a human corpse or a grave; of such the Baraita says:[206] "If a Samaritan states that there is no grave under the tree that forms a cover by its overhanging

---

[202] Mekilta R. Simeon p. 2 Midrash haGadol on Exodus, ed. Hoffmann, p. 24: רבי יוסי והגלילי אומר מפני מה נגלה הקב"ה משמי מרום והיה מדבר עם משה מתוך הסנה, מפני שהוא טהור ואין אומות העולם עושין אותו עבודה זרה.

[203] Fifty years later R. Simeon b. Eleazar in Tos. 'Abod. Zar. 6. 8 stated that there were three in Palestine: חרוב שבכפר קסם ושבכפר פגשה שקמה שבראנו ושבכרמל. As four are enumerated, should we read שבכרמל?

[204] 'Abod. Zar. 3, 7: איזוהי אשרה כל שיש תחתיה עבודה זרה, רבי שמעון אומר כל שעובדין אותה, ומעשה בצידון באילן שהיו עובדין אותו ומצאו תחתיו גל, אמר להם רבי שמעון בדקו את הגל הזה ובדקוהו ומצאו בו צורה אמר להן הואיל ולצורה הן עובדין נתיר להן את האילן.

[205] Tos. 'Abod. Zar. 6, 8: הנכנס תחתיו כנכנס לבית עבודה זרה ואם היתה דרך הרבים מפסקתה הרי זו מותרת.

[206] Niddah 57a bottom; Tos. 6, 16: אילן שהוא מיסך על הארץ נאמן לומר אין תחתיו קבר לפי שאינו מעיד אלא על גופו של קבר. אלו הן השכבות אילן שהוא מיסך על הארץ Ohal. 18, 2; Tos. 9, 3.

boughs he is relied upon, as his testimony refers to the grave itself" (a biblical law which he observes). The principle underlying R. Jehudah b. Bethera's declaration that the offering brought to the idol defiles the person and the things that are with it under the same roof,[207] was extended to the idol itself, or perhaps was in this case the primary, and the sacrifice the extension. But it is not evident how old the principle itself is, and when it was for the first time applied by any teacher to practical life.

It is an interesting coincidence that the *Philosophoumena*, a work composed by a Christian writer of the third century, stated[208] that pious Jews are so shy of figures that they would not even pass under a gate over which statues have been placed. And Hippolytus[209] reports of the Zealots that they carried no coins on them, nor even looked at coins, because there was a figure on them; and none entered a town by a gate over which a statue was standing, because they considered it to be forbidden to walk in the shadow of a figure. In the case of the Zealots, that attitude might originally have been the outcome of their great patriotism and their hatred of Rome. But when it was formulated as a prohibition and extended to the passing under a Roman gate or in the shadow of human figures, the dictate of patriotism was changed into a religious commandment; and the sentiments of piety and strict observance might at an early date have invited the support of the levitical impurity to mark the moral abhorrence by the levitical abstention. So the figure of the Roman emperor was to the Zealot, who was, at the same time, an observant Pharisee, not only idolatrous, but also levi-

[207] Baraita 'Abod. Zar. 48b.
[208] IX 26, see Solomon Reinach in Revue des Etudes Juives 20, 1890, Actes et Conférences p. lxxxix.
[209] Refutatio haeres. IX 26; see Kohler in Harkavy's *Festschrift*, p. 8ff.

tically defiling. When R. Jehudah b. Ilai interpreted[210] Lev. 19, 4, 'Turn ye not unto the idols,' to prohibit even to look at idols, it was only a further and consistent step in the progressive injunction to abhor idols. It is reported:[211] "When בי ינאי מלכה[212] was destroyed, some Gentiles came and set up there a pillar of Hermes; later on, other non-Jews who did not worship Mercury went there, took those stones, and paved with them roads and streets. Some rabbis refrained from walking on that pavement, others did not refrain; R. Johanan said: Since R. Menaḥem b. Simai, the holy man, walked on those stones, why should I refrain? R. Menaḥem never looked at the figure on a coin." As R. Ḥiyya b. Joseph explained the strict view, as a gift offered to Mercury the stones never lose their idolatrous character again; by the other teachers they were not regarded as an offering at all. The question was discussed before the beginning of the third century, as a Baraita, quoted in the discussion,[213] proves; and it supports the lenient view. R. Menaḥem, though strict in matters of looking at the figure of the emperor on a coin,[214] relied on the Baraita.

Such holiness on the point of figures was not, as in the case of the Zealots, actuated by patriotism, but by religious considerations. Immediately after the discussion about the prohibition to stay in the shadow of the Asherah, several incidents are reported.[215] "Gamaliel Zuga, and R. Simeon b. Lakish, leaning on him, came to a figure; when the former asked the master, whether they should

[210] Sifra Lev. 19, 4, 87a §10; Shabb. 149a bottom; Jer. 'Abod. Zar. III 42c 1: אל תפנו אל האלילים... רבי יהודה אומר אל תפנה לראותן.
[211] 'Abod. Zar. 50a.
[212] See S. Klein, *Palaestina-Studien* I, 1923, 2, 8.
[213] 'Abod. Zar. 50a ff.; Tos. 6, 14: נכרי שהביא אבנים מן המרקוליס וחיפה בהן דרכים וסרטיאות מותרות, ישראל שהביא אבנים מן המרקוליס וחיפה בהן דרכים וסרטיאות אסורות.
[214] Jer. 'Abod. Zar. III 42c 1 ff.; b. Pesaḥ. 104a; Büchler, *Types*, 49, 3.
[215] Jer. 'Abod. Zar. III 43b 70 ff.

pass before it, he said: Pass before it, and blind its eyes. R. Yiṣḥaḳ b. Mathnah and R. Johanan, leaning on him, came to the figure of a Bulé;[216] when the former asked the master whether they should pass before it, he said: Pass before it, and blind its eyes. R. Jacob b. Idi and R. Joshua b. Levi, leaning on him, came to the figure אדורי[217a]; when the former asked the master whether they should pass before it, he said: Nahum, the most holy man, passed, and you should not pass? Pass before it, and blind its eyes." In another context the following is reported:[217] "R. Johanan, leaning on R. Jacob b. Idi, noticed that R. Eleazar b. P'dath was hiding himself from him, and he expressed to his disciple his annoyance at R. Eleazar's deliberate slight. In walking on, they passed by a school, and R. Jacob remarked that there R. Meir once expounded. In continuing their walk, they came to a figure,[218] and R. Jacob asked the master whether they might pass before the idol אדורי? R. Johanan answered: Why should you pay it respect by heeding it at all? Pass before it, and blind its eyes. To this R. Jacob remarked: So R. Eleazar acted rightly in not passing before you."[219] As in the instances of the coins and the pavement, so in this of the idolatrous figures, Nahum b. Simai, as also the context shows, had to consider religious grounds only which went

[216] The incident occurred in Tiberias, see Bacher, *Agada der pal. Amoräer* III, 100 4; Klein in הצופה מארץ הגר IV, 1914, 57. 62. 63, 1, and MGWJ 64, 1920, 125. On the other hand, it might be doubtful whether the incident with R. Eleazar happened in Sepphoris or Tiberias; but R. Meir's school to which R. Jacob referred was in Tiberias, Jer. Ḥagigah II 77b 24, cf. Sifre Zuta Num. 19, 10, 133 Horovitz; Jer. Sotah I 16d 45. Consequently, the figures mentioned stood in the streets of Tiberias.

[217] Jer. Berak. II 4b 30.

[218] So in the parallel in Midr. Samuel 19, 4, 52a; cf. Ginzberg, *Yerushalmi Fragments*, p. 6. 204, and Buber's note on Midr. Samuel, p. 52a, 17. The expression: blind its eyes, is explained by Frankel to mean: close your eyes and ignore it, as if it did not exist; so also Jastrow, *Dictionary*, p. 999b. The same is found again in Rosh haShan. 24b where Samuel told R. Jehudah who had a figure in his signet: Blind its eyes, and Rashi explains it: spoil its shape. In 'Abod. Zar. 30a Rabbah b. R. Huna was carrying wine in a boat; on seeing a serpent approaching, he said to his attendant: Blind its eyes; the man took some water and poured it upon the serpent, and it withdrew.

[219] The meaning of the last remark is not clear to me, as the idol was regarded by the teachers as useless and unworthy of attention.

even beyond the prohibitions in the Mishnah; as might be assumed, he not only avoided the contraction of the levitical impurity arising out of the passing under idols, but would not even look at them. If, in this instance, he passed before the figure, there was no occasion for his contracting the defilement incidental to idols. But his lenient attitude in this instance in no way weakens the explicit evidence of the Mishnah, Baraita and Tosefta that passing under an idol or entering a heathen temple defiled levitically.[220]

10. *The levitical impurity of all images before the year 70.*

The only question that remains to be answered is whether the levitical impurity ascribed by R. Jehudah b. Bethera to idols and their temples and sacrifices represents an earlier opinion, or perhaps even an institution of Temple times. From various passages in the Bible it is clear that, before the conquest by the Israelites, the land of Canaan was, in the opinion of the biblical writers, thoroughly impure on account of the idolatry of the inhabitants and their immorality. So Ezra 9, 11 expresses that judgment in strong terms: "The land, unto which ye go to possess it, is an unclean land through the uncleanness of the peoples of the lands, through their abominations, wherewith they have filled it from one end to another in their filthiness."[221] If the Israelites were to practise these abominations, their deeds would have the same effect, and defile the land;[222] and the prophets had, unfortunately, occasion for the complaint that their contemporaries actually defiled the land

---

[220] Cf. also 'Abod. Zar. 17a bottom: When once R. Ḥaninah and R. Jonathan were on the road, they came to two paths one of which opened toward the entrance of a heathen temple, and the other to that of an immoral house. One of the teachers said: Let us go to the entrance of the heathen temple, for the evil spirit of idolatry is dead. No levitical impurity is meant here, as they did not enter the temple.

[221] Cf. Lev. 18, 24-30.

[222] Lev. 18, 24. 28. 30; Deut. 24, 4; cf. Lev. 20, 3; Num. 35, 33. 34; Deut. 21, 23.

with their idolatry.[223] After the exile the spirit of idolatry no longer troubled the community, and if any revivals recurred,[224] Ezra's determined dissolution of the mixed marriages removed the dangerous missionaries of heathen cults from Judea; for Malachi 2, 11, which was spoken before that measure, saw in the foreign women daughters of a strange god. The consistent religious separation of the community from its non-Jewish neighbors cleared away every vestige of idolatry, and there seems to have been no cause for anxiety lest the country might be again defiled by any form of heathen worship. The foundation of Hellenistic cities by Alexander the Great and his successors brought no new danger to the religious life of the Jews, as those towns, just like those on the coast of Philistia, lay in heathen territory. Only when Antiochos IV Epiphanes desecrated the Temple in Jerusalem, and set up altars in its streets and in the towns of Judea, was the confidence and security of the religious leaders shaken and their fear roused, as the land was again defiled by heathen altars and idolatrous sacrifices. The countermeasures of Mattathias and his sons, as reported in I Macc., clearly indicate their view of the effect of the altars on the land. "And Mattathias and his friends went round about, and pulled down the altars, and they circumcised by force the children that were uncircumcised";[225] and already Dr. Rawlinson remarks on that action: "An idolatrous altar was a pollution to the holy land." And it was neither barbarity nor intolerance, when "Judas turned aside to Azotus, to the land of the Philistines, and pulled down their altars, and burned the carved images of their gods, and took the spoil of their cities, and returned into the land of Judah.[226] And Jonathan burned Azotus, and

[223] Jer. 3, 1. 2. 9; 2, 7; Ezek. 36, 17. 18; 37, 23.
[224] Is. 65 and 66.5
[225] I Macc. 2, 45.
[226] I Macc. 5, 68.

the cities round about it, and took their spoils; and the temple of Dagon, and them that fled into it, he burned with fire."[227]

It was only a natural reaction that, after that experience of heathen desecration, the religious leaders of the Jews should have watched even more intently over the purity of the Temple and its sanctity and the purity of the country from idolatry. They knew that the prophets had declared that the images of gods set up in the Temple defiled it,[228] and now the image placed there by Antiochos, and the sacrifices brought upon the idolatrous altar, had polluted the sanctuary. The Jews were now taught rather to give up their lives than allow any idol, or even the image of a man, to be set up in the Temple; and that accounts for their determined and unanimous attitude, and their readiness to sacrifice their lives, when Caligula ordered Petronius to place the emperor's figure in the sanctuary in Jerusalem. But the prohibition to set up there the image of a god or of a man to be worshipped was extended to more harmless figures, even if they were not connected with any form of worship at all. But there is no information extant as to whether the strong opposition against all images was the immediate outcome of the Maccabean cleansing of the Temple and the country from the pollution of idolatry. Shortly before Herod's death, two scholars of Jerusalem impressed it as a sacred duty upon their disciples to break down the golden eagle fixed by the king over the eastern gate of the Temple, and, if necessary, to give their lives for the vindication of the law of the fathers which was violated by the king, "for it was unlawful that there should be in the Temple images, figures, or similar

---

[227] I Macc. 10, 84; 11, 4. In II Macc. 12, 26 Judas attacked Carnaim and the temple of Atergatis; *Antiquit.* 12, 8, 4, 344.
[228] Jer. 7, 30; 32, 34; Ezek. 5, 11.

representations of any animal whatsoever."[229] It is possible that this extension of the law only originated under the Roman rule in Palestine to prevent the setting up of the figure of any Roman conqueror or ruler, or of Roman emblems, on the Temple Mount; or perhaps it was only passed under Herod whose many buildings of a purely heathen character outside his country filled the teachers with the fear lest he might plan the erection of similar buildings and statues in Jerusalem.

In the case of the Roman eagle to which Jewish patriotism objected not less than religious feeling, the Temple was concerned, and to some extent, it accounts for the prohibition. But the same revulsion was again revealed in the days of Herod in connection with trophies in the theatre, erected by the king in Jerusalem, and they were very strongly resented by the Jews as contrary to the law. Josephus reports: "But above all the rest, the trophies gave most annoyance to the Jews; for as they thought them to be images, enclosed within the armor that hung round about them, they were sorely displeased at them, because it was not the custom of their country to pay honor to such images.[230] They cried out with one accord, out of their great uneasiness at the offences of which they thought he had been guilty, that although they should think of bearing all the rest, yet would they never bear images of men in their city, meaning the trophies, as it was contrary to the laws of their country."[231] Here it is in the city of Jerusalem where no such images must be tolerated according to the Jewish law. And we find that in a similar case and in identical circumstances the Jews of Jerusalem and of Judea in a body, were just as ready to sacrifice their lives, when neither the Temple

[229] *Wars* I, 33, 2, 650; *Antiquit.* 17, 6, 2, 151.
[230] *Antiquit.* 15, 8, 1, 276.
[231] *Antiquit.* 15, 8, 2, 276. 277; Schürer, *Geschichte* II 90.

nor the Temple Mount, nor anythng connected with its religious life was in question, but again the city of Jerusalem. When Pilate, the governor of Judea, had secretly, at night, a number of the emperor's images, wrapped signa, brought into his temporary residence in Herod's palace in Jerusalem, the Jews not only protested and begged, but fell down before him in vast numbers, exposed their necks bare, and cried out that they were sooner ready to be slain than that their law should be transgressed; for their laws did not permit any kind of image to be brought into the city.[232] Undoubtedly, patriotism and the hatred against the tyrannical rule of the Romans helped to confirm the Jews in their determined resistance; but how could they refer the Procurator to any law so definitely, and where was the prohibition to be found that demanded their lives in such an emergency? And yet, there can be no doubt that the teachers who guided them on that religious rule, impressed upon them the duty to sacrifice their lives, in unbending obedience to a definite law which they could have pointed out to the governor, if he had asked for it, though the Torah forbade figures only in connection with the worship of God.[233] As in both cases, that of the trophies and the other of the signa, the city of Jerusalem was to be protected from the coming in of the images of human beings, some verse in the Bible referring to the purity of Jerusalem and its sanctity must have been interpreted to that effect.

When Vitellius, the legate of Syria, was marching with his legions against Aretas, the king of the Arabs, to Petra in the year 37 C. E., and intended to pass from Ptolemais through Judea, the leaders of the Jews went to meet him, and begged him to change his direction, as the Jews

---

[232] *Wars* 2, 9, 2, 169 ff.; *Antiquit.* 18, 3, 1, 55; described by Philo, *Legatio and Caium* 38.
[233] Exod. 20, 4. ff.; Deut. 5, 8; Lev. 26, 1; Deut. 4, 16-19.

were not permitted by their law to allow the images on the standards to be carried through their country.[234] Here the prohibition referred to the whole of Judea; and it is fairly clear that it was to be kept free from even the remotest suggestion of idolatry. The teachers found it stated in Ezek. 36, 17. 18 that Palestine's soil had, in the days of the prophet, been defiled by bloodshed and idolatry, and that such impurity had brought the exile; when God will again gather Israel and bring it to its land, the impurity of idolatry will be purged away.[235] As, accordingly, the restoration of the people depended on the purity of the soil of the country, the teachers laid the greatest stress on keeping away not only the images of idols, but also those of all men; and, especially, since the advent of the Romans, and even more so, since the institution of emperor worship, their care extended to all possible manifestations of idolatrous thought which might pollute the soil of Judea. The special stress laid on Jerusalem in that connection suggests that the peculiar sanctity of the city of the Temple would have been affected by the presence of those images, that is, it would have been defiled. Whether that meant levitical defilement, is not easy to prove, as no information on the point has come down. Two references in I Macc. are instructive illustrations of the relevant concept. When Simeon had conquered Gazara, he drove out the inhabitants, "and cleansed the houses wherein the idols were, and so entered into it with songs and thanksgiving. Yea, he put all uncleanness out of it, and placed such men there as kept the law."[236] The cleansing appears to be of the same purport as the removal by King Josiah of all the idolatry which his father Manasseh

[234] *Antiquit.* 18, 5, 3, 120. 121.
[235] Ezek. 36, 25; 37, 23.
[236] I Macc. 13, 47. 48; cf. 4, 36, 41. 43.

had set up in Jerusalem and in Judah;[237] but it characterizes idols and their worship more distinctly as impure things. When Simeon had taken the Akra, "and when he had put them out from there, he cleansed the tower from pollutions."[238] As Professor Rawlinson notes, "here, too, idolatry had been practised, and purification was necessary, before the place could be a fit dwelling for Jews." In the description of the religious persecutions in Judea under Antiochos IV Epiphanes, Assumptio Mosis, 8, 4 says: "And others among them shall be punished by tortures and fire and sword, and they shall be forced to bear in public their idols, polluted as they are like those who keep them." The author describes the idols and their worshippers as polluted, and it seems that his idea of their impurity, about the year 1, was very near that of Lev. and the prophets and R. Jehudah b. Bethera, if not identical with it, as, unlike I Macc., he characterizes also the worshippers as polluted, evidently by their idols. The statement of Hippolytos[239] that the Zealots considered it forbidden to walk in the shadow of figures, could have referred neither to Jerusalem nor to any other place in Judea, as no gate with a statue placed over it would have been tolerated there. As the Zealots were Galileans, the cities of Sepphoris and Tiberias, with their many buildings and structures in the Hellenistic-Roman style erected by Herod Antipas, afforded them sufficient opportunities for their strict observance. But as they were in religious matters Pharisees, the religious side of their attitude might have been discussed and formulated for them by the teachers in Jerusalem on the principle of the levitical impurity of all works of sculpture. And it is not improbable that there existed before the year 70 a Mishnah that con-

[237] II. Chron. 34, 5. 8.
[238] I Macc. 13, 50.
[239] Above p. 67.

tained directions for the attitude of the Jews who lived among non-Jews in cities like Caesarea,[240] Ashkelon and Skythopolis, to idols and idolatry.[241]

The destruction of Jerusalem, and the conditions created by the Romans after their complete reconquest of Judea in this province, gave to the teachers occasion for new rules about the attitude of the Jew to idolatry. For, according to their custom, the Roman administrators built in Judea not only forts and camps, and military settlements and offices of administration, but also public baths, theatres, circuses, and race-courses,[242] as well as temples; and all such buildings and structures were adorned not only with the emperor's statue or bust, but very often with the images of various gods. So already R. Johanan b. Zakkai warned his contemporaries, especially religious and political zealots, not to interfere with the places of

[240] Cf. Tos. Ḥullin 2, 13; b. 39b about a Jew in Caesarea who brought a sacrifice to a heathen god.

[241] The only definite evidence of a discussion of the subject are two statements of Nahum the Mede who, according to R. Nathan, a teacher of Babylonian noble origin in Galilee in the middle of the second century, was before the year 70 a member of a civil court in Jerusalem (Kethub. 105a Baraita; Tos. Baba bat. 9, 1), and who immediately after the destruction of the Temple gave a decision about their vow to some Nazirites who had arrived from Babylonia. In a discussion between Naḥum and other teachers about the rule that a Jew must not deal with a heathen even on the day preceding his idolatrous festival in the Baraita in Tos. 'Abod. Zar. 1, 1; Jer. I 39a 56; b. 7b נחום המדי אומר יום אחד בגליות לפני אידיהן אסור, אמרו לו נשתקע הדבר ולא נאמר, Naḥum said that in the diaspora one day before the festival of the heathens business dealings are prohibited; the scholars, however, remarked to him that that view had disappeared, and had never been expressed. This clearly shows that the contemporary scholars must have, before that discussion, given attention to that subject. In Abod. Zar. 7b: תניא אידך נחום המדי אומר מוכרין להן סוס זכר חקן במלחמה, אמרו לו נשתקע הדבר ולא נאמר, in the Baraita Naḥum said that it was permitted to sell the Gentiles an old male horse in wartime; but the scholars remarked to him that that view had disappeared, and had never been expressed. (In 'Abod. Zar. 1, 6 ben Bethera holds a view near to that of Naḥum; as his own name is not given, he may be the older R. Joshua b. Bethera who reported several incidents from Jerusalem before the year 70, 'Eduy. 8, 1; Menaḥ. 103b). Again we see that the relations between Jews and non-Jews were discussed by the teachers before the year 70, in this instance restricting the sale of every kind of horses for war purposes.

[242] R. Gamaliel II, before the year 120, says in ARN 28, 43a that the Roman government consumes (our property) במכסאות במרחצאות ותרטייאות וארנוניות, by tolls, public baths, theatres, and annonae. See, however, the various readings in Schechter's note.

Roman worship:[243] "Be not hasty to pull down the high places of the Gentiles, that thou shouldst not have to rebuild them with thy hand; pull not down such of bricks, for they might tell thee to rebuild them of stones; nor such of stones, for they might tell thee to rebuild them of timber." Not only the public bath in 'Akko had a statue of Aphrodite;[244] but there was for R. Ishmael an occasion to discuss the stones of Mercury,[245] and R. Akiba, in a discussion with R. Eliezer, advised the scholars to avoid the utterance of the correct names of the heathen gods, and to call them rather by some abusive perversion of them.[246] And Zonén asked R. Akiba how it was that some persons affected with diseases went into certain idolatrous temples, and came out sound?[247] Jamnia, the seat of the central school and of the chief religious council under R. Johanan b. Zakkai and his successor, R. Gamaliel II, was an important granary of the military and civil Roman administration,[248] and must have had other public buildings with statues and images. As some Jews were in Roman service and associated with the officials, and imitated them in dress and outward appearance, even when their heathen character was undeniable, R. Jehudah b. Bethera

[243] Midr. Tanna'im Deuter. p. 58, no. 4; 2 ARN 31, 33b ff.; Tos. 'Abod. Zar. 1, 19; Bacher, *Agada der Tannaiten* II, 425, 3: אל תבהל לסתור במות גוים שלא תבנה בידך, שלא תסתור של לבנים ויאמרו לך עשם של אבנים, של אבנים ויאמרו לך עשם של עץ.

[244] R. Gamaliel's visit there surprised a certain Proklos b. Philosophos, and he asked the rabbi for an explanation, 'Abod. Zar. 3, 4.

[245] 'Abod. Zar. 4, 1; Baraita 50a.

[246] Baraita 'Abod. Zar. 45b ff.; Jer. III 43a 67-73.

[247] 'Abod. Zar. 55a. Bacher, *Agada der Tannaiten* I, 294, 3 points out that Zonen's observation referred to the healing by incubation in the temple of Asklepios or Serapis (Suetonius, Vespasian, 7; Tacitus, Historiae 4, 81; Dio Cassius 66, 8, to whom should be added Chrysostomos, Contra Judaeos I, about the temple of the Matrona in Antioch-Daphne). It is strange that Strabo (Reinach, *Textes d'auteurs Grecs* 99. 100, 1) attributed to the Jews the practice of incubation in the Temple of Jerusalem in connection with obtaining prophecies. As Schürer, *Geschichte* III, 31. 35, has proved the existence of temples of Asklepios and Serapis in various cities of the Philistine coast, Zonen might have observed the practice of incubation in Ashkelon, Caesarea, or Ptolemais.

[248] Tos. Dammai 1, 13. 14; Jer. III 23c 63; Gen. r. 76, 8.

opposed the custom on religious grounds.[249] But the teachers must have been afraid, lest the crushing catastrophe of the year 70, and the consequent terrible misery and starvation might have made some weaker Jews pliant for the insistent temptations emanating from the Roman officials.[250] For that reason, R. Jehudah b. Bethera, and, to some extent, also R. Akiba, in order to confirm the weakened resistance, impressed upon the Jews the gravity of the sin committed, and the levitical impurity contracted, by entering an idolatrous temple, by walking under a worshipped tree, by drinking of libation wine, by eating of heathen offerings, or even by visiting the Gentile's house, when any parts of such sacrifice were in it. The consideration that, since the destruction of the Temple, the contraction of even the gravest levitical impurity was of no consequence for the ordinary Jew and was not prohibited, would strongly suggest that R. Jehudah b. Bethera's and R. Akiba's rules viewed, in the first instance and mainly, the considerable number of priests, some of whom, after the destruction of the Temple, might easily have lost their religious hold. In Temple times, the defilement of the ordinary Israelite by the Gentile, whether by his touch or his spittle, prevented the Jew for the day from visiting the Temple or from participating in a sacrificial meal, and from associating with those who were purified for those sacred acts, and with priests who were purified for the service in the Temple or for eating in their homes certain dues of sacrifices and their heaveofferings.

[249] Sifra Lev. 18, 3, 86a: ובחוקותיהם לא תלכו, רבי יהודה בן בתירא אומר שלא ינקור קומי, ולא יגדל ציצית ולא יגדל בלורית,'and in their statues ye shall not walk,' forbids various kinds of self-adornment, the first before a mirror in order to attract the attention of women, then to grow a forelock and a hind lock, as all these are דרכי האמורי, heathen customs. (In the reading of RABD the author was R. Jehudah b. Bethera's colleague, R. Jehudah b. Baba; see Bacher, *Agada der Tannaiten* I. 405.) The authorities permitted the household of R. Gamaliel to wear the forelock, as they had to appear before high officials of the Roman administration, Tos. Shabb. 6, 1; Jer. VI 7d 55; b. Baba Kam. 83a; Tos. Sotah 15, 8; Tos. 'Abod. Zar. 3, 5; see Lewy, *Abba Saul* 21, 42.

[250] As a statement of R. Akiba suggests, Mekil. Exod. 15, 2, 37a.

As to the levitical impurity of the Gentile, it was instituted by the rabbis about the year 1 as a novelty going beyond the law in Lev. 15. Its first stage was the extension of the rules of the menstruous Jewess to the Gentile woman, and of the communication of her impurity to her Gentile husband; and, as she did not observe the purification demanded of the Jewess by the written law and its rabbinic interpretation, she was declared to be permanently in the levitical state of the menstruous woman. Later, the Hillelites attempted to declare the Gentile man and woman liable to the defilement by a corpse, and to be permanently so defiled; but they failed to carry their suggestion against the opposition of the Shammaites. Shortly before the outbreak of the revolution in the year 66, the two schools, to counteract sodomy between Roman and Jewish youths, resolved to ascribe to the Gentile the grave impurity of the Jew who has an issue; but the outbreak of the war prevented that rule from being applied in practice, at least no information about any actual occurrence has been preserved. The assumed levitical impurity of the Gentile affected, as the reports show, only the priest on duty, and the ordinary Jew only when purified for a visit to the Temple and for a participation in a sacrificial meal. The private associations between the Jew and the Gentile were in no way restricted, and commercial and other relations were not affected by the levitical purity ascribed to the Gentile. He could move about freely even on the Temple Mount, and proceed to the wall enclosing the inner forecourt; and it was only in the first century that that boundary was pushed back by the erection of the Soreg. Other aspects of the problem of the Gentile's levitical impurity were, incidentally, discussed here, and a number of questions bearing on the subject brought nearer solution. Yet, there are still some difficulties left which require further investigation, if only the scanty information preserved were sufficient to afford the answers.

THOSE APPOINTED FOR MONEY

On the History of the Various Juridical Authorities in Eretz-Israel in the Talmudic Period*

Gedalyahu Alon

Several sources in both Talmuds attest that certain Patriarchs used to appoint ignorant judges for pecuniary considerations. Some of these judges would wrap themselves in a Sage's cloak (*Tallit*) and wished to sit and teach with a *Meturgeman* ['Expounder'] at their side, after the manner of Torah scholars, but the Sages objected to them, disqualified them from judging, and demanded that the due honour and status be withheld from them.[1] These testimonies date from after the middle of the third century to the middle of the fourth century. Because this period is generally treated as one of spiritual and ethical decline in the world of the Patriarchate, since it had ceased giving Halakhic decisions and teaching Torah in the Great Bet ha-Midrash [Academy][2] and became wholly immersed in wielding

---

* This article follows on a lecture delivered at the First World Congress of Jewish Studies, which was held at Jerusalem during Tammuz, 5707 (1947). [The translation is by Israel Abrahams.]

1 *T.B. Sanhedrin* 7b; *T.P. Bikkurim* iii, 65d; *Midrash Samuel*, ed. Buber, p. 68. Possibly Resh Laqish's dictum in *Sanhedrin, loc. cit.*, 'Whoever appoints an unworthy judge is as one who planted an Ashera in Israel', may be linked to this question. For it was his Meturgeman who publicly denounced the judge appointed by the Patriarch on account of his ignorance.

2 Halevy, *Dorot Harischonim* (II, i, pp. 766–774; see also Dinaburg in the *Memorial Volume to Gulak and Klein*, p. 88, note 1) seeks to prove that the separation of the office of Head of the College from the Patriarchate obtained already in Rabban Simeon b. Gamaliel's day. He finds support for the conjecture in the title 'Head of the Speakers' applied to R. Judah b. Ille'ai (*T.B. Shabbat* 33b, and parallels cited *ibid.*), which according to the Talmudic explanation was given him by the Government because he had praised it, thus showing that R. Judah served as Head of the College, while Rabban Simeon b. Gamaliel as Patriarch conducted public affairs. However, the Talmudic explanation is merely a Haggada, and 'Head of the Speakers' does not mean the Head of the College, but the term is related to the procedures adopted at the College among the Sages as a whole. These procedures are referred to in the *Tosefta* (*Sanhedrin* viii, 1; *T.B. ibid.*, 17b; *T.P. Sheqalim* v, 48d): 'Every Sanhedrin that contains two members who know how "to speak" [i.e. to discuss a Halakhic matter] and all are able "to hear" [i.e. to comprehend the discussion]', etc. (cf. *Tosefta, loc. cit.*, vii, 9; *T.B. Horayot* 13b: 'Sons of Sages and disciples of Sages, when they have the knowledge to understand', etc., since these are certainly unable 'to speak'). For only certain of the Sages would take part in public discussions to elucidate the Halakhic questions raised at the College, and some of them were 'Heads of the Speakers', as we are informed in the Palestinian

the sceptre of authority and the evil that this entailed, historians are mostly inclined to regard this facet, too, as one of the symptoms of degeneration and corruption that had spread among the Patriarchs. Some explain this practice of the Jewish Patriarchs[3] by reference to the difficult conditions prevailing in the time of crisis, economic collapse, and governmental oppression, which marked the third century.

However, we must first qualify the current view that the Patriarchate was sundered from the world of the Torah and Halakhic decision during this period. Undoubtedly, already in the days of Rabban Gamaliel 'Berabbi' we see the standing of the Patriarch in the sphere of Halakha impaired in relation to the Sages,[4] and needless to say, in the period under discussion the Patriarchs appear to be subject to the contemporary Sages' ruling on religious matters, to depend on them in respect of Halakhic questions, and to act under their direction.[5] Nevertheless, this does not yet prove that the Patriarchs were devoid of Torah-learning or that their connection with the Great Bet ha-Midrash had been severed. Not only were Rabban Gamaliel 'Berabbi' and R. Judah Nesi'a I leading Torah scholars having a decisive voice in Halakhic matters,[6] but their descendants living at the

---

Talmud (*Rosh ha-Shana* ii, 58b; *Sanhedrin* i, 18c): 'Provided each one spoke in his due place, for instance, R. Ḥanina opened the discussion, and R. Joḥanan and R. Simeon b. Laqish closed it; R. Ba bar Zavda opened it, and R. Ḥiyya, R. Yassa, and R. Ammi closed it; R. Ḥaggai opened it, and R. Jonah and R. Jose closed it.'

Furthermore, L. Ginzberg (*Perushim we-Ḥiddushim bi-Yerushalmi*, Pt. III, pp. 195–196) is of opinion that when Rabban Gamaliel of Jabneh was deposed and R. Eleazar b. Azariah was appointed in his place, the two offices were separated. For in his view (and Kämpf thinks so, too, *MGWJ*, v, 155, note 2) the Sages were able to depose Rabban Gamaliel only from the headship of the College but not from the Patriarchate, which was subject to Roman authorization. However, the argument is not decisive, and the traditions, understood according to their simple meaning, attest his removal from the Patriarchate, as well. This was actually what happened (but this is not the place to discuss the subject).

3 Among recent scholars: Jawitz, *Toledot*, viii, 107–130; Marmorstein, *REJ*, vol. 64, pp. 59–66; Zucker, *Studien*, p. 167; Strack-Billerbeck, *Kommentar*, etc., II, 150; Dinaburg, *op. cit.*, p. 91; and others.

4 *T.P. Shabbat* vi, 8a: 'Rabban Gamaliel once went down to stroll in his courtyard on the Sabbath, holding a golden key in his hand, and his colleagues rebuked him on the ground that it was an adornment'. *Ibid., Ḥalla* iv, 60a: 'Rabban Gamaliel "Berabbi" wished to apply the law of *Demai* [produce concerning which there is a doubt as to whether the sacred gifts and the laws of levitical cleanness have been observed] to Syria, but R. Hosha'ya did not permit him.' (Although Halevy, *Dorot Harischonim*, II, i, p. 332, holds that this Rabban Gamaliel was the son of R. Judah Nesi'a, his opinion is predicated on his theory that the Patriarchs' knowledge of the Torah did not decline till after the time of R. Judah Nesi'a. But we cannot but regard Rabban Gamaliel here, too, as the son of Rabbi.)

5 Thus Resh Laqish gave the Patriarch a Halakhic direction (*T.B. 'Avoda Zara* 6b; *T.P. ibid*, i, 39b); so, too, did R. Ammi (*T.B. Ta'anit* 14a-b; *ibid.* 25b; *T.B. 'Avoda Zara* 33b), R. Manni (*T.P. Pesaḥim* x, 37b), and R. Abbahu (*T.P. Avoda Zara, loc. cit.*). R. Ammi was vexed at a Halakhic practice of R. Judah Nesi'a, which was contrary to his own opinion (*T.B. Mo'ed Qaṭan* 12b). The Patriarchs likewise enquired of the Sages the interpretation of certain Haggadas. However, we find a similar situation in the case of Rabban Simeon b. Gamaliel, who declared (*Tosefta Sukka* ii, 2, and the parallels in the Talmuds): 'Rabbi Jose permitted me', etc. On Rabban Simeon b. Gamaliel and his status *vis-à-vis* the Sages see below.

6 See Halevy, *op. cit.*, II, i, pp. 19–49.

end of the third century and the beginning of the fourth were also at times asked Halakhic questions[7] and some Sages were even guided by their ritual practice.[8] At times a Halakhic dispute between the Patriarch and the Av Bet Din (Head of the Court) caused perplexity and transgression.[9] We also know the testimony of Epiphanius concerning the 'apostles' who used 'to sit with the Patriarch day and night in order to advise him and to cite before him responsa regarding the laws of the Torah'.[10]

---

7 T.B. Ḥullin 51a: 'Rav Safra said to Abbaye: Has the Master seen the scholar who came from the West and said: My name is R. 'Awira... once there came before Rabbi the case of a needle... He (R. 'Awira) replied: I am the janitor *[maftîr kĕnêsiyyôt,* see Jastrow s.v.] at the meetings of scholars to His Excellency the Great Rabbi (i.e. the Patriarch; *ibid.* 54a R. Judah the Patriarch is called thus by R. Joḥanan)... and there came before Rabbi the case of a needle found in the thick wall of the reticulum... and he declared it *terefa* [an animal possessing an organic defect rendering it forbidden as food].' The case came before one of the Patriarchs at the beginning of the fourth century. Incidentally, the term *maftîr kĕnêsiyyôt* has not yet been satisfactorily explained (Lauterbach's explanation in the *Hebrew Union College Annual, Jubilee Volume* [Cincinnati, 1925], p. 217, is not clear). However, this is, at all events, connected with the Patriarch's practice to lecture in public. As regards the teaching of Torah by the (later) Patriarchs, the requisite inference may be drawn from the expression 'The School of Rabbi teaches', which frequently occurs in the Palestinian Talmud and simply refers to Baraitot taught in the college of the Patriarchs (cf. *T.B.* Berakhot 34b: 'R. Safra said in the name of a scholar of the School of Rabbi' — this is the correct reading, although there are variant versions).

8 *T.P. Yom Tov* i, 60d: 'R. Ze'ira asked Qalla Daroma, R. Judah Nesi'a's slave: Does your Master grind spices on a Holy Day?'

9 *Deuteronomy Rabba* ii, 19: 'R. Samuel bar Naḥmani said: All that the leaders do the generation does. How is this (to be understood)? If the Patriarch permits and the Av Bet Din says: The Patriarch permits, but I forbid; and the judges say: The Av Bet Din permits, but we forbid, and the rest of the people [lit.: 'generation'] declare: The judges permit, but we forbid; who then caused the entire generation to sin? The Patriarch, who was the first to transgress' (Av Bet Din here, apparently, means the Head of the College at Tiberias).

10 *Haer.* 30, 4. Epiphanius who wishes to glorify the 'apostles' (in connection with the story of the apostate Joseph) emphasizes their outstanding knowledge of the Torah and the authority they enjoyed among the Patriarchs. But it is clear that it was the Patriarch who gave the final decision in Halakhic practice. Some scholars prove the Patriarch's paucity of Halakhic erudition from *T.P. 'Avoda Zara* i, 39b: 'R. Abbahu said: ואני לא is wanting in the citation of the passage in *Or Zarua'*, Pisqe 'Avoda Zara, §96) Rabban Gamaliel 'Berabbi' asked me: Is it permitted to go to a (Gentile) fair? and I forbade him... But it has been taught: It is permitted to go to a fair and to buy male and female slaves there! Resh Laqish said: Not only may not Israelite slaves (be purchased), but even Gentile slaves... How is Resh Laqish's ruling to be explained then ? *Rabban Gamaliel was a small man and R. Abbahu wished to restrain him,* but R. Judan Nesi'a was a great man! Even so Resh Laqish (who likewise forbade Rabban Gamaliel to go to a fair) wished to curb the practice.' From this, it is argued, one can see how vast was the difference between R. Judah Nesi'a and Rabban Gamaliel who succeeded him! But the correct reading, given in *Or Zarua'*, is: 'Rabban Gamaliel was a great man... R. Judan Nesi'a was also a great man...' (see *Sha'are Torat Ereṣ Yisra'el*, p. 557). The meaning is: Although the general public is permitted to visit a fair, the rule for 'an eminent person' is made stricter so that he may serve as a deterrent and prevent the multitude from breaching the law completely — a principle that is applied in other Halakhot as well (the recension of current editions does not make sense).

Now as to his position as ruler. The status of the Patriarch in the conduct of communal and political affairs did not oust nor blur his spiritual and religious image.[11] The Sages still assigned to the Patriarch sovereign authority in the religious life of the people.[12] The Patriarchs themselves are known to have continued to care for communal needs by sending Sages to various cities of Eretz-Israel to see to the socio-religious institutions of the community in the Jewish settlements,[13] and the last Rabban Gamaliel jeopardized his position for the sake of building synagogues in the country (thus circumventing the imperial decree forbidding this) and on account of the judicial rights of which the Government had deprived the Jews.[14]

We undoubtedly hear, at this period, of acts of oppression committed by the Patriarchal House towards the Sages[15] and of the excessive exaction of money from the Jews.[16] But over and beyond the evidence of greed and callousness of individual Patriarchs, these traditions testify to the conflict between the Sages — or some of them — and the Patriarchs on public issues.[17] In other words, these

---

11 See Ginzberg, *Perushim we-Ḥiddushim bi-Yerushalmi*, Pt. II, p. 195.
12 As, for instance, the proclamation of a fast, which was not decided solely by the Sages, 'but only if the Patriarch agreed'. See *T.P. Ta'anit* ii, 65a (in Harkavy, *Teshuvot ha-Ge'onim*, §259, p. 133, the reading is: עבדין [instead of דאנן] דאינון תעניתא אילין, 'The fasts that they [not 'we'] observed', i.e. that the Babylonians keep. This accords with Samuel's dictum: 'The only public fasts in Babylonia are the Ninth of Av and the Day of Atonement' — *T.B. Ta'anit* 12b and the parallels listed *ibid.* The reason is that suggested by some of the Rishonim: Since the Babylonian fasts are not appointed by the Patriarchs, they are not treated Halakhically as proper fasts. There is no need to emend the reading, as does Harkavy.) Similarly in the case of a person placed under the ban; the Patriarch can always grant absolution, whether the one who imposed it dies, or it is not known who he is (see the episodes of Resh Laqish and Rav Judah in *T.B. Mo'ed Qaṭan* 17a, and the statement of R. Joshua b. Levi in *T.P. Mo'ed Qaṭan* iii, 81d).
13 *T.P. Ḥagiga* i, 86c and the parallels in the Midrashim: 'R. Judan Nesi'a (II) sent a message to R. Ḥiyya (bar Abba), to R. Assi, and R. Ammi that they should visit the cities of Eretz-Israel and arrange for them Bible and Mishna teachers', etc.
14 The reference is to the right to judge disputes between Christians and Jews; *C. Th.* 16, 8, 22 (*C. J.* 1, 9, 15).
15 For instance, R. Judah Nesi'a's attitude towards Jose of Ma'on, *T.P. Sanhedrin* ii, 20c–d (*Genesis Rabba* lxxx, Theodor-Albeck, p. 950) and towards Resh Laqish (*T.P. loc. cit.*, 19d. But these scholars attacked the Patriarch in public). Likewise the case of R. Mani of whom we are told 'that the members of the Patriarch's House vexed him' (*T.B. Ta'anit* 23b) and the story of how 'the servants of the Patriarchate' tortured Osha'ya Ze'ira of Ḥaverya *[aliter:* 'the youngest of the members'] (*T.B. Ta'anit* 24a; he, too, lectured publicly and blamed the Patriarchs for the tribulations suffered by the people).
16 The exposition of Jose of Ma'on was directed against the Patriarch's taking money from the people. The story of the woman that brought R. Judah Nesi'a a gift is well known and is one of the incidents against which Resh Laqish protested — *Genesis Rabba* lxxviii.
17 When Resh Laqish advised the Patriarch 'that he should not accept a gift from anyone' and even the Roman officers would not oppress him, he certainly gave him good counsel, which was in keeping with the plebeian character of this Sage. However, even if at times the collection of the contributions of the Palestinian Jews to the Patriarchate was accompanied by unworthy actions, it must be remembered that it was difficult for the Patriarch to forgo the financial means that enabled the central administrative institutions of the nation and its activities to survive. Incidentally, it

traditions primarily reflect the clashes between the Patriarchs and the Sages, particularly in the sphere of their interrelationship and views.[18] Hence it is not surprising that our sources, which emanate from the world of the Sages, present the incidents tendentiously and with some suppression of the truth.

Far greater is the need to qualify the testimony of the Church Fathers, who completely deny any spiritual virtue to the Patriarchs and compare them to 'actors in the theatre', to 'pampered women', or to 'mere youths', 'immersed in

---

appears that the landed estates that provided the material mainstay of the Patriarchate in the time of Rabbi (land that he leased from the Imperial House) were wholly, or partly, taken away from the Patriarch in the course of the changes that took place after the Severan Dynasty. Thereafter the Patriarchs were particularly in need of the support of the Jews in Eretz-Israel and the Diaspora.

This problem arose again in the reign of Julian, who wished to deliver the Jews from the burden of the ἀποστολή, against which many of them protested (see the famous letter of this Emperor). Similarly when Honorius Caesar charged that by exacting the *aurum coronarium* the Patriarch was acting as *depopulator Judaeorum*, he undoubtedly based his case on popular criticism, only the abolition of the 'coronation tax', needless to say, did not help to solve the problem of the maintenance of the administration, whose activities in Eretz-Israel and in the Diaspora were manifold at that time.

18 Jose of Ma'on's charge that 'the king takes all' and that 'the priests', in consequence, do not receive 'their gifts' from the people actually raises the question in whose custody the contributions to the Patriarchs and the Sages should be placed. For the 'Sages' Fund' was, apparently, none other than the Patriarch's 'coronation tax'. Without doubt the cause of the contention was the question under whose control these monies should be. This is one of the aspects of the struggle between the two elements in the supreme leadership — the *Bet Din ha-Gadol* [High Court] and the Patriarch — over the issue of sovereign authority. It likewise applied to R. Judah Nesi'a's demand that the Sages should contribute to the cost of building the wall of Tiberias, an impost that Resh Laqish and R. Johanan foiled (*T.B. Bava Batra* 7b–8a). The Sages claimed complete exemption from all obligations towards the city, an attitude that contributed, especially in places where there were large numbers of Sages and disciples, like Tiberias, to the aggravation of the burden borne by the townspeople (these were difficult times for the empire as a whole, including Eretz-Israel). Is it to be wondered at that the Patriarchs, on whom rested the responsibility and supervision of communal life in general, wished to avoid granting excessive privileges to the Sages as a body to the detriment of others?

It is true that some scholars hold the view that the exemption of the Sages from public taxation and service is based on an ancient Jewish usage dating from the period of the Second Temple and that the Antonine Emperors released them from governmental taxes. If that were the case the action of R. Judah Nesi'a would have to be regarded as an assault on the established rights of the Sages and an act of 'despotism'. But although Rabbi already freed the Sages from paying the 'coronation tax' (*T.B. Bava Batra* 8a), there is, to my mind, no basis for the view that in practice this tradition gradually crystallized from the days of Rabbi onwards. This subject requires elucidation, but this is not the place for it (I propose to revert to this theme in an essay entitled 'Aspects of the Political and Social History of Jewish Palestine in the Period of the Severan Dynasty' [Hebrew]).

Furthermore, the repair of the wall of Tiberias presumably occurred at a time of turmoil, when there was danger of attack (i.e. by 'robber bands') upon the city. We also find that the Sages, on occasion, acted as did R. Judah Nesi'a and imposed a monetary contribution on their colleagues at a time of trouble, and there were protests against them as well (*T.P. Mo'ed Qatan* iii, 81d: 'In the days of R. Jeremiah trouble came upon Tiberias, so he sent a request for a silver (*aliter:* golden) lamp to R. Jacob b. Bun. He replied: "Jeremiah has not yet changed his evil ways", and he wished to put him under the ban... so they banned each other.').

lewdness'.[19] For even if 'secular' dominion did not leave the Patriarchs unaffected and some of them indulged in luxuries,[20] basically this testimony is polemical and seeks to repudiate the Jewish claim that the sovereignty and priesthood[21] still remained in their possession — and would continue to be theirs until the advent of the Messiah — in the form of the Patriarchate.[22]

In their polemic they even accused the Sages of ignorance of the Torah and of wallowing in the pleasures of this world, a charge that is at any rate highly exaggerated.[23] We must therefore conclude that it is improbable that the ordination of ignorant judges for pecuniary considerations was due primarily to the cupidity of the Patriarchs. Without doubt these appointments, which continued for several generations, had a general social and historical significance. The same applies to the protests of the Sages against them.

This conclusion, it appears, is borne out by a Christian tradition of the beginning of the fifth century, which also refers to a practice similar to those previously mentioned. Palladius writes in his *History of John Chrysostom*[24] that it is the custom of the Patriarchs to change each year, or every two years, the heads of the congregations in order to enrich themselves (by receiving the appointment fee). This writer also charges the Patriarchs with cupidity, which undermines the religious administration of the Jews through the frequent changes of its leaders. But we are inclined to regard this practice — the question of the acceptance of money we shall discuss later — not as an evil innovation of the Patriarchs but as the continuation (or intensification) of the democratic tradition in the Jewish community — the appointment of the administrative authorities for one year. This usage, however, began to be impaired by occasional life-appointments, and even

---

19 Origen, *MG*, 24, 110; Jerome, in his commentary on Isaiah iii 3, Pl. 24, 59, his introduction to Hosea, Vallarsi, vol. 6, p. XXIII (ML, 25, 820). Chrysostom, *Adversus Judaeos* vi, *PG*, 48, 911–913; Epiphanius, *op. cit.*, 30, 7.
20 Rabbi's wealthy home and 'his (lavish) table' are well known (although he himself 'did not enjoy even with his little finger' anything of this world's pleasures). See the story of 'one of the members of the Patriarch's family' who became impoverished — *T.P. Pe'a* viii, 21a. In this connection mention should be made of the Patriarchs' practice, from the time of Rabbi onward, to visit Ḥammat Gader [which had hot springs], and although Sages also went with them and sometimes they went by themselves (see the sources cited in *Sefer ha-Yishuv*, א, א, pp. 45–46, and Epiphanius, *op. cit.*, p. 69), it seems that at times these visits were connected with Rabbinic conventions concerned with public matters (*T.P. 'Eruvin* vi, 23c; Ẓuri, *Shilton ha-Nesi'ut we-ha-Va'ad*, pp. 113–114, only he overstates the case).
21 Chrysostom implies that some Jews regarded the Patriarch as taking the place of the High Priest.
22 Origen initiates this polemic (*De Principiis* 4, 1, 3, Kötschau, pp. 297–298) and Theodoritus concludes it, shortly after the abolition of the Patriarchate (*PG*, 83, 61–64).
23 Origen, *PG*, 24, 110, and Jerome *passim*. Even if we assume that there was a decline in Torah-learning among the Palestinian Sages at the close of the fourth century and the beginning of the fifth (and this is by no means certain) it was undoubtedly not wholly forgotten, nor did Halakhic authorities cease in Eretz-Israel. Jerome himself testifies frequently to the numerous 'teachers' and 'illustrious teachers', who were to be found in Eretz-Israel.
24 *PG*, 47, p. 51.

more so by the tendency to establish a lineal aristocracy in the form of hereditary offices among the communal leaders.[25]

These acts of the Patriarchs and the opposition thereto of the Sages were related, it seems, to the problem of the existence of communal judicatures alongside the judiciary of the expert, ordained Rabbis. However, since we still lack a methodical presentation of the judicial institutions of Eretz-Israel in the Talmudic period, describing the different types, their interrelationship, and the structure of their organization,[26] we are therefore compelled to deal here with the main problems inherent in this theme. Needless to say, we have no intention of stating explicit conclusions, something that cannot be done definitely even after deep study, because of the nature of our sources. What follows is no more than an attempt to outline in general terms the framework of the problem — a few headings, as it were for suggested investigation.

The abstract, theoretical formulation adopted by the sources on the subject of the courts, the multiplicity of conflicting opinions and the contradictions in the Halakhic and practical traditions regarding their authority and composition, including many actual facts that ostensibly attest the temporary character of the Palestinian judicial institutions at that period, have collectively induced one scholar[27] to deny completely the existence of organized courts of a permanent and regular nature. According to Chajes we only find in the sources evidence of separate, individual judges,[28] who tried cases by special authorization and on a temporary basis, but judicial bodies were entirely non-existent.

There is undoubtedly much evidence to support this assessment, only it does not embrace the entire sphere of judicial tribunals but only a part of them. For against this testimony we learn of courts that tried the accused perforce,[29] of courts

---

[25] In the third and fourth centuries there are common in the Diaspora communal leaders who served (διὰ βίου) 'throughout their lifetime' and, similarly, μελλάρχοντες, μελλογραμματεῖς, and children archons, a fact which indicates, that there was a kind of law of heredity in public administration (see Frey, *Corpus*, Introduction, p. 78; Baron, *The Jewish Community*, I, pp. 104–105). But Theodotus already in his inscription (first century) boasts that he is the head of a congregation, the son of the head of a congregation, and the grandson of the head of a congregation (*REJ*, 1920, vol. 71, p. 46; this inscription has been translated into Hebrew by M. Schwabe in *Sefer Yerushalayim*, vol. I, p. 362 ff).

[26] Although Weinberg's article ('Organisation' etc., *MGWJ*, 1897, pp 249–262) and the presentation of Juster and Gulak, *Yesode ha-Mishpat ha-'Ivri* (Book IV pp. 23–40), and similar works, teach us a great deal, they do not provide us with a full picture.

[27] Chajes in *REJ*, 1899, vol. 39, pp. 39–52.

[28] Juster (II, p. 96, n. 2) answers that all the Sages who are represented as judging by themselves actually had others with them, and thus constituted permanent courts. But although in many instances this was undoubtedly the case, individuals also gave judgement, without holding a permanent position. See below.

[29] *Sifre Deuteronomy* §144 (ed. Finkelstein, p. 198): '"And they shall judge the people"—perforce'; *ibid.* §286 (ed. Finkelstein, p. 302): '"And they shall judge" — perforce'. See also *T.P. Sanhedrin* i, 18a: 'If an authorized judge forced (the litigants to come before him) and judged by himself (despite the law requiring three judges), his judgement is valid'.

that enforced certain acts upon the demand of one of the parties to the suit,[30] of courts 'that flagellated and imprisoned',[31] of 'court messengers who administered beatings',[32] of the seizure of the lands of debtors in their absence and against their will,[33] of courts that appointed administrators for orphans, for deaf-mutes, and for imbeciles, or themselves acted as administrators,[34] of 'the judges of Sepphoris',[35]

30 Although in regard to the Halakhot that treat of compelling one of the parties to a suit to carry out the court's decision, the nature of the enforcement is not clearly stated in the sources and sometimes the Rishonim discuss the question whether physical compulsion is implied, it is apparent that generally the actual use of force is meant; and this is inconceivable without a permanent court of justice, for example 'And these are they that are compelled to put away their wives' (*M. Ketubbot* vii, 9, 10). So, too, 'a bill of divorce given under compulsion' (*M. Giṭṭin* ix, 8; *Mekhilta*, Mishpatim, ed. Horovitz, p. 246), and Ḥaliṣa [ceremony of removing the *yavam's* shoe; Deut. xxv 5–11] carried out under compulsion (*Tosefta Yevamot* xii, 13), and the like.

31 See the Baraita in *T.B. Sanhedrin* 17b: 'Any city where the following ten things are absent... and a court that flagellates and *imprisons* (*ḥŏvĕshîn*)' — this is the correct recension and not 'imposes penalties (*'ŏnĕshîn*)', as in current editions. See *Diqduqe Soferim* and 'Pirqe Rabbenu ha-Qadosh' (Higger, *Ḥorev*, vol. vi, p. 143) and several works published subsequently. This is also the reading in the parallel dictum of Rav in *T.P. Qiddushin* iv, 66b. Indeed, the expression is quite old and so, too, is the institution itself, for we read in Josephus (*Ant.* xiii, 10, 6) that when Joḥanan the High Priest [John Hyrcanus] requested the Pharisees to pronounce sentence on one of their number who had slandered him (alleging that he was the son of a captive woman), they declared that he deserved 'stripes and fetters' — πληγῶν καὶ δεσμῶν. This is not the place to discuss the problem, dealt with by various scholars, whether this imprisonment was a punishment based on criminal law, or *poena extraordinaria*, and whether it was imposed before sentence was passed, or was 'a police measure' (see Katz, *Die Strafe im Talmud*, pp. 52–55; Gulak, *Ha-Ḥiyyuv we-Shi'budaw*, pp. 24 ff. On the specific question of *kippa* see Kantor, *Beiträge zur Lehre von der Strafrechtlichen Schuld im Talmud*; see also below, pp. 289 ff).

The existence of prisons in the Jewish cities of Eretz-Israel is not surprising, since these existed in Hellenistic cities of the East and were under the control of the municipal authorities; see Mommsen, *Das römische Strafrecht*, p. 309 (Sifre §309, *Midrash Tanna'im*, p. 188: 'It is like the case of a man who was standing and insulting a senator in the street. Said the bystanders to him: Fool that you are, do you stand and insult a senator? Could he not, if he wished, beat you, tear your garments, and cast you into prison...?'). However, it should be noted, on the other hand, that we do not find explicit reference in civil cases to *actual instances* in which beatings were administered and force was employed except by the order of the Patriarchs, or by the Sages who enforced their sentence by means of 'the servants' of the Patriarch (*Ecclesiastes Rabba* x; *T.P. Ketubbot* ix, 33a; *T.B. Nidda* 52a).

This apart, there is evidence to support the assumption that sometimes the Bet Din was unable in practice to enforce payment by debtors. This situation is to be attributed to the parallel Roman Judiciary (under the auspices of the Governor) and to the practice of the authorities to intervene in the autonomous judicature, both of the Jews and the Greek cities, despite the tradition and law that assured them independence and the right of jurisdiction.

32 *Tosefta Bava Qamma* ix, 1; *ibid. Makkot* ii, 5, and similar sources.

33 Cf. especially R. Mana's remarks to Alaxa (a Gentile) in *T.P. Ketubbot* ix, 33b and *T.P. Shevu'ot* vii, 38a on the practice of Jewish courts in the fourth century to collect by force property of the debtor for the benefit of the creditor.

34 *Tosefta Terumot* i, 1; *Ibid.* Yevamot ix, 2 ('A deaf-mute, an imbecile, and a minor... but if the Bet Din bought for them or the administrators bought for them', etc.).

35 *M. Bava Batra* vi, 7. Büchler suggests that these may have served as judges by governmental appointment (*Der Galiläische 'Am-Ha'ares*, p. 139; *The Political and Social Leaders of the*

and of Sages who were specifically designated 'judges'.[36] Perhaps the strongest evidence of permanent and composite courts is furnished by the existence of Avot Bet Din ['Fathers of the courts'] in populated localities; their chief function was undoubtedly judicial.[37]

The investigation of our sources points to the existence (or the possible existence) of the following three principal judicial systems: (1) the communal judiciary, which was independent of the central authority — the Patriarchate and the Sanhedrin; (2) the judicature of the Sages, who were experts or ordained judges; their authority derived, directly or indirectly, from the authorization of the central administration mentioned above; (3) private jurisdiction, which was provisional, in the form of arbitration.

The communal judiciary. It will appear, from our subsequent analysis, to have comprised three different forms of jurisdiction: that of the municipal

---

Jewish Community of Sepphoris in the 2nd and 3rd Centuries, p. 25, note 1). This conjecture is intrinsically different from the tradition in *Tractate Semahot* xiv, ed. Higger, p. 208, where this Halakha is attributed to 'the elders of Bet Av', an obscure expression (which cannot be discussed here), but which, at any rate, signifies a Bet Din of Sages. But Büchler's entire theory concerning Jewish judges that were appointed by the Government, including Tannaim, who tried cases, in his view, according to Roman law and not in accordance with the Halakha, is doubtful. Büchler relies on the Haggadah in *T.B. Bava Batra* 58a-b concerning R. Banna'a, who was appointed a judge by the Roman authorities. But it is not stated that he acted as judge to Jews, or where he judged. Now there is a kind of parallel to this story in another Haggada relating to R. Shila in *T.B. Berakhot* 58a (according to the correct recensions it is clear that the incident occurred in Eretz-Israel and not in Babylon, and the objection raised in *Diqduqe Soferim* is without basis, because there was a Sage of that name also in Eretz-Israel). We read at the end of that narrative in the original manuscript versions: 'They put a rod in his hand and seated him at the gateway of Rome and he served as judge.' We cannot therefore make any deductions from the sources in regard to our subject. But the whole question as to whether Jews served in the Roman judiciary in Eretz-Israel is bound up, to my mind, with the problem discussed by modern authorities on Roman law with reference to the structure of the Roman judiciary in the provinces during the period of the *principatus*. As is well known, from the time of Diocletian onwards the early Roman civil law was abolished throughout the empire (apparently in the middle of the third century). The formulary proceedings, with their inherent division between judgement *in jure* by the ruler and *in judaico* by the civil magistrate, were replaced by bureaucratic *extraordinary proceedings* of the government. Only it cannot be ascertained when the latter procedure was introduced in the provinces. There is evidence to support the premise, especially in respect of the imperial states (in contrast to those of the Senate), that the *extraordinary proceedings* were in force since the time of the early emperors. If this may be assumed — and apparently it seems correct — the possibility of Jewish citizens being appointed by the Government to serve as judges in Eretz-Israel appears to be precluded (on the existence of *judices pedanei* in the Byzantine period see Wlassak, *Zum römischen Provinzialprozess, passim;* cf. also 'the judges of Caesarea', *T.B. Sukka* 8a and the parallel passages listed *ibid.*).

36 R. Nathan, *T.B. Bava Qamma* 53a; *T.B. Bava Mesi'a* 117b; R. Jose b. Hanina, *T.B. Bava Qamma* 39a. Cf. 'the judges' grotto' *T.B. Mo'ed Qatan* 17a.

37 *T.B. Mo'ed Qatan* 17a: 'In Usha they enacted that if an Av Bet Din committed an offence he was not to be put under the ban'. In the parallel passage in the Palestinian Talmud (*ibid*, iii, 81d) we read: 'They decided by vote in Usha not to put an Elder under the ban'. Similarly in *T.B. Hagiga* 13a 'R. Zera said: The headings of chapters may be transmitted only to an Av Bet Din and to one whose heart is anxious within him' etc., the pre-eminent Av Bet Din, the Vice-President [of the Sanhedrin of which the Patriarch was the President]. The same applies to the Baraita in *T.B. Mo'ed*

administration, that of the citizens' tribunal, and that of the permanent 'judges'. The factor common to them all is that in each sector the judges were 'inexpert', and hence whenever the Talmudic sources speak of 'a Bet Din of lay judges' they may refer to one of these types of tribunals.

The judicature of the municipal administration. There is the well-known tradition of Josephus in *Antiquities* to the effect that Moses enjoined that a Bet Din of seven judges[38] be established in every city of Eretz-Israel. He further testifies that he himself appointed seven judges in every Galilean settlement, when he was made the governor of that province by the Jerusalem authorities.[39] From Josephus' own observation we learn that these judges were merely the members of the local administrative organization, and the Sages already equated them with the seven town representatives [שבעה טובי העיר *shiv'ā ṭôvê hā-'îr*, literally: 'the seven good men of the town'] mentioned in the Talmuds, who were the leaders of the urban settlement.[40] Thus we see that the town administration, in the period prior to the destruction of the Second Temple, possessed judicial powers, just as 'the city Elders' also served as judges in the Biblical era.[41]

Qaṭan (*Tractate Semaḥot* x, 3, ed. Higger, p. 185): 'when an Av Bet Din dies all the colleges *in his city* are closed'; this ruling refers explicitly to the Av Bet Din of a city. Likewise in *T.B. Sukka* 29a (*Massekhtot Derekh 'Ereṣ*,ed. Higger, p. 290): 'On account of four things the sun is eclipsed: because of an Av Bet Din who died and no appropriate mourning oration was delivered over him.' This statement is related to the many Talmudic admonitions concerning the observance of the *hespēd* ['mourning oration'] and *'ēvel* ['mourning'] for a Sage who died, every Sage being implied. The matter is elucidated by R. Samuel bar Naḥmani in *Ruth Rabba* ii: '"The father of Lecah" — the Av Bet Din of Lecah; "the father of Mareshah" — the Av Bet Din of Mareshah.' So, too, the dictum in the *Yalquṭ*, Deuteronomy, §416, taken from *Sifre Zuṭa*: 'It is like the case of an Av Bet Din who had many sons all of whom were ignoramuses *[ammê ha-'areṣ]* and only his eldest son was learned in the Torah. In his will he assigned to each one his share... (To the eldest) he said: Let it suffice you that you take my place.' Unquestionably the passage speaks of the Sage of a city (although Büchler, *Der Galiläische 'Am-Ha'ares*, p. 174, n. 136, seeks to prove that this dictum refers specifically to the Av Bet Din who was Vice-President. As proof he adduces the fact that the Av Bet Din gives his office as a heritage to his son, for only administrative offices were hereditary, not posts concerned with Halakhic decisions. But this distinction is incorrect; see below, the article 'The Sons of the Sages', p. 436). A similar position of Av Bet Din was filled by R. Osha'ya, under whom were 'judges' who transgressed (*Ecclesiastes Rabba* ii, 16), and it is certainly possible that the 'Av Bet Din' R. Joshua b. Uanania (*T.B. Bava Qamma* 74b) must have held this position on a municipal level. This also applies to 'Aqavya whom the Sages proposed to appoint an Av Bet Din in Israel (*M. 'Eduyot* v, 6). See M. Guttmann, *Mafteaḥ ha-Talmud*, I, p. 82, who points to the tradition in *Ruth Rabba*, and Albeck, *Zion*, 1943, p. 91, who posited the possibility of the position of local Av Bet Din applying to R. Joshua b. Ḥanania and 'Aqavya.

38 iv, 8, 14; *ibid.* 38.
39 *Wars* ii, 20, 5; *Life* §14.
40 Weyl, *Die jüdischen Strafgesetze bei Flavius Josephus*, p. 15. Although the term שבעה טובי העיר is found only in the Babylonian Talmud (*Megilla* 26a), the Palestinian Talmud also mentions שבעת מבני העיר, 'seven burghers of the town', who stand at the head of the community (*Megilla* iii, 74a). Also the epithet טב קרתא, 'town representative' is found in the Palestinian Talmud (*Ta'anit* iv, 68d; so, too, *Lamentations Rabba* v, 12, and *Midrash Samuel* xxxii, ed. Buber, p. 141).
41 Menes, *Die vorexilischen Gesetze Israels*, pp. 91–92; Ring, *Israel's Rechts- leben*, pp. 78–79; Sulzberger, *JQR*, N.S., Vol. III, pp. 48–49, 61 ff; Nicolsky, *ZAW*, 1930, pp. 156–158. Josephus'

Of the period after the Destruction we have no explicit evidence, it seems, of the existence of this type of district judicature; only it is not an improbable assumption that it continued to function also at this period. The local settlement and its administration were, to a large extent, a stable factor amid the upheavals that accompanied the war against Rome and followed it, although at times, to be sure, they also suffered in the time of crisis. Generally speaking the Roman authorities were tolerant towards the autonomous rule of the urban settlements in Jewish Palestine, primarily because an established local management could help to furnish their requirements in the administrative and financial sphere. There is no reason, therefore, to negate the hypothesis that the judicial powers of the local administration were not abolished, at least for given areas of Eretz-Israel, even in the Talmudic period.

The citizens' tribunals. Most of the sources that speak of lay persons connected with judicial proceedings, or with matters of a legal nature, generally refer to any citizens who have no public standing in their locality. These are the 'members of the congregation' [בני כנסת *běnê kěneset*], i.e. the ordinary members of the community, who are contrasted with the 'experts'.[42] But our sources do not explain how these judges were appointed and what authority they and their rulings had in the local administration.

Our survey does not, of course, include actions of a judicial or religio-judicial character that do not involve the settlement of a dispute between parties, or the passing of a sentence of conviction that is enforceable, as for example the selection of arbiters entirely by those concerned, which requires no communal organization or supervision to speak of. But a judicial institution dealing with cases between plaintiffs and defendants is apparently inconceivable — if we exclude arbitration, with which we are not concerned here — unless we assume control and supervision by the public authority to ensure submission by the defendant to litigation and its verdict.[43]

---

testimony concerning the municipal judicature is supported by the tradition in *The History of Susanna* (i, 5): καὶ ἀπεδείχθησαν δύο πρεσβύτεροι ἐκ τοῦ λαοῦ κριταί ἐν τῷ ἐνιαυτῷ ἐκείνῳ ('And the same year there were appointed two of the elders of the people to be judges'). Although this verse does not state expressly that these 'elders' were members of the urban administration, this can be seen from v. 29: καὶ ἀναστάντες οἱ δύο πρεσβύτεροι καὶ κριταί ('Then the two elders and judges arose'). Cf. vv. 34, 41 (see especially the version of Theodotion in v. 41, πρεσβύτεροι τοῦ λαοῦ κ. κριταί 'elders of the people and judges'). But it is still uncertain where and when the book was written and what its original language was.

42 *M. Bekhorot* iv, 2; *Tosefta Sanhedrin* i, 2; *ibid. Bekhorot* iii, 25. Although Lauterbach, like Büchler, takes these *běnê kěneset* to be associates of Rabbinic scholars (*Hebrew Union College Annual, Jubilee Volume*, 1925, pp. 216–218), the real meaning of the expression is that given in the text; see above, p. 211, n. 62 (= *Meḥqarim*, vol. I, p. 162, n. 62).

Undoubtedly the Rishonim are correct in stating that three lay judges can enforce their decision (see below, the views of scholars who wish to identify them invariably with arbitrators).

43 The Rishonim are undoubtedly correct. Three non-ordained judges can force the parties to accept their jurisdiction (but see below, the views of scholars who always seek to identity these judges as arbitrators).

We can posit such control vested in the hands of the entire community represented by 'the assembly of the townspeople [מעמד אנשי העיר] *ma'ămad 'anshê ha-'îr*]', which took unto itself — at least in certain places — supreme authority in the administration of public affairs, both in theory and in practice.[44] The citizens, or some of them, were required and authorized to act as judges in private matters, when they were called upon to try a case by the parties to the dispute or by the plaintiffs.[45] But it is possible that it was the local administration that supervised the citizens' judicial role mentioned above. In that case the municipal authority saw to it that the law was carried out and compelled those judged liable to obey the verdict. Since those judges were not permanent nor belonged to a closed group of administrators, it appears that the composition of these tribunals of changing judges was left undecided, even in respect of fixing the lower limit.[46] It would consequently seem that it is this judicial authority to which the Halakha — ostensibly

---

44 *Ma'amad 'anshê ha-'îr* is referred to in this precise form only in a Baraita in the Babylonian Talmud (*Bava Meṣi'a* 78b; 106b) and in the Gemara (*T.B. Megilla* 26a). Furthermore, in the parallel passage to this Baraita in the Tosefta (*Megilla* i, 5) this assembly is not mentioned at all. The Tosefta likewise makes no mention of the Halakha cited in the Gemara (*ibid*, iii, 1), but makes the sale of the sacred objects of the town depend specifically on the stipulations of the town administrators. Nevertheless, the substance of the Halakha concerning the primacy of 'the citizens' over the administrators is also found in the Palestinian Talmud (iii, 74a): 'With what case are we dealing? If they accepted (an administrative authority) over them, even one (may act). If they did not do so, even many (cannot act)...' Most of the Rishonim explain that the reference is to the assent of the townspeople to the action of the administration in selling sacred articles (in consonance with the discussion in the Babylonian Talmud). But Me'iri interprets the passage in relation to the election of administrators, which was in the hands of the townspeople as a whole. Be this as it may, the power of the latter *vis-à-vis* the administration is clearly stated here. But it is well known that in the course of the second century the ἐκκλησία progressively disappears in the Hellenistic cities of the East as a factor in administration and legislation. The fact that municipal government was placed in the hands of the affluent classes under imperial law (in the period of the Severans) also conduced to the weakening of 'the assembly of the townspeople' even in the Jewish settlements of Eretz-Israel, which were not organized in the form of πόλεις ['cities'].
45 It seems that the courts of the Essenes acted similarly; it is thus implied by Josephus (*Wars* ii, 8, 9), who attests that they did not pass sentence with fewer than a hundred judges (only these judges did not deal with civil suits). Apparently he does not refer to permanent judges but to any 'members of the congregation'. This citizens' tribunal is probably to be regarded as a development of communal judgement, for we still find traces of 'a community; judging' even in the post-Biblical period. Thus we read in Sirach (xxiii 24) that an adulteress αὕτη ἐκκλησίαν ἐξαχθήσεται — 'she shall be led into the assembly' (i.e. for punishment. But can inferences be drawn from a book of proverbs? Perhaps the author is merely using an ancient formula). Also in the story of Susanna the people assemble for judgement, only we do not find them actively participating in the trial. Herod likewise 'handed over' to the community the trial of capital cases and the latter actually carried them out (*Wars* i, 27, 6; *Ant.* xvi, 11, 6–7, and elsewhere). It seems that Herod wished to abide by ancient tradition and to show that he observed it (or renewed it?). See above, 'Par'irtin', p. 84 (= *Meḥqarim*, I, 6, 73).
46 That civil cases require three judges was already taught by R. Akiba (*Tosefta Shevu'ot* iii, 8), but Rabbi calls for five (*ibid.*; *Tosefta Sanhedrin* i, 1; *T.B. ibid.* 3b). The Amoraim of Eretz-Israel differed, as we know, from those of Babylon in regard to judgement given by two, the former disqualifying the decision and the latter validating it (*T.P. Sanhedrin* i, 18a; *T.B. ibid.* 2b; *T.B. Ketubbot*

so surprising — refers in two or three passages, when it rules that each of the parties has the right to demand the appointment of additional judges even during the course of the legal proceedings right to the end.[47]

A third type of communal judicature consisted of permanent 'judges', who were apparently appointed from among the city's nobility and wealthy citizens. This fact is not to be explained on a Halakhic basis,[48] for 'all are eligible to adjudicate in civil cases' and the demand for 'such as can marry (their daughters) to priests' applies only to capital cases.[49] But just as many of the town leaders were men of standing and noble lineage,[50] so it is not surprising that these judges were chosen

---

22a. See the similar dispute with reference to the benediction of the common grace [zimmûn] in *T.B. Berakhot* 45a and *T.P. ibid.* vii, 11a).

47 *Sifre Deuteronomy* §12 (ed. Finkelstein, pp. 19–20): 'If one of them saw that his opponent was winning the case, he would say: I am able to bring (more) witnesses, I have (more) evidence; when I argue my case tomorrow I shall add more judges.' In *Tosefta Sanhedrin* i, 4 we read: 'More judges can always be appointed until the conclusion of the case.' So, too, *T.P. Sanhedrin* iii, 22d (see ed. Finkelstein, *ibid.*, note 1).

Apparently the Baraita in *T.B. Sanhedrin* 23a, 'The perspicacious in Jerusalem [נקיי הדעת, בירושלים, 'the clear-minded of Jerusalem'] acted thus... and they would not sit in judgement unless they knew who would sit with them', refers to the type of Bet Din under discussion; for citizens had the right to refuse to act as judges, when they were not sure that their would-be colleagues were worthy (נקיי הדעת בירושלים) are not to be identified with יקירי ירושלים ['the noble ones of Jerusalem'] and to be regarded as aristocrats and dignitaries, as does Klein, *Madda'e ha-Yahadut*, vol. I, pp. 75–77). The expression 'clarity of mind' simply means 'understanding', 'knowledge of life' (see *T.P. Ma'aśerot* ii, 49d 'R. Ze'ira said: R. Joshua has a clear mind. R. Mani retorted: Are all other people then fools?' So, too, *T.P. Terumot* viii, 45d, with reference to the serpent, who drops venom into liquids: 'This wicked creature has a clear mind and does not drink hot water that has been cooled.' But undoubtedly no inferences are to be drawn from this Baraita in regard to the practice in Temple times for the added reason that the relevant sentence is wanting in the *Mekhilta*, Mishpaṭim, pericope 2, ed. Horovitz-Rabin, p. 322).

48 Dinaburg, *op. cit.*; the question of the judiciary is not to be identified with the appointment of administrators.

49 However, we possess evidence that at first care was taken to appoint as judges only 'such as can marry their daughters to priests'. Thus we are told in the Mishna (*Qiddushin* iv, 5): 'Also any whose name was signed as a witness in the old archives at Sepphoris' (...חתום בערכי — this is the reading in most recensions and appears to be correct; another version is: חתום עד). Some of the Rishonim explained it to mean 'signed as a judge'. This explanation is possible, although ערכי is probably to be understood in the sense of ἀρχεῖον (Gulak, *Dinê Qarqa'ot*, pp. 46–47). It is similarly taught in the Tosefta (Sanhedrin vii, 1): 'Rabban Simeon b. Gamaliel said: Formerly a woman's *ketubba* ['marriage contract'] was signed only by priests, Levites, or Israelites who can marry their daughters to priests.' But even the expression '[those who can] marry their daughters to priests' does not imply the status of real nobility, but refers to Israelites who were born of absolutely lawful wedlock (of which marriage to priests constitutes Halakhic proof); this is, therefore, a religio-national criterion that goes beyond a social test. At any rate, the Halakha in the course of its development validated 'disqualified' citizens as judges (even proselytes, the Palestinian Talmud states — *Yevamot* xii, 12c top, and likewise *T.B. Sanhedrin* 36b — were permitted by some authorities to adjudicate in civil cases; see below, pp. 436 ff.).

50 There are undoubtedly intimations of this also in the Halakha (see Dinaburg, *op. cit.*), just as even the presumption of inheritance is expounded in the Halakha. But this represents only the view of

from among them, because judgeship of this kind symbolized (and vouchsafed) high status in the community.

The image of such a judge emerges from the tradition in the *Sifre,* Numbers, *Be-ha'alotekha,* §79 (ed. Horovitz), p. 76: ' "And he (Jethro) said to him (Moses): I will not go" — He said to him: If I did not return on account of (my) chattels, or on account of (my) land — for sometimes a man has land but no chattels, or he has chattels but no family — but I have land and chattels and family, *and* I was *a judge in my town,* if I did not go (home) on account of my land, I would go on account of my chattels, and if I did not go on account of my chattels, I would go on account of my kindred.'

However, another important factor contributed strongly to the appointment of rich men as judges: they were able to find the time for public service without taking payment. The fact that a judge was prohibited from taking fees for his judgement,[51] and that there was no fixed salary for public administrators in general,[52] as well as for important communal functionaries in the cities, conduced to judicial work being placed in the hands of men of means, 'the *batlanin*' ['men of leisure'].[53]

---

a certain school; other traditions depreciated these things (I intend dealing with the question in the article 'The Sons of the Sages').

51 *M. Bekhorot* iv, 6. But in *Tosefta ibid.,* iii, 8 (cf. *T.B. Ketubbot* 105a; *T.P. Sanhedrin* i, 18b): 'He who is suspected of taking a fee and giving judgement... all the judgements given by him... are void. But one gives the judge a fee for his judgement [i.e. the professional fee to compensate him for loss of work]... although they said: Contemptible is the judge who takes his fee.' Is it far-fetched to suggest that just as this Halakha, which permits the taking of payment for judgement, contains evidence of the country's deteriorated economic position, so it also attests the aim to validate the judicature of people (and Sages) who do not belong to the affluent class?

52 *Tanna de-vê Eliyyahu* (ed. Friedmann, p. 54): 'There was a small town in Eretz-Israel... and they hired unto themselves the Sage *[Ḥākhām]*' etc. However, even if we ascribe this work to Eretz-Israel (I am personally inclined to this view; it was possibly written at the end of the Byzantine period), the subject-matter of the dictum apparently indicates that the reading of the *Yalkut:* 'And they hired a *ḥazzan* (attendant, official, supervisor) for themselves' is the correct version. The same applies to the parallel instance of the appointment of the Babylonian by Resh Laqish as a *ḥazzan* in Basrah (*T.P. Shevi'it* vi, 36d) mentioned in *Deuteronomy Rabba,* ed. Liberman, pp. 60–61, from which it follows he was appointed and allocated a fixed salary, and in this tradition he is not mentioned as having exercised any judicial function (as in T.P.). Indeed, the other functionaries enumerated there (teacher, scribe, etc.), as is known, did receive emoluments from the community.

53 Scholars have been extensively preoccupied in attempting to clarify the nature of the 'ten men of leisure' mentioned in *M. Megilla* (i, 3; see most recently, *JQR* 1943/4, pp. 93 ff). It would seem first of all, however, that these individuals did not constitute some kind of *council* of public leaders. Furthermore, the Halakha — 'Which is considered a large town? — One that has ten men of leisure. One that has fewer is considered a village' — only refers to a locality where at least ten rich men reside, who are able to free themselves from their businesses. This is a socio-economic indication of the multitude of inhabitants of a city. Yet others rightly wanted to regard them as men needed for the performance of public duties (such as Torah and prayer), since from them emanated the individuals who were engaged in public affairs (*T.B. Megilla* 5a; *Sanhedrin* 17b; *T.P. Megilla,* i, 70b).

It seems that already in the first generation after the Destruction the Sages discussed the problem, in the manner in which it is apparently reflected in the dispute between R. Joshua and R. Eleazar of Modi'im in the *Mekhilta* (Massekhta da-Amalek, Jethro, section ii, Horovitz, p. 198): '"Moreover, thou shalt provide... able men", that is, wealthy people, people of means; "such as fear God", that means those who fear the Omnipresent when sitting in judgement; "men of truth", these are people of trust; "hating unjust gain", these are men that are averse to accepting fees for given judgement — this is the view of R. Joshua. R. Eleazar of Modi'im said: "Moreover, thou shalt provide ... able men", that is people of trust; "such as fear of God", those who arbitrate litigations, "men of truth", like R. Hanina b. Dosa and his associates; "hating unjust gain", those who are disdainful of their own money — if now they are contemptuous of their own money, how much more so of that of others.' The same applies to the subsequent dispute: '"And let them judge the people at all seasons" — R. Joshua said: Men who are free from work shall judge the people at all times. R. Eleazar of Modi'im said: Men who are free from work *and occupy themselves with the Torah* shall judge the people at all times.'

It is not unwarranted to perceive in these differences of opinion the disputes of the Sages concerning the kind of judges required for their own days. R. Joshua emphasizes, as a decisive factor in the choice of judges, their economic position, which enables them to find time for public service and makes no mention whatsoever of their preoccupation with Torah study.

At the time of his death, Rabbi Prof. Abrahams had translated the article and notes till here. The rest has been completed by another hand.

R. Eleazar of Modi'im, in contradistinction, attaches less importance to this factor and emphasizes Torah study and saintly conduct as the essential precondition for judgeship. Here, then, we have before us two contradictory Tannaitic evaluations of the qualifications of the 'secular' aristocracy for judicial authority.

This negative attitude towards prevailing conditions is apparently given caustic expression by another contemporary Sage.[54] In *Deuteronomy Rabba,* MS Munich (Buber, *Bet Talmud,* IV, p. 278) and MS Oxford (Lieberman, pp. 13–14), we read: 'What does *hirba etkhem* (lit. 'has made you great') [mean]? You find that Ben Azzai said: A Jew's dog is better than a Jewish judge. How? One man came and said to another: Exchange with me. Will you take this kid and give me that dog? He said to him: Yes. As they were standing, someone else came and said to him: Take two for yourself. Another came and said: Take three. Still another came and said: Take four for yourself. They would not agree. They came to trial to a judge and related the case to him. The judges began saying: Let them divide the dog among the four of them, and let each take a quarter of the dog (while the Sages say: The verdict should be in favour of the first only). But they divided it among the four men. So it happens that justice is perverted, and one receives an ear more than

---

54 We certainly cannot be positive that Ben Azzai uttered these words exactly as transcribed.

the next. What happens to the judges? They destroy their lives and the lives of their children and everything they have. What caused this (to happen) to them? That he gave more to one than to the other. Alas, a dog's ear is worth more than their judges.[55] Hence, "the Lord your God has made you greater than your judges".' The caustic language this tradition uses against these 'Judges of Israel' makes it clear to us that the Sages had the upper and powerful classes in mind and not the simple citizens who undertook to conduct lawsuits only occasionally. The Sages objected to these judges because they were ignorant (that is to say, they did not judge in accordance with the Halakhic norms), and just as in other Tannaitic Halakhic traditions, the insistence is repeated that only judges 'expert in law' be appointed.[56]

A similar accusation, presumably, appears in a Baraita quoted in *Sifre Deuteronomy*, §17 (ed. Finkelstein, pp. 19–20): '"You shall not respect persons in judgement" — (this is directed at) the person appointed for the placement of judges. Lest you say: This person is pleasing, I shall assign him a judgeship; this person is mighty, I shall assign him a judgeship; this person is my relative (*qerovi*),[57] I shall assign him a judgeship; this person knows Greek, I shall assign him a judgeship; this person knows all languages, I shall assign him a judgeship. It is found that he acquits the guilty, and convicts the innocent, not because he is wicked, but because he is ignorant. Scripture regards him as if he had respected persons in judgement.' Several scholars in recent times have explicated this tradition as being directed against the Patriarch (or his authorized agent), who would appoint the judges to their seats in the communities.[58] Nevertheless the expression 'appointed for the placement of judges' and the entire passage itself, which sets down the above-mentioned qualifications of the candidates, makes their

---

55 It stands to reason that what we have here is a popular maxim. The Haggada, however, wished to interweave it with circumstances providing an excuse for the usage (the legally unjustified award of a dog's ear is the excuse for the exaction of retribution from the judge). This approach is adopted by the Haggada in other instances as well, as in the incident, for instance, involving R. Eliezer recorded in *Genesis Rabba*, xlii: 'And his cow fell and broke (its leg). He said: It was for my good that my cow broke its leg'; similarly in *T.P. Horayot* iii, 48a, where the remark, too, is a popular maxim. The same applies to *T.B. Shabbat* 116b: 'She brought him a golden lamp... R. Gamaliel said to him: An ass came and knocked down the lamp.' The lamp was introduced into the narrative in order to furnish a pretext for the emergence of the proverb (*T.P. Yoma* i, 38c, 'The donkey kicked over the Menorah.').
56 *Midrash Tannaim*, pp. 97, 161.
57 Lieberman (*Sinai* IV, p. 233) wishes to regard *qerova* as 'precentor', for the holder of this office is sometimes associated with a '*poetan*' in the Haggada, that is to say, he received his appointment in recognition of his public service and fitness. First of all, however, the recension *qerovi* should be retained, and moreover we find no *qerova* among the Tannaim (even though R. Eliezer b. R. Simeon is accorded this title in Midrashim). Nor do we learn of any permanently serving precentor until Amoraic times (the Haggada concerning R. Eliezer b. R. Simeon being unreliable in its present form). See §144 — '"You (the judge) shall not pervert judgement" — You shall not say: Such a man is pleasant; such a man is *qerovi* [my relative].' Consequently *qerovi* is to be taken in its plain sense.
58 Guttmann, *MGWJ*, 1936, p. 353; Dinaburg, *ibid.*, et al. So Rambam in his Code and in the *Sefer Hamiṣvot* (See Finkelstein, *op. cit.*, p. 28, n. 15).

conjecture far-fetched in my mind. What is dealt with here is, presumably, the making of local appointments (by the municipal administrations, which assigned the selection of city judges to one of its members), the appointments being determined solely by personal and social criteria, without knowledge of the Torah, i.e. the teachings of the Sages, being a prerequisite.[59]

The aforementioned traditions censure these judges for their lack of attachment to, and preparation for 'lawsuits conducted according to the Halakha'. Nevertheless many Baraitot make the grave accusation of moral corruption against the 'Judges of Israel' and testify against them that they pervert justice, favour persons and take bribes — and hold them responsible for the troubles that beset Israel and for delaying the advent of the Messiah.[60] Even though similar condemnations are found in the tradition of the Sages, of the 'Elders' who do not practice what they preach, take bribes and show favouritism in lawsuits,[61] it is nevertheless clear that the above-mentioned statements refer only to the 'wicked judges' who were not learned Sages, the strong-armed, power-wielding and upper-class individuals in the settlements.[62] The truth of these testimonies is certainly not to be denied. It is only natural for the pedigreed class to give rise to social corruption, as the Sages averred (especially in the particular, political circumstances following the Bar Kokhba rebellion, in that and subsequent generations). Nevertheless we may safely ascribe a certain measure of polemical exaggeration to these statements, since they constitute a protest against the existence of powerful judges of the aristocracy of wealth and parentage, who did not, generally, belong to the realm of the learned in Torah.

How did these unqualified judges (*hedyoṭot* [lit. 'commoners']) try their lawsuits? After all, only very few laws are explicitly stated in the Torah, and these are insufficient to constitute a legal system of any kind.

Firstly, some of them must certainly have possessed some familiarity with the teachings of the Sages pertaining to monetary cases, which they must have tried

---

59 Cf. Büchler, *Manhige Ṣippori*, p. 30.
60 *T.B. Shabbat* 139a; *Sanhedrin* 98a; *Tosefta Soṭa* xiv, 3–4; *T.B. ibid.* 47b. Dinaburg's conjecture, *ibid.*, p. 99, that 'those who forced their goods upon the householders' were the Sages, who were judges, is far-fetched; although the expression, which is also found in *T.B. Shabbat* and was voiced by R. Judah in reference to the sons of Eli, is not altogether clear, it may reasonably be held to apply to power-wielding individuals who were not Sages. See Büchler, *Manhige Ṣippori*, p. 27.
61 *Ruth Rabba*, lxxxi, 2; *Deuteronomy Rabba* lxxxii, 9, etc. Most of these evidences date from the Amoraic period. About the same time (that of the first Amoraim), Origen complained at the Bishops, 'Elders' and ministers being ignorant boors, who love pecuniary gain, are corrupt, devour the flesh of orphans, sell the church for money, and rush after glory (Commentary on Matthew); Lommatzsh, *op. cit.*, Vol. IV, p. 202. See also, Harnack, *Die kirchengeschichtiiche Ertrag* usw., Texte und Untersuchungen, 1916,1, p. 114.
62 See in detail, Büchler, *The Political and Social Leaders* etc. This scholar by far exaggerates the depravity of the city judges. He also denies the existence of judges who were Sages in Galilee prior to the Bar Kokhba rebellion, which is unsubstantiated. He also fails to mention the rivalry existing in the world of the Sages themselves in respect of the exercise of judicial functions by the urban upper classes, which we have pealt [sic] with.

to learn or else they must have relied for assistance on the legal opinions of the Sages and their disciples, whom they consulted. This much may be inferred from R. Eleazar b. R. Simeon's attack upon the 'disciples of the Sages who were relatives of the judges', obviously for their having assisted their relatives, affording them guidance in trying cases — and also from the Baraita which forbids 'the teaching of monetary laws to the ignorant'.[63] Yet certainly many of these 'ignorant judges' would have no truck with the Halakha and its exponents. It stands to reason, then, that they must first of all have rendered their decisions in conformity with precedents, with 'local custom', some sort of 'common law'. Secondly, their verdicts must in the main have been based on 'equity' and on their appraisal of the facts, but not according to any defined legal procedures.[64] Consequently, in all likelihood, a whole system of popular civil law became crystallized in the course of time, side by side with the official Halakha of the Sages.

The fact that these courts generally lacked all connection with the laws of the Sages emerges, it seems, from the sources. In *T.P. Sanhedrin* iii, 21a, it is stated of an Halakha in our Mishna: '"Each party may reject the judge of the other..." (which the Palestinian Talmud takes to refer to the selection of the court to try the case by the litigants, see below) — Resh Laqish said: They said this of the courts in Syria, but not of cases tried by Torah law; R. Johanan said: Even in Torah lawsuits.' Resh Laqish sought to restrict the right of the parties to disqualify a judge or judicial tribunal proposed by the other party (see below) to courts of unqualified judges only, of which the 'Syrian courts' furnish an obvious example. Now these courts existed parallel to the 'lawsuits' conducted by the Sages according to the Halakha, and this parallel functioning can only be explained by the fact that the former did not base their judgements on the laws of the Sages.

It appears that the substance of this distinction is also evident in the tradition we cite here. In *T.P. Sanhedrin* i, 18a, we read: 'Two men came to R. Jose b. Ḥalafta. They said to him: (Try our case) on condition that you judge according to Torah law. He said to them: I don't know Torah law, but may He Who knows (human) thoughts exact retribution from those men. Will you accept what I shall say to you?' The commentators have found this seemingly obscure passage difficult to explain. It appears, however, that here the Sage had two alternatives, either to try the case as a 'qualified expert' (*Mumḥe*) or else as an unqualified judge (*hedyoṭ*) who would not be liable to suffer the penalties that misjudging a case in Torah law would entail.[65] The litigants had demanded that R. Jose try the case as an 'expert'.

---

63 *T.B. Shabbat* 139a. Mar Zutra's observation, *ibid.*; 'These are the disciples of the Sages who teach communal laws to ignorant judges'; *Mekhilta de R. Simeon b. Johai*, p. 97.

64 Büchler, *Manhige Ṣippori*, p. 21. He regards it possible, however, that the 'heads of the settlements' exercising judicial functions were judges appointed by the Roman government.

65 Büchler, *ibid.*, p. 21, holds that these litigants refused to be tried by Torah law, since they rejected the teachings of the Sages, somewhat after the manner of the Sadducees. This elucidation fits in with his general view (which is groundless) of the Galilean *Ammê Ha'areṣ* who were especially hard natured. Nevertheless, the tradition cited below does not lend any credence to this explanation of his.

He, however, evaded the issue by claiming that he 'did not know' how to judge otherwise than by his personal evaluation, after the manner of the unqualified judge (since he had been approached by them to act as judge, he was acceptable to them as [having the authority of] three [judges] — *Tosefta, Sanhedrin* iv, 1). His evasion and sharp retort stemmed from his realization of their hidden intention, to reserve the right to themselves to appeal his verdict, and have it annulled as erroneous, if either of them was dissatisfied. Hence he would only consent to officiate as an unqualified judge, whose decision is irrevocable, even when he is mistaken.[66]

Their stipulation was based on the Halakha that the erroneous verdict of a qualified judge can be reversed, while that of an unqualified judge cannot,[67] the view of R. Joseph in the Talmud (*T.B. Sanhedrin* 33a): 'In the case of a *Mumḥe* we reverse (the verdict); in the case of a non-*Mumḥe* we do not.'[68]

---

66 The tradition concerning R. Jose's behaviour is appended to the opening of the discussion in this way: 'And it follows R. Jose.' That passage, however, is truncated and its content obscure. See Ginzberg's suggested reconstruction of the text (*Jubilee Volume in honour of Israel Levi* [Hebrew], pp. 407–409): '... "Before them" — to the best of them, which teaches that one does not teach monetary laws to the ignorant'. The *No'am Yerushalmi* suggests a similar reading: <'"Before them" — and not before the unqualified'>. Yet the passage still remains unclear. At all events no arguments can be adduced from R. Jose's tradition to refute our explanation. Certainly the very dread of passing judgement, and often the complexity of 'Torah' jurisprudence could well have impelled the Sage-judge to recoil from becoming involved in the gravity, and often the complexity of Torah jurisprudence.

The large measure of freedom accorded the unqualified judge, not bound by Torah law, to pronounce judgement in accordance with what is 'right and good', could also have induced the Sage to try cases not as a *Mumḥe*. It is not far-fetched, in my opinion, to assert that R. Joḥanan's dictum (*T.B. Bava Meṣi'a*, 30b): 'Jerusalem was only destroyed because they based their judgements on the law of the Torah' is relevant here. Certainly the Babylonian Talmud poses the question: 'Should they then have judged with unqualified judges?' ('by force' — Rashi). The Talmud amends the statement to 'They based their judgements on Torah law and did not go beyond the requirements of the law'. Yet the entire observation needs no emendation, and the Talmud fits in perfectly with the tradition *ab initio*. R. Joḥanan protested against them — both litigants and judges — needing to depend on the strict particulars of the Torah of the Sages, and refusing to conduct their trials within the freer judicial framework that approximated more closely to the 'good' of the unqualified judges.

67 Our explanation agrees partially with the view of R. Jacob, the author of the *Ṭurim* (*Ṭur, Ḥoshen Mishpat*, Hilkhot Dayyanim, xii, 6). The latter, however, holds the view that R. Jose wanted them to submit to arbitration. It stands to reason, however, that the enforcement depended upon the consent of the parties, as the wording shows: 'Go out and settle' (*Tosefta, Sanhedrin* i, 6; *T.B. ibid.*, 6b; *T.P. ibid.*, i, 6b. Cf. *Mekhilta, Massekhta da'Amalek*, Jethro ii, Horowitz p. 190; ' "And his friend" — this is the law which has a compromise (*peshara*), that the two of them become tempered [*nifsharin*] to each other like friends'). Now R. Jose rebukes them: 'Will you accept upon yourselves what I say?' even where the verdict would not be to their advantage. If so, then why did he curse them? Because they did not come before him for arbitration, but for him to judge them, did they deserve to be cursed?

68 The reversal of a verdict in monetary cases, which is mentioned in the teachings of the Tannaim, is also referred to by Josephus in regard to the seven judges of the city (Ant. iv, 7, 14): ἢ ἄλλην τινὰ αἰτίαν προφέροι καθ' ἣν οὐ καλῶς ἐλέγχει αὐτοὺς ἀποφηναμένους ('Let judges have power

The juridical authority of the ordained Sages. A relatively large amount of source material pertaining to this field is available. Moreover, we have in our possession definitions of sorts for ordination, texts of certificates of appointment, as well as evidence of the development of ordination through its various stages. Contemporary scholars, too, have produced research studies on the subject.[69] Nevertheless, we still possess no comprehensive presentation of the history of the *Semikha* and the structure of the courts headed by *Mumḥim*. We also lack sufficient documentation in the sources to compile them.

Ordination possesses one basic significance: the co-option of the Sage to the Sanhedrin (and the Great Bet Midrash).[70] The expression *Yashav Biyeshiva* (took his seat in the Academy) used synonymously for *Ḥakham,* Sage or Rabbi (or 'was given his seat in the Academy') proves as much.[71] The same connotation applies

---

to pronounce what sentence they think fit, always provided that no one denounces them for having received a bribe or of not having pronounced aright.') Contrastingly, he testifies of the Essenes (*Wars* ii, 8, 9) that they never reverse any court verdict. Possibly the obscure tradition appearing further on in the Palestinian Talmud has some bearing here: 'We were taught there: If one had judged a case and pronounced the guilty guiltless and the guiltless guilty... What he has done is irrevocable... and he must pay from his pocket... R. Ba in the name of R. Abbahu: When they said to him: You are as acceptable to us as three [judges] on condition that you judge us in accordance with Torah law, and he erred and delivered his verdict in accordance with his own appraisal, he must pay from his pocket because he acted presumptuously in trying the case on his own assessment, for we have been taught: Do not judge alone, for no one may judge alone, except the One.' I regard 'Torah law' here as having the same connotation as in the case of R. Jose. R. Abbahu's remark purports to protest against the judge who consents to conduct a trial on his own properly and in accordance with the Torah of the Sages and does not humble himself to judge like the 'unqualified' (once they had accepted him as equivalent to three judges). For R. Abbahu always warned against judging on one's own, even a *Mumḥe* (although it is stated of him further that he himself had conducted a lawsuit singly, once the parties to the trial 'had accepted him over them', as the Baraita transcribed there in his name has it, *ibid.* Do we have conflicting traditions before us?).

In the parallel in the Babylonian Talmud, *Sanhedrin* 6a, however, we find: '...since they said to him: Judge us according to the Torah', the significance of the stipulation being that he should not err. Yet it is easy to discern that the content represents a change from the main substance of the original Palestinian tradition.

Another version of this discussion is found in the *Sefer Hama'asim Shel Bĕnê Ereṣ Israel* (*Tarbiz* I, 3, p. 10): 'What is it that we have been taught? Having judged the case... what he has done is irrevocable and he must pay from his pocket? You say that he judged in accordance with his own, appraisal, and they had accepted this, but in such matters as he traduces the Torah...' — the language is obscure.

69 See, most recently, Albeck, *Zion* (1943), pp. 85–93.
70 A certain scholar has, however, recently written that the 'appointment of Elders' is not to be regarded as entailing membership in the Sanhedrin (A. Weiss, *Proceedings of the American Academy for Jewish Research,* 1944, p. 273). Yet, except for the sole passage that he deals with, and which is not decisive for our discussion, as he admits, such membership is certainly included in the signification of ordination.
71 *Tosefta, Demai,* ii, 8, and the parallels in the Talmudim: *T.B. Nedarim* 62a; *Yoma* 78a, etc. Even the expression: 'On the day that they appointed R. Eleazar to the Academy' (*M. Zevaḥim* i, 3; *Yadayim* iii, 5) does not essentially convey anything else than ordination. Although this testimony of our Mishna apparently contradicts that referring to the appointment of R. Eleazar B. Azaria

to the term *Yashav berosh* (or *Hushav berosh*), which never meant anything else than ordination (the last expression stems from the practice of the 'sages' to sit on higher seats than their 'disciples').[72] The actual conferring of membership in the Great Bet Din entailed, *ipso facto,* the authorization to try lawsuits, as well as other 'rights and privileges' conferred on the Sage. Insofar as the law is concerned, two elements are involved here: (a) the certification of professional competence (in the language of the Babylonian Talmud, 'learned and able to reason logically');[73] (b) the granting of authority 'to give rulings' (taking authority — *neṭilat reshut*).

These sources, however, also make mention of appointment not involving 'taking one's seat in the Academy' but as being the direct granting of authority to perform certain specific public functions alone. This aspect of ordination as appointment to public office is especially evident from what we find to have existed from Rabbi's days and onwards, the separation of functions previously included in ordination in general, and the granting of certification for single specific duties.[74] (The same would apply to appointments granted for limited periods of time, which confront us first in the third century.)[75] This last manifestation is a wide deviation from the earlier frame of reference of *Semikha,* which was essentially: the concentration of the communal authority of the Sages within the Sanhedrin. Such a development, however, proves how great was the real worth of ordination in actual practice; it constituted direct certification for public office in the settled areas of the country. And this fact of itself is tied up with the growth of the element of 'rulership' in ordination, which corresponded to the increase in the power and quality of the *ordaining authority.*

From here we are led to the investigation of the nature of the ordaining authority. Apparently this is clearly established by that famous tradition (end of the third century) in *T.P. Sanhedrin* (i, 19a), which scholars have used as the basis for their

---

'on that very day' as Patriarch, our explanation still stands, although here is not the place to deal with the topic. Similarly, too, the expression 'And they appointed him to the Academy' in reference to Menaḥem b. Sugnai in *Tosefta Eduyot* iii, 2, also signifies ordination. (His ordination was conferred on the occasion of his evidence on a question of Halakha, and is similar to R. Joḥanan's conferring ordination on R. Jose b. Ḥanina, *T.B. Sanhedrin* 30b).

72 The episode involving R. Eleazar Ḥisma and R. Joḥanan b. Gudgada (in the Babylonian tradition, *Horayot* 10a; the parallel, *Sifre Deuteronomy* xvi has 'R. Joḥanan b. Nuri') whom 'R. Gamaliel appointed at the head' (the Talmudic version) does not signify that they were appointed 'supervisors in the House of Study' (as Bacher holds, *Aggada der Tannaiten,* I, p. 360, n. 1; i *Studien usw.,* pp. 13–30; Finkelstein in his notes to *Sifre,* p. 26) but that they received ordination by the Sages instead (like the wording of the *Sifre*: 'And R. Gamaliel appointed them to the Academy'). That they thereby obtained their livelihood (according to the Babylonian tradition, but not mentioned in the *Sifre*) was part of the general practice of supporting ordained Sages (especially); see below.
73 That the deciding factor in the performance of judicial functions is the qualification of knowledge emerges from Ben Sira's remarks, xxxviii, 33–34; xxxix, 1 ('On the seat of the judges they shall not sit', etc., and the same occurs in the Greek version).
74 See especially *T.P. Ḥagiga* i, 76c–d, and its parallel in *Nedarim* x, 42b.
75 *T.P.* ibid.; *T.B. Sanhedrin* 5b.

concurring conception of the metamorphosis in ordination during the course of generations. Here is the text: 'Said R. Ba:[76] At first each would ordain his own disciples — such as R. Joḥanan b. Zakkai who ordained R. Eliezer; R. Eliezer, R. Joshua; R. Joshua, R. Akiba; R. Akiba, R. Meir and R. Simeon... They reverted and accorded honour to this House (the Patriarchal family). They declared ordination conferred by a Bet Din[77] without the ratification of the Patriarch to be void; while ordination by the Patriarch without the approval of the Bet Din to be valid. They reverted and instituted that no Bet Din should ordain without the approval of the Bet Din.'

Of the three stages in the history of ordination as viewed by this tradition, we shall briefly survey the middle one, the concentration of ordination in the hands of the Patriarch, first. As is known, scholars differ on when this state of affairs first came into being. Some assign the event to the days of Rabban Simeon b. Gamaliel, others to the time of Rabbi.

As I see it, the first view has no ground to stand on. First, we find Rabbi granting ordination in many instances, while nowhere is there any mention of the Sanhedrin of his time doing likewise. As for Rabban Simeon b. Gamaliel, we never find him granting ordination at all, even though in his days, *Mumḥim* were appointed by the Bet Din.[78] Secondly, although Rabbi controlled the Sages (as well as the nation as a whole) with a firm hand, nevertheless it is reasonable to assume that Rabban Simeon b. Gamaliel needed the Sages and was even subordinate to them, even though he was successful in the course of time in providing himself with a position of supremacy in the Sanhedrin. This fact, which is variously manifested, is not to be accounted for in terms of the personality of the Patriarch only. In those days the Patriarchate became weakened *vis-à-vis* the nation and even the realm of the Sages.[79] Finally, the opinion is current among scholars that Rabban Simeon b. Gamaliel secured recognition for his Patriarchate from the Roman government, and furthermore that it was he who was the true founder of the Patriarchate, wielding unlimited and recognized power.[80] This view, it appears, is totally unsupported by the sources. We never find R. Simeon b. Gamaliel being accepted by the government or dependent upon the ruling power (as in the case of his successor, Rabbi, and his predecessor, R. Gamaliel). This is presumably more than a coincidence. Its cause lies in the political position of Eretz-Israel, which suffered discrimination in the days of the Antonines. At that time the government could *tolerate* the existence of the Patriarchate but could not recognize it officially.

---

76 In R. Judah of Barcelona's *Sefer Hashetarot* (ed. Halberstadt), p. 133, the reading is 'R. Abba b. Bina'.
77 As is known, Maimonides (Laws of Sanhedrin iv, 5) has: *Av Bet Din*. This is the reading of the *Midrash Hagadol*, MS, *Numbers* Pineḥas. Guttmann (*Mafteah* I, p. 89) accepts Maimonides' version. There are no grounds for doing so, however (our reading is also accepted by Rishonim).
78 *M. Sanhedrin* iii, 1; *Tosefta ibid.*, v, 1; *T.B. ibid.*, 23a.
79 I intend to deal with this point in the future, in my above-mentioned article, *Qavvim*, etc.
80 Dinaburg, *ibid.*, p. 88; Zucker, *op. cit.*, pp. 151–153.

We revert to the first period. It can be inferred that until the time of Rabbi, ordination was entrusted neither to the Patriarchate nor to the Sanhedrin, but was conferred by individual Sages, who ordained their disciples as Rabbis but not as members and delegates of the Great Bet Din. For at that time no direct relationship obtained between ordination and the central authority. Essentially ordination signified testimony to the professional competence of the candidate. This conception is to be found, as is known, in the Babylonian Talmud which regards the *Mumḥe Larabbim* (qualified to try cases as a sole judge) as one who had acquired expertise in Torah knowledge without having 'obtained authority' (*T.B. Sanhedrin* 5a).

Yet many finer points compel us to cast considerable doubt on the veracity of this evidence. Certainly, the tradition is apparently reinforced by what is related of R. Akiba in the Talmud — that he ordained his own disciples[81] — and the same applies to R. Judah b. Bava who also conferred ordination.[82] The episode involving R. Judah b. Bava, however, occurred at the time when neither Patriarchate nor Sanhedrin existed, 'in the generation of forcible conversion' (immediately subsequent to the Bar Kokhba rebellion). It is not to be wondered at, then, that this Sage arose and rescued Jewish jurisprudence from extinction. Furthermore, the very substance of this tradition concerning R. Judah b. Bava's ordination of Sages is subject to doubt.[83] It is not even known when R. Akiba ordained his disciples.

---

81 *T.P. Sanhedrin* i, 19a; *T.B. Sanhedrin* 14a.
82 *T.B. ibid.*
83 First of all, the Talmud itself has noted the contradiction between the traditions ascribing the ordination of R. Meir and R. Simeon to R. Akiba and to R. Judah b. Bava (the explanation advanced by the Talmud is merely an attempt at harmonization, and so unacceptable). All the evidence concerning the death of R. Judah b. Bava at the hands of Roman legions, however (at the time when he was engaged in conferring ordination), is doubtful. We have been taught in a Baraita quoted in the Babylonian Talmud (*Soṭa* 48b; *Sanhedrin* 11a; *Canticles Rabba* lxxxviii, 10): 'And they sought to say the same of R. Judah b. Bava, but the hour was too turbulent, since no funeral orations were delivered over those slain by the government.' (In MS Munich, *Soṭa*, 'since funeral orations are not delivered...' alone appears. In Sanhedrin, however, the text is the same as we have given it.) Hence the text in its original form does confirm that he was slain by the Romans. So, too, is his name listed in *Midrash Pss.* ix (Buber ed., 45a) and in *Lamentations Rabba*, in the comment on the verse: 'The Lord has swallowed up unsparingly...', among those suffering martyrdom at the hands of the Romans. Yet we are disposed, first, to assume that two earlier traditions have been combined here; the one having, 'the hour was turbulent' and the other explaining that 'no funeral orations were delivered'. 'The hour was turbulent' conveys that prevailing abnormal political conditions prevented the Sages in general from performing certain specific acts, but does not denote any Halakhic obstacle directly affecting the person in question, such as 'No funeral orations are delivered over those martyred by the Roman government', which referred to his case specifically. We may therefore infer that the first reason accounts for the other. In the parallel in *Tosefta Soṭa*, xiii, 5 and in *T.P. ibid*, ix, 24b, we only have the reading: 'But the hour was turbulent.' Is it then far-fetched to assume that tradition did not know of R. Judah b. Bava meeting his death in the manner reported in the Babylonian Talmud? This assumption is supported by the tradition in the Palestinian Talmud, *ibid.* a, and *Tosefta Bava Qamma* viii, 13, which explicitly testifies that he died a natural death in his home because he violated the prohibition against raising a sheep in

Possibly, he did so immediately after the defeat of Bar Kokhba. But this apart, R. Akiba was, after all, one of the most prominent members of the Sanhedrin, and ordination by him could well have been considered as ordination by the Sanhedrin itself, which had vested the authority in him to do so (either explicitly or tacitly). The general assumption that the Head of the Great Bet Din would confer ordination on behalf of the Sanhedrin, and not personally as the teacher of the ordained, should rightfully be accepted as applying to the third period, as we shall see later on.

At all events, we find Rabban Gamaliel conferring ordination in the Jabneh period (and the indication is that it was he who made the decisions)[84] and also R. Akiba calling R. Ṭarfon 'qualified for the Bet Din', which would signify that he had certainly been ordained in the name of the Great Bet Din. The same expression, however, is reiterated by R. Meir and his colleagues,[85] which indicates that even in the generation of Usha, the main object of ordination was for membership in the Sanhedrin.

Furthermore the very tradition itself relating to R. Abba also reinforces our doubts. What this tradition conveys principally is the evolution of the relationship between the Patriarchate and Sanhedrin in respect of ordination. In the second period, the Patriarchate attained exclusive authority (this is substantiated by the facts), while in the third, a compromise of some sort was effected, a balance between the two contending elements for supreme control. It is reasonable to assume then, that even the first period represents a particular stage in this process; that is to say, at first ordination was completely entrusted to the Sages in the form of the Sanhedrin. During the next epoch, it rested exclusively with the Patriarchate, while finally the two authorities combined. This pattern is reasonable (although the main substance of the evidence fits the situation subsequent to the Bar Kokhba rebellion and continuing till the time of Rabbi, rather than the time of Rabban Gamaliel of Jabneh). This cannot be said of the tradition in its original form, since at first glance it would be incapable of explaining how the right of ordination, which originally had no connection at all with the central authority, should later become the exclusive province of the Patriarchate, and why, after it had reverted to the Sages, it did not accrue to them in their individual capacities but as the Bet Din.

Hence the tradition under discussion is highly suspect in respect of the first period. Nevertheless, its wording undoubtedly reflects certain concrete facts. First

---

his house. Certainly it is possible to argue that this last tradition is derived from the rule of the Babylonian Talmud (*Temura* 15b; *Bava Qamma* 80a) that wherever it is reported that 'It happened that a certain pious man...' the reference is to R. Judah b. Bava or R. Judah b. Il'ai, and that its first version is the same as in *T.B. Temura, ibid.*, and *Bava Qamma* 80a: 'It happened that a certain pious man...' At all events there were Sages who did not ascribe R. Judah b. Bava's death to the Romans, and even more so is the tradition of his having conferred ordination on that occasion questionable.

84 This is the incident of the appointment of R. Eleazar Ḥisma and R. Johanan b. Nuri. See above, n. 72.
85 *M. Sanhedri*n, iii, 1; *Tosefta* v, 1; *T.B. ibid.* 23a.

of all, it may reasonably be assumed that in the period immediately following Bar Kokhba's rebellion (and this lasted for a long time) and until the Patriarchate became reestablished and the standing of the Sanhedrin, too, had become stabilized once more, it was possible for individual ordination to become current practice, and then not to disappear entirely even after the positions of the Great Bet Din and Patriarchate had become normalized. Yet even the discriminating investigation of the situation and opinions prevailing in the time of R. Abba can provide us with an explanation of the form the tradition has taken, as we shall see presently.

The evidence furnished by that tradition of the third period, that ordination was entrusted in general to two authorities, the Patriarchate and the Sanhedrin, is substantiated by the sources in our possession. Most of the ordinations that are mentioned were granted by the Patriarch.[86] On several occasions, however, it was the Sages, as we learn, who did the conferring.[87] Yet the Patriarch undoubtedly

---

86 T.P. Ḥagiga i, 76d; Nedarim x, 42b; T.P. Terumot xi, 48b, and the parallel, Shabbat ii, 4d; Ketubbot, i, 25a and the parallel, Ruth Rabba, vii 8: 'R. Pineḥas said: ..."From this we learn that this House appoints Elders at their banquet halls".' And in Sifre Zuṭa ed. Horowitz, p. 271: 'It teaches that every Elder to whom the head of the generation dealt honour...' (in speaking of the ordination of Sages).

87 Soṭa 40a: 'The Rabbis decided to appoint him (sic, MS Munich), R. Abbahu, at the head.' In T.P. Eruvin viii, 28b, in the name of R. Ḥiyya (b. Abba): 'When we ordain Sages, we shall appoint you with them' (and it makes no difference to our discussion whether the remark was made 'in jest' or 'seriously').

It is in place here to deal with the passage in T.B. Yoma 88a–b which poses the question to us: 'Rabba b.b. Ḥana said: They asked R. Eleazar: Must an Elder who is a member of the Academy obtain permission to declare a firstborn animal permitted, or must he not?... R. Isaac b. Ḥaqola (the correct reading) rose to his feet and said: I saw R. Jose b. Zimra, who was both an Elder and a member of the Academy, and was superior to the grandfather of this one, yet obtained permission to declare a firstborn permissible. ...' This tradition confirms that the Patriarchs possessed the exclusive right to grant permission to rule on firstborn animals (a matter to which Patriarchs paid the most meticulous attention in granting ordination, T.B. Sanhedrin 5a and T.P. Ḥagiga i, 76c, and the parallel in Nedarim). This would seem at first sight to remove the right of ordination entirely from the Sages' province, for it stands to reason that the status of the 'Elder who was appointed to the Academy' was not at all dependent upon any 'securing of permission' from the Patriarch (as was the right to declare a firstborn permissible). The conclusion follows explicitly from the dictum of R. Idi b. Avin, ibid.: 'This matter was left for the House of the Patriarch in which to distinguish itself', which implies that all other areas of authority did not require the Patriarch's assent. From here it follows that the consent which, according to the tradition of R. Abba, had to be given by the Patriarchs for appointment to the Bet Din was not accepted by all (or not always).

However, R. Abba himself denies the entire tradition transmitted by Isaac b. Ḥaqola (further in the same section). It is also necessary to examine the passage in order to determine the date when this took place. For it is known that R. Jose b. Zimra's teacher married off his son to the former's daughter (Ketubbot 62b). Hence it follows that the event in question occurred during the time of Rabbi and this implies that the Sages were not dependent upon him for their ordination. The fact, however, that there is much evidence testifying to the right of ordination being concentrated in the hands of the Patriarch, taken together with what we know of R. Isaac b. Ḥaqola that he was a disciple of R. Judah Nesi'a (the first) — supports the identification of 'his grandfather' as R. Judah Nesi'a II's paternal grandfather and so indicates that the episode took place in the days of R. Judah

held the upper hand.[88] This is most convincingly established by the tradition in *T.P. Horayot* iii, 48c:[89] 'They sought to appoint Elders. From where do they make the appointments? From Tiberias — from the South? R. Simeon said: "Judah shall go up." R. Mana said to him: This (Scriptural verse) speaks of war, but for ordination (it is) "those who see the face of the king" who sit first in the kingdom - this teaches that ordination is vested in the Patriarch' (who had his seat in Galilee).[90]

Yet many facts indicate, apparently, that even in the last period ordination was still at times held to lie within the province of the individual Sage. First, we read in many instances in the Babylonian Talmud of R. Joḥanan conferring ordination on his disciples,[91] and the Palestinian Talmud gives evidence of R. Joshua b. Levi doing likewise to his disciples.[92] To these testimonies we must add the evidence of the Babylonian Talmud (*Sanhedrin* 5a) concerning Rabba b. R. Huna, who 'received his authority from his father, and R. Huna had received his from Rab, and Rab from R. Ḥiyya, which shows that the Rabbi could ordain his disciples without any direct connection with the Bet Din or Patriarch.

Nesi'a I. (In that event, R. Jose b. Zimra must have been extremely old at the time or else was it, possibly, his grandson who is mentioned here?)

88 The fact of the matter under discussion: The opposition of the Sages to the nomination of judges by the Patriarchs can testify to this. (There is no doubt however, that our sources only bring the opinions of some of the group opposed to the Patriarchate, such as Resh Laqish, to light.) Nevertheless, a view currently held by scholars (see most recently, Dinaburg, *op. cit.*, p. 97) seeks to ascribe the entire regulation restricting the Patriarch's power to the cases where they received remuneration for conferring ordination. This explanation is without any basis in the sources nor is it a reasonable assumption. The denial of the Patriarchs' exclusive right in granting ordination and its being made dependent on the Bet Din stems from the earlier protracted rivalry between the Patriarchate and the Sanhedrin for control, and was facilitated in the third century by the growing power of the Sages and by the distinction drawn in practice (not in principle) between headship of the Academy and the Patriarchate.

89 *Ruth Rabba*, iv.

90 Insofar as the rivalry between the Sages and the Patriarch in the appointment of judges is concerned, it would be worthwhile to take account of Diocletian's *Rescript*, the subject of Dinaburg's research-study. Now since that document requires somewhat detailed clarification, I shall deal with it in an appendix to this article.

91 It follows from *T.B. Sanhedrin*, 14a, apparently, that it was R. Joḥanan who was granting ordination. The wording, 'that he was not among them' (and similarly further on), and also 'that they ordained him', or 'they did not ordain him' — would tend to convey that ordination was performed by more than one person at a time (the Sages in general, the Bet Din). So, too, *ibid.* 30b. In the parallel, *T.P. Sanhedrin* iii, 21d, however, 'the elevation of R. Simeon b. Yakim to a higher level' is spoken of. This expression is not altogether clear. It may perhaps refer to ordination (Albeck, *op. cit.*, p. 87). The same applies to *ibid.* 5b (R. Joḥanan's observation to R. Shemen = R. Simeon b. Abba. In the parallel, *T.P. Ḥagiga* i, *Nedarim* x, the individual doing the conferring is not R. Joḥanan but R. Judah Nesi'a). Resh Laqish's appointment of a 'lecturer, judge' etc. in Basra with R. Joḥanan's assent (*T.P. Shevi'it* vi, 36d) should be added to what is said here. On the other hand, this conclusion can neither be deduced, nor drawn from R. Zeira's remark in *T.P. Megilla* iv, 75b: 'He appointed him Sage'.

92 *T.P. loc. cit.*

Still insofar as R. Johanan and R. Joshua are concerned, these testimonies apparently directly contradict the essential evidence of R. Abba, that a Bet Din might only confer ordination with the consent of the Patriarch (certainly no individual Sages could do so), for his consent to these appointments is not mentioned. Now since R. Abba was a younger contemporary of these Sages (it is reasonable to assume him to be the first R. Abba), we must perforce admit that he could not be completely mistaken in recounting the deeds of his Rabbis. Hence we must explain R. Johanan to have made his appointments in his capacity as head of the Great Bet Din (in Tiberias), with its approval and that of the Patriarch as well. We must assume this because of the close relationship that obtained between R. Johanan and the Patriarchal dynasty. This consent need not have been given in each individual instance; the Patriarch could have issued a general authorization to him.[93]

The same applies to Rabbi Joshua b. Levi. His ordination of 'all his pupils' has some connection, apparently, with his position as head of the 'Great Academy' of Lod and with the standing of the Academy itself and the 'Sages of the South' in the third (and fourth) centuries. The significant role played by that city in the lives of the Jewish Eretz-Israel and in the world of the Sages (and Patriarchs) from the end of the Tannaitic period onwards is common knowledge.[94] So, too, was the rivalry between the Sages and their Academy in Lod on the one hand and the Sages of Galilee on the other — a rivalry which extended even into the domain of ordination — well known.[95] In fact the Great Academy seems, as it were, to have split (and with it, of course, the Sanhedrin) into two: Tiberias and Lod.[96] The 'subordination' of the South to the overall authority of the central administration was maintained essentially through the former's dependence on the Patriarchs.[97] Yet it was only right that the Patriarchs in turn should grant the same recognition and authority to the South as they had given to the Galileans. R. Joshua b. Levi's ordination of his students might likely be attributed to the strong stand taken by the Academy in Lod. Yet this authority, too, was derived principally from the

---

93 Meiri puts it so: (*Sanhedrin,* p. 73): 'The Exilarch or Patriarch has the right to authorize one of the Sages to grant permission to others on their own.' And this is what R. Johanan said to R. Shemen: 'Behold you have our authorization...' (the *makhtir* [one who crowns, confers] with whom Rabbi consulted).
94 It similarly played an important role even in the period prior to the Bar Kokhba rebellion.
95 The history of the relations between the southerners and the Galileans in the second and third centuries is known in particular from the writings of scholars. It is not in place here to clarify this in detail.
96 The duplication and separation of the '*Sanhedra'ot*' took place in the days subsequent to the abolition of the Patriarchate by the well-known order of the last of the Theodosians, C. Th. 16, 8, 29. There *Judaeorum primates qui in utriusque Palaestinae Synedriis nominantur* is spoken of, where the first Palestine (the 'South', with its seat in Caesarea) is referred to, as well as the second (with its seat in Beisan, Galilee).
97 Cf. the practice of the Patriarchs of the third and fourth centuries to contract marital unions with the heads of the Sages in Lod, for instance R Joshua b. Levi (*T.B. Qiddushin* 33b) and Ben Pazzi's house (*T.P. Shabbat* xiv, 13c; *Horayot* iii, 48c; and see also *T.P. 'Avoda Zara* iii, 42c).

(overall) Bet Din (established in Tiberias) and the consent of the Patriarch. This should be taken for granted since Rabbi Joshua b. Levi's family relationship with the Patriarchal House precludes us from regarding him as instigating any provocative action against the Patriarch in ordaining Sages.[98]

As for the Babylonian tradition, it first of all conflicts with the Halakha set down in the Palestinian Talmud (*Bikkurim* iii, 65d) that 'Elders' were appointed outside Eretz-Israel, even by Eretz-Israel authorities, only on condition that they return, yet R. Huna (as well as his son) lived out all his days in Babylon, and the same applies to R. Joshua b. Levi's Halakha quoted in the Babylonian Talmud (*Sanhedrin* 14a): 'There is no ordination outside of Eretz-Israel', even where the authority wishing to confer the ordination had himself been ordained by a Sage in Eretz-Israel (as the Talmud itself understands, *ibid.*). Yet this passage itself contradicts this Halakha for, according to that same tradition, Rav was ordained by R. Ḥiyya,: and the continuation of that passage teaches that Rabbi ordained him directly (testimony that is in essence substantiated by the Palestinian Talmud, *Ḥagiga* i, 76c; *Nedarim* x, 42b).[99] Hence this doubtful evidence is unreliable.

It is nevertheless a reasonable conclusion that, as a whole, the records telling of Rabbis ordaining their disciples are trustworthy. First the practice allowed certain circles among the Sages to give expression to their disposition to preserve their individual freedom as against the tendency to centralization which had become increasingly prevalent in the entire world of the Sages in the form of authorization by the Sanhedrin and Patriarchate. Just as we find evidence in the remaining areas (Halakha and Halakhic decisions) of this rivalry between the aim to subordinate the Sages to the authority of the leadership and the demand for complete independence on the part of the Halakhists, so can the vestiges of these traditions furnish evidence of the striving on the part of some of the Sages to retain their individual independence in the area of jurisdiction. Secondly, in practice non-ordained Sages tried lawsuits and even held permanent appointments in this area in certain cities. Furthermore the Patriarch himself (and the Bet Din) was accustomed to send non-ordained judges to the smaller cities.[100] What

---

98 *Qiddushin ibid.:* 'It is not fitting that I should stand up before my son... but the honor of the Patriarch's House [requires it].'
99 Albeck (*op. cit.*, p. 90) seeks to resolve this last contradiction in a manner that, to me, seems farfetched. (It is not in place here to delve into the subject in all its details.) The entire substance of the passage in *Sanhedrin* is a 'composite', its elements being drawn from divergent sources (Cf. Şori's attempt at an analysis, *op. cit.*, pp. 184 ff).
100 Levi, who was delegated by Rabbi to serve as lecturer and judge, etc. in Simonia (*T.P. Yevamot* ii, 13a, and the parallels in the Midrashim; the tradition in *T.B. Yevamot* 105a probably does not give adequate mention to the circumstances surrounding the event) was never ordained. The same would apparently apply to the 'Babylonian' sent by Resh Laqish and R. Jobanan to Basra. It is to be assumed that discharging juridical functions without ordination entailed, in principle, non-participation in the Sanhedrin, and, in practice, lesser independence and authority than was enjoyed by the ordained, (although we are unable to prove this from actual events).

those judges (permanent or occasional) were in practice required to possess was sufficient knowledge to judge in accordance with the prescriptions of the Torah, which would be attested to by the Rabbi (and could be regarded as something similar to 'ordination'), but their authority in law cases was inferior to that of the ordained Sages.

Furthermore, the consolidation of the ordination procedure was dependent first of all on the organizing and strengthening of Jewish jurisprudence as a whole, and even more upon the growing supremacy and control of the central authority over the population of Eretz Israel. These two prerequisites were not automatically equally guaranteed in all generations and localities. Sometimes the knowledge of law had become weakened even when the period was not one of forcible conversion; nor did the control of the central authority over the population increase in strength all at once, and probably also not in all localities simultaneously. Under these circumstances 'a free judiciary of Sages' based on their specialized knowledge could well find a place for itself, by freeing itself from the mastery and rulership of the supreme leadership. Especially from the time of Rabbi onwards, however, the general development moved in the direction of strengthening the power of the centre and particularly the Patriarchate, and the improvement of its position and influence in the settled areas. Concomitant with this development, ordination became increasingly crystallized as an authorization granted by those who wielded supreme control: the Patriarch and the Bet Din.

The principal powers delegated to the ordained were: (a) To offer theoretical public instruction in the House of Study and the community (the discourse);[101] (b) to issue practical Halakhic rulings to individuals; and (c) to try lawsuits. In all of these instances, ordination generally signified nothing more than the granting of absolute, recognized authority, but in practice authority was not denied to the non-ordained to deal with these matters by withdrawing from them the preferential rights accorded to the ordained. Now when the first element ceased appearing in the ordination formulas in the Talmudic sources, the trying of lawsuits became instead the chief feature of ordination.

Even though the giving of practical Halakhic decisions was a less significant feature of ordination than the power to adjudicate, it is not to be excluded to the extent that scholars are accustomed to assert (especially in the time before

---

101 In *Sifre*, Pineḥas cxl (ed. Horowitz, p. 186) and *Sifre Deuteronomy* §cccv, 'Give Joshua a *Meturgeman* who will question, expound and deliver Halakhift rulings' etc. Since Tannaim had expounded that Moses' 'ordination' of Joshua was of the same nature as the ordination of the Sages, this passage furnishes us with evidence for our topic. (In his above-mentioned article, Albeck has stated his view that every appointment entailed being assigned to head a minor Academy. Hence he has cited this passage as evidence for his approach. Yet even if such an implication can be read into the text before us — for ordination in general did entail the heading of an Academy in addition, as was explained above — in this article as it is, the *Derasha Barabbim* is taken to include public discourses as well, and not to refer to the studying with groups only. As for interpreting 'sitting at the head' as 'heading a House of Study', see our article itself, above, for another approach.

Rabbi). It is known that the tradition of the Palestinian Talmud testifies of Rabbi that he was the first to institute 'that no student render Halakhic decisions'. What is referred to here is undoubtedly the obtaining of authority from the central administration (the Patriarch) in the form of ordination, and not as the Babylonian tradition has it: from the disciple's rabbi.[102] From here it would seem to follow that until the days of Rabbi, the giving of Halakhic decisions was not dependent upon ordination, as many of the most recent scholars presume. Yet, even though the sources show that 'disciples' were accustomed to issue such rulings in the Jabneh period,[103] certainly there is no proof from here of the lack of any official, preferred status for ordained Sages even in the area of Halakhic decisions. For non-ordained Sages were not in practice precluded from adjudicating law suits, although they were regarded as not completely competent to try such cases.

Yet several items of evidence prove that (complete) authority to decide questions of law was dependent upon ordination in the generation of Jabneh. So we learn in a Baraita: 'Distinguished disciples like Simeon b. Azzai are fit to decide matters of law.'[104] This teaches that legal decisions did not lie within the province of any and all disciples, but of Sages. Furthermore, R. Judah b. Bava testified fo himself: 'I am one of those capable of deciding points of law' etc.[105] Here, too, presumably complete authority to render such decisions was confined to the 'Sages', while in *practice* even the non-ordained who possessed sufficient scholarship to be able to render decisions were considered fit and permitted to do so. Our assertion may be deduced with some certitude from *M. Bekhorot* (iv, 4), where R. Akiba said to R. Tarfon, who had erroneously declared a firstborn permissible: 'You are absolved, since you are an expert (*Mumḥe*), and whoever is an expert for the Bet Din is absolved from reparation.'[106] It follows, then, that there is a distinction between the expert and nonexpert (not-ordained) in rendering legal decisions, just as there is in law suits.[107] Perforce, then, deciding points of law also constituted an element of ordination, even before Rabbi's day. In practice, however, even the non-ordained would give rulings and at times the boundary

---

102 *T.P. Shevi'it* vi, 36c; *Giṭṭin* i, 39c; *T.B. Sanhedrin* 5b.
103 *Tasefta Kil'ayim* i, 3–4.
104 *Tosefta Horayot* i, 1 and the parallels in the Talmudim. Even though the Halakha speaks here of dependence on the Great Bet Din in Jerusalem, nevertheless this no longer applied to the post-Destruction usage and reality.
105 *Tosefta Terumot* v, 10. In my opinion 'those fit to render decisions' denotes a special level, some kind of permanence among the Sages. The topic deserves a study of its own, which is not in place here.
106 From Rabbi's generation onwards, however, we find that the granting of authority to rule firstborn animals permissible was the exclusive prerogative of the Patriarchs and they were extremely particular in granting it to Sages alone.
107 To what extent serious limitations were imposed in the field of rendering decisions during the days of R. Gamaliel may be seen from the incident involving R. Joshua's nephew, Hanania, who gave a ruling. R. Gamaliel objected and sought to punish him, until it became apparent that the author of the ruling had been R. Joshua, *T.B. Nidda* 24b.

between the decision of a 'disciple and of a Sage was effaced, till Rabbi arose and categorically denied disciples the right to render decisions.[108] Nevertheless, the essential distinction of ordination became restricted to the area of jurisdiction, since it is there that full public authority becomes requisite in order to oblige and compel the litigants to comply with the verdict. This is not so in respect of giving legal decisions which generally remain optional and dependent upon the attitude of the individual.

Essentially, ordination did not signify the assignment of any concrete functions in practice, but merely the competence to perform them. Hence ordained Sages are found studiously avoiding judicial functions,[109] and recommending 'withdrawal from litigation'. Their motive was either the realization of the excessive liability entailed in rendering legal judgement or else the desire, in general, to avoid becoming preoccupied with communal needs — which would distract them from Torah study.[110] Sages confined their world to the study and dissemination of Torah and regarded any connection with public affairs as lying outside their purview and duty.[111] Moreover, the 'judge' was permitted to excuse himself from judging a case even after the trial had begun, in such cases where he might possibly suffer physical hurt at the hands of a violent litigant, were the latter to lose the case.[112]

---

108 That Rabbi's regulation was not maintained in its original form subsequent to his time is apparently indicated by R. Abba's statement, as well as R. Abbahu's in the name of R. Huna and Rav (*Sota* 22a), who speak of 'students who are qualified to rule and do not' and 'disciples who are not, and do. (It stands to reason that being qualified to rule does not imply ordination, but represents a status similar to 'those who are fit to rule'.)

109 *Tanḥuma*. Mishpatim 2.

110 R. Ishmael b. R. Jose in *M. Avot* iv, 7. See also *Avot de-R. Nathan*, version II, xxxiv; ed. Schechter xxxviii, 2. Even the remark of R. Simeon in *T.P. Sanhedrin* i, 18a: 'Blessed be the Allpresent that I do not know how to judge' must not be taken as pertaining to the earlier tradition, 'In the days of R. Simeon b. Joḥai monetary cases were taken away from Israel', and so implying that R. Simeon had studiously avoided becoming appointed by the Roman government to try cases according to their law, once the Jewish legal system had been proscribed, as recent scholars have averred. The remark signifies instead that the Tanna in question (who is renowned for demanding that the life of the moment, including the performance of *mitzvot* and good deeds, be set aside in favour of a complete communion with Torah learning, the 'eternal' life) praises himself as not being expert in (practical) laws, and hence is exempt from the obligation to become preoccupied with judicial functions for the benefit of the community. (His observation is in no way connected with the previous tradition, except insofar as the name is the same: R. Simeon b. Joḥai).

111 The sources are many, and Dinaburg has already adduced several in his above-mentioned study. The subject, however, requires systematic treatment on its own. Insofar as the exercise of judicial functions is concerned, however, attention deserves to be drawn further to *Tanḥuma* (Mishpatim) where the disciples of R. Assi comfort and praise him for his deeds, since he 'kept himself far removed from judging' 'and did not allow himself to be appointed over the public' and he replied: 'Perhaps I shall have to render account for having been fit to try Jewish lawsuits', etc. Cf. *Exodus Rabba* xxx.

112 *Tosefta Sanhedrin* i, 7 and the parallels in the Talmudim (the recension appearing in the body of the article being the correct one).

Yet, presumably, ordination was often tied up directly with the assignment of official duties to the person on whom it was conferred. This is proved, ostensibly, by the recurring formula found among Tannaim, 'appointed over the community', or 'the Bet Din appointed him over the community' (*Deuteronomy Rabba* i, 3: 'An Israelite who has been appointed Sage or judge of the community'),[113] which signifies ordination. The same would apply to those testimonies in the sources which prove that appointments brought wealth and a livelihood in their train.[114] Certainly no fixed salary or remuneration is referred to. Instead, the remark is to be understood in terms of the communal practice of providing the Sage living and officiating in the community with greater or lesser material support. The statement in *Exodus Rabba* xxvi, 9 bears this out: 'R. Nehemiah said:... As long as one is but an ordinary scholar (*ḥaver*), he has no concern with the community and is not punished on their account. Once he is appointed as their head and dons the cloak of leadership he shall not say: I live for my own benefit; I do not care about the community. Instead the whole burden of the community is on his shoulders. If he sees anyone acting violently against his neighbour or committing a transgression, and does not try to prevent him, he is held punishable.'[115]

It seems that the communal and local implications of ordination which had become current began spreading and crystallizing from the time of Rabbi onwards.[116]

Were the appointments dependent upon the ratification of the community? We apparently possess the answer to this question. In *Sifre Deuteronomy* §13 (ed. Finkelstein, p. 23) we find: '"And I shall make them heads over you" — you might think that if you appoint them they are appointed, and if not, not. Scripture teaches: "And I shall make them heads over you." If I appoint them they are appointed, and if not, not...' This homily on Moses' appointments certainly reflects the opinion of the expositors towards the appointment of 'Elders' in their time.[117] Yet, at all events,

---

113 *Tosefta Ta'aniyot* i, 50, and the parallels in the Talmudim; *Tosefta Bava Qamma* vii, 13; *Sifre Deuteronomy* §306. These 'Parnassim' were not the heads of cities and communities but spiritual leaders (as opposed to the view of Dinaburg, *op. cit.*, p. 85 on Sages who occupied permanent, civil administrative posts). Cf. Ginzberg, *Perushim*, etc., Introduction, pp. lxiii–lxiv; *ibid.* I, pp. 403–406. (His view that, in the Palestinian sources, 'Parnas' signified 'a secular appointment' only is inaccurate.)
114 *Sifre Deuteronomy* §81; *T.B. Sota* 40a; *Horayot* 10a-b.
115 In the parallel, *Midrash Pss.*, ed., Buber, however, it is not clearly so.
116 Certainly in the Babylonian tradition already R. Eleazar Ḥisma and R. Joḥanan b. Gudgada had received emoluments for heading the Academy. In Sifre, however, the whole discussion between R. Joshua and R. Gamaliel concerning R. Joshua's poverty is missing. The same applies to R. Neḥemiah's above-mentioned statement in *Exodus Rabba* which the Tanna need not necessarily have made verbatim in that form.
117 In his *Legends of the Jews*, Vol. III, p. 72; Vol. VI, n. 164, Ginzberg writes that, in contradistinction to this tradition, it is to be inferred from Josephus, *Ant.* iii, 4,1 (which speaks of the qualities of the judges Jethro advised Moses to appoint) that 'the people had to ratify the appointments made by Moses'. Where he deduced this from is not clear to me. Apparently he derived it from the passage: οἱ δὲ δοκιμασθέντες ὑπὸ τοῦ, πλήθους παντὸς εἶναι ἀγαθοὶ καὶ δίκαιοι κτλ ('known

to the extent that ordination in practice entailed appointment to public office, there was some reason for it. Apparently, the sources portray divergent opinions, for we read so in the Palestinian Talmud (*Ta'aniyot* iv, 68a) of the testament of Rabbi to Rabban Gamaliel, his son: ' "And appoint R. Ḥanina b. Ḥamma its head." And why did he himself not make the appointment? Said R. Derusai: "Since the people of Sepphoris cried out against him (in Sepphoris)." And because of a (vain) protest, we do (as they wish)? Said R. Eliezer b. Jose: "Because he raised an argument against him (Rabbi) in public".' The first Amora lays down, then, that because of the opposition of the inhabitants of Sepphoris, appointment was withheld from R. Ḥanina, who should automatically have served as *Parnas* (leader) of the community in that city (as he did after Rabbi's death). Yet the anonymous tradition in the Palestinian Talmud questions this supposition and rejects it.[118]

The need for the populace to assent to the appointment of Sages in their own localities, however, is indirectly substantiated also by R. Isaac's dictum (*T.B. Berakhot* 55a): 'A leader is not appointed over a community without it being consulted.' Similarly, we read in the tradition preserved in *Midrash Hagadol* (Leviticus, ed. Rabinowitz, p. 168): '"And gather all the congregation..." and furthermore all communal office is only (conferred) in the presence of the entire congregation.'

What may be decisive here is the tradition of the Palestinian Talmud, *Yevamot* xii, 13a concerning Levi b. Sisi, whom Rabbi 'gave' to the inhabitants of Simonia to serve them as lecturer and judge, etc., for they dismissed him immediately on their own authority and did not at all require the consent of the Patriarch[119] (Levi, however, was not ordained).

    amongst the entire people as good and righteous'). This, however, has nothing to do with the selection of judges but with their reputation as fit and faithful men.
118 That ratification by the populace was a prerequisite may perhaps be derived from the tradition in *Sifre Zuṭa* (ed. Horowitz, p. 321): '"And you shall place him before Eleazar the priest and before all the congregation" — that he should be [acknowledged] a *Mumḥe* by Eleazar, the priest, and all the congregation' (as is well known, everything pertaining to ordination was deduced from Joshua). An allusion to this may perhaps be found in the remark in *Sifre* Beha'alotekha §92 (and similarly in *Sifre Deuteronomy* x): 'It teaches that one does not occupy a seat in the Academy beneath... till people talk favourably of him and say: "That particular man is fit and righteous and deserves to be a Sage".' (As for the preceding Midrash: '"Whom you know to be the Elders of the people and officers over them" — you have to know if they are selected before Me,' it is reasonable to adopt the reading of R. Meir Ish Shalom, 'Before the people', as is found in the *Yalkut*. If so, we have a Halakhic tradition before us teaching that at least tacit consent on the part of the public is required.) As for the communal activities of the Patriarchs and Sanhedrin in general, the texts of the Baraita in the *Tosefta Sanhedrin* ii, 10: 'The year is not intercalated nor public action undertaken except on condition that they are acceptable to the majority of the public' should be contrasted with the divergent recension in the Talmudim.
119 Indeed, exactly as in the manner that the men of Terbanat had dismissed the scribe of their city, since he had been accustomed to read the Ten Commandments in conformity with the Halakha and prohibitions laid down by R. Ḥanina, and not with the view of the members of the community (*T.P. Megilla* iv, 75b).

It therefore appears that although, in principle, the right to appoint to office rested with the Patriarch (and the Sanhedrin), in practice the ordained Sages would not serve as judges in the cities without the consent of the inhabitants.[120]

The arbitrators. All the information we possess concerning the institution of arbitration is contained in a single Halakha in Mishna and Baraita dating from the time of R. Meir and his colleagues. Furthermore, the text of the Mishna seems to prove that arbitration was the sole authorized procedure in lawsuits, for so we find in the Mishna: 'Monetary cases are to be tried by three. Each litigant chooses one...' This tradition, then, knows of no other method of conducting law suits except by arbitration. These facts led more recent scholars to propound the view that the institution of arbitration only became established in the generation following the Bar Kokhba rebellion because the Roman government had proscribed the trying of law suits by Jews. At that time, when the regular courts had been forcibly abolished, the Jews found a loophole, namely private, occasional jurisdiction.[121]

This view cannot, it seems, be sustained. First we read of R. Johanan already making statements (*T.P. Mo'ed Qatan* ii, 82a) which ostensibly attest to the

---

According to Klein, however (*MGWJ*, 1934, pp. 170–171), Levi was at first only taken on trial in Simonia. The questions posed to him by the local inhabitants were for the purpose of testing him. The view, however, which maintains that the candidate for Sage-judge was tested by his 'discourse' during the Talmudic epoch is not substantiated by other sources and is not supported even by the tradition of the episode before us. Had they 'constructed a large platform and placed him on it' in order to test whether he was suitable to be a judge or not, Levi would not have been able to offer the excuse for having forgotten his learning at that time to Rabbi 'that his spirit had become proud', for then 'dread of the public' (stage fright) rather than pride would have been the cause.

120 Courts composed of Sages and *hedyotot* (commoners or non-ordained Sages) combined did in fact exist. This state of affairs was considered Halakhically valid on account of the requirement that even an ordained Sage abstain from being a sole judge, even according to those who considered him fit | to do so in principle (see *T.P. Sanhedrin* i, 18a-b). Hence, R. Ḥiyya coopted 'one disciple' when he conducted a trial (*T.P. ibid.,* b). This is to be learnt from R. Ishmael b. R. Jose's remark in *M. Avot* (iv, 8): 'Do not be a sole judge for none may judge alone except One; do not say, "Accept my view", for they are entitled to, but not you.' This Mishna presents the case of a Sage sitting together with two unqualified judges trying a lawsuit, and warns of the rights of the other two judges in determining the verdict. Some of the Rishonim give a similar interpretation. It may be possible, perhaps, to follow Gulak (*Yesode Hamishpat Ha'ivri,* IV, p. 33) in deriving the competence of such a composite Bet Din to try monetary cases by comparison (*hekesh*) with the procedure in the annulment of vows, which, according to R. Judah (*T.B. Bekhorot* 37a) is dispensed by three [judges], only one of whom is required to be an ordained Sage. (This requires further study.) The following tradition, however, forces us, apparently, to assume that the Sages rebelled against such a state of affairs. For, in practice, this constituted a compromise between the jurisdiction of the Sages and that of the 'commoners', one that resulted from the struggle between the competing judiciaries. In *Tanḥuma* Shofetim, ed. Buber (p. 30), we read: 'Another explanation: "You shall not pervert judgement" — this is an admonition to the Sage not to let sit next to him someone unfit to judge. If he did seat such a one, it is tantamount to his having planted an *Ashera...*' Here then is a protest against Sage-judges who co-opted actual 'commoners', couched in the same language used by those opposing the Patriarchs for appointing ignoramuses as judges.

121 Gulak, *op. cit.,* IV, pp. 30–32. Cf. the miscellany, *Hamishpat Ha'ivri* (1936), p. 199 for the debate on this issue between the Sages of Jerusalem.

existence of arbitrators even in his days.[122] Furthermore, R. Meir himself and the Sages of our Mishna and Baraitot speak of judges 'qualified for the Bet Din', that is to say they were aware of the existence of the courts of the Sanhedrin in their time. Certainly, we could posit that arbitration first came into existence at the time when the permanent courts were in abeyance but that its existence persisted even after the regular courts were reinstated.

Nevertheless it is far-fetched to make arbitration in Israel dependent on adverse circumstances alone. This institution existed among many ancient (and modern) peoples, side by side with the central and local, established judiciaries, and there is no reason to deny its existence among Jews in normal times. Yet the explicit assertion of the Mishna cannot lightly be set aside, and it recognizes the existence of arbitrators alone, a state of affairs which cannot possibly be ascribed to the entire Talmudic epoch.[123] Nevertheless no deduction may be drawn from one Mishna. The Halakha clearly sets down 'each party chooses one' etc. as the exposition, so to say, of the Halakha, 'Monetary cases are to be tried by three', a statement transcribed from the first Mishna, as if in order to explicate it. 'How is this? Each (litigant) chooses one (judge)...' We sometimes, however, do find dicta in the Mishna directly attached to earlier Halakhic generalizations apparently as their complete elucidation, and opening with, 'How is this?' — whilst in fact this is only a method of tying in traditions which deal with one or more specific details related to the general Halakhot themselves. The Mishna attaches them to the earlier tradition because they contain something novel or some dispute.[124] This then is a device of literary editorship and not a really, but only an apparently, exhaustive exposition of the generalization. Here, too, in our Mishna, the same relationship obtains between the 'explication' and the basic Halakha. The general rule, 'Monetary cases are to be tried by three judges' is not exhaustively explained, but a tradition is appended to it which sets down the differing opinions of Tannaim concerning one of the forms assumed by a three-judge court, i.e how this court is constituted. This tradition knew of no discussion or doubt on the part of the Sages pertaining to the permanent courts.

The juridical authority of the non-ordained, as contrasted with the ordained, Sages. It is found that the very Halakha in which the existence of courts of non-ordained is accepted as such discriminates between the authority of the

---

122 The very words of R. Jeremiah b. Abba in *T.B. Bava Meṣi'a* 20a; *Bava Batra* 168a.
123 Indeed scholars are to be found who have the view that no permanent courts of the three judges ever existed in the Talmudic epoch, but only courts of arbitration instead (Ginzberg, *MGWJ*, 1912, pp. 303–304. See Frankel, *Der gerichtliche Beweis*, p. 89. Similarly, Fassel, *Das rabbinische Gerichtserfahren* par. 235. Cf. M. Bloch, *Die Civilrechtprozessordnung*, p. 11, n. 13; Sidon *Magazin*, 17, 207).
124 Such as *M. Giṭṭin* v, 6: 'There was no *sicaricon* in Judea for those killed in the war; from (the termination of) the killing of war there has been *sicaricon*. How is this? If one bought from the *sicaricon*, and then bought it over again from the owner, his purchase is void' etc. Here there is no direct comprehensive explication of the law of *sicaricon* but the selection of an example of a specific problematic detail of that Halakha.

non-ordained as compared with the ordained Sages, and restricts the juridical functions of the former. And there are divergent views.

The classical tradition,[125] as is known, withdrew the adjudication of 'penalty cases' (where the amounts to be paid are punitive and do not coincide with the value of the loss sustained) from the jurisdiction of non-ordained judges, since these cases require the authority to enforce the judgements, and this was withdrawn from those without ordination by order of the Patriarch or Sanhedrin. Yet it also happened that the fields denied to the non-expert were extended to cover even 'robbery and assault suits', including damages (or certain classes thereof) and only the adjudication of money disputes arising from business relations (obligations between the parties) were left to the judicial authority of the non-ordained.[126] Furthermore, in principle, the current Halakhic tradition even removed the right from these courts to try cases of 'admissions and loans', and only allowed them to judge these cases in practice on the general (assumption) that these judges were 'acting as the agents' of the ordained judges (that is to say, theirs was only a delegated authority granted by the highest body in law, the Sages or the Sanhedrin or Patriarch).[127]

Did these Halakhot and their like constitute the real factors in the judicial functioning of the local administrations? Or were they stated as requirements only? It stands to reason that originally these courts did not restrict their judicial authority. Just as there were Sages who intended to deprive them of all authority in all fields, so, too, were there public figures in the cities, who completely divested themselves of any dependence whatsoever on the jurisdiction of the Sages and Sanhedrin. It was possible, however, in the course of time, for that very conflict caused by the existence of two parallel judiciaries in the settlements to have produced some proposal for the defining of the boundaries between them. Such an equilibrium could only have been conditional upon an upsurge of power among the Sages, and even more so upon the strengthening of the Patriarchate, and an increase in its influence in the social life-patterns of the settlements of Eretz-Israel.

The Halakhic sources afford a clear insight into the rights of the litigants to choose judicial tribunals or the judges of which these were composed. A dispute among Amoraim is mentioned in the Babylonian Talmud (*Sanhedrin* 23a). It first interprets the statement in the Mishna, 'Each party chooses one', etc., to refer to the choice of court — as to whether the parties have the right to object to a court proposed by the other side only when it is composed of nonexpert judges or even when it is composed of experts. The tradition does acknowledge the distinction in question between the judicatures (even though our Mishna is definitely dealing with the composition of a court of arbitrators, as the conclusion of the passage

---

125 *T.B. Sanhedrin* 14a, 13b, 8a, and all passages which deny the right to judge penalty cases outside Eretz-Israel (since the diaspora judges are *hedyotot*, unqualified).
126 *T.B. Sanhedrin* 2b; *Bava Qamma* 84a–b.
127 *Bava Qamma, ibid.; Giṭṭin* 88b (from their stance against the judges in Babylon, we learn of their attitude to the 'unqualified' in Eretz-Israel).

shows).[128] Yet even the Palestinian Talmud (*Sanhedrin* iii, 21a) records a difference of opinion among Amoraim on the subject. For so Resh Laqish expresses himself: 'They said this of the (Gentile) courts of Syria, but not of Torah lawsuits.' R. Johanan (is of the opinion): 'even in Torah lawsuits'. This dispute is identical with the first in the Babylonian Talmud: In Resh Laqish's view, once he is summoned, the defendant has no right to demand that he be tried by another court, except where the court consists solely of non-experts. In R. Johanan's view he may object even where ordained judges alone comprise the court.[129]

Tannaim had, however, differed on this point earlier. For so we are taught: 'Each party may reject the judge of the other — this is R. Meir's view. But the Sages say: When? — At the time that he adduces proof that they are relatives or unfit, but if they were recognized as experts (*Mumḥin*) by the Bet Din he may not disqualify them'. The commentators explain our Mishna as tied to the preceding Halakha: 'Each party may choose one'. Hence, here too the Tannaim would be differing as to whether, in their opinion, each litigant may reject the arbitrator chosen by the other side. It seems that this explanation cannot be sustained. First, such a right would contradict the first Halakha: 'Each side may choose one.' Furthermore, we are taught in a parallel Baraita (*T.B. Sanhedrin* 23a): 'One may go on rejecting judges until he undertakes that the case be tried before a Bet Din publicly recognized as expert.' The selection of courts must then be referred to. The wording of our Mishna, too, 'at the time when he adduces proof that they are relatives, unfit, fit, *Mumḥin*,' teaches, apparently, that judges are the subject of discussion, that is to say: a college of judges and not individual arbitrators proposed by the litigants.[130] Hence it stands to reason that R. Meir and the Sages also differ in regard to the right of the litigants to choose their judicial tribunals. But our Mishna does not explicitly draw any distinction between unqualified judges and Sages.

---

128 The Babylonian Talmud's explication of the first Halakha as referring to the selection of courts can only have resulted, it seems to me, from the proper reference of a tradition associated with our Mishna having become forgotten — and this was the second Halakha. (*T.P.* immediately proceeds to expound 'This party chooses one for itself' in its plain sense.)

129 That this is the significance of the divergent opinions of Resh Laqish and R. Johanan is also substantiated by the continuation of the discussion, 'How? They said: Two men had a lawsuit in Antioch...' Here the Talmud adduces an example of the preference of one of the litigants for a court outside the city. (R. Johanan denied him this right, since he would force ['tear away'] his opponent to travel afar. See R. Johanan's remarks in *T.B. Sanhedrin* 30b on the tradition of R. Safra.) The preceding passage, 'So is the Mishna: This one may disqualify... but not his judge', which is obscure and has puzzled the commentators, may perhaps be based on the Halakha which speaks of the disqualification of the arbitrating judge. Yet even so this does not constitute any substantiation of the discussion that follows.

130 It is certainly possible to advance the forced explanation that the wording refers to repeated disqualifying, in the manner of the Baraita in the Babylonian Talmud: 'Indeed he may continue to disqualify...', which is not stated in the Mishna as such. The Talmud, apparently, gives this explanation, since it proceeds to raise the query: 'Has he then the power to disqualify judges?' Now if our Mishna is taken to be dealing with arbitrators nominated by the litigants then what

However, an examination of the parallel Baraitot (and the Mishna itself) leads us to discover this difference. What is surprising first of all is the wording of the Mishna: 'But if they were fit, or recognized by the Bet Din as qualified', for if one is unable to reject the unqualified (when they are neither related nor unfit), is it necessary to state that one may not reject the qualified? Now we read in a Tosefta (and also in the parallel in the Babylonian Talmud), *ibid.:* 'It is not in his power to disqualify the recognized, expert judge' (the 'fit' is not mentioned), which teaches that the Sages concede that he has the right to reject non-ordained judges. Secondly, we read in another Baraita in the Talmud: 'He may go on rejecting until he accepts upon himself a publicly recognized, qualified Bet Din, so the words of R. Meir.' According to this tradition, then, even R. Meir agrees that qualified judges may not be rejected. Perforce, then, there must have been conflicting traditions in the Academies of other Tannaim in respect of the dispute between R. Meir and the Sages. One of these traditions takes the dispute to refer to unqualified judges alone: R. Meir upholds the right to disqualify them, and the Sages deny it. According to the other, these Tannaim differed in respect of qualified judges, and R. Meir upholds the right to reject even them. The first being the main tradition ('when he adduces proof that they are relatives or unfit, but if they are fit...'), the Mishna nevertheless finally concludes by inserting the later tradition as an addition, 'or qualified'.[131] So it follows that the Sages adopted conflicting attitudes. Some denied the right of choice even where the courts consisted of unqualified judges, and others upheld it in this instance, while others extended this right even to courts of ordained judges. (In the days of the Amoraim, the Halakha was finally established that the litigants did possess this right. They [the Amoraim] differed, however, concerning the courts of the Sages. In this instance Resh Laqish denied, while R. Joḥanan upheld the right).[132]

is surprising? The same applies to the answer given by R. Joḥanan: 'This was taught of Syrian lawcourts', which signifies permanent courts (of unqualified judges) but not arbitrators. As to single judges, see above n. 131. The disqualification of a proposed court, however, could result from the rejection of one of its judges. The conflicting opinions of those Tannaim on the rejection of witnesses makes the interpretation of this Halakha as referring to arbitrators appear even more far-fetched.

131 As is known, the Halakha distinguishes between unqualified (*hedyoṭot*) and ordained, qualified (*Mumḥin*) judges, even in judging singly, although the Sages of Eretz-Israel (in part) were still protesting against judges conducting lawsuits singly at the end of the third century. Gulak (*op. cit.,* IV, p. 36), however, holds the view that the Halakha which recognizes the right of *Mumḥin* to judge singly first appeared only at the beginning of the era of the Amoraim. Yet R. Ishmael b. R. Jose's admonition in *M. Avot,* 'Do not judge alone' tells of a previously existing situation (or at least, an existing custom in practice). The same applies to the evidence of R. Simeon the flax merchant in the *Tosefta* (*Bava Qamma* viii, 14 and the parallels in the Talmudim) on 'my father's house which was destroyed because they judged monetary cases singly' (hence even prior to Bar Kokhba, and it seems that there is mention of it dating back to Temple times). So we must assume that the institution of single judges trying cases may have possibly stemmed from an ancient tradition.

132 I refrain from making any comparisons between the structures and mutual relations of the judicial authorities in Eretz-Israel prior and subsequent to the Talmudic epoch, and also of the diaspora

It is in place now, perhaps, to sum up some of the topics we have dealt with so far, to a lesser or greater extent.

We have seen that, already during the generation of Jabneh there was a dispute among the Sages concerning the jurisdiction of unqualified (judges of the wealthy classes and parentage). Those who upheld this right, who esteemed the abilities of these classes because of their economic standing in conducting public affairs, regarded them as fit to judge, while others denied their competence on the grounds of their lack of Torah knowledge. Even though our sources complain against 'corrupt judges' of that generation,[133] the main opposition of the Sages to these 'Israelitish judges' was not on account of their socio-moral turpitude but because of their ignorance. The Tannaitic traditions, which should be ascribed to the latter half of the second century, on the other hand, frequently denounce judges for unethical conduct, for perverting justice, and for corrupting the entire generation.

These complaints reveal a social situation which arose especially and reached its peak of intensity after the Bar Kokhba rebellion. The collapse of the central authority, the enfeebled Patriarchate and Sanhedrin, which failed to regain their previous strength (of Jabneh days) until Rabbi's days, greatly reduced the juridical powers of the Sages (their influence on the general life of the population also declined considerably in that period). On the other hand, the political conditions that arose after the war paved the way for the ascendance and seizure of power by certain elements among the wealthy and pedigreed in the country. Certainly through them and among them, those circles ('collaborators') arose on whom the government could rely for its own purposes and so give them the authority over the population in the communities. These tax-gatherers and (great) treasurers, which the sources of the generation following Bar Kokhba mention a great deal, certainly stemmed from these circles, and they gave their support to the ruling power in the cities of the land. Even the prolonged economic impoverishment of the country from the time of the Antonines, which helped to weaken the traditional social structure of the settlements and their institutions as well, was able to serve as a factor in strengthening the above-mentioned circles and increasing their power in the communities.[134]

The Tannaim, who censured these judges-leaders for their moral depravity, certainly uncovered much of the grave state of affairs of their times. By striking out against the judicial functioning of these uppermost classes, the Sages were also attacking them for their conduct of public life in general, which at all events brought evil and harm upon the community. Yet it stands to reason that these accusations, as true as they may have been, nevertheless are tied up with the rivalry between the Sages and the power-wielding classes in Eretz-Israel for influence

---

judicial authorities (especially Babylon) in the same era, since these demand a study on their own. We still lack a complete and trustworthy presentation of the subject. It would similarly have been fitting to make comparisons with the judiciaries of other peoples (especially those of the Ptolemies, since the papyri certainly furnish us with considerable source material) but this task must be undertaken on its own.

133 In *Esther Rabba*, Petiḥta 9 and *Midrash Abba Gorion (initio)*, it is ascribed to Rabban Gamaliel.
134 I shall revert to this in my Article, *Qavvim* [never written — ed.].

on public life, a situation first drawn to our attention by the late Dr. Büchler.[135] We may therefore justifiably assert that the generalizations indulged in by the Tannaim do not completely reflect the true state of affairs. Certainly the rich also had their noble individuals who were solicitous of the welfare of the community and who helped shore up the beaches after the Rebellion. The same applies to the Sages: It cannot be asserted that all of them categorically denied the right of these circles to assume communal leadership and judicial functions, even though that generation evinced a negative attitude towards them on the whole.

This socio-ethical consideration ought not to blind us to the antagonism among the ranks of the Sages to the 'unqualified' officiating as judges, since the Sages aimed at a uniform jurisprudence based exclusively on the law of the Torah. There were some, however, who approved the existence of such judicatures and accorded them recognition to a greater or lesser extent. This fact enabled the emergence of a set of accepted rulings, for the purpose of regulating relationships between the courts of the non-expert judges and of the qualified, and which inclined towards giving preferential treatment to the latter, and establishing some balance of power between the various judicatures in the country.

In the judicial world of the Sages, a rivalry obtained between the two combined and competing central elements, the Patriarchate and the Sanhedrin, in respect of the authority in making appointments. This rivalry, which was merely one manifestation of the constant struggle of these two elements for control of the supreme leadership, was decided once and for all at the end of the second and the beginning of the third century (the time of Rabbi) in favour of the Patriarchate. Yet that outcome did not, most probably, eliminate the power of the Sages completely, nor still the desire of the Sages once again to lay claim to a position of strength *vis-à-vis* the Patriarchate. Consequently the practice finally came into being which aimed at creating a balance between the Sanhedrin and the Patriarchate, by awarding the right of ordination to either party with the consent of the other.

To revert to the first topic. The appointment of non-qualified judges on the part of the Patriarchs first of all meant that the problem of recognition for judiciaries in the settlements and of a civil legal system for 'commoners' had finally been solved. We have seen before that, from the time of the Sages of Jabneh and onwards, the attitudes of the Tannaitic world toward the standing of these courts had become polarized; some upheld, while others denied, their authority. In awarding these judges 'ordination' the Patriarchs were only confirming the existence of an ancient social tradition, even though it had elicited protests from many of the Torah scholars.[136] Secondly the elevation of local judges to the level of the

---

135 See also Dinaburg in his above-mentioned study, p. 89, although I am unable to concur with all his remarks.
136 We find objections raised against unworthy appointments already at the end of the second century. *Midrash Tannaim*, p. 8: 'R. Simeon b. Eleazar says: There is not a single Academy, no member of which will go to Gehinnom, but the last Academy will all go to Gehinnom' etc. Did some similar situation exist to some extent as early as in Rabbi's days?

ordained was likely to abolish the rivalry between the one judicial authority and the other in regard to their respective realms of authority. From now on, the courts of the 'commoners' were equal to those of the Sages, and were able to try all civil cases (including penalties, etc.). This fact meant the removal of a complicated and quarrelsome factor from urban Jewish life.

This recognition afforded by the Patriarchs is significant mainly for its regulation and strengthening of the 'democratic' tradition in the judicial world, the granting of power to civil judicatures. In actual practice, however, these appointments were mainly allotted to the ruling classes in the cities, i.e. the country aristocracy. The opposition of the Sages to the appointment of such judges was also a link in the chain of their rivalry with the powerful classes in the cities of Eretz-Israel for influence in (and control of) the settlements.

Granting 'ordination' to city judges drawn from the ruling strata meant, on the other hand — together with the imposition of organizational supervision over the local, civil courts on the part of the central administration — the inclusion of the country aristocracy, the governing circles in the settled areas, in the social and national structure, which became increasingly stabilized during the course of generations in Eretz-Israel, with the Patriarch at the head,[137] for recognition of this judicial authority entailed obedience to the supreme leadership, and cooperation with it in reinforcing its rule over the nation (as well as its standing with the Roman government).

---

137 We have no substantial information on the relations between the Patriarchate, Sanhedrin and municipal authorities in respect of the subordination of the latter to the central authority, in the area either of adjudication or administration, prior to the end of the second century. Logically, we may well assume as almost certain that the control of the central body did not extend over the settlements in these areas. (We are unable to deal in this article with the subject of the relationship obtaining between the city judges and the local administration on the one hand and the supreme authority of the nation on the other during the days of the Second Temple.) One tradition, however, is capable of teaching us apparently that the Patriarchs had the power to depose heads of cities (or communities) in the generation subsequent to the Destruction. So we learn in a Baraita (*Rosh Ha-Shana* 22a; *T.P. ibid.*, i, 57b) of Rabban Gamaliel that he removed the head of Gader from office. (There are still scholars who retain the reading in this form, thereby identifying the locality as Gader in Transjordan. So, Klein '*Ever Hayarden Hayehudi*, pp. 30–31; *Sefer Hayishuv*, s.v. *Gader*. This, however, is impossible, since the Sabbath is not set aside for witnesses coming to give evidence on having seen the new moon, except from a 'walking [distance] of a night and a day', and Gader is farther than this from Jabneh. Horowitz [p. 92] has previously rejected this view. He, however, takes it to be the Gederah mentioned in Joshua xv, 36. To me, it appears that the locality is Gezer, and we have already found Greek sources substituting Gader for Gezer Γάξαρα, Γάδαρα, see Schurer, *Geschichte*⁴, I, p. 339. In MS Leyden the Palestinian Talmud has גנ and above it a letter that, in my mind, is only to be read as ו. Other references in our sources also testify to the existence of a Jewish settlement in Gezer after the Destruction.) This 'head' was certainly a leader of the community and so these functionaries were obviously subordinate to the Patriarch. Although the tradition in the Mishna repudiates this testimony, yet in many respects, the authority of the centre, which gained in strength from the days of Rabbi onwards over the settlements, existed already in the time of the Patriarchate of R. Gamaliel and disappeared afterwards, till it was reinstated at the end of the second century and thereafter.

What led to this act was the prevailing historical situation, the development that occurred especially during the days of the Severan emperors. We discern the tendency of the Patriarchate already in Rabbi's days to base its strength on the economically powerful classes in the country.[138] Such conduct on the part of the Patriarch certainly did not merely arise from personal predilection. These classes had produced from among themselves an elite (the most 'patriotic'), the instrument for promoting social life in the communities of the country. Support of public institutions, provision of funds for public needs, was derived in abundant measure from them. In the days of the Antonines, after the Bar Kokhba rebellion, Jewish Palestine was crushed, populationwise, economically and socially. Public institutions, such as community schools, synagogues, etc. had disappeared altogether or become enfeebled. With the beginning of the Severan dynasty, economic conditions began to improve. The restoration of public life to normalcy, however, was only made possible by the support of the wealthy classes. They served, then, as a necessary basis for the rehabilitation process of the Jewish population.[139]

Yet another factor also operated here. In the period under discussion, the process of the consolidation of the ruling status of the wealthy elements in the cities of the Roman Empire reached its culmination. Henceforth the State granted them additional legal rights in the colonies (which had become transformed in the course of time into legally endorsed hereditary rights of these families). There came into being that defined, crystallised class of βουλενται, *curiales,* as opposed to the plebs, who had lost the right to participate in city government. Burdensome responsibilities and obligations, however, were also forcibly thrust upon these classes. The Bouleute were compelled to assume the responsibility for the administrative and financial obligations of the populations of the cities and their environs. The combination of additional privileges and heavy responsibilities led to the centralization of communal supervision and caused the administration of the cities to fall into the hands of the above-mentioned class.

Certainly, in theory, this development only pertained to communities organized in the form of the πόλεις. Three 'cities' of this type were added in Eretz-Israel during the rule of the Severan dynasty, most (or a large minority) of the populations of these cities being Jews (Lod - Diospolis; Emmaus - Nicopolis; Bet Guvrin - Eleutheropolis). Moreover, the continuation of the process must be assumed to have occurred even in the larger settlements, which had obtained

---

138 *T.B. Eruvin* 85b: 'The son of Bonyin once visited Rabbi. He said to them: Make room for the owner of 100 maneh. Another person came. He said: Make room for the owner of 200 maneh. R. Ishmael b. Jose said before him: This one's father owns a thousand ships at sea and also judges a thousand towns on land. He said to him: When you come to his father, say to him: Do not send him in such clothes to Rabbi, since Rabbi respects the rich, while R. Jacob respects the saintly.' (This is the recension of the Geonim, as the tradition itself testifies, and this is apparent from the discussion, *ibid.* 86a — that honour was bestowed on them because they brought benefit to the public by supplying its needs. See Koenigsberger, *Haqedem,* II, p. 153.) Cf. the evidence of Ben El'asa's son-in-law's wealth.

139 To clarify this matter requires a detailed study, which would not be in place here.

a broad measure of autonomy, although they did not rank officially as πόλεις (cities). This situation most likely helped to make the rich elements of the settlements the basis of the organized national structure in Eretz-Israel.[140]

On the other hand, Rabbi also instituted a number of regulations designed to consolidate the realm of the Sages.[141] Although these actions of his led to the enforcement of the mastery of the Patriarchs and some denial of the freedom of the former,[142] nevertheless it was he who facilitated the increase of their influence in the cities, their appointment as communal leaders and the consolidation of their rights.

The reinforcement of the communal status of the Sages, however, brought about an intensified religious educational endeavour on their part in the towns (in cooperation with and under the supervision of the Patriarchate) in Torah study which became immeasurably intensified. There ensued a certain saturation of spiritual influence within the broad strata of the nation, a rejuvenation as it were, effected by the Torah scholars (and stimulated by the Patriarch).[143] All these efforts enhanced the power of the Sages and prepared the way for their powerful position in the future, both *vis-à-vis* the 'secularized' wealthy elements and the Patriarchate itself.

Rabbi's practice of including those circles in the organizational structure of the nation was continued by the succeeding Patriarchs. From now onwards, the Bouleute and the *Ḥaverim*[144] (or 'heads' or 'Elders') constituted the two bodies

---

140 This does not detract from the deeds of the Patriarchs directed at times at depriving the leadership of these elements in the diaspora communities of any permanence, according to the evidence of Palladius, p. 381 above.
141 We do not hear of the Sages being exempted from taxes (only the occasional?) until his day, in the manner that they had been exempted from the Coronation Tax by the Patriarch (*Bava Batra* 8a).
142 For instance, the ordinance: 'A student shall not give Halakhic decisions', or his decree that the Sages should not give instruction to their disciples in the market place (but in the House of Study instead; *T.B. Mo'ed Qaṭan* 16a), and 'the high-handed conduct of the Patriarch and casting bitterness among the disciples' in general which he commanded to his son.
143 There are conclusive proofs testifying to the widespread teaching of Torah in the settlements by Sages despatched there by the Patriarchs, from the days of Rabbi onwards, concomitant with the upsurge of Torah study in the world of the Sages themselves during that period. One need only recall all the traditions referring to the Sages 'who went out to the towns' (which began in the reign of the Severan dynasty and continued) or 'who were sent to traverse' the cities of the land. Perhaps it is in place here to consider Origen's evidence. He reiterates in several places that he saw 'many Jews who study Torah constantly, from infancy to old age', and uses similar expressions.
144 See, e.g., *T.P. Nedarim*, vi, 40a, and *Sanhedrin* i, 19a, and the parallels in Midrashim: '"The craftsmen and smiths a thousand" — R. Berekhia said in the name of R. Ḥelbo: These are the associates (Sages), while the Rabbis say: These are the Bouleute.' The passage reveals the duality existing in public administration in the view of these Amoraim (cf. *Massekhet Soferim* xix, 9–10: Associations of Elders and Bouleute; the 'good men' of the city and the associates), just as other statements deal with the comparison of the rights of 'those who help the public', the monied (and the 'performers of *mitzvoth*') with the rights of the 'Torah scholars' and with the question as to who is the more important (see, for instance, *Sifre Deuteronomy* §47, ed. Finkelstein, p. 106

assuming the leadership of the communities in the settlements. Each of its field (civil and spiritual) was joined with the Patriarchate and operated under its supervision.[145]

The opposition of the Sages to the appointment of ignorant judges also brought about the first clash between the two elements in civil leadership, perhaps more violently at first. This was occasioned by the growing power of the wealthy classes and the increased strength of the Sages, who sought to prevent the former from interfering in what they considered exclusively their province. Yet it is feasible to regard this protest, too, as an expression of the opposition to the Patriarchate itself, for the manner in which it had assumed control by basing itself upon the power-wielding classes. Certainly moral and religious-social self-assertion was involved here as well. It was only right for the Sages to protest against the 'secularization' likely to ensue from the assignment of judicial functions to 'commoners' drawn from among the heads of the settlements, and against the corruption existing in that world, both of which were liable to lead to the perversion of justice. The Patriarchs, however, who were alive to the needs of the nation at the

---

in reference to the charity treasurers and the Elders). Cf. for the rivalry between the Bouleute and the Sages for superiority in the Patriarchal House, *T.P. Shabbat* xii, 13c; *Horayot* iii, 48c (Büchler, *Manhige Ṣippori*, p. 135. Cf. also Baron, *The Jewish Community*, I, p. 119).

145 Here, too the sources reveal the separate realms and the problem of which of the two was superior. In *T.P. Horayot*, iii, 48b we read: 'R. Joshua b. Levi said: [As between] the head and the Elder, the Elder takes precedence, for if there is no Elder there can be no head' etc. The nature of the 'head' is not explained properly here (the continuation of the passage is not sufficiently clear for our purposes). Further on, however, *ibid.* c, 'R. Joshua of Sikhnin in the name of R. Levi: Because Moses foresaw by means of the Holy Spirit that Israel would become entangled *(sic)* in the kingdoms, and their heads would stand by them, he gave the heads priority over the Elders.' Hence the functions of the 'heads' were social and political. The same conclusion emerges from the statement in *Midrash Tannaim*, ed. Hoffman, p. 213: ' "Heads of..." — Scripture tells us that when the heads enter to take counsel below, they sustain the Kingdom of Heaven above, as it is said, "Heads of and these are none other than great men' (the great men of the city, the civic leaders). This, however, is the recension of the Geonim (*Halakhot Gedolot*, Warsaw, 124b; *ibid.*, Berlin, and *Teshuvot Hageonim*, ed. Koronel, Nos. 117 and 703; Lyck, No. 2) and the *Seride Yerushalmi*, p. 286: 'The head and the Elder — the head takes priority over an Elder who is not a head.' This recension might likely support the view held by scholars that ordinary Sages served as leaders of the communities. However, our recension seems to be the correct version. For so we read in *Midrash Tanḥuma*, ed. Buber, end of *Shemot* (p. 17): 'Hah! They indeed consult with the Elders. So Moses "called to the Elders of the people" and afterwards "to the heads and judges": When does Israel have heads? — When they have Elders.' Our Midrash which serves as a parallel to the passage in the Palestinian Talmud undoubtedly supports the recension we have before us (which draws a distinction between the authority of the heads and that of the Elders), which is explained after the manner of the commentators: 'Who is not a head' — that is to say that Israel cannot attain to orderly and effective political and civil administration unless it has Elders, although Ginzberg, *Perushim* etc., III, p. 113, takes 'Heads' to mean Sages, and identical with Elders (the tradition ascribed to R. Akiba in the Talmud, *Pesaḥim* 112a, and Rabbi, *Pirqe Rabbenu Hakadosh*, see ed. Higger, *Horeb*, V, p. 133: That a person should not reside in a city, the Head of which is a *Talmid Hakham* — reveals the same duality and the same attitude of withdrawal from all preoccupation with public affairs evinced by some of the Sages).

time, who, more than most of the Sages, grasped the full compass of public affairs and who, more than the latter, were capable of sensing and adapting themselves to the requirements and circumstances of the hour, were also mindful of the discharge of their own function: The inclusion and balancing of the ruling elements and their subordination to the supreme leadership, and their involvement in the government of the nation.[146]

What results emerged from this development? It seems that the actions of the Patriarch were vindicated. The power of the central authority continued to increase. The joining of the 'heads of the cities' to the rule of the Patriarchate enhanced its authority, but in like manner helped to stimulate the process of the penetration of the influence of the Torah scholars among the local population and with it the stabilization of the religious-spiritual world of the masses.[147] Yet it seems that, in practice, the appointment of unqualified judges by the Patriarchate encouraged the predominance of Torah lawsuits — i.e. the judgement by the Sages. Through their dependence on the supremacy of the Patriarchate the two authorities came closer to one another and proceeded towards integration.[148]

---

146 There can be no reasonable doubt that the dependence of the Sages on the supremacy of the Patriarchs also increased the power of their own realm, by ensuring consolidation and order. It seems, indeed, that this is the meaning conveyed by R. Mana's remark in *T.P. Pesaḥim* vi, 33a: I heard from R. Yudan and all the rabbis: Why are the courts below (the House of the Patriarch) accustomed to insist on honour? So that disputes should not proliferate in Israel.' Such disputes were certainly liable to erupt too frequently in the realm of the Sages. (The question and answer before us concerning the reason for the Patriarchate insisting on being honoured also implies the negation, in principle, of any assumption of power and privilege by the Patriarchate. It teaches that their control did not stem from the fact of power or by right, but was exercised for the benefit of the public alone, and only endured because of the endorsement of the Sages at such time as they alone deemed fit.)

147 Just as we find Rabbi himself appointing officials (Parnassim), so do we find the Sages making appointments, *T.P. Pe'a*, viii, 20a, here, too, presumably with the assent of the Patriarch — Bacher, *Die Aggada der Palaestiner Amoraim*, II, p. 153. (We read of R. Ḥiyya b. Abba, among others, appointing archons. According to Lieberman's opinion, *Tarbiz*, II, ii, p. 235; *JQR*, 1943/44, p. 230, n. 20, the heads of the diaspora communities are intended here. This may be possible and even probable. R. Ḥiyya tarried in many diaspora communities, perhaps as an emissary of the Patriarch. Nevertheless, Lieberman's proof, based on the fact that we do not find archons in the sense of heads of communities in our sources except in reference to diaspora communities alone, is not conclusive. For so we read in *Midrash Yelammedenu*, as quoted in *Arukh*, s.v. "*Erekh Alef*', *Sefer Halikkutim*, ed. Grünhut, Numbers xix, 1: ' "And he saw the heads of the people" — [teaches] that he came to each single group and took remuneration for the Parnassim separately and for the archons separately.' It is far-fetched to assert that by using the term archon, the observation was directed especially at the diaspora population. It should further be noted that the name *'arkhuna* among the Samaritans is commonly used to designate the head of the community.) After the abolition of the Patriarchate, however, we find the 'Sanhedrins of the two Palestines' appointing 'great men' in the cities of the land (C. Th. 16, 8, 9).

148 The attempts of the 'ignorant judges' to deliver public discourses and to clothe themselves in the 'garment' certainly arises from the fact that the ordained Sages were accustomed to behave in this manner. Our method of inquiry, however, leads us to learn from here of the inclination of the

Quite possibly, too, this unification of the judicial systems, which the Patriarchs endeavoured to bring about in Eretz-Israel, also helped, in some measure, to bring about the acknowledgement of the suzerainty of Eretz-Israel in the area of jurisdiction, which took the form of subservience to the judicial authority of the Patriarchate on the part of the diaspora communities of the Roman Empire and which was initiated and continued progressively during the third and fourth centuries.[149]

What, then, is meant by 'taking money from the appointees'? We certainly recall the 'selling of office' which received wide mention in the tradition of the Roman Empire (and so too in our sources in reference to the High Priesthood at the end of the Second Temple period).[150] We should by no means absolve the Patriarchs from all social and moral taint (social developments in general in the Roman Empire at the end of the third and during the fourth century were likely to encourage the rise of arbitrary rule and despotism in the world of the Patriarchate). It is probable, however, that the above mentioned practice in itself is based on a tradition of urban life. It is known that immediately prior to the period under discussion Greek citizens were accustomed, on being elevated to 'honorary office' (ἀρχαί) in their cities or to other positions of prestige, to pay sums of money to the city treasury for public needs (*summa honorari*). It is, accordingly, not at all far-fetched to assume that a similar practice existed in at least some of the cities of Jewish Eretz-Israel. From the time the 'appointments' became the prerogative of the Patriarchs, however, these sums, which had previously been contributed to the local treasury by city inhabitants upon their being appointed 'judges' in their localities, were now by right handed over to the central authority which had made the appointment, i.e. to the general treasury controlled by the Patriarchs.[151]

Here, too, the polemical language used by the Sages opposed to the appointment of unqualified judges was likely to obscure the tradition underlying the conduct of the Patriarchs and to obliterate its social background and organizational significance, thus unfairly to deprive the Patriarchs of the justification for their conduct.

---

ignorant to approach more closely to the world of the Sages and to combine Torah knowledge with judicial functions.
149 The dependence of the diaspora judiciaries on the Patriarch's establishment of their supremacy is tied up with their control of the administration of the communities as a whole, a fact which is found in Roman legal sources and in the literary sources cited in this article.
150 Cf. above, pp. 65 ff.
151 The same applies to the contributions of the leaders of the diaspora communities under Roman suzerainty. which were transmitted to the Patriarch, according to the evidence of Palladius.

Appendix

ON DIOCLETIAN'S RESCRIPT, C. J. m, 13, 3.

We have dealt above with the continuing struggle between the Patriarchate and the Sages on the appointment of judges, even after the 'compromise' reached between them, a matter stressed by Dinaburg as well. That scholar, however, wanted to infer from Diocletian's Rescript written to 'Judah' that this controversy had become so intense that the struggle of the Patriarch against Sages appointing judges without his consent led to the intervention of the Roman government, with the Emperor pronouncing his verdict against the Sages. For many reasons, it is difficult to sustain Dinaburg's conjecture. Even if the argument raised by scholars against the commentators who wished to regard our document as relating to the Jewish law-courts is discarded — viz. the absence of any mention of Jews in the text — it still remains doubtful whether the Emperor could speak of *qui judicio praeest,* of someone, anonymous, as possessing official power, if he had Jewish judges (authorised by the Patriarch and not by him) in mind, and whom the government had not endowed with judicial authority (except over Jews). Moreover, if this document refers to the conflict between the Patriarchate and the Sages on the right to appoint judges, how can it refer without qualification to those appointed by the Sages (the Bet Din) as chosen by the consent of private persons as axiomatic, for the entire issue (submitted, according to Dinaburg, by the Patriarch to the government) was: Who are to be the judges considered authorised and duly appointed — those appointed by the Patriarch or those ordained by the Bet Din? It follows, then, that the main point at issue is missing from the Emperor's reply. It is also somewhat far-fetched to give the expression *consensu privatorum* the interpretation suggested by Dinaburg: 'with the consent of other people' (i.e. the Sages). Its plain sense, it seems to me, is similar to *consensus partium*, of the parties to the trial. This is, it appears, substantiated especially by the clause, *qui nulli praeest judicio.* For if the reference is to the appointment of overall judges by the Sages (without the authorization of the Patriarch), is it possible to say that prior to their appointment they did not possess the status of heads of lawcourts ? It is accordingly much more reasonable to interpret this document as dealing with courts of arbitration chosen by the litigants from amongst the unqualified who do not judge by consent of the government and has nothing at all to do with the Jews.

True, the name, Judah, ostensibly inclines one to assume that we are dealing here with a Jew. Nevertheless, I see no difficulty in Juster's assumption that he was a Christian governor in one of the Hyparchies. For we learn from many sources of Christian governors, officers and court officials in Diocletian's day, all the time until he began persecuting them. At all events it may be worthwhile to dwell on the inscription published by L. Wickert, in his article, *Vorbemerkungen zu einem Supplementum Ostiense des Corpus Inscriptionum Latinarum* in *Sitzungsberichte der Preussischen Akademie usw.*, 1928, This inscription was written by *Ordo Augustalium* of Ostia and here is its text: *M. Aurel[io] f. Ter.*

p. a. sui - - - Scythop[oli] p[an] tomim[o sui] temporis] primo in O[riente - - -] to approbato a[b impp. Valeriano e]t Gal... ex provincia e[- - -. .post] mortem patr[is s]ui Jud[ae; item de] curioni civitat[iu]m Ascalo[nito]narum et Damascen[or] um. Huic s...ndus ordo Augustalium non propter memoriam pat[ri]s eius, sed et propter plenam [ipsius per] itiam postul[antibus omnibus pariter civibus...

The reconstructed text *Jud[ae; item de] curioni* was taken over by the author from Wilken (who mentions Judah, the chronographer of the days of Septimus Severus known from Eusebius' *Ecclesiastical History*). While another reconstruction suggested itself first to him at the time, he finally rejected it (see *ibid.* p. 41, n. 3). Now, first of all, it is necessary to examine whether it is reasonable to assume that M. Aurelius, the Pantomime, son of Judah, was a Jew. Certainly we do find a Jewish mime in the time of Nero (Josephus, *Life* 3). Yet that a Jewish Pantomime should have risen in the third century (the inscription most certainly is to be dated between 253–260; see *ibid.* p. 40), to serve honorarily, because of his preeminence as an artist, as a member of the municipal council of Ashkelon (which hated Jews) and of Damascus is much too far-fetched. Nor, for the same reason can he be regarded as a Christian.

The inscription, however, also clearly informs us that Judah the father as well served in a capacity similar to that of the son, and that the latter went from Beisan to Ostia to replace his own father, who had died (hence the honour of the father is alluded to first), as the author explains (p. 42). Perhaps the conjecture is not farfetched that the father was the *citharoedus* praised in the inscription at Dessau (ILS No. 5233) for his accomplishments in *Sebasia aput Damascum III, Actia aput Bo[s]tram II, Pithia Karthaginis,* etc. It is almost definite that this Judah could not be regarded as Jewish. Yet there is nothing strange, in my mind, in a non-Jew (Semitic), a native of Beisan being called by a name inherited from Jews in that city and its surroundings (or perhaps he was an apostate?).

So we do have some support in our hands for regarding the Judah of Diocletian's Rescript as a pagan Gentile.

Dinaburg, however, also relies for his conjecture upon the document in *Codex Theodosianus* II, 1, 10, which speaks of Jewish judication, *apud Judaeos vel patriarchas* (among the Jews or Patriarchs). This scholar accordingly discerns two distinct types of courts in Eretz-Israel (in the eyes of the authority): Those officially recognized ('among the Patriarchs') and those not officially recognized ('among the Jews'), and assigns the beginnings of these two authorities to the same document of Diocletian, whose above-mentioned decision was responsible for the rise, from then onwards, of courts not appointed by the Patriarchs and regarded by the Empire as 'private'. It seems, however, that we cannot assume any rivalry existing between the courts of the Patriarchs and the Sages elsewhere than in Eretz-Israel. We have not heard as yet that the rivalry extended into the diaspora, and had gained ground there, becoming a permanent reality, till it became necessary for it to be mentioned in Roman legislation (the order under discussion does not elaborate and speaks generally of Jews in the Empire).

The principal substance of our document makes it reasonable to assert that only one type of court existed among Diaspora Jewry, and this consisted generally of the heads of the community, but that it went by several names. Some referred to it (in Gentile language, and chiefly in the Empire) as being *apud Judaeos* ('among the Jews') and some called it after the judges, 'of the Patriarchs' (i.e. minor patriarchs, the heads of the communities. That such courts existed is in my mind incontrovertible[1]). In our document, the combining of the two names by the conjunction *'vel'* into a single term is not surprising (or perhaps the reference is to the Bet Din of the members of the community, 'commoners', side by side with the leaders of the community?).

---

1 The *interpretatio* gives this version of our passage: *Sane si apud maiores legis consentientes ambae partes* etc., which is identical with 'the law-court of the heads of the communities'.

Part II
Rabbinic Culture – Tradition and Self-Invention

THE DAVIDIC DESCENT OF HILLEL*

Israel Levy

Translated by Erin Brust

It is believed that Hillel, the head of the family of Patriarchs, was a descendant of David; this is what all the historians affirm.[1] Krochmal himself, who was not kind to the dynasty of the *Nasi*, does not question the validity of this opinion.[2] Only Mr. [Emil] Schürer seems to have been constrained by some scientific scruple when he included this assertion in the collection of legends that surround the life of the great Babylonian sage.[3]

Such unanimity can be explained only by the power of the testimony that attributes to Hillel this illustrious origin. These texts must be singularly probative if they are to cause us to dismiss the numerous objections that the assertion raises.

In effect, nothing, in the life of Hillel or the lives of his descendants, during more than a century, suggests that they boasted such a lineage.

Hillel's entrance onto the scene of history, if we suppose that the account is authentic (and it certainly is not in all of its parts),[4] is as an obscure personage without credibility. A meeting, presided over by the elders of Bathyra, was called to resolve a question about the temple service: Hillel did not attend. He was sought so that the opinions of Shemaiah and of Avtalion might be learned from him. In response, he resorted to a logical argument after which the assembled exclaimed: "You see very well that there is nothing to learn from this Babylonian!"

As modest as Hillel is supposed to have been, it is likely that, had he known of his Davidic descent, he would not have failed to speak of it, if only to destroy the

---

* This translation was completed by Erin Brust and reviewed by Christine Hayes. The translation of primary sources is based on the version that appears in the original article with a footnote indicating those that are paraphrastic or inexact. Full bibliographic information for secondary sources cited in the article has been added at the end of the article by Christine Hayes. Comments and corrections by Hayes are set in square brackets and marked (CH).

1 Herzfeld, III, 257; Graetz, III, 222; Geiger, *Das Judenthum und seine Geschichte* I, 99; Goitein, *Magazin*, 1884, 5; Weiss, *Dor Dor ve Dorshav*, I, 155.
2 *He-Ḥaluts*, II, 69.
3 *Geschichte des jüdischen Volkes*, II, 296.
4 See the very rigorous discussion of this passage in Chwolson, *Das letzte Passahmahl Christi und der Tag seines Todes* (St. Petersburg 1892).

disfavor that attached to his Babylonian identity. This [Davidic] descent would surely have established him as without equal.

Might it be supposed that Hillel feared he would awaken the jealousy of Herod? For this to be the case, it would be necessary first of all to prove that he lived under this king. The text that is relied upon to affirm this is devoid of all historical character. Incidentally, secrets of this kind cannot be kept. Given the frequent relationships between the Jews of Palestine and those of Babylonia, there would surely have been some individual indiscreet enough to betray Hillel's *incognito* and reveal the illustrious personage shining in their midst. In this period, when the Israelites were impatiently awaiting a "son of David," Hillel would have become, even in spite of himself, the center of national hopes and the cause of a movement of rebellion.

If Hillel remains absolutely silent about his descent, his son pushes discretion further yet: during his entire lifetime, he does not speak a single word about it that would be passed down to his posterity, and we can attest to his existence through only one obscure text.[5]

His grandson, Gamliel, who is perhaps his son,[6] emerges from the shadows and appears in full light. Not only talmudic sources, but also the Acts of the Apostles (5:34–39; 22:3) portray him as a renowned personage, honored by all people, but makes no allusion to his Davidic descent.

It might be supposed that the Acts would have feared that in relating this trait, the glory of Jesus, whom genealogists also linked to the king of Israel, would be diminished. The contrary could just as well be supported: the author who makes Gamliel speak so favorably of a disciple of Jesus, and who accords such uncommon accolades to a Pharisee, would not have passed up the chance to place Gamiliel's courageous intervention into even greater relief.

The son of Gamliel plays a primary role during the siege of Jerusalem. He takes sides against the zealots, and Josephus refers to his intervention with approval.[7] In his autobiography, the historian speaks of Gamliel's very illustrious birth. But of a Davidic ancestry, he says not a word. The talmudic texts are not any more generous with information on his account.

Will we be happier in regard to his son, Gamliel II, the first of the Hillelites, who was called to preside over the counsel of the Jews?

The details of his life are more abundant. A glaring example of his well-known authoritarian character is seen in his humiliation of R. Joshua. Gamliel, abandoned by all, is reduced to resigning from his post and sees another Rabbi named president of the Academy.[8] Throughout this conflict, one waits in vain for any mention of the title "descendant of David," which would have elevated Gamliel's

---

5 b. Shabbat 15a.
6 Lebrecht has already cast doubt on the existence of Simon, in Geiger's *Judaische Zeitschrift*, 11, 278, *pace* Herzfeld, *Monatschrift*, 1854, 222.
7 *Jewish War*, 4, 3, 9; *Life*, 38, 39, 44, 60.
8 b. Berakhot 27b; y. Berakhot 7c.

prestige and disarmed those present. Neither Gamliel nor the rabbis who dismiss him seem informed of this illustrious ancestry.

A passage from b. Baba Metsia (59b), if one is to believe Rashi, would show, however, that the family of Gamliel of Yavne already glorified the latter as a descendant of David. It is recounted that Imma Shalom, Gamliel's sister, once said: "I received a tradition from the house of my father's father that all the gates (of heaven) are closed, except for those of wounded feelings" (i.e., God always listens to the complaints of the unfortunates who are treated with severity.) According to Rashi, Imma Shalom was referring to David who expresses this idea in the Psalms and whom she called the ancestor of her family.

One must admit that the evidence is very weak. It is on this point that the Tosafot reject Rashi's view and say that Imma Shalom simply invoked a traditional family maxim. They make the irrefutable argument that Gamliel himself uses the same phrase in connection with a tradition that does not in any way trace to David or to the Psalms.

The son of Gamliel II does not allow the supposed secret to transpire, any more than his father does. Here too, in many circumstances, one waits in vain for him to adopt this peerless nobility: he never says a word. Yet he too was very infatuated with his Patriarchal title and would prove to be possessive of his prerogatives. The following text recounts this anecdote about him: When R. Simon b. Gamliel was there (at the Academy), everyone stood before him; upon the entrance of R. Meir and of R. Nathan, they behaved in the same way. "Should there, therefore, be no difference between them and me?!" said Simon b. Gamliel. And so it was that he established this rule.[9] On that day, R. Meir and R. Nathan were absent. The next day, seeing that no one stood before them as usual, they inquired as to the reason. They learned of the rule established by Simon b. Gamliel. R. Meir thus said to R. Nathan: "I am *hakham* and you are *ab bet din*; let us do the same to him (or: prepare questions for him); let us question him on *Uqtsin*, and as he will not know how to respond, we will depose him. I will then be *ab bet din*, and you, you will be *nasi*." R. Jacob b. Karsi, having heard them and wanting to avoid a scandal, went to instruct Simon b. Gamliel on the questions that they would pose to him. The next day, the *nasi*, invited by Meir and Nathan to deliver a lesson on *Uqtsin*, knew how to extricate himself. He said to them, "If I had not been prepared you would have exposed me to humiliation." And he ordered that they be excluded from the Academy. Thereupon they began to formulate difficult questions which they sent in writing to the Academy; some were resolved, but others were not. The answers to the latter questions they then passed on to the school. R. Yosi said: "How is it that Torah is outside and we are inside!" R. Simon b. Gamliel decided that Meir and Nathan should be allowed to return but that, as punishment for their audacity, their opinions would not be reported in their name; rather, instead of Meir, one should say: "*the others*" and, instead of Nathan, "*some people.*" The two rabbis

---

9 Which changed the customary habit.

heard in a dream that they should be reconciled with the *nasi*. Nathan took the first step; Meir did not agree to do so, saying that dreams signify nothing. Upon receiving him, Simon b. Gamliel said to Nathan: "The honored title of your father (the Exilarch in Babylonia) made you *ab bet din*. Does it also entitle you to the powers of the *nasi*?"[10]

Let us grant, for the sake of argument, the historicity of this interaction. In this case, had Simon b. Gamliel known of his own glorious genealogy, he would not have made the mistake of contrasting it to that of the Exilarch.

It will be recalled that in reliance on this account, Mr. [Adolf] Büchler wrote in his *Revue des Etudes Juives*, an article of uncommon ingenuity on "The Conspiracy of R. Meir and R. Nathan against the Patriarch."[11] Our learned colleague wanted to find in the *aggadah* some vestiges of remarks made by the conspirators against the Patriarch. The principle that guides him is the idea that since the Patriarch is a descendant of David and, consequently, Judah, all of Meir's attacks against one or the other of these biblical heroes are directed at the Patriarch.

Mr. Büchler neglected, first of all, to meet all of the difficulties which the story in the Babylonian Talmud raises. This account is, first of all, of a rather late date, since it was written in Babylonian Aramaic. It is thus only an oral tradition, and one must not place too much weight on its language. In addition, this tradition has a tendentious character; its goal is to provide a historical explanation for the rule according to which the expression "others" designates [a teaching by] R. Meir and "some say" designates [a teaching by] R. Nathan. Finally, and more serious, is the fact that the Palestinian Talmud ignores all of the details of this episode as reported by the Babylonian Talmud. It says only that the people, who had a custom of standing before Meir, having learned of the new rule, wanted to apply it to R. Meir, and that he left in anger, indignant that he was to be stripped of an honor to which he was accustomed.[12]

Most important, Mr. Büchler neglects to establish in the first instance the validity of the premise of his reasoning. "Concerning the origin of the Patriarch, he says (p. 64), we know, from a scroll found in Jerusalem, that his ancestor Hillel, the founder of the dynasty, descended from King David."

We will see below that this scroll could have been written only in the time of Rabbi, son of our Simon. Moreover, Mr. Büchler, in his later work, full of ideas and erudition, returned to his previous opinion and claimed that the name of Hillel that appears in this scroll alongside that of R. Ḥiyya, contemporary and rival of Rabbi, designates none other than Rabbi.[13]

"According to the book of Ruth, iv, 20," adds Mr. Büchler, "the first royal

---

10 b. Horayot 13b. [Levy's translation of rabbinic sources here and throughout the article, is both abbreviated and paraphrastic (CH)].
11 Volume 28, p. 60 and following.
12 y. Bikkurim 65c.
13 Büchler, "Die Priester und der Cultus," p. 41.

ancestor of David, and also of the house of the Patriarchs, was Naḥshon b. Amminadab, who can be considered the ancestor of this dynasty, as an obscure passage from b. Sanhedrin 12a demonstrates: "The descendants of Naḥshon wanted to fix the new moons, but the Romans prohibited it." We see, therefore, that the Patriarchs often recalled that they were descended from Judah; otherwise the meaning of this statement would have been incomprehensible."

The event recounted in this passage from b. Sanhedrin took place *more than a century* after Simon b. Gamliel, and therefore long after the rise of the idea of the Davidic origin of the Hillelites which, we will see, is mentioned during the administration of Rabbi. "The Patriarchs" here thus refers to the Patriarchs *starting from Rabbi*.

"It is necessary," Büchler concludes, "to remember above all that Hillel descended from the tribe of Judah, a fact uncontested elsewhere, because, in the Talmud, a second passage repeats this tradition."

This second passage pertains to a statement allegedly uttered by Rabbi Judah; it therefore has no value for an earlier time. The "fact is uncontested" only beginning with Rabbi [Judah] but not before.

It is not our plan to discuss the hypotheses of our learned colleague and to see whether he has been misled by his imagination and by his love of stratagems into discovering attacks against the Patriarch in Meir's words. These conjectures are much too hazardous to be turned into premises of backwards reason that would be formulated along these lines: "insofar as Meir surely wanted to impugn the Patriarch by speaking of Judah, son of Jacob, then the Patriarch was, to everyone's knowledge, a descendant of Judah through David."

Thus, from Hillel to Simon b. Gamliel II, there is no allusion to the Davidic ancestry of the family, neither from their own mouths, nor from the mouths of their contemporaries. Such silence would be inexplicable if the fact had been verified or if the tradition had been well attested. Could it be that the Patriarchs and their contemporaries organized a conspiracy of silence so as not to awaken the suspicions of the Roman government? The matter requires further consideration: would the Roman government grant official recognition to a functionary exercising an authority as great as that of the Patriarchate, if it harbored the fear that by virtue of its descent from ancient kings, it could ever become the focal point of national hopes? That the Exilarch attributes to himself the same noble lineage, did not concern the Persian government; it was not in Babylonia that an insurrectional movement, a messianic agitation, was feared.[14] Palestine, on the contrary, was always expecting the Redeemer. The Bar-Kokhba Revolt is sufficient proof

---

14 Even in the 3rd century, when the ranks of the Jews on the banks of the Euphrates were multiplied and enlarged by the influx of exiles from Judea, and the rabbis spoke openly of their messianic hopes, King Shapur revealed by means of a joke how amused he was by their illusion and how little he thought of their vain expectation. "You maintain," he said to Samuel, "that the Messiah will come mounted on a donkey; I will send him a white horse of mine!" (b. Sanhedrin 98a).

of that. Would Rome itself identify for the Jewish patriots the flag around which to rally and maintain their illusions, by reviving yet again the prestige of a *son of David*?

If in fact, through a tacit agreement, the rabbis had avoided *in public* all incriminating remarks that might be recounted to the Romans, they would not have maintained such discretion in their conversations preserved in the Talmud, or in their conduct towards the Patriarchs, and, in any case, popular preachers would not have been prohibited from alluding to the existence of a possible *messiah*.

The Roman authority could allow the Patriarchs this conceit after the definitive quashing of the national party and after Simon b. Gamliel II pledged submission to the Empire. It is, in effect, during the patriarchy of Judah ha-Nasi, son of Simon b. Gamliel II, or Rabbi, that the idea that the Hillelite dynasty is linked to David first appears. But this new idea manifests itself only timidly; it is not yet definitively formulated but is still in process, and those it most concerns still do not dare give it precise contours.

It appears in the texts that we will cite forthwith.[15]

It is said that Rabbi wanted to marry his son to a daughter of R. Hiyya. At the moment of the drafting of the marriage contract, the young girl died. "Was there something unsuitable with this union," cried Rabbi? The families were investigated, and it was found that Rabbi descended from Shefatyah ben Avital[16] and R. Hiyya from Shimei, a brother of David.[17]

We will not yet discuss this text; we want first to continue the enumeration of passages that reveal the same tendency.

The Palestinian Talmud (y. Kilayim 32b) recounts: "Rabbi was very humble. He used to say: 'I would do anything except what the elders of Bathyra did for my ancestor [Hillel]; they relinquished the dignity of the Patriarchate and conferred it upon him. If R. Huna, the Resh Galutha, were to come up here [to Palestine], I would set him above me because he descends from Judah and I from Benjamin, he through the male line and I through the female line.' Once, R. Hiyya told him, 'The Exilarch is outside.' Rabbi became upset. [R. Hiyya added,] 'It is his coffin

---

15 A *baraita* (b. Sanhedrin 5a) says that the words in Gen 49:10 "*The scepter shall not depart from Judah*" apply to the Exilarch in Babylonia who exercises authority over Israel, and the continuation of the verse "*nor the ruler's staff from his descendants* [lit. between his feet (CH)]" applies to the descendants of Hillel who teach the Torah in public. But since there is no way to date this text, nothing can be deduced from it. If one wishes at all costs to find an approximate date for the redaction of this statement, it would have to be declared contemporaneous with the dialogue between R. Judah and R. Hiyya, for, in accordance with the Talmud and the linguistic usage in force precisely in the time of R. Hiyya, this *baraita* puts the Patriarchs beneath the Exilarch. This is the sense of Rabbenu Tam, who rightly links this passage to the parallel in Palestinian Talmud tractate Kilayim. However, according to Rav Safra, in b. Horayot 11b, R. Hiyya already relies on this *baraita*; but this assertion in the Talmud is not certain.

16 The son of David and Avital, 2 Samuel 3:4.

17 b. Ketubot 62b.

that has come.' Rabbi replied, 'Go and see who wants you outside!' and [when he went out] he [Rabbi] excluded him from the Academy."

This account is reproduced in Genesis Rabbah 33.

This remark by Rabbi is, it is true, obscure; how precisely he can claim to descend from Benjamin, which would preclude a Davidic descent, is not easily understood. In addition, he speaks only of Judah, and not of David. But we will forgo a verdict on these points, easily recognizing in these words the affirmation of an idea that will be spelled out in the following text.[18]

"Rabbi Levi says:[19] There was found in Jerusalem a genealogical scroll containing these words:[20]

> Hillel descended from David
> R. Ḥiyya the Great from Shefatyah ben Avital
> The family of Kalba from Kaleb
> That of Ben Tsitsit, the carpet maker, from Abner
> Ben Ḥubsin from Aḥav;[21]
> The family of Yatsah from Asaf;
> The family of Jehu from Sepphoris;[22]
> The family of Yannai from Eli;
> R. Yosi b. Ḥalafta from Yodanab the Rechabite;
> R. Nehemiah from Nehemia Hatirshata."

It is this text that is invoked endlessly to affirm the Davidic origin of Hillel, and more credence is accorded to it because it is cited in two places. However, regarding these two citations, one is simply the copy of the other. In chapter 98 of Genesis Rabbah, a chapter which, as Zunz demonstrates, is much more recent than the rest of the book, we find only a reproduction of the passage from the Palestinian Talmud, including even the incomprehensible sentence that we have highlighted.

The scroll hardly accords with the anecdote cited above that correctly had Rabbi descending from Shefatyah b. Avital. It accords even less with another account in which it is claimed that in Rabbi's day, some wanted to decree that

---

18 y. Ta'anit 68a; Genesis Rabbah 98.
19 In the Palestinian Talmud's version, the order of the names is not the same; moreover, instead of Yatsah, there is Yatsaf, a very similar reading; instead of קוביסין בן כובשין, בית כובשין; instead of "the house of Jehu," "ben Judah." Büchler, "Die Priester und der Cultus im letzten Jahrzehnt des jerusalemischen Tempels," p. 42ff., tried to extract from this passage whatever authentic historical information it might contain. He believes that this document suffered some interpolations, among others, the reference to Hillel who, he says reasonably enough, is here named in lieu of Judah the Patriarch.
20 These words are preceded in Genesis Rabbah, by the following phrase: "They counted and asked: From whom is Hillel [descended]?" Needless to say, this addition is a historical error.
21 Might this be ישוע בן קבסין who is referred to in y. Pesaḥim 33a?
22 This section is incomprehensible. The other personages are connected to a biblical hero; in regard to these, a mere indication of the place of origin is given.

Babylonian families would have to submit to a genealogical investigation, and that Rabbi subsequently exclaimed: "You are putting thorns in my eyes."[23] If his Davidic ancestry had been attested in a valid document, and had been as unanimously accepted as is commonly believed, Rabbi would not have had, as indicated in this account, such fear of these investigations.

But this scroll discovered in Jerusalem, according to Levi, raises many other difficulties. One finds here, pell-mell, the names of individuals and rabbis from the first, second and third centuries, and even some contemporaries of Levi!

Büchler assumes a primitive base, containing only the names of heroes of the rebellion, such as Tsitsit, to which were successively added the names of other individuals.[24] But he himself recognizes that in any case, the name of Hillel had nothing to do with the earliest kernel of this chronicle.

In any case, this chronicle, even in its (hypothetical) primitive condition, was only a popular document, produced in an aggadic manner. Kalba descends from Kaleb, because of the analogy between the two names; similarly Yatsaf from Asaf. In the supposedly more recent section, the same genealogical procedures are followed: Nehemiah descends from the contemporary of Ezra, because he bears the same name. This is not a historical document; it is simply an aggadic composition, a popular fantasy. That Levi should be the one to announce this discovery is self-explanatory: Such a heraldic parchment would be especially appealing to an aggadist of his caliber.

Based on all of these data, it can be concluded with certainty that the idea of the Davidic ancestry of Hillel originated during the Patriarchate of Rabbi.

It is even possible to surmise the circumstances that favored, if not created, this ennoblement of the Patriarch.

One is struck by the presence of the name of R. Ḥiyya in all the instances in which this conception appears.[25] R. Ḥiyya derived from Babylonia and was the parent of the Exilarch, reputed to be a descendant of David. He was, at the same time, a distinguished sage who, more than once, put Rabbi to shame. His renown must have cast a shadow over the Patriarch; his distinction of descent from David must have caused him to offend even more. This state of inferiority inspired in some well-meaning genealogist the intention to rectify this wrong.[26] With the best

---

23 b. Qiddushin 71a.
24 "Die Priester und der Cultus," p. 41.
25 It is quite remarkable that it is the same R. Judah who asks the same R. Ḥiyya: "If I, the *nasi*, had lived in the time of the Temple, would I have had to offer the sacrifice imposed upon the *nasi* (i.e., the king)?" And R. Ḥiyya replied to him: "No, for your rival (who is higher than you) is a Babylonian." As a result, you cannot compare yourself to the king. And Rabbi Judah accepted this view to such an extent that he replied, "Nevertheless, the kings of Israel, like the Davidic kings, offered this sacrifice, independently of one another" (b. Horayot 11b). Here again R. Judah accepts his inferiority as compared to the Exilarch.
26 Who knows whether there is not found even in the name הלל an allusion to his Davidic ancestry. Does הלל, "he sings the Psalms," awaken the memory of the author of the Psalms? These popular etymologies which are readily mocked have created many other traditions.

faith in the world, perhaps, this "proto-D'Hozier"[27] added the name of the ancestor of the Patriarchs, Hillel, to the list on the famous scroll. "Hillel descended from David," he is of royal family; whereas R. Ḥiyya is connected to David only through Shefatyah who played no role in history and whose descendants never furnished kings of Israel: small nobility!

Rabbi had no reason to oppose this glorious investiture. Nevertheless, he seems to have been embarrassed, as he was not yet fully entered into his role. Ḥiyya, who without a doubt, had good reason not to share the sentiments of the friends of the Patriarchate, was happy to tease him by speaking of his rival and authentic descendant of David, the Exilarch. In the presence of Ḥiyya, Rabbi was obliged to mute his pretentions and accept descent from the king of Israel only through the female line.

Is it in order to once more enhance his nobility that Rabbi conceived of the plan to marry his son to the daughter of R. Ḥiyya? We do not know, and we do not wish to create a novel. At the very least, the account that tells us of this marriage retains the memory of a muted rivalry between the two sages and of the resentment that Rabbi felt on account of the reputation of R. Ḥiyya. It is this that is the explanation for the proposed investigation that would have revealed that the nobility of Ḥiyya did not compare to that of the Patriarch. The author of this account, aided only by memories, doesn't know that the famous scroll of Levi correctly attributes to R. Ḥiyya the ancestry that he assigns to Rabbi. The name Shefatyah survived only in his memory; he placed it where he could.

We do not conceal the speculative nature of our attempted reconstruction of the genesis and history of this tradition. But we believe that we have demonstrated, and here lies the only goal of this study, that it was born only in the time of Rabbi Judah the Patriarch, that is to say, more than two centuries after Hillel, and that it is not based on any authentic document.

References

Büchler, Adolphe. "La Conspiration de R. Nathan et R. Meir contre le Patriarche Simon Ben Gamaliel," *Revue des Etudes Juives* 28 (1894), 60–74.

Chwolson, Daniel. *Das letzte Passahmahl Christi und der Tag seines Todes* (St. Petersburg, 1892).

——. "Die Priester und der Cultus im letzten Jahrzehnt des jerusalemischen Tempels," in *Jahresbericht der isr. theologischen Lehrallstalt* (Vienna, 1895).

Goitein, Gabor. "Das Leben und Wirken des Patriarchen Hillel" in *Magazin für die Wissenschaft des Judentums* (Berlin: Verl. d. Jüdischen Presse, 1884).

Grätz, Heinrich. *Geschichte der Juden von den ältesten Zeiten bis auf die Gegenwart* (Leipzig: O. Leiner, 1853–76).

Herzfeld, Levi. *Geschichte des Volkes Jisrael von der Zerstörung des Ersten Tempels bis*

---

27 [D'Hozier was a 17th–18th century French historical commentator who compiled armorials and genealogies of French nobility (CH)].

zur Einsetzung des Makkabäers Schimon zum Hohenpriester und Fürsten, 3 vols., 1847 (Nordhausen, 1855–57; abridged edition, 1870).

——. "Chronologische Unsetzung der Schriftgelehrten von Antigonus aus Socho bis auf R. Akiba" in *Monatsschrift für Geschichte und Wissenschaft des Judentums* (ed. Z. Frankel; Leipzig, 1854).

Krochmal, Nahman. "Toldot Rabbi Yehudah na-Nasi" in *He-Ḥaluts* 2 (Lemburg, 1953), 63–93. Reprinted Jerusalem: Makor, 1993.

Lebrecht, Fürchtegott. "Der Jüdische Senator in Rom" in *Jüdische Zeitschrift für Wissenschaft und Leben* (ed. A. Geiger; Breslau, 1875).

Schürer, Emil. *Geschichte des jüdischen Volkes im Zeitalter Jesu Christi* (Leipzig: J.C. Hinrichs, 1886–1890).

Weiss, Isaac Hirsch. *Dor Dor ve Dorshav* (Vienna: Herzfeld and Bauer, 1871–91).

THE ANCIENT JEWISH SCHOOL SYSTEM*

Wilhelm Bacher[1]

Translated by Eva Kiesele

From one of our ancient sages, who helped to restore Judaism in Palestine after Rome's victory over Jerusalem, a prayer, which he used to say upon leaving the house of study, has been preserved:[2] "I give thanks to You, my God and God of my Fathers, that You have set my portion among those who sit in the synagogues and houses of study, and not among those who sit in the theater and the arena. I labor and they labor; I persist and they persist; but I labor for the sake of paradise, and they labor for the pit of perdition."

This prayer lends vivid expression not only to the deep satisfaction that the pious Torah scholar finds in his profession, but also to the opposition between Jewish culture and Greco-Roman culture. The theater of the Greeks and the arena of the Romans, these two institutions of the pagan lust for life, which the Jews of Palestine could observe even in the cities of their own country, were in their eyes the most distinctive feature of pagan education, with its spirit so flagrantly contradicting the religion and mores of Israel. For them, theater and arena were the incarnation of this spirit.

An ancient exegesis therefore applies the scriptural prohibition[3] against walking in the statutes of the nations to the theater and arena.[4] The "seat of scoffers," against which the first verse of the book of Psalms warns, denotes, in the reading of the acclaimed second century teacher R. Meir, the theater and arena.[5]

---

* This translation was completed by Eva Kiesele and reviewed by Elisa Ronzheimer. The translation of primary sources is based on the version that appears in the original article with a footnote indicating those that are paraphrastic or inexact. Comments and corrections are set in square brackets and the author identified by initials: EK = Eva Kiesele and CH = Christine Hayes.
1 Lecture held on January 8, 1902 at the Society for the Collection and Preservation of artistic and historical monuments of Judaism in Vienna.
2 Neḥunya b. HaQanah, y. Berakhot 4:2, 7d; for a different version, see b. Berakhot 28b.
3 Lev 18:3.
4 Sifra § Aḥarei Mot 13.
5 t. Avodah Zarah 2:6; Avot de-Rabbi Nathan 6, 28; cp. b. Avodah Zarah 18b.

A contemporary of Meir has the prophet Elijah explain that earthquakes occur because the earth has to bear theaters and arenas while Israel's sanctuary is lying in ruins.[6] A Palestinian preacher of the 3rd century recognizes Esau in the abominable fool whose ungodly disposition is castigated in the fourteenth psalm: Esau, i.e. Rome, whose abominations – the ubiquitous idolatrous temples, theaters and arenas – fill the globe.[7] Another preacher has the congregation of Israel speak in the words of the prophet:[8] *"I did not sit in the company of merrymakers, in the theater and arena of the pagans, in order to rejoice with them."*[9] And a third predicts the future triumph of Judaism over paganism by saying that the time will come when theater and arena will become places for the promulgation of Israel's Torah.[10]

Just as the Jews of Palestine saw Greco-Roman culture with its splendor and its vices, its gaiety and its immorality, manifested in theater and arena, they saw their own ancestral culture embodied in the synagogue and the house of study. The synagogue as the site of communal worship and public instruction for the assembled congregation, the house of study as the site of education for the young and collective study for the adults; both institutions are creations of a unique Jewish culture. It was their joint responsibility to safeguard and perpetuate Judaism.

Today, from a distance of two millennia, the contemplation of world history teaches us to recognize more clearly than did our predecessors in earlier epochs wherein lay the unique character of Jewish culture, and how long it was successful at asserting itself in its homeland over the culture of the Greeks and Romans. Today, we will not attribute to the culture of ancient Israel elements that it did not possess. We will not, as earnest thinkers in antiquity and the Middle Ages did in all seriousness, make the prophets and sages of Israel into the teachers of the Greek philosophers and scientists. Rather, we will acknowledge that Israel's destiny was *not* to produce arts and sciences, and that in these areas it was to receive, not give. Through its religion and its ethic alone, the latter inseparably connected to the former, did Israel become an inventive cultural people, and a light unto the nations. The illumination of thought by the true knowledge of God, the cultivation of sensibility, the heightening of the sense of duty, the sanctification of life and its tasks through a morality that springs from true knowledge of God – these are the essential constituents of Israel's unique culture. And it is through them that Judaism was called to become the teacher of the peoples and to induce the moral transformation of humankind.

The first creative period of Israel's civilization produced the sacred literature. This literature did not, however, become a dead memorial of the past. Rather, it

---

6 Nehorai, y. Berakhot 4:2, 13c; Shoher Tov on Ps 18:8.
7 Samuel b. Naḥman, Shoher Tov on Ps 14:1.
8 Jer 15:17.
9 Abba b. Kahana, Pesiqta deRav Kahana 119b.
10 Yose b. Ḥanina, b. Megillah 6a.

continued to live and stir new life in and among the people from whom it had emerged. From the commandments and narratives of the Torah, from the speeches of the prophets, from the words of wise men and poets welled forth the same spirit that had animated the authors of this literature. The new cultural period, rooted in the engagement with and inquiry into the ancient literature – this period, named after the Second Temple, brought forth as its unique product *Torah scholarship*. Concurrently, it produced the institutions designed to provide the entire nation with access to this scholarship: the synagogue and the house of study.

At a time when numerous transformations and harrowing events determined the external history of the Jewish nation, a silent process took place internally, as both institutions evolved and gained strength. Over the course of the Second Temple period, Persian rule is superseded by that of the Greeks, Egyptian by Syrian; the tyranny of Antiochus entails the Maccabean campaigns and victories; the new national kingdom is vanquished by the all-consuming brute force of the Romans. The procurators' oppressions provoke the last courageous battle, and along with the capital and the sanctuary, the remnants of national sovereignty are reduced to rubble. Yet the synagogue and house of study emerge from the ruins as mighty fortresses[11] of a new form of existence, and as true cultural venues for the development and perpetuation of the spirit expressed in them.

It is therefore a reference to historical fact, not just a thoughtful interpretation of a biblical saying, when a great Babylonian teacher of the fourth century paraphrases the beginning of the ninetieth psalm as:[12] "Lord, you have been our refuge through all generations, in the synagogues and houses of study." Even in times of greatest distress, the feeling of being godforsaken could not arise as long as synagogues and houses of study were active. "Where is God to be found?" asked a highly esteemed leader of the Palestinian Jews at the end of the third century with reference to a prophetic saying.[13] And he replied: "In the synagogues and the houses of study!"[14] His contemporary, the spirited scriptural interpreter Rabbi Isaac, coined the bold statement: "Whenever Israel gathers in the synagogues and houses of study, the divine glory is present with them."[15] The spiritual awakening emanating from the synagogues and houses of study was found in the words of

---

11 [Cf. Ps 46:2. Bacher might be alluding to Martin Luther's famous periphrasis of Ps 46 ("Eine feste Burg ist unser Gott") rather than to the psalm itself. "The Marseillaise of the Reformation," as Heinrich Heine described Luther's hymn in his *On the History of Religion and Philosophy in Germany* (1834), became a paean of the emerging German national movement during the 19th century and bore even stronger nationalistic connotation at the time Bacher was writing. Cf. M. Fischer, *"Religion, Nation, Krieg: Der Lutherchoral 'Ein feste Burg ist unser Gott' zwischen Befreiungskriegen und Erstem Weltkrieg,"* Populäre Kultur und Musik, Band 11 (Münster, New York: Waxmann, 2014) (EK).]
12 Rava, b. Megillah 29a.
13 Isa 55:6.
14 Abbahu, y. Berakhot 5:1 8d.
15 Pesiqta deRav Kahana 193a-b.

the Song of Solomon,[16] allegorically placed in the mouth of the congregation of Israel: "*I am sleeping, but my heart wakes!*"[17]

It was piously assumed that already the pagan seer Bilaam glorified the synagogues and houses of study in his praise[18] of the tents of Jacob and dwellings of Israel.[19] In the same vein, a statement about their unrivaled importance for the Jewish people was attributed to a second century pagan philosopher. He was Oenomaus of Gadera, a friend of Rabbi Meir. His statement is rendered in the following *aggadah*.[20] "Once the pagans came to Oenomaus the Gaderian and asked him: How can we overcome this people [the Jews]? He replied: Walk around and observe their synagogues and houses of study. As long as the light voices of school children resound from these, you will not be able to do them any harm. For thus they were told by their forefather:[21] '*The voice is Jacob's voice, but the hands are the hands of Esau.*' As long as the voice of Jacob can be heard from the synagogues and houses of study, the hands of Esau – Esau is Rome – have no power over him.'"

From the story, this, too, is apparent: the synagogues were regarded above all as institutions of education. And this they were, not only because here the assembled congregation drew insights from the scriptural readings and their subsequent explanations, so that Philo describes them as houses of study where "the Jews engage every sabbath in ancestral philosophy and in which every kind of virtue is taught;"[22] but also because they served as institutions of learning in the proper sense of the word, since elementary youth education was usually delivered in the synagogue in that ancient period.[23] The age-old custom of German Jews to call the synagogue 'school' is therefore historically appropriate even with respect to antiquity.

For the ancient Jewish homilists, from whose polyphonic paeans I have cited some voices, synagogue and house of study form a unity. They belonged together inseparably and complemented each other as institutions as well. At a time when the Jews were deprived of the external conditions of a sovereign national existence, they found in them a means to preserve their unique culture and to move on to the new form of existence destined for their life among the nations. Above all, however, it is the house of study which, as the leading historical factor in the transition to this new form of existence, proved efficacious in an unprecedented way.

For during the first few centuries after its loss of political sovereignty, the Jewish people presents to the historical observer the picture of a national

---

16 Song 5:2.
17 Song Rabbah ad loc.
18 Num 24:5.
19 b. Sanhedrin 105b.
20 Genesis Rabbah 65:20; Lamentations Rabbah proem no. 2. Pesiqta deRav Kahana 121a (Abba b. Kahana).
21 Gen 27:22.
22 Philo, *Life of Moses* III, 27.
23 See below.

collectivity whose greatest interest was study, learning and teaching; a collectivity who guarded as its sole national good the object of study – the literature and the traditions of the fathers; a collectivity, moreover, whose leading class – though accessible to every man – was the clergy, and whose only visible authority was the house of study.

The ancient Jewish school system, from which this focal point of the entire national existence emerged, therefore constitutes an important subject for all historical inquiry into Israel's past. The way in which the Jewish school system developed in Second Temple Palestine, its organization and dominant characteristics, and what must be recognized as its pedagogical goal and output – all this I wish to sketch briefly in the following exposition.

I

No reports have come down to us about the very beginnings of the ancient Jewish school system as it evolved in Palestine during the Second Temple period. The Chronicler's history (comprising the books now located separately at the end of our Hebrew Bible: Chronicles, Ezra, and Nehemiah), from which we glean historical information about the first two centuries after the Babylonian exile, contains but a single occurrence of the word that will later designate students of all levels, *talmid*.[24] It refers to the singing schools in the sanctuary in Jerusalem, in which appointed masters, the psalm singers, trained the levitical choirs.

Yet this chronicle has preserved for us other valuable notes and reports that allow us to identify the origins of the ancient Jewish school system. It tells of Ezra, the scholar of Scripture who devoted himself to inquiring into God's Torah and to teaching statutes and law in Israel.[25] It provides a vivid account of the first public class that Ezra himself, aided by learned assistants, taught in Jerusalem. This memorable first of Tishrei in the year of 445 B.C.E., when Ezra with the Levites at his side read the Torah and explained it to the assembled people,[26] can be considered the ancient Jewish school system's day of birth. For the subject matter of this class held by Ezra, the Torah, remained the principal subject of the pedagogic activity cultivated in the schools of Jerusalem and Judaea in Ezra's wake.

We know nothing about the foundation of these schools. But we may assume that Ezra himself began to implement a key element of his life mission of teaching Torah in Israel. Among the institutions that tradition attributes to him, the founding of schools is not mentioned.[27] However, one passage in the Babylonian Talmud (even though it is deemed apocryphal)[28] notes that Ezra ordained that

---

24 1 Chr 25:8.
25 Ezra 7:10.
26 Neh 8:1–8.
27 b. Bava Qamma 82a.
28 b. Bava Batra 21b–22a.

there should be appointed *school teacher next to school teacher*, such that the competition amongst colleagues should increase wisdom. This note does not lack some inner truth, for the school system of Palestine was justified in regarding Ezra as its founder. Common parlance has immortalized this merit of his as well. The word *sofer*, which characterizes Ezra's profession, namely the Torah scholar, as one who is κατ' ἐξοχὴν occupied with the *sefer*, the book, still designated the school teacher in later centuries. At the same time, it also served to denote the ancient scholars, the successors of Ezra and earliest perpetuators of his work.

Tradition calls these Torah scholars of old *the men of the Great Assembly*,[29] in memory of that decisive assembly that took place a few weeks after Ezra's first public class in Jerusalem, and during which the representatives of the entire nation solemnly committed to observe Moses' teaching.[30] The men of the Great Assembly for their part expressed a maxim[31] that we may consider the foundational principle of the ancient Jewish school system: *Educate many students!* To offer the opportunity of study to many, to expand the circle of the school, is the task this maxim assigns to the leading men.

We can recognize the same principle in a narrative in Chronicles.[32] We read that King Jehoshaphat sent out a council composed mainly of Levites, a kind of teaching commission, in order to give instruction from the book of the Torah to the people in all cities of the country. Thus the author of Chronicles has Jehoshaphat accomplish the task which Ezra and his successors had defined for themselves; ascribing the realization of his, the eager Levite's, own ideal to a glorious past, as so often happens.

An extremely interesting tradition, which offers in lapidary brevity the history of public youth education in Palestine, tells us that this ideal of a pedagogical institution spanning the entire country, each and every town in Judaea, now slowly came to be realized. The source behind this tradition is Rav, the greatest authority of third century Babylonia and a great friend and supporter of the school system; but it definitely goes back to an ancient Palestinian tradition. The tradition says:[33] "At first, each father taught his own son; if one had no father, he did not receive instruction at all. Then they ordained that schools should be instituted in Jerusalem, to which even the children from the provinces had to be taken. Later on, each district received its own school. But the students entered school at a more mature age of sixteen or seventeen, and if the teacher was strict, they rebelled and quit. Finally, Joshua ben Gamla ordained that teachers of children should be appointed in each town, and that the children should enter school at the age of six or seven."[34]

---

29 *Anshei knesset ha-Gedolah.*
30 Neh 9:1.
31 m. Avot 1:2.
32 2 Chr 17:7.
33 b. Bava Batra 21a [an abridged paraphrase (EK)].
34 The words "in each district" are lacking in several mss. and ancient quotations, and entered the talmudic passage on analogy with Esth 8:17 (cp. 9:28).

As artificially constructed as the history of the school system in Palestine may seem, it is undoubtedly based on a kernel of historical truth. The memory of a gradual introduction of public schooling is preserved here: first in the capital, then in the suburbs of the districts, eventually in all towns of the country. The statement about the district schools employs a rare term for the district.[35] From Nehemiah's records we know that it was used for the districts of Judea under Persian rule.[36] The same term is to be found in yet another tradition, about the institution of courts for the various districts and cities.[37] This word points to the Persian era very clearly. The institution of courts and the foundation of schools in the districts thus seems to belong to the Persian era, to the century following Ezra.

But according to the concluding statement of our tradition, the final decree about the school system of Palestine was ordained only half a millennium after Ezra. And its initiator was one of those last high priests of the Second Temple who replaced one another in rapid succession and about whom history has almost only inglorious news to report. But can we really imagine that such a decisive measure as the introduction of general youth instruction originated with such a person and in such an era? The era during which Joshua b. Gamla – or b. Gamliel – served as high priest for all but two years[38] was a time of fateful disquiet. The yoke of tyrannical procurators weighed heavily on the country, and the people were on the verge of the great desperate battle against Rome. Was such an era suitable for the implementation of a nation-wide measure of peaceful cultural efforts? If it really originated with Joshua b. Gamla, could the decree have been implemented and borne fruit during the subsequent years of war, such that, thanks to it, Torah was not forgotten from Israel, as the tradent of that tradition says? And, what is more, would a holder of the high-priestly office, long deprived of its reputation and disconnected from the leading forces of the nation – would a high priest have led to victory the basic tenet of the Pharisees (the heirs of the ancient scribes), by generalizing education of children?

In light of such historical improbability an emendation of the wording of the tradition so as to put this eminent task into its true historical context is justified. A confusion of names, I dare to presume, has taken place here. The tradition originally referred not to Joshua b. Gamla but to an earlier bearer of the same name, to Joshua b. Perahya.

Joshua b. Perahya officiated as head of the Torah scholars during the time of the high-priestly ruler John Hyrcanus. He was the leading figure of the great faction which appeared then, for the first time in history, under the name Pharisees, and which had to relinquish its influence and its power to the Sadducees only towards

---

35 *pelekh*.
36 Neh 3:9, 12, 14–18.
37 b. Makkot 7a; t. Sanhedrin end of chapter 3. Cf. t. Bikkurim 2:8 on the offering of first fruits by groups from each district.
38 In the years 63–65.

the end of Hyrcanus' reign. Judea's religious and national revival, initiated by the revolt of the Maccabees and their victories, reached its apex at this time. Such a period was uniquely suitable for a measure so attuned to the spirit of Pharisaism as was the expansion of schooling across the entire country. Moreover, the only statement by Joshua b. Peraḥya that has come down to posterity makes him appear to be a uniquely apt initiator of an educational measure. His maxim, as we read it in the Sayings of the Fathers,[39] concerns one's studies and says: "Provide yourself with a teacher and get yourself a fellow disciple!" This saying does not lack significance for the wider history of the ancient Jewish school system. Here we encounter for the first time those two terms that came to be standing expressions for the teacher and the colleague. "*Rav*," the master, teacher, became an honorific title for scholars in the form "*rabbi*." And the other word, "*ḥaver*," which denotes a companion or fellow in general, but a fellow disciple specifically in Joshua b. Peraḥya's statement, likewise acquired independent significance later on, as people applied it to the members of the learned council or the sages as such.

If we follow this hypothesis – bold, as I myself admit, yet justified by considerations of plausibility with regard to times and men – and assume that not the high priest Joshua b. Gamla but his predecessor by two hundred years, the Torah scholar Joshua b. Peraḥya, instituted the general education of youth in Palestine, we can also comprehend another tradition, which until now has resisted reconciliation with the tradition discussed and emended above. According to this other tradition,[40] it was Simon ben Shetaḥ who decreed that children had to attend school. In other words, he instituted general and mandatory instruction of the youth. But Simon b. Shetaḥ was Joshua b. Peraḥya's disciple and his successor as head of the Torah scholars. It was Simon b. Shetaḥ who, once the deadly persecutions of the Pharisees by Alexander Yannai had come to an end, restored the influence of his faction, and restored Torah to its pristine glory, as an ancient report has it.[41] Under the peaceful reign of Queen Salome Alexandra and under the powerful leadership of Simon b. Shetaḥ, Torah scholarship began to flourish. The Pharisees gained power, and the vast majority of the nation bowed to their influence. It was once again a suitable period to consolidate the school system. What Joshua b. Peraḥya had begun, and the woeful years of persecution under Alexander Yannai had not let reach full implementation, was now initiated anew by Simon b. Shetaḥ. His decree can count as the renewal and amendment of his teacher's and predecessor's decree.

We may now embrace the idea that the general instruction of youth in Palestine was introduced not just in the nick of time during the last days of Jerusalem, as we had to believe until now, but that by then this institution had already been in place for two centuries. It emerged as a result of the enormous influence that the

---

39 m. Avot 1:6.
40 y. Qiddushin end of chapter 8 (32c, d).
41 b. Qiddushin 66a.

Pharisees had gained during the days of the Hasmonean monarchy; and at the same time, it was an inexhaustible source of their ever increasing moral impact. With this idea alone, we can further reconcile the reports about the Jewish educational system from two witnesses of the last centuries of the Second Temple. The Alexandrian Philo says about his coreligionists' attachment to their religion:[42] "Conceiving of their laws as divine revelations and having been instructed in them from their earliest years, they carry the likeness of the commandments enshrined in their souls." And Josephus, the historiographer of those days, says:[43] "More than for anything else we strive to educate our children." He further writes:[44] "Ask any one among us about the laws, and he will recite from memory all their stipulations with even greater ease than his own name. Since we study the laws from the awakening of consciousness on, they are etched into our souls, as it were."

II

Whenever the Jewish circles of Palestine commemorated the former capital and its splendor during the centuries following the destruction of Jerusalem, its school system also became the object of nostalgic recollection. They recounted[45] that immediately before the disaster there had been 480, or according to a more precise notice 394, synagogues in Jerusalem, and that each synagogue was accompanied by two schools, an elementary one for instruction in the Bible and an advanced one for classes in the transmitted teachings. Furthermore, they reminisced about the "great house," alluding to a biblical expression[46] to refer to the house of study of Yoḥanan ben Zakkai, the last great Torah scholar around whom disciples had gathered in Jerusalem.

This recollection from the last days of Jerusalem presents our most important data on the organization of the ancient Jewish school system before the destruction. The house of study of Yoḥanan ben Zakkai was the preeminent school, at which lads and men listened to the master's words, sought his guidance, answered his questions, or stimulated each other in their learning as they jointly explained and discussed the subject matter, shared their individual insights, raised questions and objections, debated and disputed. This house of study continued the activity of the houses of study of Hillel and Shammai, of Shemaya and Avtalion and the earlier heads of the scholars. It was destined to become the safe haven of Judaism in Palestine and the origin of a new upsurge.

During the time of terror, as the Roman army was besieging the doomed capital, Yoḥanan ben Zakkai moved his house of study to Yavneh. There it began

---

42 *The Embassy to Gaius* 31.
43 *Against Apion* I, 12.
44 Ibid., II, 18.
45 R. Hoshaya, y. Megillah 73d, y. Ketubbot 35c; Lamentations Rabbah proem no. 12; ibid., on 2:2; Song Rabbah on 5:12; b. Ketubbot 105a.
46 2 Kgs 25:9.

to fulfill its historical mission. After decades of fruitful activity, it was relocated to other places during the tempestuous disquiet of the Hadrianic era and finally found its permanent location on the shore of Lake Tiberias. The history of this house of study, together with the history of the other houses of study in Palestine and Babylonia, constituted the center of gravity of Jewish history for a long time to come. Historiography names the whole period as the era of the *tannaim* and *amoraim* after the members of these houses of study.

While the heartbeat of the Jews' historical existence pulsed in the great house of study, the school dedicated to the education of children continued its silent activity, and uninterruptedly accomplished the cultural work incumbent on it. The two levels of this school arose from its educational objective. Children were supposed first to be introduced into the sacred literature, to learn to read and comprehend the Bible; and then to acquire proficiency in the continuously growing body of traditional explanations, statutes, and teachings preserved by oral transmission. The twofold division of Torah into written and oral Torah[47] entailed a twofold division of the school. The aforementioned tradition about the schools of Jerusalem calls the first level "*beit ha-sefer*," the house of the book, and the upper level "*beit ha-talmud*," the house of study. The first term commonly signifies a school; the second term is not customary elsewhere and is replaced by the usual term for the house of study, *beit ha-midrash*. Corresponding to the two levels of instruction, there were also two types of teachers: Bible teachers, designated by the old term "*soferim*," and teachers of the Tradition or *Mishnah*, called "*mashnim*." Each community was obliged to appoint both categories of teacher. In the second century, in order to admonish his contemporaries, Simon bar Yoḥai said with regard to the desolate state of Palestine: "If you see cities in the Land of Israel that are entirely ruined, know that this is their punishment because they did not pay teachers to instruct the children in Bible and Tradition." In the third century, the Patriarch commissioned three outstanding members of the house of study of Tiberias with the supervision of youth education in the Palestinian cities and let them appoint teachers of Bible and Tradition wherever necessary.[48] In the course of this inspection, the three scholars came to a community that employed watchmen for the fields but no teachers. The scholars thereupon informed the citizens that the true guardians of the city were the teachers of children.[49] An ancient exegesis relates the psalm about those who know the right way and to whom God will show his salvation,[50] to teachers of Bible and Tradition who instruct children with abiding devotion.[51]

An interesting Talmudic report about the merits of Rabbi Ḥiyya, a contemporary of Judah I, confirms that some communities were lacking a teacher of

---

47 See b. Shabbat 31a; Sifre on Deuteronomy 33:10; Sifra on Lev 26:43.
48 Ibid.
49 Ibid.
50 Ps 50:23.
51 Leviticus Rabbah p. 9, very beginning.

children.[52] He used to prepare scrolls from the hides of stags he had hunted, and write the five books of the Pentateuch on them. Then he taught one boy out of five one book, and obliged each of them to teach the other four what he had learned. In the same way, he taught six boys the six orders of the *Mishnah*. This procedure (reminiscent of the mutual, so-called Bell-Lancaster method of teaching),[53] which the industrious scholar applied in other locations as well, earned him the emphatic praise of the Patriarch.

According to a well-known saying about the different stages of human life,[54] a child should receive training in the Bible from his fifth year and training in Tradition from his tenth year. However, an old decree attributed until now to Joshua b. Gamla sets the beginning of mandatory schooling at the sixth or seventh year. Among the rules which the great Babylonian authority Rav gave to a teacher, we find the prohibition to admit children under six years of age.[55] A popular rule related[56] by another Babylonian sage, Abaye, also gives the sixth year as the beginning of one's first education.

A formal upper limit for mandatory schooling did not exist. But it seems that the thirteenth year – the age of majority in religious law[57] – functioned as such. In a story about the joint education of Jacob and Esau, the aggadist Rabbi Levi, prospering in the third century, imagines that they entered and exited the school house together until their thirteenth year. Then their ways parted: Jacob sought the houses of study, Esau the idolatrous temples.[58] In a statement about the different stages in human life, the fifteenth year is given as the onset of advanced study, designated by the term "*talmud*." Josephus claims to have completed his first studies at the age of fourteen. As he relates in his autobiography,[59] he was so advanced in his erudition as a boy of fourteen that the high priests and nobles of the city would come to visit him in order to hear from him particularly meticulous interpretations of the law. Josephus did not attend a public school, however. As the child of a noble family in the capital, he and his brother were taught by private teachers. Generally, our sources make frequent mention of private teachers. But we hear similar things also about the son of Joseph the carpenter in Nazareth, who was to become the founder of Christianity. A childhood narrative has the

---

52 b. Ketubbot 103b; b. Bava Metsia 85b.
53 [Under the system of teaching developed by the British educator Joseph Lancaster (1778–1838), more advanced students taught their less advanced classmates, while the teacher only instructed the former. It enjoyed considerable popularity across Europe and the United States in the 19th century, as it served to provide the poor masses with rudimentary education. Cf. G.L. Gutek, *An Historical Introduction to American Education*, 3rd edition (Long Grove, IL: Waveland Press, 2013), p. 79 (EK).]
54 m. Avot, end of chapter 5.
55 b. Bava Batra 21a.
56 b. Ketubbot 50a.
57 m. Avot end of chap. 5; Genesis Rabbah p. 63 (Elazar b. Simon).
58 Genesis Rabbah p. 63; Tanḥuma Buber § Toledot 2.
59 *Life* chap. 2.

twelve-year old, on pilgrimage to Jerusalem with his parents, sitting in the Temple building amidst the sages, listening to them and raising questions; and all who listened to him were astonished by his understanding and his answers.[60]

A touching example of someone who lacked the benefits of education in his youth and made up for it at a mature age is the great Akiva, whose was a youth in the mid-first century. Although the narrative dates to a later period, it provides insight into the ways of learning and teaching and adds to our notions of the ancient Jewish school system:[61] Akiva was already forty years old and had not learned anything yet. One day he was sitting at the well in Lod and saw a stone lying on the well, hollowed out by the water. He asked, 'Who hollowed out this stone?' They answered him, 'The water that falls onto the stone, day after day.' It suddenly occurred to him: 'If water can hollow out the solid stone, should the words of Torah, which are hard as iron, not be able to affect my heart?' Immediately he resolved to study. He went to a school with his son and asked the instructor to teach both of them. Father and son would sit together, each grasping one end of the writing tablet on which the letters of the alphabet had been written in normal order and also in various groupings; and they were initiated into the basics of reading. Then Bible instruction began with the third book of the Torah. Once Akiva had mastered the sacred Scripture, he went to Yoḥanan ben Zakkai's famous disciples Eliezer and Joshua, and asked them to introduce him to the Tradition. Whenever Akiva learned a sentence from the Bible, he secluded himself and contemplated the meaning of each and every letter. In the same manner, he later reflected on the traditional teachings. Then he raised questions and objections to his teachers. Thus Akiva slowly acquired the entire body of knowledge and became the greatest master of Torah in Israel.

Two details of this narrative deserve special attention: the use of tablets as the primary pedagogical tool, and the commencement of biblical instruction with the third book of Moses. The tablets on which the alphabet was written in various groupings of letters are mentioned in other sources as well.[62] Introduction into the secrets of the alphabet was naturally a starting point for literacy education, no doubt accompanied by instruction in writing. Occasionally we find an allusion to the fact that the teacher would guide the student's hand in writing.[63] In the well-known anecdote about Hillel teaching a proselyte, Hillel also starts with the alphabet, and convinces the disbelieving student of the authenticity of a certain tradition by demonstrating to him the need for transmitted knowledge about the

---

60 Lk 2:41ff.
61 Avot de-Rabbi Natan, chap. 6 (ed. Schechter p. 29). [Bacher's presentation of the story is paraphrastic (CH).]
62 See Tanḥuma as quoted by Dr. Zarua, cited in Friedmann's introduction to the Mekhilta, p. XXXIV [The reference is to *Mekhilta de R. Ishma'el. Der älteste halachische und hagadische Midrasch zu Exodus. Nach den ältesten Druckwerken hrsg., mit kritischen Noten, Erklärungen, Indices und einer ausführlichen Einleitung versehen* by Meir Friedmann, (Vienna, 1870) (EK).]
63 Song Rabbah on 1:2.

meaning of the letters and their proper order. In addition to the tablets, small scrolls with individual portions of the Pentateuch served as pedagogical tools.[64] They say of one teacher that he misused a Torah scroll by cutting out sections for class instruction.[65]

Concerning the use of Leviticus in elementary education, it was a very old custom to begin the reading of the Bible in school with this book. Already in the third century, an important sage can explain this custom only homiletically:[66] "The sacrifices (the regulations of which form the core of the book) are pure, and the children are pure; let the pure occupy themselves with things that are pure." Presumably the custom dated back to the schools in Jerusalem, where the children of priestly families were taught. They would have been introduced first to the statutes about sacrifices and the sanctuary, which were of particular importance to them.

III

Occasional remarks like the ones discussed above make up the whole of the source material offering us insight into the ancient Jewish school system. I allow myself to present a few more that are especially characteristic.

The synagogue usually served as the site of youth education, while adults gathered in the house of study. A third century homilist glosses the prophet [Jeremiah]'s lamentation about the children and young men cut off from the streets and squares[67] with the words: "but not from the synagogues and houses of study."[68] For the child belongs in the synagogue, the young man in the house of study. In the hyperbolic description of Bar Kokhba's capital, where schooling did not cease even during the siege, we find the following information:[69] In Beitar there were 400 synagogues; in each synagogue taught 400 teachers and each teacher taught 400 children. (Incidentally, one of the school rules of the Babylonian sage Rava limits the maximum number of students per teacher to twenty-five.)[70] About one famous sage, Joshua ben Levi, it is said that he would take his little grandson to the synagogue, i.e. to school, himself.[71] More commonly, however, mothers would take their children to the synagogue. This is reckoned among the great merits of women.[72] A homilist from the third century warns the mothers not to dodge their duty under the pretext that the child lacks

---

64 See n59.
65 y. Megillah 75b.
66 R. Assi, Pesiqta deRav Kahana 60b; Leviticus Rabbah p. 7; Pesiqta Rabbati p. 16.
67 Jer 9:20.
68 Lamentations Rabbah on Lam 1:9 (Abba b. Kahana).
69 b. Gittin 58a.
70 b. Bava Batra 21a.
71 b. Qiddushin 30a.
72 b. Berakhot 17a (Rav).

the necessary skills for study.[73] Some anecdotes relate how sages passing by the synagogues of Sepphoris or Tiberias overheard a verse recited by some school children, and attributed a profound meaning to the event.[74]

Besides the publicly appointed instructors teaching in the synagogues there were also those who taught in their own homes. For this reason the school children were also called the 'children of the teacher's house.'[75] The children's comings and goings and the classroom noise might have bothered the neighbors. Therefore, the residents of the courtyard in which the home that was to be transformed into a school was located, were legally authorized early on to protest against the house-cum-school, just as they could protest against any other neighboring nuisance, and their protest was answered.[76]

The *hazzan* served in ancient times as the teacher's assistant.[77] He was the official in charge of the synagogue and its utensils; only later, in the post-Talmudic era, did his title become the designation for the prayer leader.[78] In a strange complaint about intellectual decline in his own days, which he relates causally to the destruction of the sanctuary, Yohanan ben Zakkai's student Eliezer ben Hyrcanus characterizes the teacher's rank in the hierarchy of the sages as follows: "Since the sanctuary has been destroyed, the sages have fallen to the level of school teachers, the school teachers have fallen to the level of the *hazzanim*."[79] Sages of great repute often served as teachers, whether private or public. The inhabitants of one small town turned to the Patriarch Judah I with a request that he recommend to them one of his disciples to serve as judge, preacher, teacher, and *hazzan*.[80] He recommended to them Levi bar Sisi, who was ranked among the best from the Patriarch's school. Apparently it happened not infrequently that small communities appointed a single official for all of the aforementioned functions. Thus the community of Bostra asked Shimeon ben Laqish in the third century to recommend to them a scholar who would be able to serve, besides various other tasks, as a teacher.[81] From the fourth century, the Talmud tells us of an interesting controversy between two reputable sages about the qualification of a teacher of children. One holds that vast knowledge in a teacher takes priority over less knowledge combined with thoroughness; the other endorses the opposite view.[82]

---

73 y. Hallah 57b (R. Shimeon).
74 See Genesis Rabbah 52 (R. Hiyya b. Abba); Shoher Tov on Ps 93 towards the end (Haggai).
75 *Tinoqot shel beit-rabban*.
76 m. Bava Batra 2:3; b. Bava Batra 21a-b; t. Bava Batra chap. 1.
77 m. Shabbat 1:3.
78 See Qohelet Rabbah on 7:5 and 9:15; Soferim end of chap. 10 and beginning of chap. 11; Pirqe deRabbi Eliezer, end of chap. 13.
79 b. Sotah 49a-b.
80 y. Yevamot 13a; Genesis Rabbah p. 81.
81 y. Shevuot 36d top of the page.
82 b. Bava Batra 21b (Rava and R. Dimi).

It must be mentioned that the average teacher did not assume high social standing, at least if a tannaitic rule of marriage accurately reflects an attitude actually held in dominant Palestinian circles. The rule states:[83] A man who wishes to get married should sell all his possessions so that he can marry the daughter of a disciple of the sages, i.e. of a scholar. If he cannot find one, he should marry the daughter of a great man of the time, meaning, a man excelling in piety and charity. If he cannot find such a one either, he should choose the daughter of a synagogue assistant. If even this is impossible, he should marry the daughter of a custodian of alms; if he cannot find even such a one, the daughter of a teacher of children.

The high esteem of the profession's importance and distinction did not pose a contradiction to the school teacher's subordinate position in the social hierarchy, as clearly marked at least in this important context. The profession was considered so superior over others exercised in order to make a living, that a material reward for the professional was out of the question. But for obvious reasons, school teachers had to accept some remuneration for their efforts; and hence, a number of alternative arguments were found for the right of teachers to demand payment for their activities. Some suggested that the teacher received the money not for his classes but for watching over the children during the time of class;[84] others, that pay was granted for the physical strain which the teacher incurred during Bible instruction as he signaled and rehearsed the phrase divisions of the Bible verses.[85] A third view justified the teacher's payment as a compensation for the time he could have spent on other profitable occupations instead.[86]

It was considered a great merit to contribute to the remuneration of teachers. Posterity praised the example of Rabbi Akiva: his friend Rabbi Tarfon once gave a large sum of money in order to purchase land so that its revenue would provide them with a living during their joint studies, but Akiva distributed the money to needy teachers of Bible and Mishnah. When Tarfon inquired about the estate, he showed him the recipients, and remarked that documentation for the expense was to be found in David, in the words of the Psalm:[87] *"his good deed endures forever."*[88] A fourth century homily states:[89] A bachelor who resides in a city and contributes to the payment of Bible and Mishnah teachers fulfills a duty that ought to be incumbent on him only once he founds a family and sends children to school. God's word from the Book of Job may be applied to him:[90] *"Whosoever has given me anything beforehand, I shall repay him."* In reward, sons shall be born to him who will benefit from the classes.

---

83 b. Pesaḥim 29b.
84 b. Nedarim 37a (Rav).
85 Ibid. (R. Yoḥanan).
86 y. Nedarim 38c, bottom of the page (R. Yudan b. Ishmael).
87 Ps 112:9 [Bacher translates צדקה as 'Wohltat'. I follow his rendition (EK).]
88 Leviticus Rabbah p. 34, end; Pesiqta Rabbati p. 25 (126b); Kallah.
89 Tanḥuma; Leviticus Rabbah p. 27; Pesiqta deRav Kahana 256.
90 Job 41:3.

In the Babylonian houses of study, they praised as the paragon of a noble and altruistic sense of duty a certain teacher whose prayer once proved more efficacious than a fast ordained by the most acclaimed sage of his day:[91] Once Rav came to a place that had been suffering from a persistent drought. He held a fasting service, yet the desired rain did not fall. When the prayer leader stepped down and spoke the words "He causes the wind to blow," the wind began to blow. And when he continued and spoke the words "and causes the rain to fall," rain fell. Rav asked the successful supplicant about his occupation. He replied: I am a teacher of children and teach the children of the poor just like those of the rich; I do not take fees from anyone who cannot afford the tuition. Children, however, who willfully stay away from school I allure with presents and coax them until they are willing to study.

The following Palestinian anecdote is equally telling.[92] The great Tiberian master Rabbi Yoḥanan once found the teacher in a certain village asleep. Confronted about his lapse, the teacher apologized and said that he was fasting. Yoḥanan said: If it is prohibited to fast while fulfilling a duty towards humans because it compromises one's performance, how much more illicit is it to fast if a duty towards God is being compromised. In the same vein, Jeremiah's exclamation[93] was applied to a teacher not rigorously striving to accomplish his obligation: *"Accursed is the one who is slack in doing the work of the Lord!"*[94]

In the spirit of biblical pedagogy,[95] the ancient Jewish school could not forego corporal punishment as a means of correction. But its excessive use was frowned upon. The aforementioned Yoḥanan, entirely forbade Bible and Mishnah teachers any corporal punishment of their students during the hot days of summer.[96] We are told the following anecdote from the 4th century.[97] The maidservant of a noble Tiberian home passed by a synagogue and noticed how a Bible teacher beat a child more than necessary. She exclaimed in shock, 'May this man be banished!' The man, so unexpectedly under a ban, came before Rabbi Aḥa and inquired about the validity of such a ban. He received the answer that he should regard himself as banished, because his impermissible action had merited him the same. Rav, whom we have mentioned already a few times, interpreted the psalm[98] *"Do not touch my anointed ones"* as referring to school children.[99] Most likely, he was targeting the abuse of the teacher's right to chastisement.

---

91 b. Taanit 24b.
92 y. Demai 26b.
93 Jer 48:10.
94 b. Bava Batra 21b.
95 See Prov 13:24.
96 Lamentations Rabbah on 1:7, end.
97 y. Moed Qatan 81d.
98 Ps 105:15.
99 b. Shabbat 119b.

We do not read of the interruption of schooling by longer vacations. Rather, it was held as a fundamental principle transmitted by the house of the Patriarch[100] that the education of children was not to be interrupted even for the building of the Temple. But by the end of the third century, the Bible and Mishnah teachers in Palestine were obliged to release the students from the last morning and first afternoon periods during the hottest summer months.[101] On the other hand, another report from the same time has it that a reputable scholar from Tiberias resented his children's teacher for taking three days off during the grape harvest.[102]

As even the Church Father Jerome chose to emphasize,[103] class began early in the morning and was interrupted by a lunch break. In an aggadic composition of the 4th century we find an image clearly taken from life: the mother washes the child's face before he goes to school, and cheerfully strides towards the returnee from school.[104] Another composition lets Qohelet's words[105] resound as a heavenly voice over the children leaving school and rushing home for lunch: "*Go, eat your bread with pleasure; for God has approved what you do!*"[106]

Our sources contain an unusually rich number of the most beautiful statements about the school's proper task, namely learning and teaching, and about the relations between teachers and students as well as among classmates and fellow students, the latter being uniquely important in the ancient Jewish school system. Unfortunately, I will have to abstain from relating even a fraction thereof. The same holds for the rules about the art of teaching, which centers around the exceedingly demanding mnemonic instruction in the Tradition. Only one fine observation of didactic physiognomy, if I may say so, shall be mentioned:[107] according to this observation, the face of the instructor displays a different expression for each of the four subjects as follows – a serious, solemn face for Bible instruction, a calm face for teaching *Mishnah*, a vivid, emotional one for Talmud, and a cheerily smiling one for aggadah.

IV

The book of Psalms contains a composition that we may well consider the poetic manifesto of the ancient Jewish school: Ps 119. Curious in its form – an eightfold acrostic of the alphabet in eight times twenty-two verses – the psalm is even more curious in its content. Despite its extraordinary length, it expresses a

---

100 Ibid.
101 Lamentations Rabbah on 1:3, end (Shmuel b. Naḥman); Shoḥer Tov on Ps 91:6 (Shmuel b. Isaac).
102 b. Ketubbot 111b (Shimeon b. Laqish).
103 On Isa 19:14. Cited in S. Krauss, "A zsidók Szt-Jeromos müveiben." *Magyar-Zsidó Szemle* [= Hungarian-Jewish Quarterly (EK)] 7 (1890), p. 339n1.
104 Pesiqta Rabbati 43, end (Tanḥuma b. Abba).
105 Qoh 9:7.
106 Qohelet Rabbah ad loc. (Aḥa).
107 Pesiqta deRav Kahana 110a; Pesiqta Rabbati c. 20 (101b); Soferim 16:2.

single sentiment: devotion to God's word, ardor for God's Torah and its statutes. Whoever composed this psalm, the guiding concept of an educational system, towards which Judaism had been developing ever since the days of Ezra, had already sparked a spirited enthusiasm in his heart.

The compositional monotony of this longest of all psalms seems to herald that grandiose monocentrism in which the ancient Jewish school system flourished. At all its stages, it only ever pursued one goal: the study of Torah. The word Torah, though, designates not just the Torah of Moses (the Pentateuch), but the Jewish teaching in its entirety as its adherents conceived of it, the sum total of anything that came down from the fathers in written or in oral form. In this wider sense, Torah – in which Bible and Tradition merged into an organic whole – constituted the sole object of study. This holds true for the house of study as much as for the education of children in school. Proficiency in the Bible presents the didactic objective of the first level, mastery of the Tradition the objective of the second. A decisive difference separated the two levels: in one, *texts* were *read*; in the other, the material was *taught orally*. Hence the Bible, the subject of the first level, is called *miqra*, 'what is read;' and Tradition, the subject matter of the second level, is called *Mishnah*, 'the recited' or 'what is repeated in learning or in teaching without the help of written texts.' This distinction was so essential and so diligently observed that the idea of a prohibition emerged, according to which the written teaching was not to be recited, and the oral teaching was not to be taught from a written copy, nay, not even to be written down at all. Yet natural difficulties obstructed the perfect implementation of this prohibition. Eventually, the ban had to yield to the necessity arising from an impulse of tradition towards self-preservation, and the oral teaching evolved into a vast body of literature.

The Bible teacher was obliged to use the most correct copy, and to exert the greatest care and precision in his reading, accentuation, and parsing of the sacred texts. Their diligence and exactitude let the Bible teachers of the ancient Jewish schools, who usually also prepared the copies of the Bible, fulfill a truly historical mission. If the *Urtext* of our Hebrew Bible in the form in which it was once defined has maintained its integrity; if we can read this text according to a tradition that ultimately goes back to living language use; if, thanks to this tradition, we have been able to discern the varieties (*Sprachformen*)[108] of ancient Hebrew down to the finest nuances, and to identify the laws of the language; if this language research has guided our understanding of the sacred Scripture in the proper direction – then our gratitude for these facts, which are so important both for the history of scholarship and the history of religious progress, is due to those selfless and abiding preservers of the sacred texts: to the Bible teachers of the ancient Jewish school. Carrying out their duty, they accomplished the preservation in its

---

108 [The German "Sprachform" can refer to morphology as well as to linguistic registers. Bacher's sentence allows for both readings (EK).]

purity of the greatest treasure of human culture, the life-giving font of religion and morality.

A legal stipulation that even minors, i.e. boys under thirteen, are authorized to read out the Pentateuchal and prophetic portions in the synagogue and to recite the Targum (the translation into the Aramaic vernacular), attests to the degree of proficiency that the Bible instruction imparted.[109] The fourth century Church Father Jerome speaks with great astonishment of the biblical erudition of Palestinian Jews, and especially emphasizes[110] that they familiarize themselves with the contents of Scripture from their early years. Thus, for instance, they are as quick in enumerating the characters of biblical history from Adam to Zerubbabel as if they had been asked for their own name. The liturgical sermons that were delivered to the congregation in those days likewise attest to a familiarity with the biblical text that the homilists could take for granted in their audience. A rich variety of such sermons has come down to us.

The study of Tradition, the subject matter of the second level in youth education, had ramified into three disciplines already earlier. Together, these constituted *Mishnah* in the wider, older sense of the term. The names of these three fields, whose definition is attributed in an isolated remark to the men of the Great Assembly,[111] sound familiar to anyone versed in the literary monuments of the relevant period: *midrash*, *halakhah*, and *haggadah*. Everyone knows, and even if only from Heinrich Heine's delightful poem about Yehuda Halevi,[112] that *halakhah* and *haggadah* – or *aggadah*, as the word is usually pronounced – together constitute the content of the Talmud. And *midrash* refers in its standard usage to a number of exegetical-homiletic writings closely connected to the Talmud in origin and nature.

However, during the centuries when the aforementioned literature, Talmud and *Midrash*, was not yet extant as literature proper but thrived as an ever developing and growing body of tradition in the houses of study and among the sages and their disciples, these three terms denoted the three subdivisions of the Tradition. *Midrash* was the name for the exegesis and interpretation of the sacred texts, inasmuch as it served to deduce and justify the individual rules and regulations of the religious law. *Halakhah* – or more precisely, the plural *halakhot* – signified the religious decrees and stipulations themselves in a form dissociated from their basis in biblical exegesis and condensed into an independent tradition. *Haggadah*, finally – or more precisely, the plural form *haggadot* – meant the interpretation of biblical texts that do not pertain to religious law. *Haggadah* was thus based not only on great portions of the Pentateuch, in particular the narrative ones, but also on all the other biblical books. Its tendency is best characterized by a very old

---

109 m. Megillah 4:5f.
110 In the Letter to Titus 3:9 (in Krauss ibid.).
111 y. Sheqalim, beginning of chap. 5.
112 [In his *Romanzero* (EK).]

saying:[113] If you want to know the world's creator, study *aggadah*; for it teaches you to know God and cling to his ways.[114]

People liked to relate the three branches of Tradition to the three divisions of the Bible, and took delight in this symmetry in the organization of the whole of national eruditon. It was said that *miqra* – Scripture – consists of Pentateuch, Prophets, and Hagiographa; and *Mishnah* – Tradition – of *midrash, halakhah,* and *aggadah*.[115] But over time the parlance changed, and *Mishnah*, originally denoting the entire body of Tradition, became the name of its middle branch, of *halakhot*. By the beginning of the third century, the Mishnah of the Patriarch Judah I was recognized as the definitive, systematic representation of this branch – as the codified religious law, as it were. It was elevated to the status of (canonical) textbook for instruction as well as for the lectures and debates at the house of study. Now the Talmud, the elucidation and discussion of the Mishnaic statements, moves to the fore. With the newly assumed position of the *Mishnah* in its narrow sense, Torah scholarship, and thus the body of knowledge cultivated in school and house of study, was now divided into the disciplines *miqra, Mishnah, Talmud, aggadah*.[116] In the imagery of the well-known biblical expression, the Talmud becomes the ocean into which the diverse streams of knowledge and inquiry flow.

In its monocentrism and uniformity, the ancient Jewish school was the fitting product of the distinct intellectual culture which Judaism brought forth during the time of the Second Temple and continued to develop in the four centuries following the latter's destruction. While foreign knowledge frequently made its way into this culture, such elements never reached independent significance and did not exert a transformative effect on the national school system. A contemporary of Rabbi Akiva famous for his mathematical skills once expressed his view[117] that astronomical and mathematical knowledge are but secondary additions to wisdom, i.e. to the study of the law. This view applies to all external knowledge in relation to the "autochthonous" scholarship taught in the ancient Jewish school. Jewish scriptural scholarship could certainly not forego such contributions; in fact, it exerted an outright attraction upon all kinds of knowledge! Since the religious law covered all matters of individual and collective life, be it agriculture or the entirety of jurisprudence, its ongoing development and refinement down to the smallest details entailed that no area of human knowledge remained alien to *halakhah*. A profound understanding of animal anatomy was as important to *halakhah* as the observation of celestial bodies and the calculation of their orbital periods. Nothing that has ever occupied the exploratory urge and pondering of the

---

113 Sifre on Deut 11:22 (§49).
114 On the three branches of Tradition see more in *Revue des Études Juives*, XXXVIII, 211ff.
115 See Pesiqta deRav Kahana 105a-b; Tanḥuma on Ex 19:1.
116 See. y. Peah 17a, bottom, and the parallel Leviticus Rabbah p. 22, beginning (Joshua b. Levi); Soferim 16:3.
117 m. Avot, end of chap. 3.

human intellect, or has been conceived by human fantasy, remained outside of the sheer infinite range of ideas that *aggadah* opened up to the learner. The exegesis of two biblical chapters, the first chapter of Genesis and the first one in the prophet Ezekiel, even formed a framework for speculations on natural philosophy and metaphysics, cultivated as esoteric teaching by the most eminent teachers of the law. Yet all this vast knowledge that was integrated into Jewish Torah scholarship and rendered its great literary monument, the Talmud, an inexhaustible treasure trove of the most diverse pieces of information, altered neither the idiosyncratic nature of this scholarship nor the character of the school system in which the latter was cultivated.

The monocentrism of the ancient Jewish school guaranteed one of the main conditions of its success, the focus of all instruction on one main subject. To the nature of its object it owed an advantage that any educational institution must envision as its ideal: it influenced the students' moral-intellectual disposition and educated them for life. For the original purpose of the knowledge it imparted and nurtured was religious enlightenment and ethical perfection. It was aimed to imbue the learner with knowledge of God, with the lessons of justice and altruism, and to foster in him the virtues of duty, self-renunciation, and humility. As its masters once solemnly declared,[118] the study of Torah obtains its true significance only by virtue of its guidance towards proper action, towards the practice of good deeds.

* * *

During nearly a millennium of continuous activity – from Ezra to the completion of the Talmud – the ancient Jewish school system has transformed the Jewish people and influenced the development of Judaism and its adherents in a decisive way. The monocentrism of this school system, dedicated to the cultivation of the religious documents and traditions, manifested with increasing clarity the historical fact that it was Israel's destiny to live on as a people of religion, as a community called to cultivate the ancestral religious truths. And while the process of detachment from the external conditions of national existence unfolded steadily and in providential consequentiality over the course of this millennium, Israel gained an intellectual homeland in the study of Torah. The leading men and the wider community, who willingly followed them, clung to this homeland with an enthusiasm and selfless dedication usually only elicited by fervent patriotism. In the soul of the Jewish people, this millennium awakened, and fostered as a steadfast quality for times to come, an urge that was the most precious fruit of the ancient Jewish school system: the urge to learn. This urge impacted the evolution of Jewish intellectual life in two different ways. Inwardly, the urge took root in the heritage of the past, immersed in the traditional literature, the intensive study

---

118 b. Qiddushin 40b; Song Rabbah on 2:14; y. Pesaḥim 30b; Sifre on Deut 11:13.

of which led people to cling to the old monocentrism and exclusivity as befits its origins. Outwardly, however, the urge to learn, the thirst for knowledge, turned to the foreign cultural influences and pushed toward intimate contact and amalgamation with the intellectual endeavors of the non-Jewish cultural world. The inner history of Judaism rests to this very day on both currents, on the struggles arising from their clash and on the attempts to reconcile them.

The ancient Jewish school system in its uniformity and exclusivity is irrevocably consigned to history. Yet even under altered cultural conditions we must still embrace the great goal that it pursued and achieved to a degree unequaled in its time. Any institutions within the Jewish collectivity which have come to replace the ancient Jewish school system must strengthen the knowledge of our sacred literature and our traditions and make them accessible to many. Thus may the intellectual spirit that created and preserved them throughout millennia be kept alive in our midst; and the feeling of connectedness with the workings of this spirit in our history shall not dwindle. The Society, which lists the collection and preservation of the historical monuments of Judaism among its objectives, serves the same goal. The Society, too, may claim the glory of being an institution striving – in its own way and its own more limited sphere of action – to keep the intellectual spirit of Judaism alive and nurture the feeling of connectedness with its millennia-long history. So if I today, in this august company, chose to commemorate the erstwhile and, in its own way, perfected institution dedicated to the accomplishment of this goal – the ancient Jewish school – then I believe to have contributed for my part to fulfilling the tasks of this meritorious Society.

8

THE DERASHAH AS THE BASIS FOR THE HALAKHAH AND THE PROBLEM OF THE SOFRIM*

E.E. Urbach

Translated by Christine Hayes

The dual form in which the tannaitic Torah was transmitted, that of *midrash halakhah* and that of the Mishnah, Tosefta and *baraitot*, raises a host of challenges that have occupied talmudic research since its inception, from the days of R. Nahman Krochmal and R. Zechariah Frankel to the present day. The history of research reflects not a little the battle of beliefs and opinions in Israel since the Enlightenment. It appears that there are two questions which scholars – according to the particular approach they adopt – view as interconnected. The first is whether exegesis of Scripture served as a source for *halakhah*. The second is whether learning proceeded by connecting laws to scriptural verses, or whether laws were learned in an abstract manner.

The term "*divre sofrim*" [words of the scribes] used in the sources to refer to the Oral Torah, and the explanation for the term given in the *gemara* of b. Qiddushin 30a ("For this reason, the early ones were called scribes [*sofrim*] – because they used to count [*sofer*] all of the letters in the Torah") led R. Nahman Krochmal to base his theory on a "period of the scribes" which lasted from the time of Ezra until Simon the Righteous. But nowhere do we find the expression "the *laws* of the scribes" (*hilkhot sofrim*), because they did not at that time study the laws in an abstract way, according to R. Nahman Krochmal. Rather they occupied themselves with the explication of Scripture. "Teachers of the laws [*halakhot*] began only in the time of Simon the Righteous; after dealing extensively with the Torah, they discovered limitations and details in the laws of the commandments and in actual cases that were not included in the initial conception of the law – not in the

---

* This translation is by Christine Hayes. Full bibliographic information for secondary sources has been added by Christine Hayes, as well as comments and corrections in square brackets identified by author (CH). Mishnah = the Mishnah of R. Judah ha-Nasi; *mishnah* = (1) a mode of learning as distinct from *midrash*; (2) an individual passage of mishnah; (3) halakhah formulated independently of Scripture. Urbach uses *mishnah* in all three senses.

writings of the Torah nor in the interpretations of the scribes, and they reached conclusions through deduction and reasoning. And since these matters could not be included in the study of Scripture through interpretation or allusion, they therefore established the style of abstract formulation ... and they called it *halakhot*." For the most part, Frankel, Hoffman and Lauterbach also took this approach. They differ only on the date of the transition from the earlier study method to the new method of abstract law, and accordingly also on the historical causes that brought about this change. Lauterbach[1] could be considered as bringing into this camp, to which Weiss also belonged, Oppenheim and Bassfreund, who conjectured regarding the two modes of learning as follows: from the *midrash* to *mishnah* and from the *mishnah* back to *midrash*. Lauterbach presented lengthy arguments for dating the transition from the earlier to the new mode of learning, to the year 190 B.C.E. When Lauterbach says in reference to the "first mishnah" (*mishnah rishonah*) in m. Avot that it is an artificial reconstruction of the historical process, he is attributing his own fault to others.

An extreme opponent of this approach was Y.Y. HaLevy[2] who objected forcefully and in general distorted the words of those who preceded him. The source of *halakhah*, in his view, was tradition: not even the simplest exegesis was ever relied upon. Rationalizations and debate are not the basis of the *mishnah*. Harsh decrees, persecution and wars led to uncertainty in explaining the basis for the *mishnah*, "Again it was forgotten until Hillel arose and set it on its foundation [i.e., re-established it]" (b. Sukkah 20a); the statements of the *tannaim* from Hillel and onward are nothing more than explanations of the basis of the *mishnah*. These explanations contain much exegesis (*drashot*) and debate, but even then doubts were not resolved by means of exegesis.

Two contemporary talmudic scholars who have dealt with this question adopt a mediating compromise position. But their compromise positions are diametrically opposed. In "Introduction to *Midrash Halakhah*,"[3] J.N. Epstein holds, like Halevy, that *midrash supports* the *halakhah* but does not *create halakhah*; the *halakhah* is supported from Scripture, but *halakhah* is not found or created by exegesis. In this, he relies on the words of R. Ḥai Gaon in his responsum:[4] "Thus we see that it is not proof but rather a *midrash*, and the matter is essentially a *halakhah* ..." (and see b. Yevamot 72a); but in addition, Epstein says with a clarity that leaves no room for doubt: "by this method, the method of *midrash*, the scribes taught Torah and by this method, they transmitted to their students the traditions and laws conveyed together with the written Torah." According to Epstein, this was the

---

1 "*Midrash* and Mishnah"; The article appeared in *Jewish Quarterly Review* 5, 6 (1915–1916) and is not included in the collection *Rabbinic Essays*, 1951: 163–256.
2 *Dorot HaRishonim* part 1, vol. 3, p. 292ff., vol. 5, p. 467ff., and see Shlomo Zeitlin, "The Halaka: Introduction to Tannaitic Jurisprudence," *Jewish Quarterly Review* (1948), p. 15.
3 J.N. Epstein, *Mevo'ot leSifrut haTannaim* (Jerusalem, 1957), p. 501f., and see there references to the literature on this issue.
4 *Teshuvot haGeonim*, ed. Simḥa Assaf, p. 102, ʃ14.

scholastic method of instruction. Here too, Geonic traditions may testify in support of this opinion. In his *Iggeret*, Rav Sherira Gaon says:[5] "And Sifra and Sifre are expositions [exegesis] of biblical verses, and [show] the allusions to *halakhah* in Scripture; originally, in the second Temple period, in the days of the earlier sages, this was the way they studied" [in contrast to the tannaitic period when the laws were studied in collections independent of Scripture]. This method of instruction [studying laws alongside relevant biblical verses] lasted until the time of Yosi ben Yoezer. In his time, following the decrees of Antiochus, the transition to the new method of instruction occurred, that of *mishnah*. While there may also have been external causes, fundamentally and "quite certainly" the cause was the multiplication of *halakhot* and secondary *halakhot* that were linked to Scripture by only the weakest of connections. From the time of Yosi ben Yoezer, the method of *halakhah*, or "*mishnah*" replaced the method of *midrash*.

In his article, "Halakhot ve-haDrashot"[6] Hanoch Albeck makes a sharp distinction between the question of study methods and the question of the sources of the *halakhah*, and even the latter issue he restricted by asserting that there are *halakhot* whose source is most certainly not in Scripture or exegesis and which are merely supported by it. The question is only whether there are *also halakhot* that were derived by means of a scriptural exegesis. Albeck wants to prove that even in earliest times, when the Great Court was in existence, when a question about a new case came before the court for which there was no existing tradition, Scripture was certainly expounded and discussed, and only in this way was a ruling produced. When they had decisive expositions, they would determine and fix the law according to the exposition [or exegesis of Scripture]. There is no difference between "the early tannaitic authorities and the later *tannaim* or even between the *tannaim* and the *amoraim*."

Despite the many differences between the approaches we have presented here, in one respect they have something in common. Each one is based on only a part of the sources, and to the extent that they try to respond to sources that appear to support the opposing viewpoint, their solutions are forced. Making do with forced solutions of this kind is aided and abetted by the lack of any reasonable attempt to obtain clarity on questions regarding the emergence and growth of the Oral Torah against the realities of the governing and judicial institutions in various periods and to determine the *sitz-im-leben* of the various forms of the *halakhah*. Therefore, both Albeck and Halevy – each in accordance with his own approach – see scriptural exegesis as a perpetual and constant source of *halakhah* in every period. It is a fact that the laws that come to us from the time of the Pairs and from the time of the early *tannaim* are transmitted only in the form of decrees (*gezerah*)

---

5 *Iggeret Rav Sherira Gaon*, ed. Lewin, p. 39, French version; in the Spanish version: "in the days of the earlier sages."
6 In *Alexander Marx: Jubilee Volume on the Occasion of his Seventieth Birthday* (New York, 1950), pp. 1–8.

and ordinances (*taqqanah*), deeds (*maaseh*) and testimonies (*edut*), and tradition (*masoret*) whose source is custom (*minhag*). The decree and ordinance have their source in the appropriate principal authority, whether the high priests, grandees and elders, the Great Assembly or the Sanhedrin. Their number was much greater apparently than what would appear to be the case based on the laws that are explicitly labeled "ordinances" and "decrees." It suffices to mention the laws introduced with the formula, "At first, [*barishonah*] it was the case that ... [but later] he ordained" or "at first, they would [do X] ... [but later] they ordained [Y]," or "At first, there were ... [but] when [some factor] increased, they ordained ..." There is no difference between these formulations and, "At first they would say ... then they retracted and said." More than 60 *mishnayot* and *baraitot* are taught with this formulation. These include ordinances that predate the Hasmonean period and that were rejected and annulled by new ordinances owing to a change in objective circumstances. Many *halakhot* are taught in their final form in one source while another source preserves their earlier stages. And we can infer from the explicit cases to the less explicit cases and conclude that a similar process occurred also for other *halakhot*, that were preserved in only one version.[7]

The second source of *halakhah* is the *ma'aseh* (case), i.e., the decision of the court or a sage in a case that is brought before him. The decision becomes a precedent, a ruling, a *halakhah*. Traditions about such cases are "testimony." It can be demonstrated that all of the testimonies taught in our sources – even those that have been disconnected from the original case and are taught as an abstract *halakhah* – have their basis and source in an actual case. One example will suffice: in m. Eduyot 7:3–5 we read:

> R. Zadoq testified concerning [a mixture in which] flowing water was greater than dripping water that it was fit [i.e., subsumed under the category of flowing water.] There was a case in Birat HaPilya and the case came before the sages and they declared it valid. R. Zadoq testified

---

7 I will cite two examples. In m. Bava Metsia 2:6 we learn: "And for how long must one announce [that one has found a lost object]? Until his neighbors know about it – the words of R. Meir. R. Judah says: when three festivals [have passed] and for seven days after the last festival ..." But the Tosefta there (2:17) reads: "At first, they would make an announcement about it for three successive festivals and for seven days after the final festival. After the Temple was destroyed, they enacted a ruling that one should made an announcement about it for thirty days. But from the time of the danger and onward they enacted a ruling that one should inform his neighbors and relatives and acquaintances and townspeople about it, and that is sufficient." And see b. Bava Metsia 28b. Also m. Bava Metsia 2:7 "If [a claimant] states the lost item but not its identifying marks, one should not give it to him; And as regards a [known] deceiver, even if he states its identifying marks, one should not give it to him as it is said [literally], '*Until the asking of your brother concerning it*' (Deut 22:2) – [i.e.,] until *you* inquire of your brother to find out whether or not he is a deceiver." But in t. Bava Metsia 2:16: "At first, anyone who came along and stated the identifying marks of an object would take it. When deceivers multiplied, they enacted a ruling that the claimant should state the identifying marks and bring proof that he is not a deceiver."

concerning water that flowed through a channel of nut leaves that it was valid. There was a case in Oholiya and the case came before the court of the Chamber of the Hewn Stone and they declared the water fit.

But in m. Miqva'ot 5:5, only this is said: "R. Tsadoq testified concerning [a mixture in which] flowing water was greater than dripping water that it was fit" – with no reference to a case.[8] And in m. Parah 6:4 "If he placed his hand or foot or vegetable leaves so that the water should [be led to] flow into the jar it is unfit, but if leaves of reeds or nuts, it is fit. This is the principle: an object that is susceptible to impurity – it is unfit, and an object that is not susceptible to impurity – it is fit." Here not only has the case itself disappeared but also the characteristic features of testimony, about which we know only by virtue of the basic *mishnah* in Eduyot: "R. Ḥama b. Abba said in the name of R. Yoḥanan: This *mishnah* was taught on the basis of the testimony of R. Zadoq" (b. Zevaḥim 25b).

The power of testimony was considerable. "Do we dispute testimony?" is an objection found in the Palestinian Talmud (y. Yevamot 12a) and the response is, "We may dispute the substance of testimony," which means that one can *deny* the substance of testimony by means of contradictory testimony but one cannot *dispute* it.[9] However, at the end of the tannaitic period, the authority of cases was limited: "The [operative] *halakhah* may not be derived from theoretical learning or from a practical case unless it is said in reference to it that it is a practical ruling" (b. Bava Batra 130b). However, the matter was still an open question even in the days of the *amoraim*, a phenomenon like that which is found in the history of Roman law in connection with the *res iudicata* prior to the declaration by Justinian: *Non exemplis sed legibus iudicandum est* ["one should judge in accordance with the laws, not examples/cases"] (C 7.45.13).

The origins and emergence of custom are always obscure, but it owes its validity to the strength of its being the "custom of the majority" and the "custom of generations," i.e., *halakhah*, in accordance with the Sifra's usage.[10] In the same way, Ulpian says: *Mores sunt tacitus consensus populi longa consuetudine inveteratus* ["customs are a tacit consensus among the people, established by long habit"].[11] Likewise it is said in Sofrim 14:18: "The people acted in this way, for no *halakhah* is established until it is customary practice, and as for the

---

8 And see H. Albeck, *Meḥqarim al 'arikhat haMishnah* [German], p. 5.
9 In my view, this is how the case involving Aqaviah ben Mehalalel (m. Eduyot 5:6) is to be understood. The sages were divided over the substance of the testimony because of testimony that they had regarding the case of Karkemit [a freed slave girl] and the decision of Shemaya and Avtalion. See m. Niddah 25b: "In the name of our Masters it was testified: 'An aborted fetus [*sandal*] must have facial features [to be deemed valid].' R. Bibi b. Abaye said that R. Yoḥanan said, 'It was on the testimony of R. Neḥunya that this *mishnah* was taught.'" Rashi explains: "He testified concerning it in the study house and it was the only testimony." See also t. Niddah 4:7 and y. Niddah 3:4.
10 Sifra § Emor pereq 13 and see also pereq 17.
11 See C.K. Allen, *Law in the Making*, p. 81ff.

saying 'custom annuls *halakhah*,' it refers to the custom of the elders [*vatikin*]." However, custom can also win general applicability pursuant to the court or the *nasi* or an elder who follows it and serves as an exemplar, in which case there is no difference between establishing a custom (*hinhig*) and enacting a ruling (*hitqin*).[12]

The institutional character of early law is confirmed by two distinguishing qualities: the absence of dispute and its anonymity. Neither exegetical dialectic nor rational argumentation determines the law, but authority. This authority was the authority of tradition, and therefore the patriarchs and the heads of the court are frequently mentioned, with some enactments and decrees being attributed to their names. As Rav Sherira Gaon wrote already in his *Iggeret*:[13] "This was the situation: the early sages were not known by their names, except for the patriarchs and the presidents of the court, because there were no disputes among them. Instead, they knew clearly all the explanations of the Torah" [trans., Rabinovich]. In my view, the Gaon does not mean that there were no differences of opinion, but rather that such opinions were within the general rubric of *halakhah* and there was no need to remember or mention them. And Rav Sherira himself explains it this way in another place: "The earlier sages, prior to the destruction of the Temple, did not need this [an orderly and uniform arrangement of the laws], because they were involved with the Oral Torah. They did not spell out the reasons for well-known matters, as is done in written Torah; rather, they knew and thought over their rationales in their hearts, and each one taught these to his students as a man teaches his companion, using whatever words he chooses ... *The sages enjoyed sovereignty, without distress or fear, and the heavens helped them. The underlying principles of the Torah were as clear to them as the Law given to Moses at Sinai. There was no confusion or dispute among them*" [trans., Rabinowich; emphasis, Urbach].

The Gaon relied on the well-known *baraita*: "Rabbi Yosi said: 'Originally there were no disputes in Israel; rather, the court of seventy-one convened in the Hall of Hewn Stone; and two courts of twenty-three convened, one at the entrance of the Temple Mount, and one at the door of the Temple Courtyard. Other courts of twenty-three convened in the Jewish cities. If a question arose,

---

12 "R. Gamliel acted with disregard to himself [his dignity]; everyone acted as R. Gamliel did" (t. Niddah 9:17; b. Moed Qatan 27b); "Todos of Rome taught the people of Rome to observe the custom of ..." (t. Yom Tov 2:15); and even the performance of a private action by a sage could be considered as establishing the *halakhah*. See t. Demai 5:24 where, in response to the statement by R. Akiva, "And have I established a law in Israel? I [only] tithed my own vegetables!" R. Gamliel says, "Know that you have [indeed] established a law in Israel by tithing your own vegetables." And only in the days of the *amoraim* was a distinction made between custom and *halakhah*; y. Megillah 1:5: "R. Ba in the name of R. Yirmiyah in the name of R. Simon in the name of R. Joshua b. Levi: the *halakhah* is according to R. Simon b. Gamliel. R. Huna the Great of Sepphoris said: R. Ḥanina of Sepphoris established the custom of acting as R. Simon b. Gamliel did – "established the custom" is said, not "[established the] *halakhah*." See b. Taanit 26b and Ḥayyim Oppenheim, *Bet Talmud*, vol. 2, p. 148; and see Meir Ish-Shalom [Friedmann] in his Introduction to *The Mekhilta d'Rabbi Ishmael* (Vienna, 1870).

13 See the *Iggeret of R. Sherira Gaon*, ed. Lewin, p. 8.

etc ... but when the disciples of Shammai and Hillel increased in number, disputes multiplied in Israel, because these disciples had not studied sufficiently. As a result, the Torah became two Torahs."[14] And also, as for the statement by Samuel (b. Temurah 15b): "All the 'grape-clusters' [students] who arose from the days of Moses until Yosi b. Yo'ezer learned Torah like Moses our Teacher; from that time onward, they did not learn Torah like Moses our Teacher" – this means only that up to the time of Yosi b. Yo'ezer they learned decided law without disputes.[15] And it seems to me, that the same meaning lies behind the Gaon's response regarding the "men of deeds": "And as for your question about the men of deeds, know that from the time of Moses our Teacher until Hillel the Great there were 600 orders of *Mishnah* which the Holy One, blessed be He, gave to Moses at Sinai, and from the time of Hillel onward the world decreased and weakened and the honor of Torah grew weaker and only 6 orders of Hillel and Shammai were established and those who established them were the men of the *mishnah* (not the early authorities) and not the men of deeds who were earlier."[16]

---

14 Ibid., p. 22. And see t. Sanhedrin 7:1; t. Ḥagigah 2:9; b. Sanhedrin 88b; y. Sanhedrin 1:4 and Maimonides, *Hilkhot Mamrim* 1, 4.

15 Epstein (*op. cit.*, p. 505 n47) correctly rejects the explanation of Lauterbach, p. 187ff. which holds that this refers to the method of *midrash*. But in my view there is no reason to understand the comment regarding Yosi b. Yoezer's testimony to the effect that "they called him Yosi the Permitter" [as an indication of] "disputes alongside the laws" about which he testified (Epstein, ibid., p. 510). Epstein identifies two additional early laws which are accompanied by a dispute in t. Makhshirin 4(3):3–4: "Ḥilfata ben Qunya says: "Baalbeki garlic is susceptible to impurity because they sprinkle it with water and then twist it." The sages said: "If so, let it be impure for Ḥilfata ben Qunya and pure for the rest of Israel. Joshua b. Peraḥiah says: Wheat which comes from Alexandria is susceptible to uncleanness because of their irrigation wheel." The sages said: "If so, let it be impure for Joshua b. Peraḥiah and pure for the rest of Israel." But what does it mean that the terminology of legal dispute does not appear here? Z. Frankel dealt with the difficulty in the *baraita*, *Darkhei haMishnah*, p. 35, and very surprising remarks were made by R. Tsa'ir, *Toldot haHalakhah* 4, p. 171. It seems to me that the ensuing *halakhah* clarifies the previous ones. In *halakhah* 5 it is said: "R. Yosi said: at first, the first fruits of cucumbers and gourds which were in Sepphoris were considered to be susceptible to impurity because they clean them off with a sponge when they pick them, [but then] the people of Sepphoris agreed not to do so." The change in custom of the Sepphoreans led to the annulment of the *halakhah*. In the case of the two previous laws, the sages were not of the same generation as Joshua or Ḥilfata so as to be able to dispute with them. Rather, they were sages of the generation or generations after and the meaning of their statement is this: if so, if that is the reason, then they are susceptible to impurity during the time of the sage who made the enactment because of the irrigation wheel (ἀντλία), but it turns out that not all Egyptian fields are irrigated in this way (see Ludwig Blau, *Papyri und Talmud in gegenseitiger beleuchtung* [Leipzig, 1913], p. 18, which shows that in the papyri they made a distinction between the βεβρεμένη, the ground flooded by the Nile and the ἐπάντλητος). Therefore, it is said in connection with Ḥilfata's statement: If so, if the reason is "because they sprinkle it with water" then the law is cancelled because only in the days of Ḥilfata were things so, but not in our time. And as for the formulation "the sages said" see Z. Frankel, *Darkhei haMishnah* (Leipzig, 1859), p. 287 and Y.N. Epstein, *Sefer haZikkaron leGulak ve-Klein* (Jerusalem, 1942) p. 252ff.

16 *Sha'arei Teshuvah*, 20.

The men of deeds were the first elders, as in m. Yadayim 4:3: "[the law regarding] Egypt is an enactment of the elders."[17]

This conception of the early *halakhah* as institutional, i.e., as the product of intentional legislation and as a result of court rulings – sharpens the question of the role of exegesis as the source of *halakhah* and the means of its production. In order to answer this question we must first provide a brief clarification of two terms, the term "*darash*" (and *midrash, derashah*) and the term "*sofrim*."

In his article "On the development of technical terms for the interpretation of Scripture" (*Lehitpathut hamunahim hamiqtsoi'im leperush hamiqra*), Isaac Heinemann[18] demonstrated that the use of the verb "*darash*" in its various forms in the Bible does not refer to philological investigation, to "*darash*" in our sense, but rather to preservation, the attempt to establish (*qiyyum*). The situation is no different in Ben Sira 32:18 "he who *doresh* the Lord will accept instruction and those who rise early will receive approval; he who *doresh* the Torah will be filled with it, and he who is hypocritical will stumble on it" [trans., Wright, *NETS*]. *Derisha* of Torah is parallel to *derisha* of God. [Urbach may understand the term to mean "preserve" or "establish" in both cases (CH).] The use of the word *darash* in the exegetical sense is found only from the time of Shemaya and Avtalyon, who are called the "great *darshanim*." In connection with this subject, M.H. Segal's claim[19] that traces of Torah exegesis are found in the Septuagint and that midrashic exegesis is found in Chronicles[20] and even in other books, is beside the point. The question is not whether interpretations can be found, and even exegeses of the *derash* type, but rather whether this kind of exegesis was already designated by a special term. And it is none other than Ben Sira's exhortation (51:23): "dwell in a house of instruction" (translated by his grandson as ἐν τῷ οἴκῳ τῆς παιδείς) that proves that the term is not defined in an exegetical sense, but rather points to any kind of inquiry and study, even that of Ben Sira who did not engage in the study of Torah in the midrashic mode.

For reasons that will be adduced below, I explain the phrase *doresh torah* in the Damascus Document: "and the lawgiver is *doresh torah*" (8:10), "and the star is the *doresh torah* who comes from Damascus" (9:13), in connection with the term *sofrim*. Recently Yeḥezkel Kaufman wrote on the question "Was there a Period of the Scribes?"[21] In my view, he is correct when he states that there is no evidence for a period of the scribes; the talmudic tradition nowhere hints to a period like this and attributes nothing to that time; and yet in establishing this fact, the

---

17 On "the commandment of the elders" [*mitsvat zakenim*] (b. Sukkah 46a), see Hirsch Mendel ben Solomon Pineles, *Darkah shel Torah* (Vienna, 1861), p. 38.
18 *Leshonenu* 14:182–189.
19 Segal, M.H., "Miscellanies: גרש, מדרש, בית מדרש," *Tarbiz* 17 (1946) 194–96, [Hebrew] p. 194.
20 See Y.A. Seeligman, "Voraussetzungen der Midrasch-Exegese," *Supplements to Vetus Testamentum* I (1953): 150–181, p. 150f.
21 *Toldot haEmunah haYisraelit miYeme Kedem ad sof bayit sheni*, 8 vols (Tel Aviv, 1937–56), vol. 4:1, p. 481.

question of the position/status of the *sofrim* and their place and function at various stages of the Second Temple and tannaitic periods, remains unanswered.

The first task of the scribe was simply that of writing and copying the holy books. This is the sole meaning of the statement, "For this reason, the *rishonim* [lit. "first ones"] were called scribes—because they counted the letters in the Torah." The "*rishonim*" were not sages at all, but rather the first scribes.[22] The *rishonim* were also teachers of Scripture, and several mishnaic teachings[23] attest to this usage. In my view, it is found already in Sirach 38, the famous chapter about the "sage," or aristocratic leader, which is incorrectly taken as evidence for the claim that the scribe may be identified with the sage. Sirach opens his chapter with the verse, "A scribe's wisdom (*hokhmat sofer*) is in the opportunity for leisure [lit. increases wisdom], and he who does less business, it is he who will become wise" (38:24) [trans. Wright, *NETS*]. Commentators have already pointed to the parallel rabbinic statement: "The jealousy of scribes increases wisdom" (b. Bava Batra 21b-22a) which means, that jealousy and competition between instructors and teachers increases the wisdom of the students. Segal (*op. cit.*, p. 255) explains correctly that the wisdom of a scribe (*hokhmat sofer*) refers to the craft of the scribes, but he errs in identifying the sage with the scribe and speaking of the craft of the scribe-sage. The meaning [of the verse in Sirach] is that the craft of the teacher increases wisdom, but the one who was wise and the one who becomes wise is the "one who has less business." This sage is the one that "they will seek out for a council of the people" [Sirach 38:32]; he will be raised up in the assembly, he will sit on the judge's seat, he will serve among nobles, he will appear in front of rulers, he will travel in foreign lands after meditating on the law of the Most High, he will seek out the wisdom of all the ancients and he will be occupied with prophecies [Sirach 38–39]. The sage is a person of the highest rank, [like] the elders and the nobles ... Not so the scribe. As for the area of the scribes' activity and their methods, a parallel may be found in the Greek grammarians, the Homeric commentators who worked in Alexandria in the third century B.C.E.[24]

---

22 In rabbinic Hebrew we do not find such a use of the term *rishonim* standing alone, but always as an adjective for a prior noun. M. Yoma 3:11: "Concerning the *rishonim* it is said that the memory of a righteous man is a blessing," and the reference is to Ben Gamla, Ben Qatin, and Monobaz mentioned in mishnahs 9 and 10; m. Tamid 7:2: "They [the priests who performed the service] would come and stand on the steps of the vestibule. The *rishonim* stood to the south of their brother priests ..." the reference here is to the priest who clears the inner altar, the priest who clears the *menorah*, and the priest who handles the firepan, all mentioned in chapter 6. In b. Qiddushin 30a, there is no connection between the term and what precedes it and Rashi has already commented: "the word stands alone." It seems that the term comes from a source in which scribes and others are referenced and then in the continuation it is said "therefore, the *rishonim* ..." This original meaning is what Onqelos intends when he translates the word "*mehoqeq*" [staff] (Gen 49:10; Num 21:30; Deut 33:21) with "scribe."
23 m. Nedarim 9:2; m. Qiddushin 4:13; and see y. Ḥagigah 1:7; *Leviticus Rabbah* 9:2; and see Z. Frankel, *Mevo le Yerushami* (Breslau, 1870), 118b.
24 See S. Lieberman, *Hellenism in Jewish Palestine* (New York, 1950), p. 26f.

In these scribal circles of interpreters and elucidators of the Torah, exegesis (*derashah*) was born. The first expositions consisted only of interpretations of difficult words on the basis of comparison with parallel verses. These interpretations were initially formulated in this way: "'and acts unfaithfully against him' [Num 5:11]: "unfaithfully" refers only to lying, as it says [in verse X] ... and as it says [in verse Y] ..."[25] or in this way: "this verse is written here and it is interpreted in the book of Job."[26] Hence the name "*dorshe reshumot*" [Urbach does not explain how he understands *reshumot* in this phrase but possibly as lists of verses ripe for comparison because of some similar feature (CH)]. But the comparison of parallels occasions interesting analogies, the transfer of things explained in one place to another place, the determination that certain words and expressions are redundant, and the awareness of verses that contradict one another. These expositions (*derashot*) brought with them answers to questions and thus solutions to problems that are not explained in the Torah, and defined and clarified details of the observance of the laws. But "matters whose principal law is from the Torah and whose interpretation is from the words of the scribes" achieved recognition as laws only to the extent that the interpretations confirmed and established the traditions and ordinances, testimonies and precedents of the sages [and not because they were generated by exegesis of Scripture (CH)].

The distinction between scribes and sages resembles the well-known distinction in the history of early Roman law between the jurist, who decided and fixed the law, and the early legal commentator. There is no more striking proof of the status difference between the sages and the scribes than the fact that while the "early ones" (*rishonim*), members of the Sanhedrin and the courts, did not accept – and it was prohibited for them to accept – payment for their work, "those who corrected the books of Ezra received their wages from the Temple fund."[27] It seems that these book correctors in Jerusalem were scribe-priests. A hint of this difference may also be detected in the statement of R. Joshua b. Levi: "The Men of the Great Assembly held 24 fasts over those who wrote Scripture, *tefillin*, and *mezuzot*, that they not become wealthy, for were they to become wealthy they would not write."[28] As regards the Men of the Great Assembly themselves there was no such fear, because they were rich and viewed their function as that of the nobility and representatives. In the letter of Antiochus III from the year 190 B.C.E. (Josephus, *Antiq.* 12.3.8), the priests and scribes of the sanctuary

---

25 Sifra § Ḥova, parashah 11, and see S. Lieberman, *Hellenism*, p. 49f.
26 *Mekhilta* § Amaleq, 1; and see W. Bacher, *Erkhe midrash* (Tel Aviv, 1922) 1, p. 125.
27 y. Sheqalim 4:2; and see the variants in the edition of Abraham Sofer, p. 41 and in the comment of R. Meshullam there; b. Ketubot 106a: "Those book correctors in Jerusalem used to take their wages from the Temple funds." And whatever the function of the "*gozre hagezerot*" (those making decrees), who also took their wages from the Temple funds (ibid., 105a), they were certainly not members of the Sanhedrin or even judges, according to Weiss, *Dor Dor veDorshav*, p. 193; Sidney Hoenig's remarks in his book *The Great Sanhedrin* (New York, 1953) are strained.
28 b. Pesaḥim 50b.

(οἱ ... γραμματεῖς τοῦ ἱεροῦ)[29] are mentioned alongside the *gerousia* (γερουσία). In 1 Maccabees, the assembly of scribes (*knesset sofrim*, συναγωή γραμματείων) appears before Bacchidus and [the priestly] Alcimus, but they are neither the older leadership represented by Alcimus and his people nor the new leadership which is founded with Judah Maccabeus. [The priest] Elazar, about whom it is said (2 Macc 6:18), that he was one of the "first scribes" (*sofrim rishonim*) was a kind of teacher-educator. Josephus is familiar with the Greek term [ἱερογραμματεῖς], or scribe-priests (*Wars* 6:291). In the New Testament there is much talk of "Pharisees and scribes" and it would appear that they are not identical, even though it is difficult to determine the original meaning of these terms owing to modifications over the course of the gospels' transmission. However, one variant is significant. In Matthew 26:3 participants in the consultation over the execution of Jesus, held in the house of the high priest, are "high priests and the elders" (οἱ ἀρχιερεῖς καὶ οἱ πρεσβύτεροι), but in Mark 14:1 and Luke 22:2 only "high priests and scribes" (καὶ οἱ γραμματεῖς) are mentioned.[30]

All available evidence proves that the position of the scribes was that of copyists of the holy books, keepers of the tradition, teachers and expounders of the Torah, and there are hints that the earliest scribes were linked to the Temple and were apparently priests. It is perhaps no coincidence that Jonathan ben Uzziel translates "priest and prophet" as "priest and scribe."[31] These priest-scribes were of a lower status then those priests who took part in the government and sat in the Sanhedrin, in the court of the priests, and who were called "sons of the high priests." Notably, we have a tradition about early exegesis that is connected with the priests: "This is the exposition expounded by Jehoiada the high priest: '*it is a guilt offering, he is certainly guilty before the Lord*' (Lev 5:19). This is the general rule: whatever is offered for an act of sin or guilt, must be brought with burnt offerings, the meat for God and the hides for the priests. [The Kaufman ms. of the *mishnah* continues: In this way the two verses are established: '*a guilt offering for the Lord*' (Lev 5:15) and '*a guilt offering for the priests*' (Lev 5:18) (CH)] And it says '*the guilt offering money and the purification offering money were not brought into the house of the Lord; they were for the priests*'" [2 Kings

---

29 In his article mentioned above [see n1], pp. 193–200, Lauterbach relies on this for his theory concerning the end of a period of anarchy that supposedly prevailed from 270 to 190 B.C.E., during which the study of Torah became the inheritance of both sages and ordinary individuals. But there is no basis for this view in the sources. By the same logic one could argue that the period prior to Simon the Righteous was a period of anarchy.

30 Hans Zucker, *Studien zur jüdischen Selbstverwaltung im Altertum* (Berlin, 1936), p. 41 and p. 77 n1 claims the two titles are identical, but this claim flows from the assumption that the term "scribes" once indicated the general category of sages, and thus he attempts to prove that the title "scribes" was still (!) in use.

31 Isa 28:7; Jer 6:13; 14:18; 18:18: "*For instruction shall not perish from the priest, nor counsel from the wise* (חכים), *nor the word from the prophet* (ספר). And see Büchler, *Priester und Kultus*, pp. 188–89, who following the Targum goes so far as to suggest that the Gospels [also] originally read "priests and scribes."

12:17] (*m. Sheqalim* 6:6). When "Ben Bukhri testified at Yavne that a priest who pays the shekel does not commit a sin, R. Yoḥanan b. Zakkai said to him: 'Not so! Rather, a priest who does not pay the shekel, commits a sin.' The priests, however, used to explain the following verse to their advantage: '*every meal offering of the priest shall be entirely turned into smoke; it shall not be eaten*' (Lev 6:16). Now [they reasoned] since the *omer* and the two loaves and the showbread are ours, how could they be eaten?" (m. Sheqalim 11:4; [sic; the text actually appears in b. Menahot 21b, 46b, and b. Arakhin 4a (CH)]). R. Yoḥanan b. Zakkai contradicts the accepted law here and says that it is no more than an exposition (*derasha*) of the priests.[32]

With the spread of Torah study among many social strata, the number of scribes and expounders grew in all circles, and sages who were members of the courts and the Sanhedrin also adapted the wisdom of the scribes to their purposes. But the recognition of exegesis as a source of law was a gradual process. It began and grew stronger as the structures of internal government weakened and were undermined, and the authority of the Sanhedrin was removed.

The only ones to win the title of great expounders (*darshanim gedolim*) were Shemayah and Avtalyon, one of whom demanded a hatred of lordship and a distancing from the ruling authority and the other of whom warned the sages to be cautious in their words lest they incur the penalty of exile by the government.[33] And yet they did not want to expound Scripture so as to teach that the festival offering overrides the Sabbath. Judah b. Durtai and his son Durtai withdrew and went and dwelled in the south, expressing astonishment over the [inaction of the] two great men of the generation (b. Pesaḥim 70b). This withdrawal of sages who promoted exegesis as a source of law is worthy of attention. Megillat Taanit tells of a similar separation of sages in a previous generation: "On the 17th day,

---

32 An exposition expounded in the time of the Temple and subsequently rejected is also found in a *baraita*: "The shops of the Bene Ḥanan were destroyed three years before the destruction of the Land because they used to exempt their produce from the tithe by expounding the verse (Deut 14:22–23) '*You shall surely tithe [all the increase of your seed] ... and you shall* eat' – [implying but not if] you sell it; and '*all the increase of your field*' [implying and not the purchaser's]" (Sifre Deuteronomy 105; y. Peah 1:5; and see also b. Bava Metsia 88a: "Why were the shops of Beth Hini destroyed? Because they based their actions on Scripture" and Rashi explains, "They found permission in Scripture for something prohibited by the rabbis"). Joseph Derenbourg, *Essai sur l'Histoire et la Geographie de la Palestine* (Paris, 1867), p. 446 speculates that the Bene Ḥanan shopkeepers were priests; and Büchler, *Priester und Kultus*, pp. 188–89 views the shops of the Bene Ḥanan as the location to which the Sanhedrin was exiled forty years before the destruction of the Temple (b. Avodah Zarah 8:2; b. Rosh haShanah 31a), but there is no proof for this identification and certainly one cannot find here any proof for the existence of two Sanhedrins, as Büchler does.

33 According to an explanation attributed to "some say" in Avot deR. Natan 11; and it is said of the teachers of Avtalyon, Simon b. Shetaḥ and also Judah b. Tabbai, that they fled from king Yannai (y. Berakhot 7:2; Ḥagigah 2:2). And see Ḥ. Albeck, his additions to *Shishah Sidrei Mishnah: Seder Neziqin* (Jerusalem, 1959), p. 494.

the gentiles rose up against the refugee scholars[34] in the land of Chalcis in Bet Zabdai, but they were saved."[35] In the Hebrew commentary on the scroll it is said: "When King Yannai [Alexander Janneus] descended to kill the sages, they fled from him, turned to Syria and dwelt in the province of Chalcis. The gentiles of that place gathered against them, attacked them murderously, caused much depredation among them and inflicted a great and deadly blow, and there was left of them a remnant. These went to Bet Zabdai and remained there until dark, and then fled from there." One might connect the incident of the refugee scholars with the refugee scribes mentioned in the blessing "On the righteous" in the standard liturgy. The blessing makes mention of "righteous ones, saints, and elders of your people, the house of Israel."[36] In his book on the Damascus Document, Ginsberg[37] wanted to find in Megillat Taanit an allusion to the Damascus Document's reference to the flight of the members of the sect, at whose head was "the staff who is the interpreter of Torah" [CD col 6 line 7; interpreting Num 21:18], as well as an allusion to the solemnizing of the covenant "without entering the Temple to kindle his altar in vain ... they should take care to act in accordance with the exact interpretation of the law" [ibid. lines 12, 14]. In my view, those who fled were a scribal faction – teachers and interpreters of the Torah. Their reliance on exegesis as a source of law made it easier for them to cut themselves off from the institutions in Jerusalem. In Damascus, an extreme faction formed, which sought a complete break with all of the institutions in Jerusalem, the sanctuary and the Sanhedrin, and came to base their entire lives on the power of the expounder of Torah to interpret the Torah "until the Teacher of Righteousness arises at the end of days" [ibid., lines 10–11]. These expositions generated precisely those laws that distinguished the sect from the sages. The prohibition of marriage with a niece was derived by a

---

34 [Urbach reads פליטת ספריא as "refugee scholars" following one of the scholiasts. For a discussion of the variants, scholia, and scholarly opinions, see Vered Noam's *Megillat Taanit: ha-nusaḥim, pishram, toldotehem* (Jerusalem, 2003) ad. loc. (CH).]
35 For various interpretations of this passage, see Lichtenstein, "Die Fastenrolle eine Untersuchung zur Jüdisch-Hellenistischen Geschichte" *Hebrew Union College Annual*, 8/9 (1931–32), p. 293.
36 In his Siddur *Higayon Lev* (Königsberg, 1845), Eliezer Landshut already hypothesized that the blessing "On the righteous" was formulated during the persecutions of Antiochus. If we are correct in our hypothesis that the phrase "refugee scribes" is a late addition from the time of King Yannai, then perhaps the prayer for the righteous proselyte can be understand as a polemic against the mass conversion that was carried out by Yannai. However, Rav Saadyah Gaon's version of the blessing and its Palestinian version, does not contain "refugee scribes," and Elbogen supposes that these words, found in the Ashkenazic and Sefardic versions, are late. But the question is: what prompted this innovation? It seems to me that we must distinguish between the formulation of the prayer itself and its formulation after it was fixed in the standard liturgy, but we cannot expand on this point here. On the versions of this blessing see Ismar Elbogen, *Der Jüdische Gottesdienst in seiner geschichtlichen Entwicklung* (Leipzig, 1913), p. 52; and Louis Finkelstein, "The Development of the Amidah," *Jewish Quarterly Review* 16 (1925–26), p. 158.
37 Louis Ginsberg, *Eine unbekannte jüdische Sekte* (New York, 1922), p. 373f. A different interpretation is given by Chaim Rabin, *Zadokite Documents* (Oxford, 1954), p. 23 but he emends and fills in the written text without sufficient justification.

syllogistic argument (*heqqesh*): "But Moses said: 'Do not approach your mother's sister, she is a blood relation of your mother' [cf. the MT of Lev 18:13–14]. The law of prohibited marriages, written for males, applies equally to females, and therefore to the daughter of a brother who uncovers the nakedness of the brother of her father, for she is a blood relation" (ibid. col. 5 ll. 9–11) ... From the verses "*male and female he created them*" [Gen 1:27] and "*two by two they came into the ark*" [Gen 7:9] one derives the prohibition of bigamy. The centrality of scriptural exposition is emphasized also in the Community Rule (10:6–8): "and in the place in which the ten assemble there should not be missing a man to interpret the law day and night ... And the Many shall be on watch together for a third of each night of the year in order to read the book, explain the regulation, and bless together."[38] Even if we do not, like Ginsberg, resolve the question of the identity of the sect by reference to the events conveyed in Megillat Taanit, we nevertheless have three attestations of separatists (*perushim*) whose separation is linked to a demand for basing their *halakhah* exclusively on scriptural exegesis.

We are also able to trace the process by which exegesis arose and was finally accepted as a source of *halakhah* of equal value to the other sources of the *halakhah*. The stages of this process may be clearly recognized in the reservations expressed by various tannaim regarding the expositions and words of the scribes. The reservations of the Bene Batyra to the expositions of Hillel when he came up from Babylon are well-known: "And even though he sat and expounded for them the entire day they did not accept it from him until he said to them, 'May [harm] befall me if I did not hear this from Shemayah and Avtalyon.'"[39] We have

---

38 N. Wieder, "The Term קץ in the Dead Sea Scrolls and in Hebrew Liturgical Poetry" *Journal of Jewish Studies* 5:1 (1953), p. 158, devotes a special article to the "Interpreter of the Law" in the scrolls, but he focuses on the eschatological character of the Interpreter of the Law. In his view, he is a prophet similar to Moses, whose arrival was anticipated to occur before the arrival of the messiah. But his claims are highly imaginative and do not convince. Regarding the latter's comparisons to Philo, Paul Winter has correctly written a sharp criticism in "Covenanters of Damascus," *Jewish Quarterly Review* 45:1 (1954), p. 39.

39 Pace Halevy, *Dorot HaRishonim* part 1, vol. 3, p. 307 and Epstein, *Mevo'ot*, p. 511, there is a basic contradiction in the idea of exegesis as a source of law. In a *baraita* in b. Shabbat 19a the exposition of "until it falls" [Deut 20:20 referring to the fall of a besieged city] as applying "even on the Sabbath" is attributed to Shammai. However, according to the Erfurt ms. of the Tosefta, the expounder is Hillel, while in Sifre Deuteronomy pisqa 204, the expounder is anonymous, and in pisqa 103 we read: "And we do not commence the siege of a city on Sabbath, but rather three days before; and if they surround them and it happens to be the Sabbath, the Sabbath does not halt the battle. This is one of three things expounded by Shammai the Elder ..."; similarly, y. Shabbat 1:8; see Saul Lieberman, *HaYerushalmi Kifeshuto*; however, in Midrash Tannaim, p. 123, this exposition is attributed to R. Ye'asya. And the phrase "Shammai expounded" [*darash*] does not necessarily refer to exposition of Scripture. The use of *darash* without connection to Scripture is found in b. Pesaḥim 42a, b. Ketubot 49a, b. Gittin 43a. When it is said that "Hillel expounded ordinary language" (t. Ketubot 4:9, p. 264; similarly, in the subsequent baraitot, 10–13 and their parallels), it refers to the fact that Hillel, and sages who behaved like him, did not expound the language of documents so much as he took it into consideration and upheld what was written in them.

already seen above, R. Yoḥanan b. Zakkai's reservations about the exegesis of the priests; and the words of R. Joshua in m. Sotah 5:2 also hint at reservations of this kind: "On that day, R. Akiva expounded: 'and every earthen vessel into which any of them falls – whatever is in it shall be impure' [Lev 11:33]; it does not state 'is impure' but 'shall be impure,' that is, to make others impure. This teaches that a loaf of bread which is impure in the second degree makes [items it contacts] impure in the third degree. Rabbi Joshua said: who will remove the dust from your eyes, R. Yoḥanan b. Zakkai, since you say that another generation is destined to pronounce pure a loaf which is impure in the third degree, on the ground that there is no verse in the Torah according to which it is impure [following Kaufman ms.: Is not R. Akiva your student? He adduces a text in the Torah according to which it is impure (CH)], for it is written: 'whatever is in it shall be impure.'" Rabbi Yoḥanan b. Zakkai was of the opinion that the loaf at the third degree was impure, but he suspected that a generation committed to establishing everything on the basis of an exposition of Scripture would be inclined to annul this law. R. Joshua's words allude to this; and in m. Nazir 7:4, R. Joshua also rejects a *qal veḥomer* argument (*a minore ad maius* argument), for which there is no refutation, because [the law is established on the basis of] a tradition: "R. Akiva said, 'I argued before R. Eleazer: if in the case of a bone the size of a barleycorn which does not defile a man by overhang, a Nazarite who touches or carries it must cut off his hair, then all the more so in the case of a quarter log of blood which does defile a person by overhang, a Nazarite should cut off his hair on account of contacting it or carrying it.' He replied to me, 'What is this Akiva? We do not make a *qal veḥomer* argument in this case!' And when I came and told these things to R. Joshua he said to me, 'You have spoken well, but they have declared the *halakhah* thus [independent of any exegesis].'"[40] Regarding a whole series of laws R. Joshua says, "The scribes have produced an innovation (*ḥiddush*) and I cannot refute then."[41] What is the meaning of the phrase "the scribes have produced an innovation," the like of which we find nowhere else? In my view, it means that even though the scribes innovate here, i.e., a law is based on exegesis and not on tradition – and that is an innovation – he has no refutation and he accepts it. It is clear that it is R. Joshua who formulates these laws in this abstract form [without a scriptural base] and he makes his comment in regard to all of them.[42] R. Joshua's words here stand in opposition to his statement in m. Keritot 3:9: "R. Joshua said, 'I heard that in the case of one who eats, in a single act of forgetfulness, from one sacrifice that is divided among five dishes, he is liable for sacrilege for each and every one and it seems to me that

---

See Shlomo Zeitlin, *op. cit.*, p. 17 and Alexander Guttman, "Foundations of Rabbinic Culture," *Hebrew Union College Annual* 23 (1950–51), part 1, p. 453f.

40 And see H. Albeck, *Shishah Sidrei Mishnah: Seder Nashim* (Jerusalem, 1954), additions, p. 379.
41 m. Kelim 13:7; m. Tevul Yom 4:6; t. Tevul Yom 2:12.
42 See for now J.N. Epstein, *Mevo'ot*, p. 401.

the matter [you are discussing can be determined by] a *qal vehomer* argument ...' R. Akiva said, 'If this is an accepted *halakhah* we will accept it, but if it is a logical deduction, then there is a rebuttal'" (and see m. Yevamot 8:3). Support for my interpretation of R. Joshua's words is found in an exegesis that appears in the Palestinian Talmud: "[The eastern gate of the wall around Jerusalem is referred to as] 'the gate of the foundation' because there they founded the *halakhah*; [and it is referred to as] 'the new gate' because there the scribes innovate the law." Even though this is merely an exegesis of names [of the gate in question], it attests to an awareness of the distinction between the basic *halakhah* and "the innovations of the scribes."[43] The connection between exegesis and the scribes is also striking in m. Sotah 2:1. When Rabban Gamliel begins to expound, he turns to the sages and says, "Scribes, permit me to explain this as a kind of *homer*"[44] [b. Sotah 15a] (and see Sifre § Naso,' Piska 8), for the scribes would expound *hamurot*.[45] In early sources, the phrase "words of the scribes" still has the meaning of exposition, and m. Orlah 3:10 attests to this: "New produce is prohibited from the Torah everywhere, and the prohibition of *orlah* is a *halakhah*, and the law of mixed kinds is from the words of the scribes." Regarding the new grain [which is said to be prohibited from the Torah] it is written: "And you shall eat neither bread nor parched corn nor fresh ears until this day, until you have brought the offering of your God; it is a statute forever throughout your generations in all your dwellings" (Lev 23:14). The term *halakhah* [which describes the prohibition of *orlah*] is explained by Samuel as "the laws of the land," which is to say custom, and by R. Yoḥanan as, "a *halakhah* to Moses at Sinai," which is to say tradition (b. Qiddushin 38:2). As for the words of the scribes [which is the basis for the prohibition of mixed kinds] – that is the exegesis transmitted by R. Yoḥanan: "'you shall not let your cattle mate with a different kind; you shall not sow your field with two kinds of seed; neither shall you wear a garment of two kinds of stuff mingled together' (Lev 19:19). Mixed kinds of seeds are analogous to [mixed kinds of clothing and] mixed kinds of animals. Just as mixed kinds of clothing and mixed kinds of animals which do not depend on residence in the land and yet are observed both in the land and abroad, so also mixed seeds even though they do depend on residence in the land are observed both in the land and abroad."

However, this distinction between *halakhah* and the words of the scribes becomes weaker with the proliferation of expositions ... After the destruction of the Temple the sages began "to be like scribes" (m. Sotah 9:16). R. Neḥuniah b. haQaneh would expound the entire Torah by means of *klal u-ferat* [generalization and exclusion arguments], and Naḥum of Gamzo expounded it by means of

---

43 y. Eruvin 5:1; and see y. Sanhedrin 113a; Leviticus Rabbah 4:1; Ecclesiastes Rabbah 3:16.
44 [For Urbach's understanding of *homer*, see the next note (CH).].
45 See the discussion of *dorshe reshumot* above. Rashi's explanation is to be preferred above all others, that *homer* is a kind of ornamentation that connects two things. The *dorshe hamurot*, like the *dorshe reshumot*, interpreted and expounded by stringing verse to verse, by means of "this is none other than ..." and by analogies, as in the exposition of R. Gamliel.

ribbuy u-miut [amplification and restriction], and expounded every *"et"* [definite object marker] in the Torah.[46] R. Zechariah b. Qatsav also belonged to this group of sages. When R. Akiva expounded thus: "[Scripture does not say in Num 5:29] 'she is defiled' [but rather] 'and she is defiled' [to teach that] just as she is prohibited to her husband so also she is prohibited to her paramour," R. Joshua said to him: "that is how Zechariah b. Qatsav used to expound" (m. Sotah 5:1). R. Joshua also explicitly disputed with R. Nehuniah b. haQaneh from Emmaus and placed in opposition to his exposition not what his ears had heard but what his eyes had seen, which is to say, evidence about the letter which was sent by R. Shimon b. Gamliel and R. Yohanan b. Zakkai (Midrash Tannanim, p. 175). However, R. Akiva, the student of R. Eliezer and R. Joshua,[47] chose the path of his other teachers – Nahum of Gamzo and R. Nehuniah b. haQaneh – and tipped the scales in the direction of extreme exegetical freedom despite the reservations of his colleagues. R. Ishmael limited exegesis by means of *gezerah shavah* [verbal analogies] in two ways: one may not argue from a verbal analogy on one's own authority and one does not expound an analogy unless there is a free [i.e., semantically unnecessary] element [in the verse]. R. Ishmael says "they are [just] repetitions of the

---

46 m. Hagigah 12:1; m. Pesahim 22:2; m. Shevu'ot 26a; Genesis Rabbah 1:13.
47 It would appear that some of the disputes between R. Akiva and his teachers that seem to turn on the exegesis of Scripture, are formulated this way under the influence of a *derash* by R. Akiva, while the opinion attributed to his teachers did not have its source in exegesis. Some examples cited by H. Albeck, *Mehqarim*, will suffice; m. Terumot 6:6: "R. Eliezer says, 'They may compensate [for appropriated *terumah*] with one kind [of produce] for another kind [of produce] as long as the payment is from a superior kind for an inferior kind.' But R. Akiva says, 'They may not compensate except from the same kind. Thus, if one ate cucumbers grown in the year before the Sabbatical Year, he must wait for the cucumbers of the following year and make compensation from them.' R. Eliezer derives his lenient ruling from the same source from which R. Akiva derives his stringent ruling, as it is said: *'And he shall give to the priest* the holy thing,' (Lev 22:14) i.e., whatever is fit to be holy – this is the view of R. Eliezer. But R. Akiva says, *'And he shall give to the priest* the holy thing,' i.e., the holy thing which he ate." While the exegesis of R. Akiva teaches his *halakhah*, the exegesis of R. Eliezer is insufficient for teaching that "one makes payment from a superior kind for an inferior kind." T. Terumah 7:9 lacks the scriptural exegesis altogether. See Saul Lieberman, *Tosefta Ki-fshutah: A Comprehensive Commentary on the Tosefta* (New York, 1955–88), vol. 1, p. 403. In Sifra § Emor 6:6 the exegesis is cited as support for the view of R. Akiva only, and not for the view of R. Eliezer. It would appear that "[R. Eliezer derives his lenient ruling] from the same source ..." is a later explanation that connects the dispute to R. Akiva's prooftext. It seems that the dispute in m. Yevamot 12:3 developed in the same way: "If she [a woman undergoing the shoe removal ritual to release a levirate bond] removed the shoe and recited [the necessary words] but did not spit, R. Eliezer says her ritual of release is invalid but R. Akiva says her ritual of release is valid. R. Eliezer said: *'Thus shall it be done'* (Deut 25:9) – anything that is an action [and is not performed] impairs [its validity]. R. Akiva said: A proof is from there [i.e., that very verse]! *'Thus shall it be done* to the man' – anything that is an action that is to be done to the man [impairs its validity and the spitting is done on the ground, not at the man, hence the ritual is valid without it].' Clearly, R. Eliezer takes the verse in its plain sense and requires no exegesis, since the words *"thus shall it be done"* refer back to the shoe removal and spitting, and only R. Akiva expounds [the verse to support the view] that [the absence of] spitting does not impair [the validity of the ritual].

language" or "the Torah speaks in the [ordinary] language of humankind."[48] He even complained against R. Akiva: "and because you expound 'daughter' [vs.] 'and daughter' we should take her out to be burned?"[49] Similarly R. Eleazer b. Azariah responded to R. Akiva: "Even if you draw out your speech the entire day saying 'with oil' 'with oil,' I will not listen to you, but rather a half log of oil for the thanksgiving offering and a quarter log of oil for the nazirite and 11 days between two periods of menstrual impurity, and each is a *halakhah* to Moses at Sinai [and not derived from forced exposition of Scripture]."[50] In the eyes of R. Akiva and his students, "the entire Torah is a *halakhah* to Moses at Sinai" (b. Niddah 45a) whether ordinances or decrees, traditions or deeds, and even expositions; according to them "words of the scribes" points to the entire Torah of the sages, including decrees and enactments.[51] On the one hand, the laws – whether their source be in tradition, custom, cases or testimony – received their authority from Scripture, and on the other hand, even "the minutiae (*diqduqe*) of the scribes and what they are yet to innovate" were already transmitted to Moses at Sinai and were now none other than tradition.[52] This change in the meaning of the term "words of the scribes" is also reflected clearly in the exegetical explanations of the name

---

48 See David Hoffman on *Midrash haTannaim* in *Mesilot leTorah haTannaim* (Tel Aviv, 1928), pp. 5–9.
49 b. Sanhedrin 51b, and see b. Zevaḥim 12:1.
50 b. Menaḥot 89a, and see b. Niddah 73a: "According to R. Akiva it is based on a verse; according to R. Elazar b. Azariah it is a *halakhah*."
51 The teaching of R. Meir, m. Parah 11:5; m. Tohorot 4:11 – the teaching, apparently, of R. Yosi as in *mishnah* 10 there. T. Taanit 2:10, the teaching of R. Meir; t. Eduyot 1:1, is evidently repeated in the generation after R. Elazar b. Azariah. "Secondary degrees of relationship are [prohibited for marriage] from the words of the scribes" (m. Yevamot 2:3–4) – this is an explanation for "*asur mitzvah*" [prohibited by virtue of a commandment] or for "*asur qedushah*" [prohibited by virtue of holiness], see b. Yevamot 20a. According to the Bavli's sugya, the prohibition of secondary degrees of relationship is an ordinance (*gezerah*) and only Rava finds an allusion to it in the Torah. According to the Palestinian Talmud: "R. Huna learned all of them from these verses." In m. Yadayim 2:3 [correction: 3:2 (CH)], however, it is said following a debate between R. Joshua and the sages [about secondary degrees of ritual impurity]: "We do not learn words of Torah from the words of the scribes, nor words of the scribes from the words of Torah, nor words of the scribes from [other] words of the scribes." There is some doubt whether this is the teaching of the sages in disagreement with R. Joshua, since in connection with another dispute in t. Tevul Yom 1:10, "R. Yosi said, 'See concerning this law, how the early fathers debated it and drew inferences from the words of the scribes for the words of the Torah and from the words of the scribes to [other] words of the scribes'" (and see Lieberman, *Tosefet Rishonim*, part 4, p. 164). The early fathers are R. Eliezer and R. Joshua! See also t. Eduyot 1:5 and t. Miqvaot 5:4, and see Rambam's *Commentary on the Mishnah* to m. Kelim 17:12: "Lest you err, they declared its minimum quantity from the words of the scribes on the known principle that all of the minimum measures are *halakhot* to Moses at Sinai. Because whatever is not clear in the language of the Torah is said to be from the words of the scribes, and even those matters that are *halakhot* to Moses at Sinai." And see J.N. Guttman, "Torah baTalmud," *Festschrift in honor of Schwartz*, p. 5f.
52 b. Megillah 19:2; y. Peah 2:4, and see my article "*Mashma'ut ḥadatit shel hahalakhah*" in the volume "*Arkhe haYahadut* (Tel Aviv, 1953), p. 25.

"scribes." If the explanation "that they used to count all of the letters of the Torah" was appropriate for the first scribes, then R. Abbahu's words,[53] viz., "why *sofrim*? Because they made the Torah into numbers: five who do not give *terumah*, five who do not give *hallah*," are consistent with the "words of the scribes" as a term referring to the entire Oral Law ... This signification is even more obvious in the words of R. Aha: "'And Ezra the priest and scribe' (*sofer*; Neh 8:9). What is the meaning of *sofer*? Just as he used to count (*sofer*) the words of the Torah, so he would count the words of the sages."[54] In the following statement "They said of R. Yohanan b. Zakkai that he did not neglect Scripture, Mishnah, Talmud, *halakhah*, and *aggadah*, the minutiae (*diqduqe*) of Scripture and the minutiae (*diqduqe*) of the scribes" (b. Sukkah 28a), and in R. Yohanan's statement, "This teaches that God showed Moses in advance all the minutiae of the Torah and all the minutiae of the scribes and that which the scribes would innovate" (b. Megillah 19b), the word "scribes" [*sofrim*] already signifies the generality of sages. But a reminder of their basic function remains in the [phrase] "minutiae of the scribes," and only at a later stage [can one speak of] "the innovations of the scribes."

The method we have proposed regarding the status and function of the *sofrim* and regarding exegesis as a source of *halakhah*, would appear to be contradicted[55]

---

53 y. Sheqalim 5:1.
54 ibid.
55 For our argument, there is no obligation to discuss scholarly proofs that new laws were produced through exegesis from *mishnayot* and *baraitot* of R. Akiva, his colleagues and students, so we will deal with only two cited by H. Albeck, in "Halakhot ve-haDrashot," p. 2, and relating to the time when the Great Court was in existence. In m. Sanhedrin 11:2 it is said that a rebellious elder who came to the court at the entrance to the Temple mount would say: "Thus have I expounded and thus have my colleagues expounded; thus have I taught and thus have my fellows taught." According to this passage, it seems that they taught through exegesis. But in the continuation of the *mishnah* it is explicitly said: "If they had heard, they tell him"; "if he returned to his own city and repeats and teaches it as he used to teach, he is exempt but if gives instruction as to what is to be done, he is liable." It seems therefore that practical *halakhah* was not dependent on exegesis but rather on oral transmission and majority rule. As a side note, the *mishnah* in Sanhedrin was apparently formulated at a later time, because the section from "there were three courts there" to "if he returned to his own city" has no connection to the case of the rebellious elder and flows from a source like the well-known *baraita* of R. Yosi (see above n13): "Originally there were no disputes in Israel ..." This tradition appears in four sources and in three of them it is said: "he goes to the court in his own city; if there is no court in his town he goes to the court near his town; if they had heard, they tell him and if not ... they go to the court in the Chamber of Hewn Stone ... the question is posed and if they had heard, they tell them and if not they take a vote and if a majority declares impure, they declare it impure and if the majority declares pure, they declare it pure." It is only in b. Sanhedrin 88b that we find "'Thus have I expounded and thus have my colleagues expounded; thus have I taught and thus have my fellows taught." It seems that these words were added under the influence of the *mishnah*'s formulation, as was noted already by Abraham Weiss in "On the Nature of the Court of Seventy-One" in *Louis Ginzberg: Jubilee Volume on the Occasion of his Seventieth Birthday* (New York, 1946), 189–216 [Hebrew], p. 204. T. Sanhedrin 9:1, on the procedure for reaching a verdict, appears to be stronger proof: "And on the next day they would come together in pairs and eat little and discuss the relevant biblical text all night. If he was a murderer they would

by the well-known and widely accepted view that the disputes between the Pharisees and the Sadducees were disputes over the connection between scriptural proofs and *halakhah*. But in fact, a close examination of the tradition regarding the dispute between the two sects confirms our method. In Megillat Taanit it is said: "On the fourth of Tammuz the book of decrees was removed" and in the Hebrew scholion: "Because a book of decrees was written and set before the Sadducees – these [are liable to] death by stoning, these [are liable to] death by burning, these [are liable to] death by execution, these [are liable to] death by strangulation. When they were sitting and someone would ask [about a punishment] and they would show him in the book, he would say to them 'from where in Scripture [do you know] that this one is liable to death by stoning, and this one to death by burning and this one to death by execution and this one to death by strangulation?' And they wouldn't know how to adduce a proof from Scripture. The sages said: Doesn't it say, '*according to the instruction that they will teach you*' etc. (Deut 17:11) which teaches that *halakhot* are not written in a book?" A second comment connects with what is reported in the scroll as the view of the Boethusians in their interpretation of such phrases as "*an eye for an eye*," and "*and they shall spread the garment before the elders of the city*" (Deut 22:17) – [that these are to be taken] literally. But what is the connection between this [second] view and the [statement that] "a book of decrees was written and set"? Moreover, the first comment [cited above] has two components. The first is that they "didn't know how to adduce a proof from Scripture," and the second is "that *halakhot* are not written in a book." And it is only the second of these claims that bears any connection to the case of the "book of decrees that was written and set." The statement that they "didn't know how to adduce a proof from Scripture," is not an objection to the book of decrees referred to here. The four types of capital punishment that are taught in our *Mishnah* are also in this style [i.e., the style of] a book of decrees: "these [are liable to] death by stoning, these [are liable to] death by burning, these [are liable to] strangulation." And despite all of the expositions one is hard pressed to say that there is biblical proof for death by strangulation.[56] R. Abraham ibn Ezra has already written (on Lev 20:9) "and there is a general rule regarding the modes of capital punishment that we require tradition because we cannot derive them from Scripture." The Sadducees did not deny the need for rules and *halakhot* that are not explicit in the Torah, but they did claim that the only obligatory laws and decrees were those written and set forth, and not the

---

discuss the passage about the murderer, and if he had committed a sexual misdeed they discussed the passage on sexual sins ..." However, in a *baraita* in the Palestinian Talmud 5:2, we find only: "And they discuss all night." Even if we see the Tosefta's version as primary, we still can't say in this case that they reached the verdict by examining the scriptural passage, but rather that they occupied themselves with the passage.

56 Mekhilta § Mishpatim, 5 (Horowitz-Rabin ed., p. 267); and see Torat Cohanim 9:11 and A. Büchler, "Die Todesstrafen der Bibel und der jüdisch-nachbiblischen Zeit" in *Monatschrift für Geschichte und Wissenschaft des Judentums* 5 (1906), p. 539f.

received oral tradition; and it seems to me that this is what Josephus meant when he said (*Antiq.* XIII, 10.6): [λέγον ἐκεῖνα δεῖν ἡγεῖσθαι νόμιμα τὰ γεγραμμένα, τὰ δ' ἐκ παραδόσεως τῶν πατέρων]: "They say that only the written laws [the translators add: in the Torah of Moses] have validity but not those that were received from earlier generations [the forefathers]."

The position of the sages was that none of the ordinances and decrees, traditions and teachings were to be written down or made into "written Torah." There is in "writing and depositing"[57] the creation of a kind of new Torah, alongside the Torah of Moses. It seems to me that this provides an opening for understanding the response of the Sadducees to King Yannai in the well-known *baraita* in Qiddushin 66a. They advised the king to crush the Pharisees: "If you will listen to me, crush them." And in response to the king's question, "and what will become of the Torah?" They replied "There it is rolled up and deposited in the corner. [Whoever wishes to study it, let him go and study!]." This response has no meaning and I would hypothesize that the text should read "it is written and deposited." Indeed, I have found that this is the version in *Aggadot haTalmud* (Cassuto, 1511) and in a manuscript of *Aggadot haTalmud* and in Spanish mss and printed editions.[58] I would venture to say that the phrase "in the corner" is a late addition in the spirit of a later time. The Sadducees claimed that there was no need for a living oral tradition when there was a "book, written and deposited."

I am well aware that this view contradicts many of the theories and approaches constructed by scholars concerning the nature of these two parties, which see in one a conservative party and in the other a progressive liberal party, an aristocratic and a plebeian party, but the basis for these views in the sources is generally weak and thus also the explanation of the great difference in the approaches that they presented. Aristocrats and plebeians, conservatives and liberals were also found among the Pharisaic sages.

It is a fact that the authentic disputes between the Sadducees and the Pharisees such as the debate over the water libation [ceremony at Sukkot], the day after the Sabbath [as the base for counting the days of the *omer*], the beating of the willow [at Sukkot], and even the placement of the incense [on the firepan by the high priest entering] the Holy of Holies [on Yom Kippur] do not have their origin in exegetical differences,[59] i.e., in bringing proof from Scripture. This is also the case

---

57 See S. Lieberman, *Hellenism in Jewish Palestine* (New York, 1962), p. 86.
58 Parma ms. of *Aggadot haTalmud*, de Rossi 156; Spanish edition in the British Museum. The British Museum ms. 2419 contains a deletion and correction. I consulted the photographs of the Machon leHotsa'at haShas.
59 As for the first items here, even scholars who champion the priority of the midrashic method of study [over the abstract mishnaic method] concede that these were old traditions, and as for the last item here, the Rambam has already noted in *Hilkhot Avodat Yom haKippurim* 1, 7: "The sages learned from oral tradition that one places the incense [on the firepan] only in the shrine." This approach is followed by R. Leszynsky, *Die Sadduzäer* (Berlin, 1912), p. 61: and see the contrary view of J.Z. Lauterbach, "A Significant Controversy between the Sadducees and the Pharisees,"

in the arguments between R. Yoḥanan b. Zakkai and the Sadducees. There were certainly Sadducean scribes who were occupied themselves with the minutiae of the scribes and the interpretation of Scripture. It is possible that with the spread of exegesis and with a conception of its role as a source of *halakhah*, differences of opinion on exegetical matters were also revealed, but as we have seen these were also found within Pharisaic circles and it was not the fundamental and principal point of dispute.

Hebrew Union College Annual 4 (1927), pp. 173–205 and now in *Rabbinic Essays* (Cincinnati, 1951), p. 51f. See also H. Albeck, *Shishah Sidrei Mishnah: Seder Moed*, vol. 2 (Jerusalem, 1958), p. 215 and what I have written in "Ha-Yehudim be-'Artzam bi-Tequfat ha-Tannaim" in *Beḥinot be-viḳoret ha-sifrut* 4 (1953), p. 76 [sic; The article's page range is 61–72 (CH)]. Interestingly, it is in fact the Sadducee who accuses his father: "All your days, you expounded [that this is the practice] but you did not *do* it ..." and his father answers him: "Even though we expound [that this is the practice], we don't *do* it." By contrast, there is a striking preference for decisions based on authority in the story of R. Yoḥanan ben Zakkai in a *baraita* in b. Rosh haShanah 29b: Bene Batyra "said to him, 'Let us discuss [whether the shofar should be blown in Yavneh when the New Year falls on the Sabbath].' He said to them: 'Let us sound the shofar and then we will discuss it.' After they sounded it they said to him, '[Now] let us discuss it.' He said to them, 'The horn has already been sounded in Yavneh and after an action has been performed it is not open to retraction.'" R. Yoḥanan ben Zakkai's response is reminiscent of the saying by the Roman Cato: *Rem tene verba sequentur* ["grasp the subject, and the words will follow"]. See H. Jordan, *M. Catonis librum de re rustica quae extant* (Lipsiae, 1860), p. 80. See also Schultz, *op. cit.*, p. 38. [Note that there does not appear to be a previous citation of a work by Schultz (CH).]

INTRODUCTION TO THE HALAKHIC MIDRASHIM*

David Hoffmann

A supplement to the annual of the Berlin rabbinical seminary 5647 (1886–87)

Translated by James Redfield

I. Halakhic Midrash

1. All teachers of the law up to the time of R. Judah ha-Nasi and his older students[1] are usually designated *tannaim*. The teachings that they stated, or those attributed to them, are designated *mishnayot* (singular: *mishnah*), if they were included within certain collections.[2] Among the *mishnayot*, we distinguish between the widely received Mishnah of R. Judah ha-Nasi ("the Mishnah" *par excellence*) and the rest of the *mishnayot* that were less widely known (as *mishnah ḥiṣonah, matnita baraita*, or simply *baraita*) and hence held no such authority as the received Mishnah. The overwhelming majority of *mishnah*-teachings (*mishnayot* and *baraitot*) deal with the teachings of the law, and are therefore "*halakhic mishnayot*"; the contents of some, however, are aggadic, in that they comprise not legal determinations but scriptural exegeses, narratives, ethical and other aphorisms.

---

* This translation was completed by James Redfield and reviewed by Elisa Ronzheimer. Common transliterations of Hebrew as well as translations in square brackets, have been added by Christine Hayes. Comments and corrections are also set in square brackets and the author identified by initials: JR = James Redfield and CH = Christine Hayes.

1 A definite date for the beginning of the period of the *tannaim* is not easy to determine. Greek authors of the Second Temple period do not know the name "*tannaim*" and instead call the teachers of the law σοφισταί, γραμματεῖς, φαρισαίοι, etc. (*soferim, perushim, ḥakhamim*). However, usually, all the teachers mentioned in the Mishnah, beginning with Simon the Just (Avot 1:2) are called "*tannaim*."

2 Not all statements of the *tannaim* belong to the Mishnah or the *baraitot*; some of these were preserved for us only by the *amoraim*; these qualify only as *memra* (מימרא, amoraic statement).

The halakhic *mishnayot* either present the law as quite independent of holy Scripture and are dubbed "*halakhot*" (הלכות), or they derive the legal determinations from a scriptural passage. In the latter case, the *tanna*'s teaching is called "*midrash*" (מדרש).[3] Here is just an example of a *mishnah* in the forms of *halakhah* and *midrash*.

Halakhah:	Midrash:
One who slaughters an animal and finds in it afterbirth, if he is not sensitive, may eat it; afterbirth that has partially emerged may not be eaten. m. Ḥullin 4:7 (Mishnah Ḥullin 77a)	"[whatever is] in the beast, that you shall eat' [Lev 11:3] -- to include the afterbirth. I might say that even if it has partially emerged [it is permitted]. The verse therefore says "that [you shall eat" -- and not the partially emerged afterbirth]. (Sifra Shemini 3:1 (= Talmud)

On the other hand, there are many *halakhot* not derived from Scripture, where we cannot speak of *midrash* at all. Only for legal determinations that originated in the written Torah, was the scriptural proof usually presented; as a result, a *midrash* also existed for that kind of *halakhah* among the *tannaim*.

2. Like our Mishnah,[4] *mishnah*-collections arranged by the *tannaim* were usually divided into six orders when their function was simply to order and fix the *halakhot*. Other than our Mishnah, the only such collection that we still have is the Tosefta. The Tosefta is not, however, an independent collection of *halakhah* but consistently relies on our Mishnah. That said, in the time of the *amoraim*, there were also many other independent *halakhah* collections, e.g. the great *mishnayot* of R. Hoshaya, bar Qappara, and others,[5] often referred to in Palestinian sources, as well as the numerous *baraitot* cited in the Babylonian Talmud. In contrast to these collections, others which presented the *halakhot* derived from Scripture alongside their scriptural source were, naturally, organized according to the text of the Pentateuch; these *mishnah*-collections were called Midrashim.[6] These works further aimed to exposit and interpret Scripture.

---

3 In b. Qiddushin 49a, there is indeed a dispute as to whether or not "*mishnah*" should be understood as *midrash* or as *halakhah*. There, however, the discussion concerns only "*mishnah*" in the narrower sense. That said, it is beyond doubt that both *midrash* and *halakhah* are understood as belonging to "*mishnah*" in the broader sense as well, for a "*tanna*" was supposed to know the *midrashim* as well as the *halakhah* (b. Qiddushin 49b).

4 In the Babylonian Talmud, the Mishnah of R. Judah ha-Nasi is called "our Mishnah."

5 See y. Horayot 3, 48c, Midrash Rabbah to Qohelet 2:5, 6:2, 12:3; to the Song of Songs, 8:2 and to Lamentations, Petiḥta 23; Pesiqta deR. Kahana, Ekhah ed. Buber 122a; Midrash to Psalms 1:2.

6 [An upper case M and no italics is used when referring to the standard midrashic collections (the Halakhic Midrashim), and a lower case m with italics is used when referring to *midrash* as a literary genre or mode of exegesis (CH)].

As Genesis contains only little law, there is no halakhic *midrash* to this book. By contrast, there are various Halakhic Midrashim to the other four books of the Torah. Of these, the following have been preserved until our own time: 1. The Mekhilta to Exodus; 2. Sifra deBe Rab or Torat Kohanim to Leviticus; 3. the Sifre deBe Rab to Numbers and Deuteronomy.[7] Another halakhic *midrash* to Numbers, called Sifre Zuta (the little Sifre) is cited so often in the compilation "Yalqut Shimoni" and elsewhere that it is also preserved in large part. The rest of the Halakhic Midrashim which, as we shall see, were also at the disposal of the *amoraim*, have not reached us and were no longer known—with just one exception—after the completion of the Talmud.

3. Some of the halakhic *baraitot* that are cited in the Babylonian and Jerusalem Talmuds belong to collections of *halakhah*, others to collections of *midrash*. Therefore, a halakhic *baraita* can be a "*halakhah-baraita*" or a "*midrash-baraita*." In line with what we have said above, a *midrash-baraita* can be very easily recognized in that it either cites the scriptural text immediately at the outset,[8] or otherwise makes it plain in the course of discussion that it means to derive the *halakhah* from Scripture. However, in the *halakhah* collections, in *our* Mishnah, and in the Tosefta, there are not a few sections whose midrashic quality is striking,[9] just as, on the other hand, longer or shorter halakhic statements have been included in the midrashic collections without scriptural proof.[10] This alone shows at least that the redactors of one collection often borrowed fragments from another; as the final redactor of the Midrashim already had many halakhic collections before him, so older *midrashim* served as the basis for even the oldest collection of *halakhah*—our Mishnah.[11] In the Talmud, the *midrash-baraita* is cited in just the same way as the *halakhah-baraita*, with an obligatory formula such as תני, תנא, תניא, תנו רבנן or, especially in the Yerushalmi and also in the Bavli, מתיבי, תא שמע, and the like, with no further qualification. Of the extant Midrashim, the Sifra is cited most frequently in the Talmud, as is the Sifre to Deuteronomy; less often are the Sifre to Numbers and, even more rarely, the Mekhilta. But in the Talmuds, very many *midrash-baraitot* are mentioned that do not appear in the surviving Midrashim, from which one can only conclude that still more Midrashim were available to the Talmud, as will now be further demonstrated in detail.

4. Halakhic *midrash* derives *halakhah* from Scripture by means of specific rules (*middot*). *Midrash* itself was also frequently called *middot* (מדות, Aramaic

---

7 The Midrashim listed here do also contain *aggadah* (a great deal, in the case of the Mekhilta and the Sifre). Hence these really ought to be distinguished from the rest of the Midrashim by the name "Tannaitic Midrashim." That said, the designation "Halakhic Midrashim" is also suitable, insofar as these are the only ones primarily dedicated to the *halakhah*, and the beginning of these collections (Exodus chap. 12; Numbers chap. 5) suffices to show that their object is primarily the *halakhah*.
8 In the Yerushalmi, the *midrash-baraitot* are often introduced by *ketiv* and then the scriptural verse.
9 See e.g. m. Sotah 8:9, Sanhedrin 10:5–6, t. Zevaḥim I:8, 12:20.
10 See e.g. Sifra § *Vayyiqra*, 1:9–13.
11 See my discussion in "*Die Erste Mischna Und Die Controversen Der Tannaim*" (Berlin, 1882), p. 5 ff.

מכילתא).¹² These rules were either a) grammatical and exegetical rules;¹³ b) interpretive rules for certain words and letters or, generally, for superfluous words, suffixes, or prefixes;¹⁴ c) logical rules for how a *halakhah* can be deduced from other legal determinations through logical conclusions.¹⁵ In the Midrashim, this sort of argumentation is called "*din*" (דין). Quite often, against the derivation of a teaching from Scripture (according to rules (a) and (b)) is found the objection: והלא דין הוא ["and is it not logical (which renders the scriptural derivation unnecessary)?]. Yet this leads immediately to further argumentation ("To what, then, *does* this passage from Scripture refer?!")¹⁶ According to the Baraita of R. Ishmael (printed at the head of editions of the Sifra), Hillel expounded seven interpretive rules (*middot*). As R. Ishmael teaches: "The Torah is investigated according to thirteen *middot*."¹⁷ R. Eliezer, the son of R. Yosi the Galilean, transmits thirty-two rules for the *aggadah*, many of which are also valid for the *halakhah*.¹⁸ That said, many passages in the Talmud indicate that the *middot* were handed down directly

---

12 See Leviticus Rabbah 3:1, טוב מי ... טוב מי ששונה שני סדרים ורגיל בהם ממי ששונה הלכות ואינו רגיל בהם ששונה הלכות ורגיל בהם ממי שהוא שונה הלכות ומדות ואינו רגיל בהן ... טוב מי שהוא שונה הלכות ומדות ורגיל בהם ממי שהוא שונה הלכות ומדות ותלמוד ואינו רגיל בהם = "Better is one who studies two orders and is skilled in them than one who studies laws [*halakhah*] and is not skilled in them ... better is one who studies laws and is skilled in them than one who studies laws and their derivation from Scripture (*middot*) and is not skilled in them ... better is one who studies laws and their derivation from Scripture and is skilled in them than one who studies laws and their derivation from Scripture and the rhetorical underpinnings (Talmud)." From this passage we see clearly that one would first learn the *halakhah*, then their derivation from Scripture (*middot*) and finally their rhetorical underpinnings (Talmud).
13 e.g. an interpretation of the passive Nifal form (Sifra § *Shemini* 5:1) or an explanation of the words בהמה and חיה in their narrower and broader senses (ibid., 2:8).
14 e.g. that the articles ה, מן, etc., delimit the sense of a term so that the formulation found at the end of a certain type of sacrifice (עולה היא, מנחה היא, etc.) is inclusive in one context but exclusive in another.
15 The analogical conclusion (מה מצינו) and the *a fortiori* conclusion (קל וחומר).
16 In the Midrashim, very often the words חקים ומשפטים of the Torah are explained by the following addition: החקים: אלו המדרשות והמשפטים: אלו הדינים (see e.g. Sifra § *Beḥuqqotay* 8:10; Sifre § *Re'eh* 59). It is not unlikely that here by דינים is meant *halakhah* that are derived by logical conclusions (דין), whereas those derived through other interpretive rules (דרש) are designated מדרשות. Hence מדרשות and דינים can be said to encompass nearly all laws of the Oral Torah.
17 If we actually count the *middot* of R. Ishmael, we find 16. Only R. Abraham ben David combines them as follows: 1) both of the בנין אב rules; 2) מכלל שצריך לפרט ומפרט שצריך לכלל; 3) דבר הלמד מעניינו ודבר הלמד מסופו. In the 1862 Vienna edition, R. Abraham ben David's subdivision is wrong. The correct division is found in *Kelale Shmuel* (in *Sefer Tummat Yesharim*, Venice 1613) chap. 40.
18 See Dr. J. Hildesheimer: "The tractate *Netivot Olam*, the third in the [five-part] work *Sefer Keritut* by R. Samson ben Isaac of Chinon critically emends and interprets it in detail after a thorough comparison of sources," in Supplement to the Third Report on the public Rabbinical Seminary at Eisenstadt, (Haberstadt 1869). The Baraita on the Thirty-Two Middot of R. Eliezer, as well as the Thirteen Middot of R. Ishmael, is quoted verbatim in the work of the Karaite Judah Hadassi, from which many errors in the other editions can be corrected.

from Sinai. In order to account for certain differences, however,[19] one might be permitted to assume that the *tannaim* abstracted some of these rules from specific received interpretations and reformulated them in various ways. If we study the statements in halakhic *midrash*, we find a number of interpretive rules that those *tannaim* do not count among the received *middot* for various reasons. Although it is extremely important for our understanding of the tradition to be perfectly clear about the rules that halakhic *midrash* uses to examine Scripture, it will be necessary to bracket that question in these remarks, as the various midrashic sources do not deploy all the rules in the same way. Hence, that study must be preceded by an elucidation of the various works of halakhic *midrash*. Most of the Halakhic Midrashim are attributed to the schools of R. Ishmael and R. Akiva, and the differences between these Midrashim are indeed associated with the diverse views of these *tannaim*.

II. R. Ishmael and R. Akiva

1. Elsewhere, we have shown how the later *tannaim* often debated the wording or the construal of an earlier *mishnah*.[20] For R. Ishmael and R. Akiva, we refer here only to M. Eruvin 1:2; Bava Batra 3:1; Bekhorot 6:6; Oholot 3:5; Negaim 1:2, 12:3; Niddah 6:12; Zavim 1:2. Although it may well be that for the *halakhot*—where, in most cases, the Sinaitic tradition had been firmly established—differences can be reduced to fewer cases, still, varying opinions must have arisen often about the proper way to derive the *halakhah* from the words of Scripture. In fact, we also find very many disputes between R. Ishmael and R. Akiva in, precisely, the halakhic *midrash*. The Talmud cites a great many differences of this kind, while the Jerusalem Talmud in particular frequently alerts us to the differences in midrashic method between R. Ishmael and R. Akiva by noting when a teaching is derived from Scripture that it is acceptable only according to R. Akiva, whereas, according to R. Ishmael, it must be deduced in another way (עד כדון כר׳ עקיבא כר׳ ישמעאל וכו׳).[21] By comparing a variety of Talmudic passages, the following differences in perspective between R. Ishmael and R. Akiva come to light with regard to their methods of halakhic *midrash*.

---

19 See b. Shevuot 26a on כלל ופרט [*kelal u-ferat*] and רבוי ומיעוט [*ribbuy u-miut*]. In y. Peah 1, 16c and Sotah 9, 23d there is a dispute about דבר שיצא מן הכלל לידון בדבר החדש which is not (as one would think from the Pene Moshe) identical to that found in b. Zevaḥim 49a-b. In y. Terumot 11, 47d, the Talmud (מקשן) concludes that according to R. Eliezer, כלל ופרט וכלל הכל בכלל, but the view is rejected.
20 See "The First Mishnah," p. 37ff.
21 See y. Berakhot 7, 11a (see Midrash Shmuel 13); Peah 1, 16c; Maaser Sheni 1, 52d; Orlah 2, 62a; Shabbat 7, 9d; 14, 15b; 19, 17a; Eruvin 3, 20c; Pesaḥim 1, 27a; 2, 29c; 9, 36c; Yoma 8, 45a; Rosh haShanah 3, 58d; Megillah 4, 74d; Ḥagigah 2, 77a; 3, 79b; Yevamot 1, 2b; 6, 7b; 8, 8c; 8d; 10, 11a; 11, 11d; Sotah 5, 20a; 20b; 7, 21d; 8, 22b, 23a; Nedarim 1, 36c; Gittin 8, 49b; Qiddushin 1, 59a; 59d; 2, 62a; Sanhedrin 3, 21c; 7, 24c; 24d; 25a (twice); Shevuot 1, 32d; 4, 35b, 7, 38b; 38c, Horayot 1, 45c.

a) R. Akiva often produces a teaching from the scriptural text by means of profound interpretive rules, whereas R. Ishmael comes to the same teaching from a simple logical conclusion or derives it from the explicit words of Scripture. See y. Berakhot 7, 11a; Orlah 2, 62a (R. Akiva deduces with a שוה גזירה [*gezerah shavah*], R. Ishmael with a ק"ו [*qal vehomer*]); Shabbat 7, 9d (R. Akiva by means of גז"ש [*gezerah shavah*], R. Ishmael from נדה היא); Gittin 8, 49b (R. Akiva from ונתן מ"מ,[22] R. Ishmael from an exegetical interpretation of ידה as רשותה); Pesaḥim 9, 36c (R. Akiva from איש איש, R. Ishmael from *binyan av*).

b) R. Akiva applies the interpretive rules in certain cases where, according to R. Ishmael, they ought not be applied. According to R. Ishmael, the *gezerah shavah* should only be used where Scripture plainly furnishes a superfluous word (*mufneh*) for this purpose; R. Akiva, by contrast, permits *gezerah shavah* even where no *mufneh* is available.[23] See y. Yoma 8, 45a; Sanhedrin 7, 24d; but also b. Niddah 22b, Yoma 81a and Yevamot 70b.[24] Further, R. Akiva permits these teachings derived from midrashic rules to be applied to other cases, by means of the same or other rules, while according to R. Ishmael, this practice (למד מן הלמד; [*lamed min halamed*, "a conclusion derive from a derived conclusion")] would not be permissible. In the Babylonian Talmud (b. Zevaḥim 49b ff.), this axiom is acknowledged to be definitive only for *qodashim* [sacred matters] and there only as far as היקש [*heqqesh*] goes, whereas for certain other rules of derivation it is doubtful. In any case, however, a broader range of derivations is permitted for *ḥullin* [profane matters]. There, the dispute between R. Ishmael and R. Akiva is confined to a single form, *hemennu ve-davar aḥer*; see b. Zevaḥim 57a. In the Yerushalmi, on the other hand, R. Ishmael and R. Akiva debate *ḥullin* [profane matters] and there we learn that unlike R. Akiva, R. Ishmael assumes the axiom of אין למדין מן הלמד [*ein lamedin min halamed*, "we do not derive a conclusion from a derived conclusion"] for various other forms: a *gezerah shavah* from a *gezerah shavah*, y. Yevamot 11, 11d; a *binyan av* from a *gezerah shavah*, y. Yevamot 8, 8c;

---

22 R. Akiva's proof is found in Sifre Deuteronomy 269 (cited in b. Gittin 77a), which comes from his school. Similarly, R. Ishmael's deduction is found in Mekhilta § *Mishpatim* par. 13, which pertains to his school. Along the same lines, in, e.g., Sifra, רובע ונרבע etc. is deduced from מן הבהמה etc., whereas in R. Ishmael's midrash, it is deduced from כי משחתם בהם; compare b. Temurah 28.

23 This controversy accounts for the fact that the expression מופנה להקיש ממנו ולדון גז"ש ["available for drawing a *heqqesh* or constructing a *gezerah shavah*"] appears only in R. Ishmael's school, but not in R. Akiva's.

24 In b. Niddah 22b, R. Akiva's view is not cited, which is quite surprising; instead there is a debate between R. Ishmael and the sages (or R. Eliezer, according to b. Yevamot 70b), whether a *gezerah shavah* with an "available term" in only one location can be refuted. There is a difference of opinion between the *amoraim* Samuel and R. Elazer about אינה מופנה כלל ["when the term of comparison is not available in either location"] as to whether one can deduce from it at all; in any case, such a deduction may indeed be refuted (משיבין). So if, as R. Elazar (b. Niddah 23a) holds, according to R. Ishmael and R. Eliezer, אינו מופנה כלל למידין ["where there is no available term we may make a deduction"] then R. Akiva in the Yerushalmi must hold: אפילו אינו מופנה כלל למידין ואין משיבין ["even where there is no available term we may make a deduction and may not refute it"].

a *heqqesh* from a *binyan av* and a *heqqesh* from a *gezerah shavah*, y. Qiddushin 1, 59a (see *Qorban Edah* there).²⁵ Finally, there is a well-known dispute wherein R. Ishmael's rule of *kelal u-ferat u-kelal* ("a general term followed by a particular term followed by a general term") is apprehended by R. Akiva as a *ribbuy u-miut ve-ribbuy* ("an inclusion followed by an exclusion followed by an inclusion") according to which rule the extent of the law is substantially broadened (b. Shevuot 26a).²⁶

2. c) Other than his famous thirteen *middot*, R. Ishmael also pronounced a *middah* intended not to widen but to contract the domain of legal interpretation. As it says in Sifre § *Naso* 2: "This is a *middah* of the Torah: whatever is taught in one place and repeated in another is repeated because something was lacking in it."²⁷ This statement does belong to R. Ishmael, as the Babylonian Talmud cites it several times (see b. Sotah 3a) in the name of a *tanna* of the school of R. Ishmael with the words: כל פרשה שנאמרה ונשנית לא נשנית אלא בשביל דבר שנתחדש בה ["whatever was repeated was repeated only for the sake of a new element that was added"]. According to this teaching, the Torah occasionally repeated an entire section of the law in order to add *one* new determination to it, and it is therefore unnecessary to derive yet another novelty from *every* repetition. For example, the passage on the guilt offering for theft in Lev 5:20–26 was repeated by the Torah in Num 5:5–8, in order to teach the new determination there (v. 8) that in certain cases of theft the priest is to be compensated. R. Akiva, however, opposes

---

25 The *baraita* cited by the Talmud (Zevaḥim 57a) is found in Sifre Numbers 118 (ed. Friedmann p. 39a), and there R. Ishmael states generally that one ought not to derive [from a derived conclusion] למד מן הלמד, without speaking directly of היקש [*heqqesh*]. However, that the Sifre to Numbers, which comes from the school of R. Ishmael (as will be shown below), does *not* distinguish in this respect between היקש [*heqqesh*] and other *middot* or between profane matters and sacred matters, may be clearly seen in Sifre § *Ḥuqqat* 127 (Friedmann 46a), where not even a *binyan av* is derived from a *qal veḥomer* in profane matters. Already R. Hillel, the Rabad and *Zera Avraham* were surprised by this contradiction between Sifre and the Babylonian Talmud, without coming to an answer. The explanation of the Malbim [Meir Leibush ben Yehiel Michel Wisser], against the reading in the Yalqut and the early commentators, does not take the Yerushalmi into account: "In y. Qiddushin 1:2 an objection is raised from a *baraita* taught by R. Ishmael holding that one may make a deduction from a derived conclusion, and it is taught in the name of another sage as if to say he [R. Ishmael] doesn't really hold this view, and in fact we find in b. Zevaḥim 41a another *tanna* from the school of R. Ishmael who holds that something derived from a *heqqesh* can then be used to derive a conclusion by *qal veḥomer* even in sacred matters, but in the Yerushalmi and Sifre R. Ishmael teaches this *baraita* also in the name of another sage and doesn't hold this view himself. And all of this appears forced to the Bavli; the gemara maintains that there are two *tannaim* following the view of R. Ishmael and the point of difference is that according to one *tanna* there is not a great dispute between R. Ishmael and R. Akiva. It is also possible that R. Ishmael retracted in his later years as we find in other places, in m. Kilayim 3, and see the Yerushalmi ad loc., and see also b. Shabbat 27a, where according to Abbaye two *tannaim* of the school of R. Ishmael dispute, and see also b. Megillah 23a and b. Zevaḥim 57b."
26 On the difference between the two forms see at length, Rashi to Sanhedrin 45b and 46a.
27 Here, as in the Talmud, R. Elijah of Vilna reads: "it is repeated only for the sake of the new element in it."

this teaching with the words "כל מקום שנאמר בה לאמר צריך לידרש"[28] ["wherever the word 'saying' is written, one must expound"] or, as R. Elijah of Vilna reads, כל מה שנאמר בה צריך להדרש ["everything written in it must be expounded"]. Accordingly, an interpretation would have to be sought for every repetition in the passage Num 5:5–8 (see Malbim there and to Sifra § *VaYiqra* 3). In b. Sotah 3a, too, R. Akiva is opposed to R. Ishmael's application of this rule. This is why so often in the Sifra, many *derashot* are derived from a single phrase. On this, Malbim notes (*Ayelet haShaḥar* 242, see there): "The commentators of the Sifra believed that all expositions were derived from one and the same word; therefore, they were forced to base their teachings on a ה or ו or the like, so that it may seem that the fundamental teachings of tradition hang upon spiders' webs. Truly, however, the Sifra only derived one exposition from each passage, and where more than one is found in [connection with] the same passage, it is certain that the interpreted expression is repeated as often within the same section or elsewhere in the Torah as the sum of the expositions, which the Sifra collected and assembled only in the first instance where they occur." However, the Sifra is not able to interpret all repetitions. With regard to, for example, the dietary laws from Lev 11 that are repeated in Deut 14, it must concede to the axiom of R. Ishmael that is stated in another *baraita* as follows: למה נשנו בבהמה מפני השסועה ובעופות מפני הראה ["why was the list (of animals) repeated (in Deuteronomy)? The quadrupeds on account of the *sha'asuah* (not mentioned in Leviticus) and the birds on account of the *ra'ah*"].[29] Nevertheless, the students of R. Akiva himself want to derive new teachings from repetition in these passages, insofar as possible: כל היכא דאיכא למדרש דרשינן ["wherever we can interpret we do interpret"] (b. Bechorot 6b).

3. d) R. Akiva uses certain superfluous words and letters that are not especially significant in ordinary human language in order to derive *halakhot* in holy Scripture, because in his view, unlike humans, holy Scripture would not have used superfluous words or sounds without a special purpose. לשנות רבויים הן ("They are expressions of expansion") – this is the teaching of R. Akiva (y. Shabbat 19, 17a).

---

28 If this reading is correct, then R. Akiva would have required a definite interpretation of these repeated sections only where לאמר is present, as according to b. Pesaḥim 42a, a literal and precise observance of the divine word is emphatically required (as bar Qappara seems to mean by לא יומרו הדברים, in the reading of R Ḥananel and several mss.; see, however, y. Nazir 5, 53d). According to this, it would be easier to explain why the Talmud itself brings forward these rules of R. Ishmael in the name of R. Akiva (b. Shevuot 19a), for there, the discussion concerns a section where לאמור is not present. Regardless, R. Akiva does seem to adduce this teaching in several other cases and secures an expanded range of application for the axiom כל היכא דאיכא למדרש דרשינן ("wherever we can interpret, we do interpret)" b. Berakhot 6b) through deeper examination.

29 This *baraita*, which is also cited in b. Ḥullin 63b, did not appear in the Sifre editions. Only Friedmann included it in his edition, following the *Yalqut* (Friedmann p. 95a). It is probably a *baraita* from the school of R. Ishmael, as it appears with a statement of Immi ben Judah = Immi ben Aqavyah, a *tanna* who, as will be shown below, does not appear in the Midrashim of the school of R. Akiva. Below it will also be shown that the Sifre to Deuteronomy, on the other hand, at least beginning with § *Re'eh*, originally belongs to the school of R. Akiva. Therefore, our *baraita* was probably added to Sifre later on.

By contrast, R. Ishmael contends: לשונות כפולין הן ("They are repeated expressions") or: דברה תורה כלשון בני אדם ("the Torah speaks according to the language of humans"), Sifre Numbers 112 (Friedmann p. 33a) and the Yerushalmi *loc. cit.* and in many other passages. Therefore, R. Ishmael was obliged to reject many legal derivations of R. Akiva and support the relevant determinations in other ways, through logical rules, *gezerah shavah*, or explicit scriptural passages. The axiom "the Torah speaks according to the language of humans" was deployed especially by R. Ishmael against R. Akiva in order to classify the following expressions not as expansions or special legal determinations: the infinitive preceding the finite verb, e.g. "*hikkaret tikkaret*" (b. Sanhedrin 64b, b. Keritot 11a); the doubling of an expression, e.g. "*ish ish*" (b. Yevamot 71a, y. Pesaḥim 9, 36c), "*ish eḥad ish eḥad*" (y. Sotah 7, 21d); repetition of an expression by a synonym, e.g. ודבר ואמר (y. Sotah 8, 22b); the combination of a verb and a verbal noun (y. Nedarim 1, 36c, see Malbim *Ayelet haShaḥar* 36); a *vav* (ו'), e.g. פקדו ופקדו (y. Sotah 8, 23a).

If we take a glance at the Midrashim from the schools of R. Ishmael and R. Akiva, however, we learn that controversies of this sort also extended to other expressions. Very often in the Sifra, for instance, the prefix to a collective term, מן [*min*, of, from], is interpreted so as to exclude a certain individual in a category from the law, see Sifra ויקרא (Malbim *Ayelet haShaḥar* 51). In b. Temurah 28a-b, moreover, regarding the famous *derashot* of the Sifra מן הבהמה להוציא את הרובע והנרבע מן הבקר להוציא את הנעבד מן הצאן להוציא את המוקצה ["'of the quadrupeds' – this excludes an animal who sexually penetrated (a woman) or was sexually penetrated by a man; 'of the herd' – this excludes one that has been used for an idolatrous purpose; 'of the flock' – this excludes one that was set aside for idolatrous purposes"] it is noted that the *tanna* from the school or R. Ishmael derived these teachings from another passage, and that he indeed applied this מן [*min*, "from, of"] to other teachings, rejecting, on the other hand, the Sifra's interpretation of "of the goats," "of the sheep," and "of the herd," with the words: אורחיה דקרא לאשתעויי הכי, "It is the way of Scripture to express itself thus," which is similar to the axiom "the Torah speaks according to the language of humans." Hence R. Ishmael does not always want the מן [*min*, "from, of"] to be interpreted conclusively. In practice, no such interpretation is found in the Midrashim of the school of R. Ishmael; see Mekhilta to Ex 12:4, Sifre to Num 15:3. Indeed, the Sifre to Num shows clearly in another passage that he tries to avoid this kind of legal derivation. A *baraita* on Num 15:19 in the Yerushalmi (interpreting מלחם ולא כל לחם; ["some of the bread and not all of the bread"]) proves that only five kinds of grain are liable for *ḥallah*. Then, however, a *baraita* of R. Ishmael is introduced which derives this teaching from a *gezerah shavah* (see b. Menaḥot 70b). The first *baraita*, which interprets מלחם ["from the bread"] comes from the school to which the Sifra also belongs. The Sifre Numbers 110 follows the view of R. Ishmael and does not stress the word מלחם.[30]

---

30 Of course מן ["of, from"] is not only interpreted so as to entirely exclude a part of the collective

Phrases like "*ḥattat hi*," "*minḥah hi*" ("it is a purification offering," "it is a cereal offering") etc., which seem to be superfluous in various laws, are always used in the Sifra as a way to derive two teachings in the tradition, whereby the first term (e.g. "cereal offering") is used as an expansion (רבוי) while the second term ("it is") is a limitation (מיעוט). (See 55 examples of this interpretive mode in Malbim *Ayelet haShaḥar* 135). The Midrashim of R. Ishmael are unaware of interpretations of this kind, which is easy to see if one contrasts Sifra to Lev 5:11 with Sifre to Num 5:15 [*minḥah qenaot hi*, "it is a cereal offering of jealousy"]: the latter seems to openly reject an interpretation like the Sifra's with the words "the sense of the matter is that it is a cereal offering of (i.e., expressing) jealousy." Further, in the Sifre, the "*minḥah qenaot hi*" of Num 5:18 is not interpreted.

A third example: The words "*zot torah*" or "*zot ha-torah*" ("this is a law" or "this is the law") are always used by the Sifra for expounding (Malbim, *Ayelet haShaḥar* 569). In the Talmud, too, we find such *midrash-baraitot* to "*zot torat ha-qenaot*" ("this is the law of jealousy," Num 5:29) and "*zot torat na-nazir*" ("this is the law of the Nazirite," Num 6:21) but the Sifre does not contain them. The Sifre contains, rather, a *midrash* to "*ve-zot torat ha-nazir*" ("this is the law of the Nazirite," Num 6:13). On the other hand, in the Sifre, the concluding statements "this is the law of jealousy," "this is the law of the Nazirite" are always associated with a dispute between R. Yoshia and R. Yonatan (a student of R. Ishmael). According to R. Yoshaya, the verse teaches that the commandments of this section are also valid for the altar [when the tabernacle was situated] in Nob and Gibeon; by contrast, R. Yonatan says that it is simply a concluding formula for the verse from which no new teaching can be deduced (see Malbim, *Naso*, 76 and *Ba*, 87). If we now consider that R. Yoshaya also follows R. Akiva with regard to his interpretation of the expression "*ish ish*" (in Sanhedrin 85b), whereas R. Yonatan contends that "the Torah speaks according to the language of humans," then we must consider R. Yonatan's explanation of "*zot ha-torah*" ["this is the law"] as a further consequence of his view, and conclude that the teaching "the Torah speaks according to the language of humans" was granted a further extension by certain students of R. Ishmael,[31] and had a significant influence on the formation of the *midrash*.[32]

---

term from the law; where, by contrast, in the same section of the Sifre, "*mi-reshit arisoteiḥem*" ["from the first of your dough"] is explained as "*mi-qtsatah ve-lo kulah*" ["some but not all of it"], this is not a *derash* but the plain meaning of the words.

31 One should also note that, for example, in the anonymous Sifre Num 23, it is taught: "The Torah uses two [synonymous] expressions for the same thing" [examples of such synonyms are cited (CH)].

32 Just as R. Yoshaya, though an exemplary student of R. Ishmael, follows R. Akiva with regard to this question, other students of R. Akiva adopted the view of R. Ishmael in certain cases. Thus, R. Simon (b. Ketubot 67b), R. Yosi (b. Zevaḥim 108b) and R. Meir (= "other," b. Keritot 11a). The many differences among various *tannaim* are extensively discussed in Tosafot to Sotah 24a s.v. ורבי יוחנן where it emerges that R. Ishmael accepts the principle "the Torah speaks according to the language of humans" everywhere, while R. Akiva adopts the opposite approach everywhere (see

4. e) In their exposition of holy Scripture, R. Ishmael and R. Akiva also seem to have used different methods. R. Akiva always displayed an incredible intellectual depth in his scriptural exegesis, and did not, to all appearances, follow the simple meaning of the scriptural text. Hence R. Akiva's explanations of Scripture often come across as exceptional and can only be comprehended upon thorough investigation. Many verses that the early sages could not interpret, many *halakhot* that could not be adequately supported, were explained and supported by R. Akiva with astonishing sagacity (b. Pesaḥim 22b, 96b; Bava Metzia 62a; Qiddushin 66b; Sotah 27b; Zevaḥim 13a; Menaḥot 29b; Sifre Numbers 75; Gittin 67a and Rashi there; y. Nazir 3, 52d). In contrast, R. Ishmael tends to try to explain Scripture according to the simple meaning of the words. He prefers even to apply the axiom "the Torah speaks in the language of humans" to his scriptural exegesis as licensing only those explanations that can be immediately comprehended by ordinary human understanding.

Examples: R. Ishmael always apprehends the words "*lah yittamma*'" ("for her, he may defile himself," Lev 21:3), "*le'olam bahem ta'avodu*" ("you may take them for slaves in perpetuity," Lev 25:46), and "*ve-qinne' et ishto*" ("and he is jealous of his wife," Num 5:14) as a simple permission; by contrast, for R. Akiva, they are imperatives (Sotah 3a). R. Akiva derives the traditional determination that relatives are disqualified from giving testimony from Deut 24:16; R. Ishmael, by contrast, selects another passage where this interpretation more closely approximates the simple meaning of the words (y. Sanhedrin 3, 21c). There is a dispute about the "*ki yarḥiv*" etc. [the passage from Deut 12:20–28] in b. Ḥullin 16b and 17a. According to R. Ishmael, this section is intended to permit free enjoyment of meat consumption (without offering it as a sacrifice), whereas according to R. Akiva, here we have only a prohibition of the meat of non-slaughtered animals. As Rashi explains, and Rambam and Rashba prove from *midrashim*, the difference between these views also extends to Lev 17 which, according to R. Ishmael (as the simple meaning of the words instructs), prohibits any slaughter in the desert outside the sanctuary, whereas according to R. Akiva, it speaks only of sacred animals.[33] R Akiva often revealed a more profound comprehension of the scriptural word when he, for instance, explained יְטַמֵּא = יִטַּמָּא (y. Sotah V, 20b), or תִשְׁכַּב

---

also *Mishneh laMelekh*, Hilkhot Deot 6:7 and Hilkhot Mamrim 5:1). In Sifra § *Qedoshim*, R. Yosi expresses a mediating position. In the Yerushalmi, only R. Ishmael and R. Akiva are named as representatives of the two views. The difference is rendered most apparent in the midrashic works that emerged from the schools of these *tannaim*. One will rarely find an anonymous statement in the Sifre to Numbers or the Mekhilta in which a halakhic teaching is derived from the appearance of an infinitive before a finite verb form, or a reduplicated word, whereas such derivations are found in great quantity in the Sifra (Malbim, *Ayalet HaShaḥar* 35) and also in the Sifre to Deuteronomy (60, 94, 105, 117, 119, 214, 222, 225, 228). Further details will be provided in connection with the individual midrashic works.

33 See Maimonides, *Hilkhot Sheḥitah* IV, 17–18, according to whose approach the view of R. Akiva departs less from the plain sense.

תְּשָׁכַב = [treating passive verbs as active verbs and vice versa] (Sifra § *Qĕdoshim*, see Malbim there, 109 and 114). The plain exegesis would surely accord with R. Ishmael, but a thorough investigation would endorse the words of R. Akiva (see Malbim § *Shemini* 131 and Hirsch, *Jeshurun* III, p. 410 ff.) R. Akiva's deep and keen-eyed exposition of Scripture thus found support in the scriptural text for certain *halakhot* that were formerly valid only as Sinaitic traditions, and thereby expanded the domain of *midrash* quite significantly. The *midrashim* of R. Akiva, so admired by his contemporaries, eventually gained quite general recognition, and one can also recognize his methods in certain other *midrashim*.

THE PHARISEES
A Historical Study

By Solomon Zeitlin, Dropsie College

There is an extensive literature on the Pharisees. This is due to the fact that Jesus, according to the Synoptic Gospels, had disputations with them. In Acts it is stated that Paul said he was a Pharisee.[1] The Church Fathers, in their references to the Pharisees, always assumed a hostile attitude towards them. Christian theologians, Protestants and later Catholics after the Reformation, in their studies on the life of Jesus and the origin of Christianity dealt with the Pharisees. Hence to this day we have a vast literature on the Pharisees written by Christian theologians. There are also studies on the Pharisees written by Jewish theologians.

The general view is that the Pharisees, *Perushim*, were so called because they separated themselves from the *Ame ha'aretz*[2] to avoid not only the uncleanliness of the pagans but also that of their own people who did not scrupulously observe the laws of purity. It has been held that the *Perushim* and the *Haberim* were identical.[3] Although this view is generally entertained by the Christian as well as the Jewish theologians it is historically untrue and should be disregarded. No reference is made in the entire tannaitic literature of antagonism between the *Perushim* and the *Ame ha'aretz*. There are many references to the antagonism between the *Haberim* and the *Ame ha'aretz* and these were only in regard to the laws of purity and impurity, and the laws affecting agriculture,[4] like the laws of tithe. There is no mention

---

[1] Acts 23.6.
[2] Cf. W. O. E. Oesterley, *A History of Israel*, 1932, p. 317; G. F. Moore, *Judaism*, pp. 56-62; E. Schurer, *Geschichte*, v. 2,
[3] J. Klausner, היסטוריה של הבית השני 3, p. 118-122.
[4] Cf. Mishne Demoi, 2.2-3.

whatsoever of antagonism between these two groups with regard to other precepts and laws. The reason for this is that in the early tannaitic literature the term *Ame ha'aretz* has the connotation of farmers.[5] The urban dwellers, who were scrupulous in their observance of the laws of purity and also in connection with the laws of agriculture, organized themselves as a group known as *Haberim*. They suspected the *Ame ha'aretz*, the farmers, of not observing the laws of purity and impurity,[6] and also the laws in relation to agriculture.[7] They suspected the *Ame ha'aretz* of not giving the necessary tithe to the Levites.[8] Hence they did not associate with the *Ame ha'aretz* nor did they partake of meals with them.[9] To repeat—there is no reference in the entire tannaitic literature of disputations between the Pharisees and the *Ame ha'aretz*. This literature records disputations between the Sadducees and the Pharisees.

It has also been held that the Pharisees separated themselves from the Essenes.[10] This view likewise is untenable since there is no reference in the entire tannaitic literature to any discussion between the Essenes and the Pharisees. If the Pharisees separated from the Essenes, *Hasidim*, we would find record of controversies between them. There is no mention in the tannaitic literature of any dialogues between the Essenes, *Hasidim*, and the Pharisees, while we do find dialogues between the Sadducees and the Pharisees.[11]

It has also been suggested that the term *Perushim* has the connotation of interpreters, interpreters of the Pentateuch.[12] There is no foundation for this view. The Term *Perushim* in

---

[5] See S. Zeitlin, "The Am Haarez" *JQR*, 1932, pp. 45-61.
[6] M. Toh. 7.5; 8.1; Tos. ibid. 8.2,3,4; 9. 11.
[7] M. Demoi, 2. 3; 6. 9; Tos. 2. 2,15,17.20, 21, 22.
[8] Cf. Tos. Sotah 13.10; Yer. ibid. 9.11. מקצתן מעשרין ומקצתן אין מעשרין.
[9] Cf. M. Demoi, 2.3. ואינו מתארח אצל עם הארץ.
[10] J. Klausner, ibid. 3. p. 118; Moore, *op. cit.*. pp. 60-62.
[11] See Mishne Yad. 4.6,7. S. Zeitlin, הצדוקים והפרושים.
[12] Cf. Moore, *op. cit.*

the sense of party, group or a philosophy is not found in the entire tannaitic literature. If indeed the name *Perushim* was adopted by a certain group because they interpreted the words of the Pentateuch, or because they were scrupulous in observance of the laws of purity and separated themselves from those who did not observe these laws, their name would appear in the tannaitic literature, since it was produced by them. We frequently find the expression, "The sages said" [13] of "The sayings of the Soferim," [14] but we never find "The Pharisees said" or "The sayings of the Pharisees". There are no halakot given in the name of the Pharisees.

The foregoing discussion leads us to the conclusion that the term Pharisees, *Perushim*, was not the name adopted by a group of people who followed a certain philosophy. Pharisees, *Perushim*, was a nickname applied to them by their adversaries. Who were their adversaries? The answer is the Zadokites, Sadducees.

The question now confronting us is—when did the conflict between the Sadducees and the Pharisees come about? In other words we must ascertain when the Pharisaism came into being as a philosophy in opposition to the ideas and ideologies of the Sadducees. The general view is that the Pharisees came into being early in the Hasmonean period. [15] There are difficulties in the acceptance of this view. First— What ideological forces brought about the genesis of the Pharisees? The Hasmonean were not of the Zadokite family. Furthermore how could the Sadducees nickname those who opposed them *Perushim*, Pharisees, separatists? From whom did they separate? At that time the Pharisees were in the ascendancy in influence and power while the Sadducees were in decline. Moreover the main contention between these two groups was the question of the validity of oral law.

Speaking historically we cannot assume that the question

---

[13] ‏חכמים אומרים‎.
[14] ‏אין דנין דברי תורה מדברי סופרים‎.
[15] Schurer, *op. cit.* Moore, ibid., Klausner, *op. cit.*

of the validity of the oral law arose in the early Hasmonean period. The Judean community had been in existence for centuries. The Pentateuch was canonized after the return of the Judaeans from Babylonia centuries before the Hasmonean period. What then brought up the question of the validity of oral law at such a late period after the canonization of the Pentateuch? We believe that it came at the time that the Pentateuch was canonized. The Pentateuch does not contain all laws. At the time of the canonization of the Pentateuch the Judaeans had many laws not included in it.[16]

In the writings of the prophets as well as in the Hagiographa there are references to customs and laws that are not found in the Pentateuch. In the book of Jeremiah it is stated that when the prophet bought a field from Hanamel he wrote a deed in the presence of witnesses who affixed their signatures.[17] There is no mention in the Pentateuch of the requirement of a deed and witnesses in the transfer of real property. In the book of Ruth it is said that Boaz told his kinsman that he would have to marry Ruth when he purchased the field from Naomi, "in order to restore the name of the dead to his inheritance." It is further stated that this was the custom, "In former times in Israel concerning redeeming and exchanging, to confirm a transaction, the one drew off his sandal and gave it to the other, and this was the manner of attesting in Israel." [18] This custom of transferring immovable property by the symbolic act of drawing off the shoe is not mentioned in the Pentateuch. From the book of II Kings we learn that if a man did not pay his debts, his creditor had the right to take him into servitude. If he died and left the debt unpaid the creditor could enslave his children. It is said in this book that a woman cried to the prophet Elisha, "Your servant, my husband, is dead and you know that your servant feared Yahweh, but the creditors come to take my

[16] Cf. S. Zeitlin, "The Halaka," *JQR*, 1948,
[17] Jer. 32. 9-10.
[18] Ruth, 4.7.

children to be slaves." [19] This law is not mentioned in the Pentateuch. It is stated in the book of Haggai that God told the prophet to examine the priests on the laws of sanctity and impurity. "Ask now the priests Torah (law) saying 'If one bare hallowed pledge in the skirt of his garment, and with his skirt do touch bread or butter, or wine, or oil, or any food, shall it become holy? and the priests answered and said No.' Then said Haggai, 'If one that is unclean by a dead body touch any of these, shall it be unclean?' And the priests answered and said, 'He shall be unclean' ". [20] These two laws about which Haggai questioned the priests are not found in the Pentateuch, but apparently the prophet thought that they should be familiar with the laws of sanctification and defilement.

It is evident from the book of Genesis that among the early Hebrews a man had to purchase his wife from her father. Jacob paid Laban in manual labor for the privilege of marrying his daughters. [21] David paid King Saul two hundred foreskins of the Philistines for the right to marry his daughter Michal. [22] The Pentateuch makes no mention of a writ in connection with marriage. However such a document is recorded in the Elephantine papyri. [23] We learn from the book of Tobit that when Raguel gave his daughter Sarah to Tobit he called her mother "and wrote an instrument of cohabitation."[24]

Hence it is evident that at the time of the Restoration and the canonization of the Pentateuch there were in vogue many laws and customs which were not found in the Pentateuch. The unwritten laws were as old and perhaps older than some of those embodied in the Pentateuch. The sages of the Talmud recognized this when they said that, "In the days of mourning for Moses thousands of Halakot were forgotten." [25]

[19] II Kings, 4. 1.   [20] Hag. 2. 11-13.
[21] Gen. 29. 15-28.
[22] I Sam. 25-27.
[23] Cowley, *Aramaic Papyri of the Fifth Century B.C.*
[24] Tobit 7. 11-14.
[25] Tem. 16. שלשת אלפים הלכות נשתכחו בימי אבלו של משה.

It was at the time of the canonization of the Pentateuch that there arose a difference of views, ideology, in regard to the *Halakot*. One group maintained that only the laws recorded in the Pentateuch are binding and had to be followed, while the customs which had come in vogue among the people, *i.e.* oral law, are not binding. The other group maintained that the customs, oral law, are as binding as the laws given in the Pentateuch. Those two diverse ideologies could only arise when the Pentateuch was canonized and the question of binding of the unwritten law confronted the people.

The validity of the unwritten law has been considered by all peoples. Sophocles made Antigone justify the burying of Polynices, against the order of King Creon, on the basis of "the immutable unwritten laws of god. They were not born today nor yesterday; they die not and none knoweth whence they sprang." [26] Aristotle said that customs are more sovereign than the written laws. [27] Cicero has well remarked that law had its origin ages before any written law existed or any state had been established. [28] Philo, who lived centuries after the Restoration and in a Greek environment, wrote in his book *The Special Laws* "For customs are unwritten laws, the decisions approved by man of old, not inscribed on monuments or leaves of paper, which the moth destroys, but on the souls of those who are partners in the same society." [29]

Taking into consideration that the law givers of all the peoples revered the unwritten law it can hardly be assumed that there was a group among the Judaeans who entirely

[26] ὥστ' ἄγραπτα κἀσιραλῆ θεῶν νόμμα δύνασθαι θνητὸν ὄνθ ὑπερδραμεῖν...

[27] ἔτι κυριώτεροι καὶ περὶ κυριωτέρων τῶν κατὰ γράμματα νόμων οἱ κατὰ τὰ ἔθη εἰσιν. *Politics*, 3. 1287b.

[28] ...*quae saeclis omnibus ante nata est quam scripta lex ulla aut quam omnino civitas constituta. Laws*, I. 6,

[29] ἔθη γὰρ ἄγραφοι νόμοι δόγματα παλαιῶν ἀνδρῶν οὐ στήλαις ἐγκεχαραγμένα καὶ χαρτιδίοις ὑπὸ σητῶν ἀναλισκομένοις ἀλλὰ ψυχαῖς τῶν μετειληφότων τῆς αὐτῆς πολιτείας. 4. 28.

ignored the value of the unwritten law. No state, large or small, can function only on written laws and ignore the unwritten law. All peoples had unwritten laws.

Josephus, in his account of the rift between John Hyrcanus I and the Pharisees, wrote, "The Pharisees passed on to the people certain regulations handed down by the traditions of the fathers and they were not written in the Laws of Moses, for which reason they are rejected by the Sadducaean group, who hold that only those laws should be considered valid which were written down, and that those which came down by tradition of the fathers need not be observed." [30] Josephus, in *Antiquities*, describing the different sects which existed in Judaea, wrote that "They (Sadducees) do not regard the observation of anything besides what the law enjoins them. They consider it a virtue to have frequent disputations with the teachers of learning." [31]

From Josephus it is evident that the Sadducees rejected the "traditions of the fathers", *i.e.* the unwritten law. Likewise from the tannaitic literature we learn that the Sadducees rejected the unwritten law. Thus we seem to contradict our observation that all peoples have unwritten laws besides the written laws and that no state could exist without unwritten laws. Our observation is supported by the prophetic books and by the Scriptures from which we have the right to deduce that the Judaeans when they returned from Babylonia followed customs which were observed by the people, *i.e.* unwritten laws. What then was the conflict regarding the observance of unwritten laws to which Josephus referred and is substantiated by the tannaitic literature?

[30] νῦν δὲ δηλῶσαι βούλομαι ὅτι νόμιμά τινα παρέδοσαν τῷ δήμῳ οἱ Φαρισαῖοι ἐκ πατέρων διαδοχῆς ἅπερ οὐκ ἀναγέγραπται ἐν τοῖς Μωυσέος νομοις καί διὰ τοῦτο ταῦτα τὸ τῶν Σαδδουκαίων γένος ἐκβάλλει λέγον ἐκεῖνα δεῖν ἡγεῖσθαι νόμιμα τὰ γεγραμμένα τὰ δ' ἐκ παραδόσεως τῶν πατέρων μὴ τηρεῖν, *Ant.* 13. 10,6 (297).
[31] .... φυλακῇ δὲ οὐδαμῶς τινων μεταποίησις αὐτοῖς ἢ τῶν νόμων πρὸς γάρ τοὺς διδασκάλους σοφίας ἣν μετίασεν ἀμφιλογεῖν ἀρετὴν ἀριθμοῦσιν. 18. 1,4(16)

The difference between these two groups was that one group, while accepting the unwritten law considered that no person could be punished for non-observance of it, that it was not on a par with the written law. Another group maintained that many of the unwritten laws should be on a par with the written laws and should be made statutory laws, thus that new laws could be deduced from them, just as new laws were deduced from the written laws, the Torah. Any one who transgressed the unwritten law would than be as liable to punishment as if he had transgressed the written laws. [32] This was indeed an evasion of the accepted view.

Aristotle, who held that customs are more sovereign than the written laws, wrote, "The written laws involve compulsion, the unwritten do not." [33] In other words he held that a person cannot be punished if he transgressed the unwritten laws. These were valuable for society but were not binding. Philo said, as was noted before, that the unwritten laws are the decisions approved by men of old and that they are inscribed on the souls of those who are partners in the same citizenship. He wrote, "Praise cannot be duly given to one who obeys the written laws, since he acts under the admonition of restraint and the fear of punishment. But he who faithfully observes the unwritten deserves commendation, since the virtue which he displays is freely willed." [34] Thus Philo held that one who transgresses an unwritten law cannot be punished. In other words the unwritten laws are not binding. Most likely Philo copied Aristotle's view as he usually echoed the Greek philosophers.

The clash of the different views on the binding of the oral law on man could not have arisen during the Hasmonean period when the Judaean community had been in existence

[32] Cf. M. Sanh. 10.4. חומר דברי סופרים מדברי תורה.
[33] ... Τὰ μὲν οὖν γεγραμένα ἐξ ἀνάγκες τὰ δ' αγραφα οὔ ἄλλον δὲ τρόπον εἰ παρὰ τὰ γεγραμμενα ... *Rhetoric* 1.14.
[34] ὁ μὲν γὰρ τοῖς ἀναγραφεῖσι νόμοις πειθαρχῶν οὐκ ἂν δεόντως ἐπαινοῖτο νουθετούμενος ἀνάγκῃ καὶ φόβῳ κολάσεως ὁ δὲ τοῖς ἀγράφοις ἐμμένων ἑκούσιον ἐπιδεικνύμενος τὴν ἀρετὴν ἐγκωμιων ἄξιος, *Special Laws* 4.28.

for many centuries. It could come only after the Pentateuch was canonized. Then the question arose—have the laws which were in vogue among the people but were not embodied in the Pentateuch the validity as the Pentateuchal laws and are they as binding? One group, the conservative, headed by the high priests of the family of Zadok, held that the unwritten laws are not on a par with the Pentateuchal laws. Another group, particularly the natives of Judaea and not those who had returned from Babylonia, held that the unwritten laws were on a par with the Pentateuchal laws. Later the followers of this group held that the unwritten laws were more important than the laws of the Pentateuch and even favored them above the Torah. [35] According to the prophetic books of Haggai and Zechariah two men headed the return of the exiles to Judaea. One was Joshua, of the family of Zaddok, the grandson of the High Priest Seraiah, who had been killed by the Babylonians, the other was Zerubbabel, of the Davidic family, grandson of King Jehoiachin. From these books we also know that there was a clash between the two men, rather a clash was between the two factions headed by them. Those who maintained that the new community should be organized on a religious basis were the followers of Joshua, while those who believed that the Judaean community should be organized under civil authority were the followers of Zerubbabel, who was a scion of the family of David. Thus the clash was between the followers of the priestly family, the Zadokites, and those who were followers of the Davidic family. Apparently Zerubbabel and his followers contemplated the use of force against their opponents. The prophet Zechariah said to him, "This is the word of Yahweh unto Zerubbabel, saying: 'Not by might nor by power, but by My spirit' said Yahweh"[36] Zechariah tried to affect a reconciliation between Zerubbabel and Joshua. When the Judaeans remaining in Babylonia sent gold and silver

[35] ‏חביבים מדברי תורה‏· Yer. Sanh. 10.4.
[36] 4.6.

to Jerusalem, Zechariah stated in the name of Yahweh that crowns were to be made for both men. He further declared, "the counsel of peace shall be between them both." [37] The prophecy was not fulfilled. Peace was not established between the two leaders nor harmony between their ideologies.

The followers of Joshua were victorious. [38] The defeat of Zerubbabel and his disappearance did not, however, eradicate the view that the new community should be headed by a secular leader, by a scion of the family of David, rather than by a high priest of the family of Zadok. This view had many adherents, particularly among those who were not among the former exiles but had remained in Judaea. After the Restoration a profound change took place in Judaean religion which revolutionized the history not only of the Judaeans but the entire western world. From the prophetic books we learn that King Solomon built a House for Yahweh. [39] It was termed the House of Yahweh throughout the Bible. When the Babylonians conquered Judaea they burned the House of Yahweh. [40] We also know from the books of Ezra and Nehemia that the people who returned from Babylonia built a House for Yahweh. [41] However, in the tannaitic literature as well as in the apocryphal books and in the writings of Josephus the term House of Yahweh does not appear. The term given is Sanctuary, [42] the Sacred House, sometimes simply the House [43] but never House of Yahweh. This is not a matter of change in terms but a change in the entire idea of God among the Judaeans. Originally Yahweh was an ethnic God of the people, descendants of Abraham,

---

[37] 6. 13.

[38] The forces which brought about the victory of Joshua over Zerubbabel will be dealt with in my forthcoming book *The Rise and the Fall of the Judaean State*: Published by The Jewish Publication Society of America.

[39] Cf. I kings 6.1.

[40] II Kings 25. 9; Jer. 52. 13.

[41] Cf. Ezra 3.8; Neh. 10.36.

[42] בית המקדש.

[43] הבית.

Isaac and Jacob with whom Yahweh made a covenant to be their God and their children to be His epople. When Yahweh took the children of Abraham, Isaac and Jacob out of bondage in Egypt he thus became the God of their descendants. [44] The Judaeans who were the descendants of Abraham, Isaac and Jacob became the chosen people of Yahweh. Foreign people could not join the Judaeans, no converts could become part of the Judaean community or accept its religion. There is no reference to proselytism in the Pentateuch. The word *ger*, there, has the connotation of sojourner in the Pentateuch, one who lived in a foreign country. The Pentateuch refers to the children of Israel as *gerim* who lived in the land of Egypt.[45] There were, however, those who opposed these ideas, maintaining that Yahweh is not only the God of the Judaeans but the God of all peoples. The prophet Amos said, "O children of Israel? saith Yahweh, have not I brought up Israel out of the land of Egypt and the Philistines from Caphtor and Aram from Kir?" [46] What the prophet Amos said was that Yahweh takes care of other peoples besides Israel.

In the prophecies which have come down to us under the name of Isaiah there is a challenge against the building of a House for Yahweh. It is said, "Thus saith Yahweh heaven is my throne and the earth is my footstool. What is the house which you would build for Me and what is the place which will be My rest?" [47] These words were uttered not as a prophecy but as a challenge to those who returned from Babylonia and began to build a house and called it the House of Yahweh. The prophet protested against the building of a House for Yahweh, He is everywhere.

It is understandable that the views held that the oral law is on a par with the Pentateuchal laws, that the leadership of the new community should be vested not in the hands of

[44] Cf. Lev. 26. 13, 45; Deut. 4.20, 6.20; 29,24; Judg. 2. 12; 6.8-9. S. Zeitlin, "Judaism as a Religion," *JQR*, 1943, pp. 331-332.
[45] Cf. Ex. 23.8; Lev. 19.34, 25.6.
[46] 9.7.
[47] Is. 66.1.

the high priest but that a scion of the family of David should rule, and that Yahweh is not only the God of the Judaeans but the God of all the peoples was considered heretical in the eyes of the high priestly family, the *Zadukim*, Sadducees. Those who held these heretical views were nicknamed *Perushim*, Pharisees, separatists, separated from the Judaean people, from God. The word *Perushim* was a nickname created by *Zadukim* as a term of reproach and contempt.[48] Those who separated from the uncleanliness of the people of the land, the pagans, were signified by the term נבדלים separatists.[49] Those Judaeans who did not conform with the norm laid down by the high priestly family, the *Zedukim*, were called פרושים separatists, who had separated from the people of Judaea.

If, as we maintain, the *Perushim*, Pharisees, came into being shortly after the time of the Restoration and the name given them was one of opprobrium, why does not their name found in the book of Ezra? The name Pharisee first occurs in *Antiquities*—where Josephus relates the history of Jonathan the Hasmonean.[50] This is readily explained. The book of Ezra is tendentious (showing its genuineness) giving all the credit to those who returned from exile and ignoring those Judaeans who remained in the land after Babylonia had conquered the country. As was noted before, not only the poorest class remained but many members of the military class as well as many of the royal family.[51] The prophets Haggai, Zechariah and Malachi were Judaeans, they were not of those who returned from exile. The encouragement and prophetic words to the returned exiles came from the prophet Isaiah, a Judaean.[52]

At that time the arch enemies of the Judaeans were the Samaritans. Their name is ignored in the books of Ezra and

[48] Cf. S. Zeitlin, הצדוקים והפרושים.
[49] Cf. Ezra 7.21; 9.1.
[50] 13. 5, 9(171-173); *Jewish War*, 2.8,
[51] Cf. II Kings 25.22-25; Jer. 40.6-14; 41.1.
[52] Is. chs. 48-52.

Nehemiah. In the book of Ezra it is said that when the people who had returned from exile began to build the House for Yahweh the adversaries of Judah and Benjamin heard that the children of the exiles were building a Temple to Yahweh and offered to join them. [53] The author does not indentify the adversaries. We learn from Josephus that they were the Samaritans. [54] Sanballat was the leader of the Samaritans, who strove to prevent the building of the House for Yahweh. His name does not occur in the book of Ezra. Nehemiah does mention a man named Sanballat but does not identify him as the head of the Samaritan group. The books of Ezra and Nehemiah ignore mention of those who were their enemies. They even ignored mention of those Judaeans who had remained in the country. They passed in silence all those opposed to their views. They ignored mention of those who did not follow the doctrines laid down by the leaders who had returned from exile and by the high priestly families, the *Zadukim*. That is the reason there is no reference to the heretics *Perushim*, Pharisees in the books of Ezra and Nehemiah.

The leadership, religious as well as secular, of the new Judaean community was held by the high priest of the *Zadokite* family. [55] The Pharisees had no voice in managing the new community. After the triumph of the Hasmoneans, who were victorious over the Syrian oppressors, they also succeeded in the removal of the high priest of the *Zadokite* family from leadership. The Pharisees who supported the Hasmoneans were now in the ascendant. Josephus, in relating the history of Jonathan, the Hasmonean, made reference to the three sects which now dominated the Judaean community.

Though during the long period from the time of Ezra to

---

[53] Ezra 4.1. וישמעו צרי יהודה.

[54] *Ant.* 11. 4, 3 (84).

[55] Ibid. 4,9(111), For the high priests were at the head of affairs until the descendants of the Hasmonaean family came to rule as kings. Οἱ γὰρ ἀρχιερεῖς προεστήκεσαν τῶν πραγμάτων ἄχρις οὗ τοὺς 'Ασαμωναίου συνέβη βασιλεύειν ἐκγόνους.

the Hasmonean the Pharisees did not dominate the life of the Judaeans, nevertheless their influence in shaping the Judaean religion was of great significance. As was noted before in the biblical books the Sanctuary was called the House of Yahweh but there voices against such nomenclature since Yahweh is the God of the universe, He is everywhere, no house can be built to him. Ben Sirach, who wrote Ecclesiastes, circa 200 BCE, in writing about the Babylonians who captured Jerusalem, said that they burned the Sanctuary. [56] He did not say that they burned the House of Yahweh as is stated in the biblical books. In speaking of about Zerubbabel and Joshua, he refered to them as those "who in their time builded the house and set up a holy temple to the Lord." [57] He does not call it the House of Yahweh as it is called in the biblical books. Again, in his glorification of the High Priest Simon, son of Onias, he wrote, "who in his life repaired the house again, and in his days fortified the temple." [58] The author of the first Book of Maccabees, in describing the desolation and profanation of the Temple by the forces of Antiochus Epiphanes, did not call it the House of Yahweh but Sanctuary. Similarly, in his account of the victory over the Syrians, he also called it the Temple, not House of Yahweh. [59] This change of nomenclature is not only a change of terms but has a wider meaning indicating a change in the ideology of the Judaeans toward their religion.

A story about the Pharisees is given in the Talmud. It is stated that one Sadducee said to John Hyrcanus I (in the Talmud he is called Jannaeus) that the Pharisees were not loyal to him. He inquired how he could find it out and was told that he should give them an oath, an oath of allegiance. One man by the name of Judah said to John Hyrcanus, "Too much for you the crown of kingdom, [60] leave the crown

[56] 49.6,   [57] Ibid. ναὸν.
[58] 50.1.
[59] I. Mac. 4. 41, 48.
[60] Kid. 66. רב לך כתר מלכות Cf. Num. 16.7. רב לכם בני לוי. Cf. also *Ant*. 13. 16, 5(291),

of priesthood to the descendants of Aaron," *i.e.* the true children of Aaron, the descendants of Zadok. [61]

John Hyrcanus I, who had been a follower of the Pharisees, now became angry with them and left them, joining the Sadducees. This passage recording the rift between him and the Pharisees is significant. The story begins with the statement that one man, a Sadducee, told Hyrcanus that the "Pharisees" were not loyal to him. The Sadducees called their opponents Pharisees. [62] However, at the end of the story, where the Talmud itself relates the consequence of the rift, the name Pharisees is not mentioned but sages is given. [63] This again shows that the term Pharisees was never applied by the sages to themselves but only by the Sadducees. At the end of his life John Hyrcanus contemplated declaring himself king. This was opposed by the Pharisees who maintained that the crown of the kingdom belonged to a scion of David. Some of their extremists even thought that Hyrcanus was not a true heir of the high priesthood, not being a scion of Zadok. Josephus also wrote about the rift between the Pharisees and John Hyrcanus I. Josephus named the Sadduceean spokesman Jonathan while the Talmud has Eleazar. The critic of Hyrcanus was named Eleazar by Josephus while the Talmud named him Judah. According to Josephus Eleazar told Hyrcanus, "If you wish to be righteous give up the high priesthood and be content with governing the people." [64] This does not contradict the talmudic statement that his critics were against his contemplation of becoming king. Josephus plainly said that he should be content with having the title of leader of the people, the title which was given his father by the Great Synagogue.

The word *Perushim* in the Talmud had the connotation of separatists, those who made a point of separating themselves

---

[61] Cf. I Mac. 7. 14.
[62] לבם של פרושים עליך.
[63] ויבדלו חכמי ישראל בזעם.
[64] Ant. Ibid. καὶ μόνον ἀρκείτω σοι τὸ ἄρχειν τοῦ λαοῦ.

from particular objects for some reason. The Talmud states that after the destruction of the Second Temple there were many *Perushim* who separated themselves by not eating meat nor drinking wine as a sign of mourning for the Temple. [65] The Talmud also refers to a man named Judah and his son who separated themselves from the academy and settled in the south. [66] The Mishne in Hag., which gives different degrees of impurity has "The garments of the *Am Haretz* are unclean to the *Perushim*" i.e. those who separate themselves from uncleanliness. "The garments of the *Perushim* are unclean to those who eat *terumah*, teruma is more sacred than maaser. The garments of those who eat teruma are unclean to Hallow things. [67] This Mishne, as indicated by the previous Mishne, deals with the degrees of purity and impurity and not with groups. [68]

The Talmud also makes reference to seven types of *Perushim*, those who separated themselves to show their exclusiveness and piety. The Mishne calls them the plague of the *Perushim*. [69] The seven types enumerated in the Talmud, who separated themselves from the rest of the people, were consciously dishonest. [70] One of them—a man who walked with closed eyes, stumbled and hurt himself, saying that he did this so as not to look at women. [71] This as well as the other six types of *Perushim* were those who separated themselves from the rest of society to show that they were superior in piety and more devoted to the precepts of God. These

[65] Talmud B.B. 60 כשחרב הבית בשניה רבו פרושין בישראל שלא לאכול בשר ושלא לשתות יין.
[66] Pes. 70 תניא יהודה בן דורתאי הוא ודורתאי בנו והלך וישב לו בדרום.... אמר רב אשי ואנן טעמא דפרושים ניקו ונפרש.
[67] M. Hag. 2.4. בגדי עם הארץ מדרס לפרושין בגדי פרושין מדרס לאוכלי תרומה בגדי אוכלי תרומה מדרס לקודש בגדי קודש מדרס לחטאת.
[68] Ibid. 5. הטובל לחולין והוחזק לחולין אסור למעשר טבל למעשר והוחזק למעשר אסור לתרומה טבל לתרומה והוחזק לתרומה אסור לקודש טבל לקודש והוחזק לקודש אסור לחטאת.
[69] M. Sotah חסיד שוטה ורשע ערום ואשה פרושה ומכות פרושין.
[70] Yer. ibid. זו מכת פרושין נגעו בו.
[71] Bab. ibid. 22. פרוש נקפי זה המנקוף את רגליו.

types of men were stamped as the plague of the *Perushim*, separatists from society.

In the Talmud it is related that when Jannaeus Alexander was on his death bed he told his wife not to fear the *Perushim*, Pharisees, nor the non-*Perushim* but to beware of those persons like *Zimri* who are wicked and present themselves as righteous like Phinehas, grandson of Aaron who killed Zimri.[72] It was perfectly proper for Jannaeus Alexander, who was a Sadducee, to call his opponents *Perushim*, Pharisees.

The name, *Perushim*, originally coined as a term of reproach and contempt, became at a later time one of respect. An analagous use of contemptuous terms in names may be found throughout history. In the eighteenth century there came into existence a sect named Hassidim. The Jews who opposed their theories were nicknamed by them *Mitnagdim*, a term of contempt. The opponents of the Hassidim did not called themselves *Mitnagdim*, but did so at a later date and it ceased to be a term of contempt. In the sixteenth century reformers arose against the pope. The catholics termed them protestants, a name of contempt. Later the term Protestants was adopted by all Christians who opposed catholicism. The Friends were nicknamed Quakers by other Christians. In later days, however, many Friends so called themselves. History is replete with examples of this nicknaming propensity. Similarly the word *Perushim* became one of respect and its original meaning was lost. Josephus who used the term probably did not know how it arose.

Jannaeus Alexander before his death advised his wife to beware of the "tainted", *i.e.*, hypocrites. Unscrupulous people often join a popular movement merely to further their own interests. Assocation with a distinguished group casts its aura of respectability upon questionable characters. Certainly evil and designing persons joined the Pharisees for

[72] Sotah 22, אמר ינאי מלכא לדביתיה אל תתיראי מן הפרושין ולא ממי שאינן פרושין אלא מן הצבועין שדומין לפרושין שמעשיהן כמעשה זמרי ומבקשין שכר כפנחס.

their own purposes. Undoubtedly there were many hypocrites among the Jews of that period as there were among other peoples.

Pious and humble men who abandoned worldly affairs attired themselves in black garments and walked slowly with downcast faces.[73] The wearing of black signified humility and piety. (The wearing of black garments is still considered a symbol of piety.) Dishonest men, in order to make people believe that they were righteous and trustworthy, wore black clothes. Species of hypocrisy prevailed in those days. *Tephilin* contained Pentateuchal passages and hence could be worn by those who observed the physical laws of cleanliness and were spiritually pure.[74] The wearing of them by a person indicated that he was pious and observed the laws. However, in many cases, the wearing of *tephilin* gave rise to hypocrisy. In the Palestinian Talmud it is related that a man who wore *tephilin* refused to return a sum of money that had been placed with him and he denied ever having received it. The man who had intrusted the money to him said, "I had confidence in the *tephilin* which you wore."[75] He made this statement because *tephilin* were worn only by pious people. Not all the Judaeans during the Second Commonwealth wore *tephilin*. It seems that even during the Middle Ages not all the Jews wore *tephilin*.[76]

The Pentateuchal injunction that "It shall be for a sign unto thee upon thy hand, and for a memorial between thine eyes"[77] may have had its origin as phylacteries but lost its original significance during the Second Commonwealth. To render *tephilin* by the term phylacteries is erroneous.[78] The

---

[73] Cf. Ben Sirach 19.23, ἔστι πονηρευόμενος συγκεκυφὼς μελανίᾳ.
[74] Cf. Shab. 49; Yer. Ber. 2.3.
[75] Ber. Ibid. עובדא הוה בחד בר בש דאפקיד גביה חבריה וכפר ביה אמר ליה לא לך הימנית אלא לאלין דבירישך הימנית.
[76] ואין תימא על מה שמצוה זאת רפויה בידנו שגם בימי חכמים היתה רפויה Tosafot Shab. 49.
[77] Ex. 13. 9; Deut. 6.8.
[78] See below p. 122.

Greek word φυλακτήρια phylacteria has the meaning of talisman, protective charm. The wearing of *tephilin* is not for the purpose of a protective charm but to remind the wearer of the power of God.

The Pharisees as leaders of the people sought to solve their religious problems. They offered to explain why the virtuous suffered and the wicked prospered. The Pharisees formulated the concept of the future world, teaching that the soul was incorruptible, that it held an immortal element and that reward and punishment were in store for those lived virtuously and wickedly respectively. They held that the body was a prison for the soul and that after death the soul would be released from it. [79] Some of these views were held by other peoples but the Pharisees either adopted them and shaped them according with their views or developed them independently.

The Pharisees held that men were the children of God and were under His Providence. Although they thought that every deed depends on fate and God, they believed in the freedom of man to act as he thinks, that he can exercise his will and act virtuously or evilly. But they also maintained that there was some cooperation of fate with men's deeds. The Sadducees denied both resurrection and providence, [80] neither of which is mentioned in the Pentateuch. They believed, however, that God takes care of the Jewish people as a whole but not as individuals.

The differences between the Sadducees and the Pharisees about the idea of God went much deeper. The Sadducees, who followed the Pentateuch literally, maintained that Yahweh is the God of the Judaeans only, that he is the creater of heaven and earth, superior to all other gods, that He is an ethnic God, that He is the God only of the descendants of Abraham, Isaac and Jacob who cannot worship other gods. They held that other peoples could not join the Judaeans and

[79] *Ant.* 18. 1, 3(12-15).
[80] Ibid. 13.5,9(171-173).

worship Yahweh. They did not recognize proselytism. The Pharisees, on the other hand, believed that Yahweh is the God of the universe, of all peoples and that anyone could join Jews and worship him. Thus the Pharisees favored proselytism.[81] This view had already been propagated by some of the prophets. The very pronunciation of Yahweh was changed, it was no longer pronounced as it is written. The Talmud states that while it is written *yod he* it is pronounced *alef dalet*,[82] in other words it is written Yahweh but pronounced *Adonai* to indicate that the God of the Jews is not an ethnic God but the God of the universe. Some of the biblical books have the word *Adonai* preceding Yahweh. The traditional pronunciation is *Adonai Elohim*, the Lord God. We are, however, confronted with the problem: If the original pronunciation of these four letters *yod he waw he* was to be pronounced *Elohim* why was it not so written? The word *Elohim* occurs frequently in the Bible. As a matter of fact the Septuagint renders these two words κύριος κύριος Lord Lord.[83] Those who rendered the biblical books into Greek read it *Adonai Adonai*.

The expression ארני יהוה is found only four times in the Pentateuch. In Deuteronomy 3. 23, where Moses began to beseech God to let him enter the land beyond the Jordan in the words אדני יהוה tradition rendered the words Lord God. Again in 9. 26 where Moses prayed to God not to destroy the children of Israel in the words אדני יהוה here again tradition renders the words Lord God. It is a probability that in these two places where the word אדני יהוה preceded Yahweh it should be read אֲדֹנִי[84] and should be rendered my Lord Yahweh. In Exodus 23.17 the text has פני האדן יהוה which tradition renders the Lord God. The Septuagint renders it the "lord

---

[81] חביבים גרים.
[82] Yer. Sanh. 10.1. נכתב ביוד הא ונקרא באלף דלת.
[83] Cf. Is. 22. 12, 16; 30. 15; 40.10; 65.13; Jer. 7.20. Those who rendered the biblical books into Greek read it *Adonai Adonai*. Some Greek manuscripts of Ezekiel have *Adonai*.
[84] Cf. Numb. 11. 28; 12. 11. Cf. also Gen. 15. 2; 8.

thy God." [85] The authors of the Septuagint had the reading in the Pentateuch פני יהוה אלהיך. This reading is partially substantiated in the Sifre.[86]

The expression of *Adonai* Yahweh occurs frequently in the Bible, sometimes only Yahweh without the addition of *Adonai*, and in a few instances only *Adonai*. In the book of Ezekiel *Adonai* Yahweh predominates, while in the book of Joel *Adonai* Yahweh does not occur, only Yahweh.

It seems that the word *Adonai* was added in the Bible when the Judaeans no longer considered Yahweh an ethnic God but the God of the universe. They no longer pronounced Yahweh as spelled but *Adonai*, Lord of the universe. Only the high priest in the Temple pronounced the name of God as it was written. How he pronounced the four letters we do not know. All the theories advanced as to how the four letters were pronounced are only guess work. Neither can it be explained why in some books of the Bible we find *Adonai* Yahweh, in some Yahweh, and in some passages only *Adonai*. We may, however, say with certainty that in the Pentateuch, the oldest, most sacred and revered book, the expression *Adonai* Yahweh does not occur.

With the successful revolt of the Hasmoneans the Pharisees gained great power. Their domination in the matters of religion can be said to have begun. Now they endeavored to put their views into practice. First they sought to democratize the institutions of the Judaeans, beginning with the Temple.

According to the Pentateuchal law sacrifices were brought to the Temple every day, morning and afternoon. The Sadducees, who consisted of the wealthy class and who sought to monopolize the Temple, maintained that the daily sacrifices should be considered private matters so that any individual could provide the lamb slaughtered in his own name. Only the rich could afford the luxury of such a sacrifice. They

---

[85] Κυρίου τοῦ θεοῦ σου.
[86] והלא כבר נאמר את פני האדון יי אלהיך ומה תלמוד לומר אלהי ישראל.

could either bring a lamb for the daily sacrifice or offer to the Temple treasury the necessary money for purchasing it.

The Pharisees, on the other hand, from the time of the establishment of the Judaean community maintained that religion should not be a matter of interest to a few people but that it should be so to all persons, which meant that all should participate in the religious ceremonies, Israelites as well as the priests. Hence the Pharisees now established the rule that the daily sacrifices should be provided by the entire Judaean community. The money for their purpose now came from the funds of the Temple treasury to which every Judaean had contributed his equitable portion.[87]

But the Pharisees were not entirely satisfied and sought to further democratize the institution of the daily sacrifice. They wanted the entire people to participate in the slaughtering of the daily sacrifice in the morning and the afternoon. To this end they instituted the following arrangement: The Israelite inhabitants of each city, town and village were divided into twenty-four divisions called *Maamadot* (communal divisions). The members of each *Maamad* were to go to the Temple to take part in the ceremony of the slaughtering of the daily sacrifices. The members of these communal divisions represented the entire inhabitants of Judaea. But not all Israelites of the division could go or wished to go to Jerusalem. Therefore it was arranged by the Pharisees that those who remained at home should gather in their respective cities and towns on the days on which they were supposed to be in the Temple and read portions of the Pentateuch relating to the sacrifices.[88] The synagogue, which became a vitally important institution in the religious life of the people, is a later development of the *Maamadot*.[89]

The Pharisees were not satisfied only to democratize the services in the Temple and to make it an institution for the

[87] Cf. Men. 65; S. Zeitlin, הצדוקים והפרושים.
[88] M. Tan. 4.2; S. Zeitlin, ibid.
[89] Cf. S. Zeitlin, ibid. p. 13.

entire people but they endeavored to adjust religion to life. They therefore modified many laws, the written and the oral. They strove to bring these into consonance with life. The Sadducees opposed all modifications. Tannaitic literature records many instances where they complained against the Pharisees because of their innovations. The Pharisees utilized many occasions to demonstate the validity of their views.[90]

The Pharisees gained full control over the religious life of the Judaeans in the later days of the Second Commonwealth. Josephus wrote that when a Sadducee was appointed judge he had to follow the Pharisees' views, otherwise the people would object to him.[91] The teachings of the Pharisees became normative Judaism. The Sadducees now became the heretical group. History reverses itself. Originally the Sadducees were the orthodox, strict in observance of the Pentateuchal law and opposed to the oral law. The Pharisees, *Perushim*, had been the separatists, dissenters, had been regarded as heretics, innovators. Later the Pharisees became the orthodox, whose views the people followed. The Sadducees, *Zadukim*, were now regarded as heretics because they did not adhere to the views of the Pharisees. The term *Zaduki* now became a nickname for heresy, a term of reproach and contempt.

The Synoptic Gospels tell of controversies and conflicts between Jesus and his disciples with the Pharisees. These disciples called the Pharisees hypocrites. It is to be deplored that this unjustifiable nomenclature for the Pharisees should be attached to them and be so given in the dictionaries. A historical injustice has thus been perpetrated upon them.

In the charges and counter changes between the Pharisees and Jesus and his disciples are reflected their diverse philosophies concerning the nature of society. The Pharisees as leaders of the Judaeans were responsible for their welfare and they had to take note of their deeds. A person could be punished only if he committed a transgression of the law.

[90] Ibid. p. 18.
[91] *Ant.* 18. 1,4(17); Ibid. 13.10, 6(298).

A court had to have evidence in order to condemn a person. It could not punish one for wishing to commit a crime. Jesus and his disciples, being idealists, dreamed of establishing a utopian society. They believed that a person should never even in his mind transgress the law. They did not take into consideration the weaknesses of humanity. In the Sermon on the Mount it is said, "Ye have heard that it hath been said an eye for an eye a tooth for a tooth, but I say unto you that ye resist not evil but whoesoever shall strike thee on the right cheek turn to him the other also. And if any man will sue ye at the law and take away thy coat let him have thy cloak also." [92]

The law of talio stated in the Pentateuch was not to be enforced by the state since injuring a person was not considered a crime against society, it was a private delict. This was a matter to be settled between the litigants. The injured person could demand whatever satisfaction he desired even to the extent of removing the eye of the person who caused the loss of his eye. Talio was the ultimate and extreme satisfaction which the plaintiff could exact. However he might take compensation with money. [93] The Pharisees felt the need of the abolishing of the law of *talio* and did abolish it. According to the newly enacted law the injured man had the right only to demand monetary satisfaction for the loss of his eye, [94] for the pain and suffering, for medical care, for disability and for humiliation. This form of retribution has been followed in the courts of all civilized peoples. Jesus, as a moralist, appealed to the people that they should not only not demand satisfaction by *talio* but that they should not resist evil at all. They should be meek to their oppressors; if one smites a person

---

[92] Mat. 5. 38-42.

[93] Cf. *Ant* 4. 8, 35(280). "He that maimeth a man shall undergo the like, being deprived of that limb whereof he deprived the other, unless indeed the maimed man be willing to accept money; for the law empowers the victim himself to assess the damage that has befallen him and makes this concession, unless he would show himself too severe."

[94] Cf. Talmud M.K. 83.

on the cheek the injured man should turn the other cheek to be punished twice. This may be great moral teaching but could a society really function on such principles? Have the followers of Jesus ever practiced this way of life? Not only have the Christians made war against non-Christians but they have made war against each other. The literal words an eye for an eye (modified and abolished by the sages during the Second Commonwealth) was followed more among the Christians than the teachings of the Sermon on the Mount.

We have the right to maintain that some controversies between the Pharisees and Jesus and his disciples could not have occurred during their lifetime. The Gospel according to Mark relates, "Then came to gather unto him the Pharisees and certain of the scribes, which came from Jerusalem. And when they saw some of his disciples eat bread with defiled, that is to say with unwashed hands, they found fault for the Pharisees and all the Judaeans, except they washed their hands oft, eat not, holding the tradition of the elders." [95] The institution of washing the hands before a meal was instituted at the earliest a few years before the destruction of the Temple, [96] long after the time of the crucifixion of Jesus. Thus, historically, such a controversey could not have occurred during the time of Jesus. The statement, according to the Gospel of Mark, "For the Pharisees and all the Judaeans, except they wash their hands oft, eat not," is an anachronism to say the least. At the time of Jesus for a Judaean who was in the status of uncleanliness the washing of the hands was not sufficient to become clean, he had to be submerged in water. [97] A person who was not defiled could eat without washing the hands.

Matthew states that Jesus accused the Pharisees of being hypocrites, "They make broad their phylacteries," [98] he said,

---

[95] Mark 7.3.
[96] S. Zeitlin, "The Halaka in the Gospels" *HUCA*, 1.
[97] Cf. ibid.
[98] Mat. 23.5

and added, that they wanted to be called rabbis.[99] The *tephilin* are not phylacteries. To repeat, they were not used as a talisman, a charm for protection against evil spirits.[100] The author of this passage did not know the meaning of *tephilin*, thinking that they were phylacteries. Furthermore the term *rabbi* came into vogue after the destruction of the Second Temple.[101] The title rabbi was not used by the Judaeans at the time of Jesus. This is anotner anachronism which may shed light on this passage.

It cannot be denied that the disciples of Jesus were strongly opposed to the Pharisees and considered them adversaries, and in the heat of arguments they accused their former teachers, the Pharisees, of being hypocrites for not accepting Jesus as the Messiah. The Pharisees, on the other hand, considered the disciples of Jesus transgressors and deceivers who wanted to destroy Judaism as it was propagated by them throughout the centuries. No historian writing on the Pharisees can rely solely upon the denunciations of them in the Gospels. In order to write about the Pharisees one must be well versed in the literature of their own creation, the tannaitic.

It has been maintained that the Pharisees were narrow nationalists, in contrast to the prophets who were universalists. Such a view betrays lack of knowledge of the tannaitic literature and the essence of Phariseeism. The canonization of the prophetic books, Isaiah, Jeremiah, Amos and Micah, making their views fundamental for Judaism, was accomplished by the Pharisees. They were responsible for abolishing the term "House of Yahweh" and substituting the term "Sanctuary." They thereby emphasized that the God of Israel is universal, that no house could contain him, that he is everywhere. The Pharisees were far from being narrow nationalists. They were the first to maintain that anyone, regardless of race, can be converted to Judaism since Judaism is a universal religion.

[99] Ibid. 7. [100] See above p. 114.
[101] See S. Zeitlin, Who Crucified Jesus? Pp. 139-140.

On the other hand a theory has been advanced that the Pharisees were truly Hellenized. This view likewise betrays total lack of knowledge of the Pharisaic literature. It cannot be denied that many views held by the Pharisees, such as the resurrection of the soul, believing in reward and punishment after death, were held by other peoples. This does not prove that the Pharisees were Hellenized. Ideas permeate the world due to the progress of civilization. One people does not necessarily copy from another. If it should be granted that the idea of resurrection was adopted by the Pharisees from other people this does not indicate that they were thoroughly Hellenized. The idea of the resurrection of the spirit was not the only foundation of Phariseeism. The Pharisees, as we have endeavored to show, were the heirs of the prophets who stressed the idea of the universality of God. The Pharisees encouraged proselytism and opposed theocracy. They held that a scion of the family of David should be the secular ruler of the people. This view later developed into the idea of a Messiah, the anointed of God. They emphasized particularly that the oral law is binding and on a par with Written Law, i.e., making the oral law statutory law.

In order to establish a legal system by which the Pentateuchal laws could be interpreted, to make them in consonance with life, and in order to make the oral law statutory, the Pharisees employed hermeneutic devices like *kal wa-homer* inference *a minori ad maius*, from the less important law to the more important; and *gezerah shawah*, inference by analogy of words. It has been contended that these hermeneutic devices are good illustrations of the thoroughly Hellenistic framework of Pharisaic thought. This again shows a lack understanding of tannaitic literature. It should be noted that Hillel was not the originator of the principle of *a minori ad maius*. It is already found in the Pentateuch. [102] Hillel only

[102] E.g., Gen. 44.8, הן כסף אשר מצאנו בפי אמתחותינו השיבנו אליך מארץ הן בני ישראל. Cf. also Ex. 6.12. כנען ואיך נגנב מבית אדניך כסף או זהב לא שמעו אלי ואיך ישמעני פרעה.

perfected the three hermeneutic devices, (The Tosefta made reference to seven hermeneutic devices [103] but they are a later development of the three.) and employed them to make the unwritten law statutory. Not only the Sadducees opposed this method but also the school of Shamai did not adopt it. As a matter of fact even in a later time the school of Shamai did not employ the hermeneutic device of *gezerah shawah*. [104]

To utilize the rabbinic literature for the study of the Pharisees one must analyze it critically. Not all rabbinic literature can be used for the history of the Pharisees. There is a vast difference between the tannaitic and the amoraic literature and between the Palestinian and Babylonian. The later rabbinic literature is not a source for the history of the Pharisees. Many writers who have dealt with the Pharisees employed the later Babylonian literature and thus they distorted the history of the Pharisees.

To cite an example: The *Megillat Taanit*, which was composed circa 65 C.E., records that on the 28th of the month of Tebet the Synagogue sat in judgment and that a semiholiday was declared. Besides the aramaic text of the *Megillat* there exist also commentaries or scholia in Hebrew, explaining the events mentioned in the Megillah. The scholium on this event interpreted it that on that day the Pharisees were victorious over the Sadducees, that the Sadducaean Sanhedrin was abolished and therefore a holiday was declared on that day. The scholia on the *Megillat Taanit* were composed during the Middle Ages and hence have no value whatsoever on the history of the Pharisees. To use the scholia as a source for the history of the Pharisees is tantamount to the usage of Rashi's commentary on the Talmud as a source for the history of the Second Jewish Commonwealth and of

---

[103] Tos. Sanh. 7.11.
[104] See M. Bezah 1.8, אמרו בית שמאי גזירה שוה חלה ומתנות Cf. however Tos. ibid. אמרו בית הלל גזירה שוה חלה ומתנות From internal evidence we may say with certainty that the reading of the text, as recorded in the Tosefta is the original text.

the Tannaim. Such a method is not historical, to say the least, and is confusing and misleading.

In order to write on the Pharisees one must also deal with the history of the Judaeans during the Second Commonwealth. Parties are not created in a vacuum. They do not arise as the result of a whim of a leader or leaders. They are the result of political, social, economic and religious forces. Parties are indeed the creation of the people and in turn mold its history. Both are interwoven. To fully comprehend the Pharisees and their theological development one must follow step by step the history of the Judaeans. The history of a people may have a zig zag deviate course but the main characteristics always remain. This is also true of parties. Parties adapt themselves to ever changing historical forces but their main characteristics remain.

The Sadducees, it will be recalled, were those who after the Restoration opposed Zerubbabel and the effort to establish the Judaean community on a secular basis. They sought the establishment of a theocracy and favored Joshua, of the family of Zadok. When the Judaean state was established they supported Jannaeus Alexander, who was not of the Zadokite family, for the kingship and high priesthood. On the surface this would seem anomalous. In reality the ideology of the Sadducees had not changed. They had followed Joshua because they believed that he would serve their interests. They had been in favor of theocracy because it would give the high priest full authority over the Judaean community. They now supported Jannaeus Alexander although he was not of the Zadokite family, because of their ideology. They saw in him their ideal who, by his military genius, had placed the Judaean state on a firm foundation. They approved his policy of conquest to add more territory to Judaea for they were strongly nationalistic. They always believed that the Judaeans were the chosen people of God. However. when proselytism did became the norm of Judaism proselytes were not condidered in the eyes of the Sadducees on a par with the native Judaeans—they were considered half Judaeans.

The Sadducees, who regarded the unwritten law as not binding, however, followed them when they became statutory. But they always opposed the unwritten law which was based on tradition and any new laws which were based on inferences from the Pentateuch. The essential characteristics of the Sadducees with regard to religion, people and law remained the same throughout history.

The Pharisees, who opposed theocracy, believed that the kingship of the people should be vested in a scion of the family of David, and hence were opposed to Jannaeus Alexander. They did not hold that the Judaeans are the chosen people of God.

After the civil war which raged between the sons of Jannaeus Alexander, which was really one between the Sadducees and the Pharisees, the latter dedicated themselves solely to the advancement of religion. They were quietists.

The reign of Herod and the oppression of the Romans brought about two offshoots from the Pharisees. Josephus named one (followers of) the Fourth Philosophy.[105] The other whom Josephus called deceivers, wicked,[106] were really the Apocalyptic Pharisees. The former were militant, nationalistic and followed the principle that terror must oppose terror. Later they were called Sicarii because they concealed a *sica*, dagger, under their garments.[107] The Apocalyptic Pharisees, like the Sicarii, preached the gospel of no lordship of man over man and equality of men; they held that the only ruler

[105] *Ant.* 18. 1, 6(23-25). Josephus named the "Fourth Philosophy," because this group came fourth after the Sadduccees, the Pharisees and the Essenes.

[106] *Jewish War*, 2.13, 4(258-259). "Besides these there arose another body of villains, with purer hands but more impious intentions, who no less than the assassins ruined the peace of the city. Deceivers and impostors, under the pretence of divine inspiration fostering revolutionary changes, they persuaded the multitude to act like madmen, and led them out into the desert under the belief that God would there give them tokens of delieverance."

[107] *Jewish War*, ibid. (254-257).

over men is God. They differed from the Sicarii in opposing terror and violence. They preached love, "If anyone seeketh to do evil unto you do well unto him and pray for him." [108] This was their watchword and guide. They believed that God, either through himself or a Messiah, who would be a scion of the family of David, by a miraculous act would annihilate their oppressors. Since the salvation of the people would not come through arms but by act of God the Apocalyptists declared themselves messengers of God, claiming that they had supernatural power by which to smite the Romans and save the Judaeans. They held that the suffering of the people was the chastisement of God, that they are his beloved children and that He would never forsake them. They believed He would restore Jerusalem to its glory and proclaim His kingdom. The Pharisaic Apocalyptists were the forerunners of Christianity. The Pharisees saw dangers in the views and deeds of the adherants of the Fourth Philosophy and the Apocalyptists.

The view that the Judaeans, the Israelites, are the chosen people of God was emphasized in the Pentateuch and in other books of the Bible and, as noted before, was held by the Sadducees. When the Christians became entrenched they maintained that they were the true Israelites and are the chosen people of God. [109] Hence the Judaeans abandoned the name of Judaean and called themselves Israelites and maintained that they are the chosen people. [110] They now called their land, originally called Judaea, *Eretz Israel*, the Land of Israel. This was done to combat the contention of the Judaean Christians.

The view that the Jews are the chosen people was both the result of the Sadduceean influence and a reaction against

[108] See The Testament of the Twelve Pariarchs (The Testament of Joseph) 18. 2.

[109] Cf. Origen, *Against Celsus*, 5. 42, 50; Tertullian, *Adversus Iudaeos*, 3.

[110] Cf. ibid., S. Zeitlin, "Judaism as a Religion," *JQR*, 1944, pp. 88-91.

Christianity. After the destruction of the Second Temple the Sadducees, as a group, ceased to exist but some of their views were not entirely eradicated. One strong exponent of the view that the Jews are a chosen people was Jehudah ha-Levi (1085-1142). He held that although the Torah was given to the Jews, its acceptance was free to every one. Nevertheless he maintained that those who were not of the Jewish race, even though they embraced Judaism, could never acquire the gift of prophecy. He said that since Judaism is the historic, ethnic religion of the Jewish people anyone who embraced the Jewish religion becomes a member of the Jewish people and would be rewarded for his deeds but he would never be equal with those who are racially Jews. [111] Judah ha-Levi stated that when God revealed himself on Mount Sinai and gave the Torah to the Children of Israel; He did not say "I am the God who created the Universe but I am the God who brought you out of the land of Egypt." [112] He adhered to the view of the Sadducees who followed the Pentateuch literally and maintained that Yahweh is the God of the children of Israel because he took them out of the land of Egypt. The view of "peoplehood" held by many contemporary Jews is in accordance with that held by the Sadducees. The Pharisees strongly opposed the view that the Jews are a chosen people. They held that Judaism is the chosen religion.

In the liturgy of the festivals are recited the words, "Thou didst choose us from among all peoples; Thou didst love and favor us." [113] Here the view of chosen people is stressed. This again is due both to the influence of the Sadducees and the reaction against Christianity. However, when a person who has become a convert to Judaism, regardless of his race, yellow or negro, when he is called to the Torah he

[111] *Kusari*, 27, וכל הנלוה אלינו מן האומות בפרט יגיעהו מן הטובה אשר ייטיב הבורא אלינו אך לא יהיה שוה עמנו מפני שאנחנו נקראים הסגולה מבני אדם.

[112] וכן פתח אלהים דבריו אל המון ישראל אנכי ד אלהיך אשר הוצאתיך מארץ מצרים ולא אמר אני בורא העולם ובוראכם.

[113] אתה בחרתנו מכל העמים אהבת אותנו ורצית בנו.

makes the following blessing, "Blessed art Thou, Adonai, our God, King of the universe, Who has chosen us from all peoples. [114] Hence a person not of the Jewish race, who might be of the yellow or negro race, when called to the Torah proclaims himself as being one chosen above all other peoples. This is the Pharisaic view that the God of Israel is the God of the universe and that the whole human race are his children. Judaism is the chosen religion. Anyone who accepts Judaism is the spiritual descendant of Abraham, Isaac and Jacob. The Pharisees opposed the idea of a chosen race and the view of "peoplehood."

The Pharisees molded Judaism. Judaism of today is based on their teachings. Their view that the Pentateuchal and the subsequent oral law should be interpreted and amended in consonance with life made the Jewish religion a living one. Their maxim that law was for man, not man for the law, [115] gave substance to the life of the people, and made it possible for them to withstand the calamities which almost annihilated them. Their view of the universality of God not only had an impact on western civilization but made possible the survival of the Jewish people.

The nations of antiquity that were conquered by different empires have disappeared from the historical arena because they had ethnic gods. Their gods were conquered and they as ethnic peoples disappeared. The Jews were conquered by the Romans; their national life was destroyed, their land was taken away from them for a while but the Jews have not disappeared from the historical arena. This is primarily due to the teachings of the Pharisees—the universality of God, that God is everywhere and is not bound to one particular country. In the hearts of the Jews Judaea, Eretz Israel, was always considered the Holy Land, the Land of Israel, the land that always belonged to them. They never abandoned the hope that a new state would be reestablished in the land of Israel.

[114] ברוך אתה אדני אלהינו מלך העולם אשר בחר בנו מכל העמים ונתן לנו את תורתו׃

[115] Yoma 86. היא מסורה בידכם ולא אתם מסורים בידה׃

Part III
Rabbinic Contexts

THE MARTYRS OF CAESAREA

Saul Lieberman

The vast field of Talmudic literature fared ill at the hands of the historians. The historians were no Talmudists; the Talmudists were no historians. The former either entirely ignored the Rabbinic sources or misused them. Every single passage of Talmudic literature must be investigated both in the light of the whole context and as a separate unit in regard to its correct reading, meaning, time and place. Thanks to the modern methods of investigation which have begun to exert their influence on the work of the very small circle of Talmudic scholars, their researches often result in quite exact conclusions in the domain of history. The simple rule should be followed that the Talmud may serve as a good historic document when it deals in contemporary matters within its own locality. The legendary portions of the Talmud can hardly be utilized for this purpose. The Palestinian Talmud (and some of the early Midrashim) whose material was produced in the third and fourth centuries contains valuable information regarding Palestine during that period. It embodies many elements similar to those contained in the so-called documentary papyri. The evidence is all the more trustworthy since the facts are often recorded incidentally and casually. The Rabbinic literature has much in common with the non-literary papyri and the inscriptions.

Although the following paper cannot serve as a classical example of the above statement, since the nature of the subject-matter has sometimes compelled the author to resort to a probable conjecture, the reader can nevertheless learn that Talmudic literature is a valuable source for the events of its own time.[*]

I.

Our information on the life of the Jews in Caesarea in the third and fourth centuries is derived in the main from Rabbinic sources.

---

[*] Unless otherwise specified all the dates mentioned in this article are C. E. The English translations of the Greek text of M. P. are mainly borrowed from Lawlor and Oulton. In the translation of the Syriac version I followed in the main W. Cureton.

But the Rabbis did not write history; they did not intend to leave behind records of the events which affected Jewish life. They taught and explained the law; they instructed the people to behave morally and piously, and only incidentally mentioned facts and events bearing on Jewish life in Caesarea.[1] Thus any additional Caesarean source of that time may shed more light on this obscure period.

Happily we possess a contemporary literary work composed by an inhabitant of this city in which the writer reports facts and events of which he was an eyewitness, or had first-hand information. This is the work of Eusebius of Caesarea which is known by the name *De Martyribus Palaestinae*.

The shorter Greek recension[2] of this work follows the eighth book of Eusebius' Ecclesiastical History in most of the printed editions. A Syriac version of the longer recension[3] was published by W. Cureton in 1861 from a manuscript bearing the date 411.[4] The complicated and difficult problem of the relation of these two recensions to each other and to the *Historia Ecclesiastica*[5] is of no great importance for our subject. It should however be pointed out that the Greek original of the Syriac version was almost certainly written by Eusebius himself[6].

The longer version abounds in minute details which were of special interest and value to the people who were familiar with the scenes of action, and "it was written mainly for the instruction of the Christians of Caesarea"[7]. And what can be more valuable or trustworthy than an account written by a witness for people who were in a position to judge the facts by their own information? At least one aspect of the life of Caesarea, reflected in the treatment of the local Christians in the beginning of the fourth century, is fully available. The behavior of the Roman government, of its officials and their victims is clearly mirrored in these accounts. When we analyze the information supplied by the Rabbinic sources of the time and compare it with the records of Eusebius we see how remarkably they supplement one another.

In the third and fourth centuries Caesarea was a center of Jewish learning. Many Jewish sages resided and taught there;[8] among them was the famous Jewish scholar, R. Abbahu, an older contemporary of Eusebius. He was the head of the Rabbinic academy in Caesarea and one of the pillars of the Palestinian Talmud. A learned and cultured person,[9] he was also an influential member of the commu-

---

1 See S. LIEBERMAN, *The Talmud of Caesarea*, p. 13 ff.
2 Preserved in the group ATER of the mss. of the *Hist. Eccles.*
3 Greek fragments were published in *Analecta Bolland.* XVI, 129 ff. and printed by Schwartz in his edition underneath the shorter Greek text.
4 See CURETON's Preface, p. V, n. c.
5 See N. G. LAWLOR, *Eusebiana*, p. 279 ff.; *ibid.* p. 285 ff.
6 See LAWLOR, *ibid.* p. 179.
7 LIGHTFOOT as quoted by LAWLOR, *ibid.* p. 180. This is, of course, true for the Greek original as well.
8 See BACHER, Die *Gelehrten von Caesarea in MGWJ* 1901, p. 302 ff.
9 See his biography by S. G. PERLITZ in MGWJ 1887, p. 60 ff.; BACHER, Die *Agada der Paläst. Amoräer*, II, 88 ff.; *Jewish Encyclopedia*, I, p. 36; comp. also LIEBERMAN, *Greek in Jewish Palestine*, p. 21 ff.

nity, who frequently came in direct contact with the government.[10] His connection with the government is particularly well illustrated in a passage in TP[11] where it is told that a woman named Tamar complained to the proconsul of Caesarea of the decision of the Tiberian Rabbinic court which condemned her. The Rabbis of Tiberias asked R. Abbahu to intercede in their behalf. He replied in a cryptic letter that he had already appeased three *lictores*[12] but had not succeeded in "sweetening" Tamar, who persisted in her "bitterness".[13] Thus, the connections of R. Abbahu with the *officium* of the proconsul in Caesarea are well attested.

TB[14] bears witness to his good relations with the *Minim*. It is related there that R. Abbahu praised the great scholarship of Rab Safra before the *Minim*, whereupon the latter exempted him from paying taxes for a number of years. But when R. Safra failed to explain a difficult passage in the Scriptures they were annoyed with him. Herford[15] assumes that the *Minim* were Jewish Christians[16] and were therefore interested in the Bible. It is, however, hard to believe that R. Abbahu was on good terms with Jewish-Christian apostates. It is also unlikely that *Jewish Christians*, apostates from Judaism should grant a Rabbi exemption from taxes only because of his learning.[17] The simple meaning of the text is that the *Minim* were Gentile[18] Christians. Scholarly intercourse between Jews and Gentile Christians in Caesarea was practiced long before the time of R. Abbahu. Origen used to consult the Jews on Scriptural matters, and his contemporary R. Hoshaiah

---

10 Comp. TB *Kethuhoth,* 17a and parallels; BACHER, *ibid.* p. 94, n. 5 and n. 6.
11 *Megilla,* III. 3, 74a.
12 The text reads ליטורין which was variously interpreted. See KRAUSS, *Lehnwörter* etc. p. 301 *s. v.* לאיטור. Comp. also M. SCHWABE in *Tarbiz,* vol. I. fasc. 3, p. 111, n. 1. The explanation of Mussafia that the word means *lictores* was disregarded by Jewish scholars; but his interpretation can hardly be doubted. These *lictores* are members of the *officium* of the proconsul of Caesarea. They were in a position to withdraw the complaint of Tamar from the office before it came to the notice of the proconsul. The Rabbis frequently mention the officials of the *apparitio*. They know the *exceptor* (See KRAUSS, *Lehnwörter* etc. p. 410^b), the *speculator* (ibid. p. 409^b), the *quaestionarius (ibid.* 514^b), the *commentariensis (ibid.* 510) and other members of the *officium*. These officials are very common in the documents of the Christian Martyrology (See E. LE BLANT, *Les persécuteurs et les martyrs* etc. p. 304 ff). The latter talk indiscriminately of the *spiculatores, lictores, exceptores* and *commentarienses (ibid.* p. 304–305). It is by way of bribing the *spiculatores* and the *exceptores* that the Christians obtained the protocols from the archives of the judge *(ibid.* p. 4, n. 3), and it is quite natural that R. Abbahu applied to the *lictores* for help in withdrawing the complaint of Tamar.
13 It seems that the *lictores* agreed to withdraw the complaint on condition that Tamar should not object to it.
14 '*Abodah Zarah,* 4a.
15 *Christianity in Talmud* etc. p. 270.
16 Comp. also his article in *Jewish Studies* (in memory of GEORGE A. KOHUT), p. 359 ff.
17 HERFORD's (*Christianity* etc., p. 268) suggestion that the *Minim* engaged R. Safra as their teacher has no basis whatever in the text of the Talmud. Nor is there any hint to the effect that the *Minim* engaged R. Safra as an assistant in collecting the imperial revenue, an opinion erroneously attributed by HERFORD (*Ibid.* p. 269) to BACHER.
18 Comp. S. LIEBERMAN, *Greek in Jewish Palestine,* p. 141, n. 196.

(of Caesarea) discussed religious questions with Christians.[19] In R. Abbahu's time the school of Christian instruction founded by Pamphilus functioned in Caesarea, where texts of the Scriptures were diligently studied.[20] Eusebius himself discussed his Biblical interpretations with Jewish authorities,[21] and he expressly mentions his Jewish teacher.[22] It is therefore no wonder that the Gentile Christians in Caesarea had a special respect for the Rabbis, who were well versed in the Scriptures.

But when did the incident with R. Safra take place? When were the Christians of Caesarea in a position (as contractors or collectors) to exempt a scholar from taxes? When did R. Abbahu have the friendly discussions with the Christians?[23] Since the activity of R. Abbahu in Caesarea was mainly concentrated in the time of Diocletian and his Caesars, it is pertinent to ask whether the incident with R. Safra occurred before, during or after the persecutions of the Christians by Diocletian and Galerius.

It is accepted among Jewish scholars that R. Abbahu died long after the Edict of Toleration was promulgated (311). Frankel remarks[24] that R. Abbahu was already "a great man" in 312, and it seems that he places his death much later than 312.[25] But there are few Rabbis whose death can be dated with such exactness as that of R. Abbahu.

Before we establish the time of his death let us try to estimate the approximate time of his birth. We read in the Midrash:[26] וימלוך תחתיו יובב בן זרח מבצרה. אמר ר' אבהו ... כבר היתה מלכות עקורה מאדום ובאת בצרה וסיפקה לה מלכים וכו'. *"And Jobab the son of Zerak of Bozrah reigned in his stead* (Gen. XXXVI. 33). R. Abbahu said ... 'Kingship had already been uprooted from Edom (=Rome), whereupon Bozrah came and supplied her with kings, etc'." It is clear that this saying could be uttered not later than 249 when Philippus Arabs,[27] a native of Bostra, was still reigning in Rome jointly with his son. The "legal" dynasty of the Severi finished with the murder of Alexander Severus (235). The Thracian peasant Maximinus[28] usurped the purple, and was killed (238); the two emperors, Balbinus and

---

19 See BACHER, *Die Agada der Pal. Amor.* I, p. 92; KRAUSS, *JQR* V (1893), p. 139 ff.
20 See below p. 421.
21 See his com. *on Is.* XXXIV. 1, *Migne, PG* XXIV, 361[b]; *ibid.* XXII. 15.19, 249c. Comp. KRAUSS in *JQR* VI (1894), p. 84 ff.
22 *Ibid.* XXXIX. 1, 361[b].
23 Comp. BACHER, *ibid.* p. 96–98. The story told in TB (*'Abodah Zarah*, 28a) about a Christian physician who wanted to poison R. Abbahu seems to disagree with the Palestinian tradition (See TP *ibid.* II. 2, 40d).
24 *Mebo Hayeruschalmi*, 63[b].
25 The writer in the Jewish *Encyclopedia*, I, 36a puts his death around 320.
26 *Bereshith Rabba*, LXXXIII. 3, 998[6].
27 KRAUSS, *Monumenta Talmudica*, V, p. 61, correctly surmised that R. Abbahu referred to this king.
28 On the social and economic situation of the Roman empire of that time see ROSTOVTZEFF, *The Social and Economic History of the Roman Empire*, p. 387 ff. 401 ff. and notes, *ibid.* p. 615; *idem*, *Musée Belge*, XXVII (1923), p. 236 ff.

Maximus, elected by the Roman Senate were murdered in their turn by the praetorians after a reign of three months. Gordian the Third did not occupy the throne more than half a dozen years; he was murdered by his own soldiers (244). What wonder then that the Jews saw in it a sign from Heaven, an omen that kingship was going to be uprooted from Edom (Rome)?[29] Bostra, on the other hand, supplied Rome with a king who intended to establish a new dynasty!

In the reign of Decius, when the purple returned to a Roman Senator, and especially during the subsequent anarchy, the remark of R. Abbahu would have had no justification. If we suppose that the latter was at least around twenty when he applied the verse of the Bible to the reign of Philippus we can place his birth about 229.[30] Thus R. Abbahu was more than seventy years old at the beginning of the persecutions (303), and it is natural to expect his death at that time or somewhat later.

Eusebius gives us the key to the solution of this problem. He describes a miracle that happened in Caesarea between the middle of November and that of December 309. He says:[31]

Αἰθρία ἦν καὶ λαμπρὸς ἀὴρ καὶ τοῦ περιέχοντος κατάστασις εὐδινοτάτη. εἶτα ἀθρόως τῶν ἀνὰ τὴν πόλιν κιόνων οὐ τὰς δημοσίας ὑπήρειδον στοάς, δακρύων τινὰ τρόπον οἱ πλείσυς σταλαγμοὺς ἀπέσταζον ... λῆρος ἴσως καὶ μῦθος εὖ οἶδ' ὅτι δόξει εἶναι τό ῥῆμα τοῖς μεθ' ἡμᾶς, ἀλλ' οὐχ οἷσπερ ὁ καιρὸς τὴν ἀλήθειαν ἐπιστώσατο.

"It was fine weather, the air was clear, the state of the atmosphere very calm. Then all at once many of the pillars of the city which support the public porches let fall drop by drop as it were tears ... I know well that my word will seem, perchance, idle talk and a fable to those who come after us, but not to those who have had its truth accredited on the spot." Eusebius' story is a report of a witness of the time and place of the miracle. The Syriac version[31a] states that "some of the people who saw it are still alive." The truth of the story is well attested. We find unexpected corroboration of the fact in Rabbinic sources. We read in the Babylonian Talmud:[32] כי נח נפשיה דר' אבהו אהיתו עמודי דקסרי דמעי [32a] "When

---

29   It was asserted that a similar feeling dominated the Roman soldiers when they heard that Caracalla was murdered, and they had no more Antoninus as emperor. *Ingens maeror obsedit omnium pectora, quod Antoninum in re publica non haberent, existimantium quod cum eo Romanum esset imperium periturum.* (Hist Aug. Diadum. I. 2).
30   The period in which R. Abbahu's teachers, colleagues and pupils lived does not contradict this date.
31   M. P. IX. 12.
31a CURETON, p. ל"י.
32   *Mo'ed Katan*, 25[b].
32a So mss. See RABBINOVICZ, *Var. Lect.* 87 n. 40.

R. Abbahu died the pillars of Caesarea shed tears."[33] Some mediaeval authorities[34] interpreted the passage not as the account of an actual incident but as the phrase of a eulogist who bewailed R. Abbahu by calling upon the pillars of Caesarea to weep over his death. However the Palestinian Talmud disproves this interpretation. There it is stated:[34a] כד דמך רי אבהו בכן עמודיא דקיסרין. אמרין (read: אמרון) כותיא לית אינון אלא מריעין (read: מדיעין) אמר לון ישראל ידעין רחיקייא כמה דקריביא מריעין (read: מדיעין) ידעון (read: "When R. Abbahu died the pillars of Caesarea wept. The Kuthim (= Samaritans) said: 'They are only perspiring.'[35] The Jews said to them: 'May the distant ones perspire as the near ones are perspiring".[36] The Palestinian Talmud cites it as a fact and not as a phrase of the eulogist.

It is very remarkable that Jewish scholars who noticed the passage of Eusebius took it only as a parallel to the Talmudic story. M. Joël[37] says clearly: "In der Deutung des Factums unterscheiden sich *die Zeiten* (my italics) und die Menschen." This seems also to be the opinion of Levy and Bacher.[38] Yet there is no doubt that both Eusebius and the Rabbinic source refer to the same facts.

From the words of the sources we see that the inhabitants of Caesarea took the drops of water on the pillars as a miraculous manifestation, as a phenomenon that was not known to them before, and it is therefore impossible to admit that the same wonder occurred twice in the same town within no more than a quarter of a century. It is clear that the Jews and the Christians refer to the same occurrence. The Jews were sure that nature shed tears over the death of R. Abbahu, the Samaritans (of whom R. Abbahu was the bitterest enemy, see below) took them

---

33 The Syriac *M. P.* relates that the pillars emitted spots as if they were of blood; הוא. ודמא...דמא. דמן כאפא...בדמות דמעא שחלא הות. (Comp. also below n. 35). LAWLOR and OULTON (I, p. 375, n. a) emend (on the basis of the Greek and the Menaea) דמא into דמ[ע]א. But TB *ibid.* tells (immediately after our passage): *At the death of* R. *lose the roof gutters at Sepphoris ran with blood.* TP '*Abodah Zarah* (III. 1, 42c) *repeats the story and explains* : אמריו דיהב נפשית על גזורתא. "*Some say because he risked his life for the sake of circumcision*" (See *Tosaphoth Mo'ed Katan*, 25[b], *s. v.* שפעו). This is probably the source of *Midrash Tehilim* (IX. 19, ed Buber p. 89) which numbers R. Jose among the Ten Martyrs. Thus the miracle of the appearance of blood was associated with the sympathy of the inanimate objects with the martyrs, exactly the same as in the case of Eusebius.

34 ME'IRI and RAN *ad loc.* in the "*Harry Fischel Institute Publications,*" pp. 143, 68. R. Salomo b. Ha-jathom (p. 119 bottom) explained that the pillars *perspired* (read: הזיעו instead of הזיפו) and looked like weeping.

34a '*Abodah Zarah ibid.*

35 The Rabbis probably transmitted the words of the Samaritans literally, the verb as they used it. In the Syriac translation of Luke (XXII. 44) we read *(Palest. Syr. Lect.*, London 1899, p. 79) ואתעבדת דעתה: היך שליאן דאדם. Comp, below n. 39.

36 *I. e.*, let the Samaritans perspire like the pillars (which mourn and display sympathy over the death of R. Abbahu).

37 *Blicke in die Religionsgeschichte* etc. I. p. 9.

38 *Agada der pal. Amor.* II., 103 n. 3.

as drops of perspiration,[39] and the Christians saw in them nature's reaction to the atrocities of the persecutors.

Now we can fix the death of R. Abbahu (at the age of approximately eighty) on a bright autumn day in 309.[40] R. Abbahu's connections with the government, with the men of the proconsul's *officium,* with Christian scholars and tax collectors should be placed in the time before and during the persecution but not after them.

The Christians seem to have been numerous and powerful in Caesarea in the time of Diocletian; their relations with the Jewish leaders of the community were tolerably good. But there was another minority problem in Caesarea at that time, one which reached its crisis with the persecutions. The Samaritans constituted the largest minority in that city.[41] This follows from TP[42] which implies that only together did the Jews and the Gentiles form a majority over the Samaritans.[43] The final break between the Jews and the Samaritans seems to have taken place at the time and as a result of the persecutions.

Many diverse reasons have been offered for the excommunication of the Samaritans,[44] but the main reason is disclosed by the Palestinian Talmud:[45] על ידי עילא, "on a pretext." The formal reasons were only an excuse; there were intrinsic causes for it. As one of the formal grounds it was alleged that the Samaritans were suspected of worshipping a dove on Gerizim.[46] The Talmuds, however, did not take this charge seriously. TB quotes it in the name of a Babylonian Rabbi (III/IV c.) and TP ascribes it to "some one" (ואית דבעי מימר)! The Babylonian Rabbis probably drew the information from a polemical source. The Samaritans accused the Jews of practising idolatry in the Temple,[47] and the Jews retorted[48]

---

39 Among the omens which foretold the death of Commodus his biographer records *(Hist. Aug. Com.* XVI. 5) that "In *the Minucian Portico a bronze statue* of *Hercules sweated for several days".* (Herculis signum aeneum *sudavit* in Minucia per plures dies). Comp. also *Pap. Ox. X.* 1242, 1. 51–52 (ἡ τοῦ Σαράπιδος προτομή...αἰφνίδιον ἵδρωσεν) and C. B. Welles in the *Transactions and Proceedings of the American Philological Association,* vol. LXVII (1936) p. 13. Welles refers to Joannes Lydus, De ostentis, Proem. 8. Comp, also *"The Itinerary of R. Benjamin of Tudela",* ed. Grünhut (Hebrew), p. 915. The existence of this superstition does not invalidate the credibility of the Talmudic sources and Eusebius. The contemporary evidence of the latter and the life-like controversy of the Jews with the Samaritans recorded by the Rabbis cannot be discredited. It may incidentally be noted that many of the miracles recorded in the *Hist. Aug. ibid.* are very similar to those related by Joseph. Bel. *Jud.* VI. 5. 3. 288–300. *Comp.* Tac. *Hist.* V. 13.
40 See Appendix, I.
41 A fact overlooked by scholars, as far as I know.
42 Demai, II. 1, 22°.
43 המינין האסורין בקסרין ... הרי אלו נשביעית היתר בשבוע שני שבוע דמאי ... ויהו ודאי ? ישראל מתקנין וגוים פטורים. ישראל וגוים רבים על הכותים.
44 TP. *'Abodah Zarah,* V. 4, 44d and TB *Hullin* 6a.
45 *Ibid.*
46 TP and TB *ibid.*
47 See Montgomery, *The Samaritans,* p. 91. n. 32.
48 TP *ibid.;* Bereshith Rabba, LXXXI. 3, 974⁴.

by charging that the Samaritans worshipped idols on Gerizim.⁴⁹ The Palestinian Rabbis repeated this Babylonian opinion on the vague authority of "some one," but they themselves admitted that the Samaritans were outlawed ע"י עילא, "on a pretext." Among other reasons TP (ibid.) tells: ואית דבעי מימר כד סליק דיקליטינוס מלכא להכא גזר ואמר כל אומייא ינסכון בר מן יודאיי ונסכין כותייא ונאסר יינן "And some propose this explanation: When Diocletian came here he issued an edict decreeing: All nations except the Jews must offer libations. The Kuthim (Samaritans) complied and [therefore] their wine was declared forbidden." Graetz⁵⁰ remarked that the Talmud here refers to the persecutions of Diocletian, condemning the Samaritans because they did not suffer martyrdom for the sanctification of His Name. Halevy⁵¹ justly objected to Graetz's view, contending that the Samaritans did not offer libations of their own accord but under threat of death, and in this case they do not deserve to be outlawed on account of their transgression of the Law. He, therefore, surmises that the Samaritans were in a position to avail themselves of the privileges of the Jews by identifying themselves with them. But they did not utilize the opportunity, and by offering libations they silently forfeited all claims to be regarded as Jews. This opinion is hardly tenable. The Samaritans did not worship idols. As a matter of fact they were very conservative and clung tenaciously to the precepts of the Bible. They would have never failed to avail themselves of the *privilegia Judaica,* if they had been in a position to do so. If they *willingly* worshipped idols under the very eyes of the Jewish community in Caesarea, the Rabbis would not have had to look for reasons to excommunicate them; they would never have admitted that the Samaritans were outlawed only on a pretext. It is therefore evident that the local governors who frequently enforced the imperial decrees at their own discretion and who knew the differences between the Jewish and Samaritan communities in Caesarea did not exempt the Samaritans from libations⁵² to the gods of the state. They sacrificed under duress, and the Palestinian Talmud did not therefore regard these Samaritan libations as a serious reason for their excommunication, and treated it merely as the opinion of "some one." All the grounds for the break attributed here to the "some one" are among the latest anonymous strata of the Palestinian Talmud.

The item referred to in the Talmud is, according to Graetz,⁵³ the promulgation of the fourth edict of Diocletian⁵⁴ in 305. It seems more plausible that the Talmud referred to the enactment of the edict in Caesarea, when registers of all the citizens were drawn up, and heralds summoned all men, women and children

---

49 See MONTGOMERY, *ibid,* p. 320.
50 *Geschichte,* IV³, p. 279, n. 1.
51 *Doroth Harishonim,* IIᵃ, ch. 25, p. 340, n. 46.
52 See MONTGOMERY, *ibid.* p. 93, but the reading of the text (ORIGEN., *Contra Celsum* II. 13) he refers to is doubtful.
53 Above n. 50. Comp. also MARMORSTEIN, *Revue des Études Juives,* IIC, p. 26. I cannot share his view.
54 *M. P.* III. 1.

to assemble in the temples and offer libations to the idols (306).[55] The people of Palestine probably heard that the Caesar Maximin Daia visited Caesarea shortly afterwards (November 20, 307), celebrating the birthday[56] there with a beastly and gruesome spectacle.[57] The Jews subsequently confused Maximin with Diocletian who had already abdicated at that time. At any rate it is hardly possible to admit that Diocletian visited Palestine when his Fourth Edict arrived there.[58]

Happily, another passage in TP, combined together with a Christian inscription, sheds light on this difficult problem. According to the opinion of R. Johanan,[59] the Jews are allowed to transact business with the heathen on the *Saturnalia* and *Kalendae* if the latter do not observe them. It seems that already in the time of R. Johanan (middle of the III c.) the heathen of Palestine were rather indifferent to the rites of idolatry and, therefore, the Jews were sometimes permitted to transact business with them on their festivals. This was especially true in Caesarea in the beginning of the fourth century. In a city where the majority of the population consisted of Samaritans, Jews and Christians the heathen appear to have entirely neglected the idolatrous ceremonies.

Eusebius[60] cites an order by Maximin (fifth edict, 309) to the effect "that care should be taken that all the people in a mass, men with their wives and household, *even babes at the breast*[61] (ὑπομάζιοι παῖδες) should offer sacrifices and libations ... and the unbelieving heathen found fault with the absurdity of what was done, on the ground that it was harsh and unnecessary (for to their mind the thing was disgusting and burdensome)." Lawlor and Oulton[62] justly remarked: "It was a call to the heathen to observe the customs, so generally neglected, of their nominal religion. It may have been the part of the edict to which they objected as unnecessary and burdensome."

Now we shall be able to understand the obscure passage in the Palestinian Talmud to which it was referred above. It reads:[63] ר' אבהו בעי והדא טקסים דקיסרין מכיוון דסוגייא שמריין כפלחין היא הדא טקסים דדוקים[64] צריכה. The commentaries, dictionaries and modern scholars completely misunderstood both the words and the

---

55 *Ibid*. IV. 8.
56 Of Diocletian. See the notes of Lawlor and Oulton, II. p. 327.
57 *M.P.* VI.1.
58 See Lawlor etc. *ibid.*, p. 324, and comp. Lactantius, *de mort. persec.* XVII.
59 TP *'Abodah Zarah*, I. 2, 39°. Comp. TB *ibid.* 8ª and 65ª.
60 M. P. IX. 2–3.
61 Comp. Cyprian *de lapsis* 25 and 26 (On the libation of minors, see *Texte aus Aegypten*, ed. Meyer, No. 15 1. 10). In a city like Caesarea, where the Samaritans formed the largest minority (see above), it was well understood, for the latter used to initiate their sucklings in religious rites. See Prof. A. Halkin's article in the *Proceedings of the American Academy for Jewish Research*, vol VII., p. 47 and my remarks in ספר קרית vol. XV., p. 57.
62 Vol. II., p. 330.
63 *'Abodah Zarah*, I. 2, 39°.
64 So *Cod. Leyden*, an obvious mistake for דוקוס. The usual spelling of *dux*, both in Aramaic and Syriac, is דוכוס, *or* דובס *but* דוקוס is also found. See Payne Smith, *Thesaurus, s. v.* דוקאס and דוקוס.

meaning of the passage. Some scholars[64a] altered the word טקסיס into טיכוס, τεῖχος, wall; some[64b] explained it to mean order, arrangement, and some[64c] translated it "garrison." The word דוקים on the other hand was understood as a name of a place.[64d] And after all these explanations the passage offers no sense.

But in truth the phrase needs no emendation whatever. We now know from papyri, inscriptions and literary sources[64e] that in the fourth century τάξις had quite a definite meaning, namely, *officium*. Thus it is clear that טקסיס דקיסרין means ἡγεμονικὴ τάξις, the *officium* of the governor of Caesarea, and טקסיס דדוקום means the δουκικὴ τάξις, the *officium* of the *dux Palaestinae*.

The correct translation of the passage is: "R. Abbahu said: 'The [members of the] *officium* of Caesarea (i. e. of the proconsul), since many of them are Samaritans,[65] are considered as people who observe the ceremonies [of Saturnalia and Kalendae] but the [status of the] *officium* of the *dux*[66] is doubtful.' " Here R. Abbahu explicitly states that the Samaritans are worshippers of idols in the plain sense of the word. This could only have had any meaning in the time of the persecutions. The heathen were heedless of their ceremonies, and, according to the opinion of R. Johanan (see above), the Jews could be allowed to transact business with the *officium* of the proconsul on the Saturnalia and the Kalendae. But the Samaritan members of the *officium*, who were afraid of losing their positions and feared suspicion of their indifference to the State religion, did not disregard the required ceremonies and did not fail to worship idols on these two festivals. Therefore R. Abbahu prohibited dealings with the *officum* (of the proconsul) on such days.

The decision may have concerned his own person. We have seen above[67] that he was on good terms with the officials of the proconsul and sometimes "appeased" them. In the interests of such relations R. Abbahu may have formerly (i. e. before the persecutions of Diocletian) followed the general practice of sending gifts to the *officium* of the proconsul on the Saturnalia.[68] But subsequently he had to

---

64a LEVY II, 184, KOHUT IV, 71 and others.
64b KRAUSS, *Lehnwörter* etc. 267 and *Additamenta ad librum Aruch Completum*, p. 206.
64c JASTROW 535.
64d See previous notes. Add ספר הישוב, Jerusalem 1939, p. 35. The word טקסיס is translated there (under a question mark) "holiday"!
64e See below n. 66.
65 The Rabbinic sources usually call them "*Kuthim,*" but the name שמריי is also employed (See TP *Abodah Zarah*, V. 4, 44d; *Bereshith Rabba*, LXXXI. 3, 974²; *ibid.* XCIV. 7, 1178[4,6] and elsewhere). The Samaritans used this name for themselves, saying: *"We observe the holy Law and are called Observers"* (MONTGOMERY, *Samaritans*, p. 318. Comp. also Z. BEN-HAIM, *Tarbiz*, vol. X, p. 340 n. 38). R. Abbahu hinted here with biting irony that the "Observers" are worshippers of idols.
66 δουκικη τάξις. See PREISIGKE, *Wörterbuch* etc. vol. *III (Aemter)*, p. 168b, DESSAU *apud* CALDER, *Expositor,* 1909 (vol. VII), p. 308, n. 2.
67 P. 397
68 As the Christians did, see TERTULLIAN, *de fuga*, XIII (end); comp. also *idem, de idolatria*, X. For the Jewish practice see TB '*Abodah Zarah*, 64[b] (bottom), 65[a].

decide against it because of the Samaritan officials who were to be treated like idol-worshippers of the old stamp.

But it is very interesting that the Caesarean Rabbi clearly realized the difference between the degree of duress under which the members of the *officium* of Caesarea (ἡγεμονικὴ τάξις) worshipped and that of the *taxis* of the *dux* (δουκικὴ τάξις). He is more lenient with regard to the latter than to the former. As a matter of fact the whole weight of R. Abbahu's statement seems to lie in his doubt regarding the status of the worshippers in the δουκικὴ τάξις.

This distinction throws more light on the famous inscription of Julius Eugenius.[69] We learn from it that according to a late edict of Maximinus the Christian officials of the ἡγεμονικὴ τάξις were ordered to offer sacrifices without the option of leaving the service; they had to remain therein.[70]

W. M. Calder has demonstrated by force of good arguments[71] that στρατευσάμενος and στρατεία in our inscription could refer only to military and not to civil service. The new edict of Maximin concerned only the army but the old laws regarding the civil officials remained in force; they were to be dismissed.[72] The distinction in the Palestinian Talmud between the *officium of Caesarea* and that of the *dux* can be a distinction only between the civil and the military offices, for in those countries where the institution of *dux* was introduced all the cohorts were under his command.[73] Under this arrangement the offering of libations was absolutely incumbent only upon the members of the δουκικὴ τάξις. The members of the ἡγεμονικὴ τάξις could resign their posts and, as private citizens, remain loyal to their faith. The Caesarean Rabbi ruled on the basis of the respective status of the civil and military officials in connection with the character of their worship of idols.[74]

The officials of the governor would be dismissed if, as Christians or Samaritans, they refused to offer sacrifices, but thereafter as private people could easily avoid the worship of idols on the Saturnalia and the Kalendae. Since the Samaritan officials held on to their posts despite their knowledge that as government officials they would have to attend and participate in idolatrous rites and ceremonies, R. Abbahu regarded them as voluntary worshippers of idols. On the other hand, the officials of the δουκικὴ τάξις, as military officers, were *now* forbidden to leave

---

69 *Monumenta Asiae Minoris Antiqua*, ed. CALDER, I, 170. Comp. the bibliography in the *Journal of Roman Studies*, X, 1920, p. 44. Add: H. GRÉGOIRE, in *Byzantion*, VIII, p. 68–69.
70 Μ. Ἰού. Εὐ[γέ]νιος Κυρίλλου Κέλερος Κουησσέως βουλ. στρατευσ[ά]μενος ἐν τῇ κατὰ Πισιδίαν ἡγεμονικῇ τάξι... ἐν δὲ τῷ μεταξὺ χρόνῳ κελεύσεως [φ]οιτησάσης ἐπὶ Μαξιμίνου τοὺς Χρ[ε]ιστιανοὺς θύειν καί μὴ ἀπα[λ]άσσεσθαι τῆς στρατεί[α]ς...
71 *Expositor*, 1909 (vol. VII), p. 319 ff. Comp. also RAMSAY, *Luke the Physician*, p. 342 ff.
72 See EUSEBIUS, *Hist. Eccl.* VIII. 2. 4; M. P., Introduction. The "scourging" mentioned by LACTANTIUS (*de mort. pers.* X) refers to the "household" of the palace.
73 The ἡγεμονικὴ τάξις of Pisidia, which apparently did not have a *dux* at that time, included soldiers and military officers. See CALDER, *ibid.* p. 309 ff.
74 Since R. Abbahu died in 309, the question regarding the officials of the δουκικὴ τάξις was raised by him between 307 and 309. This may solve the doubts of RAMSAY, *Luke the Physician*, p. 345.

the service, and consequently R. Abbahu was unable to decide whether to regard their participation in the festival rites as voluntary or not.

This explains the distinctly negative attitude of R. Abbahu towards the Samaritans. Their officials in Caesarea, afraid of losing their posts, offered sacrifices and libations even when they had a way of avoiding it (by resigning from their positions). They did it for mercenary reasons. Not in vain did R. Abbahu reproach the Samaritans:[75] "אבותיכם לא קילקלו מעשיהם, אתם קילקלתם מעשיכם "Your fathers did not corrupt their ways but you have corrupted your ways." In face of the Christian acts of martyrdom the eagerness of the Samaritan officials to cling to their positions seemed shameful and disgraceful. From their behavior the Caesarean public inferred that the Samaritans offered not compulsory but voluntary libations. Hence the opinion of the "Some" (see above) in the Palestinian Talmud. The Samaritans were then finally outlawed and excommunicated by the Jews.

To sum up: Caesarea of the time of the persecutions had a small heathen minority; the overwhelming majority consisted of Samaritans, Jews, Christians and, probably, "Fearers of Heaven" (θεοσεβεῖς). The heathen minority was quite indifferent to the rites and ceremonies of its nominal religion. The social life of the community was complicated by the "Samaritan problem," the group with whom the Jews were on bad terms at that time. The relations between the heathen and the Jews and the Christians were tolerably good.

II.

A natural question arises. What was the attitude of the Jews at that time towards the Christian martyrs in Palestine? Eusebius twice[76] mentions that the Jews were present at the place where the Christians were tortured,[77] but he says nothing about a provocative attitude of the Jews towards the oppressed, persecuted Christians. If there had been any animosity on their part against the latter, Eusebius,[78] a contemporary eye-witness, would not have failed to mention it.[79]

We have good evidence to the effect that far from remaining indifferent to the fate of Christian martyrs in Caesarea the Rabbis approached this question from the point of view of Jewish law.

---

75 TP *Abodah Zarah* V. 4. 44ᵈ.
76 M. P. VIII. 1 and the passage quoted in the following note.
77 M. P., p. 32: חלף יחודיא בעלדבבא מצלא הוא. סגיאא גיר מנחון בהו עדנא כריכין הוו לה. "*He prayed for the Jews, the enemies, for many of them at that time stood around him.*" Comp. also M. P. VIII. 1, quoted below.
78 He did not forget to record the behavior of the Smyrnaen Jews during the martyrdom of Polycarp in the II century *(Hist. Eccl.* IV. 15, 26–29, 41, 43), a fact which was known to him only from the Epistle of the Smyrnaens. He would, therefore, not have overlooked any misconduct of the Jews of his own time and city if there had been any.
79 Comp. Juster, *Les Juifs dans l'empire Romain.* I, 52 n. 4; 53, n. 1.

In the beginning of the fourth century Christianity was no longer the creed of Jewish heretics,[80] for it had long become the faith of the Gentiles. The persecutions of the Christians were not limited to the denial of Jesus,[81] but required actual worship of idols. In the legal formulations of the previous edicts of persecution it was clearly stated that punishments would be directed against: *eos qui se cultores Dei confiterentur,*[82] "Such as professed to be *fearers of God."*

The Jews saw simple "Fearers of Heaven" among the Christian martyrs. They were probably present at the Stadium of Caesarea[83] when Agapius of Gaza was tortured. They heard him expounding his views. In his long confession[84] there is only one single allusion to the life of Jesus; to all the rest any orthodox Jew could subscribe. The Jews saw him, a Gentile, refusing to offer libations to the idols, declaring: I am going to die in order "to bear witness to you all, to the end that you may know and worship the one and only God, Creator of heaven and earth[85] etc."

What were the feelings of the Jews in this and similar cases? Eusebius himself discloses them. He tells us[86] that in a certain town of Palestine[87] the Jews were present at the trial of the Christians. "They watched that amazing contest and surrounded the court of justice on all sides ... they were the more agitated and rent in their hearts[88] when they heard the heralds of the governor crying out and calling the Egyptians by Hebrew names etc."[89] Eusebius is here a very trustworthy witness of the fact that the Jews were "agitated and rent in their hearts" at the terrible scene of trial.

Their feelings can be very easily understood. The Gentiles refused to sacrifice to the idols and suffered terrible tortures because of their refusal. What is the Jewish legal point of view? The question was brought before the Rabbinic academies. We read in TP:[90] ... ר׳ אבונא בעא קומי ר׳ אימי גוים מהו שיהו מצווין על קידוש השם ר׳ נסא בשם ר׳ לעזר שמע לה וכו׳ "R. Abuna asked R. Imi:[91] 'Are the Gentiles bound to

---

80 Whose beliefs were a threat to the integrity of Judaism, and with whom no Jewish Rabbinic authority could compromise. These were always considered by the latter as the greatest enemies of Judaism.
81 Comp. JUST. MART., *Apol.* 1. 31; EUSEB. *Hist. Eccl.* IV. 8, 4.
82 ULPIAN, *as quoted by* LACTANTIUS, Div. *Inst.* V. 11. See LE BLANT, *Les persécuteurs* etc., p. 51 ff.
83 See above n. 1.
84 M. P., ed. CURETON, p. כ״ב, Assem, and Menaea, but missing in the Greek short recension VI. 4.
85 *Ibidem.*
86 M. P. VIII. 1, according to the Syriac version and the Menaea.
87 On the name of the town see below.
88 CURET. p. כ״ט: פקעין הוו דין יתיראית ונפשתהון מצטרין הוי
89 *Ibid.* In the sixth year of the persecutions, i. e. in 309.
90 *Shebi'ith,* IV. 1, 35a and parallel. Comp. TB *Sanhedrin,* 74ᵇ.
91 Rabbis of the III, IV c.

sanctify His Name'[92]... R. Nassa in the name of R. Eleazar[93] learned it etc." The passage in TP comes from the school of Caesarea.[94] It was not a purely academical question but a problem coming directly from the stadium of that city.

Although the decision was that Gentiles were *not bound* to suffer martyrdom for the sanctification of His Name, it was only a release from a duty but not an order not to do it. What did the Rabbis think of the Gentile who did not avail himself of the exemption and did suffer martyrdom for His Name? All pious Gentiles were promised their share in the future life;[95] those of them who suffered for their good deeds were especially singled out,[96] and there can be no doubt that the pious Gentiles who suffered martyrdom for their refusal to offer sacrifices to idols were deemed deserving of one of the noblest ranks in the future world. Moreover, it seems to me that we have a direct allusion in Rabbinic literature to the status of those martyrs.

We first have to establish the correct name of the city where "the Jews surrounded the court of justice on all sides and were rent to their hearts etc."[97] The Greek[98] does not mention it; the Menaea names this city Diocaesarea. But the Syriac version[99] records: אית דין מדינתא חדא רבתא סגיאא באנשותא בארעא דפלסטינא וכולהון עמוריה יהודיא הוו. ומתקריא בלשנה ארמיא לוד ויונאית מתקריא דיוקסריא. "There is a certain great and populous city in the land of Palestine all of whose inhabitants are Jews. It is called *Lod* in the Aramaic tongue, and in Greek it is called Diocaesarea." Cureton[100] is of the opinion that Diocaesarea (= Sepphoris, צפורי) is a mistake for Diospolis,[101] and that the scene took place in Lod (= Lydda). Lawlor and Oulton[102] accept the reading Diocaesarea (= Sepphoris). They refer to the *Chronicle* (p. 320) from which it appears that the population of Diocaesarea was entirely Jewish. But the same source provides similar information about Diospolis. From Rabbinical literature we know that both cities had a predominantly Jewish population at that time.

However there seems to be internal evidence that the city in question was not Sepphoris but Lydda[103] as maintained by Cureton. Ninety-seven confessors, who

---

92 I. e. to suffer martyrdom for the sake of the sanctification of His Name.
93 This R. Eleazar is R. Eleazar the Second (See Frankel, *Mebo Hayerushalmi*, 111[b] and I. Lewy, *Interpretation des I Abschnittes des paläst. Talmud-Traktats Nezikin,* Vorwort, p. 18, n. 2). He was a contemporary of R. Nassa (See TP *Gittin,* V. 1, 46[c]), i. e. fl. in the first half of the IV c.
94 The preceding sentence in TP is explicitly recorded in the name of "the Caesarean Rabbis." R. Nassa likewise was a Caesarean Rabbi. See Lieberman, *"The Talmud of Caesarea",* p. 11.
95 *Tosephta Sanhedrin,* XIII 2, 434[10] and elsewhere.
96 See TB '*Abodah Zarah,* 10b; *ibid.* 18a; *Midrash Tehilim,* IX. 13, ed. Buber p. 89 and elsewhere.
97 See above p. 410.
98 *M. P.* VIII. 1.
99 Cureton, p. כ"ט.
100 P. 65.
101 On p. י"ב it is spelled: דיופולס
102 II. p. 328–329.
103 The Syriac version uses the old Semitic names of the places more frequently than their Greek equivalents. M. P. I. 1 (Assem. See Cureton, p. 52) has אורשלם instead of the Greek *Aelia.*

were Egyptians sent from their native land to Palestine, had their fate foredoomed in advance. They were subsequently condemned to labor in the copper-mines of Phaeno. Since the way from Caesarea to Phaeno led via Lydda,[104] the proconsul Firmilian naturally passed through that city together with the assembly of the confessors on their way to Phaeno, and tried once more to break their determination by the trial in Lydda. This city was the crucial station on the ὁδός βασιλική from where the confessors could either return to Egypt as free people or continue to Phaeno as convicts. The choice of Lydda as the scene of the last trial[105] was based on psychological considerations. But to argue that Firmilian took ninety-seven men with him to *Palaestina Secunda,* to a Jewish town in Galilee, is to assume a hardly understandable procedure. There are therefore good reasons for accepting the reading Lod as the genuine one.

It seems that the trial of the confessors in Lydda and the terrible tortures they withstood before the eyes of the Jews who "surrounded the court of justice on all sides and were agitated and rent to their hearts" at that sight left its traces in the contemporary Rabbinic writings. We find a very obscure oracle in the Midrash:[106] ר' אהא הוה מתחמד למיחמי אפוי דר' אלכסנדרי. איתחמי ליה בחלמיה. הראהו ב' מילין. הרוני לוד אין לפנים ממחיצתם. ברוך שהעביר חרפתן של לוליאנום ו פ פ ו ס ואשרי מי שבא לכאן ותלמודו בידו "R. Aha longed to see the face of R. Alexandri [in a dream]. He appeared to him in his dream and showed him *two*[107] things: There is no compartment beyond that of the martyrs of Lydda;[108] blessed be He Who removed the shame of Lulianus and Pappus and happy is he who came here [to the next world] equipped with learning."[109] The last part of the vision is quite understandable. R. Aha was comforted to hear that the man who dies in possession of learning, the man whose doubts are solved by his learning, is happy in Paradise. But the first part of the vision is very obscure. According to the commentaries the martyrs of Lydda were Julianus and Pappus, the famous two brothers who suffered martyrdom in the

---

Ibid. (CURET. p. ד twice; *ibid.* p. ל"ה twice): בישן instead of Scythopolis. *Ibid.* X. 2 (CURET. p. ל"ח) : בית גוברין instead of Eleutheropolis (but p. ה אלותרפולס:).
104 See LIEBERMAN, *The Talmud* of *Caesarea,* p. 14.
105 Ammian. Marcel. (XIX. 12.8) relates: "As the theatre of torture and death (of those who were suspected of high treason) Scythopolis was chosen, a city of Palestine which for two reasons seemed more suitable than any other: because it is more secluded and because it is midway between Antioch and Alexandria from which cities the greater number were brought to meet charges." (transl. of Loeb Class. Libr.). For these very two reasons (in our case publicity and not seclusion was desirable) we have to prefer the reading Lod.
106 *Koheleth Rabba,* IX. 10, ed. Romm 24ᵇ.
107 Counting the martyrs and the "Shame" as one thing. (See below).
108 I. e. nobody occupied a higher place than they in Paradise.
109 In TB *Pesahim,* 50ᵃ, (and its parallel) a similar vision is ascribed to R. Joseph the son of R. Joshua b. Levi (III c.), but the Palestinian *Ruth Rabba* (Ch. III, beginning) does not mention the martyrs. This proves that we have in TB a later combination of two different stories. *Koheleth Zuta, ad loc.,* p. 122–123 follows the later tradition of TB. Comp. also יחוסי תנאים ואמוראים s. v. זבדי בן לוי ed. FISHMAN, p. 56. The author quotes our Midrash and not *Koheleth Rabba!* For further details see *Appendix* III.

first half of the second century; the "shame" refers to their martyrdom and the "removal of the shame" to the punishment of their persecutor.[110] It is difficult to understand why the martyrdom of these two men was styled "shame" and why R. Aha's mind was disturbed by a fact which happened about two hundred years previously. However the reading in our editions is a correction by the author of מתנות כהונה who quotes it in the name of an old book. The genuine reading is in *ed. pr.*:[111]

הראהו ג' מילין הרוגי לוד אין לפנים ממחיצתם בדור [112] שהעביר חרפתו של לוליאנוס ואשרי וכו'[113]. "He showed him *three* things: There is no compartment beyond that of the martyrs of Lydda; blessed be He Who removed the shame of Lulianus and happy is he etc.' " According to this true reading the martyrs of Lydda and the "shame" etc. are two entirely different things. Moreover, there is no hint of Pappus; only Lulianus is mentioned.[114] But who is this Lulianus, and what is the shame connected with his name?

It seems to me that this Lulianus is none other than Julianus[115] the Roman Emperor (361–363), and that the "Shame of Julianus" is an abbreviated euphemism for the shame brought upon the Jews by their consent to his decision to rebuild the Temple in Jerusalem.[116] Jewish scholars[117] frequently asked why the Rabbinic sources did not explicitly mention Julian's promise to rebuild the Temple. Graetz[118] correctly conjectured that the Rabbis were not too enthusiastic about the restoration of the former Jewish splendor by a heathen emperor. The Third Temple will be rebuilt by the Messiah and not by a Roman heathen.[119] Our R. Aha seems to have been of a different opinion; he maintained that the Temple will be rebuilt before the advent of the kingdom of the house of David.[120] Bacher[121] correctly saw in it an allusion to his agreement to the undertaking of Julianus. It was after Julian's death (363), when it was clear that his undertaking failed, that R. Aha

---

110 See *Megillath Ta'anith*, end, scholion, and the sources mentioned in Prof. Finkelstein's article in *Essays and Studies in Memory of L. R. Miller*, p. 38, n. 7.
111 Pesaro and Constantinople.
112 Read: ממחיצתם. ברוך.
113 Ed. Venice 1545, f. 84ᶜ reads: הראה ב' מילין, הרוגי לוד אין לפנים ממחיצתם בדור שהעבירו חרפתו של לוליאנוס ואשרי וכו'. BENVINISTE (*Oth Emeth*, ed. Salonica, f. 114ᵇ) quotes the variant ברוך (to the word בדור) but records no other variant to this passage.
114 The wrong addition of Pappus to Julianus is quite understandable; these two names are very frequently associated in Rabbinic literature, see *Bereshith Rabba*, LXIV. 10, 710; TP *Shebi'ith*, IV. 2, 35ª and above n. 35.
115 See *Appendix*, II.
116 See J. BIDEZ, *La vie de l'empereur Julien*, p. 306 and notes ibid.
117 See BACHER in *JQR*. X, 1898, p. 168.
118 See BACHER, *ibid*.
119 Comp. *Pesikta Rabbathi*, ed. FRIEDMANN, f. 160ª. See also *Rashi, Sukka*, 41ª (bottom), whose explanation is a quotation from *Tanhuma*, as it follows from *Tosaphoth Shebu'oth*, 15ᵇ (.top). For the expression used by this *Midrash*, comp. *Sifre* II, 352, ed. FINKELSTEIN, p. 410³ ff.
120 TP *Ma'aser Sheni* V. 2. 56ᵇ.
121 *Ibid*. p. 169–170 and *Agada der Paläst. Am*. III, p. 111–112.

saw the vision; "Blessed be He Who removed the shame of Lulianus,"[122] for a Jewish Messiah will rebuild the Third Temple and not a Gentile king. R. Aha himself subsequently formulated his opinion succincty:[123] ממי דרך כוכב מיעקב. דרך כוכב ועתיד לעמוד מיעקב *"There shall come forth a star out of Jacob'* (Num. XXIV. 17). Out of whom shall the star come forth and remain permanently? Out of Jacob." This saying was probably uttered after his vision.

Thus we see that two points of the vision were contemporary questions which disturbed R. Aha personally, and it is reasonable to seek the third point (the martyrs of Lydda) in the same direction. We can presume *a priori* that it was a hard and perplexing question which troubled the Jewish sage.

Our R. Aha was a Lyddan Rabbi,[124] born in the last decades of the third century. He may have had first-hand information of the trial of the Egyptian confessors (in 309) in his native town. Perhaps he himself, as a youth, was present at the terrible spectacle and witnessed the sympathy which the Jewish crowds showed towards the martyrs. The problem might have disturbed his mind for a long time.

He was very old when he saw the vision. The failure of Julian's promise was already known to him, and therefore the dream could not have occurred earlier than June 363, probably a few months later. Ammian. Marcell. relates[125] that comets were seen at Antioch in broad daylight (*et visa sunt interdia sidera cometarum*) shortly after the death of Julian. He talks as an eye-witness, for he says that he was in Antioch at that time, and he tries to explain the phenomenon. At any rate this was the rumor current then in the orient. The Palestinian Talmud[126] records: "The star (Mercury?) was seen at midday when R. Aha died."[127] If we take these legends seriously[128] we may assume that the death of R. Aha shortly followed that of Julian. The "shame of Julian" has just now been removed, the doubts of R. Aha regarding the martyrs[129] of Lydda were finally solved, and he

---

122 Dr. Johanan Lewy demonstrated the motives and plans of Julian, which dictated his decision to rebuild the Temple (Hebrew quarterly Zion vol. VI. p. 22 ff.). I fully accept his conclusions and there is no wonder that the Jews considered their consent "a shame."
123 TP *Nedarim*, III. 12, 38ᵃ. Comp. Bacher, *ibid.*
124 See TP *Sanhedrin*, I. 2, 18ᶜ⁻ᵈ and elsewhere. Comp. Bacher, *Agada etc.*, III p. 106 ff.
125 XXV. 10. 2.
126 *'Abodah Zarah*, III. 1, 42ᶜ.
127 כד דמך רי אחא איתחמי כוכבא בטיהרא. Comp. also TB *Mo'ed Katan*, 25ᵇ and Rabbinovicz *ad loc.* p. 87 n. 50.
128 A similar legend is related on another occasion. We read in the *Hist. Aug.* (Pert., XIV 3): "*On the day before he died, very brilliant stars were seen near the sun in the day-time*" (Stellae etiam iuxta solem per diem visae clarissimae ante diem quam obiret). Comp. also the Christian legends in Migne PG XXXIII, 1169; *ibid.* 1176 ff.; H. Grégoire, *Revue de l'Université de Bruxelles*, vol. 36 (1931), pp. 254–255.
129 The original has הרוגי "the slain." The Egyptian confessors were not slain, but "*they were deprived of the use of their left feet ... their eyes were dug out with the sword and then finally destroyed by fire.*" (Comp. Lact. *de mort. pers.* ch. XXXVI.). The term הרוגי could easily be applied to them (Comp. TB *Hullin*, 35ᵇ and parallels).

was comforted to see the last part of his vision: "Happy is he who came here equipped with his learning."

III.

The history of the Jews in Palestine is rich in martyrs and martyrdoms. In the time of Antiochus Epiphanes the Jews, though suffering tortures and death, remained faithful to the precepts of the Law. After the destruction of the Second Temple the Jewish prisoners endured tortures and death and did not utter a single word contrary to the law.[130] In the time of Hadrian they did not betray the Law in the face of threats of death and tortures of vengeance.

The Jews took their martyrdom calmly and as a matter of course. They tried to avoid it, going so far as to disguise their nationality by dressing as non-Jews.[131] But when they were discovered and had to face the worst, they submitted to martyrdom quietly. They sanctified His Name by showing that they loved Him with all their soul (see Deut. VI. 5). The names of the simple people who suffered tortures and death for the sanctification of His Name are not known. The dates of the martyrdom of the great, learned Jewish leaders were not transmitted to posterity (we find them only in the later writings). The Jews did not commemorate those days; there was no martyr-cult in Israel.

Apparently there were no Jewish martyrs in Palestine during the persecutions by Diocletian and Galerius. Yet the Jewish victims in the time of Hadrian, according to the Rabbis of the II–IV centuries, suffered tortures very similar to those described by Eusebius in M. P. The martyrs of both religions were tormented in the same city (Caesarea), by the same Roman government. The difference of almost two centuries did not change conditions greatly in the procedure of the *apparitores* in Caesarea.

S. Krauss published two useful articles bearing on our subject. One, in which he collected much material from the Talmuds and Midrashim, deals[132] with the tortures of the body mentioned in ancient Rabbinic literature.[133] In the other he presents the Talmudic and Midrashic material bearing on the tortures of

---

It goes without saying that the interpretations regarding the Martyrs of Lod and the Shame of Julianus are entirely independent. Whereas the former is only a probable conjecture, the latter is almost a certainty.

130 Joseph., *Contra Ap*. I. 8. 43: ἤδη οὖν πολλοὶ πολλάκις ἑώρανται τῶν αἰχμαλώτων στρέβλας καὶ παντοίων θανάτων τρόπους ἐν θεάτροις ὑπομένοντες ἐπὶ τῷ μηδὲν ῥῆμα προέσθαι παρὰ τοὺς νόμους καὶ τὰς μετὰ τούτων ἀναγραφάς.

131 *Bereshith Rabba*, LXXXII. 8, ed. Theodor-Albeck p. 984⁶. Comp. also Suet. *Domitian*. XII.

132 Hebrew quarterly דביר, I. p. 88 ff.

133 Krauss (p. 104) quotes the Rabbinic Aggada which charged Manasseh with the assassination of Isaiah by means of sawing his body, remarking that this kind of torture as an actual punishment is not referred to anywhere else in Rabbinic literature. This statement is not correct. In *Bereshith Rabba* (LXV. 22, 742⁵) this cruelty is mentioned. Comp. also Le Blant; *Les persécuteurs* etc.,

the famous "Ten Martyrs."[134] In the latter he made an attempt to compare the Rabbinic records on the Jewish martyrs with those of the various Christian *acta martyrum*. However, Krauss did not discriminate well between Tannaitic (II c.), Amoraic (III–V c.) and later Midrashic sources. His investigations are mainly concentrated around the later Midrashim. These have little historical value for our purpose, since they utilized material from earlier Midrashim concerning individual martyrs, which they related to the traditional number of the Ten Martyrs and embellished them with the usual Aggadic elements.[135] The only trustworthy accounts are those of the Tannaitic and Amoraic works. It is to be highly regretted that the Tannaitic sources have only very scanty material on this subject.[136] The stories of martyrdom are reported by them occasionally and incidentally, only for the purpose of teaching a moral lesson,[137] and their silence on details is not decisive. The Amoraic writings provide more ample information.

However, the difference between them and the Tannaitic presentation of such stories is very instructive. We read, for instance, in Sifre:[138]

כשתפסו את ר' חנינה בן תרדיון נגזרה עליו גזירה לישרף עם ספרו. אמרו לו נגזרה עליך גזירה לישרף עם ספרך... אמרו לאשתו נגזרה על בעלך גזרה לישרף ועליך ליהרג...אמרו לבתה נגזרה גזרה על אביך לישרף ועל אמך אמר ליהרג ועליך לעשות מלאבה...עמד פילוסופוס [139] על אפדכיא [140] שלו אמר לו מרי אל תזוח דעתך ששרפת את התורה שממקום שיצאת חזרה לה לבית אביה, אמר לו למחר אף דינך כיוצא באלו, אמד לו בשרתני בשורה טובה שמחר יהא חלקי עמהם לעולם הבא

"When R. Haninah b. Teradyon was seized [while teaching the Law] sentence was passed on him to be burnt with his Book (i. e. the Torah). They informed him: 'Sentence has been passed upon you to be burnt together with your Book'... they informed his wife: 'Sentence has been passed upon your husband to be burnt with his Book and on you to be executed' ... they informed his daughter: 'Sentence has been passed on your father to be burnt, on your mother to be executed, on you to "do work" ' (i.e. to be prostituted)[141]... Then one philosopher stood up before

---

p. 295, n. 4 and the figure *ibid.* For the torture by means of a copper μίλιον (KRAUSS, *ibid.*, p. 110) see LE BLANT, *ibid.* p. 292 and the figure on that page.

134 השלח Vol. XLIV (1925), p. 10–22, 106–117, 221–233.

135 See Prof. FINKELSTEIN's article on the Ten Martyrs in *Essays and Studies in Memory of L. R. Miller*, p. 29 ff. Comp. n. 33, above ch. I.

136 See *Mekhilta Bahodesh*, VI. ed. HOROVITS, 277[7]; *ibid. Mishpatim* XVIII, 313[5] (and parallels in *Aboth deR. Nathan*, ed. SCHECHTER, p. 114 and *Semahoth* ch. VIII. Comp. *Appendix* IV); *Sifre* II, sect. 307, ed. FINKELSTEIN, p. 346 and *Tosephta Sota*, XIII, 319[5]. See also *Midrash Haggadol, Genes.*, p. 510 (Comp. the wording of R. *Hiyya B. Abba's* statement with that of *Shir Hashirim Rabba* II. 7).

137 Comp. *Mekhilta Mishpatim*, *ibid.*

138 *Ibid.* The story is related quite incidentally on account of the verses cited by the martyrs.

139 The majority of mss. read: פוליסופוס, πολύσοφος, very wise.

140 An Aramaic form of איפרכוס. Comp. *Koheleth Zuta*, VIII. 4 *(Yalkut ibid.* 989): איפרכיא באיש.

141 *Midrash Haggadol Genes.*, ed. SCHECHTER, p. 420. quotes from the Sifre: שיעשו ביך מלאכת בשבה: the *Exempla* of the Rabbis (GASTER, p. 41) read ועליך לעשות מלאכה בשבת "*On you to do work on Saturday*"! The Yemenite sources misunderstood the expression מלאכה. This word when used in connection with a woman had a definite meaning, as above, in Palestine. It meant: [σώματι]

the proconsul[142] and said: 'My master do not become proud [of the fact] that you burnt the Scroll of the Law, for it has returned to the place whence it was issued, to its Father's house.' He said to him: 'Tomorrow you will be punished like them.' He retorted: 'You have announced good tidings to me; tomorrow my share will be with them in the future world.' "

The final redaction of this text took place either at the end of the second or at the beginning of the third century. Thus, the source used by the Sifre was most probably contemporary with the event (during the fourth decade (?) of the second century), and is most authentic as regards the details of the execution. If we analyze the single elements of the story we find there nothing unusual in the Roman practice. R. Hanina was sentenced to be burnt alive (together with his book)[143] for having taught the Law. This penalty was frequently inflicted on the Christian Martyrs.[144] His daughter was condemned to prostitution, a punishment often mentioned by the Christian Church Fathers.[145] Finally a certain "philosopher" expressed sympathy for the martyr, and was threatened with death—nothing unusual.

But the Babylonian Talmud[146] describes in detail the execution of our saint. Three elements attract our attention in the account recorded in TB: first, that the Jewish sage was consumed by a slow fire and had wet tufts of wool placed over his heart; second, that his disciples advised him to open his mouth in order to let the fire enter the inside of his body, but he refused; third, that the executioner voluntarily threw himself into the fire.

The first detail was frequently practiced on the Christian martyrs of Palestine at the beginning of the IV c.[147] Urbanus, the governor of that country, had the feet of Apphianus wrapped in cotton soaked in oil and set them on fire.[148]

The second detail is very interesting. Le Blant[149] has already called attention to the habit of Christian martyrs tortured by fire of opening their mouths in order to

---

ἐργάζεσθαι This is clearly evident from *Bereshith Rabba*, LXXXVII. 7, 1072². The parallel sources state explicitly that the daughter was condemned to a house of infamy. Comp. however TB *Megilla* 12b.

142 Literally: "before *his* proconsul". The philosopher was a member of the *consilium* over which the proconsul presided.
143 Comp. *Mekhilta, Bahodesh*, VI: מה לך יוצא לישרף על שקראתי בתורה '*Why are you being, lead out to be burnt? Because I read the Tora.*" Comp. also TP *Ta'anith* VI, 69ª and our conclusions at the end of this chapter.
144 Comp. LE BLANT, *Les persécuteurs* etc., p. 65 ff.
145 See LE BLANT, *ibid.* pp. 171, 176, 206; LAWLOR and OULTON, *Eusebius*, II, p. 326; F. AUGAR, *Die Frau im römischen Christenprocess*, p. 40 ff. Our source shows that this sentence was practiced under Hadrian.
146 A "*Baraitha*" in '*Abodah Zarah* 18ª.
147 See *M. P.* III. 1; KRAUSS *in* השלח XLIV (1925), p. 228.
148 *M. P.* IV. 12; KRAUSS, *ibid.*
149 *Mélanges d'archéologie et d'histoire*, V (1885),p. 102 ff.; idem, *Les persécuteurs* etc., p. 239 ff.

put an end to their sufferings.[150] However, R. Hanina did not open his mouth to the flames; he preferred to endure the terrible pains and not to return the deposit of the King until He Himself chose to take it.

As to the third scene, the death of the executioner, there is an open divergence between the Sifre[151] and the Talmud.

From the comparison of the two scenes portrayed in the above sources it may seem that the later one is colored by the contemporary procedure. However, there is no doubt that the display of cruelty of the Caesarean *apparitores* did not change much during the almost two centuries separating the Jewish from the Christian martyrs.

The great R. 'Akiba was beyond any doubt the most famous and the most popular Jewish martyr. Many legends have been woven around his death;[152] we shall however quote only the oldest records of his martyrdom. We read in the Palestinian Talmud:[153] ר' עקיבה הוה מיתדין קומי טונוס (ט)רופוס הרשע אתת ענתה דקרית שמע שרי קרי ונחך, אמר ליה סבא, סבא או חרש את או מבעט בייסורין את וכו' "R. 'Akiba was tried[154] before the impious Tineius Rufus.[155] The time for reciting the Shema' arrived. He commenced to recite it and became very joyful. 'Old man, old man', said he (i. e. Rufus), 'art thou a magician or dost thou defy torture'?[156] etc." He was detained in prison for a long time. According to a later source[157] he was confined there for *two*[158] years. During that time his disciples had access to him,[159] and he contrived to teach them the Law there. Even the governor himself used to conduct discussions with R. 'Akiba,[160] in which he was always worsted by the

---

150 *M. P.* XI. 19: PRUDENTIUS. *Peristeph. Hymn.* III, 159–160. Hananiah, Mishael and Azariah in the furnace are portrayed in the early Christian pictures as standing with open mouths amidst the flames; see LE BLANT, *ibid.,* p. 291. Comp. also LUCIAN, *de morte Peregrini* 21 (end).
151 Here it is the philosopher, a member of the *consilium* (above n. 11), who protested against the sentence. Some hundred and fifty years later (298) St. Cassianus, the shorthand-writer of the court, threw down his note books in protest of the sentence pronounced over St. Marcellus. He declared to the judge: *iniquam eum dictasse sententiam.* (RUINART, *Acta Sincera*,[2] p. 305).
152 See *Midrash Mishle,* IX. 2, ed. BUBER, p. 61 and the sources referred to by KRAUSS, *ibid,* p. 108.
153 *Sota,* V. 7, 20[c] and parallel.
154 But TB *Berakhoth* 61[b] records: והיו סורקין את בשרו במסרקות של ברזל "*And they combed his flesh with iron combs.*" This seems to have been the most common torture in Caesarea at the beginning of the IV c. The Syriac version of M. P. mentions these cruel סרקא very frequently. See ed. CURETON (translation), pp. 6[16], 15[31], 22[25], 28[28], 38[21], 40[35] 41[8], 45[18] and 47[33].
155 See SCHÜRER, *Geschichte,* I[4], p. 467.
156 The Christian martyrs were also accused of defying torture by means of sorcery. See LE BLANT, *Les Persécuteurs* etc., p. 217.
157 *Midrash Shir Hashirim,* ed. GRÜNHUT, f. 5b.
158 The text has 'ב as noted by the editor *ad loc.* The scribes have subsequently resolved the abbreviation to עשרים (see below there). The earlier sources *(Tosephta Sanhedrin,* II. 8, 417[2]) seem to imply three years, but the meaning is not quite clear. See TB *Sanhedrin,* 12a.
159 See TB '*Erubin,* 21b, *Pesahim,* 112a (in the name of a "*Baraitha*", probably of the III c.).
160 *Bereshith Rabba,* XI. 5. 92[5]; TB *Sanhedrin,* 65b; *Pesikta Rabbathi,* XXIII, ed. FRIEDMANN, f. 119[6]; *Tanhuma Terumah,* 3; *ibid. Tazri'a,* ed. BUBER, p. 35 (all the sources apparently not earlier

wisdom of the latter. Subsequently the treatment of R. 'Akiba became harsher, and the Rabbis had to outwit the guards in order to get legal decisions from him.[161] When the difficulties increased four hundred denarii had to be expended in order to obviate them.[162]

The great saint breathed his last in prison during the month of Tishri[163] and by a miracle his body was removed from there and brought to eternal rest in the vicinity of Caesarea.[164] TB[165] is the first source to inform us that he died of being tortured by means of iron combs at the hands of the proconsul of Caesarea.

Pamphilus, the teacher of Eusebius, was undoubtedly the most distinguished and learned man among the Christian martyrs of Caesarea.[166] He founded a school of Christian instruction in that city, collected a big library and was particularly interested in the establishment of the authentic text of the Bible; he created a center of Christian learning, and copies of the Bible were brought there from different churches for the purpose of fixing the correct text.[167] He was thrown into prison around November (the latter Teshri), 308 and kept there about two years.[168] During his imprisonment the governor Urbanus "made a trial of his wisdom by questions and answers"[169] or "tested his knowledge of rhetoric and philosophy."[170]

All that time he continued his regular activity of transcribing and correcting the Scriptures,[171] and his pupils were able to visit him.[172] This tolerant attitude on the part of the Roman officials did not save him from the tortures of the combs.[173] He was executed[174] in 310, and his body was buried in honor after having been miraculously preserved from carnivorous wild beasts.[175]

---

    than the IV c.). There is, however, no hint in the sources that the discussions took place during R. 'Akiba's imprisonment.

161 See TP *Yebamoth*, XII. 6, 12^d; Comp. TB *ibid.* 105^b (the sources are not later than the III c.).
162 TB *ibid.* 108^b (not later than the III c.).
163 *Midrash Mishle*, IX. 2 (ed. BUBER, p. 62); *Halakhoth Gedoloth*, ed. HILDESHEIMER, p. 194 (on the time of the source see the following note).
164 *Midrash Mishle, ibid.* (original source not earlier than the IV c.).
165 See above n. 23 (The source seems to be a later "*Baraitha*", III c.?). Comp. also TB *Menahoth*, 29^b.
166 *M. P.* VII. 4–5.
167 See *M. P.* V. 2; *ibid.* ed. CURETON, p. 37 ff.; SCHWARTZ in PAULY-WISSOWA, *Real-Encyclopädie*, VI. 1372, 1373; J. STEVENSON, *Studies in Eusebius*, p. 23 ff.; LAWLOR and OULTON, *Eusebius*, vol. II, p. 331–332.
168 M. P. XI. 5. On the exact time see LAWLOR, *Eusebiana*, p. 199.
169 *M. P.* Syriac version, ed. CURETON, p. 25^{13}.
170 *Ibid.* Greek version, VII. 5.
171 See LAWLOR and OULTON, *Eusebius*, vol. II, p. 224–225; *ibid.* p. 331. Comp. also H. B. SWETE, *An Introduction to the Old Testament in Greek*, p. 77.
172 See STEVENSON, *Studies in Eusebius*, p. 54 ff.
173 *M. P.* VII. 6.
174 *Ibid.* XI. 7.
175 *Ibid.* XI. 28.

What a striking parallel to the account of R. 'Akiba's life and death in the prison of the same city![176]

However, although the tortures and the means of executions of the Christian and Jewish martyrs (during the Hadrianic persecutions) were very similar, the judicial procedure in the trial of these two groups differed considerably. Mommsen[177] maintained that originally no special law was in force against Christianity and that the Christians were nominally charged under the *Lex Majestatis* with refusal to render the religious honor due to the emperors, but actually prosecuted under the vague power of *coercitio* which entitled prefects, governors and other high officials to act summarily against any person considered to be dangerous.

Other scholars[178] are of the opinion that a special law against Christianity was issued by Nero, which read something like: *Non licet esse Christianos*. Tertullian[179] states that the Roman law said: *Non licet esse vos*. Origen[180] asserts: *Decreverunt (reges terrae) legibus suis ut non sint Christiani*. The Edict of Toleration[181] declared: denuo *sint Christiani*.[182]

It is clear that in the second century the mere name of Christian was already a crime *(nomen crimen est)* regardless of the moral behaviour of the bearer. But unlike all other criminals the Christian had the choice of repentance. If he sacrificed to idols or to the statue of the emperor he was immediately acquitted, in accordance with the special rescript of Trajan[183] (in 112). This was the regular practice[184] of the judges, as can be seen from the various *acta martyrum*. They disregarded the confession of the Christians if the latter followed their prompting to recant. A few grains of incense were enough to dismiss the case.

But what was the legal formulation of the persecutions of the Jews during the reign of Hadrian? Mommsen's theory[185] that the Jewish nation was dissolved after the revolt (in 70) was totally refuted by Juster.[186] The Jews continued to

---

176 The most important details of R. 'Akiba's martyrdom are provided by third century sources, and therefore could not be influenced by the narratives about the Christian martyrs under Diocletian. On the other hand, the details of Pamphilus' martyrdom are well attested by authentic contemporary sources, and they could not be borrowed from the description of the death of the great Jewish Martyr. We may therefore conclude that we have here two independent accounts which display the similar procedure of the Caesarean *apparitores* during almost two centuries.
177 In his famous article *"The Crime of Religion in Roman Law"*, Historische Zeitschrift, 1890, vol. LXIV. p. 389 ff.
178 See, for instance, PAUL ALLARD, *Histoire des persécutions pendant les aeux premiers siécles*, p. 165 ff.
179 *Apol.* IV
180 *Homil.* IX *in Jos.*
181 LACT., *de mort. pers.* 34.
182 ALLARD *ibid.*, p. 165 nn. 3, 4, 5. Comp. also n. 2.
183 PLIN., *Epist.* X, 97.
184 From the second century on.
185 *Historische Zeitschrift*, 1890, p. 421 ff.
186 *Les Juifs dans l'empire Romain* II, p. 19 ff.

be recognized as a nation and not only as *collegia cultorum*. The question then is, did the anti-Jewish laws of Hadrian proscribe the name Jew, reading something like: *Non licet esse Judaeos?* Or did they abrogate the *privilegia Judaica*, declaring the Jewish religion a *religio illicita* and punishing the transgressors in conformity with the imperial law? The answer is provided by the Rabbinic sources.

From both Jewish and non-Jewish sources it appears that Hadrian's prohibition of circumcision preceded the Jewish rebellion,[187] a view accepted by modern Jewish and non-Jewish scholars.[188] Schürer[189] rightly observed: "The prohibition of circumcision was not limited to the Jews and was not immediately directed against them. When, under Antoninus Pius, the Jews were again allowed to circumcise their children, the prohibition still stood good against non-Jewish peoples. It was therefore originally a general order. The special feature of this legislation was not that it aimed at the rooting out of Judaism, but that it placed circumcision on the same level with castration and punished its practice accordingly (under *lex Cornelia de sicariis*). The prohibition was not, therefore, first of all directed against Judaism, but it is at the same time quite evident that Judaism would receive from it a deadly wound." There can be no doubt that the prohibition was one of the causes which stimulated the Jewish rebellion.[190] It is after the full outbreak of the rebellion that the reaction of Hadrian resulted in the proscription of most Jewish rites and practices.

We know that thereafter the Jews were forbidden to observe the Sabbath,[191] to eat unleavened bread on Passover,[191] to take the *Lulab* on *Sukkoth*,[192] to sit in the *Sukka*,[193] to read the scroll of Esther on *Purim*,[194] to light candles on *Hanukka*,[195] to observe the laws of tithes,[196] show-fringes,[197] *Tephilin*,[198] *Mezuza*,[199] mourning customs,[200]

---

187 *Mishna Shabbath* XIX. 1; TB *ibid*. 130a. TP *ibid*. 17a, TB *Yebamoth* 72ª; SPART. *Hadr.* 14. Comp. S. RAPOPORT, *'Erekh Millin s. v. Adrianus*.
188 SCHÜRER, *Geschichte*, I³, p. 674 ff.; JUSTER, Les *Juifs dans l'empire Romain*, I, p. 226 and notes *ibid*.
189 *Ibid*. English translation I. 2, p. 292.
190 This reason is given by SPARTIAN. See above n. 56.
191 *Mekhilta, Bahodesh*, VI; TP *Hagiga* II, 1. 77ᵇ; TB *Taanith* 18ª and *Me'ila* 17ª. Comp. Jos. *Bel. Jud.* VII. 3. 3, 52–53 (for an earlier period).
192 *Mekhilta, ibid*.
193 *Tosephta Sukka* I, 192¹⁹ and parallel.
194 *Ibid. Megilla* II, 223¹⁵ Comp. 221²⁷ and parallels.
195 TB *Shabbath* 21ᵇ, as correctly understood by PINELES, *Darka Shel Tora*, p. 47.
196 *Mishna Ma'aser Sheni* IV. 11.
197 *Vayyikra Rabba* XXXII, 1.
198 *Mishna 'Erubin* X, 1; *Megilla* IV, 8; TB *Shabbath* 49ª.
199 *Tosephta Megilla* IV, 228⁴ (and parallels); TB *Yoma* 11ª.
200 *Semahoth* IX, ed. HIGGER 175¹, see variants *ibid*.

divorce,[201] marriage on Wednesday,[202] ritual immersion[203] (after menstruation), reading of *Shema'*,[204] study of the law,[205] and ordination of Rabbis.[206]

We have seen above that the prohibition of circumcision preceded the Jewish rebellion. It is pertinent to ask whether all the enumerated restrictions were enacted during and after the rebellion, or whether some of them were decreed prior to it.

It seems that not all of them were published simultaneously. We read in Tosephta[207]: "Rabbi Meir said: We were once sitting before R. 'Akiba in the House of Study[208] and we recited the *Shema'* [in such a low voice] that it was not audible to our own ears, on account of a *quaestor* who was standing at the door etc". It is evident from this passage that the study of the Law was not as yet forbidden; R. 'Akiba met together with his disciples in the House of Study. The *quaestor* watched them only to prevent them from reciting the *Shema'* but apparently was not concerned with their study of the Law.

It seems, therefore, that the recitation of *Shema'* was forbidden before the other restrictions were enacted. The reason is quite obvious. The first verse of the *Shema'* (Deut. VI 4) reads: *God is our Lord, God is One*. This sounded like a direct challenge to the ambitions of Hadrian. At a time when discontent with the Emperor's religious policy began to brew in Palestine, the Jewish acclamation εἷς θεὸς μόνος acquired a revolutionary meaning. Hadrian may have seen in it a protest against his ambitions,[209] a watchword to defy his divine authority.[210] It is quite reasonable to assume that the prohibition to recite the *Shema'* was the precursor of the other restrictions.

We know further that in the time of R. 'Akiba it was already forbidden to teach the Law publicly.[211] But I doubt that it was then a prohibition *per se*. We read in the Babylonian Talmud[212]: "The wicked government once decreed against the Jews[213] that they should not engage in the study of the Law (publicly?). Pappus b. Judah came and found R. 'Akiba collecting assemblies and teaching them the Law." This is the reading of the editions. But the correct text is found in the best

---

201 *Mishna Kethuboth* IX. 9.
202 *Tosephta ibid.* I. 260[17] (and parallels). See Pineles *ibid.* (referred to above n. 64), p. 47.
203 TB *Me'ila* 17a.
204 *Tosephta Berakhoth* II, 4[21].
205 *Ibid. 'Erubin* VIII, 147[20], *Sota* XV, 322[13], *Mekhilta Bahodesh* VI, *passim*.
206 TB *Sanhedrin* 14[a].
207 *Berakhoth* II, 4[10].
208 *So ed. princ.* and *Cod. Vienna*.
209 On εἷς θεός as an acclamation see E. Peterson, εἷς θεός, P. 227 ff., pp. 271 (εἷς Ἰουλιανός), 305, n. 1.
210 The εἷς θεός acclamation was subsequently a regular feature in the Christian martyrology. See Peterson, *ibid.* p. 183 ff., p. 189 ff.
211 Minor tract *Kalla*, end: R. 'Akiba taught under an olive tree, *etc*.
212 Berakhoth 61[b]. The source is a "*Baraitha*" of the second or the early third century.
213 See Rabbinovicz, *Variae Lectiones ad loc.*, p. 355.

mss. of the Talmud:[214] "The wicked government once issued a decree that the Jews should not engage in the study of the Law, and that he who engaged in the study of the Law would be stabbed by the sword.[215] Pappus b. Judah came and found R Akiba expounding [the Law] and collecting assemblies, etc."

At first glance the order of the sentence in the editions is quite logical: R. 'Akiba collected assemblies in order to teach them the Law. But the original and genuine reading of the mss.[216] implies that there were two transgressions: teaching of the Law and collecting assemblies.

One of the first measures preceding a general persecution was the prohibition of political associations. This was the course of action adopted by Pliny regarding the Christians.[217] It seems that the Talmud has preserved here the official terminology of the decree. In the Edict of Toleration[218] the Christians were accused of *per diversa varios populos congregarent*. Eusebius of Caesarea[219] renders it: ἐν διαφόροις διάφορα πλήθη συνάγειν, "They were collecting various assemblies in divers places." πλήθη συνάγειν is the exact equivalent of [220] להקהיל קהלות of which the Rabbinic Sages[221] were accused. Both the Rabbis and Eusebius quoted the official terminology of Caesarea.

Thus we should divide the decrees of Hadrian into two categories. The first (the prohibition of circumcision, reciting of *Shema‘* and collecting assemblies to teach the Law) emanated from Hadrian's general policy and were not immediately directed against Judaism. The second, comprising the restrictions issued during and after the Jewish rebellion when most of the Jewish rites were proscribed, aimed at the destruction of Judaism proper. The Roman government was aided by Jewish advisers who informed it of various details of the Rabbinic laws,[222] and the Jews were accordingly ordered to transgress them. The punishment was merciless and cruel, as we shall see presently.

Indeed the Rabbis employed different terms for the two different stages of the Hadrianic persecutions. The earlier was named סכנה, *Peril*. It is used in the

---

214 *Codd. Oxf. and Paris*. See Rabbinovicz *ibid*.
215 It is noteworthy that the decree threatens with the sword and not with fire as was later the case. See above n. 12.
216 It is also corroborated by the Yemenite tradition in the *Exempla of the Rabbis*, ed. Gaster, p. 16 and by TB *'Abodah Zarah* 17ᵃ in the editions and mss. Comp. also *Acta Saturnini, Dativi*, etc., 12.
217 *Epist. X.* 96: *post edictum meum, quo secundum mandata tua hetaerias esse vetueram*. On the prohibition of associations, see the literature referred to by Lewy in Zion (Hebrew) vol. VIII, p. 63 ff., 66 n. 230 and p. 73.
218 Lact., *de mort. pers.* 34.
219 *His. Eccl.* VIII. 17.7.
220 On πλῆθος = קהלה see M. Schwabe in *Kedem* I, 1942, p. 92.
221 R. 'Akiba and R. Hanina b. Teradyon, see TB *'Abodah Zarah* 17ᵃ.
222 TP Hagiga II 1, 77ᵃ. The Roman governor himself was credited by the *Aggada* (*Pesikta Rabbathi*, ed. Friedmann f. 120ᵃ) with sound knowledge of Rabbinic law.

Mishna[223] and is prevalent in the *Baraithoth*.[224] Although subsequently it was applied indiscriminately, it *originally* designated only the first stage of the persecutions. It was *dangerous* to perform the Law. Regular punishment in accordance with the Roman decrees was inflicted upon the transgressors. Because he collected assemblies to teach the law, R. 'Akiba was sentenced to death by sword.[225] But it so happened that before his execution the hour for the recital of *Shema'* arrived, and the saintly hero began to recite it in defiance of the special decree which proscribed it. It was a direct challenge to the divinity of the Emperor (see above), and iron combs were applied to prevent R. 'Akiba from his recitation.[226] He did not mind the tortures and gave up his ghost with the word אתד, εἷς.[227] The tortures were applied to him only as a preventive measure, to keep him from reciting the *Shema'*. The entire execution was performed in accordance with the unjust and cruel imperial law.

As pointed out above this stage of the persecution was styled *Peril*.[228]

The later term found in the *Baraithoth* and regularly used in the Talmudim and Midrashim is שמד, destruction, extermination. It designated both the eradication, *extirpatio*,[229] of the spirit and the physical extermination, ἐξώλεια,[230] of the nation. The Jewish rebellion was drowned in fire and blood and all kinds of illogical pretexts were used to exterminate the nation physically.[231] Most of the Jewish rites and ceremonies were then forbidden and the most cruel tortures were applied to the Jews. There was no "legal" regulation of the penalties. Jewish life and property were entirely in the hands of the Roman proconsul and his officials. They acted summarily against all the Jews of Palestine under the power of *coercitio* and vented all their fury on the unhappy nation. There is no record from that period of sentences against the Jews involving exile,[232] imprisonment or work in the mines. The only sentence was death. This proves that the normal imperial law did not at that time operate in Palestine in respect of the religious crimes of the Jews. Everything depended on the arbitrariness of the local administration.

---

223 *Ma aser Sheni* IV, 11; *Shabbath* XIX. 1; *'Erubin* X.1; *Megilla* IV.8 and *Kethuboth* IX.9.
224 *Tosephta* 4[21], 147[26], 192[19], 223[15], 228[4], 260[17], 374[17], *passim*.
225 The sword was the fate of the two earlier martyrs. See *Mekhilta, Mishpatim* XVIII (and parallels in *Aboth deR. Nathan*, ed. Schechter, p. 114) and *Tosephta Sota* 319[6].
226 See above n. 23.
227 On εἷς as an acclamation see Peterson. εἷς θεός, pp. 180 ff., 253, 271.
228 Eusebius (*Hist. Eccles.* VIII. 17. 8) renders the Latin of the Edict of Toleration pertaining to the persecutions of the Christians By: πλεῖστοι μὲν κινδύνῳ ὑποβληθέντες, Many indeed were subjected to *peril*.
229 A regular Roman term for the uprooting of foreign religions. See Lewy in *Zion* vol. VIII, p. 82 and n. 8 *ibid*.
230 Appian *(de bel. civ.* II. 90) calls Trajan: ἐξολλύντα τὸ ἐν Αἰγύπτῳ Ἰουδαίων γένος.
231 See *Eka Rabba* III. 58, ed. Buber p. 139; *ibid*. p. 155.
232 For the post-Hadrianic period comp. TB *Shabbath* 33[b].

And herein lies the main difference between the persecution of the Jews at that time and that of the Christians. To be a Jew[233] was not a crime, and when a Jew confessed in court: *Judaeus sum,* he could not be sentenced for it, nor could he be condemned for his creed. Only the positive performance of a proscribed Jewish rite or ceremony was considered a crime. And although the performance of most of the Jewish rites and ceremonies became illegal,[234] it seems that specific edicts were issued to prohibit every important Jewish practice in particular, and different punishments were imposed for various practices.[235]

We read, for instance, in the Babylonian Talmud:[236] "The wicked government once decreed that whoever performed ordination should be put to death, as well as he who received ordination, the city in which the ordination took place should be demolished, and the boundaries wherein it was performed uprooted etc." The wholesale punishment of the crime is a typical example of the punitive measures applied under the power of *coercitio,* and is in accordance with the political character of the crime.[237] Indeed, when R. Judah b. Baba[238] was caught in the act of performing ordination, "the enemy did not stir from the spot until they had driven three hundred iron spear-heads into his body"[239], i. e. he was killed by the soldiers on the spot without even a nominal trial, an obvious application of military law on the field in time of war.

But what was the procedure at that time if the accused Jew was granted the privilege of a nominal trial in court? We turn once more to the unique, authoritative story referred to above. We read in the Babylonian Talmud:[240] "They brought R. Hanina b. Teradyon [to court]. They asked him: 'Why did you engage in the study of the Law?' He replied: '*As God my Lord ordered me*' (*Deut. IV* 5). *They immediately sentenced him* to be burned alive, his wife to be executed and his daughter to be committed to a house of infamy". The subsequent *Baraitha*[241] describes the terrible tortures which were inflicted on the martyr in course of his execution. We learn from these sources that, unlike the Christian martyrs, our saint was not offered the choice of recanting, but was sentenced to a cruel death *immediately* he confessed the crime. His answer: as God my Lord ordered me incensed the judge

---

233 For a man born in that faith.
234 It seems that only the specifically Jewish practices or national festivals (like *Hanuhka* and *Purim*) and civil institutions were proscribed, but prayer, celebration of holidays in a general way (rest from work, better meals) etc. were not forbidden. Only the typically Jewish "superstitions" were banned but not the general religious rites practiced by Gentiles as well in their heathen worship.
235 *Mekhilta, Bahodesh* IV, end; *Vayyikra Rabba* XXXII. 1; TB *Shabbath* 49ª.
236 *Sanhedrin* 14ª.
237 Ordination of Jewish judges granting them the right to impose fines on their correligionists.
238 There is some doubt regarding the man (See *Tosephta Baba Kamma* VIII, 362¹⁶; TP *Sota* IX. 10, 24ª and comp. Midrash *Shir Hashirim* ed. Grünhut p. 5), but the truth of the story itself is not thereby invalidated.
239 TB *Sanhedrin* 14ª.
240 TB '*Abodah Zarah* 17ᵇ, bottom.
241 TB *ibid.* 18ª.

who saw in it a direct defiance of the authority of the Emperor, and he therefore condemned him to a cruel death and all his family to perish with him. The tortures of the martyr, unlike those of the Christians, were not admonitory but vengeful.

Our R. Hanina was not the only Jewish martyr on whom the Roman officials vented their cruelty. From the Palestinian Talmud[242] we infer that the tongue of one of the Jewish martyrs was cut out.[243] This cruel act was performed both on Christian martyrs[244] and on political criminals.[245]

Although the Jewish sources do not explicitly record admonitory tortures during the Hadrianic persecutions,[246] it is hard to believe that the Roman magistrates did not in the long run avail themselves of cruelties for that purpose. After their thirst for vengeance was satisfied an alteration of method seemed a natural consequence. It is reasonable to assume that they attempted to eradicate the Jewish "superstition" by forcing the martyrs to abandon their faith.[247]

Moreover, Schlatter[248] noted that there is no clear evidence to the effect that Hadrian compelled the Jews to worship idols. He required of them only to abandon their Law, not actually to practice idolatry. This is partly true. No record exists in Rabbinic literature of a decree by Hadrian ordering the Jews to worship idols. The condemned Jewish leaders were not offered the alternative of sacrificing to idols, but there can be no doubt that the Roman officials, in their relentless efforts to destroy Judaism, tried to compel the Jews to do homage to the pagan gods or, at least, to offer divine honors to the emperor.

Indeed we read in *Tosephta*:[249] "Altars[250] which were set up by Gentiles during the persecutions may not be used even when the persecutions are over." Another statement provides even clearer proof of Roman attempts to force the conversion

---

242 *Hagiga* II. 1, 77ᵇ. Comp. TB *Kiddushin* 39ᵇ.
243 The stories mentioned in the later Midrashim are not taken into account here. Comp. however TB *Hullin* 123ᵃ, *'Abodah Zarah* 11ᵇ.
244 Romanus of Caesarea. See EUSEBIUS M. P. II. 3.
245 SUET. *Calig.* 27 (end) and DIO CASSIUS LIX. 10. For tortures of political criminals see MOMMSEN, *Le droit pénal Romain* II, p. 239 seq.
246 The story of Miriam and her seven sons (Midrash *Eka Rabba* I. 16; TB *Gittin* 57ᵇ and parallels) is borrowed from the accounts of the persecutions of Antiochus Epiphanes, as rightly observed by SCHLATTER, *Die Tage Trajans und Hadrians*, p. 8 ff. Comp. also TP *Shebi'ith* IV. 2, 34ᵃ (and parallel).
247 R. Hiyya b. Abba (fl. in the last quarter of the third century) described (*Shir Hashirim Rabba* II. 7) the terrible tortures of the "Generation of the [Hadrianic] destruction". He added that he himself would readily give his life for the sanctification of His Name, provided he were executed immediately, but that he feared he would not be able to stand the tortures they endured. In the light of this supposed change of policy on the part of the Roman officials the meaning or this statement gains added importance. He was ready to sanctify His Name if death followed immediately, but feared that he might succumb to the demands of the Romans, if torture were applied. Comp. also TB *Kethuboth* 33ᵇ and *Tosaphoth ibid.*
248 *Ibid.*
249 *'Abodah Zarah* V, 468²⁶. Comp. also TB *ibid.* 54ᵃ.
250 בימסיות, as in *ed. princ*, and *cod. Vienna.*

of Jews. The *Mishna*[251] teaches: "If a punitive expedition[252] has entered a town in peace time all the open jars [of wine] are forbidden but the sealed ones are allowed." Thereupon the Palestinian Talmud[253] observes: "During the persecutions (literally: the destruction) all (i. e. both open and sealed jars) are forbidden, for inevitably some Jew was compelled to worship".[254] This clearly implies that during the persecutions the Gentiles erected special altars to compel the Jewish masses to worship and to offer libations to idols.[255] The Romans then followed the same procedure as during the persecutions of the Christians.

But since the fragments of the Jewish *acta martyrum* preserved in Talmudic literature do not record this Roman practice, and since the above mentioned sources make no mention of the punishment for the refusal to worship idols[256] it may be safely assumed that this policy of compulsion was an arbitrary creation of the local authorities who sought to break the "obstinacy" of the Jews by all the means in their power. It was as a result of this same arbitrary policy and vague authority of *coercitio* that a soldier threatened the disciples of R. Joshua that he would compel them to worship idols, הריני משמד אתכם.[257]

We conclude with the following summary. The legal basis of the Hadrianic persecutions was provided by a series of decrees which consecutively proscribed most of the Jewish practices by specific mention of each rite and ceremony, and imposed various punishment for their transgression. Since most of the decrees were issued during and after the Jewish Rebellion, the Roman proconsul had the right to act summarily against all the Jews of Palestine under the power of *coercitio*. The Jews were not condemned either for being Jews or for their creed, but only for the positive performance and observance of Jewish rites. If a Jew was caught in the act of fulfilling the Law he was convicted and no escape was *originally* open to him. If he dared challenge the authority of the Emperor cruel tortures were inflicted upon him, and, as a political criminal, drew vengeance on his family as well. But the final aim of the Roman authorities was to pacify the country. They adopted the usual policy; after thousands of cruel executions they began to relax. They resorted to admonitory tortures and similar measures. The Jew who recanted was probably pardoned. The Romans themselves, weary of the

---

251 *Ibid.* V. 8.
252 בולשת, διογμῖται.
253 *Ibid.* V. 8, 45a.
254 I. e. to offer libations, with the result that even Jewish wine was then considered, like that of the Gentiles at that place.
255 Comp. also TB *Shabbath* 130a; *Tosephta ibid.* 128[18].
256 It is possible that later on the authorities adopted an administrative measure of pacification by pardoning the Jew who was caught in the act of observing the Law if he offered sacrifices to the idols.
257 *Bereshith Rabba* LXXXII. 8, 985. To avoid the annoyance of the Romans the disciples of R. Joshua dressed as non-Jews. Similarly, another Jew sold pork in his shop (*Tanhuma Balak*, ed. Buber, p. 145 and parallels) to pass as a non-Jew.

innocent bloodshed, inaugurated a period of so-called pacification, a time termed by the Rabbis שלפי השמד.[258]

Finally, a few words are in order about the attitude of the Gentiles towards the Jewish martyrs. It was stated at the beginning of this chapter that the Jews took their martyrdom calmly and as a matter of course. The simple Jew who was a victim of the Hadrianic persecutions did not philosophise[259] with his executioner but submitted to martyrdom quietly and untheatrically, ἀτραγῳδῶς.[260] The Gentiles were unwilling to acknowledge the courage of the Jewish martyr. In the initial act of accusation they tried to impute criminal charges to him,[261] a practice adopted by the Romans towards (the Christians as well.[262] They were subsequently able to allege that the martyr died as a criminal.

It seems to me that an interesting fragment of a polemical source to this effect is preserved in Midrash Tanhuma.[263] We read there:[264] "The [Gentile] people who witness [the execution of the martyrs] say: 'They (i. e. the martyrs) are *full of decay*, crimes are on their bands, and for this they are executed, and die because of their *corruption*',[265] but they do not know that the lot of the martyrs is in *the eternal life* etc." This Jewish view of the lot of the martyrs was known to the Gentiles. Tacitus[266] says about the Jews: *animosqne* proelio aut *suppliciis peremptorum aeternos putant. "They believe that the souls of those killed* in battle or *by the executioner* (i. e. הרוגי מלכות) *are immortal."* The whole idea of interpreting the word חלד in Ps. XVII. 14 was probably suggested by the Gentile claim that the Jewish martyrs are φθορᾶς, full of corruption.[267] To this the Jews cleverly retorted that the Gentiles do not know that the souls of the martyrs are ἄφθαρτοι,[268] immortal and eternal.

---

258 On שלהי see the Talmudic dictionaries s. v.
259 In one case it was the judge who challenged the Jew to argue *(Sifra Emor* IX. 5, 99d, and parallels), and the latter merely answered a question. Comp. also *supra* n. 115. Many retorts of Jewish martyrs during the persecutions of Antiochus Epiphanes have probably no more historical value than some of the discourses recorded by the early historians. On the defiant replies of the heathen martyrs to their judges comp. ROSTOVTZEFF, *The Social and Economic History of the Roman Empire,* p. 520, n. 17.
260 On the attitude of the enlightened pagans towards the Christian martyrs see MARC. AUR. XI. 3. Comp. P. ALLARD, *Histoire des persécutions pendant les deux premiers siècles* etc. (Paris 1892), p. 393–394; A. D. NOCK, *Conversion,* p. 197 (comp. *ibid.,* p. 299).
261 R. Eleazar b. Perata was accused of both being a teacher of the Law and a robber (TB *'Abodah Zarah* 17b).
262 See W. M. RAMSAY, *The Church in the Roman Empire,* p. 293–294.
263 *Ki Thavo* 2. The translation follows the *ed. pr.* Comp. ed. BUBER, V, p. 47, n. 19. The editor totally misunderstood the text.
264 The author of the statement is a sage of the third century.
265 An interpretation of *Ps.* XVII. 14: ממתים מחלד.
266 *Hist.* V. 5.
267 Comp. MAXIMUS THE GRAMMARIAN's epithets of the Christian martyrs (*Augustin. epist.* XVI. 2.).
268 On the play of these two Greek words in ancient literature see R. REITZENSTEIN, *Historia Monachorum etc.* (Goettingen 1916), p. 26, n. 3.

Appendices

I (to p. 402)

Eusebius[269] tells us: "The customary rains, indeed, and showers of the then prevailing winter season were withholding their usual downpour upon the earth, and an unexpected famine broke out, and on top of this a plague and an outbreak of another kind of disease. This latter was an ulcer, which on account of its fiery character was called an *anthrax*.[270] Spreading as it did over the entire body it used to *endanger greatly* its victims[271] ... while the rest of the inhabitants of the cities under his rule were so terribly wasted by both the famine and the pestilence, that two thousand five hundred Attic drachmas were given for a single measure of wheat (ἑνὸς μέτρου πυρῶν)[272] ... and others again injured their bodily health, and died from *chewing small wisps of hay*[273] etc."

From the description of the season of the rains it is evident that Eusebius talks of Palestine, or at any rate includes Palestine among the lands stricken by hunger and plague (in the winter of 312–313). Lawlor and Oulton[274] seem to question a few of Eusebius' assertions. They remark: "The famine cannot have been due to the failure of the winter rain. Scarcity from that cause would not take place till the harvest of the following year etc." This argument is not sufficient to refute the clear statement of Eusebius: absence of the customary rains creates an immediate panic. The peasant and the grain dealer instantly withdraw the grain from the market in expectation of the future hunger, and scarcity and famine break out directly after the drought.

They further remark[275] about the price of 2500 drachmas for a measure of wheat: "The sum mentioned here would therefore be about £100, which seems an impossible charge for a measure of wheat—however large the 'measure' may have been." The learned authors lost sight of the fact that the famine took place at a time of inflation.[276] Two thousand five hundred drachmas were equal to 2500

---

269 *Hist. Eccl.* IX. 8.
270 The Syriac translation (ed. WRIGHT p. 368) calls it גמורתא.
271 ἄνθραξ προσαγορευόμενον ... σφαλερούς ἐνεποίει τοῖς πεπονθόσι κινδύνους. The Palestinian Talmud (*Shabbath*, XIV. 4, 14d and parallel), in a passage apparently taken from the Caesarean academy, refers to this disease הדא גומרתא סכנה. "*This anthrax* (comp. the preceding note) is *a dangerous disease.*"
272 The Syriac translation (ed. WRIGHT, p. 369) reads: דחד מ ו ד י א דחטא בתרין אלפין וחמשמאא מעין מתיהב הוא. BAR HEBRAEUS, *Chronography*, (ed. BUDGE, vol. I. 58) writes: "*God admonished the earth with famine and pestilence [so severely] that a modius of wheat was sold for two hundred and fifty menîn.*"
273 σμικρὰ χόρτου διαμασώμενοι σπαράγματα.
274 *Eusebius*, vol. II, p. 297–298.
275 P. 298.
276 On the traces of this inflation on Palestine see LIEBERMAN, *Greek in Jewish Palestine*, p. 5. Comp. also *Tanhumah, Terumah*, ed. BUBER, p. 92.

denarii,[277] which at that time (313) had the value of something more than one *aureus*.[278] The "measure"[279] which Eusebius mentions was probably a small part of an artaba, and the price of more than an *aureus* for "a measure" of wheat[280] in time of a famine is not surprising at all. Moreover, the record of Eusebius that people used to eat "hay" at that time is corroborated by a contemporary of his. We read in the Midrash:[281] אמר ר' יצחק על הדורות הללו הוא אומר ואכלת את עשב השדה שאדם משליף משדהו ואוכלה עד שהיא עשב "R Isaac (III–IV c.) said: [The verse] *Thou shalt eat the grass of the field* (Gen. III. 18) refers to the present-day generations, when a man plucks from his field and eats it while it is still herbage."

TP[282] relates that in the time of R. Abbahu the Jews had to offer prayers for rain. This statement does not disprove the clear evidence that R. Abbahu was not alive any more at the time of the previously mentioned famine. Absence of rain at the beginning of the season was not infrequent in Palestine, and prayers for it do not prove that there was a drought during the whole season. In the case of R. Abbahu the prayers seemed to have been answered.[283] Nor was drought accompanied by pestilence very rare in that country.[284] It is, however, probable that our case of plague and drought is referred to in TB,[285] where it is related that "In the time of R. Judah the Prince (III–IV c.) there was distress;[286] he ordered thirteen fast-days but their prayer was not answered etc." The personalities who figure in this case[287] were active in 313, and the tradition tells us[288] that the prayers to remove the misfortune were ineffective.

II (to p. 413)

In TP[289] it is recorded:

"When the והא לוליינוס מלכא כד נחת לתמן נחו' (נחתון read:) עמיה מאה כ' ריבוון. Emperor Lulianus *came down* to Babylonia[290] (lit. "to there") there *came down*

---

277 See A. Segré, *Byzantion*, XV, (1940–1941), p. 249, n. 1.
278 See Segré, *ibid.* p. 263.
279 See above n. 4. Comp. Julianus, *Misopogon*, 369a-b.
280 Comp. Segré, *ibid.* p. 261. See also Joseph., *Ant.* XIV. 2.2 (28).
281 *Bereshith Rabba*, XX. 10, 194.
282 *Ta'anith*, I. 4, 64a.
283 See TP *ibid.*
284 See TB *ibid.* 8b.
285 *Ibid.* 14a-b.
286 This "distress" meant something additional to the drought (plague?). See Tosaphoth ad loc. and מראה הפנים ad TP *Ta'anith*, I.7, s. v. באילין. Comp. the reading in Ginzberg's *Genizah Studies*, I, p. 406, 1, 3.
287 R. Judah III and R. Ami etc.
288 TB *ibidem*.
289 *Nedarim*, III. 3, 37d.
290 = Persia.

with him[291] one hundred and twenty myriads [of people]." Zunz[292] correctly surmised that the Talmud refers to the expedition of Julian against the Persians, an opinion subsequently supported by Bacher.[293] However, Graetz[294] preferred the reading of the parallel passage in TP[295] which records דוקליטיאנוס, Diocletian, instead of לולייגוס Lulianus. His opinion was accepted by modern scholars.[296]

But there is no doubt that the reading Lulianus is the only genuine one.[297] In addition to the arguments adduced by Bacher, there is internal decisive evidence in favor of this reading. The army which Diocletian's Caesar, Galerius, led to Persia was comparatively small;[298] its numbers could hardly impress the orientals. On the other hand the expedition of Julian against the Persians included an army almost three times greater[299] and was led by the emperor himself. The orientals greatly exaggerated its number. The "Syriac Stories,"[300] describing the different parts of this army and their numbers, set the total at about four hundred thousand.[301] The narrator adds that these numbers did not include the people of the villages who joined the army when *it came down* to Persia.[302]

Although these stories have little historic value for the time of Julian, they afford good evidence of the exaggerated estimates of Julian's army, which circulated among the Orientals at the beginning of the VI century, the time of the composition of the Roman,[303] and probably also during the V century. They talked about immense hosts of people who *came down with Julian to Persia*.

The Palestinian Rabbis got their information from Babylonian (= Persian) sources; it is no wonder that the latter, desiring to emphasize that they were greatly outnumbered by the Romans, swelled the size of the enemy army to fantastic numbers.

Thus, the reading לוליאנוס is beyond any question, and the Talmud refers to the expedition of Julian into Persia. The name לוליאנוס given in the vision of R. Aha is not only the same name but the same person.

---

291 See below n. 34.
292 *Die gottesdienstlichen Vorträge der Juden*, ed. BRÜLL, p. 56.
293 *JQR* X (1898), p. 172.
294 *Geschichte*, IV³, p. 459.
295 *Shebu'oth*, III. 9, 34d.
296 KRAUSS, *Monumenta Talmudica*, V, p. 59. But comp. *ibid.* p. 79 note.
297 In Syriac texts of the VI c. the emperor Julian is called לוליגוס; see the Index of HOFFMANN, *Julianos der Abtruennige*, p. XIII, s. v. לוליגוס; LOEW *apud* KRAUSS, *Lehnwörter*, II, p. 310.
298 About twenty five thousand. See GIBBON, *Decline and Fall etc.* I, ch. XIII, p. 678. Comp. KRAUSS, ibid.
299 *Zosim*. (III. 13.2) gives the number of 65.000.
300 Edited by HOFFMANN. See above n. 29.
301 *Ibid.* p. 162: והוא מנינא דחילא דאתסים למעבר עם קסר לארעא דפרסיא תלתמאא ותשעין והמשא אלפין. "*And the number of the host ready to pass into the land of the Persians with Caesar, was 395 thousand.*" Comp. also BAR HEBRAEUS, *Chronography*, ed. BUDGE, I, p. 62.
302 סטר מן חלוטא דאתלויו להון כד נתחין...דלא עלו למנינא.
303 See NÖLDEKE, *Zeitschrift d. deutsch-morgenland. Gesellsch.* XXVIII, p. 283; BAUMSTARK, *Geschichte der syrischen Literatur*, p. 183.

III.

'Ανελήφθη. 'Ο κοινωνὸς ὁ κατὰ τόπον.

איתנגיד. חבר עיר. חבר מדינה (!)

On p. 413, n. 34, the version recorded in the Palestinian Midrash was prefered to that of the Babylonian Talmud. Since the incident took place in Palestine it is reasonable to accept the testimony of the Palestinian source. In support of our view a second Palestinian Midrash was also quoted there.[304] Interestingly enough internal evidence further proves that the original wording of the story has been preserved in the Palestinian source which does not mention the martyrs in the vision of R. Joshua b. Levi's grandson. TB[305] records: דרב יוסף בריה דר׳ יהושע בן לוי חלש ואיתנגיד[306] כי הדר, אמר ליה אבוה מאי חזית? א״ל עולם הפוך ראיתי עליונים למטה ותחתונים למעלה ... ושמעתי הרוגי מלכות אין אדם יכול לעמוד במחיצתן וכו׳ "R. Joseph the son of R. Joshua ben Levi fell sick and gave up the ghost.[307] When he recovered his father asked him: 'What did you see'? He said: 'I saw an inverted world; the exalted were low and the low were exalted ... And I heard that none can stand within the compartment of those martyred by the State.'" The text in the Palestinian Midrash[308] reads:

ר׳ מיאשה בר בריה דר׳ יהושע [בן לוי][309] נשתקע שלשה ימים בחליו לאחר שלשה ימים נתיישבה דעתו. אמר לה אבוי, הן הוית? אמ׳ ליה, בעולם מעורב הייתי. אמר ליה, ומה חמית תמן ? אמר ליה הרבה בני אדם ראיתי כאן בכבוד ושם בבזיון.

"R. Meyasha the grandson of R. Joshua b. Levi was made unconscious by his illness for three days. After three days he regained consciousness. His father said to him: Where were you'? He replied: 'In a confused world.' He asked: What did you see there?' He answered: 'I saw many people who were held in honor here and are in disgrace there.'" The Midrash does not mention the martyrs at all.

---

304 *Ibid.*
305 *Pesahim,* 50a.
306 See RABBINOVICZ, *Variae Lectiones, ad loc.;* idem, *Baba Bathra,* p. 45, n. 300. Comp. the *Geonic Responsa,* ed. HARKAVY, p. 179 and the *Commentary on the Sepher Yezirah* by R. JUDAH of BARCELONA, p. 24 and p. 25, *Pirkei de-Rabbi* ed. GRÜNHUT p. 48, ed. SCHÖNBLUM f. 28a.
307 So RASHI: גוע ופרחה רוחו R. HANANEL (and other commentaries): כאילו פרחה נשמתו."As if *he gave up* the ghost," i. e. fainted (Comp. *Aruch Completum s.* v. נגד I *and* נגד V.). The word איתנגיד is used as a euphemism for the death of the righteous by the *Targumim* of the Pentateuch *(Gen.* XXV. 8, 17; XXXV. 29; IL. 33). Comp. TB *Baba Bathra,* 16b (bottom) and *Nahmanides ad Gen.* XXV. 17. *Pirkei de-Rabbi (ibid.)* translated איתנגיד with לאותו העולם נמשך.Comp. below n. 30. It is noteworthy that this word does not occur (in our sense) in the Palestinian Talmud and the early Midrashim.
308 *Ruth Rabba,* III. 1.
309 See below.

As for the text, it is defective. The complete passage was preserved by R. Samuel Jama[310] who records:[311]

ר׳ מיאשה בר בריה דר׳ יהושע בן לוי נשתקע בחולי׳ אנליפתין ג׳ ימים לאחר ג׳ ימים נתיישבה דעתיה וכו׳.

The words אנליפתין נ׳ ימים—Ἀνελήφθην for three days—were omitted by the scribes (of the manuscript, or manuscripts, from which our printed editions were published) in accordance with their usual practice in case of foreign words.[312] What does אנליפהין ἀνελήφθην mean here? No Talmudic dictionary lists it. Perles[313] explains it to mean "he recuperated."[314] This explanation is totally untenable. It requires considerable alteration of the following sentence of the text. Secondly,[315] the passive of ἀναλαμβάνω never occurs in Greek in the sense of recovering. It may above all be asked why the Rabbis employed an inflected form of a Greek verb in the middle of an Aramaic sentence? It has already been observed[316] that "Almost every foreign word and phrase have their *raison d'etre* in Rabbinic literature." The use of ἀνελήφθη in this passage could be justified only if it could be proved to have been an every-day technical term conveying a well-known concept.

A very instructive article by Prof. H. Grégoire sheds light on this passage. He[317] elucidated certain words and phrases which he shows to have belonged to the Montanist terminology. He has republished[318] an inscription of the sixth century, found near the Lydian Philadelphia which reads:

Ἀνελήμφθη ὁ ἅγι[ο]ς Πραΰλι[ος]
ὁ κοινωνὸς ὁ κατὰ τόπον...

We shall subsequently return to this inscription; let us first deal with the term ἀνελήφθη. Prof. Grégoire pointed out[319] that, in addition to this occurrence, the term is found only twice among the thousands of Christian inscriptions. The oldest is the inscription of Julia Euaresta[320] which mentions: μετὰ τῶν ἁγίων

---

310 XII. c.
311 In his אגוד, *Jubelschrift ... Grätz*, Hebrew part, p. 25.
312 See Lieberman, *Greek in Jewish Palestine*, p. 152 and n. 43 *ibid.*
313 *Festschrift Adolf Schwarz*, p. 294.
314 Previously accepted by me in *Hayerushalmi Kiphshuto*, I, p. 187.
315 *Greek in Jewish Palestine*, p. 6.
316 As I learn from Prof. Grégoire.
317 *Byzantion*, II. 1925, p. 329 ff.
318 *Ibid.* p. 330.
319 *Byzant.* X, (1935), p. 248.
320 Found in Rome on the Via Latina. De Rossi, p. CXVI.

ἀνελήμφθη. De Rossi[321] designates it as *antiquissima* (i. e. third c.). The second is found in Dioskomè:[322] ἀνελήμφθη τὸ πεδίον Ἀντίπατρος etc.[323]

The first two of the inscriptions quoted above display their Montanistic character clearly, and H. Grégoire after convincing argumentation concludes that the last is also of Montanistic origin. Thus the existence of ἀνελήφθη as a technical term (= died)[324] on Montanist grave inscriptions is a well established fact.[325] The term was not invented by them. It occurs very frequently in Jewish Greek texts and especially in the Apocalyptic literature.[326] But subsequently the term disappears almost entirely from Jewish sources. It is therefore reasonable to assume that it was rather current among the Judeo Christians, who were always under the influence of the Jewish Apocryphal and Apocalyptic writings. True to their general practice[327] the Jews ceased to use it after it was monopolized by the Christians. The Montanists borrowed it from their Judeo-Christian brethren, just as they did in the case of the Heavenly Jerusalem[328](Pepouza).

Since R. Joshua b. Levi had Judeo-Christian neighbors,[329] he and other Jews of the neighborhood could naturally be expected to be familiar with the term ἀνελήφθη.[330] The original narrator in the Midrash happily used this current term in his neighborhood instead of "died" because it suited his idea perfectly; the subject of the little tale did not actually die. He was taken up, ἀνελήφθη,[331] but returned. The Midrash resorted here to the current terminology of the locality.

---

321 *Ibidem.*
322 RAMSAY, *Cities and Bishoprics* etc. II, p. 561.
323 Fifth century? See RAMSAY, ibid.
324 GRÉGOIRE (Byzantion, II, 331) takes the formula ἀνάληψις Πέτοου (Recueil, I, 260) as the death of Peter. In the *Ps. of Solomon* (IV. 20) ἀνάληψις is applied to the death of the wicked. But the word seems to be either a mistranslation from the Hebrew or a scribal error. Comp. the notes of RYLE JAMES *ad loc.*
325 The opinion or PETERSON *(Römische Quartalschrift,* XLII, 1934, p. 173 ff.) notwithstanding. Prof. GRÉGOIRE calls my attention to EUSEBIUS (Hist. *Eccles.* V. XVI, 14.) who expressed himself about Theodotus, the Montanist: ἀναλαμβανόμενον εἰς οὐρανούς.
326 See the long list by CHARLES, *The Apocalypse of Baruch* (1896), p. 73, n. 7.
327 A. APTOWITZER *(Tarbiz,* II, 270ff.) has shown that the vision of the heavenly Jerusalem and Temple which will in the future be established in this earth is a purely Jewish idea, yet it does not occur in any early Rabbinic source; according to him it was eliminated by the Rabbis because it was exploited by the Christians. It reappears in later Rabbinic sources compiled in Moslem countries. Similar examples can be found in my *"Yemenite Midrashim"* (Hebrew), p. 15 ff. Comp. also *Greek in Jewish Palestine,* p. 189. n. 30.
328 Comp. preceding note.
329 TB *Berakkoth* 7a and TP *Shabbath* XIV. 4, 14d.
330 Although the Judeo-Christians of Palestine spoke Aramaic at that time, the prayers and the biblical lessons were recited in Greek (as appears from EUSEBIUS, M. P. ed. CURETON, p. 4. See *Greek in Jewish Palestine,* p. 2), and, of course, the same language was utilized for the sacred terminology which was employed on the tomb-stones.
331 A good illustration of the use of our word in this *Midrash* is offered by a Greek fragment of the *Ascension of Isaiah* (ed. CHARLES, London 1900, p. 142). It records that Isaiah fell into a trance (ἐν ἐκστάσει) and he was thought to be dead, but when the king took his hand he learned that

The translation of ἀνελήφθη by איתנגיד[332] is quite correct. Ps. Jonathan (Gen. V. 24) renders the 'Ἀνάληψις of Enoch:[333] איתנגיד וסליק לרקיעא. It is also noteworthy that איתנגיד (designating "died") reappears on the fifteenth century tombs of the Yemenite Jews[334] who frequently preserved ancient traditions.[335]

Thus, it is clear that איתנגיד is a translation of ἀνελήφθη hut not the reverse. The original is preserved in the Palestinian Midrash; this proves the authenticity of that source. It does not record the question of the Martyrs in the vision of R. Joshua b. Levi's grandson. We can reaffirm our statement that the vision about the Martyrs was not connected with the name of R. Joshua b. Levi's grandson (III c.) but only with the name of R. Aha (IV c.). The Babylonian Talmud combined two different stories into one.

* * *

Moreover, we may assume that the title of Praylios[336] κοινωνὸς ὁ κατὰ τόπον is borrowed from the Jews. Prof. Grégoire[337] has elucidated the meaning of the Κοινωνός. The emperor Justinian banished the prelates and the priests of the Montanist church from Constantinople. He mentions:[338] τῶν καλουμένων αὐτῶν πατριαρχῶν καὶ κοινωνῶν ἢ ἐπισκόπων κτλ. H. Grégoire further refers to Jerome[339] who writes: Apud nos apostolorum locum episcopi tenent: apud eos episcopus tertius est! Habent enim primos de *Pepusa Phrygiae patriarchas,* secundos, quos appellant κοινωνοὺς[340] atque in tertium, paene ultimum gradum episcopi devolvuntur. From the Latin translation of the edict of Justinian we learn that the equivalent of the Κοινωνός was *socius.*[341]

Thus, the Κοινωνός, *socius,* was a high dignitary in the Montanist church ranking next to the Patriarch. The title Patriarch was most probably borrowed by

---

he did not actually die, but was taken up (οὐκ ἀπέθανεν, ἀλλ' ἀνελτίφθή). Comp. also HIERON., *Epist.* XXII. 30 (MIGNE PL XXII. 416): Cum subit o *raptus in spiritu* ad tribunal iudicis pertrahor. "Suddenly I was spiritually taken up and dragged before the tribunal of the Judge" (ed. Isid. HILBERG, *CSEL* L1V [1910], p. 190, 8).

332 TB. *Pesahim,* 50a Comp. *Pirkei de-Rabbi,* quoted above n. 307.
333 In Greek we should render it: ἀνελήφθη καὶ ἀνέβη εἰς τὸν οὐρανον. It shoul d be not ed t hat וסליק לרקיעא has no equivalent in the Hebrew text.
334 S. D. GOITEN, *Joseph Halévy's Journey in Yemen,* Hebrew, p. 114; Arabic, p. 61. It is very noteworthy that the Yemenite sources (Midrash *Haggadol Gen.,* p. 429; The *Exempla of the Rabbis,* ed. GASTER, p. 18) r ead in BR LXV (end), 7433: איתנח ונגוד instead of נתנמנם, fell into a trance.
335 See *Hayerushalmi Kiphshuto,* I, p. 520; *Yemenite Midrashim,* p. 16 ff.; *Greek in Jewish Palestine,* p. 189, n. 30.
336 See above p. 439.
337 *Byzantion,* II, 332 ff.
338 *Cod. Just.* I. V. 20.
339 *Ep.* XLI. 3 (ed. HILBERG, *ibid,.* p. 313, 14 ff.).
340 Mss. *caenonus* AIID, *cenonos* B, *cenonas* ς.
341 See GRÉCOIRE, *ibid.* p. 333–334.

the Montanists from the Jews, as suggested by H. Grégoire.[342] It seems that the κοινωνός[343] similarly was taken from the same source.

The Rabbinic writings frequently mention the term חבר עיר.[344] Ancient authorities[345] as well as modern scholars[346] disagree as to the meaning of this word. There is ample evidence in the Rabbinic sources that the phrase refers to a group of people in charge of religious and charitable functions;[347] the חבר עיר is then something like κοινὸν τῆς πόλεως. But, on the other hand, there is authentic evidence[348] that חבר עיר refers to an individual. And, indeed, the earliest authorities explain חבר עיר to mean the most prominent man in learning and wisdom, who exercises certain religious and social functions.[349] The term is therefore very similar to κοινωνὸς τῆς πόλεως.

In our opinion it is impossible to translate חבר עיר by the same word in all places. The existence among the Jews of an institution like κοινὸν τῆς πόλεως and an individual like κοινωνὸς τῆς πόλεως is quite certain. Both were called חבר עיר (perhaps differently vocalized), and both existed probably at the same time. The Κοινωνός of the Montanists seems to be the counterpart of the חבר עיר of the Jews, who was the religious (and to a certain extent the social) leader of the community.

We have now to reexamine the meaning of חבר in the famous inscriptions on the Maccabean coins, which read:[350]

כהן גדול וחבר היהודים

Perhaps the exact translation would be: ἀρχιερεὺς καὶ κοινωνὸς τῶν Ἰουδαίων.

Finally, it should be noted that a grave and misleading[351] error crept into Schulthess' Lexicon Syropalaestinum[352] s. v. He lists חבר מדינא as meaning *civis, πολιτικός*. The only occurrence cited by him is from a fragment of the translation[353] of the vita S. Antonii.[354] The passage relates that S. Antonius' manners were not uncouth like those of a man who grew up and became old on a mountain, but that

---

342 *Byzantion*, VIII, p. 76.
343 κοινωνὸς ὁ κατὰ τόπον would be rendered in Aramaic: תברא דאתרא. Comp. סרבא דאתרא in TP *'Abodah Zarah* I. 1, 39b.
344 Almost all of the sources which mention it are of the second century.
345 See 'Arukh *s. v.* חבר.
346 See Krauss, *Jahrbuch der Jüdisch-Literarischen Gesellschaft*, XVII (Frankfurt a. M., 1926), p. 195 ff.; Ginzberg, *A Commentary to the Palestinian Talmud*, III, p. 410 ff.
347 See Ginzberg, *ibid.* p. 421–425.
348 *Tosephta Megilla*, IV, 228².
349 See *Aruch Completum*, III, p. 337a and n. 3.
350 Madden, *the History of Jewish coinage* (London 1864), p. 62–77. The bibliography and the different commentaries were collected by Schürer, *Geschichte* etc. I⁴, p. 269 n. 25.
351 See Ginzberg, *l.* c. (above n. 41), p. 426.
352 P. 59.
353 *Palestinian Syriac texts* by Lewis and Gibson, London, 1900, p. 104.
354 Migne PG XXVI, 945a.

he was courteous and urbane. (Οὐκ... ἄγριον εἶχε τὸ ἦθος, ἀλλὰ καὶ χαρίεις ἦν καὶ πολιτικός). The Palestinian Syriac renders the last sentence: אלא מלא הוא חסד חבר מדינא This makes absolutely no sense. There is an obvious mistake of one letter. The last two words have to be read כבר מדינא [355] and not חבר מדינא [356] The translation is: "He was full of grace like an *urbanus.*" The same connection between בן מדינה and πολιτικός is found in the Mishna,[357] where פוליטיקון (or פוליטיקין) provides a play of words in conjunction with בני מדינה.[358] The correction of the Syriac text is positively certain. We may conclude: The word חבר מרינא as quoted by Schulthess does not exist.

IV

εἰς κόλπον (ἐν κόλπῳ) Ἀβραάμ בחיקו של אברהם

On p. 417, n. 5, we referred to *Aboth deR. Nathan* and to the minor tract *Semahoth* where the stories of the martyrdom of R. Simeon b. Gamaliel and R. Ishmael are related. In the eighth chapter of *Semahoth* we have a collection of almost all the early martyrdoms mentioned in the *Tannaitic* and Talmudic writings. We do not know the original source (or sources) from which it drew, but the account agrees on the whole with the earlier, *Tannaitic,* sources; the details mentioned in the Talmud are missing there. It seems therefore that its readings are sometimes preferable to those of the Talmud. On the other hand it represents a later formulation than that of the *Tannaitic* works.

According to the above *Aboth deR. Nathan*[359] R. Ishmael said to R. Simeon b. Gamaliel: כשתי [360] פסיעות ואתה [361] נתון בצד אבותיך "In two steps and you will be at the side of your ancestors." Instead of בצד אבותיך *Semahoth*[362] reads בחיקן של צדיקים, "In the bosom of the righteous." This phrase seems to be borrowed from the later terminology of the martyrs. *Midrash Ekah,*[363] in relating the story of the Mother of the Seven,[364] tells us that the mother urged her youngest son to die for

---

355 A Hebraism for הֵיךְ בַר.
356 It seems to be a mere misprint, for the editors have in the corresponding Greek text (p. 105). ὡς πολιτικός instead of καὶ πολιτικός of ed. MIGNE.
357 *Terumoth,* II. 5.
358 The explanations by Löw (*Flora der Juden,* II, 129) of בני מדינה and by SACHS (*Beiträge,* II, 195) of פוליטיקוס are wrong.
359 Version II, ch. 41, ed. SCHECHTER, p. 114.
360 So in *Neveh Shalom,* ed. TAUSZIG, p. 39. Comp. also *Menorat Ha-maor* IV, ed. ENELOW, p. 189.
361 So *Cod. Parma.*
362 *Ibid.,* ed. HIGGER, p. 153.
363 I. 16, ed. BUBER, p. 85. Comp. also *Pesikta Rabbathi* 43, ed. FRIEDMANN f. 180b.
364 IV *Maccab.* VIII. 3 ff.

His Name, telling him [365] ואתה ניתן בחיקו של אברהם אבינו "Thou wilt be placed in the bosom of our father Abraham," εἰς τὸν κόλπον τοῦ Ἀβραάμ τοῦ πατρὸς ἡμῶν.[366]

On the Christian epitaphs[367] the formula ἐν κόλποις (or εἰς κόλπους) Ἀβραάμ καὶ Ἰσαὰκ καὶ Ἰακώβ occurs very frequently. It was already observed by Le Blant[368] that both the *Euchologium* and the Christian epitaphs used here the terminology of the Martyrs. But it appears that the Christians were wont to mention the bosoms of all the three patriarchs,[369] whereas the Jews referred to the bosom of Abraham only.

In the collection of M. G. Lefebvre,[370] among the dozens of inscriptions where the bosoms of all the patriarchs[371] are mentioned, one reads:[372] ἀνάπαυσον αὐτὸ[ν] ὁ Θ(εό)ς εἰς κόλιπον[373] Ἀβραάμ.

Thus, the "bosom" mentioned in *Semahoth* betrays the later martyr-terminology, which is still absent in the earlier *Aboth deR. Nathan*.

Finally we may add that not only do we find in Jewish and Christian martyrology parallel incidents and similar terminology but also the same slogans.

The Babylonian Talmud[374] records that R. Eleazar b. Perata was charged[375] with studying the Law and committing theft.[376] He was asked by the judge: "Why have you been studying [the Law] and why have you been stealing?"[377] Our sage pleaded innocent saying: אי סייפא לא ספרא ואי ספרא לא סייפא, "He who is a warrior is not a scholar, and if he is a scholar, he is not a warrior." Since the text is not vocalized it can also be translated: "If the sword, then not the book, and if the book, then not the sword."[378] R. Eleazar pointed to the inconsistency of the charge which accused him of being both a student and a robber, and he was acquitted.

---

365 The term appears once more in Talmudic literature (TB *Kiddushin* 72b) in a different meaning (as appears from *Bereshith Rabba* LVIII 2, ed. THEODOR, p. 620 and parallels). Comp. also *Pesikta deR. Kahana* in *Beth Talmud* ed. WEISS vol. V, p. 168; ed. BUBER F. 25b n. 79.
366 Comp. *Luke* XVI. 22 and "*Kommentar*" *ibid.*
367 Especially in Nubia and Egypt. See DUMONT *in Bull. de Corresp. Hell.* I, 1877; p. 321, and H. I. BELL, *Studies presented to F. Ll. Griffith*, p. 202.
368 *Manuel d'épigraphie Chrétienne* etc., p. 87 n. 3, and p. 88 n. 1. Comp, also *ibid.* pp. 5, 83.
369 See also R. JAMES, *The Testament of Abraham*, Cambridge 1892, p. 128 ff.
370 *Recueil des inscriptions gerecques-chretiennes d'Egypte*.
371 NN 48. 67, 107, 541, 563, 564, 608, 623–625, 629, 635, 636, 641, 642, 645–647, 649, 652, 654, 655, 657–661, 664–668, 790, 805, 1157, 1173.
372 N 622.
373 Comp. LEFEBVRE *ibid.* No. 625.
374 '*Abodah Zarah* 17b.
375 Probably in the fourth decade of the second century.
376 The original Palestinian version most probably told that he was accused of being a λῃστής, a robber, the usual Roman name for the Jewish nationalist fighters.
377 Διὰ τί ἐλῄστευσας; "Why did you become a robber?" was the question put by the ἔπαρχος to Bulla the Robber. (DIO CASSIUS (LXXXVI) LXXVII. 10. 7).
378 Comp. *Sifre* II, 40 (end), ed. FINKELSTEIN, p. 84² and KRAUSS in *Haggoren* (Hebrew) IV, p. 28 and n. 9 *ibid.*

Eusebius[379] relates that the Roman soldier Marianus, stationed in Caesarea, confessed himself a Christian.[380] He was given three hours for consideration, after which he was expected to make a definite statement regarding his views. Meanwhile the bishop of Caesarea, Theotecnus, took hold of him and brought him near the altar. He raised a little the soldier's cloak and pointed to the sword, then pointed to the book of the gospels, and bade him choose between the two. The sword and the book[381] are incompatible.

ABBREVIATIONS

b	– *ben, bar* (son of).
BR	– Midrash Bereshith Rabba.
JQR	– The Jewish Quarterly Review.
MGWJ	– Monatsschrift für Geschichte und Wissenschaft des Judentums.
MP	– De Martyribus Palaestinae, by Eusebius.
R.	– Rabbi.
TB	– Talmud Babylonicum.
TP	– Talmud Palæstiniensis.

S. Lieberman.

---

379 *Hist. Eccl.* VII. 15.
380 In the seventh decade of the III c.
381 The play of words in the slogan rather suggests an Aramaic origin.

To Professor S. A. Cook of Cambridge

תורה ללמדה זו היא תורה של חסד

RABBINIC METHODS OF INTERPRETATION AND HELLENISTIC RHETORIC[1]

DAVID DAUBE, Cambridge, England

THE way in which the Rabbis built up the colossal system of Talmudic law by means of an exegesis of the relatively few provisions contained in the Bible is still a mystery. To outsiders, the whole development appears arbitrary, a mass of sophistic and involved deductions governed by no coherent first principles and serving no valid communal needs. Orthodox Jews affirm that the methods used by the Rabbis and the results reached by them are of Sinaitic origin: God revealed them all to Moses during the forty days Moses stayed with him, and Moses, though not writing them down, transmitted them to Joshua, Joshua to the elders and so on. This dogma goes back to the Talmud itself and, as we shall see, it made good sense in that period; but, as proposed today, it amounts to an admission that the evolution cannot be justified on rational grounds. Some liberal Jewish scholars, on the other hand, have tried to shew that the Rabbis were guided by pure logic.[2] But that is hardly more convincing. No real attempt, however, has so far been made to understand the growth of Talmudic law against its historical background, and to investigate the relationship with other Hellenistic systems of law, such as the Greek ones or the Roman. The reasons for this failure are not far to seek. Apart from the usual difficulties where several fields of study are concerned, the modern expo-

---

[1] One of four lectures on Talmudic law delivered at the London School of Oriental and African Studies in the Winter 1948-9.

[2] Adolf Schwarz's works are the outstanding example of this sort.

239

nents of Greek and Roman law are often quite unaware of some of the mainsprings of their systems, namely, the conventions among the ancient jurists as to types of arguments admissible or inadmissible, the relative weight of arguments and the like. But it is precisely in this province of 'legal science' that may be found the really important points of contact between the Talmud and other Hellenistic creations.

The thesis here to be submitted is that the Rabbinic methods of interpretation derive from Hellenistic rhetoric.[3] Hellenistic rhetoric is at the bottom both of the fundamental ideas, presuppositions, from which the Rabbis proceeded and of the major details of application, the manner in which these ideas were translated into practice. This is not to detract from the value of the work of the Rabbis. On the contrary, it is important to note that, when the Hellenistic methods were first adopted, about 100 to 25 B. C., the 'classical,' Tannaitic era of Rabbinic law was just opening. That is to say, the borrowing took place in the best period of Talmudic jurisprudence, when the Rabbis were masters, not slaves, of the new influences. The methods taken over were thoroughly hebraized in spirit as well as form, adapted to the native material, worked out so as to assist the natural progress of Jewish law. It is the kind of thing which, *mutatis mutandis*, happened at Rome in the same epoch. Later on, from A. D. 200, in 'post-classical,' Amoraic law, the development was in several respects more autonomous, less open to foreign inspiration, yet at the same time there was a distinct lack of vitality and originality, the most prominent tendency now being ever greater specialisation. However, in its beginnings, the Rabbinic system of hermeneutics is a product of the Hellenistic civilisation then dominating the entire Mediterranean world.

Let us begin by recalling a few matters concerning date and geography. It is to Hillel, the great Pharisee who flourished about 30 B. C., that we owe the oldest rules in accordance with which Scripture is to be *nidhrasheth*, 'interpreted.' He himself says that he learned them from his teachers Shemaiah and

[3] See some provisional observations by the present writer in Law Quarterly Review 1936, 265 f., Journal of Roman Studies 1948, 115 ff., Cambridge Law Journal 1949, 215.

Abtalion;[4] and, indeed, they are the first Rabbis to be called *darshanim*, 'interpreters of Scripture.'[5] The Talmud represents them as proselytes. The historicity of this feature has been doubted; but it is agreed that, if they were not natives of Alexandria, they studied and taught there long enough to go on using Egyptian measures even after settling in Palestine.[6] So there is a *prima facie* case for a direct connection between Hillel's seven norms of interpretation and Alexandria, a centre of Hellenistic scholarship.

The historical situation in which Hillel found himself may next be considered. For centuries before him, Scripture had been subjected to the most scrupulous philological analysis, each word and sentence being inspected with a view to establishing its exact sense and grammatical status.[7] But treated in this conservative manner, the Bible yielded comparatively little law; and it is not surprising that a large body of law, religious and secular, grew up in addition to that contained in Scripture. This non-Scriptural law consisted of various elements. Some of it indeed

---

[4] Palestinian Pes. 33a, Babylonian Pes. 66a.

[5] Bab. Pes. 70b, a passage all the more reliable as it is a Sadducee who describes them as such, and probably in a sneering tone: 'It is curious that these wonderful interpreters of Scripture did not realize....'

[6] Graetz, *Geschichte der Juden*, 5th ed. by Brann, vol. 3, pt. 2, 711 ff.

[7] Bab. Kid. 30a says that *sopher*, 'scribe,' originally meant 'one who counts:' the ancient scribes counted all the letters in the Bible. Whatever the original meaning of the word, there is no reason to doubt the information concerning the activity of the early scholars. We can go further. Most, if not all, of the early *gezeroth shawoth* (inferences from analogy, in accordance with the second of Hillel's norms of interpretation) are based on expressions which occur only in the two passages concerned and nowhere else in the Bible (Schwarz, *Die Hermeneutische Analogie*, 61 ff.). Thus the Mekhiltha tells us that from the use of *'asher lo' 'orasa* in Ex. 22.15 (16) and Deut. 22.28 it follows that the penalty is 50 shekels for seduction (Exodus) just as for rape (Deuteronomy). The phrase *'asher lo' 'orasa* occurs only in these two verses. It is safe to conclude that there existed, before Hillel, collections of ἅπαξ λεγόμενα, δὶς λεγόμενα etc. The norm of *gezera shawa* would have been impracticable without them. How far even this old, narrowly grammatical and lexicographical analysis and statistics may have been influenced by Greek ideas we need not here decide. In Rome, Varro, about 100 B.C., wrote monographs about synonyms, about the formation of words, about rare words in Plautus. He followed Greek models.

was still almost Scriptural: the meaning of an obscure verse would be fixed, a very inconvenient precept would be credited with a somewhat more desirable meaning, the claims of flagrantly inconsistent ordinances would be settled. But a great part was avowedly novel, extensions of Biblical provisions designed to deal with fresh cases or also, in the words ascribed to the men of the Great Synagogue, 'to make a fence around the Torah.'[8] In either case, what was the ground of recognition of this vast body of non-Scriptural law? It was the authority of the people promulgating it. The correctness of a decision was guaranteed by the character and learning of him who delivered it. Significantly, the *dibhere sopherim*, the 'sayings of the ancient scribes,' are never supported by any arguments. The wise man simply knows the true import of a Biblical commandment or the proper supplement to add.

The non-Scriptural law was aptly termed 'the tradition received from, or handed down by, the fathers,' πατέρων διαδοχή or παράδοσις τῶν πατέρων, *qabbalath ha'abhoth, masoreth ha-'abhoth*.[9] From Akiba's statement, about A. D. 120, that 'tradition is a fence around the Torah,' we may gather that the extensions for the purpose of ensuring strictest observance of the Biblical law were regarded as the chief component of the non-Biblical;[10] and it may be remarked, in passing, that this adage is surely

---

[8] Mishnah Ab. 1.1.

[9] Josephus, Ant. 13.10.6, Targum on Job 15.18. A synonym is παράδοσις τῶν πρεσβυτέρων, occurring in Matthew 15.2, Mark 7.3, 5; it would correspond to *masoreth hazzeqenim* (cp. *dibhere hazzeqenim*, e. g. in Pal. Berakhoth 3b).

[10] Mishnah Ab. 3.14. Certainly, for Akiba, *masoreth* had come to signify, more specifically, 'the tradition concerning the exact state of the sacred text' (see Bacher, *Älteste Terminologie*, 108, *Tradition und Tradenten*, 3). But for one thing, it must not be forgotten that this particular branch was of such importance for him precisely because — in opposition to Ishmael — he used technicalities like the presence or absence of the optional accusative sign for deriving fresh law; hence 'the tradition concerning the state of the text' so to speak swallowed up the tradition of the fathers in general, it more or less represented the entire oral Law. For another thing, the adage 'tradition is a fence around the Torah' is doubtless older than Akiba, dating from a time when *masoreth* had its original, wider sense. The point of Abhoth 3.14 is the putting together of this maxim with 'tithes are a fence around riches' etc.

indebted — however indirectly — to Plato's praise of 'ancestral customs which, if well established, form a cover around the written laws for their full protection.'[11] The trouble was that important groups refused to consider the tradition binding, above all, the Sadducees (but also the Samaritans). For them, the text of the Bible was of God, but nothing beyond it. The Pharisaic 'fence' they rejected and even ridiculed. When the Pharisees insisted on purification of the golden candlestick in the Temple in case it had contracted some uncleanness, the Sadducees commented: 'Look how they purify the light of the moon!'[12]

Josephus has an interesting remark: the Sadducees, he says, hold it a virtue to dispute against their own teachers.[13] Evidently, they had taken over from the Hellenistic schools of philosophy the ideal of working out any problem by unfettered argument and counter-argument. Their encounter with Jesus in the New Testament provides support: they attempt to reduce to absurdity the belief in a resurrection of the body, and the point they make might well figure in a philosophical dialogue of the time.[14] It is worth noting that very similar arguments — also in the form of 'teasers' — are attributed by the Talmud to the citizens of Alexandria[15] and (which comes to the same thing) to Queen Cleopatra.[16]

[11] Laws 7.793B (πάτρια νόμιμα ἃ καλῶς ἐθισθέντα πάσῃ σωτηρίᾳ περικαλύψαντα ἔχει τοὺς τότε γραφέντας νόμους).

[12] Tosephtha Hag. 3.35, Pal. Hag. 79d. The Samaritans, as they disallowed any 'interpretation,' and yet found it impossible to go on sticking to the text in its literal form, were driven to the only alternative — emendation; see the present writer's discussion in *Zeitschrift für die Alttestamentliche Wissenschaft* 1932, 152. The Rabbis saw through this: cp. e.g. Bab. Sota 33b.

[13] Ant. 18.1.4.

[14] Matthew 22.23 ff., Mark 12.18 ff., Luke 20.27 ff.

[15] Bab. Nid. 69b ff.: Does Lot's wife, a pillar of salt, convey uncleanness? (Strictly, she is a corpse.) Does the child raised from the dead by Elisha convey uncleanness? When the dead are raised, will they need sprinkling on the third and seventh days, having been in contact with a corpse? The Talmud terms these scoffing questions *dibhere boruth*, 'sayings of a vulgar nature.'

[16] Bab. Sanh. 90b. The Queen admits that the dead will rise but wonders whether they will be naked or dressed? Bacher, *Agada der Tannaiten*, vol. 2, 68 (followed by Strack and Billerbeck, *Kommentar zum Neuen Testament*,

There were, then, these diametrically opposed views: the Pharisaic, according to which the authority of the fathers must be unconditionally accepted, and the Sadducean, according to which the text alone was binding, while any question not answered by it might be approached quite freely, in a philosophical fashion. In this situation, Hillel[17] declared that Scripture itself included the tradition of the fathers; and that it did so — here he took a leaf out of the other party's book — precisely if read

vol. 1, 897), thinks that 'Cleopatra' must be emended because she was not contemporary with Meir, A. D. 150, to whom she is represented as talking. But Talmudic legend was never afraid of anachronisms, and whoever wanted to indicate that Meir's opponents were Alexandrians, i. e. addicts to Greek philosophy, might find Cleopatra particularly suitable in view of the rather improper flavour of the question. A most unsavoury story is told about her in Bab. Nid. 30b.

[17] The Talmud is fully aware of the decisive role played by him; he is compared to Ezra in Bab. Suk. 20a, Sota 48b. The four legends in Bab. Shab. 30b f. are designed to illustrate (*inter alia*) four cardinal teachings of his: (1) every question deserves a well-reasoned answer, (2) tradition must inevitably command some authority, (3) by applying the norms of interpretation, the entire Law might be inferred from a single, ethical principle, and (4) the tradition of the fathers contains nothing but what follows from Scripture on proper exegesis. Ad (1): Somebody asks Hillel questions like 'Why have the Babylonians such round heads?,' to which he replies 'A weighty question — because they have no skilful midwives.' Ad (2): A gentile undertakes to become a convert if he need submit only to the written Law. The severe Shammai rejects him, Hillel accepts him. The first day, he teaches him the Hebrew alphabet; the second, he reverses the order of the letters. The proselyte protests, whereupon Hillel tells him that if he trusts him as to the alphabet, he might do so as to the oral Torah. Ad (3): A gentile undertakes to become a convert if he can be taught the entire Torah while standing on one foot. Shammai rejects him, Hillel accepts him. He teaches him 'What is hateful to you, do not to your fellowman:' all the rest, he says, is interpretation. Ad (4): A gentile undertakes to become a convert if he will be made High Priest. Shammai rejects him, Hillel accepts him. In the course of his instruction, Num. 1.51 is reached: 'And the stranger that cometh nigh shall be put to death.' Hillel explains that even King David is a 'stranger' for this purpose, whereupon his pupil, by a *qal wahomer*, an inference *a minori ad maius*, deduces the utter unfitness of a proselyte. He then returns to Shammai to ask him why he dogmatized instead of drawing his attention to Num. 1.51: once he (the convert) knew that verse, and the method of *qal wahomer*, he himself (the convert) agreed with the traditional attitude, he himself shuddered at his original request.

as, on the most up-to-date teaching of the philosophical schools, a code of laws ought to be read. There existed, he claimed, a series of rational norms of exegesis making possible a sober clarification and extension of legal provisions. If they were applied to Scripture, the opinions expressed by the fathers would be vindicated, would turn out to be logical, not arbitrary; and in fact, he contended, some measure of traditional, Rabbinic authority would always remain indispensable — not everybody was in a position to judge the merits of a doctrine approved by the experts.[18] While this part of his program was addressed to the Sadducees, he pointed out to his own group that his hermeneutics, if they vindicated the tradition of the fathers, must themselves enjoy a degree of sanctity and be put to further use: the tradition of the fathers (he urged) had evidently been evolved along these lines all the time. His first public debate before the Pharisaic officers — on the question whether the paschal lamb might be slaughtered even if Passover fell on a Sabbath — culminated in the demonstration that what he concluded from the Bible by means of his system of interpretation coincided with the traditional ruling. It was then that the Pharisees made him their leader and accepted his innovation.[19] Let us just note that the very setting of this historic debate was that of the 'disputatio fori.'[20]

Hillel, by introducing this system into Talmudic jurisprudence, accomplished two things. He not only created the basis for a development of the law at the same time orderly and unlimited,[21] but also led the way towards a bridging of the gulf

---

[18] See the legends numbered (2) and (4) in the preceding footnote. According to Pal. Pes. 33a, Hillel went from Babylonia to Palestine in order to get it confirmed that the results of his interpretation agreed with tradition. Jesus' reply to the question about resurrection (see above, p. 243) is twofold: he not only propounds a theological argument — there might be a rejoinder to that — but also quotes a verse from Scripture to be taken as alluding to a quickening of the dead.

[19] Pal. Pes. 33a, Bab. Pes. 66a.

[20] That ancient Roman 'interpretation' assumed the form of a public debate is stated in D. 1.2.2.5. A vivid illustration may be found in Cicero, De Or. 1.56.240; see below, p. 246 n. 24.

[21] The possibilities of the new method were clearly seen from the outset,

between Pharisees and Sadducees. On the one hand, he upheld the authority of tradition. Actually, in a sense, he increased it: as, for him, the traditional decisions were all logical, necessary inferences from the Bible, they were equal in rank to the latter. He went as far as to speak of two Toroth, a written one and an oral one[22] — an idea governing all subsequent thought. On the other hand, his modern, scientific technique and, above all, the very conception of the oral Torah as deriving from, and thus essentially inherent in, the text implied a profound appreciation of the Sadducean standpoint and must have brought over a good many who embraced it. Clearly, his work in this field was not the least of his achievements in the service of unity and peace.

We may now examine the main ideas underlying Hillel's program.

First, the fundamental antithesis he tried to overcome was that between law resting on the respect for a great man, on the authority of tradition, and law resting on rational, intelligible considerations. This antithesis is common in the rhetorical literature of the time. His contemporary Cicero distinguishes between arguments from the nature of the case and arguments from external evidence, that is to say, from authority. An example of the latter type would be the decision: 'Since Scaevola said so and so, this must be taken as the law.'[23] In 137 B. C., Cicero reports, P. Crassus, after first 'taking refuge in authorities,' had to admit that Galba's 'disputation' founded on arguments from analogy and equity led to a more plausible result.[24]

---

as emerges from legend (3), above, p. 244 n. 17: all Law might at a pinch be deduced from one principle.

[22] Bab. Shab. 31a. Shammai also used these terms: in this respect, there was no disagreement between him and Hillel. The equality of the oral Torah is strikingly brought out by the fact that the principle from which, in Hillel's view, the entire Law might be deduced, 'What is hateful . . .' (see legend (3), above, p. 244 n. 17), belongs, not to Scripture, but to traditional ethics.

[23] Top. 2.8, 4.24 ('quae autem adsumuntur extrinsecus, ea maxime ex auctoritate ducuntur, ut si respondeas: quoniam P. Scaevola dixerit, id tibi ius videri'). Cp. Aristotle, Rhet. 2.23.12, Quintilian 5.11.36.

[24] De Or. 1.56.240 ('Galba autem multas similitudines afferre multaque pro aequitate contra ius dicere; atque illum ad auctores confugisse, ac tamen

Secondly, Hillel claimed that any gaps in Scriptural law might be filled in with the help of certain modes of reasoning — a good, rhetorical theory. Cicero has much to say about 'ratiocination,' by which 'from that which is written there is derived a further point not written,'[25] while Auctor ad Herennium defines 'ratiocination' as the method to be applied where 'the judge has to deal with a case not falling under a statute of its own, yet covered by other statutes in view of a certain analogy.'[26]

Thirdly, the result of such interpretation was to be of the same status as the text itself, was to be treated as if directly enjoined by the original lawgiver. This view also can be parallelled. Of a certain institution, Gaius tells us that it is called 'statutory' because 'though there is no express provision about it in the statute (the XII Tables), yet it has been accepted through interpretation as if it had been introduced by the statute.'[27] Another time he even omits the 'as if,' representing as laid down by the XII Tables a rule in reality deduced from that code by its interpreters.[28] As is well known, the term *ius civile* was occasionally employed for the body of law evolved by interpretation.[29] This reflects a stage where the law evolved by interpretation was so different from, and so much fuller than, the statute law to which it attached that it had practically buried the latter and usurped its place.

concessisse Galbae disputationem sibi probabilem videri'). Of course, it was also possible to 'dispute,' 'interpret a statute,' so as to reach results in conflict with equity; D. 50.16.177, 50.17.65.

[25] De Inv. 1.13.17 ('ex eo quod scriptum est aliud quod non scriptum est inveniri'); cp. 2.50.148 ff.

[26] 1.13.23 ('cum res sine propria lege venit in iudicium, quae tamen ab aliis legibus similitudine quadam occupatur'); cp. Aristotle, Rhet. 2.23.1 ff., Quintilian 7.8.3 ff.

[27] 1.165 ('quae tutela legitima vocatur, non quia nominatim ea lege de hac tutela cavetur, sed quia proinde accepta est per interpretationem atque si verbis legis introducta esset'); cp. 3.218. The term *iura condere* may have originated as describing the activity of the ancient interpreters: see G. 4.30.

[28] 2.42: 'fundi vero et aedium biennio, et ita lege XII tabularum cautum est'. The XII Tables, as Gaius doubtless knew, mentioned only *fundus*, the interpreters, reasoning from analogy, added *aedes*; Cicero, Top. 4.23, Pro Caec. 19.54.

[29] D. 1.2.2.5, 12.

Fourthly, Hillel's assumption of 'a written Torah and an oral Torah' is highly reminiscent of the pair νόμοι ἔγγραφοι and νόμοι ἄγραφοι or *ius scriptum* and *ius non scriptum* (or *per manus traditum*). It is superfluous to adduce references, but it may be worth noting that the terms νόμοι ἄγραφοι and *ius non scriptum* do not always signify the natural law common to all men. They frequently signify the traditional, customary law of a particular community as opposed to its statute law.[30] Plato, in the same section where he describes the customs of the fathers as a protective covering around the written laws, says expressly that 'what people call customs of the fathers are nothing else than the sum of unwritten laws.'[31] They are even used of the law created by the interpreters of statutes.[32] Since, on the other hand, Hillel's 'oral Torah' was still of a wide range, embracing ethics as well as law in the narrow sense, his dependence on Hellenistic philosophy seems beyond doubt.

Fifthly, there is an idea which at first sight looks the exclusive property of the Rabbis, for whom the Bible had been composed under divine inspiration: the lawgiver foresaw the interpretation of his statutes, deliberately confined himself to a minimum, relying on the rest being inferable by a proper exegesis. (It is this idea which gradually led to the doctrine that the oral Law no less than the written is of Sinaitic origin: God, by word of mouth, revealed to Moses both the methods by which fresh precepts might be derived from Scripture and all precepts that would ever be in fact derived.) But even this is a stock argument of the orators. Cicero observes that the application of a statute

---

[30] Aristotle, Rhet. 1.13.2 (λέγω δὲ νόμον ἴδιον μὲν τὸν ἑκάστοις ὡρισμένον πρὸς αὐτούς, καὶ τοῦτον τὸν μὲν ἄγραφον τὸν δὲ γεγραμμένον, κοινὸν δὲ τὸν κατὰ φύσιν), also D. 1.1.6.1, 1.3.32 *pr.*, I. 1.2.3.9. That *ius scriptum* as understood in the *Digest* is not quite the same as statute law in the modern sense need hardly be mentioned. The term *per manus traditum* is, of course, always confined to the custom of a certain people; cp. Livy 5.51.4, D. 29.7.10.

[31] Laws 7.793A (οὓς πατρίους νόμους ἐπονομάζουσιν οὐκ ἄλλα ἐστὶν ἢ τὰ τοιαῦτα (ἄγραφα νόμιμα) ξύμπαντα. In the Statesman, ἀγράμματα or ἄγραφα is regularly paired off with πάτρια; e. g. 295A, 298D f.

[32] Cicero, De Inv. 1.13.17, 2.50.148, Quintilian 7.8.3, D. 1.2.2.5, 12; see above, p. 245 n. 20, p. 247 nn. 25, 26, 29.

to a case not mentioned in it may be justified by pleading that the lawgiver omitted the case 'because, having written about another, allied one, he thought nobody could have any doubt about this one,' or that 'in many laws many points are omitted which, however, no one would consider as really omitted, since they can be deduced from other points that are put down.'[33] Auctor ad Herennium advises him who wishes to go beyond the letter of a law to 'extol the appropriateness[34] and brevity of the author's style, since he put down only as much as was necessary, but deemed it unnecessary to put down what could be understood without being put down;' only by going beyond the letter are we giving effect to 'the will of the author.'[35] When Sabinus extended a mode of assessment prescribed in the first chapter of the *lex Aquilia* to the third where it was not prescribed, he maintained that 'the lawgiver thought it sufficient to have used the relevant word in the first chapter.'[36] The Romans inherited the idea from the Greeks. Lysias, for instance, asserts that the lawgiver who declared punishable the use of certain offensive words meant to include all equivalent ones.[37] If one wonders how Greeks

---

[33] De Inv. 2.50.150 f. ('idcirco de hac re nihil esse scriptum quod, cum de illa esset scriptum, de hac is qui scribebat dubitaturum neminem arbitratus sit.... multis in legibus multa praeterita esse quae idcirco praeterita nemo arbitretur quod ex ceteris de quibus scriptum sit intellegi possint'); cp. 2.47.39 f., 2.50.152, De Leg. 2.7.18.

[34] Cp. *commodissime* in Cicero, De Inv. 2.50.152, cited in the preceding footnote.

[35] 2.10.14 ('laudabimus scriptoris commoditatem atque brevitatem, quod tantum scripserit quod necesse fuerit, illud quod sine scripto intellegi potuerit non necessario scribendum putaverit... contra eum qui scriptum recitet et scriptoris voluntatem non interpretetur'); cp. 2.12.18.

[36] G. 3.218: 'nam legislatorem contentum fuisse quod prima parte eo verbo usus esset.' Note the close similarity in expression to Auct. ad Her. 2.10.14, 2.12.18, cited in the preceding footnote. I. 4.3.15 says: 'nam plebem Romanam, quae hanc legem tulit, contentam fuisse'. Possibly, Tribonian no longer understood the doctrine of interpretation underlying Sabinus' remark and believed that the omission in the third chapter was to be explained by the character of the *lex Aquilia* as a plebiscite, the *plebs* being a careless and lazy lawgiver.

[37] Contra Theomn. I 8 (περὶ ἑνὸς εἰπὼν περὶ πάντων ἐδήλωσεν); cp. also (despite important differences) Aristotle, Rhet. 1.13.13, 17, in turn dependent on Plato, Statesman 294A f.

and Romans could talk in this 'religious' way, it should be remembered that there had been periods when their ancient legislations also enjoyed a semi-divine standing, much as the Bible did among the Jews.

Sixthly, it is the task of a lawgiver to lay down basic principles only, from which any detailed rules may be inferred. Just so, Cicero, in the imaginary role of a legislator, announces that 'the statutes will be set forth by me, not in a complete form — that would be endless — but in the form of generalized questions and their decisions;' and according to Suetonius, Caesar planned to replace the embarrassing mass of statutes by 'a few books, containing what was best and necessary.'[38]

Seventhly, it is the task of a lawgiver, if he wants to regulate a series of allied cases, to choose the most frequent and leave the others to be inferred on the ground of analogy.[39] Just so, Cicero argues that the edict directed against violence with the help of men 'brought together' covers the case where men had assembled uninvited and were then made to participate in some violence; the edict is framed in this way because 'normally, where numbers are needed, men are brought together,' but 'though the word may be different, the substance is not, and the same law will apply to all cases where it is clear that the same principle of equity is at stake.'[40] In opening that half of his *Digest* where he discusses *leges* and *senatusconsulta*, Julian explains that neither 'can be formulated so as to comprise all cases that may

---

[38] Cicero, De Leg. 2.7.18, referred to above, p. 249 n. 33 ('leges a me edentur non perfectae — nam esset infinitum — sed ipsae summae rerum atque sententiae'); cp. 2.19.47 ff., Aristotle, Rhet. 1.13.12 ff., Nic. E. 5.10.4 ff., Plato, Statesman 294A f. Suetonius, Div. Jul. 44.2 ('optima quaeque et necessaria in paucissimos conferre libros'); cp. the use of *necessarius* in Auct. ad Her. 2.10.14, quoted above, p. 249 n. 35.

[39] It is not certain that this idea goes back to Hillel's time, but it cannot be much later: see Mishnah Edhuyoth 1.12, where the School of Shammai accounts for a traditional ruling, which they desire to extend, by saying that it speaks about 'what happens normally,' i. e. gives only the principal example. By Ishamel's age, the idea was fully established.

[40] Pro Caec. 21.59 ('quia plerumque, ubi multitudine opus est, homines cogi solent, ideo de coactis compositum interdictum est; quod etiamsi verbo differre videbitur, re tamen erit unum, et omnibus in causis idem valebit in quibus perspicitur una atque eadem causa aequitatis').

occur at any time, but it is sufficient that the most frequent happenings should be regulated.'[41]

Hillel's jurisprudence, then, i. e. his theory of the relation between statute law, tradition and interpretation, was entirely in line with the prevalent Hellenistic ideas on the matter. The same is true of the details of execution, of the methods he proposed to give practical effect to his theory. The famous seven norms of hermeneutics he proclaimed, the seven norms in accordance with which Scripture was to be interpreted, hitherto looked upon as the most typical product of Rabbinism, all of them betray the influence of the rhetorical teaching of his age.

The first of these norms is the inference *a fortiori*, or *a minori ad maius* — in Hebrew *qal wahomer*, 'the light and the weighty.' Ex. 20.25 gives permission to build the altar of stone, brick or anything else.[42] By means of a *qal wahomer*, it is concluded that, since the material may be chosen in the case of this most important object of the Temple, it may *a fortiori* be chosen for the other, less important objects. The second, third and fourth norms in Hillel's plan are various kinds of inferences from analogy. For example, just as the daily sacrifice, which Scripture says should be brought 'at its appointed time,' is due even on a Sabbath, so the Passover lamb, which Scripture also demands 'at its appointed time,' must be slaughtered even if Passover falls on a Sabbath.[43] Rhetorical parallels abound. 'What applies to the *maius*,' says Cicero, 'must apply also to the *minus*, and *vice versa*. Again, what applies to one thing must apply to that which is equal.'[44] To discover the meaning of a problematic

---

[41] D. 1.3.10; see Lenel, *Palingenesia*, vol. 1, 464 ('neque leges neque senatusconsulta ita scribi possunt ut omnes casus qui quandoque inciderint comprehendantur, sed sufficit ea quae plerumque accidunt contineri').

[42] At least that was what the Rabbis took to be the force of 'if' in 'And if thou wilt make me an altar of stones:' Mekhiltha *ad loc*. For the present purpose, it is immaterial whether or not this view is tenable.

[43] Pal. Pes. 33a, Bab. Pes. 66a, Num. 28.2, 9.2. The writer refrains from being more explicit about Hillel's second, third and fourth norms because their original nature and history has not so far been appreciated, but it would lead too far afield here to go into them. For a certain aspect of the second, *gezera shawa*, see above, p. 241 n. 7.

[44] Top. 4.23: 'quod in re maiore valet valeat in minore, item contra;

phrase, its 'normal force,' the 'usage of language' and the 'analogies and examples of those who have used it thus' will have to be considered;[45] and the definition should not 'clash with the usage in the writings of others, certainly not with that in other writings by the same author.'[46]

It might perhaps be objected that it is so natural to argue *a fortiori* or from analogy that the parallels cannot prove any borrowing on Hillel's part. Postponing this problem for a moment, we would draw attention to the arrangement of his norms: first *a fortiori*, then analogy. One could imagine the reverse order. But it is interesting that, right from Aristotle,[47] wherever in rhetorical literature the methods of interpretation are set forth in a tabulated form, this is the order we find. We have already quoted Cicero: 'What applies to the *maius* must apply to the *minus*, and *vice versa*; what applies to one thing must apply to that which is equal.'[48] Auctor ad Herennium declares that the first thing to be asked when filling the gaps of the law by 'ratiocination' is 'whether anything comparable has been laid down concerning greater, smaller or equal matters.'[49] There is a standard sequence, and it is observed in Hillel's list.

Still deferring the question of the naturalness of his first four norms, let us proceed to the fifth, which is more complicated, the rule of 'the general and the specific,' *kelal upherat*. It says that if the range of a statute is indicated both by a wider and a narrower term, it is the one put second that counts; that is to say, if the narrower term comes second, it restricts the wider

item quod in re pari valet valeat in hac quae par est.' As an illustration of the latter argument he adduces the extension of the XII Tables' rule concerning usucapion of *fundus*; see above, p. 247 n. 28.

[45] Part. Or. 36.123, 126 ('communis verbi vis,' 'consuetudo sermonis,' 'similia exemplaque eorum qui ita locuti sunt').

[46] Part. Or. 37.132 ('discrepare cum ceteris scriptis vel aliorum vel maxime eiusdem').

[47] Rhet. 2.23.4 f.

[48] Top. 4.23; see above, p. 251 n. 44. Cp. 18.68, De Or. 2.40.172, De Inv. 1.28.41, 2.17.55; also Quintilian 5.10.86 ff. There are one or two exceptions to the rule, but they can be shewn to be secondary.

[49] 2.13.18 ('in causa ratiocinali primum quaeretur ecquid de rebus maioribus aut minoribus aut similibus similiter scriptum aut iudicatum sit').

one, while if the wider one comes last, it includes and adds to the narrower one. Lev. 1.2 ordains that 'ye shall bring your offering of the beasts, of the oxen and sheep;' the general term 'beasts' is restricted by the following more specific 'oxen and sheep' — so wild animals are excluded.[50] By way of contrast, Ex. 22.9 (10) fixes the liability of a man charged by another with the custody of 'an ass, an ox, a sheep or any beast;' here the specific terms 'ass, ox, sheep' are covered and added to by the following more general 'any beast' — so the regulation extends to wild animals as well.[51]

The latter half of the norm, about the order specific — general, is fully given by Celsus (who was particularly interested in hermeneutics): 'it is not unusual,' he tells us, 'for a statute first to enumerate a few cases specially and then to add a comprehensive term by which to embrace any special cases.'[52] The rule underlies certain older decisions, for instance, one by Q. Mucius. A will provided that 'X shall be my heir if he ascends the Capitol; X shall be my heir,' and Mucius held that 'the second clause should prevail, since it is fuller than the first.'[53] However, the other part of this norm of interpretation, i. e. that concerning the order general — specific, also seems to have been familiar to the earlier classical Roman jurists. A man, in conveying land, gave an assurance that 'it was first class (free from servitudes) and he had not allowed its legal position to deteriorate (had not allowed any servitudes to be imposed).' Proculus held that only the second, narrower clause was binding: 'though the first clause alone, without the addition of the second, would mean the

---

[50] Siphra *ad loc.*

[51] Mekhiltha *ad loc.*

[52] D. 9.2.27.16: 'non esse novum ut lex specialiter quibusdam enumeratis generale subiciat verbum quo specialia complectatur.' Celsus is discussing the *lex Aquilia*, which, as we saw above, p. 249, Sabinus also treated on approved rhetorical lines. In non-legal prose, the summing up of a detailed exposé was, of course, a recognized stylistic device. Cicero, in De Inv. 2.5.18, uses almost the same words as Celsus: 'denique, ut omnia generatim amplectamur....'

[53] D. 28.5.68, from Pomponius on Mucius, but doubtless going back to the latter ('si ita scriptum fuerit "Tithasus si in Capitolium ascenderit heres esto, Tithasus heres esto," secunda scriptura potior erit; plenior est enim quam prior').

complete absence of any servitudes, yet I believe the second clause releases him sufficiently to limit his responsibility to such servitudes as were imposed through himself.'[54] The specific term, the *perat*, which comes second, restricts the general one, the *kelal*, which comes first.

To turn now to the question we have put off: can it be argued that the first four norms of Hillel are so natural that the rhetorical parallels constitute no evidence of a genetic connection? For one thing, the argument is greatly weakened by the existence of parallels to the fifth norm, of 'the general and the specific,' which is rather subtle (not to mention the Hellenistic colouring of Hillel's doctrine of the role of interpretation as a whole). But even the first four are not so very simple. If we take as illustration the inference *a fortiori* — to be sure, any layman might reason thus: 'Here is a teetotaller who does not touch cider; he will certainly refuse whisky.' Three points, however, must not be overlooked. First, the deduction will not always be made in this direct, almost technical manner; more often than not there will be some twist somewhere. Secondly, the ordinary person will rarely perceive the exact nature of his deduction. There is a considerable difference between merely using various modes of deduction and being aware of using just these modes, defining, distinguishing and tabulating them. Thirdly, the recommendation of a series of such modes of deduction as an instrument — or indeed, as the only satisfactory instrument — with which to build up a complete legal or theological system manifestly involves a further step. Medieval Icelandic law is of a high standard; if the norms of exegesis here discussed were so natural,

---

[54] D. 50.16.126: 'si, cum fundum tibi <mancipio> darem, legem ita dixi "uti optimus maximusque esset" et adieci "ius fundi deterius factum non esse per dominum praestabitur," amplius eo praestabitur nihil; etiamsi prior pars "ut optimus maximusque sit" liberum esse significat eoque, si posterior pars adiecta non esset, liberum praestare deberem, tamen inferiore parte satis me liberatum puto ne quid aliud praestare debeam quam "ius fundi per dominum deterius factum non esse."' For <mancipio>, see Lenel, *Palingenesia*, vol. 2, 164. The present writer has changed the current punctuation of the text, which takes no account of the doctrine of interpretation behind it. It is unfamiliarity with this doctrine which explains the large scale excisions and emendations proposed by some modern scholars.

we should expect to find them there, but there is no trace of them. Actually, it is by no means clear to what extent our modern lawyers are consciously applying a coherent system of hermeneutics.

A comparison between the Old Testament and the New is instructive. Both contain inferences *a fortiori*; the Old Testament cases were already collected by the Rabbis of the Talmud (occasionally, indeed, their eyes were too sharp). But there is a difference. The Old Testament cases are popular, the New Testament ones technical. A good Old Testament instance is the reply of Joseph's brothers when accused of the theft of his cup: 'The money which we found in our sacks' mouths we brought again unto thee — how then should we steal silver or gold?'[55] Apart from a slight irregularity in the structure of the argument — an action, 'we brought again,' in the premise, an omission, 'we did not steal,' in the conclusion[56] — it is relevant to note that the statement occurs in the course of a dispute concerning facts, namely, the guilt or innocence of Joseph's brothers. It is a far cry from here to the methodical elaboration of law and theology by means of the norm *a minori ad maius*. This stage, however, is reached by the time of the New Testament. According to Matthew, Jesus, asked about healing on the Sabbath, answered: 'What man shall have one sheep, and if it fall into a pit on the sabbath, will not lift it out? How much better then is a man than a sheep! Wherefore it is lawful to do well on the sabbath.'[57] According to Luke, he argued: 'Doth not each man on the sabbath loose his ox for the watering? And ought not this woman, being a daughter of Abraham, whom Satan hath bound these eighteen years, be loosed?'[58] These are academic, 'Halakhic'

---

[55] Gen. 44.8.

[56] A perfectly straight inference *a fortiori* would run either 'we did not retain the money found, still less did we steal' or 'we brought again the money found, still more did we refrain from stealing.'

[57] Matthew 12.10 ff.

[58] Luke 13.14 ff. It is interesting that the mode of reasoning is the same as in Matthew 12.10 ff., a *qal wahomer*, though the substance of the argument is not a little different. The argument of Luke 14.3 ff., on the other hand, is very close to Matthew 12.10 ff. in substance, but there is no longer an obvious *qal wahomer*. If we did not know Matthew 12.10 ff. and Luke 13.14 ff., we

applications of Hillel's first rule of exegesis. No less significant an example may be met with in Paul's theological discourse: 'While we were yet sinners, Christ died for us; much more then, being now justified by his blood, we shall be saved from wrath through him.'[59] The technique is exactly the same as that of the Roman jurists, whose 'ratiocination' respecting the *lex Aelia Sentia* is recorded by Gaius. The statute laid down that the property of certain *dediticii* should on death be treated like that of citizen freedmen. The jurists, however, decided that the *dediticii* were not thereby given the citizen freedmen's power of making a will: seeing that even Junian Latins, superior in status to *dediticii*, were incapable of making a will, it could not have been the lawgiver's intention to grant this facility to 'men of the very lowest rank.'[60]

The point is that Hillel's system — and not only the first four norms[61] — is 'natural' in the sense of 'grown out of intelligent

---

should probably see in Luke 14.5 a reasoning from analogy: as one may help a beast, so one may a man.

[59] Romans 5.8 f.; much more = πολλῷ μᾶλλον, *multo magis*. John 13.14 is curious. According to the prevalent reading, Jesus, as Lord and Master, sets an example, ὑπόδειγμα, to be imitated by his disciples; this idea recurs in many passages of the New Testament. But D Θ it sy insert πόσῳ μᾶλλον before καὶ ὑμεῖς ὀφείλετε, thus turning the argument into a technical *qal wahomer*: if the Master performs this servile duty, *a fortiori* the disciples must do it.

[60] 3.75: 'pessimae condicionis hominibus.' Note the ascription of the result to the will of the lawgiver; cp. above, pp. 248 ff. The term *incredibile* is technical in rhetorical hermeneutics: *verisimile* or *credibile* designates what may be presumed, in view of all circumstances or on 'ratiocination,' to be the import of an arrangement or law, *incredibile* what cannot be regarded as such. See e. g. Cicero, De Inv. 2.40.117, D. 12.4.6.*pr.*, 15.1.9.4, 15.1.57.2, 18.1.39.1, 19.1.13.22, 20.1.6, 20.4.13, 28.6.41.5, 30.1.47 *pr.*, 34.2.8, 34.5.24, 35.1.25, 35.1.36.1, 48.19.41, 50.16.142, 50.17.114. Later the exclusion of *dediticii* was based not on an inference *a minori ad maius*, but on an entirely different argument: Ulp. 20.14.

[61] The fifth, 'the general and the specific,' is applied, more or less consciously, in innumerable cases in modern law. The *Travellers' Guide*, handed to those spending a holiday abroad, forbids you 'to cash cheques on your sterling account, to borrow currency or to enter into any other agreement to obtain foreign currency' — clearly a provision which 'specialiter quibusdam enumeratis generale subiciat verbum quo specialia complectatur.'

observation, consistent and useful.' (So, presumably, is the theory of relativity.) But (like the theory of relativity) it is not 'natural' — not even the first four norms — in the sense of 'obvious, readily hit upon by any student of these matters.' It is the naturalness of the rhetorical categories and methods in the former sense, their soundness as doctrine and in practice, which accounts for their adoption, in one form or another, in so many parts of the Hellenistic world. Recently, it has been shewn that Philo was acquainted with them, and the conclusion has been drawn that he was influenced by Palestinian Rabbinism. But it is far more likely that he came across them in the course of his general studies at Alexandria. We have before us a science the beginnings of which may be traced back to Plato, Aristotle and their contemporaries. It recurs in Cicero, Hillel and Philo — with enormous differences in detail, yet *au fond* the same. Cicero did not sit at the feet of Hillel, nor Hillel at the feet of Cicero; and there was no need for Philo to go to Palestinian sources for this kind of teaching. As we saw, there are indeed signs that Hillel's ideas were partly imported from Egypt. The true explanation lies in the common Hellenistic background. Philosophical instruction was very similar in outline whether given at Rome, Jerusalem or Alexandria.

It is not necessary to dwell on the remaining norms of Hillel, beyond noting a clear parallel to the seventh, the rule that an ambiguity in the law may be settled by adducing the context, *dabhar hallamedh me'inyano*. The commandment 'Thou shalt not steal' is interpreted as referring to theft of a person, not of property, since it appears together with other capital crimes against a person, namely, murder and adultery.[62] Cicero writes: 'It ought to be shewn that the ambiguous passage becomes intelligible from what precedes and comes after it.'[63] It may well have been this norm of interpretation which Celsus had in mind when he declared, in discussing *leges dotis*, that 'it was not in accordance with the science of the civil law to judge or give

[62] Mekhiltha *ad loc.*, Bab Sanh. 86a.
[63] De Inv. 2.40.117 ('ex superiore et ex inferiore scriptura docendum id quod quaeratur fieri perspicuum').

an opinion on the basis of a mere fragment of a *lex*, without inspecting the whole.'[64]

A few remarks may be added about terminology. We have already pointed out that, just as the Romans succeeded in latinizing the rhetorical notions they used, so the 'classical,' Tannaitic Rabbis succeeded in hebraizing them. There was no slavish, literal rendering. In fact, it is fascinating to watch the transformation the Hellenistic concepts underwent as they were freely adapted to the Jewish milieu. To take a small example, we mentioned above the introduction by Hillel of the antithesis 'a written Torah and an oral Torah,' an antithesis owing much to that of νόμοι ἔγγραφοι and ἄγραφοι or *ius scriptum* and *non scriptum* or *per manus traditum*. Yet look at the Hebrew term for 'oral Torah:' *torah shebbe'al pe*, 'Torah by mouth.' The words *'al pe*, 'by mouth,' frequently signify 'by heart,' 'from memory,' and this meaning is certainly relevant. But for the Rabbis of the Talmud, a good many other ideas were evoked by the phrase. We need only consider passages like the following: 'According to the mouth of the Lord they rested, and according to the mouth of the Lord they journeyed; they kept the charge of the Lord according to the mouth of the Lord in the hand of Moses;'[65] again, 'The Torah of thy mouth is better unto me than thousands of gold and silver; give me understanding that I may learn thy commandments;'[66] or again, 'This book of the Torah shall not depart out of thy mouth, but thou shalt meditate therein day and night, that thou mayest observe to do according to all that is written therein.'[67] The latter verse in particular must have been in Hillel's mind when he coined the antithesis in question (or in the mind of whoever coined it about that time). It advocates the constant study, interpretation, of Scripture,[68] for the sake

[64] D. 1.3.24; Lenel, *Palingenesia*, vol. I, 141 ('incivile est nisi tota lege perspecta una aliqua particula eius proposita iudicare vel respondere'). On Celsus, see above, p. 253.

[65] Num. 9.23; cp. Josh. 22.9, Ex. 17.1, 38.21, Num. 3.51, Ezra 1.1, II Chron. 36.22.

[66] Ps. 119.72 f.

[67] Josh. 1.8.

[68] Exactly what the original author meant by this does not here matter. The Rabbis understood the verse as referring to the kind of study they

of being able scrupulously to fulfil all precepts. When we remember the function of 'a fence' around Scriptural law assigned to the tradition of the fathers in the age of Hillel, and when we consider that the verse quoted enjoins constant interpretation by saying that 'the Torah shall not depart out of thy mouth' and describes as the object the keeping of all 'that is written therein,' we can hardly doubt that here is a main root of Hillel's contrast between the 'written Torah' and the 'Torah by mouth.' The Hellenistic scheme has been completely Judaized.

Nevertheless there are instances of the Greek or Latin terms being still noticeable in the Hebrew. In some cases, this is almost inevitable. Rules concerning deduction from analogy will naturally operate with concepts like ὅμοιον in Greek — as when Aristotle explains this method as 'the comparison of like with like, when both of them come under the same genus but one is more familiar than the other'[69] — *simile* or *par* in Latin — as when Cicero says that 'the doubtful matter to be deduced must appear similar to one as to which there is certainty'[70] or that 'like is compared to like'[71] — *shawe* in Hebrew.[72] Again, rules concerning general and specific laws could scarcely avoid expressions like καθόλου — κατὰ μέρος (καθ' ἕκαστον), γενικόν (περιέχειν, περιλαμβάνειν) — ἴδιον, *generale* (*complecti*) — *speciale* (*singula*), *kelal* — *perat*. However, on occasion, the Rabbis employ words less obviously suitable, when it is worth searching for the possible Greek or Latin model. The sixth of Hillel's norms is called *keyotse' bo bemaqom 'aher*, literally, 'as what is going out with it in another passage of Scripture.' The verse 'When Moses held up his hand Israel prevailed'[73] is taken

---

practised. It is noteworthy that the verb *hagha*, 'to meditate,' is actually used as denoting 'to deduce a further law from an existing one' in Pal. Meg. 72b.

[69] Rhet. 1.2.19 (ὅμοιον πρὸς ὅμοιον, ὅταν ἄμφω μὲν ᾖ ὑπὸ τὸ αὐτὸ γένος, γνωριμώτερον δὲ θάτερον τοῦ θατέρου).

[70] De Inv. 2.50.150 ('ut id de quo quaeritur rei de qua constat simile esse videatur').

[71] Top. 10.43 ('par pari comparatur').

[72] Occurring in the second of Hillel's norms and several other Tannaitic rules of interpretation.

[73] Ex. 17.11.

as meaning that Israel prevailed when directing their thoughts on high; 'as what is going out with it thou shouldest say, Make a serpent and set it upon a standard and every one that seeth it shall live[74] also means that they were healed when directing their thoughts on high.'[75] The phrase *yotse' bo* (in Aramaic *naphiq be*), 'going out with it,' in this sense of 'corresponding to,' is rare. Its use in the norm under discussion may well be due to συμβαίνω, which signifies not only 'to correspond to,' but also 'to follow from reasoning.'[76]

Another case seems to be the familiar *(shen)ne'emar*, '(as) it is said.'[77] Like '(as) it is written,' it exclusively introduces quotations from Scripture — never an oral tradition. It is tempting to explain this by the influence of ῥητόν which, in rhetorical works, though literally 'what is said,' has the technical sense of 'the written document to be subjected to interpretation.'[78] The Roman orators translated it by *scriptum*.[79] The Rabbis, in addition to *kathubh* (Aramaic *kethibh*), 'it is written,' evolved a term more faithfully rendering the Greek: *ne'emar*, 'it is said.'

[74] Num. 21.8.

[75] Mishnah R. H. 3.8.

[76] See Plato, Gorg. 479C (συλλογίζομαι τὰ συμβαίνοντα ἐκ τοῦ λόγου), Phaedo 74A (κατὰ πάντα ταῦτα συμβαίνει τὴν ἀνάμνησιν εἶναι ἀφ' ὁμοίων), Aristotle, Nic. E. 7.12.1 (οὐ συμβαίνει διὰ ταῦτα), Demosthenes, Contra Aristog. I 792A (ἐκ γὰρ ὧν νῦν ὅδ' ἀξιοῖ ταῦτα συμβαίνει — the conclusion drawn is involved but, if the rhetorical scheme underlying it is recognized, makes perfect sense). Other terms deserving consideration in this connection are διεξέρχομαι περί τινος, 'to expound' (e. g. Plato, Laws 9.857E) and even the Latin *(per)venire* (e. g. Cicero, De Inv. 2.50.148 f., 152 — see above, p. 247 n. 25).

[77] It does not figure in Hillel's norms, but that it goes back to his epoch may be seen from ἐρρέθη in Matthew 5.21, 31, Romans 9.12; cp. εἴρηκεν in Hebrews 4.3, ῥηθέν in Matthew 1.22, 2.17, 23, 4.14, 8.17, 12.17, 13.35, 22.31, 24.15, and εἰρημένον in Luke 2.24, Acts 2.16, 13.40, Romans 4.18.

[78] The fact that later scholiasts emphasize that the spoken word also may form a ῥητόν only confirms the original limitation. See also the next footnote.

[79] They soon noticed that *scriptum* in this technical sense might consist in a purely verbal utterance; see e. g. Quintilian 7.5.6. Cp. the preceding footnote.

In conclusion, attention may be drawn to four points that should be borne in mind when these matters are pursued in greater detail.

First, the influence of Hellenistic philosophy was not confined to the period of Hillel. It had started before; and it went on afterwards, in an increasing degree, for a long time. The systems of interpretation advocated by Ishmael and Akiba some 150 years later can be understood only against the background of the rhetorical teaching of the time. Josiah, a disciple of Ishmael, about the middle of the 2nd century A. C., favoured the method of *seres*: a verse at first sight illogical may be made logical by re-arranging its parts. In Num. 9.6 ff., we are told that certain men brought a problem 'before Moses and before Aaron' and that Moses transmitted it to God, thus obtaining the correct solution. Josiah explains[80] that the passage cited must be rearranged: the men evidently came first before Aaron, who did not know, and then before Moses, who approached God. The name of the method is curious, the literal meaning of *seres* being 'to castrate.' It becomes intelligible, however, when we remember that τέμνειν also signifies 'to castrate,' 'to divide logically,' 'to distinguish,' τομή 'castration,' 'logical division,' 'distinction,' 'precision of expression,' 'caesura.' Even ideas which *prima facie* one would incline to put down as peculiarly Rabbinic may turn out to have been, if not borrowed from rhetoric, at least supported, helped on, by it. The oral Torah, in the eyes of the Rabbis, is the particular glory of Israel; the gentiles cannot grasp the secret, mysterious way Scripture is interpreted.[81] Cicero, as an argument in favour of 'interpretation,' i. e. of following the spirit rather than the letter of a statute, refers to the lawgiver's decree that judges must be of a certain rank and age, capable not only, as anybody would be, of reciting a statute, but also of discovering its intention: 'if the author of a statute committed his work to simple men and primitive judges, he would diligently put down every detail, but since he knows how well qualified the judges

---

[80] Siphre *ad loc.*
[81] Tanhuma Wayyera par. 6 on Gen. 18.17.

will be, he does not add what he deems to be obvious.'[82] It is the same thing in a Roman dress.[83]

Secondly, the influence of Hellenistic philosophy was not confined to the domain of interpretation. Such fundamental matters as the distinction between *mishpatim*, rational, natural laws, 'commandments which, were they not laid down, would have to be laid down,' and *huqqoth*, inexplicable laws, 'commandments which the evil impulse and the heathens refute,'[84] are not of purely Jewish origin; and even the teaching that 'you have no right to criticize the *huqqoth*'[85] was probably a commonplace before Plato. He has a profound discussion as to how far it is proper 'to be wiser than the laws'[86] — this sounds like a reference to an earlier slogan —, and Aristotle advises us, if our case is favoured by a statute which, though still technically in force, is clearly obsolete, to argue 'that there is no advantage in being wiser than the physician, for an error of the latter is less harmful than the habit of disobeying the authority; and to try to be wiser than the laws is precisely what is forbidden in the best of them.'[87] Students of Roman law are familiar with the statements by Julian, 'It is impossible to give reasons for everything that our forefathers laid down,'[88] and by Neratius, 'Wherefore it is not

---

[82] De Inv. 2.47.139 ('demonstrabit illum scriptorem, si scripta sua stultis hominibus et barbaris iudicibus committeret, omnia summa diligentia perscripturum fuisse; nunc vero, quod intellegeret quales viri res iudicaturi essent, idcirco eum quae perspicua videret esse non adscripsisse').

[83] Needless to say, an advocate using Cicero's argument would at the same time flatter the judges. Even this element was hardly unwelcome to the Rabbis: the people would be more willing to shoulder the burden of the oral Law if that gave them a feeling of superiority.

[84] Siphra on Lev. 18.4, Bab. Yoma 67b.

[85] *Ib*.

[86] Statesman 299C (οὐδὲν γὰρ δεῖ τῶν νόμων εἶναι σοφώτερον).

[87] Rhet. 1.15.12 (οὐ λυσιτελεῖ παρασοφίζεσθαι τὸν ἰατρόν, οὐ γὰρ τοσοῦτο βλάπτει ἡ ἁμαρτία τοῦ ἰατροῦ ὅσον τὸ ἐθίζεσθαι ἀπειθεῖν τῷ ἄρχοντι καὶ ὅτι τὸ τῶν νόμων σοφώτερον ζητεῖν εἶναι τοῦτ' ἐστὶν ὃ ἐν τοῖς ἐπαινουμένοις νόμοις ἀπαγορεύεται. The argument is strongly influenced by Plato. Even the comparison with the physician occurs in Statesman 294 ff.

[88] D. 1.3.20 ('non omnium quae a maioribus constituta sunt ratio reddi potest').

correct to inquire into the reasons of what they laid down, otherwise much that is secure would be undermined.'[89]

Thirdly, if the Roman and Greek sources can help us to elucidate the Jewish side, the converse is also true. To some extent, this may have become clear already. But to take a fresh example, about 200 B. C., Aelius Paetus wrote a 'tripertita,' where 'the law of the XII Tables was given first, then the interpretation was joined to it and finally the *legis actio* was appended.'[90] Scholars are still divided as to whether there were three large parts — first the complete XII Tables, next all results of interpretation and then a list of all *legis actiones* — or whether each provision of the XII Tables (or each group of provisions) was accompanied by its interpretation and *legis actio*. Comparison of the Rabbinic material should settle the controversy in favour of the latter alternative. Aelius Paetus wrote a Midrash. The old, expositional (as distinct from the homiletical) Midrash takes the form of a running commentary on Scripture.[91] It is significant, however, that there is nothing on the Jewish side to correspond to the *legis actio*. So even here, no sooner have we noted a parallel than we are struck by the profound difference between the two legal systems.

This brings us to the fourth and last point. The next task, of course, is to conduct a thorough inquiry into the debt of Talmudic jurisprudence to Hellenistic rhetoric. The present study is only

---

[89] D. 1.3.21 ('et ideo rationes eorum quae constituuntur inquiri non oportet, alioquin multa ex his quae certa sunt subvertuntur').

[90] D. 1.2.2.38 ('lege XII tabularum praeposita iungitur interpretatio, deinde subtexitur legis actio'). The same threefold division comes earlier on in the same fragment, in the first half of 1.2.2.12 (that the part up to 'continent' goes back to an older source than the rest is suggested by the fact that the second half begins by 'aut plebiscitum' instead of 'aut est plebiscitum'), and it recurs in 1.3.13.

[91] True, the Midrash was not written down till long after the period of the 'tripertita.' But in its oral form, it certainly dates from the 1st century B. C. (The recent discovery of a homiletical Midrash on Habakkuk 1 f., possibly written down in the 1st century B. C., is significant in this connection: the first steps towards a Halakhic Midrash can hardly be later.) Moreover, the Targum, the free rendering of Scripture into the vernacular for use in liturgy, is as old as Aelius, and the rule was that each verse of Scripture was at once to be followed by its paraphrase.

a first beginning, intended to open the subject and to shew that some debt there is, but to do no more. We have merely touched the fringe. Yet it is greatly to be hoped that, once this immediate task has been carried out, with all that belongs to it (it will, for example, be necessary to answer such subsidiary questions as whether the influence was greater or smaller at different times and on different schools, and through what channels it was chiefly exercised), the second, subtler one will not be forgotten: a working out of the differences between Greek and Roman rhetoric and Talmudic rhetoric, of the factors that determined the Rabbinic selection of certain notions and rejection of others, and of the changes that the Hellenistic concepts suffered — singly and as a system — in the course of being transferred to an alien soil.

13

THE CHAIN OF THE PHARISAIC TRADITION

Elias Bickerman

I

The Synagogue had only vague and intermittent memories of the four centuries which separated Ezra and Nehemiah from Hillel and Shammai.[1] Not even the feast of Hanukkah entailed fixed historical associations. The Talmudic stories which refer to this period are mere anecdotes, full of details borrowed from various epochs and incidents, and related for the edification or amusement of the hearers.[2] But the rabbis in Tiberias or Pumbeditha were not alone in treating history in a cavalier fashion. Gentile men of letters, the contemporaries of the *Tannaim* and *Amoraim*, likewise knew nothing of history apart from isolated small facts, *exempla* which served to decorate a discourse or to illustrate some moral commonplace.[3] The rabbis told nothing more substantial than fables about Alexander the Great.[4] This is because they, in common with the rest of the world – apart from a few lugubrious scholars – preferred to read the *History* attributed to Callisthenes. For all these readers, the Seleucids coalesced into one single "Antiochus."[5] But the same is true of Dion of Prusa or Lucian; the latter attributes to Stratonice, the consort of both Seleucus I and Antiochus I, an adventure drawn from oriental fables.[6] It was in vain that the Macedonian kings in Egypt favored the Jews and extended their patronage to the arts and sciences; the rabbis mention "King Ptolemy" only in passing, when

---

[1] Cf. J. Derenbourg, *Essai sur l'histoire... de la Palestine d'après les Thalmuds et les autres sources rabbiniques*, 1867, p. 57.

[2] Cf. e.g. I. Lévy, *REJ* 35 (1897), pp. 213–223.

[3] H.-I. Marrou, *Saint Augustin et la fin de la culture antique*, 4th edn. 1958, pp. 115ff.

[4] Cf. I. Lévy, in *Jew. Encycl.* I, pp. 342–343; Idem, *REJ* 63 (1912), pp. 211–215; L. Wallach, *PAAJR* 11 (1941), pp. 47ff.

[5] S. Krauss, *REJ* 45 (1902), p. 27.

[6] Dio of Prusa, 31.113; 37.6; Lucian, *De dea Syr.* 17. Cf. E. Benveniste, *Mélanges R. Dussaud* I, 1939, pp. 249ff.; A.H. Krappe, *Byzantina-Metabyzantina* I, 1944, pp. 189–199. Lucian knows only two anecdotes from the history of the Seleucids, which he relates several times: Seleucus I gives his own wife (Stratonice) to his son, Antiochus I (*De dea Syr.* 17; *Icaromen.* 35; *De salt.* 58; *De hist. consc.* 35); and Antiochus wins a victory in Galatia (*Zeux.* 8; *De laps.* 9). Cf. also *De laps.* 10.

they speak of the Septuagint translation.[7] It is also true that Byzantine writers merge the king and the astronomer, both of whom were called Ptolemy, into one single person.[8] In order to accommodate history to the fateful number of "seventy weeks," Jose ben Halafta reduced the duration of the Persian domination to thirty-four years. The Arsacids reigned for four hundred and fifty years, but this was reduced to two hundred and sixty-six years in the official calculations at the court of their successors, the Sassanids;[9] and the Zoroastrian magi simply eliminated the Achemenids from Persian history.[10]

Under the empire, from the second century C.E. onward, the Greeks began to abandon the hellenistic literature written in the *koiné*, which however remained their spoken idiom. In the same way, the Jews neglected the Aramaic works, all those "numerous books" of the hellenistic epoch which Qoheleth mentions, although they continued to

---

[7] Bonsirven, I, 1934, p. 39; A. Geiger, *Urschrift und Übersetzungen der Bibel*, 1857, pp. 439ff.

[8] Malalas, p. 196, ed. G. Dindorf; Zacharias of Mitylene, *The Syriac Chronicle* (trans. F.J. Hamilton and E.W. Brooks), XII, p. 7. A Byzantine scholiast informs us that the sculptor Phidias was an astrologer in Syracuse and the father of Archimedes: J. Overbeck, *Die antiken Schriftquellen zur Geschichte der bildenden Künste*, 1968, nr. 739.

[9] On the Jewish computation of time, cf. I. Lévy, *REJ* 51 (1906), pp. 186ff. On the chronology of the Sassanid authors, cf. E.J. Brown, *Literary History of Persia* I, 1901, p. 119; W. Bartold, *Zapiski* of the Oriental Section of the Russian Archaeological Society 22 (1915); Mrs H. Lewy, *Journ. Amer. Orient. Soc.* 64 (1944), pp. 197ff.

[10] The methodological analogy between the Jewish chronographer who was teaching ca. 170 C.E. and the Sassanid authors (from the third to the sixth centuries C.E.) is remarkable. The basis of their calculation is identical, viz. the beginning of the current computation, i.e. of the Seleucid era, in 311 B.C.E. After this, history is sacrificed to theology. The Jews understood the seventy weeks (= 490 years) of Dan 9:26 as running from Jeremiah to the destruction of the Second Temple in 70 C.E. (cf. J.A. Montgomery, *The Book of Daniel*, 1927, p. 397). Since, according to Jer 25:11, the Babylonian exile was to last for 70 years, there remained only 420 years (490 minus 70) for the epoch of the Second Temple, i.e. from Cyrus to Vespasian. – For the Jews, the era of the Seleucids was that "of the Greek empire" (1 Macc 1:10; cf. Abel, *Comm.*, p. xlix). This means that the Greek period began in 311 B.C.E. Alexander the Great became the master of the Persian empire in the sixth year of his reign, and this led the Jewish chronographer to place six years of Alexander before the Greek domination. This meant that only 34 years remained for the Persian monarchs, i.e. 420–386 (6 + 310 + 70). Since scripture contains the names of only four kings of Persia, this reduction need not have seemed absurd. Cf. H.L. Ginsberg, *Studies in Daniel*, 1948, p. 19. – Thanks to some aberration, the Sassanid authors identified the beginning of the Seleucid era with the appearance of Zoroaster. Since a list of (mythical) kings placed this event 258 years before Alexander the Great, and his reign lasted only 14 years, only 266 years remained for the dynasty of the Arsacids, which was overthrown by the Sassanids in 227 B.C.E.

speak Aramaic. "Why speak Aramaic in the land of Israel? Let it be either the sacred tongue or the Greek tongue!" One might fancy that these were the words (*mutatis mutandis*) of Philostratus or some other master of the "Second Sophistic movement." But this purist declaration was made by their contemporary, Rabbi Judah the Prince, the editor of the Mishnah.[11]

The centuries between Alexander and Augustus were shrouded in a general oblivion, because no one was interested in remembering them; in the words of the Sermon on the Mount, "sufficient unto the day is the evil thereof." A sustained and constant effort is indispensable, if the past is to continue to live on in the memory of posterity. If this effort is lacking, for whatever reason, all that is remembered of the splendors of the past is one or other trait that can still offer edification or amusement today. For the Copts, the ancient Pharaohs had become powerful magicians.[12] Under the Caesars of Rome and Constantinople, all that kept alive the memory of the Seleucids in Antioch, their ancient capital, was the buildings they had erected,[13] since after the Roman conquest, there was no societal institution (dynasty, school, sect, etc.) that cultivated the memory of those who had been defeated.[14] For people in general, as for the Syrian sheikh whom Apollonius of Tyana met, "Antiochus and Seleucus" were merely the names of deposed figures from the past:[15] the present and the future belonged to the Romans, and one said: "for as long as Roman dominion shall endure" in order

---

[11] S. Lieberman, *Greek in Jewish Palestine*, 2nd edn. 1965, p. 21. On the repudiation of hellenistic literature, cf. e.g. W. Schmid, *Geschichte der griechischen Literatur* II/1, 1920, p. 27. The judgment of Dionysius of Halicarnassus on Polybius is characteristic (*De comp. verbi* 4; *Ant. Rom.* 1.6,2). We should note that although Qoheleth and Daniel were both written in Aramaic, they were preserved only in a Hebrew translation. Cf. H.L. Ginsberg, *Studies in Daniel*, 1948, and *Studies in Kohelet*, 1950.

[12] G. Maspero, *Études de mythologie* VII, p. 443.

[13] Malalas, pp. 200ff.

[14] It is significant that the work of Callinicus of Petra on the history of Alexandria, which became the principal source of Porphyry (and through the mediation of Porphyry, of Jerome too, in his explanation of the passages of Daniel which refer to the conflicts between the hellenistic kings), was composed for Queen Zenobia Cleopatra, who styled herself the heiress to the Ptolemies. Cf. *FGH* III, nr. 281. It is no less significant that it was the pagan Libanius, under the Christian emperors, who cultivated the nostalgic remembrance of the Seleucids (Libanius, *Or.* 11). We should note that the literature produced by the Alexandrian opposition to the Roman emperors is silent about the Ptolemies.

[15] Philostratus, *Vita Apollonii* 1.38.

to express the concept: "forever."[16] This definitive character of the regime of the Caesars, which was a dead end weighing down upon a whole world, swallowed up and cheapened the hellenistic age. Naturally enough, since the masters of the universe believed that they would hold this position forever, they felt only scorn for their hapless predecessors. Although Augustus went to the tomb of Alexander, he refused to visit the mausoleum of the Lagids, saying that he wanted to see a king, not corpses. Livy writes that the Macedonians at Alexandria and Seleucia, and in all the colonies scattered throughout the world, have degenerated into Egyptians and Syrians.[17] For equally natural reasons, the vanquished themselves did not cultivate the reputation of the deposed monarchs: those centuries were abolished and abandoned. Towards the beginning of the Roman empire, the Greeks began to turn away, deliberately and consciously, from hellenistic history, literature, and art, and to look for the rules of art and of life in classical Greece, the Greece of the Parthenon and Demosthenes.[18] For the same reason and at the same period, Jerusalem forgot the period which came after the Bible. After Herod – and especially when one contemplated the ruins of the temple – who could be interested in a Judas Maccabeus? Like everyone else, the Jew became "classical": he closed the modern scrolls and opened the Bible. The authors of the Talmud lived with David or Jeremiah, just as their contemporaries, the Greek men of letters, moved in spirit among the shades of the Athens and Sparta of the past.[19]

---

[16] F. Cumont, *Catalogue du Musée du Cinquantenaire*, 1913, nr. 133 (= *Rev. étud. anc.*, 3, p. 273), from Aemonia in Phrygia, 95 B.C.E.: τοῦτο δὲ τὸ ψήφισμα νενομοθετῆσθαι τῷ αἰῶνι τῆς Ῥωμαίων ἡγεμονίας φυλαχθησόμενον.

[17] Dio Cassius, 51.16,5; Livy, 38.17.

[18] The historical subjects treated by the Greek rhetors under the empire went no further than the death of Alexander; the Latin rhetors went as far as the empire. Seneca, *Contr.* 2.4(12); 10, *praef.* 5; Quintilian, 3.85,55; R. Kohl, *De scholasticarum declamationum argumento*, 1915, p. 106.

[19] Cf. e.g. Lucian, *Rhet. Praec.* 16: "What you need most of all is Marathon and Cynegira... talk to me of Salamis, of the Artemision, of Plataeae." Cf. H.-I. Marrou, *Histoire de l'éducation dans l'antiquité*, 1948, p. 220 (from whom I have borrowed this quotation). Herodian (3.4,2) believes that Darius III was captured by Alexander in the battle of Issus. On the ignorance of the past in the late empire, cf. A. Momigliano, *Riv. stor. ital.*, 1969, p. 297; W. Hartke, *Römische Kinderkaiser*, 1951, pp. 6–23 and 74–91. On the origins of Atticism, cf. W. Kroll, *s.v.* "Rhetorik," *RE Suppl.* VII, pp. 1105–1108.

II

We can now understand why the synagogue preserved only one single document from the post-biblical period, viz. the list of the predecessors of Hillel and Shammai. This sequence of names forms the first chapter of the treatise *Aboth* in the Mishnah. But originally, as Louis Finkelstein has recently conjectured, it was attached to the creed which is now incorporated into ch. X(XI) of the treatise *Sanhedrin*.[20] This "manifesto of the Pharisees" declares: "All Israel has a destiny in the future eternity, as it is written..." (Is. 60:21).[21] This is followed by the exceptions to this general principle, viz. the generation at the time of the flood and other exceptionally wicked persons in the Bible.[22] The document continues: "Moses was sanctified in the cloud and received Torah from Sinai, as it is written... [Ex. 26:16]. Joshua received it from Moses, as it is written... [Deut. 34:9]." The elders, the judges, and the prophets follow as intermediaries, introduced by the same formula. Then, according to the reconstruction by Finkelstein, the document names Haggai, Zechariah, and Malachi, though without referring to

---

[20] L. Finkelstein, *Introduction to the Treatises Abot and Abot of Rabbi Nathan*, New York 1950 (in Hebrew, with an English summary on pp. i–xlviii). Since I am not an expert on Talmudic studies, I translate the Hebrew text of the document (pp. 226ff.; cf. pp. xxviff.) as it is reconstructed and understood by the learned author. [English translation: Joseph I. Gorfinkle, http://www.ultimasurf.net/bible/pirkeavot/pirke-avot-1.htm]

[21] On the term *'olam-ha-ba*, cf. Bonsirven, I, pp. 310ff. [English translation: Finkelstein, *op. cit.*]

[22] Finkelstein (p. xli) regards the passage in *Sanh.* 10, "These are those who have no share in the world to come: one who says that the dead will not awaken to life, one who says that Torah is not from heaven, and an Epicurean," as a later addition made ca. 170 C.E., but I find this dating too late. This triad of heretics corresponds to the three points of controversy between the Pharisees and the Sadducees, viz. the resurrection, the oral law, and the dogma of providence. But it was only towards the beginning of the Common Era, in the philosophical eclecticism of the period, that people in general began to believe in the divine government of the universe; Virgil could still write, *nec curare deum credis mortalia quemquam* (*Georgics* 8.36). Later, when the Peripatetics had disappeared (Epictetus, *Diss.* 2.19,20; cf. also Brink, *RE Suppl.* VII, 90ff.) and the Academy had accepted the theodicy of the Stoa, only the Epicureans continued to deny providence. Josephus (*Ant.* 10.11,7, §278) quotes the prophecies of Daniel with the explicit intention of refuting the Epicureans. A renewal of their propaganda in the second century C.E. provoked a violent reaction among "right-thinking people." Alexander the false prophet anathematized atheists, Christians, and Epicureans; cf. L. Caster, *Lucien et la pensée religieuse de son temps*, 1938, pp. 84–90. – I observe *en passant* that in another clause, the document employs a Greek work, *idiôtai*, to mean "private citizens."

scripture in their case.²³ "The people of the Great Synagogue received it from Haggai, Zechariah, and Malachi. They said three things: Be patient in administering justice, form a hedge around your words, form a great number of wise men."²⁴ "Simeon the Just was one of the last survivors of the Great Synagogue. He used to say [his precept is quoted]. Antigonus of Soko received (the tradition) from Simeon the Just. He used to say [his precept is quoted]." The list continues in the same way down to Hillel and Shammai.

Altogether, the document names fourteen intermediaries in the transmission of Torah. As Finkelstein notes, this number is not accidental.²⁵ In the first Gospel, the genealogy of Jesus is made up of three chains, each of which has fourteen links (Matt. 1:17). The Chronicler counts fourteen high priests from Aaron to Azariah, the first high priest in the temple of Solomon, and then fourteen successors of Azariah down to Jaddua (1 Chron. 5:29–41 [6:1ff. in English Bibles] and Neh. 12:10). But it is precisely these parallels that allow us to grasp the novelty of the Pharisaic chain, which substitutes the professorial lineage, from master to pupil, for the natural descent from father to son. Why is this construction made? It was not necessary in order to trace the Torah of the Pharisees back to Sinai, and thus dispossess the priests;²⁶ for one single uncertain link would have sufficed to invalidate this transmission of the treasure of the faith, and there are yawning gaps in the first part of the chain. Maimonides indeed attempted to fill these in.²⁷ The

---

[23] Finkelstein notes (p. xxxvi) that the authors of the document did not count Haggai, Zechariah, and Malachi among the prophets, and this is his principal reason for dating the "manifesto" to the third century B.C.E. Nevertheless, the fact that these three prophets are named in the chain of the tradition proves that they were already "canonical" in the eyes of the authors of the manifesto. It seems more likely that they are mentioned separately in order to indicate the intermediary link between the biblical period and the links that follow. As is well known, Haggai, Zechariah, and Malachi are often grouped together in the rabbinical sources as "the last prophets"; cf. Bonsirven, I, p. 211; N. Glatzer, *Review of Religion*, 1946, pp. 122 and 129.

[24] The explanation of the term *anše keneset ha-gedolah* given in *RB* 55 (1948), pp. 397–402, is untenable, and the meaning of the maxim attributed to these "men of the Great Synaogue" remains obscure. Cf. L. Finkelstein, *JBL* 59 (1940), pp. 55–69 (= Idem, *Pharisaism in the Making*, 1972, pp. 159–174), and J. Goldin in A. Altman, ed. *Biblical Motifs*, 1966, pp. 135–158, and Idem, *HTR* 58 (1965), pp. 365–377. On the apophthegm of Simeon, cf. J. Goldin, *PAAJR* 27 (1958), pp. 43–58. On the maxim of Antigonus, cf. the following essay in this book.

[25] Finkelstein, *op. cit.*, pp. 8ff.; p. xi and esp. pp. xlivff.

[26] Cf. e.g. I. Loeb, *REJ* 19 (1889), pp. 188ff.

[27] Maimonides, *The Mishnah Torah*, ed. with an English translation by M. Hyamson,

rabbis, who said that God approved the interpretations of particular teachers,[28] had no need of this chain of transmission to prop up their authority. The list was drawn up in order to establish the lineage of *Beth Hillel* and *Beth Shammai*. For these "houses" were schools – and more than that, they were hellenistic schools.[29]

III

Plato was the first professor who took pains to perpetuate his teaching. He bequeathed his school to Speusippus, who was succeeded by Xenocrates; then Polemon succeeded Xenocrates. In this way, the "Academy" continued to exist for more than eight centuries until 529 C.E., when it was closed down by Justinian. Plato's example was followed by Aristotle, who bequeathed his "Lyceum" to Theophrastes in 322. In 306, Epicurus founded his "Garden"; in 301, Zeno founded the school of the Stoa. In these schools, which were the centers of the Platonic, Peripatetic, and other "sects" and were organized in the form of religious fraternities, the founder's teaching was transmitted from generation to generation by successive rectors of the school.[30] As early as ca. 200 B.C.E., Sotion drew up lists of these rectors. After this, the series of "successors" (*diadochoi*) has formed the framework of every history of Greek philosophy.[31] For example, a contemporary of Hillel and Shammai writes that "the school of Epicurus continued [after his death] until the first Caesar, for a period of 227 years [271–44 B.C.E.].

1937, p. 3, gives the following succession: Moses, Joshua, Phinehas, Eli, Samuel, David, etc. Later on, Ezra follows Baruch, etc.

[28] Bonsirven, II, p. 308; I, p. 271.

[29] Cf. Horace, *Carmina* 1.29,14: *Socraticam... domum*. Cf. L. Robert, *Arch. Ephem.*, 1960, p. 8, on the term *oikos*.

[30] Cf. e.g. P. Boyancé, *Le culte des Muses chez les philosophes grecs*, 1936, pp. 261–267 and 299–327.

[31] Cf. F. Susemihl, *Geschichte der griechischen Literatur in der Alexandrinerzeit* I, 1891, pp. 496–498; E. Schwartz, *RE* V, 754. R. Philippson (*Rhein. Mus.* 78 [1929], p. 344, and 79 [1930], p. 406) identifies Sotion with the teacher of Seneca who bore the same name, but this biographical question is not important in the present context; it is certain that the philosophical "successions" were an established literary genre long before the Roman period. In his last will, Epicurus speaks of his *diadochoi* (Diogenes Laertius, 10.9). Cf. F. Wehrli, *Die Schule des Aristoteles* VI, 1952, p. 65; VII, p. 113; P. Kienle, *Die Berichte über die Sukzessionen der Philosophie*, dissertation at the Free University of Berlin, 1961 (I have not been able to consult this work). On the *diadochoi* in the Roman period, cf. J.H. Oliver, *Hesperia* 36 (1967), p. 42.

During this time, there were fourteen successors."[32] People in the classical period paid great attention to this succession of rectors, because it was much more than a purely chronological list. From Socrates onward, philosophy was not some kind of technical knowledge which can become obsolete, but rather a way of living, an *ars vivendi*, which the founder of the philosophical school had discovered. In his school, his works are read, explained, and commented upon forever. His doctrine is "a great and precious possession."[33]

One cannot learn an *ars vivendi* from books alone. The philosopher lived his doctrine, and the teaching imparted in the school was also spiritual direction. The books which were published could never contain all the richness of the oral instruction.[34] Thus, when he reports that the lecture notes of Aristotle and Theophrastes had been lost after the death of the latter, Strabo supposes that from then on, the Peripatetics would no longer have been able to engage in philosophy; all they could do was to spout forth about principles. The great duty of the disciples was to transmit faithfully the doctrine of the school. Arcesilaos was reproached for having "shaken" the doctrine of Plato, whereas his predecessors, from Speusippus to Crates, were praised for having "carefully safeguarded what they had received from their predecessors." Even in the Pyrrhonian school, one referred to the opinion "of older Skeptics." They held that Euphranor had been one of the disciples of Timon: "Eubulus heard from Euphranor, who had heard it from Sarpedon, etc."[35]

IV

The Greek historians applied this idea of an academic lineage to the barbarian wisdom too. Sotion included the "barbarians" in his work on the "succession of the philosophers." The Greeks made a list of "the succession of the magi": Ostanes (who accompanied Xerxes),

---

[32] Suidas, *s.v.* "Epicurus."
[33] Cicero, *Acad.* 2.23, Cf. the note of J.S. Reid *ad loc.*; Diogenes of Oenoanda, frag. 24: μέγα τι καὶ τείμιον κτῆμα φιλοσοφία πεπίστευται.
[34] Cf. Marrou, *op. cit.*, pp. 284–288; A.-J. Festugière, *La révélation d'Hermès Trismégiste* II, 1948, pp. 34–47; W. Jaeger, *Paideia* III, 1947, pp. 194–196.
[35] Strabo, 13.1,54, p. 608; cf. Brink, *RE Suppl.* VII, p. 939; Diogenes Laertius, 4.4; Cicero, *Acad.* 1.34; Sextus Empiricus, *Pyrrh.* 1.36. On the Skeptic "succession," cf. Diogenes Laertius, 9.115–116.

Astrampsychus, Gobryes, Pazates. But since Zoroaster was placed six thousand years before Xerxes, Pliny the Elder doubted whether he could have been the inventor of the magic art: "To begin with, it would be surprising that the memory and the art itself should have lasted for such a long time, since there were no lecture notes, and also because this was not preserved by a continuous succession of illustrious masters."[36]

The hellenized "barbarians" imitated the Greek example. Towards the mid-second century C.E., in his *Manual*, Sextus Pomponius gave the succession of Roman jurists down to his own time.[37] Among the Jews, it seems that it was Eupolemus (ca. 150 B.C.E.) who conceived the idea of a "succession" of the prophets.[38] We observe that the mention of the "prophets" in the Pharisaic document also presupposes an order of succession, and Josephus has no doubts about this order: he says that whereas Moses and the prophets who came after him describe the events of their own times, the history of the post-biblical period is less certain, because "the exact succession of the prophets" is lacking.[39]

After the deaths of Hillel and Shammai, towards the beginning of the Common Era, the Pharisees too established the spiritual genealogy of their teaching. We note that, after Antigonus of Soko,[40] the succession occurs in pairs: Hillel and Shammai received the teaching

---

[36] Pliny, *Natural History* 30.4: *Mirum hoc in primis durasse memoriam artemque tam longo aevo, commentariis intercedentibus, praeterea nec claris nec continuis successionibus custoditam.* Cf. the reconstruction of the text in J. Bidez and F. Cumont, *Les Mages Hellénisés* II, 1938, p. 10; cf. *ibid.*, p. 7, and I, p. 171 n. 4.

[37] *Dig.* 1.2,35–53. Cf. B. Kübler, *RE* I, A, pp. 380–394; F. Schulz, *History of Roman Legal Science*, 1946, pp. 119–121; V. Arangio-Ruiz, *Storia del diritto romano*, 5th edn. 1947, pp. 276–281. Lucian, *Hermotimus* 77: from master to master, one goes back to the "tenth generation" (εἰς δεκαγονίαν). A cuneiform catalog of sages of the past was copied in 165 B.C.E., but it does not contain any idea of succession or tradition: J. van Dijk, in *XVIII. vorläufiger Bericht über die... Ausgrabungen in Uruk-Warka*, 1962, p. 45. A "succession" of doctors is found in Celsus, *De arte medic.*, Prooem. 8.

[38] If this were not the case, it would be difficult to see why, when speaking of Elijah, Eupolemus gives the succession Moses-Joshua, and then goes on to speak of Shiloh and Samuel. Unfortunately, his work is known only at two removes: from Eusebius (*Praep. Ev.* 9.30,447a), who copied Alexander Polyhistor. Cf. J. Freudenthal, *Alexander Polyhistor*, 1875, p. 225. – We should note that Scripture does not know this idea of succession. The prophets are sent by God when the chosen people need them (Jer 7:25). Similarly, Ben Sira mentions the prophetic succession only in the two biblical cases of Moses and Joshua (46:2) and Elisha and Elijah (48:12); Nathan simply appears "after" Samuel (47:1).

[39] Josephus, *C. Apionem* 1.8, §41: ἀπὸ δὲ Ἀρταξέρξου... μὴ γενέσθαι τὴν τῶν προφητῶν ἀκριβῆ διαδοχήν.

[40] Cf. the following essay in this book.

from Shemaiah and Abtalion, etc.[41] Naturally, the tradition went back to Moses himself, the *fons et origo* of Jewish wisdom. In the same way, Lucian's necromancer goes to a magus "who is one of the disciples and successors of Zoroaster." Writing under Hadrian, Sextus Pomponius was not content with establishing more or less correctly the chain of the "successors" of T. Coruncianus (consul in 280 B.C.E.), who had begun the systematic teaching of law in Rome: he went back to the earliest source of Roman jurisprudence, viz. to Papirius, who was said to have collected the *leges regiae* in the days of Tarquinius Superbus. Similarly, the Greek historians saw Epicurus or Zeno as the direct heirs in an unbroken succession to the Seven Sages.[42]

I am well aware of the doubts raised by modern critics about the chain of the Pharisees,[43] but I must leave it to more learned scholars to judge this dispute. It seems to me, however, that the parallels I have cited strengthen the case for the tradition. We should note that the knowledge of the doctrinal succession had a great practical significance: it eliminated the need to guarantee each individual tradition on its own. Here we may recall the situation in Islam, where, since there is no established succession of witnesses, every story (*hadith*) about Muhammad has to be authenticated by the complete series of those who have transmitted it (*isnad*). In the rabbinic schools, such a procedure was required only in exceptional instances, e.g. in a ritual debate, when the greatest rabbis did not know the tradition and a writer in public service offered the solution, which he said he had "received" from Rabbi Mesha, who had

---

[41] I should like to point out a parallel (which occurred independently to Boaz Cohen, who is a Talmudic specialist: see his *Jewish and Roman Law* I, 1966, p. 276 n. 198). When he arrives at Labeo and Capito in his "succession" of jurists, Pomponius says (*Dig.* 1.2,47): *hi duo primum veluti diversas sectas fecerunt.* After this, he always mentions two heads of schools. *Capitoni... Sabinus successit, Labeoni Nerva... huic successit... Cassius... Nervae successit Proculus*, etc. We should also note that a Greek author whose name we do not know simplified the "successions" of the philosophers. According to him, one lineage went from Thales to Socrates and his successors (including the Stoics), while the other series began with Pythagoras and continued to Epicurus. Cf. Diogenes Laertius, *Prooem.* 13–15; E. Schwartz, *RE* V, p. 755; H. Hope, *The Book of Diogenes Laertius*, 1930, pp. 134–138.

[42] Lucian, *Menipp.* 6. In order to link their teaching to ancient philosophy with Socrates as intermediary, the Stoics established the following chain: Zeno-Crates-Diogenes-Antisthenes-Socrates, although Diogenes can scarcely have been a disciple of Antisthenes. Cf. e.g. T.S. Brown, *Onesicritus*, 1949, p. 26. Besides this, such chains are the product of human ingeniousness. Pythagoras learnt from Pherecydes. That is true enough; but who was the master of Pherecydes? No one – he was a self-taught man who had got hold of the secret books of the Phoenicians (Suidas, *s.v.*).

[43] Cf. Bonsirven, I, p. 272 n. 2.

received it from his father, who had received it from the "pairs," who had received it from the prophets as a *halakah* given to Moses on Mount Sinai.[44] And we may also compare the case of Hillel, who was as yet unknown in Jerusalem and had spent a whole day in a discussion trying in vain to win support for a certain legal interpretation. Finally, he declared: "May I be punished, if my decision was not communicated to me by Shemaiah and Abtalion!" At once, his opinion was accepted.[45] This presupposed that Shemaiah and Abtalion, who were authentic links in the sequence of heads of the school, could only have expressed the correct opinion, i.e. the traditional opinion which came from Mount Sinai. This is the *ipse dixit* which the Pythagoreans employed when they quoted the opinion of their school.[46]

V

All this was an innovation at Jerusalem – and it would have been a revolution anywhere else. Unwritten laws and traditions, *opiniones quas a maioribus accepimus de diis immortalibus*, were everywhere the foundation of religious faith.[47] This oral law in Gentile societies went back to very ancient times; succeeding generations perpetuated it by transmitting doctrines and precepts from father to son. Consequently, those born into the aristocracy were the natural repository and the legitimate interpreters of the oral law. In Egypt, in Babylon, in Persia, under the Macedonian kings and under the Caesars, sacred doctrine was transmitted by succession in the hereditary clergy, although the relationship of "father" and "son" was often fictitious.[48] The language of the mysteries

---

[44] *M. Pea* 2.6. Cf. W. Bacher, *Die Tradition und die Tradenten*, 1914, p. 25; Bonsirven, II, p. 268. We find similar chains of reference e.g. in Cicero, *Cato* 12.39–41; 13.41; *Lael.* 23.88; and of course in the "narrative" dialogues of Plato, e.g. the *Parmenides*.

[45] Derenbourg, *op. cit.*, pp. 177–179; W. Bacher, *op. cit.*, pp. 1–52; L. Finkelstein, *The Pharisees and the Men of the Great Synagogue*, 1950, ch. 2.

[46] Cicero, *De nat. deorum* 1.5,10. Cf. I. Lévy, *La légende de Pythagore*, 1927, pp. 230ff.

[47] Cicero, *De nat. deorum* 3.2,5. Cf. e.g. T. Ashkenazi, *Tribus semi-nomades de Palestine du Nord*, 1938, p. 92; S. Gandz, "The Dawn of Literature," *Osiris* 7 (1939), pp. 260–522; J. Raft, *Der Ursprung des katholischen Traditionsprinzips*, 1931, pp. 179–192; A. Deneffe, *Der Traditionsbegriff*, 1931, pp. 7–16. On the transmission of the *mnēmai* from father to son, cf. Dionysius of Halicarnassus, *De Thuc.* 7.

[48] Cf. Diodorus, 1.73,5; 81,1; 2.29,4: unlike Greek praxis, παρὰ μὲν γὰρ τοῖς Χαλδαίοις ἐκ γένους ἡ τούτων φιλοσοφία παραδέδοται. Cf. Bidez and Cumont, *op. cit.* I, p. 171 n. 4; R. Reitzenstein, *Die hellenistischen Mysterienreligionen*, 3rd edn. 1927, p. 40.

and the secret books were accommodated to this requirement.[49] The Neoplatonist Proclus, a contemporary of the last *Amoraim*, learned the art of conversing with the gods from the daughter of Plutarch, who in turn had received this knowledge from his father, the hereditary hierophant of the Eleusinian cult. In fact, from time immemorial and until the end of paganism, the family of the Eumolpides was exclusively charged with conserving and interpreting the unwritten laws of Eleusis.[50] Not even the boldest spirits ventured to tamper with these august prerogatives.[51] The Athenian democracy, the most clearly egalitarian system known to the ancient world, asked the opinion of the "well born" (*eupatrides*) about the "sacred and ancestral" usages and customs. Even as late as the fourth century C.E., it was among the "well born" that the people chose the official exegete of the sacred laws.[52]

At Jerusalem, the divine law had expressly charged the priests with ensuring the correct interpretation of Torah. They were a hereditary caste who maintained the ancestral traditions, including the oral law.[53] Ca. 200 B.C.E., long before Hillel and Shammai, a number of instructions about ritual ablutions which were not contained in the law of Moses were followed in the temple at Jerusalem "in conformity with the custom of the fathers."[54] The tribe of Levi was taught by an oral tradition which was passed on from father to son, so that each new generation inherited its ancient knowledge.[55] When the term *talmid* appears in Hebrew, it designates the sons of the levites, who learn the chants in the house of the Lord "under the hand of their fathers" (1 Chron. 25:7f.).[56] According to Philo,[57] children receive from their

---

[49] Cf. E. Norden, *Agnostos Theos*, 1913, pp. 288–290; Festugière, *op. cit.* I, pp. 332–335.

[50] Marinus, *Vita Procli* 28, quoted in S. Eitrem, *Symbol. Osloenses* 22 (1942), p. 42; P. Foucart, *Les Mystères d'Éleusis*, 1914, p. 152.

[51] Cf. Euripides, *Bacch.* 201–202: πατρίους παραδοχάς, ἅς θ' ὁμήλικας Χρόνω κεκτήμεθ', οὐδεὶς αὐτὰ καταβαλεῖ λόγος.

[52] J.H. Oliver, *The Athenian Expounders of the Sacred and Ancestral Law*, 1950, pp. 14, 28, and 50.

[53] Deut 17:8–12. Cf. G. Ostborn, *Tora in the Old Testament*, dissertation, Lund 1945, pp. 89–112.

[54] Cf. my essay "A Seleucid proclamation concerning the temple in Jerusalem," above.

[55] *Testament of Levi* 13.

[56] On the expression *btlmwd* in a Qumran text (the Commentary on Nahum 2:8), cf. B.Z. Wacholder, *Revue de Qumran* 5 (1966), p. 575; I.D. Amusin, *Teksty Kumrana* I, 1971, p. 226 n. 4.

[57] *De spec. leg.* 4.150: ὀφείλουσι γὰρ παῖδες παρὰ γονέων... κληρονομεῖν ἔθη πάτρια... ἄγραφος αὐτῶν ἡ παράδοσις Cf. H.A. Wolfson, *Philo* I, 1947, pp. 188–194.

parents the unwritten heritage of the ancestral customs. Long after the destruction of the temple, priestly families were still refusing to divulge their hereditary knowledge.[58]

This historical and aristocratic principle was universally accepted. Both the Greek observers and the Jewish writers in the hellenistic period, and subsequently Philo and Josephus, agree that the law is the business of the sons of Aaron and that it is they who are to interpret the divine precepts.[59] The sectaries of the "new covenant" took a vow to obey the law of Moses as this was interpreted by "the sons of Zadok, the priests who guard the covenant and seek the will of God."[60] The very legitimacy of Zion depended on the priestly lineage: in order to demonstrate its authority, they cited "the succession of high priests, each of whom governed the sanctuary after having received this task from his father."[61]

This transmission of the *sacra* from father to son seemed natural to the Greeks, even in the hellenistic period. When one of the Ptolemies (doubtless Philopater, 221–204) commanded that a list be drawn up of those who imparted the initiation into the mysteries of Dionysus, he required them to state from whom they had received the cult, going back three generations.[62]

The Pharisees imposed on the people rules which were not written in the law of Moses, but "had been transmitted by the succession of the fathers." The Pharisees were "those who formed a separate group." It was only in their case that the fathers – the *abôth* whose maxims are handed on in the treatise which bears this name – were not ancestors, but professors.[63] Like the philosophy of the Greeks, the Torah of the Pharisees was transmitted from master to disciple, not from father to son.

---

[58] *M. Yoma* 3.11. We should note that for some of the Talmudic authors, every biblical prophet is the son of a prophet; cf. L. Ginzberg, *The Legends of the Jews* VI, p. 357.

[59] Cf. Bonsirven, II, p. 131: Hecataeus, *apud* Diodorus, 40.3; Sirach 45:17.

[60] A. Dupont-Sommer, *Les manuscrits de la Mer Morte*, 1950, p. 65.

[61] Josephus, *Ant.* 13.3,4, §78.

[62] *SP* II, 208 = M.T. Lenger, *Corpus des ordonnances des Ptolémées*, 1964, nr. 29. Cf. A.-J. Festugière, *La révélation d'Hermès Trismégiste* I, 1944, pp. 322–354. Cf. also a letter of Attalus II, in which he says that his nephew's tutor excels ἐν τῆι τῶν λόγων ἐνπει[ρία καὶ π]αραδόσει, *BE* 1968, nr. 464. Cf. Plato, *Hipp.* 228d: ἥ τ' ἔμαθε καὶ ἣν αὐτὸς ἐξηῦρεν.

[63] Josephus, *Ant.* 13.10,6, §297; 13.6,2, §408. I borrow from Isidore Lévy (*op. cit.*, p. 235) this periphrasis of the noun *perušim*.

Additional Note

The "chain" which we have just examined has a remarkable structure. The compilers of the lists of "successors" sometimes added information about these persons, in order – as Pomponius says – to demonstrate *a quibus et qualibus haec iura orta et tradita sunt*. For example, he informs his reader that Appius Claudius was one of the *decemviri*. In the same way, Iamblichus tells us something about nearly all the "successors" of Pythagoras.[64] All that the Jewish author tells us about the transmitters of the Torah is their names. Nevertheless, he quotes a maxim of each one of them, from the Great Synagogue down to and including Hillel and Shammai.[65] This selection of one single apophthegm to characterize its author reminds us of the story of the Seven Sages, each of whom dedicated to Apollo, as the "first fruits" of the wisdom he had received, an aphorism which was "short but full of meaning," e.g. "Nothing in excess!" These sentences summed up the rule of life of each of these masters of truth. They were quoted on inscriptions at Delphi, and were very popular in Greece. They were even reproduced on mosaic pavements which depicted these Sages.[66]

But the Seven Sages were thought to have been contemporaries and competitors, whereas the *diadochoi* of a school were those who handed on the wisdom of the founder of this philosophy: their role was to transmit and interpret this wisdom, not to make innovations. This is why the lists of "successors" do not contain any apophthegmata attributed to them. In the same way, it was certainly not acceptable for those who

---

[64] Cf. n. 37, above; Iamblichus, *Vita Pythag.* 36.265.

[65] J. Neusner, *The Rabbinic Tradition about the Pharisees* I, 1971, p. 21, notes that the aphorisms of the fathers are not quoted in the other Tannaitic sources. But moral precepts are out of place in these juridical or exegetical texts, so it is not surprising that these compilations do not quote them. Hillel himself is never mentioned in the Mekhilta. Simon the son of Shetach is mentioned only once: we are told that he had a lying witness in a court case put to death, and this is important for the interpretation of Ex 23:7 (*Kaspa* III, ed. Lauterbach, III, p. 170). The maxim of Abtalion is not quoted in the same commentary on Exodus, but we find his explanation of Ex 4:31 there (*Besh.* 4.1; I, p. 220). For the same reason, the maxim of the *anše keneset ha-gedolah* is quoted in the Mekhilta (*Pisha* 6; I, p. 48) and in *Sifre Deut.*, p. 25 ed. L. Finkelstein. The doctors of the law found there the precept to make "a fence around the Torah."

[66] Plato, *Protag.* 342e. Such maxims were ἐπιδείγματα τῆς σοφίας of their authors. Plato, *Hipparch.* 228d: M. Chéhab, *Bull. du Musée de Beyrouth* 14 (1957), pp. 32–34, and 15 (1959), plates XVII–XXI. On the parody of the maxims in a latrine in Ostia, cf. B. Snell, *Leben und Meinungen der Sieben Weisen*, 1938, p. 72. In general, cf. J. Defradas, *Les thèmes de la propagande delphique*, 1954, pp. 268–283, and L. Robert, *C.R. Ac. Inscr.*, 1968, pp. 422–431 and 438–442.

transmitted the oral law to add anything to it. As Josephus says,[67] the ancestral tradition which the Pharisees imposed on the people came ἐκ πατέρων διαδοχῆς, and hence went back to Moses. And this is why Jesus tells his disciples: "The scribes and the Pharisees sit on Moses' seat; so practice and observe whatever they tell you" (Matt. 23:2f.). Why then does the Pharisaic "chain" quote the maxims of each transmitter of the tradition during the post-biblical period, as if these aphorisms could increase people's confidence in the probity of the successive bearers of the unwritten Torah? I do not know, and until fresh evidence surfaces it seems to me better to abstain from conjectures on this subject. Rather, we should bear in mind the wise words of Quintilian that one of the qualities required in an interpreter of texts is: *aliqua nescire*.

---

[67] *Ant.* 13.297. The metaphor of the "chain" for the succession of masters in the Jewish tradition appears ca. 260 C.E.: Rabbi Yohanan, *P. Sab.* 1.2, p. 3a. Cf. Gerson D. Cohen, *Sefer ha-Qabbalah* (by Abraham ibn Daud), 1967, p. 91 n. 14. This image was employed at first for the genealogical succession: M. Jastrow, *Dictionary*, p. 1590.

14

PALESTINIAN JUDAISM IN THE FIRST CENTURY

Morton Smith

"R. Simeon the son of R. Jehosadak asked R. Samuel bar Nahman, 'Since I hear you are an expert in homiletic exegesis, tell me, whence was light created?' He replied, 'The Holy One, blessed be He, wrapped himself in it [i.e., the light] as in a white garment, and the splendor of his glory shone from one end of the world to the other.'"

This saying from *Bereshit Rabba*[1] might serve as an allegorical history of ancient Christianity: the God of ancient Israel clothed himself in the white garment of a Greek philosopher and became "the light of the world."

But might it not also be a history of ancient Judaism? Did not Judaism, in the same period, undergo the same Hellenization to achieve a similar expansion? Here we enter upon controversial ground.

With regard to Diasporic Judaism, there is no doubt of the Greek garment; the question is whether the deity whom it clothed was still the God of ancient Israel. Into this question we shall not enter.

As to Palestinian Judaism, there is no serious doubt that the deity was still the God of ancient Israel, but the notion that he was ever clothed in a Greek garment is a matter of dispute. This dispute concerns not only the concept of the deity, but the entire picture of ancient Palestinian Judaism. It goes even so far as to call into doubt the classical distinction between Palestinian and Diasporic Judaism. It asks whether this contrast does not reflect the present differences between two bodies of source material (the Rabbinic and the Diasporic) rather than the ancient differences between those parts of Judaism, which the sources describe. If our reports were written by extremists from the two ends of Judaism (and handed down by groups even more extreme than the writers), they may be describing the same thing in different terms, and the classical dichotomy may be due to our ignorance of the ancient average, middle ground.

Some aspects of Diasporic Judaism suggest this: Marcel Simon, in his book, *Verus Israel,* has recently emphasized that the Jews of the Diaspora, gave up the Septuagint for Aquila's Greek translation of the Old Testament—a change of

---

1 *Bereshit Rabba* 3:4, ed. Theodor, pp. 19 f.

immense significance, since it shows that they were willing to sacrifice the superior Greek style of the Septuagint in order to get a text of which the only advantage was that it preserved the peculiarities which justified Rabbinic exegesis. Harry Wolfson, in his monumental *Philo,* has demonstrated the amazing extent of agreement between Philo and the Rabbis. There is no doubt that the picture of Judaism derived from the Roman imperial inscriptions and from the remarks of classical authors agrees in its main outlines with the picture derived from Rabbinic literature.

Now this evidence of Rabbinic influence in the Diaspora is more than matched by evidence from Palestine that Judaism there was profoundly influenced by Hellenism. Just at present, the most famous body of such evidence is composed of the documents newly discovered near the Dead Sea. It is too early to attempt any detailed interpretation of these, but they certainly show many parallels with the thought of Hellenized Jews like Paul, and they prove conclusively that Greek books were in the library of this extremely legalistic, ultraconservative Jewish community. Hardly less famous are the archaeological discoveries, especially of Bet Shearim and of the synagogues. Bet Shearim was the most famous burial ground of Rabbinic Judaism. Its remains show that it was freely adorned with drawings and, less freely, even with statues carved in relief, that most of the inscriptions written there were in Greek, and that some of them contained such commonplaces as, "Be of good courage, no one is immortal." The synagogues show us a similar use of animal and human forms in high relief, and tell us that the human and, sometimes, the animal forms were later chipped away, but carefully, so that the rest of the carving would not be damaged. They show us, further, the use of conventional representations of the pagan sun god as the central ornament in the mosaic floors of a number of synagogues. This ornamentation has been known for some time, but its significance was not demonstrated until Erwin Goodenough, in his epoch-making *Jewish Symbols in the Greco-Roman Period,* pointed out the amazing parallels between these synagogue floors and the magical amulets on which the sun god frequently appears with the titles *Iao* (i.e, YHWH) and *Sabaoth.* These parallels, in turn, enabled Professor Goodenough to make an extremely strong case for his identification of Jewish sources in many sections of the magical papyri, so that we are almost forced to accept as a product of Judaism an invocation of Helios in which he is hailed as "first and most happy of aeons and father of the world."

This identification of source material is a fascinating but hazardous business which has added a great deal, if not to our absolute knowledge, at least to our plausible guesses, about the varieties of ancient Judaism. Since our concern is the Hellenization of Palestinian Judaism, we shall pass over works of doubtful origin, like the Jewish material found by Wilhelm Bousset in the Apostolic Constitutions, and turn our attention to the undoubtedly Jewish and probably Palestinian sources of many of the pseudepigraphic writings preserved by Christians. The Ascension of Isaiah contains a source from the time of Herod the Great which shows us a group of prophets living in the wilderness beyond Bethlehem, going naked, eating herbs only, and denouncing Jerusalem as Sodom. Such asceticism is certainly not in the Israelite tradition. The Assumption of Moses contains a similar denunciation of the priesthood of the Second Temple and calls its sacrifices vain, but has great reverence for the Temple itself. It also denounces a group of rulers who claim to be just, but who will not let common people touch them for fear of pollution, and who devour the goods of the poor. Other such examples could be found, but enough has been said to show that this evidence requires a careful revision of the common notion that Palestinian Judaism was substantially free of Hellenistic influence.

The first step in estimating what the Hellenistic influence actually was is to determine the extent of the use of Greek. The preponderance of Greek in the inscriptions at Bet Shearim has already been noted. They show us the state of affairs from the late second century on. For the first century, we get most information from the Jewish ossuaries, on which about a third of the inscriptions are in Greek. For the yet earlier period, the evidence has been summed up by William F. Albright, who is an ardent advocate of Aramaic influences, but who admits in his *Archaelogy of Palestine* that there was a real eclipse of Aramaic during the period of the Seleucid Empire. He remarks that scarcely a single Aramaic inscription from this period has been discovered except in Transjordan and Arabia, and that inscriptions in Jewish Aramaic do not appear until the middle of the first century before the Common Era.

It used to be argued, however, that observant Jews kept themselves apart from this Hellenized world around them, and either knew no Greek at all or, at least, knew no Greek literature, so that their thinking about religion was not touched by Greek influence. This notion, however, has now been completely refuted by the works of Saul Lieberman, *Greek in Jewish Palestine* and *Hellenism in Jewish Palestine,* which have demonstrated, once for all, that many Jews in Rabbinic circles not only knew Greek, but read the Bible in it and prayed in it. Further (and of even greater significance), they have demonstrated that the terminology for at least one of the most important forms of Rabbinic legal exegesis is derived from the Greek name for the same sort of argument: *gezera shawa* translates *sunkrisis pros ison.* Since even here, in the Holy of Holies of legal exegesis, so basic a term could be taken from Greek, it seems only plausible to suppose that the amazing string of parallels to Greek exegetic and scribal procedures, which Professor Lieberman also demonstrates, was due largely to Hellenistic influence. So we must suppose that early in its history the scribal study of the Law underwent a period of profound Hellenization. This supposition would accord with the archaeological evidence for the extreme Hellenization of Palestine during the later Persian and Ptolemaic periods, and with the belief that the upper classes of the priesthood, which then controlled the exposition or the Law, were particularly Hellenized. Perhaps it should be remarked in passing that Ben Sira made foreign travel for the purpose of study a duty of the good scribe. His opinion is clearly in accord with the practice of many Hellenistic philosophers.

We conclude, then, that Palestine in the first century was profoundly Hellenized and that the Hellenization extended even to the basic structure of much Rabbinic thought. This requires us to reconsider the question: How were those first-century Rabbis, who appear as authorities in Rabbinic writings, related to the whole of Palestinian Judaism? What part in the general history of the times did they and their scholars play?

First of all, it must be said that they were not unopposed. The Palestinian Talmud reports that at the time of the Exile there were twenty-four sorts of heretics in Palestine. Whatever the heretics believed, they certainly did not agree with the Pharisees and they almost certainly claimed to be Jews. Many of them were probably Jewish Chrisdans, and certain Christian writers (especially Justin, Eusebius, and Epiphanius) tell us something of their many varieties.

Nor was Jesus the only religious leader whose followers established separate sects. John the Baptist also started a sect: some of his followers did not transfer their loyalty to Jesus, but maintained that John had been the true prophet, Jesus the false. Jacques Thomas, in his careful study, *Le Mouvement baptiste en Palestine,* has shown that John's group was only one of a great number of sects—some Jewish, some Christian, and some, perhaps, neither—which flourished in Palestine from the first century on and were characterized not only by the use of washing as a sacrament but also by the adoption of ascetic practices and, frequently, by the belief in a supernatural being who visited earth from time to time, in various incarnations, to reveal the will of God. It should be noticed that this belief appears very early in Christianity. To Justin, for example, Jesus is not the first appearance of the Logos—it had appeared before, for example, to Abraham at Mamre. A similar belief about John the Baptist was early developed by his followers. Whether Jesus or John actually made such claims it is hard to say, but we have good reason to think that Simon Magus (a Samaritan teacher who also founded a sect and who, like Jesus, is said to have been a disciple of John) actually did claim to be a divine power come down to earth. This divine power was often described as "the true prophet," and it is probably not insignificant in this connection that both Josephus and Acts tell us of the many prophets who arose in this period and led many astray. They were not insignificant cranks with one or two followers. One of those mentioned by both Josephus and Acts had thousands of followers and was only put down by the Roman forces in a major battle on the Mount of Olives.

Of course, not all baptist sects followed this theological pattern, and John's group presents similarities also to the Essenes, whom Josephus recognized as Jews, but whose strange practices included not only ritual bathing but the use of secret books filled with magical names and of prayers addressed to the sun. We have already noticed the position which the sun came to occupy in Jewish magic and Jewish synagogues during the fourth century. That magic flourished also in the earlier periods is hardly to be doubted. Most women, according to Tannaitic tradition, practiced magic; and magic, as Professor Lieberman has remarked, was not merely a few superstitious practices, but an actual cult, of which Professor Goodenough has shown the complicated theological ramifications.

At the opposite extreme from the magicians were the Jews who had gone over entirely to Hellenistic rationalism and who were accused of being Epicureans.

Whether these were actually members of the clear-cut and hidebound Epicurean school, or merely individuals accused by popular opinion of atheism, we cannot be certain. But there is no doubt that their neighbors in rationalism, the Sadducees, were a definite sect and undeniably Jewish—they furnished many of the high priests and were an important party in the Sanhedrin. Yet they attacked as Pharisaic superstitions the beliefs in angels and spirits, the life after death, and the divine governance of human events.

Even within the Pharisees there were divisions. We know from Josephus and the New Testament of one sect, the Zealots, which appeared as a separate group early in the first century, when its members embraced doctrines requiring civil disobedience. We know from Talmudic evidence that in the conflict between the houses of Hillel and Shammai the Law became two Laws, and the later tradition which miraculously declared them both the words of the Living God is no less suspicious than the later Christian tradition which brought Peter and Paul into perfect concord.

Finally, Palestine was not devoid of Jews from the Diaspora and these, too, formed separate communities. The only synagogue inscription we have from Jerusalem comes from a Diasporic synagogue in which a Christian preached. Communities of Jews from Alexandria, Babylonia, Tarsus, Cyrene, and Cappadocia are suggested by the funeral inscriptions of Joppa. The Acts lists, as resident in Jerusalem, Jews from Galilee, Parthia, Media, Elam, Mesopotamia, Cappadocia, Pontus, the Roman province of Asia, Phrygia, Pamphylia, Egypt, Cyrenaica, Rome, Crete, and Arabia.

But all these groups which we have discussed so far were undoubtedly minority groups. (A little magic may have been practiced by almost everybody, but the adepts were probably few. As for the Pharisees, their very name—separatists—declares their relation to the whole.) The average Palestinian Jew of the first century was probably the *'am ha-areṣ,* any member of the class which made up the "people of the land," a Biblical phrase probably used to mean *hoi polloi.* There are any number of passages in which the Mishna and Tosefta seem to take it for granted that the average man passing in the street, the average woman who stops in to visit her friend, or the average workman or shopkeeper or farmer is an *'am ha-areṣ.* The members of this majority were not without religion. They certainly did not observe some rules laid down by the Pharisees, and at a later period they were said to hate the Pharisees even more than the gentiles hated the Jews; but they had their own synagogues (though the Pharisees said that anybody who frequented them would come to an early death), they kept the Jewish festivals, and they even observed some of the more serious purity regulations. So even with them we have not reached the end of the varieties of first-century Judaism, for we have said nothing of the worldly Jews—the Herodians, tax gatherers, usurers, gamblers shepherds, and robbers (by the thousands) who fill the pages of the Gospels, the Talmuds, and Josephus.

How, then, are we to account for the tradition which makes the Pharisees the dominant group? First, no doubt, by the natural prejudice of the Rabbinic material.

This point hardly needs elaboration: the sayings of the Rabbis were, of course, recorded by and for their followers. Even if the sayings were completely unbiased and the record absolutely accurate, the mere concentration of interest in the group concerned would make them bulk out of all proportion to the rest. In the second place, however, there are the statements of Josephus, attributing to the Pharisees a predominant influence with the people. To understand these we must recall the career of Josephus and the situation in which he wrote.

Josephus was a member of the priestly aristocracy and in his later period claimed to have been a Pharisee. Certainly, the alliance of aristocrats and Pharisees which was in control during the early days of the war made him commander of some Jewish forces in Galilee, though Simeon ben Gamaliel, the leader of the Pharisaic group, later tried to have him removed. When his forces were defeated he surrendered to the Romans and hailed Vespasian as the universal ruler whom Jewish tradition had prophesied would arise from Palestine. When Vespasian fulfilled this prophecy by becoming emperor, Josephus was set at liberty and taken into Roman service, first in Jerusalem as interpreter during the siege, and later in Rome. Here he wrote his *Jewish War* in the service of Roman propaganda: its purpose being to persuade the Jews of Mesopotamia that nothing could be done to help the Jews of Palestine, and to persuade Jews everywhere that the Palestinians had brought their ruin upon themselves by their own wickedness; that the Romans were not hostile to Judaism but had acted in Palestine regretfully, as agents of divine vengeance; and that therefore submission to Roman rule was justified by religion as well as common sense.

For this service Josephus has often been denounced as an apostate from Judaism. He was not. Submission to the Romans and recognition of Vespasian as destined emperor certainly did not, in and by themselves, constitute apostasy, for these very same acts are attributed by Rabbinic tradition to the leader of the Pharisaic revival, R. Johanan ben Zakkai. Clearly, then, the question of Josephus' loyalty to Judaism must be settled by other considerations. And there is positive evidence that he remained, even in Rome, an admitted and convinced Jew. He wrote a defense of Judaism against the grammarian Apion, and this at a time when defenders of Judaism were probably not in favor. In the reign of Domitian, who seems to have been hostile to Jews, he wrote his major work, the *Jewish Antiquities*, of which the main concern was to glorify the Jewish tradition. His loyalty to that tradition, therefore, is hardly to be questioned.

But to which group within the Jewish tradition was he loyal? Here a comparison of the *War* with the *Antiquities* is extremely informative. In the *War*, written shortly after the destruction of Jerusalem, Josephus still favors the group of which his family had been representative—the wealthy, pro-Roman section of the priesthood. He represents them (no doubt correctly) as that group of the community which did all it could to keep the peace with Rome. In this effort, he once mentions that they had the assistance of the chief Pharisees, but otherwise the Pharisees hardly figure on the scene. In his account of the reign of Salome-Alexandra he copies an abusive paragraph of Nicholas of Damascus, describing the Pharisees as hypocrites whom the queen's superstition enabled to achieve and abuse political power. In his account of the Jewish sects he gives most space to the Essenes. (Undoubtedly he was catering to the interests of Roman readers, with whom ascetic philosophers in out-of-the-way countries enjoyed a long popularity.) As for the others, he merely tags brief notices of the Pharisees and Sadducees onto the end of his survey. He says nothing of the Pharisees' having any influence with the people, and the only time he represents them as attempting to exert any influence (when they ally with the leading priests and other citizens of Jerusalem to prevent the outbreak of the war), they fail.

In the *Antiquities*, however, written twenty years later, the picture is quite different. Here, whenever Josephus discusses the Jewish sects, the Pharisees take first place, and every time he mentions them he emphasizes their popularity, which is so great, he says, that they can maintain opposition against any government. His treatment of the Salome-Alexandra incident is particularly illuminating: he makes Alexander Janneus, Salome's husband and the lifelong enemy of the Pharisees, deliver himself of a deathbed speech in which he blames all the troubles of his reign on the fact that he had opposed them and urges his wife to restore them to power because of their overwhelming influence with the people. She follows his advice and the Pharisees cooperate to such extent that they actually persuade the people that Alexander was a good king and make them mourn his passing!

It is almost impossible not to see in such a rewriting of history a bid to the Roman government. That government must have been faced with the problem: Which group of Jews shall we support? It must have asked the question: Which Jews (of those who will work with us at all) can command enough popular following to keep things stable in Palestine? To this question Josephus is volunteering an answer: The Pharisees, he says again and again, have by far the greatest influence with the people. Any government which secures their support is accepted; any government which alienates them has trouble. The Sadducees, it is true, have more following among the aristocracy. (We may guess that they were better represented at the Roman court and that Josephus was trying to answer this objection.) But they have no popular following at all and, even in the old days when they were in power, they were forced by public opinion to follow the Pharisees' orders. As for the other major parties, the Essenes are a philosophical curiosity, and the Zealots differ from the Pharisees only by being fanatically anti-Roman. So any Roman government which wants peace in Palestine had better support and secure the support of the Pharisees.

Josephus' discovery of these important political facts (which he ignored when writing the *Jewish War*) may have been due partly to a change in his personal relationship with the Pharisees. Twenty years had now intervened since his trouble with Simeon ben Gamaliel, and Simeon was long dead. But the mere cessation of personal hostilities would hardly account for such pointed passages as Josephus added to the *Antiquities*. The more probable explanation is that in the meanwhile the Pharisees had become the leading candidates for Roman support in Palestine and were already negotiating for it. This same conclusion was reached from a consideration of the Rabbinic evidence by Gedalyahu Alon in his *History of the Jews in Palestine in the Period of the Mishna*.[2] He concluded that the Roman recognition of the judicial authority of the Rabbinic organization in Palestine came after the fall of Domitian, but had been a matter of negotiation even in Domitian's time and, when it came, was an official approval of an authority which had already existed *de facto* for some time. This theory, and the tradition that Jewish relations with Rome underwent some strain in the latter days of Domitian, would perfectly explain the content and tone of those passages of the *Antiquities* which insist on the influence of the Pharisees with the people.

Such motivation does not, of course, prove that Josephus' statements are false, but it would explain their falsity if that were otherwise demonstrated. Without attempting conclusive demonstration, three points may be noted:

First, as we have seen, there is much evidence that during the first century a great deal of Palestinian Judaism was not Pharisaic.

Second, the influence of the Pharisees with the people, which Josephus reports, is not demonstrated by the history he records. John Hyrcanus was not afraid to break with the Pharisees, and none of the succeeding Maccabees except Salome and the puppet Hyrcanus II felt it worth while to conciliate them. As to their relations with Herod, Josephus contradicts himself; but if Herod had the support of the Pharisees it did not suffice to secure him popularity, and if they opposed him they were not strong enough to cause him serious trouble. During the first century of the Common Era, the only ruler who consistently conciliated them was Agrippa I. If, as Josephus says, they were for peace with Rome, their influence failed to maintain it. After the war broke out, they formed only one party in the coalition upper-class government, which held the initial power in Jerusalem for a short time, but was ousted by groups with more popular support. All this accords perfectly with the fact that Josephus in his first history of the war never thought their influence important enough to deserve mention.

In the third place, even Josephus' insistence on their influence "with the multitude" implies a distinction between them and the people whom they influenced. Evidently, "the multitude" were the majority and they were not Pharisees. In one instance, where Josephus speaks of the Pharisees as refusing to take an oath of loyalty to Herod, he sets the number of them at "more than 6000." The passage is not absolutely conclusive because another seems to contradict it and assert that the oath was taken, but the most plausible explanation would seem to be that which takes the passages as contradictory rather than complementary and understands 6000 as the (approximate) total number of the Pharisees. The Essenes, by the way, numbered about 4000, according to Josephus' estimate.

How, then, are we to understand the position of these 6000 Pharisees vis-à-vis the mass of the Jewish population, that is to say, in what category of the

---

2 [*Toledot ha-Yehudim be-Ereṣ Yisrael bi-Tequfat ha-Mishna we-ha-Talmud.*]

population were they classed: were they clergy or laity? Was it a profession to be a Pharisee, or an avocation?

Here the danger is obviously that of imposing modern categories upon ancient society. Many would say there is even a danger of imposing ancient categories on a part of ancient society which they do not fit, of classifying the Pharisees in categories which belong to Greek and Roman society, not to Palestinian Judaism. This charge has been brought particularly against Josephus, who consistently describes the major Jewish sects, including the Pharisees, as philosophic schools. In this he is supported by agreement with Philo and with the ancient Christian writers who describe the Jewish sects. But it is customary to say that in using this description he is trying to explain the sects to his gentile readers, who had nothing like them in their society. The easiest way to give them a general idea of what the Pharisees did was to call them "philosophers," just as, nowadays, the simplest way to explain a *guru* is to call him a "father confessor." The people who maintain this view hold not only that all Pharisees were primarily Pharisees (a very strong position) but also that the Greco-Roman society produced nothing really like them, so that, although others may have thought of them in its terms, the Pharisees themselves never did so. Now this latter position is a particular application of the general notion that Palestinian Judaism was practically untouched by Hellenistic influences. We have already seen that general notion to be false; here we may adduce a number of reasons for doubting this particular application as well.

First of all, it must be remembered that Judaism to the ancient world was a philosophy. That world had no general term for *religion*. It could speak of a particular system of rites (a cult or an initiation), or a particular set of beliefs (doctrines or opinions), or a legal code, or a body of national customs or traditions; but for the peculiar synthesis of all these which we call a "religion," the one Hellenistic word which came closest was "philosophy." So when Judaism first took shape and became conscious of itself and its own peculiarity in the Hellenized world of the later Persian Empire, it described itself with the Hellenic term meaning the wisdom of its people (Deut. 4:6). To the success of this concept within Judaism the long roll call of the wisdom literature bears witness. Further, the claim was accepted by the surrounding world. To those who admired Judaism it was "the cult of wisdom" (for so we should translate the word "philosophy" which they used to describe it), and to those who disliked it it was "atheism," which is simply the other side of the coin, the regular term of abuse applied to philosophy by its opponents.

It is therefore not surprising that Jews living, as Palestinian Jews did, in the Greco-Roman world, and thinking of their religion as the practice of wisdom, should think of the groups in their society which were distinguished by peculiar theories and practices as different schools of the national philosophy. That the groups also thought, thus of themselves is shown by a vast number of details, of which the following are a few examples. Their claim to authority was put in the form of a chain of successors by whom the true philosophy had been handed down. Elias Bickerman in his article, "La Chaine de la tradition pharisienne," has demonstrated the parallel between this list (in *Abot*) and the list alleged by the philosophic schools, and has remarked that the Greek and Pharisaic lists differed from those of the priestly "philosophies" of the barbarians in being lists of teachers, not of ancestors. He also mentions, apropos of the "houses" of Hillel and Shammai, the fact that "house of so-and-so" is a regular form of reference to a philosophic school founded by so-and-so; and he shows that both the Greek and the Jewish philosophic schools justified their peculiar teachings by claiming accurate tradition from an authoritative master. Not only was the theory of the Pharisaic school that of a school of Greek philosophy, but so were its practices. Its teachers taught without pay, like philosophers; they attached to themselves particular disciples who followed them around and served them, like philosophers; they looked to gifts for support, like philosophers; they were exempt from taxation, like philosophers; they were distinguished in the street by their walk, speech, and peculiar clothing, like philosophers; they practiced and praised asceticism, like philosophers; and finally—what is, after all, the meat of the matter—they discussed the questions philosophers discussed and reached the conclusions philosophers reached. Here there is no need to argue the matter, for Professor Wolfson, in his aforementioned classic study of Philo, has demonstrated at length the possibility of paralleling a philosophic system point by point from the opinions of the Rabbis. Now one, or two, or two dozen parallels might be dismissed as coincidental: all men, by virtue of mere humanity, are similar and life presents them with similar problems; it is not surprising, therefore, that they should often and independently reach the same answers. But parallels of terminology are another matter, and here we come back to Professor Lieberman's demonstration that some of the most important terms of Rabbinic Biblical exegesis have been borrowed from the Greek. This is basic. As indicated above, the existence of such borrowings can be explained only by a period of profound Hellenization, and once the existence of such a period has been hypothecated it is plausible to attribute to it also the astounding series of parallels which Professor Wolfson has shown to exist between the content of philosophic and Rabbinic thought.

In sum, then, the discoveries and research of the past twenty-five years have left us with a picture of Palestinian Judaism in the first century far different from that conceived by earlier students of the period. We now see a Judaism which had behind it a long period of thoroughgoing Hellenization—Hellenization modified, but not thrown off, by the revival of nationalism and nationalistic and antiquarian interest in native tradition and classic language (an interest itself typically Hellenistic). As the Greek language had permeated the whole country, so Greek thought, in one way or another, had affected the court and the commons, the Temple and the tavern, the school and the synagogue. If there was any such thing, then, as an "orthodox Judaism," it must have been that which is now almost unknown to us, the religion of the average "people of the land." But the different parts of the country were so different, such gulfs of feeling and practice separated Idumea, Judea, Caesarea, and Galilee, that even on this level there was probably no more agreement between them than between any one of them and a similar area in the Diaspora. And in addition to the local differences, the country swarmed with special sects, each devoted to its own tradition. Some of these, the followings of particular prophets, may have been spontaneous revivals of Israelite religion as simple as anything in Judges. But even what little we know of these prophets suggests that some of them, at least, taught a complex theology. As for the major philosophic sects—the Pharisees, Sadducees, and Essenes—the largest and ultimately the most influential of them, the Pharisees, numbered only about 6000, had no real hold either on the government or on the masses of the people, and was, as were the others, profoundly Hellenized.

This period of Palestinian Jewish history, then, is the successor to one marked by great receptivity to outside influences. It is itself characterized by original developments of those influences. These developments, by their variety, vigor, and eventual significance, made this small country during this brief period the seedbed of the subsequent religious history of the Western world.

15

THE RABBIS AND JEWISH ART IN THE GRECO-ROMAN PERIOD[1]

ERWIN R. GOODENOUGH, Yale University

A PERSON who presents a novel thesis in the humanities must expect a good deal of misunderstanding. The chief difficulty, indeed, is to keep one's fellow scholars within the limits proposed, since they so often reject the suggestion in a form they have exaggerated beyond anything originally set forth. Over thirty years ago I said that Philo's interpretation of Jewish laws suggested that the Jewish law courts of Alexandria were making many decisions which adjusted Jewish traditions to those in force in Roman Alexandria. My suggestion, so far as I know, is now generally accepted. At the time several scholars thought it invalid because later rabbis could be shown to have made similar adjustments in a few details, from which it was at once concluded that all Alexandrian decisions must have reflected the jurisprudence of the courts in first century Palestine. Such a nonsequitur is no longer urged.

In my *By Light, Light*, I pointed out how drenched in the language of pagan mystery religions is Philo's interpretation of the religious values of the Torah, and how it seemed to me possible, indeed likely, that some Jews in Alexandria, at least, carried out their Sabbath and Festival cultus with a feeling that in contrast to pagans, Jews had the true rites which brought mystic rewards. Again my thesis was exaggerated by others to make me mean that Philo's mystic language could not have corresponded to any reality, unless Judaism in Alexandria had been completely changed by the introduction of formal ceremonies of initiation, cult dramas, and the like. Nothing disproves such a thesis, but there was no evidence for it at all, as it was easy to show. The issue was presented as an absolute dilemma: either the mystery language meant nothing whatever, was a mere *façon de parler*, or the Jews meant by it the full machinery of the celebrations of Isis or Eleusis. It has taken a number of years for my actual thesis to be considered on its merits, and now be widely ac-

[1] No one could better exemplify the thesis of this paper, and of most of my studies, than Dr. Julian Morgenstern. His life has demonstrated how deeply one can preserve the best in rabbinic Judaism while disagreeing with much in the teaching of the rabbis; and how one can appropriate the soul of Gentile thought and scholarship and still live dedicated to the People and their God.

cepted. To feel mystic value in the Kiddush or Seder is something mystic Jews have always done. Jews who read mystic values into the words of the Torah, as did not only Philo's group but also followers of Merkavah and all mystic Jews to the Ḥasidim could hardly be expected to stop such "nonsense," as many halachic rabbis considered it, when they lifted the cup or blessed the bread. Nor did they.

Now after the increasing acceptance of my real thesis on mystic Judaism I have aroused fresh protest by suggesting that the archaeological discoveries from Greco-Roman Jewry must be taken seriously as the only evidence we have from that group as a whole. Actually, the various archaeologists who discovered the data could hardly believe their eyes, and it was not until I had published the first three volumes of my *Jewish Symbols* in 1953 that more than a small fraction of the learned world had any conception of the nature and extent of this material. The objects seemed to violate all the traditions of orthodox Judaism. The more one studied them, the more one saw that they could not be brushed aside as ornament, as some tried to do, after the analogy of the designs of the seventeenth and eighteenth century Jewish tombstones of Poland, or the cupids on marriage contracts of that same period. For, although many of the forms borrowed by Jews were the same in both periods, the Greco-Roman Jews were borrowing live forms from pagan religious life, in contrast to the largely ornamental cupids later Jews borrowed from baroque and rococo art. Jews of the later period did not put figures of Mary and Jesus, or the crucifix, on their tombs, or anywhere else, for these represented the living religion of the Gentiles about them. But Jews in the ancient world were using the living symbols of pagans of the day, not only in synagogues, but, at Dura, elaborately integrated with biblical scenes. In graves the symbols appear with the *menorah, shofar, lulav,* and Torah shrine of Jewish worship. Certainly nothing in rabbinical tradition had given us reason to expect such combinations: as that Moses would lead the Israelites from Egypt brandishing the club of Hercules; that he should be found in his basket in the Nile by the naked Aphrodite-Anahita and given to the three Nymphs to be nursed like other divine, or human-divine, babies. Rabbinic tradition had not prepared us for the goddess of Victory holding out her wreath atop the Jewish Temple; or for the cosmic bull with Gayomart and Armaiti of Iranian tradition on the temple entrance; or for Ares with Victories presiding over the Exodus. When these Jews wanted to depict the futility of contemporary paganism they could do so forcibly by showing the local gods prostrate and broken before the Ark of the Covenant, after the analogy of Dagon. But it was not their purpose when they turned the figure of the local Cavalier God into a representation of Mordecai in his triumph, or in Rome put up the dolphin and trident of Neptune along with the *shofar* and *menorah* in their tombs. The rabbis certainly held David the Psalmist in high regard, but never compared him to Orpheus, or led us to expect that he would be portrayed in a synagogue as Orpheus stilling the beasts. And so forth: the full list of the preposterous is long indeed.

Since these were all living symbols for pagans, their use by Jews involves not only the problem of rabbinic attitude toward the making of images, but of Jews' making precisely *these* images, and of introducing them not only into the synagogues and graves, but into biblical narrative itself, and among the objects used in Jewish worship. Nothing suggests that the Jews of the period ever worshiped the dolphin, any more than they worshiped the *menorah* or *shofar*. But we may assume that Jews who put the *menorah* and *shofar* on the graves at least attested their Jewish loyalty thereby. What did they attest when they put the dolphin on the grave with the Jewish objects? What did they mean by giving Moses the infancy of a demi-god, the mature power of Hercules, or by giving Mordecai the form of the Cavalier God? We must answer these questions, and all the questions raised by the other forms Jews borrowed, in one of two ways. First, we may assume that, by the fact they were Jewish, the Jews could not have meant anything at all by them, can ignore the implications of the objects represented, and simply look for gaps in the wall which the rabbis in general erected against image making and decoration. If, by this, we can show that any rabbis under any circumstances allowed any images at all, we may assume that all rabbis allowed all kinds of images everywhere, and so may see in these Jews a part of the unbroken succession of a changeless and monolithic Judaism, normative Judaism.

Although many scholars have taken substantially this line of argument, I protest that it is utterly fallacious. Basically it does not at all consider the evidence itself, the actual images and forms which these Jews made. We cannot hope to explain why the painters at Dura gave Moses the prerogatives of the divine babies, and the power of Hercules, by looking through rabbinic comments. And no amount of indignation can obscure the fact that the Jews did do this, and much else like it.

The second approach is to begin precisely with this new evidence, aware that new evidence may tell new things, do so with the a priori assumption that since Jews made the paintings, mosaics, and carvings, they might have been saying something for their Judaism which we should not have heard in the aniconic tradition of the rabbis. In reading Philo we have long had to discuss Jewish remains with such an a priori assumption about his borrowing hellenistic terms of philosophy and mystery. For we know that Hellenism profoundly affected the tone of Philo's interpretations of Judaism, to the point that the rabbis had no interest in him: we should never have heard his name if Christians had not preserved his writings. Wolfson may be right that Philo represents "native Judaism" with a Greek veneer, native Judaism which registered in his deep loyalty to the Torah, written and in practice. I have never liked Wolfson's figure of "veneer," since the Greek elements in Philo's writings do not obscure his passionate devotion to the Jewish God, Bible, and People, which have always been basic in rabbinic tradition, while a veneer is designed precisely to conceal the cheaper wood beneath it. The figure, actually, does not represent Wolfson's own conception of Philo, and I agree with him heartily that we cannot understand Philo simply from the hellenistic schools of philosophy. Philo mingled with these a passionate commitment to Jewish tradition, as direct revelation, and, as Wolfson says, thereby represents in the history of western thought a great transition which reached its highest point in the Schoolmen. Still, I repeat, the end result in Philo himself made him so different from the rabbis that they did not like him. Living in Greco-Roman civilization could profoundly affect one's Judaism. We know that another Jew rewrote the Sibylline Books to put Moses into them, also something the rabbis did not like; and that the fragments from Alexander Polyhistor found in Eusebius show a variety of other deep modifications of "normative" Jewish attitudes on the part of individual Jews. It is well recognized that to understand these writers we must begin with their texts to see what they actually say before we judge their conformities to, or departures from, traditional Judaism. I cannot understand how there can be any question that we must do the same with archaeological data. We first must discover what these Jews actually did before we consider their relation to the Judaism preserved in rabbinical writings.

What the forms themselves tell us is too elaborate a matter to rehearse in a few pages. Their relation to rabbinical tradition still remains an important problem. Rabbinic allusion to each or any of the symbols, as I shall call them for short, whether allusion in literary figures or in what rabbis say of them directly, has the greatest importance. Of many of the symbols I have discussed, however, I could find no trace in rabbinical tradition. Trained rabbinical scholars will in time find passages which I overlooked, so that in details my conclusions about different symbols can be corrected or amplified. Some symbols the rabbis did mention directly, such as the fish, bread and wine, or the eagle. Josephus and the rabbis certainly did not prepare us to find that the hated eagle was one of the most common ornaments on Galilean synagogues. That is, rabbinical mention may make the use of certain symbols in synagogues and Jewish graves more astonishing rather than less.

This is one of the many "facts" which several scholars who resist my conclusions do not discuss,[2] scholars who assume that *qua* Jewish, the archaeological data must represent an acceptable and accepted part of rabbinical Judaism. The hypothesis on which I am proceeding is that later rabbinical tradition has always correctly interpreted the Tannaim and Amoraim as deeply disliking figured representation, and allowing their use only in exceptional instances, if at all. If that is so, and yet we see that Jews of their own day commonly made such representations, then we cannot take without scrutiny the claim that those who made them were under strict rabbinic guidance and control. We ask, first, how reliable the tradition was that the rabbinical centers really did supervise world Judaism at this time; second, what the rabbis actually are recorded to have said about figured representations; third, what the Jews actually represented.

On the first of these there is no point in rehearsing the evidence here, since, so far as I know, the statements were adequately collected in the first chapter of Volume IV, and have often been discussed elsewhere.[3] The few allusions to the authority of the Patriarchs and Sages, or the Roman recognition of the Patriarch as Ethnarch, with "power like the kings of the Gentiles even to carrying out capital punishment," as Origen tells us, tell us nothing specific about actual authority. We must see evidence of the exercise of power before mere legends or declarations of it mean anything. Frey[4] has covered the ground excellently. The only trace that the Patriarch exercised power outside Palestine is an inscription from Stobi of the year A. D. 165, which demands that if anyone wanted to make alterations in the

---

[2] As, for example, Ephraim E. Urbach, "The Rabbinical Law of Idolatry," *Israel Exploration Journal*, IX (1959), 149–65, 229–45.

[3] From the extensive bibliography the following are a few of the more important titles: E. Schürer, *A History of the Jewish People in the Time of Jesus Christ*, 1890, II, i, 173, where the important text of Origen on the subject is quoted; G. F. Moore, *Judaism*, 1927, I, 234; III, 635 f.; J. B. Frey, *Corpus Inscriptionum Judaicarum*, 1936, pp. cx f.

[4] Frey, *op. cit.*, 504–507, inscription 694. He gives an excellent bibliography of the inscription, to which add A. Marmorstein in *Jewish Quarterly Review*, XXVII (1936/7), 373–84.

synagogue there he must pay the "patriarch" 25,000 dinars. But this can by no means be taken *ohne weiteres* to be the Patriarch in Palestine mentioned by Origen a century and a half later. As Frey points out, it is highly unlikely that in the desperate years of the mid-second century a Jewish official in Palestine controlled the Jews in Macedonia. We have no trace of the rabbis controlling Jewish thinking or observance outside Jewish academies. This does not prove that they had no control, but it remains that our only test of rabbinic control over the centers which produced the art is the way in which that art squares with the major rabbinic traditions and positions. I suggested that the conformity of Jewish art to rabbinic traditions up to about the mid-second century of the common era made it a likely hypothesis that the rabbis, or pre-rabbinic Sages, who hated imagery were leading popular Jewish attitudes at the time. But in the Jewish art of the next three centuries there is not a single reservation of even the most liberal Sages not flouted in the actual representations, and the general position of the '*Avodah Zarah, Mishnah* and *Gemara*', as well as of the tannaitic Midrashim, patently rejects such representations with horror.

Here is the second point, the problem of what the rabbis of that time actually did say, or preserved from earlier rabbis, about images. On this I feel Rabbi Boaz Cohen is my best guide.[5] After a brief survey of the pre-Exilic attitudes, a highly complex matter which does not affect our problem, he points out how under the Second Commonwealth, the crisis of Hellenization produced a greater vigor in the law, so that the Mosaic prohibition of images was extended to include every animate being. That the attitude was not uniform seems suggested by the story of the eagle on Herod's temple,[6] but in general Cohen's conclusion is quite similar to that I had reached for this period.

In the tannaitic period, the first two Christian centuries, the decisions of the rabbis remained very strict. Cohen's summary of their declarations follows:

> One may not make any image in relief or in the round, be it carved out of stone, wood, or any metal, of the heaven itself, or of the heavenly servants such as angels, ministering angels, *Cherubim, Seraphim, Ofanim, Ḥasmalim* and *Ḥayyot ha-Kodesh* (the winged creatures of the heavenly chariot); or of the heavenly

---

[5] "Art in Jewish Law," *Judaism*, III (1954), 165–76. He has here outlined only the basic principles, and a note says he plans a larger annotated work on the subject. This article was published simultaneously with my review of the subject in *Symbols*, IV, 3–24.

[6] I discussed this in *Symbols*, VIII, 123–25.

bodies, such as the sun, moon, stars, and the constellations (*Mazzalot*); the earth itself, as well as the mountains and the hills, seas and rivers, of any living things on earth, such as birds, beasts, creeping things, snakes, scorpions, and ferocious animals; of living things in the water, such as fish, sea-monsters, dolphins, sea worms, sea snakes (*Shabririn*), reflected images of things in the sea (*Babuah*). (Perhaps there is an allusion here to the shadow sketches known as *en skiographiois*). Similarly the things beneath the earth, such as the abyss, the darkness, and thick darkness are forbidden.

The Tannaim further excluded the making of images even for the purpose of ornament and beauty, as the Gentiles did in the Provinces.

The Tannaim even went on to interpret "Turn not to the idols" to mean that one should not so much as look at an image, even the image of a Roman official on a coin, though, I may say, everyone knew that no cultus was offered to an image on a coin. A signet ring could be used if it had no image of an idol, that is, a god to whom worship was paid, but could be used if the image was what Cohen translates as "an ordinary figure." Even such a figure could be worn only if it was represented in intaglio. One rabbi said that in Jerusalem many such representations could be found, but no human faces. The rabbis changed the law so as to make it possible for a Jew to live in a Gentile city filled with cult images, and even for a Jew to practise the arts of sculpture and design, so long as the images Jews made were sold to Gentiles. One or another of the Tannaim specified images which he considered it dangerous for a Jew to make at all: an image bearing in its hand a staff, bird, or sphere, a sword, a crown, or a ring. One can deal with a torso when found, they said, but not with an independent hand or foot, or the sun or moon, and not a dragon or a human face. Yet practically all of these are to be found in extant Jewish art, not fragments found and sold, but made directly for graves and places of Jewish worship.

The principle in all this, as it seems to me, is the close following of the Second Commandment, which had been given in two distinct parts. The first forbade making "unto thee" any graven image, etc., by which the law does not literally forbid Jews to make for Gentiles, but only that Jews make images for Jews. This distinction seems to lie behind all the rabbinic pronouncements. The second part of the Commandment forbade one to worship such images once made, whether, as the rabbis correctly interpreted, made by a Jew or Gentile.

Almost all of this could be repeated for the Amoraim, but Cohen rightly says that "when paintings became the regular feature of synagogue decoration of the time, the rabbis tactfully and tacitly bowed before the facts." (Actually, the sculptures of the Galilean synagogues of Capernaum and Chorazin have been dated confidently by the archaeologists in the last years of the Tannaim.) Cohen concludes that the Amoraim: 1) took no exception to mosaics in the synagogues; 2) allowed sculpture of all living beings except, in combination, of the four living beings of the Heavenly Chariot; 3) continued to forbid a ring with a human figure on it in relief; 4) always forbade engravings of human figures as well as sculpture of angels and heavenly bodies. Cohen takes it to represent the opinion of the Amoraim in general when a single rabbi, or a pair of rabbis, relaxed slightly to allow paintings and mosaics, "bowed before the facts." Actually the record of their bowing may well, as so often, simply have recorded a minority opinion. Granted that Cohen is entirely right, however, such bowing by no means explains what prompted Jews in the first place to make the great change. For it was indeed a great change when they began commonly to produce not only paintings, but mosaics and carvings in deep relief, in which they represented the human figure, Helios, Dionysus, centaurs, eagles, and the like, began to make them in the tannaitic period.

So we find ourselves involved in the third aspect of the problem. We must ask what were the "facts" before which the rabbis bowed, or, as Urbach puts it, "the reality with which the Sages had to reckon even if they did not approve of it." To Urbach, the "reality" is the problem of Jews' living in idolatrous cities, and making their living by manufacturing objects for Gentiles to use in idol worship. Cohen sees much more clearly that for us the more important fact before which the rabbis had to bow was that Jews were making the forbidden forms "for themselves," forms which they used (the question is, how used) in connection with their own worship of the Jewish God. For the rabbis had to face not only the "reality" of Jews living among Gentiles, but the "fact" that Jews were putting practically all the forbidden forms into their synagogues. I have all along insisted that without direct evidence to the contrary, of which not a scrap exists, we must assume that Jewish worship was never directed to these forms, not even in the symbolic sense that in bowing before the image one really bowed before the reality behind it. I have seen no evidence that Jews ever bowed before images. But the evidence is abundant that the rabbis had to bow before the presence of images in Jewish graves and synagogues.

Both of these phrases, the rabbis having to "reckon with reality," and "bow before the facts," represent my position exactly, once we have clearly in mind what were the reality and facts. There were things going on in Jewry which the rabbis "did not approve." That Jews made these forms "for themselves," and put them in their places of holiest association, violated the spirit of such Judaism as appears in Josephus and the rabbis.

The problem is not whether a few rabbis can be shown to have bowed before the situation, but what prompted Jews to introduce the forms at all. Who started such a movement, and why? Certainly not the rabbis as a group themselves. In Beth She'arim rabbis are buried in plain sarcophagi along with the sarcophagi of Jews on which were blatantly carved reliefs of the most forbidden subjects, such as that of the sun as a human face, Zeus Helios.

Another bit of evidence, by no means adequately appraised, shows that what we would call orthodox Jews had to tolerate representations they did not approve. For after the paintings were finished in the Dura synagogue some person or persons came into the building and scratched out the eyes of many of the figures in the lowest register, did it so skillfully that the desecration can be recognized only by careful scrutiny. This could hardly have been done, as Kraeling suggested, by the desperate men who wrecked the synagogue for the city's final defense of its wall, since such people, if they did not like the paintings, would presumably have shown their contempt by hitting the faces with their shovels, rather than by so meticulously picking out the eyes. A better guess at what happened lies immediately at hand. Urbach discusses the rabbinic practice of "annulling" images so that they could not be called "images" any more. He quotes the passage I had discussed in which R. El'azar bar Kappara, as he transliterates the name, beat a Gentile until the Gentile would desecrate or annul the image on a ring which the rabbi had found and wanted to keep. Any kind of defacement would do when a Gentile did it, apparently, but when in the third century Rabbi Samuel saw his colleague, Rav Judah, wearing a ring on which a figure stood out in relief, Samuel called Judah a scornful name and ordered him specifically to "put out that fellow's eye." It would seem that some one or more Jews at Dura wanted the figures in these paintings, which seemed to them scandalous, annulled. It might possibly have been the artists themselves, to take away any grounds for accusation that they had painted objects and forms for worship; but in that case it is hard to see why only figures in the lowest register were thus treated, or why in no case is the eye damaged on a pagan divinity (Orpheus, Ares, Victory, Tyche). None of these was on the lowest register. The only probable guess is that one or more Jews at Dura did not like such figures at all, thought them conducive to idolatry, and came in secretly to annul what of them could be reached by standing on the benches, did it so carefully that they would not be caught. I strongly suspect that most rabbis in the great tradition would have applauded the act, since even the more liberal rabbis, who held that all features of bird and beast might be copied, still did not allow the human countenance. The natural assumption from such evidence is that the dominant Jews at Dura liked and made the representations, or had them made, but that others in the congregation did not like them at all. Still, presumably, they tolerated one another within the same congregation. Those who scratched out the eyes clearly did not want to be caught: that is, they wanted to remain within the community. We need only look at the new state of Israel to see again Jews of all sorts, who completely disagree in their interpretation of Jewish law and worship, cooperating magnificently.

Our real question is direct and simple, however difficult to find the answer: what were the sources and inspiration of the representations we find in ancient Jewish synagogues and graves? We need not dispute whether the Jews at Dura, Randanini, Hammam Lif, Beth Alpha, and Capernaum were either "totally different" from the rabbis, or thought identically with them. Either extreme seems absurd to me. The question is whether, as we look for the incentive which demanded and produced the art, we may find it in the rabbinic tradition. I can see, at Dura for example, a few details which recall rabbinic 'Aggadah. But this by no means indicates that the artists of Dura were inspired by rabbinical ideas to make such pictures in the first place, that they must have had the stories directly from rabbis or rabbinical writings, or that all their course of thinking followed rabbinical leadings. Nothing whatever suggests that those who lived solely within the rabbinic *Denkweise* would themselves have wanted to make the paintings, or the mosaics and carvings elsewhere. A new force, a new movement in Judaism, seems to have created the new "reality," the "facts," before which the rabbis, some of them, had to bow. Since the forms themselves can be shown to have been deeply meaningful in pagan religious thinking and feeling, my "theory" is that some Jews in more direct contact with Greco-Roman civilization thought that their religion, or their lives, would be enriched by the conceptions in which these art forms had a place. They thought so with such conviction that they took the forms even into their graves and synagogues, and mingled them with their cult objects and the heroes from Holy Writ. If it is inconceivable, as it is to me, that the rabbis of whom we know would not just have tolerated, but have led such a movement, we must ask who then did lead it, and why? The personalities we shall never know (beyond names in inscriptions), but I doubt if the movement was begun by any one man. Since Jews borrowed such generally similar forms throughout the Roman world, the movement was presumably a generally popular one, somewhat analogous to the development of Reform Judaism, which had in Moses Mendelssohn rather a spokesman and organizer than an originator. The forms which Jews borrowed from pagans in antiquity suggest a movement little resembling modern Reform, except that both meant that Jews were in each case taking into their lives what seemed to them valuable from Gentile civilization. For neither of them did it mean accepting the religious cultus of the Gentiles; for both it meant accepting ideas which did not come from, or generally please the halakhic rabbis. In both cases the rabbis, some of them, only "bowed to the facts."

That this was true in the modern world we know very well. That it was true in the ancient world is my hypothetical suggestion, and to it scholars must bow until they can produce a hypothesis which better explains the facts. In any case we must all, and always, bow to the facts. Since the Jewish symbols offer a new body of evidence, indeed a new kind of evidence, it will force all of us to be at least open to new conclusions. I have no illusion that in my *Symbols* I have exhausted, or pin-pointed, the ideas which Jews took from Gentiles and illustrated with Gentile plastic forms. We cannot determine, however, what Jews had in mind when they borrowed the Gentile forms by showing that a few rabbis did not object when other Jews began to use them.

GOODENOUGH'S *JEWISH SYMBOLS* IN RETROSPECT

MORTON SMITH

COLUMBIA UNIVERSITY

VOL. XII of *Jewish Symbols*,[1] which completes the text,[2] was finished by Professor Goodenough in his seventy-first year, only a year and a half before his death. This may excuse the fact that the text is a restatement, not a reconsideration, of the previous volumes. Some new material has been noticed;[3] there is a sprinkling of references, mostly acrimonious, to remarks by critics;[4] there are a very few changes of opinion which, if followed up, might have affected the major outlines of the work.[5]

Consequently review of the present volume entails reconsideration of the work as a whole. Let us begin by restating the argument:

Religious symbols are among the objects that produce emotional reactions in their observers (make them feel secure, hopeful, etc.). The

---

[1] Erwin R. Goodenough, *Jewish Symbols in the Greco-Roman Period*, Vol. XII, *Summary and Conclusions*, New York, 1965 (Bollingen Series XXXVII). Pp. xii + 217. $6.

[2] A thirteenth volume is in preparation. It will contain maps and a general index.

[3] So especially, G. Scholem's *Jewish Gnosticism*[2] (1965), and occasionally details of the Dead Sea finds. Pp. 191–97 deal with the synagogue of Sardis, about which Goodenough received reliable information only as the volume was going to press.

[4] The only extended discussion of criticism is a two-page attack (pp. 65–67) on E. Urbach, "The Rabbinical Laws of Idolatry in the Second and Third Centuries in the Light of Archaeological and Historical Facts," *Israel Exploration Journal*, 9 (1959), pp. 149 ff. and 229 ff.

[5] I noted only the following:

p. 67: His prior supposition, that all "rabbis" were "rabbinic Jews" in the customary sense of the term, was false; some rabbis would make images for themselves.

p. 75: He discussed psychology too much from the masculine point of view. However, the data "are overwhelmingly the product of males."

p. 92: His interpretation of the symbols as referring to individual salvation neglects the meaning for the group which they probably also had, but this meaning he still cannot recognize.

Of minor corrections I noted: He concedes the Pharisees did not dominate Palestine *politically* before 70, but continues to accept Josephus' statements that they did, and reasserts his "feeling" that it was largely their religious influence which prevented the use of symbols at that time (p. 65). He was mistaken in saying the *Rübe* never appears with the lulab, and probably, therefore, in thinking it equivalent to the lulab (p. 96, n. 1). He accepts Neusner's interpretation of the *cena pura* (p. 100). The wreath on the er-Ramah synagogue was probably not empty, but contained a bust now chipped away (p. 138, n. 20). The seats around the apse at Sardis make him dubious as to the use of apses elsewhere, perhaps they were not only recesses to hold the Torah and other cult instruments (p. 194).

This list is probably not complete, but changes of opinion, even on minor matters, are few.

53

emotional reaction produced by a symbol is its "value," as distinct from its "interpretation," which is what the people who use it say it means. The value of a symbol is always essentially the same, the interpretations often change. (Thus the picture of a wine-cup produced from time immemorial its "value," a feeling of euphoria, although its "interpretation" as a reference to Christ's salvific blood began only with Christianity.) So long as an object commonly produces its "value" in the observers, it is a "live" symbol. Once the "value" is no longer commonly produced, the object is a "dead" symbol. One social group may take over symbols from another. When "live" symbols are taken over, they retain their former values, but are commonly given new interpretations. In the Greco-Roman world there was a *"lingua franca"* of "live" symbols, drawn mostly from the cult of Dionysus, which both expressed and gratified the worshipers' hope for salvation by participation in the life of a deity which gave itself to sacrificial death in order to be eaten by its followers and to live in them. The Jews took over certain of these "live" symbols. (In Palestine, before 70, because of the anti-iconic influence of the Pharisees, they took only geometric objects, vines, grapes, and the like; elsewhere — and, in Palestine, after 70, when Pharisaic influence declined — they took also figures of animals and human beings.) Since these symbols were "live" in Greco-Roman society, the Jews must have known their "values" and adopted the symbols for the sake of those "values." Therefore the Jews must have hoped for mystical salvation by participation in the life of a self-giving deity, probably through a communal meal. However, since they worshiped only Yahweh, they must have imposed, on these pagan symbols, Jewish interpretations. These interpretations, as well as the symbols' unchanged "values," may be discovered in the works of Philo (the chief remains of this mystic Judaism) and also occasionally in the other Jewish literature of the time, and in early Christian works. (The rapid development of Christian theology and art suggests they arose from similar prior developments in Judaism.) The same sources indicate the "values" and interpretations which the Jews found in and imposed on those objects of Jewish cult which they now began to use as symbols: the menorah, the Torah shrine, and so on. For "values," however, all literary sources are secondary; the symbols must first be allowed to speak for themselves. Rabbinic literature is particularly unreliable as to both the "values" and the interpretations of the symbols, since "the rabbis" were both anti-iconic and opposed to mysticism. Their religion was a search for security by obedience to a law laid down by a god essentially different from man; with this god no union was possible, and his law forbade making images. The widespread use of the mystical symbols testifies, therefore, to a widespread mystical Judaism indifferent, at best, to the authorities cited in rabbinic literature. To judge from the archeological evidence, rabbinic Judaism must have been, by comparison with the mystical type, a minor sect.

Let us now take this argument point by point and consider the reviews.[6] Those listed in ADDITIONAL NOTE 1 will hereafter be cited merely by author's name and page number. The list is probably not complete, but is a fair sample; it was compiled chiefly from *L'Année philologique*, a bibliography too often overlooked by students of the NT and of Judaism.

The fundamental point in Goodenough's argument is his concept of the "value" of a symbol as distinct from the "interpretation." He defined the "value" as "simply emotional impact."[7] But he also equated "value" with "meaning" (*ibid*.) and discovered as the "meaning" of his symbols a complex mystical theology.[8] Now certain shapes may be subconsciously associated with certain objects or, like certain colors, may appeal particularly to persons of certain temperaments. This sort of symbolism *may* be rooted in human physiology and almost unchanging. But such "values" as these do not carry the theological implications Goodenough discovered.[9] However, these implications *need* not be represented as the "values" of the symbols. One could say, "The use of these symbols indicates a religion with the concerns characteristic of mysticism. If we attempt to recover the theology of this lost mysticism we must rely on Philo, since he is the best preserved Jewish mystic of the period. This will result in Philonic reconstructions. But most of the mystical Jews were not theologians. They only felt the things which Philo tried to explain." This, I believe, was substantially Goodenough's position, albeit obscured by careless statements which occasioned objections.[10]

After this definition of "value," the next step in Goodenough's argument is the claim that each symbol always has one and the same "value." This thesis drew many protests,[11] because many symbols have apparently contradictory values. (A red light, for instance, now, on the end of an automobile, means, *keep away*; formerly, in red-light districts, it meant, *come*.) So Goodenough's position can be defended only by making the one constant value something so deep in the subconscious and so ambiv-

---

[6] See ADDITIONAL NOTE 1.

[7] *Jewish Symbols* (henceforth *JS*), XII, p. 70.

[8] Bickerman, p. 148.

[9] Dinkler, p. 333; Bickerman, p. 135; Smith, pp. 82 f.

[10] E. g., Gaster, p. 188; R. Grant, p. 292; Marcus, p. 185; Nock, p. 733; North, pp. 313; 181; Smith, pp. 82 f.

[11] Bickerman, pp. 518, 133 (with examples), 143; den Boer, pp. 68 f.; Daniélou, pp. 576, 602; Ehrlich, p. 279; Goossens, p. 252; Guillaumont, p. 484; Gutmann, p. 35; MacKenzie, p. 629, (and the converse — the experiences symbolized also differed from culture to culture, p. 265); Momigliano, p. 246; Mouterde, p. 343; Nock, pp. 532, 731 f.; Smith, pp. 172 f., 219. By contrast, Hooke, p. 119 asserted that Goodenough had "clearly vindicated" this principle (in which Hooke found justification for the methods of the "Myth and Ritual" school); this was merely the pot calling the kettle white. Cf. H. Frankfort, "The Archetype in Analytical Psychology and the History of Religion," *Journal of the Warburg and Courtauld Institutes*, 21 (1958), pp. 166 ff., especially the fourth "correction," p. 178.

alent as to be compatible with contradictory "interpretations." In that event it will also be compatible with both mystical and legalistic religion.[12] In that event the essential argument, that the use of these symbols necessarily indicates a mystical religion, is not valid.

The same conclusion follows from the upshot of the dispute over common decorative motifs (rosettes, circles, stars, etc.). That Goodenough went too far in attributing symbolic value to these motifs was an almost universal objection[13] which he dismissed as an expression of prejudice. After the argument even Nock had to admit that rosettes might be sometimes symbolic; Goodenough, that they might often be meaningless.[14] In logic, this latter admission ruins his argument. If a symbol does not have a constant value, then one cannot use the appropriation of it as proof of concern for its constant value.

The same conclusion again follows from later Jewish borrowing of Christian symbols which were unquestionably "live," but were borrowed by Jews of unquestionable orthodoxy. Gutmann observed, for instance, that medieval Hebrew manuscripts use the conventional picture of the coronation of the Virgin as a representation of God's marriage with Israel.[15] Either this "live" symbol changed its value, or its value was something so ambivalent as to be compatible with mystical Christianity and nomistic orthodox Judaism, or the Jews neglected its value and took it over as a mere decorative device. In any of these events, Goodenough's argument from the borrowing of symbols in antiquity will not hold.[16]

[12] Bickerman, pp. 250, 518, 133.

[13] Albright, p. 24; Avi-Yonah, pp. 196 f. (singling out the ivy leaf, lion mask with ring, and six-pointed rosette as nonsymbolic); Baron, p. 198; Bickerman, pp. 142 (pagan interpretations of pictures show they were nonsymbolic), 143 (so hunting scenes and doves); den Boer, p. 67; Couroyer, p. 115 (Goodenough has done well to oppose "the intellectual laziness which is too easily content with too simple explanations," but one must not deny the artist's delight in mere decoration: rosettes on ossuaries, birds and animals in mosaic patterns, are surely decorative.); Daniélou, p. 577; Dinkler, p. 334; Ferrua, p. 243; Gusinde, p. 1013; Gutmann, p. 35; Jeremias, p. 504; Landsberger, pp. 423, 450; Leon, pp. 261 f.; Nock, pp. 564 (crowns, ivy leaves, palms); 566 (the arcuated lintel); p. 731 (female heads); pp. 732 f. masks, rosettes; North, p. 180 (crudeness of execution does not preclude decorative intent; wine, food, and phalloi may be represented for their own sweet sakes and not as symbols of something else), p. 313 (gabled roof, round objects); Smith, pp. 173 f. (bucrania, lions' feet on furniture, lions' heads holding rings); Vincent, p. 106 (zigzags, leaves).

[14] Nock, p. 732; Goodenough, *JS*, XII, p. 24. On the symbolic value of simple patterns Goodenough's views now receive strong support from the material published by E. Testa, *Il Simbolismo dei Giudeo-Cristiani*, Jerusalem, 1962 (*Pubblicazioni dello Studium Biblicum Franciscanum*, x).

[15] Gutmann, p. 22, with other striking examples. Cf. Kayser, p. 60, Roth, p. 180.

[16] Goodenough's attempt, *JS*, V–VIII, to demonstrate permanent values for the symbols by collecting scraps of ancient near-eastern evidence, is utterly unconvincing. As Segert remarked, p. 159, the scope of the comparison has resulted in superficial treatment of the parallels adduced. And what of the material *not* adduced?

However, even if a symbol does not *always* have the same value, yet *within one culture* the meanings of *most* symbols are *relatively* constant (as shown by the fact that they are commonly understood). So Goodenough's supposition of constancy might be defended as roughly correct in most instances, within the limits of the Greco-Roman period.

With this partial justification we go on to the next point: The *lingua franca* of Greco-Roman symbolism, predominantly Dionysiac, expressed hope for salvation by participation in the life of a deity which gave itself to be eaten in a sacramental meal. This oversimplifies Goodenough's interpretations of pagan symbolism; he recognized variety which cannot be discussed here for lack of space. But this thesis was his main concern, and drew objections from several reviewers, notably from Nock, who was the one most familiar with the classical material.[17]

It must be admitted that Goodenough's support of this contention was utterly inadequate. What had to be established was a probability that the symbols, as *commonly* used in the Roman empire, expressed this hope of salvation by communion. If they did not *commonly* do so *at this time*, then one cannot conclude that the Jews, who *at this time* took them over, had a similar hope. But Goodenough only picked out a scattering of examples in which the symbols could plausibly be given the significance his thesis required; he passed over the bulk of the Greco-Roman material and barely mentioned a few of the examples in which the same symbols were said, by those who used them, to have other significance. These latter examples, he declared, represented superficial "interpretations" of the symbols, while the uses which agreed with his theory expressed the symbols' permanent "values."[18] The facts of the matter, however, were stated by Nock: "Sacramental sacrifice is attested only for Dionysus and even in his cult this hardly remained a living conception" (p. 734); there is no substantial evidence that the worshipers of Dionysus commonly thought they received "his divine nature in the cup" (p. 565). So much for the significance of the *"lingua franca"* of Greco-Roman Dionysiac symbolism.[19]

Here it is not possible to plead that the "values" of the symbols testify to widespread mysticism among the common people, therefore the rarity of literary references to it is unimportant. For the question is, what *are* the "values" — if any — of the symbols, and how are they known? One might think they are best known when the people who used them left inscriptions telling what they meant, next best, when they are explained in works whose authors were close to them in time and culture, and finally, though least securely, by inference from the ways the sym-

[17] Couroyer, p. 115; Mouterde, p. 262; Nober, pp. 365 f.; Nock, pp. 564 f., 571, 530 f., 733 f. "far beyond evidence or probability."
[18] Den Boer, p. 68; Mouterde, p. 265; Nober, p. 366; Nock, p. 734; North, p. 313.
[19] Cf. den Boer, pp. 86 f.; Momigliano, pp. 240, 245.

bols are used. But Goodenough ruled out the inscriptional and literary evidence which did not agree with his theories — it stated merely the users' "interpretations," of the symbols. He also passed over the evidence of usage which he found inconvenient, especially that which showed that his symbols were often used as mere decorative devices.[20] Whence, then, did he discover the "true values" of the symbols, knowledge of which enabled him to reject so much of the evidence? By intuition. "The study of these symbols has brought out their value for my own psyche . . . and I must say that the value I have found in them seems to me what made them of such great importance in antiquity. If this be subjectivism, let my critics make the most of it. In saying I am wrong, they can speak only under the influence of other symbolic impressions."[21] Not *only*. There is also the influence of the ancient evidence which Goodenough rejected. His picture of a *common* mystic and sacramental paganism must be dismissed as fantasy.

Fortunately, not all his interpretations of pagan symbols were devoted to this theme. Many concerned hope for future life, and here he made some strong cases which secured acceptance.[22] But with his failure to demonstrate the prevalence of a belief in sacramental salvation the main structure of his argument was ruined. That the Jews *commonly* took over pagan symbols for a mystic significance which those symbols did not *commonly* have, is incredible. So the borrowing of these symbols cannot *commonly* be evidence of a mystic Judaism.[23] Individual mystics there doubtless were. Philo *may* have been one (though Goodenough's interpretation of him is by no means certain; contrast Wolfson!). But

[20] Nock, pp. 566, 731 ff.; Smith, pp. 173 f. The himation and chiton combination to which he attached mystic significance (*JS*, IX, pp. 131 ff.) appears on a cobbler at work and purchasers in a clothier's shop in Ostia (W. Zschietzschmann, *Hellas and Rome*, London, 1959, pp. 194 f.); his mystic striped chiton is worn by the orchestra and assistants in gladiatorial games (S. Aurigemma, *L'Italia in Africa, Le Scoperte Archeologiche, Tripolitania*, I, *I Monumenti d'arte decorativa*, 1. *I Mosaici*, Rome, 1960, plates 143 f., 146, etc.). Note also Goodenough's dismissal of the apotropaic and sinister sides of ancient symbolism, Bickerman, p. 144, Smith, p. 173.

[21] *JS*, VIII, p. 220. See the comments of R. Grant, p. 279, and Bickerman, pp. 128, 139.

[22] Daniélou, pp. 599 f.; Goossens, p. 231. Nock's contention that during the empire Roman funerary art was, as a whole, not concerned with future life (pp. 563 f.) is hardly credible, especially for the later period, which is that of most of the Jewish material. See the cautious remarks of Momigliano, p. 245. I pass over the other themes in Goodenough's interpretation of pagan images, but call the reader's attention to Nock's (correct) remarks anent mother: In Philo, as in Judaism generally, the mother is the principle of law and punishment, not mercy; the great goddesses of antiquity were rather terrible than comforting, and maternity was rarely their most prominent attribute; many of them were worshiped principally by women. Mother's rôle as the savior of her son is, in classical religion, next to *nil* (pp. 563, 571).

[23] As Gutmann, pp. 34 f., well observed, not everything non-"normative" is therefore "mystic."

the difficulties in the supposition of a *widespread, uniform* mystical Judaism are formidable. How did it happen that such a system and practice disappeared without leaving a trace in either Jewish or Christian polemics?[24] We may therefore turn from the main argument to incidental questions.

To what extent were the motifs on Jewish material borrowed from the hellenistic world, to what extent did they come from Jewish or near-eastern tradition? Goodenough's attempt to derive the vine, lion, eagle, fish, and cup from Hellenism occasioned protests which, at least for the first two, seem partially justified.[25]

Why did the Jews borrow motifs from the pagan world? And why were certain motifs (e. g., sirens) almost never borrowed? Goodenough used the rarity of certain objects as evidence of selectivity and supposed the selection determined by their "values," an argument which won some agreement.[26] However, given the relatively small amount of preserved evidence, the absence of these motifs may be due to chance or fashion. The adoption of the ones which are found must be variously explained, as the circumstances of the individual borrowings indicate; the range of possibilities includes both thoughtless decoration and expression of hopes and beliefs also held by pagans.[27] The important thing, however, is that the same motif need not always be explained by the same motive.

The rarity of decorated material in Palestine before 70 was seen by Goodenough as a consequence of the influence of the Pharisees, and he took the increase of decoration after 70 as evidence of the decline of pharisaic-rabbinic influence. But the rabbis were more influential in Palestine after 100 than the Pharisees had been before 70.[28] Goodenough's error was based on the statements of Josephus, the reports in rabbinic literature, and the rôle of the Pharisees in the gospels. But Josephus was ignorant when he wrote the *War*, in the 70's, of the preëminence of the Pharisees which he reports in the *Antiquities*, completed in the 90's; between 80 and 90 he had evidently gone over to the Pharisees, and his

---

[24] Nock, p. 568; Daniélou, p. 574; R. Grant, p. 280.

[25] Daniélou, p. 576; Jeremias, p. 504; Landsberger, p. 109; Marcus, p. 185; Mouterde, p. 263; Segert, p. 325; Smith, p. 263. But Goodenough did not wholly deny Israelite and near eastern sources, e. g., *JS*, XII, p. 136, on the lion.

[26] Guillaumont, p. 483; Smith, pp. 171 f. (I have changed my mind).

[27] Bickerman, p. 136; F. Grant, pp. 62 f.; Gusinde, p. 1013; Momigliano, pp. 245 f. On economic reasons see Urbach, *op. cit.* (*supra*, n. 4), enlarging the suggestions of B. Cohen, "Art in Jewish Law," *Judaism*, 3 (1954), pp. 165 ff.

[28] Avi-Yonah, p. 198; Urbach, *op. cit.*, p. 151; Smith, p. 82; Roth, p. 182. J. Neusner, "Jewish Use of Pagan Symbols After 70 C. E.," *JR*, 33 (1965), pp. 285 ff., defends Goodenough by picking out slight exaggerations in Urbach's wording, then neglecting the point at issue.

later statements are propaganda for them.[29] That the reports in rabbinic literature reflect wishful thinking is generally admitted.[30] The gospels do not consistently indicate that the Pharisees were the dominant party. In Q they appear in only one passage (Luke 11 39, 42 and //). In Mark they appear only in the *Streitgespräche* (2 1—3 6; 7 1–23; 8 11–21; 10 1–12; 11 27–12 40) which are among the later elements of this gospel.[31] The extension of their rôle in the other gospels is evidence of yet later polemic, reflecting their later rise to power. In all the gospels they are almost (or wholly) absent from the passion stories, which are probably the oldest and best preserved elements. They are also conspicuously absent from all save one of the early stories in Acts. So it would be plausible to see the lack of decoration in the earlier period as due to the influence of the Sadducean aristocracy, which took Exod 20 3 literally, and the increase in the use of figures after 70 as a consequence of increasing Pharisaic influence which, as Urbach has shown,[31a] "interpreted" the prohibition of images so as to find more and more exceptions. However, other factors must be kept in mind. First, archeological evidence from Palestine before 70 is extremely limited (e. g., no synagogues); so the absence of certain motifs in that period may be happenstance.[32] Second, the change in Palestine is paralleled by the developments of Roman art in which decoration steadily increased. The sequence of fresco styles in Pompeii shows this clearly; so does the increase of pictorial mosaics in the later imperial period, the growth of florid architectural decoration, and so on. One of the major faults of Goodenough's method was his failure to relate the history of the Jewish material to the changes in contemporary pagan art.

Returning to the interpretation of the material: One of Goodenough's presuppositions was that since the Jews who produced these objects were "loyal" to Judaism they could not have worshiped any of the images. He did accept the material in the magical papyri as evidence of syncretism but was reluctant to relate it to the other images.[33] Margalioth's recovery of *Sefer ha-Razim*,[34] however, has given us a Hebrew text, written by a man steeped in the OT and the poetry of the synagogue, which yet contains prescriptions for making images and prayers to pagan deities, including Helios, who are conceived as gods

[29] M. Smith, "Palestinian Judaism in the First Century, in M. Davis, *Israel, Its Role in Civilization*, pp. 67 ff., esp. 74 ff.

[30] E. g., by Neusner himself, *A Life of Rabban Yohanan ben Zakkai*, pp. 49–61.

[31] M. Smith, "The Jewish Elements in the Gospels," *JBR*, 24 (1956), pp. 90 ff., esp. 96.

[31a] *Op. cit.*, (n. 4), pp. 154-end.

[32] Cf. Avi Yonah, p. 196: Another pre-70 menorah has turned up since Goodenough wrote.

[33] His final statement on the matter is in *JS*, XII, pp. 60 f.

[34] The Hebrew edition is now in press in Israel.

subordinate to Yahweh.[35] This text was widely copied in rabbinic circles. Accordingly it is possible that Helios on the synagogue floors represents a major deity to whom members of the congregation addressed prayers for practical purposes (though they hardly would have addressed them to *that particular* image, as few Christians would have prayed to the Christ in the mosaic on the dome of Byzantine churches).

Goodenough's supposition that the Jews gave their own interpretations to the symbols they borrowed is plausible and has been commonly accepted.[36] His reconstructions of their interpretations, however, being based on Philo, drew objections that Philo was an upper-class intellectual whose interpretations were undreamt of by the average Jew.[37] These, however, missed Goodenough's claim: Philo was merely one example of mystical Judaism, of which other examples, from other social and intellectual classes, were attested by the monuments.[38] For this reason also, objections that Goodenough misinterpreted Philo on particular points[39] did not seriously damage his argument; it was sufficient for him to show that Philo used expressions suggestive of a mystical and sacramental interpretation of Jewish stories and ceremonies.[40] The monuments *could* then show analogous developments independent of Philo. Some did, but most did not.

Beside Philo, Goodenough found evidence of mystic Judaism in occasional passages from other works of ancient Jewish literature,[41]

[35] Cf. the subordinate gods in Clement of Alexandria, ed. O. Stählin (*Die griechischen christlichen Schriftsteller*), II, pp. 256, 489, 507; III, 6, 10, 14, 41, 144.

[36] Most enthusiastically by F. Grant, pp. 62 f., who compares the Jewish reinterpretation of the hellenistic religious vocabulary.

[37] Dinkler, p. 330; Ehrlich, pp. 93, 279; Gaster, p. 188; Gutmann, p. 34; Leon, p. 262.

[38] To this Nock, p. 562, agreed.

[39] R. Grant, p. 184; Momigliano, p. 239; Nock, pp. 528, 567; Smith, p. 84. Note Momigliano's remark that Philo's symbolism was basically biblical, that of Goodenough's Jews, not so (p. 243). Nock stigmatized a string of misinterpretations: pp. 525 ff.: VI, p. 213 on *Plant.* 160 ff.; VI, p. 203 on *Vita Mos.* I, 187; VI, p. 205 on *Somn.* II, 183; VI, pp. 208 f. on *Cher.* 84 ff.; p. 528, on eating the Logos; p. 567, on esoteric worship; p. 735: VII, p. 222 on Abr. 100-102.

[40] F. Grant, pp. 418 f.; Mouterde, p. 342.

[41] Accordingly, Dinkler's objection that, except for Philo, Goodenough neglected all ancient literature from and about Judaism (p. 331) was an overstatement, and Momigliano's reference to mystic Judaism as "not otherwise documented" (p. 248) was false. H. Chadwick, "St. Paul and Philo of Alexandria," *Bulletin of the John Rylands Library*, 48 (1966), pp. 286 ff., shows the far-reaching, but independent agreement of Paul and Philo, which may have come from a common background in mystical Judaism. It must be admitted, however, that Goodenough has neglected the main outlines of the pictures of Judaism given by works other than Philo. Only occasional details, useful for his thesis, are seized on and presented out of context. And even some of these occasioned justified complaints of misinterpretation: Bickerman, pp. 532 f.; den Boer, p. 86; Nock, p. 525 on the interpretation of Josephus *Antt.* 14, 213 ff., in *JS*, VI, p. 206; Couroyer, p. 112, n. 1, on I Macc 13 29, in *JS*, VIII, p. 158; Nock,

and in early Christian writings,[42] since he argued that Christianity could not have developed so rapidly had it not drawn on theology and symbolism already developed in hellenized Judaism. Similar arguments have been advanced by other scholars,[43] and Goodenough's (accepted by R. Grant, North, and van Puyvelde)[44] presents a most probable explanation of the facts. Further support for it is to be found in Goodenough's interpretation of the symbols drawn from Jewish cult, which found wide agreement[45] in spite of the fact that he sometimes pushed it to absurdity — for instance, by his refusal to see, in representations of the Torah scroll or Torah shrine, evidence for a religion of obedience.[46]

One reason for the acceptance of Goodenough's interpretations of the symbols drawn from Judaism was that he often supported them by quotations from rabbinic literature.[47] Yet he contended that "the rabbis" were opposed not only to images but also to mysticism; their religion was that of conformity and obedience, not mystical union;[48] therefore rabbinic literature does not reveal the reasons for the popular adoption of the mystical symbols.[49] Behind this contradiction lay his enthusiasm (especially in argument) which often led him into over-

---

p. 730 on *The Rest of the Words of Baruch*, 7 18 in *JS*, VIII, p. 137; Bickerman, p. 533 on Shabbat 119a, in *JS*, V, p. 44; Nock, p. 567 on the Jewish material in the *Apostolic Constitutions*. R. Grant, p. 185, Nock, p. 568 on *Corpus Inscriptionum Judaicarum*, nos. 651 and 652, in *JS*, II, p. 146; Nock, p. 568 on *CIJ* 22, *ibid.*; Marcus, p. 45 on Dio Cassius 60, 6, in *JS*, I, p. 35, n. 7; Nock, p. 565 on πιε ζήσαις in *JS*, II, p. 117; Nock, pp. 565 f.; Ferrua, pp. 240 f. on the catacomb of Vibia and Vincentius, *JS*, II, pp. 46 ff.

[42] His use of Justin's *Dialogue with Trypho* drew a number of objections. Baron, p. 198, opined that Trypho was a straw man and therefore useless as evidence concerning Judaism (*non sequitur*); Momigliano, p. 244, declared that, even if not a straw man, he showed no knowledge of Goodenough's system of symbolism.

[43] Leroy, p. 160, referring to Strzygowski, von Sybel, Becker, and Morey.

[44] R. Grant, p. 183, North, p. 311, van Puyvelde, pp. 325, 376, with especial reference to the development of Christian from Jewish art.

[45] Daniélou, pp. 575 f.; Gaster, p. 188; Jeremias, p. 503; MacKenzie, p. 631; Nock, p. 562; van Puyvelde, p. 325. Objections: Ehrlich, p. 279, the menorah probably indicated a claim of the synagogue to succeed to the temple and house the Shekinah. Kayser, p. 57, Leon, p. 262, the menorah was merely a means of Jewish self-indentification — but Goodenough was certainly right for some instances, see M. Smith, *The Image of God*, below, n. 52. Kayser, pp. 58 f., the shofar was not blown on the day of atonement before the high middle ages (because the Seder of Rab Amram does not provide for it). Gaster, p. 189, lamps, *shalom*, and perhaps the "throne of Moses" may be better interpreted from nomistic Judaism. Marcus, p. 183, the cherubim were probably associated with Solomon's temple. Smith, p. 220, the early Jerusalem tombs and ossuaries were made for the rich among whom were many Sadducees; it is therefore unlikely that their decoration usually indicates belief in a future life.

[46] *JS*, XII, p. 76.

[47] *JS*, IV, pp. 89 f., 131 f., 162 f., 171–84, 200 ff.; X, pp. 102 f., 135.

[48] *JS*, XII, pp. 74 ff.

[49] *JS*, IX, pp. 4 ff. and Goodenough's article, "The Rabbis and Jewish Art in the Greco-Roman Period," *Hebrew Union College Annual*, 32 (1961), pp. 269 ff.

statement, but made his enormous work possible. This passionate concern for his subject was grounded in his experience: the intense religious enthusiasm of his youth (he had been not only "saved" but "sanctified") and his equally intense adult revolt against both the austerity of his Protestant background and the religion of conformity and respectability with which he collided at Yale. This personal conflict he projected onto ancient Judaism, partly as a result of his deep feeling about G. F. Moore, who aroused in him an ambivalence worthy of a father figure. Therefore, on the one hand, Moore was right; "normative" Judaism was as he pictured it, much like the normative, upper-class New England Protestantism of 1920: common-sense, respectable, law-abiding, moral, pharisaic, in a word, square. But also, Moore was wrong; "normative" Judaism was not normative. It was, like New England "society," a puritanic sect walled up in its self-made ghetto, while outside was the wonderful world of hellenized Judaism, mystic, artistic, and free.[50]

Consequently Goodenough had a personal resistance to the suggestion that any of his symbols should have come from Moore's rabbis. This was reinforced by his inability to read the rabbinic material[51] and consequent reluctance to admit its relevance. Therefore when rabbinic parallels to his interpretations were pointed out to him, he dismissed them as insignificant, and, in his final restatement, ignored their existence.[52] The resultant misrepresentation called forth many objections: that rabbinic Judaism was not uniform,[53] but contained a tradition of mystical practice,[54] as well as important hellenistic elements.[55] As Neusner said (p. 82), "The issue was not... Hellenization, but rather how to appropriate, and accommodate oneself to, Hellenization... Goodenough might have seen both the mystic groups and the rabbinic groups as *modulations* of Jewish Hellenism."

---

[50] The Christian roots of Goodenough's mystic Judaism were noted by Nock, pp. 571, 734; contrast van Puyvelde, p. 326, "Que les vues de M. Goodenough, juif convaincu, sur l'histoire du christianisme ne seront pas toujours entièrement équitable (tant il est vrai que pour juger d'une religion il faut la voire du dedans), n'étonnera pas le lecteur"! It is worth noting that Goodenough's contempt for "mere decoration" also comes from his Protestant background. If one *must* have pictures they should at least be *useful*.

[51] Contrast Willoughby's description of Goodenough as "both a competent Orientalist and an expert Hellenist at one and the same time" (p. 260).

[52] *JS*, IX, p. 7, n. 10, on M. Smith, "The Image of God," *Bulletin of the John Rylands Library*, 40 (1958), pp. 473 ff. On the menorah *JS*, XII, p. 82 is false. In Goodenough's own words, "To deny the existence of facts in this way is hardly a scholar's method of dealing with them" (*JS*, XII, p. 65).

[53] Abi-Yonah, p. 197; Bickerman, p. 131; Gutmann, p. 34; Neusner, p. 79; Smith, p. 220.

[54] Marcus, pp. 185 f.; den Boer, p. 67; Momigliano, p. 239.

[55] Bickerman, pp. 129 f.; Gutmann, pp. 23 f.; Marcus, p. 43.

There are many elements in the haggadah[56] which may have either produced or resulted from pictures. Nevertheless, it is true, as Goodenough claimed (*JS*, IV, pp. 21, 24), that rabbinic literature would never have led us to expect the decorations of Dura or Beth Shearim or the Roman catacombs.[57] Therefore it seems likely that the varieties of Judaism which produced these various expressions[58] often differed greatly from those represented in rabbinic literature. One of the major results of Goodenough's work has been to produce general recognition of this fact.[59] In the words of Jeremias, "Eine neue Welt tut sich auf, ein Stück Volksreligion, ein Judentum neben dem rabbinischen und dem essenischen, eines, das wir in dieser Geschlossenheit bisher nicht kannten."[60]

As to how the various forms of this popular religion were related to the rabbinic authorities, opinions have differed. Goodenough supposed the relation one of hostility (*JS*, XII, p. 66).[61] Bickerman thinks the conflict not proved; he compares the contrast between early Christian art and the denunciation of images by the Fathers (pp. 249, 130 f.). Hart (pp. 95 f.) and Roth (pp. 179 f.) remark that the people may

[56] Marcus, p. 186, Smith, *op. cit. supra*, n. 52.

[57] Hart, p. 95; Leon, p. 262; MacKenzie, pp. 490, 629; Marcus, p. 44; Neusner, p. 80; Smith, p. 82.

[58] Goodenough claimed that the art was homogeneous throughout the empire (IV, p. 3) and found in this homogeneity evidence for a uniform theology of mystic Judaism (*JS*, IV, p. 60). MacKenzie, p. 490, and Mouterde, p. 342, found this claim correct, but Momigliano, pp. 244 f., argued that, *after subtracting* the obviously Jewish symbols and the "merely decorative or vaguely suggestive" non-Jewish ones (victories, crowns, rosettes, etc.), the main monuments do not show a uniform system of symbols. This important question deserves a study to itself. My first impression, however, is that Momigliano is right. No doubt many of the same banal elements — vines and rosettes and wreaths and so on — turn up everywhere. But each of the main bodies of material (the Kidron tombs, the early ossuaries, Beth Shearim, the carved synagogues, the Palestinian mosaics, the Maccabean coins, the coins of the revolts, the Roman catacombs, Hammam Lif, the magical gems, Dura) seems to have its own vocabulary as well as its own style and to be saying — if anything — something peculiar to itself. (The "if anything" refers to the Kidron tombs and the ossuaries, of which I doubt that the decoration is usually symbolic.)

[59] By Avi-Yonah, pp. 197, 199; Baron, p. 197; Daniélou, p. 574; Ehrlich, p. 93; Gaster, p. 188; Hart, p. 93; Marcus, pp. 44 f.; Neusner, pp. 90 f.; Nock, pp. 561 f.; van Puyvelde, p. 324; Segert, pp. 261 f.; Smith, p. 82.

[60] Jeremias, p. 503. Yet after this Jeremias (p. 922) went on to declare that the symbols should be thought meaningless if no Jewish literary evidence could be found to determine their meaning! Clearly, the answer to the question, whether or not a picture has meaning, cannot be made to depend on the accidents of literary transmission. This sort of attitude did much to excuse (but not to justify) Goodenough's excesses in demanding that the interpretation be based on the pictures themselves, not the *testimonia*.

[61] Cf. Ehrlich, p. 278; Mouterde, p. 264; Neusner in both his review and the article cited above, n. 28. Ehrlich finds support for the position in the forced exegesis by which the rabbis had to justify the use of the symbols they did tolerate, but the rabbis also used forced exegesis to justify their own innovations.

have, then as now, admired the rabbis without obeying them (a suggestion plausible because of the development all over the Romano-Persian world, at about this time, of double standards for the laity and the religious — monks and magi and Manichean clergy alike).[62] It seems probable that all these relationships sometimes occurred, and yet others beside; some talmudic authorities are said themselves to have made images.[63]

Here again the root of error is the attempt to explain a large body of varied material by a single formula. Among the diverse groups who in the Roman empire were called "Jews" by their neighbors and came to call themselves so, the percentage of those who were much concerned about the rulings of the rabbis at Jamnia, shortly after 70, was doubtless small. Later, as Josephus shows, it increased, thanks to Roman approval. About 130 there was a drop, and the recovery was slow. Even in Galilee in the time of Rabbi, as Büchler showed,[64] relations were strained between the landowners, the patriarchal house, and the poorer rabbis; patriarchal control was far from absolute, and congregational leaders who had popular support or could buy Roman protection did much as they pleased. Goodenough's theory falsifies the situation by substituting a single, antirabbinic, mystical Judaism for the enormous variety of personal, doctrinal, political, and cultural divergencies which the rabbinic and other evidence reveals, and by supposing a sharp division between rabbinic and antirabbinic Judaism, whereas actually there seems to have been a confused gradation. Here again he is the rebellious son of G. F. Moore.

In the preface to his last volume Goodenough wrote, "Scholars have repeatedly said to me, 'At least you will always be remembered and used for your collection of material.'... I have not spent thirty years as a mere collector: I was trying to make a point." He was, and he failed. His pandemic sacramental paganism was a fantasy; so was the interpretation of pagan symbols based on it, and so was the empire-wide, antirabbinic, mystical Judaism, based on the interpretation of these symbols. All three are enormous exaggerations of elements which existed, but were rare, in early imperial times.

---

[62] Further opinions: Gutmann, p. 35 (change of rabbinic position explained by alliance of the patriarchal house with Rome — not unlikely); Guillaumont, p. 484 (Goodenough exaggerates the difference, overlooking on the one hand Philo's acceptance of the second commandment, on the other, orthodox acceptance of illustration, as evidenced in the medieval manuscripts); Landsberger, p. 424 (the material shows rabbinic tolerance); Marcus, p. 45 (G.'s claim that the Palestinian rabbis had no control of the diaspora is a "gross exaggeration"); Nock, pp. 561 f. (G. has made a good case against central control; considerable nonnormative literature may have been lost).

[63] Rabba made a homunculus, Sanhedrin 65b. The story is presumably false, but indicates what the storytellers were trying.

[64] A. Büchler, *Der galiläische 'Am ha 'Ares; The Political and Social Leaders of the Jewish Community of Sepphoris.*

Soit. Columbus failed, too. But his failure revealed a new world, and so did Goodenough's. Jeremias' praise was no exaggeration. The extent and importance of the Jewish iconic material was practically unrealized before Goodenough's collection if it.[65] Informed opinions of ancient Judaism can never, henceforth, be the same as they were before he published. So long as the subject is studied and the history of the study is preserved, his work will mark an epoch.

[65] See ADDITIONAL NOTE 2.

ADDITIONAL NOTE 1.

W. Albright, *Bulletin of the ASOR*, 139, pp. 23 f., on vols. I–III (unimportant).
M. Avi-Yonah, *Israel Exploration Journal*, 6 (1956), pp. 194 ff., on I–IV.
A. Barb, *Antiquaries' Journal*, 36 (1956), pp. 229 ff., on I–IV; 38 (1958), pp. 117 f., on V–VI; 39 (1959), p. 301, on VII–VIII.
S. Baron, *JBL*, 74 (1955), pp. 196–99, on I–III.
E. Bickerman, *L'Antiquité classique*, 25 (1956), pp. 246 ff., on I–IV; 26 (1957), pp. 532 f., on V–VI; 28 (1959), pp. 517 f., on VII–VIII; "Symbolism in the Dura Synagogue," *HTR*, 58 (1965), pp. 127 ff., on IX–XI.
W. den Boer, *Mnemosyne*, Ser. 4, 12 (1959), pp. 85 ff., on V–VI; 14 (1961), pp. 66 ff. on VII–VIII.
D. Botterweck, *Theologische Quartalschrift*, 137 (1957), pp. 210 f., on I–VI (unimportant).
F. Buck, *CBQ*, 27 (1965), p. 191, on IX–XI (unimportant).
B. Couroyer, *RB*, 67 (1960), pp. 107 ff., on VII and VIII; 72 (1965), pp. 310 ff., on IX–XI (this latter I have not seen).
J. Daniélou, *Recherches de science religieuse*, 45 (1957), pp. 571 ff., on I–VI; 48 (1960), pp. 598 ff., on VII and VIII.
C. Delvoye, *Latomus*, 14 (1955), pp. 494 ff., on I–IV; 18 (1959), pp. 484 ff., on V–VIII (unimportant).
E. Dinkler, *ThRd*, NF 21 (1953), pp. 329 ff., on I–III.
E. Ehrlich, *ZRG*, 9 (1957), pp. 277 ff., on I–VI; 12 (1960), pp. 92–94, on VII–VIII.
A. Ferrua, *Rivista di Archeologia Cristiana*, 30 (1954), pp. 237 ff., on I–III.
K. Galling, *Zeitschrift des deutschen Palästina-Vereins*, 70 (1954), pp. 182 f., on I–III (unimportant).
T. Gaster, "Pagan Ideas and the Jewish Mind," *Commentary*, 17 (1954), pp. 185 ff., on I–III.
G. Goossens, *Revue belge d'archéologie*, 22 (1953), pp. 268 f., on I–III; 24 (1955), pp. 125 f., on IV (these two are unimportant); 25 (1956), pp. 251 f., on V–VI; 27 (1958), pp. 231, on VII–VIII.
F. Grant, *JBL*, 79 (1960), pp. 61 ff., on VII–VIII; 83 (1964), pp. 418 ff., on IX–XI.
R. Grant, *ChH*, 23 (1954), pp. 183 ff., on I–III; 24 (1955), pp. 279 f., on IV; 26 (1957), pp. 292, on V–VI; 29 (1960), pp. 94 ff., on VII–VIII.
A. Guillaumont, *Revue des études anciennes*, 59 (1957), pp. 482 ff., on I–VI; 62 (1950), pp. 542 ff., on VII–VIII.
M. Gusinde, *Anthropos*, 49 (1954), pp. 1145 ff., on I–IV; 52 (1957), pp. 311 ff., on V–VI; 54 (1959), pp. 1012 ff., on VII–VIII.
J. Gutmann, *Studies in Bibliography and Booklore*, 3 (1957), pp. 33 ff., on V–VI; *The Reconstructionist*, 31 (1965), pp. 20 ff., on IX–XI.
H. Hart, *JThS*, 7 (1956), pp. 92 ff., on I–IV.
S. Hooke, *JThS*, 9 (1958), pp. 117 ff., on V–VI; 11 (1960), pp. 371 ff., on VII–VIII (unimportant).
J. Jeremias, *ThLz*, 83 (1958), cols. 502–05, on I–VI; 87 (1962), p. 922, on VII–VIII.
S. Kayser, *Review of Religion*, 21 (1956), pp. 54 ff., on I–IV.
F. Landsberger, *AJPh*, 76 (1955), pp. 422 ff., on I–IV; 78 (1957), p. 450, on VI–VII; 81 (1960), pp. 108 f., on VIII–IX.

H. Leon, *Archaeology*, 7 (1954), pp. 261 f., on I–III; 9 (1956), p. 154, on IV; 11 (1958), pp. 135 f., on V–VI; 13 (1960), p. 155, on VII–VIII (last three unimportant).
J. Leroy, *Cahiers Sioniens*, 9 (1955), pp. 157 ff.
R. MacKenzie, *CBQ*, 16 (1954), pp. 489 ff., on I–III; 17 (1955), pp. 629–31, on IV; 20 (1958), pp. 264 ff., on V–VI.
R. Marcus, *ClPh*, 52 (1957), pp. 43 ff., on I–III; pp. 182 ff., on IV.
A. Momigliano, *Athenaeum*, NS 34 (1956), pp. 237 ff., on I–IV.
R. Mouterde, *Mélanges de l'Université Saint-Joseph*, 31 (1954), pp. 341 ff., on I–IV; 34 (1957), pp. 262 ff., on V–VI.
H. Musurillo, *ThS*, 15 (1954), pp. 295 ff., on I–III; 25 (1964), pp. 437, on IX–XI.
J. Neusner, "Notes on Goodenough's *Jewish Symbols*," *Conservative Judaism*, 17 (1963), pp. 77 ff., on I–VIII.
P. Nober, *Biblica*, 36 (1955), pp. 549 ff., on I–III; 38 (1957), pp. 364 ff., on V–VI; 41 (1960), pp. 430 ff., on VII–VIII; 46 (1965), pp. 96 ff., on IX–XI (not seen).
A. Nock, *Gnomon*, 27 (1955), pp. 558 ff., on I–IV; 29 (1957), pp. 524 ff., on V–VI; 32 (1960), pp. 728 ff., on VII–VIII.
R. North, *Orientalia*, NS 25 (1956), pp. 310 ff., on I–IV; 26 (1957), pp. 180 f., on V–VI; 35 (1966), pp. 201 ff., on IX–XI.
C. van Puyvelde, *Recherches de théologie ancienne et médiévale*, 21 (1954), pp. 324 ff., on I–IV; 24 (1957), pp. 375 ff., on V–VI.
H. Rosenau, *Journal of Jewish Studies*, 8 (1957), pp. 253 (unimportant).
C. Roth, *Judaism*, 3 (1954), pp. 179 ff., on I–III.
S. Sandmel, *JBL*, 77 (1958), pp. 380 ff., on V–VI (unimportant).
Sed-Rajna, *Revue des Études Juives*, 3 (1964), pp. 533 f. (not seen).
S. Segert, *Archiv Orientální*, 23 (1955), pp. 256 ff., on I–III; 24 (1956), pp. 157 ff., on IV; 26 (1958), pp. 322 ff., on V–VI; 28 (1960), pp. 704 ff., on VII–VIII.
M. Smith, *ATR*, 36 (1954), pp. 218 ff., on I–III; 37 (1955), pp. 81 ff., on IV; 39 (1957), pp. 261 ff., on V–VI; 42 (1960), pp. 171 ff., on VII–VIII; *Classical World*, 59 (1965–6), p. 13, on IX–XI.
H. Strauss, *Judaism*, 7 (1958), pp. 178 f., on IV–VI (not seen); 8 (1959), pp. 374 f., on VII–VIII.
M. Thelen, *JBR*, 32 (1964), pp. 361 ff., on IX–XI (unimportant).
L. Vincent, *RB*, 62 (1955), pp. 104 ff., on I–III; pp. 428 ff., on IV; 64 (1957), pp. 593 ff., on V–VI.
H. Willoughby, *JNES*, 15 (1956), pp. 121 ff., on I–IV; 17 (1958), pp. 158 f., on V–VI; 20 (1961), pp. 260 ff., on VII–VIII (unimportant).
S. Zeitlin, *JQR*, 45 (1954–5), pp. 66 ff., on I (unimportant).

ADDITIONAL NOTE 2.

Almost all the collected material is contained in vols. I–III and IX–XI. Because of the importance of the collection I think it worth while to list here the more important of the items which have been challenged:

Avi Yonah, pp. 195 f., lists as "non-Jewish" the Beit Jibrin tombs, the shaft graves near the Nablus Road, the Marissa tombs, the objects in vol. III, figs. 198, 262, 268, 285, 338, the Beit Nattif lamp (I, p. 157), the Gophna sarcophagus (I, p. 138), the lamp from Ophel (I, p. 155), and that from Silat ed Dahr (I, p. 159). Fig. 82, the "fruit dish" is a bearded face.

Barb, p. 230: II, pp. 269, 273 for "Isis and Hathor" read "Isis and Nephthys"; II, p. 200, and VIII, p. 172 for "Liliam" read "Laïlam"; II, p. 221, for "stone" read "lead"; III, fig. 1198 is a copy of C. Bonner, *Studies in Magical Amulets*, pl. XXIV, fig. 5. Barb, p. 301: VII, fig. 155 is probably a recent forgery; VIII, fig. 30 has nothing to do with Christianity.

Bickerman, p. 142, on IX, p. 22, remarks that the *Passio Quatuor Coronatorum* should now be read in H. Delehaye, *Acta Sanctorum*, Nov. 3 (1910), p. 765, with D.'s commentary: Goodenough has mistranslated it; the *philosophos* was not a master of symbolism but an engineer in charge of the stone cutting.

den Boer, p. 68; Nock, p. 729: *JS*, VIII, p. 11 mistranslates Plutarch 766 B; the rendering "pudendum" instead of "meadows" is indefensible.

Daniélou, p. 601: VIII, p. 160, of G.'s two citations from Hippolytus one is apocryphal, the other, from Callixtus.

Ferrua, pp. 239 ff.: III, p. 819, the pieces of sarcophagi from the Randanini catacomb are not Jewish, neither are most of Goodenough's small objects. III, Fig. 856 is probably pagan, and so is everything from the catacomb of Vibia. It must be said that Ferrua was motivated by a concern that neither Judaism nor Christianity should "inquinare il suo patrimonio" with improper objects (p. 238). He thought the prevention of this more important than the loss of a little evidence (!, *ibid.*) and therefore resolutely ruled out as "intrusive" everything in Jewish and Christian catacombs which did not satisfy his notion of "orthodoxy" — everything "heterodox" had fallen in through the air holes! His opinions on these matters, therefore, need not be taken seriously. Compare the amusing contention of Kayser, pp. 55 f., that symbols used as Goodenough supposed should not be called "Jewish symbols" but "symbols used by Jews."

Nock, pp. 529 f.: VI, p. 82, Aristaenetus is credited with what is actually a scholiast's remark and the passage is therefore wholly misunderstood. VI, pp. 114 ff., the Syriac Liturgy of the Nile is a corrupt expansion of a Greek text in which "O holy one of God" refers to the patriarch of Alexandria. Nock, p. 735: VII, p. 213 misinterprets Origen *PG*, XIII, 1820 = *GCS*, XXXV, 57 which is mere moralizing; VIII, p. 49 misinterprets Apuleius, *Metamorphosis* 11, 8, the fowler and fisher were not in the Isiac sacred procession; VIII, p. 64, the statuette with *soter kosmou* on its phallus is of dubious authenticity.

North, p. 314, Vincent, p. 105: I, p. 81 misdates the Kidron valley tombs; they are third, not first, century B.C. This opinion, however, is an idiosyncrasy of Vincent's.

Vincent, pp. 105 ff.: I, p. 76 thinks a Roman necropolis in Jerusalem pre-Maccabean. Dickie's account of the frescoes is correct. I, p. 84, the sole example of a triple entry to the later tombs is in a fanciful restoration by Dalman. The Marissa tombs were not Jewish before the time of Hyrcanus.

Segert, p. 159: IV, p. 127 and fig. 88, *shabu'ot* refers not to *oaths* but to the feast of *weeks*.

For alleged misinterpretations of Philonic passages see above, n. 39; of passages from other Jewish texts, n. 41.

The evidence most often impugned was that of the spells and amulets, use of which was declared unjustified by Ferrua, p. 239, Dinkler, p. 336 and R. Grant, p. 185; dubious by Bickerman, p. 249, Gaster, p. 190, Mouterde, p. 342, and Leon, p. 262; justified by Barb, p. 229, van Puyvelde, p. 325, and Roth, p. 181. Nock, pp. 569 f., thought it justified in principle, but believed Goodenough had included important non-Jewish pieces. The question of principle is now settled beyond dispute in Goodenough's favor by Margaliot's discovery of *Sefer ha Razim* which demonstrates that magic of the type familiar from the Greek papyri was adopted and perpetuated by writers in the rabbinic tradition. It remains possible that some few of the pieces used by Goodenough were not Jewish in origin, but this possibility will not substantially affect the argument.

STORY AND HISTORY: OBSERVATIONS ON GRECO-ROMAN RHETORIC AND PHARISAISM*

by Henry A. Fischel
Indiana University

TEXTS CITED

AdRN: Aboth de Rabbi Nathan, ed. S. Schechter; reprinted, N.Y. 1944
BT: Babylonian Talmud (any edition)
"Cynicism": H. A. Fischel, *Cynicism and the Ancient Near East*, American Academy For Jewish Research, New York–Jerusalem, forthcoming
D.L.: Diogenes Laertius, *Vitae Philosophorum*, 2 vols., ed. H. S. Long, Oxford 1964
P.A.: Pirqe Aboth, as in Mishna (any edition)
    In parentheses: Chas. Taylor, *Sayings of the Jewish Fathers,*[2] 2nd ed., Cambridge 1897
P.T.: Palestinian (Jerusalem) Talmud (Vilna or Krotoshin, as indicated)
P.W.: Pauly, Wissowa (Kroll, Mittelhaus, Ziegler), *Realencyclopaedie der classischen Altertumswissenschaft*, Stuttgart, 1894— (in progress)
R.: (Midrash) Rabba (any edition); for Leviticus Rabba: ed. M. Margulies, 5 vols., Jerusalem 1953–1960 (Gen. R., Deut. R., not quoted)
Tos.: Tosefta, ed. M. S. Zuckermandel; reprinted, Jerusalem 1962
W.H.: C. Wachsmuth, O. Hense, *Joannes Stobaeus, Anthologium*, 5 vols.; reprinted, Berlin 1958
Arrian-Epictetus, Aristotle, Athenaeus, Cicero (and *Auctor ad Herrenium*), Dio of Prusa, Hippocrates, Julian, Juvenal, Ovid (and *Ad Liviam*), Philo, Plato, Plutarch (and *Ad Apollonium*), Quintilian, *Scriptores Historiae Augustae*, Seneca, Varro, Xenophon: the texts as in *The Loeb Classical Library*, London, are sufficient for the purposes of this essay.

THE historian who wishes to utilize ancient literature for the reconstruction of Greco-Roman and Hellenistic Near Eastern history faces formidable difficulties indeed, for in any inquiry of

---

* This is the complete text of a paper the major parts of which were read at the Eighty-first Meeting of the American Historical Association in New York, December 29, 1966, at a Symposium on "The Impact of Hellenistic Civilization on the Pharisees." The terms Hellenistic and Greco-Roman are synonymous in this essay.

this sort the wide diffusion of Greco-Roman rhetoric in ancient sources must be recognized and accounted for. Rhetoric, whether in its oral or written crystallization, was apt to color historical reports and even to create, in its own way, non-history.

The classical and Hellenistic periods of both Greece and Rome witnessed a number of vital functions carried on in this medium. Thus, in his work on *The "Art" of Rhetoric*, Aristotle—who functions here as a summarizer rather than an innovator—distinguishes rhetoric in its use for literature, ... *graphikē* ..., and for debate, ... *agōnistikē* ..., and, apparently subdividing the latter, for public use, ... *dēmēgorikē* ..., i.e., politics, and in court, ... *dikanikē* ....[1] Philosophical and religious argument from the Sophists on was increasingly expressed in this medium. The propagation of new ideas and the preservation of proven traditional values were equally the task of rhetoric. It drew disciplines such as literary criticism, grammar, and exegesis, both critical and uncritical, both new and old, into its orbit. Precisely the same situation again prevailed in Roman culture. The writer, the teacher-philosopher, the critic-grammarian, the politician, and the lawyer-administrator—amazingly often combined in the same person—expressed themselves in this literary medium. Precisely the authors in whose works the great majority of parallels to Pharisaic stances are found, are prominent examples: Cicero (106–43), Seneca (5 B.C.–65), Dio of Prusa (Chrysostom, 40–after 112), Plutarch (c.46–after 120), and Aelianus (c.170–235)—the latter two are also priests[2]—but similarly also Philo (30 or 22 B.C.–c.45) and Paul (8–68 ?).

Apart from its style and technique, Greco-Roman rhetoric[3]

---

[1] III.xii.1, 1413b. In I.ii.7, 1356a, Aristotle discusses the close relationship between rhetoric and the disciplines of dialectic and ethics.

[2] For a brief survey of their political and administrational functions see *The Oxford Classical Dictionary*, 1964. Epictetus (c. 55–135), who should be on this list, was the slave of a secretary (*a libellis*) of Nero and Domitian, Epaphroditus, but in his later life he merely taught philosophy. Cf. further E.P. Parks, *The Roman Rhetorical School as a Preparation for the Courts under the Early Empire* (Johns Hopkins University Studies in History and Political Science, 63), Baltimore 1945.

[3] The modern literature on this subject is very large. Apart from P.W., "Rhetorik," Suppl. VII, 1940, 1039–1138, and standard histories of literature, such as W.v. Christ, W. Schmid, and O. Staehlin, *Geschichte der griechischen Literatur...*, 7 vols., Munich 1920—; H.J. Rose, *A Handbook of Greek Literature...*,[4] London 1951; M. Schanz, C. Hosius and G. Krueger, *Geschichte der roemischen Literatur*, 5 vols., Munich 1914–35, under revision; J. Wight Duff, *A Literary History of Rome...*,[3] 2 vols., New York 1960-64; these are among the more important titles

is characterized by its use of a great variety of larger literary forms, such as oration, diatribe,[4] essay, symposium, epistle, biography and others. These literary forms are composite and consist of a combination of a great many smaller independent literary (or oratorical) genres and a great many social concepts, values, and ideas. Moreover, rhetorical stances heavily penetrated other literary forms, such as aretalogy, martyrology, history, and romance, even poetic (metered) forms, such as comedy and satire.

In the Roman Age the rhetor-writer less frequently consulted original works and was no longer an adherent of any particular philosophical school—though he might choose one as the preferred target of his attacks.[5] He used ready-made handbooks, anthologies and collections of various kinds, including works on the lives and opinions of the philosophers (*bioi, vitae, memorabilia, apomnēmoneumata*), gnomologies, and even school exercises, many of which were created for the specific purpose of aiding the rhetor.[6] In all probability he did not neglect to consult the rhetorical production of others.[7] It is this entire immense phenomenon which is here

---

(that also will open up the entire field): E. Norden, *Die Antike Kunstprosa*[5], Darmstadt, reprinted 1958; G.M.A. Grube, *The Greek and Roman Critics*, Toronto 1965; J.F. Dobson, *The Greek Orators*, London 1919; B.A. van Groningen, *La composition littéraire archaïque grecque...*, Amsterdam 1958; W.R. Roberts, *Greek Rhetoric and Literary Criticism*, New York 1928; M.L. Clarke, *Rhetoric At Rome*, London 1953.

[4] In modern literature this term is occasionally used for rhetoric in general but actually signifies a Cynico-Stoic treatment of a theme by means of harangue, dialogue, wit, and continued argument, later used by all popular moralists as well as by Philo, Paul and Tertullian; see P. Wendland, *Die hellenistisch-roemische Kultur in ihren Beziehungen zu Judentum und Christentum*[2,3], Tuebingen 1912; A. Oltramare, *Les origines de la diatribe romaine*, Lausanne 1926 (defines this term too narrowly); Rudolf Bultmann, *Der Stil der paulinischen Predigt und die kynisch-stoische Diatribe*, Goëttingen 1910.

[5] This accounts for the divergence in ancient as well as modern opinions on rhetorically inclined writers as to their adherence to a particular philosophical school, as, for example, on Cicero, Musonius, Demetrius, Dio, Epictetus and others. Cf. the differing classifications of the same authors with D.L., D.R. Dudley, *A History of Cynicism*, London 1937, and Max Pohlenz, *Die Stoa*[2], 2 vols., Goettingen 1955–59.

[6] Cf. E. Ziebarth, *Aus dem griechischen Schulwesen*[2], Leipzig 1914, and *Aus der antiken Schule*[2], *Kleine Texte...* 65, Bonn 1913. D. Clark, *Rhetoric in Graeco-Roman Education*, New York 1957.

[7] This general condition of prose literature makes it rather incongruous to demand from Near Eastern writers more than from their Greco-Roman counterparts, and to accuse Aristeas, Philo, Paul or Clement of philosophical eclecticism.

called rhetoric—a use of the term in the widest of all its possible meanings.

In the rhetorical creations of the Hellenistic and Roman worlds, the figure and concept of the ideal Sage, the *sophos* or *sapiens*, plays a prominent part. He is most often a founder of a philosophical school or of a scientific discipline, or a lawgiver or creative statesman. Through his actions and words, wisdom—i.e., virtue, the use of reason, and closeness to nature—is taught in an exemplary manner. His courage, presence of mind, wit, and incisiveness are proverbial, and his personality attracts disciples and converts them to his way of life. Socrates is often expressly named as the principal model for this type of Sage, and in his image many other ancient founder-sages make their appearance in rhetoric:[8] thus Antisthenes, Diogenes, Crates, the youthful Zeno (all supposedly founders of different shades of Cynicism); Cleanthes, Chrysippus and Aristippus (all frequently treated as Cynics);[9] to a lesser degree and, probably later, Thales or all the Seven Sages;[10] further, Pythagoras, Democritus, Heraclitus, Aesopus,[11] Theodorus the Cyrenaic, Pericles, and some others.[12] Finally, even for Aristotle and some of Plato's successors, especially Xenocrates, a similar tradition began to develop.[13]

---

[8] The impact of Socrates seems to have reshaped Greek biography, according to A. Dihle, a recent contributor in a long list of predecessors: *Studien zur griechischen Biographie*, Goettingen 1956 (against F. Leo, *Die griechisch-roemische Biographie nach ihrer literarischen Form*, Leipzig 1901). Rhetorization is indicated in invented dialogues, as, for example, Satyrus' Euripides *vitae* (*Pap. Ox.* 1176, ed. F. Leo, *Nachrichten Goettinger gel. Ges.* 1912, 273ff.). Since Antigonus of Carystus (*fl.* 240 B.C.), portrayal of the person and personality became more important than technical concerns. The *ēthē* of the hero is illustrated by his *praxeis.*, see U.v. Wilamowitz-Moellendorff, *Antigonos von Karystos, Philol. Untersuch.* VI, Berlin 1881. Cf. also D.R. Stuart, *Epochs of Greek and Roman Biography*, Berkeley 1928.

[9] See "Cynicism" 5.5. Zeno is the founder of Stoicism, Aristippus, of the Cyrenaic school of philosophy.

[10] Bruno Snell, *Leben und Meinungen der Sieben Weisen*³, Tuebingen 1952.

[11] The Aesopus Romance, ed. Ben Edwin Perry, *Aesopica I*, Urbana 1952, is almost entirely rhetorical *sophos* material, set in the merest pretext of an aretalogical framework.

[12] See "Cynicism" 5.5f.

[13] I. Duering, *Aristotle In the Ancient Biographical Tradition*, Goeteborg 1957. Olof A. Gigon, "Interpretationen zu den antiken Aristotelesviten," *Museum Helveticum* 15, 1958, 146–193. In the Greek anecdote on the Sage (to be discussed below) Plato is a negative figure who, in syncrisis with Diogenes, usually loses the battle of wits and herein resembles Shammai of the Hebrew anecdote: D.L. VI. 24–26; 40 (but cf. 41); 58. Similarly in the Aristippus cycle: II.69; 78; 81.

This concept of the *sophos* finally encompassed not only reason, closeness to nature, and virtue, but also a certain type of cosmopolitanism (or, rather, universalism),[14] *philanthropia*, and even a strong approximation of monotheism,[15] contributed mainly by the Cynics and Stoics. Platonic and Pythagorean elements in rhetoric provided ideas of immortality. This new synthesis was characterized by the centrality of ethics, and in it the original contributions of the schools lost their technical character and even their identity (except when they were expressly quoted as the opinion of a specific school). This synthesis included the ennoblement and refinement of the ancient customs and myths through reinterpretation, and in spite of its cosmopolitanism, it was not hostile to a glorification of *patria*. With few exceptions, it was non-dualistic, i.e., it neither condemned matter as such nor apotheosized spirit or soul *per se*. This rhetorical "system" seems thus superficially to resemble the system connected with the name of the Pharisees and their Tannaitic successors.

The Pharisaic movement (c. 165 or 135–70 A.D.)[16] and its continuation in the culture of the Tannaim (70–200)—contrary to frequent claims of their isolation and autarky—apparently have been in close contact with Greco-Roman culture. The latter

---

[14] Cynic cosmopolitanism is not more than the feeling that the Sage belongs anywhere or nowhere. The Stoic variant is the claim that man is the citizen of a world state. Rhetorical cosmopolitanism often goes farther: it stresses that human nature and fate are one everywhere and that all men are equal before the tribunal of reason.

[15] Karl Joel, *Geschichte der antiken Philosophie*, I, Tuebingen 1921, has the most complete list of the positive achievements of the philosophical schools (especially Cynicism). Some of his overstatements have been corrected by subsequent scholarship.

[16] The vast literature is accessible through Salo W. Baron, *A Social and Religious History of the Jews*², 10 vols. (in progress), New York or Philadelphia 1952—(via *Index Volume* for vols. I-VIII) 1960. Cf. Sidney B. Hoenig's recent review, "Pharisaism Revisited," *Jew. Quart. Rev.* 61, 1966, 337–353, of L. Finkelstein, *The Pharisees*³, 2 vols. Philadelphia 1962.

Many of the observations in this paper are made on the Tannaitic successors of the actual Pharisees. Although there is a considerable difference between Pharisees and Tannaim, it is usually assumed that in some aspects of their function and teaching continuity prevailed. The formation of the literary genres described in this article may have occurred as early as a generation after the death of a hero, if not in his very lifetime after the achievement of fame. Although the sources at our disposal are Tannaitic, i.e., post-Pharisaic, some of the material may thus go back to Pharisaic times. Cp. Socrates' lifetime (469–399) and the formation of his legend with his younger contemporary Xenophon (c. 430–c. 354).

seems to have been the source for a significant number of early Pharisaic-Rabbinic parallels to Hellenistic materials, discovered and discussed by, among others, Saul Lieberman,[17] Yitshak F. Baer,[18] Leo Baeck,[19] David Daube,[20] Siegfried Stein,[21] Hans (Johanan) Lewy,[22] Edmund (Menahem) Stein,[23] Elias J. Bickerman,[24] Morton Smith,[25] Rudolf Meyer,[26] A.A. (Elimelech Epstein) Hallewy,[27] and, in the field of jurisprudence, Boas Cohen.[28] Unlike earlier writers, such as Judah Bergmann[29] and Arnold Kaminka,[30]

[17] *Greek in Jewish Palestine; Hellenism in Jewish Palestine*, New York 1942 and 1950.

[18] *Yisra'el ba-'amim*, Jerusalem 1955.

[19] *The Pharisees and Other Essays*, New York 1947.

[20] "Rabbinic Methods of Interpretation and Hellenistic Rhetoric," *Hebrew Union College Annual* 22, 1949, 239–264; "Alexandrinian Methods of Interpretation and the Rabbis," *Festschrift Hans Lewald*, Basel 1953, 21–44, etc.

[21] "The Influence of Symposia Literature and the Literary Form of the Pesach Haggadah," *Journal of Jew. Studies* 8, 1957, 13-44.

[22] "Ein Rechtsstreit um den Boden Palaestinas im Altertum," *Monatsschr. fuer Geschichte und Wissensch. des Judentums* 77, 1933, 84-99, 172-180; '*Olamoth nifgashim*, Jerusalem 1960.

[23] "Die homiletische Peroratio im Midrasch," *Hebrew Union College Annual* 8-9, 1931-32, 353-371.

[24] "The Civil Prayer For Jerusalem," *Harvard Theol. Rev.* 60, 1962, 163-186; "The Maxim of Antigonus of Socho," *ibid.* 64, 1951, 153-165.

[25] "The Image of God," *Bull. of the John Rylands Libr.* 40, 1958, 473-512; "Palestinian Judaism in the First Century," in Moshe Davis, ed., *Israel: Its Role in Civilization*, New York 1956.

[26] *Hellenistisches in der rabbinischen Anthropologie*, BWANT 74, Stuttgart 1937.

[27] *Sha'are ha'aggadah*, Tel-Aviv 1963, and a number of articles in *Tarbits* (*Tarbiz*), Jerusalem (29, 1959; 31, 1961) and *Me'assef*, Tel-Aviv (5–6, 1965) on the "Aggadists and the Greek Grammarians," "Aggadic Exegesis and Homeric Exegesis," and "On Prophecy" (Heb.).

[28] *Jewish and Roman Law*, 2 vols., New York 1966. Cf. I. Sonne, "The Schools of Shammai and Hillel Seen From Within," *Louis Ginzberg Jubilee* Vol. I, New York 1945, 275-291.

The series of preceding items does not account for a host of contributions in the field of architecture, art, music, epigraphy, and political and material history by many other scholars, nor for earlier contributors whose works are still important, such as Heinrich Graetz, Emil Schuerer, Manuel Joel, I.N. Weinstein, Israel Lévy, Wilhelm Bousset, Isaak Heinemann, Samuel Krauss and many others. On A. Marmorstein below.

[29] "Die Stoische Philosophie und die juedische Froemmigkeit," *Judaica* (Festschrift Hermann Cohen), Berlin 1913, 143–166 (denies interdependence in spite of acknowledged resemblance).

[30] Among others "Les rapports entre le rabbinisme et la philosophie stoïcienne," *Rev. des Études Juives* 82, 1926, 232–252. A number of essays of this type are included in vol. 2 of his *Meḥḳarim*, Tel-Aviv 1951. It is obvious that by then this important scholar had become more cautious.

these scholars have been cautious enough not to ascribe all of the parallel material to any one Greek philosophical school. Popular Greco-Roman rhetoric (rhetoric in its widest sense) in this attempted synthesis as the actual source of such Pharisaic parallels, however, has not yet been seriously suggested in any of the previous enterprises.[31]

If such a hypothesis has any merit, a few preliminary methodological questions are in order. Before any effort is made to utilize materials of rhetorical coloration, whether Greco-Roman or Near Eastern,[32] for historiography or biography, the question of the literary genre of the material involved must be clarified.

If we find, for example, that the political fable plays a role in both cultures, we are fully aware of the fact that the animals never actually did what they are said to have done in the narrative—although the use of this particular genre and its lessons does presuppose a certain historical reality. If, however, this genre is transformed into a type of anecdote in which the clever or good animal is replaced by a Sage and the dumb or wicked animal by his antagonist (be it a member of an opposed school, or a fool, debauchee or tyrant),[33] the modern scholar has too often been

---

[31] A number of the attempts mentioned above rightly compare, for example, talmudic-midrashic exegesis or Pharisaic exercise-practice (*askēsis*) with appropriate Hellenistic sources and admit various kinds of interrelation. The question of the immediate and specific source of this adoption is, however, left open (and is, in any case, not the subject of these essays). The working hypothesis of this essay is that the Aggadists (and to some extent the Halachists) did not have to consult difficult works on the "art of rhetoric" but could gain their insight into Hellenism from the popularized form of rhetoric (which was the usual medium of the Greco-Roman writer-scholar-administrator class, too). They may have encountered this medium in its oral crystallization, since oral communication was ubiquitous in Palestine (occupational forces, Roman administration, wandering preachers, Greek colonists, Hellenistic-Jewish pilgrims, Herod's Court, Jewish evacuees from Greek cities in the Hasmonean period, etc.). But with their certain knowledge of Greek (cf. Greek marriage documents among recent finds) the availability of even one copy of a rhetorical work could go a long way.

[32] Of course, other Near Eastern literary cultures, such as the Samaritan, Phoenician-Punic, pre-Koranic Arab, (Hellenistic-) Babylonian, native Egyptian (in Greek garb), and early Christian, must have encountered Greco-Roman rhetoric, too.

[33] Reference is to the *chria*, to be discussed forthwith. The possibility of the derivation of this genre from the fable is occasionally mentioned: C.v. Wartensleben, *Begriff der griechischen Chreia und Beitraege zur Geschichte ihrer Form* (Diss.), Heidelberg 1901; W. Gemoll, *Das Apophthegm*, Wien 1924; G.A. Gerhard, *Phoinix von Kolophon*, Leipzig 1909; Sophie Trenkner, *The Greek Novella In the Classical*

tempted to consider every detail as true history. Here a habit of classical scholarship has perhaps reinforced this error, i.e., the inclusion of an anecdote of this type among the genuine works of the philosophers by the editors of sources and fragments.[34] The question as to precisely where and when Alexander the Great met Diogenes the Cynic has been discussed by serious historians on the grounds of information supplied by anecdotal literature[35] —although no one has as yet attempted to compute the strength of the sun in which Diogenes basked when Alexander offered him the fulfillment of any wish and received the now famous request to stay out of the sun.[36] When it comes to the question of what really transpired at this supposed meeting, we find quite a number of widely different witticisms in these stories, all indicative of non-historicity.[37]

In a recent study[38] the present writer has dealt with this type of anecdote, called most often *chreia* by the Greeks and *chria* by the

---

Period, Cambridge 1958; Ben Edwin Perry, "Fable" [sic], *Studium Generale* 12, Berlin 1959, 17–37.

[34] e.g., J.v. Arnim, *Stoicorum veterum fragmenta*, 4 vols., Leipzig 1921–24; H. Diels, *Doxographi Graeci*, Berlin 1879 (reprinted 1958); H. Diels, W. Kranz, *Die Fragmente der Vorsokratiker*⁷, Berlin 1954. More cautious, A.C. Pearson, in his *The Fragments of Zeno and Cleanthes*, London 1891, listed obvious anecdotes separately. To be sure, some of the aforementioned knew of this pitfall and even warned of it in their introductions, but the factual inclusion of anecdotes proved a strong temptation to the user.

[35] E.g., W.W. Tarn, "Alexander, Cynics and Stoics," *Amer. Journal of Philol.* 60, 1939, 41–70.

[36] Plutarch, *Alex.* XIV.2: "stand a little out of the sun"; D.L. VI.38: "get out of my light." On the problem of the verb in the latter see Liddell-Scott, *Greek-English Lexicon*⁹, Oxford 1940, s.v. *aposkotizō* II.

[37] Alexander, who neither entirely nor wholeheartedly followed Aristotle, would hardly have been attracted by a less sophisticated philosopher (his "meeting" with the Indian Gymnosophists notwithstanding, since the latter seems to represent the same apocryphal cynicizing tradition. See in detail "Cynicism" 16.6). Cf. also Luitpold Wallach, "Indian Gymnosophists in Hebrew Tradition," *Proc. of the Amer. Acad. for Jew. Research* 11, 47–83.

The obviousness of the stereotype of the clash between the (Founder-) Sage representing virtue, freedom, and simplicity and the Ruler as a representative of tyranny or *typhos* (vain luxury) in the cynicizing *chria* and related genres is, of course, a decisive factor in judging on the historicity of a story. Practically all conspicuous rulers have thus been affected (Xerxes, Sardanapalus, Croesus, Midas, Archelaus, Cleomenes III, Mausolus, Dionysius of Syracuse the Younger, etc.). A new set of such anti-heroes in the persons of oppressive Roman emperors appears in Near Eastern and Alexandrinian literature from the time of the Principate on.

[38] "Cynicism."

Romans.[39] In this literary genre the Sage appears in an encounter or demonstration which is most often odd and witty, if not bizarre. The most extreme form, the burlesque *chria*, is usually told of the Sages of the Cynics, and of their associates, predecessors or descendents, and the ethic involved is strongly cynicizing. Stressing the rational in man and the simple life in conformity with nature, these terse stories are entirely free of the miraculous and the supernatural.

The cynicizing *chria* with many of its major motifs, forms, and elements is found also in Tannaitic literature. Without exception, all the stories on Hillel the Elder[40]—as distinct from brief historical notes and the actual halachic-technical materials—prove to be Greek-chriic, representing either (a) a complete Greek *chria*; (b) a composite of several chriic parts; or (c) an aggregate of the smallest meaningful chriic elements (henceforth called motemes) which, in these stories, achieve narrative unity precisely in the manner of the Greek *chria*.[41] Furthermore, some Hillel *chriae* are joined to one another within a narrative framework precisely as in Hellenistic sources.[42]

---

[39] Thus in ancient headings or expressly by ancient literary critics, such as (Pseudo-?) Demetrius of Phaleron, Bassus, Quintilian, Hermogenes and Theon. A somewhat different use of the term is reflected in Harry Caplan's modern use in his edition and translation of *Rhetorica (Auctor) ad (C.) Herrenium*. There are a number of parallel terms in ancient literature for our *chriae: apophthegmata, apomnēmoneumata, exempla*, etc., see in detail "Cynicism" 8.2-3.

[40] The great Pharisaic leader, an approximate contemporary of Herod the Great (41-4 B.C.).

[41] Treated in detail in "Cynicism" V (on the atomistic structure of the *chria*). The talmudic use of the *chria* and its narrative techniques does not exclude ingenuity if not creativity in the recombination of elements and the synthesis of the new story.

[42] One of the largest collections outside the gnomologies and Stobaeus is D.L.'s account of Diogenes of Sinope (the Cynic, VI.20-81) in which he used several independent sources, among others probably a collection called *Diogenis Prasis* (The Sale of Diogenes), which was used also by Philo (four items in *Quod omn.*, 121ff.). Other such accumulations, with or without a special framework, occur throughout D.L.'s work as well as that of Plutarch (especially in his *Laconica*, in sections on Pericles and Alcibiades—both associates of Socrates—in *Mor.* 461 D, i.e., *de cohib. ira*, etc.); all of Papyrus Vienna, in W. Croenert, *Kolotes und Menedemus*, Leipzig 1906, 50-52; part of Papyrus Bouriant (ff. VI-VIII, Ziebarth, "Schule," No. 46); Cicero's *Tusculan Disputations* (e.g., I.xliii.102ff.); the bawdy Machon collection in Athenaeus' *Deipnosophistae*, cf. now A.S.F. Gow, *Machon, the Fragments*, Cambridge 1965; and all of Lucian's moving accounts of *Demonax*. An early non-burlesque accumulation is found in Xenophon's *Memorabilia* III.xiii

Others affected by chriization are Eliezer ben Hyrcanus (*fl.* 70–100; his opponent Joshua only in syncrisis with him), to a lesser degree R. Meir (second century), and, still less, his teacher Akiba (c.50–135), whose portrait, however, is affected by actual folklore.[43]

To be sure, a Pharisaic Sage could have consciously followed the example of a Greek chriic Sage. However, a considerable number of the events reported in the Pharisaic *chriae* happen *to* the Sage. The beginning of the career of the *sophos* is encouraged by ambiguous or opaque oracles (Socrates, Diogenes, Zeno, Hillel)[44] and his life's work is endorsed by an oracular encomium (Thales, Socrates, Hillel).[45] In the famous episode on Passover[46] the following Greek chriic motifs are involved, in almost all of which the Sage is passive:

(1) The Sage is a foreigner.[47]
(2) The Sage encounters natives who perform a clever trick with sheep.[48]
(3) The Sage utters what later will be (or already was) a proverb regarding the natives and their sons.[48]

---

and xiv, beginnings. The most famous talmudic series occurs in BT Shabbat 30b, partially paralleled in AdRN A, ch. 15; B, ch. 29. All accumulations, whether Greco-Roman or Tannaitic, have similar key-words or key-situations: "seeing," guests, proselytes, burials, Spartans, disturbances, the Sage-slave, etc.

[43] See Dan Ben-Amos, *Narrative Forms in the Haggadah; A Structural Analysis* (Diss.) Bloomington, Ind., 1966; the *chria* is not treated in this dissertation.

[44] Usually in the beginnings of the reports of D.L. on the individual philosophers. For Hillel: BT Sotah 21a.

[45] D.L. I.28–33; II.37. For Hillel: BT Sotah 48b and parallels; PT Sotah IX.16 (24c end, Vilna; 24b middle, Krotoshin). On this and the preceding note cf. "Cynicism" 29.1-30.3.

[46] Longest version: PT Pes. VI.1 (33a Krotoshin); medium: BT Pes. 66a; shortest: Tos. Pes. IV.1-3. Motemes (1)–(5) are found in all three in slightly different combinations and with some variants.

[47] This moteme further frustrates Kaminka's repeated attempt to identify the historical Hillel as a native of Alexandria. The *sophos* in the *chria* and the *thaumaston* (more on this below) is a "foreigner," because this stance gives him greater scope to marvel at the "outlandish" customs of the "civilized" nations and to criticize them more freely. A similar misuse of chriic material is Kaminka's identification of the floating skull of P.A. 2.7 (*ibid.*), a rhetorical item amply paralleled with that of Pompey in Egypt! Cf. A. Kaminka, "Hillel's Life and Work," *Jew. Quart. Rev.* 30, 1939-40, 107-122 and a criticism of several similar attempts in "Cynicism" 24.9.

[48] Motemes (1)–(3): D.L. VI.41. An early date for this Greek *chria* seems to be certain on the grounds of Augustus' witty allusion to D.L.'s "punchline" ("it is better to be a Megarian's ram than his son") when commenting on Herod's

(4) The Sage forgets essentials of his teaching.[49]
(5) The Sage becomes suddenly and unexpectedly the head of the academy.[50]

It would be difficult, even for a Sage, to arrange for all this, and the story must be counted as unhistorical in view of the parallel material in Greek, partly told of Thales, partly of Cleanthes and Xenocrates, and, motifs (1)–(3) as a complete *chria*, of Diogenes at Megara.

Another important branch of classical culture, consolation literature,[51] had from its very (Sophist) beginning and owing to its very purpose, strong affinities to rhetoric, presenting, as it does, a continuous argument of urgency and persuasion. Most major ancient prose writers made a contribution to it, whether in Greek or in Latin.[52] After having absorbed actual rhetorical materials,

---

treatment of his son ("I would rather be Herod's pig than his son"), preserved in Macrobius, *Saturnalia* II.iv.11 (erroneously attached to the Slaughter of the Innocents by Macrobius).

[49] E.g., Thales, D.L. I.34.

[50] Cleanthes, D.L. VII.174. Xenocrates in the later Aristotle tradition, cf. n. 13. Sudden luck in court for both: D.L. VII.169; IV.8ff.
In a completely different study, employing different methods, Professor E.E. Urbach arrives at the result that Hillel was not the Patriarch of Israel and not the permanent president of the Sanhedrium. His study is based on the inner evidence of factual bits in the talmudic sources regarding status, title and function of the Palestinian Sages, without resort to Greco-Roman literature. Cf. "Class-Status and Leadership in the World of the Palestinian Sages," *The Israel Academy of Sciences and Humanities, Proceedings* II, no. 4, Jerusalem 1966 (separate edition).

[51] Among modern treatments: Rudolf Kassel, *Untersuchungen zur griechischen und roemischen Konsolationsliteratur*, Munich 1958. Constant Martha (sic), *Études morales sur l'antiquité*³, Paris 1896, 135–189; Chas. Favez, *La Consolation Latine Chrétienne*, Paris 1937; *idem*, introductions to his editions of Seneca's *Ad Marciam de consolatione*, Paris 1928 and *Ad Helviam matrem de consolatione*, Paris 1918. Mary E. Fern, *The Latin Consolation As Literary Type*, St. Louis 1941; Mary Evaristus (Moran), *The Consolations of Death In Ancient Greek Literature* (Diss.), Washington, D.C., 1917. Still important: Car(o)l(us) Buresch, *Consulationum a Graecis Romanisque scriptarum historia critica*, Leipzig 1886.

[52] Crantor (360–268) with his exemplary *Peri penthous pros Hippoklea* (now lost, Jerome still remembered it)—the "Golden Book" (Cicero)—ushered in the post-Sophistic development. The most famous examples come from works and writers that also otherwise proved close to Pharisaic-Tannaitic items in the earlier study ("Cynicism"), such as Cicero (*Tusc. Disp.* I and III, *Ep. ad Fam.* (to or from him) IV.5; V.16, 18; VI. 3. *Brut.* I.9, etc.); Seneca, *Ad Marciam* (*Dial.* VI), *ad Helviam* (*Dial.* XII), as in n.51; *ad Polybiam* (*Dial.* XI); Ep. 63, 81, 93, 99, 107; (Pseudo-) Plutarch, *Ad Apollonium*; poetic: (Pseudo-) Ovid, *Ad Liviam*. The Church Fathers adopted the classical *consolatio* almost intact.

the *consolatio* entered the mainstream of rhetoric through a wide diffusion of its stories, arguments, and motemes, many of which became attached to the Sage.[53] Thus, on the occasion of a tragic event, usually death but also exile,[54] the Sage comforts or is comforted himself. A whole series of stories tells us that two children of the same hero died on the same day: so with Pericles, Anaxagoras, L. Paullus, Lucius Bibulus, a priestess of Juno, and others; so with R. Meir,[55] R. Ishmael,[56] and, according to one version, R. Akiba.[57] Not only this framework but also the arguments of comfort and the similes involved in a number of Tannaitic parallels suggest a common rhetorical background for this genre also.[58]

A third area of rhetorical literature suggests still another *sophos* genre, as yet little explored and little understood.[59] In rhetoric, especially in the popular doxographic works and their Tannaitic counterparts, a body of legends on the schools seems to have been current. It consists of stories or statements on the following subjects:

(1) The number of the Sage's pupils, whether few or many, and whether received with a "smiling face" or driven away with a stick—both motemes being claimed for Shammai, Hillel's contemporary and opponent in chriic (and halachic) syncrisis![60]

(2) A typology of learning, i.e., different characteristics found in teachers or disciples, the final sources of which seem to be Plato's

---

[53] The present writer has begun to trace these in Tannaitic literature.

[54] Ironical, on a monetary loss: Juvenal, *Satires* XIII. In the aretalogy: in prison, Apollonius consoles the inmates, Philostratus, *Life of A. of Tyana* VII.26. According to Seneca (after Posidonius) *Ep.* 95.65, the Sage-Philosopher needs, for the teaching of "average" practical virtue, not only "praeceptio" (principles) but also "suasio," "consolatio" (*logos paramythētikos*) and "exhortatio."

[55] Midrash Mishle 31; AdRN A, ch. 24.

[56] BT Moʻed Katan 28b.

[57] BT Moʻed Katan 21b. In (post-BT) Semahoth 8, however, only one son is mentioned. W. Bacher, *Die Agada der Tannaiten*¹, Strasbourg 1884, p. 305, n.3, tries to dissolve this discrepancy as a misreading of Akiba's speech, in which he mentions several sons in a simile. However, the gradual penetration (or the memory) of rhetoric stances creates precisely such discrepancies ("Cynicism," *passim*). The death of two sons as a simile occurs in Lam.R. (Proems) II; as a memory of Aharon's two sons in Lam. R. 20.1.

[58] The story of R. Meir's marriage to Beruria, the comforting she-Sage of one story, seems to be a variant of the purported quasi-experimental marriages of the Cynic philosophers to similar spouses, among them Hipparchia and Arete, D.L. VI.96–98; II.86.

[59] Dealt with in "Cynicism" 32.1–33.2.

[60] BT Shabbat, *loc. cit.*, versus P.A. 1.15 (1.16). On syncrisis see F. Focke, "Synkrisis," *Hermes* 58, 1923, 327-368.

Theaetetus and Hesiod's Ages of Mankind, as applied by the Cynic Bion (c. 325-255).[61]

(3) The *diadochē* of the school leaders, usually seven following each other, i.e., a rhetorical-doxographic pattern.[62]

(4) The two simultaneous leaders who are supposed to have headed the academies.[63]

(5) Difficult questions, *akousmata* or *erōtēmata* (*problēmata*) and their answers, usually of an ethical nature, requiring the definition of the *summum bonum*. Iamblichus distinguishes three different forms in his *Life of Pythagoras*, 18.81-82 (Deubner).

(6) Near-"unanswerable" questions, *apora*, or *aporiai* (*aporiae*), and their final answers ("Of what are there more, of the living or of the dead?").[64]

(7) The *sophos*, as a "hero" of virtue, possessing immense, encyclopedic knowledge, including the ability to write fables.[65]

---

[61] *Theaetetus* 191-195; Stobaeus XXXI.97 (vol.II, p. 218 W.-H.); D.L. VII.37; Cicero, *Part. orat.* VI.21, *de orat.* II.88.360; *Auctor ad Herren.* III.17.30 (Shakespeare, Hamlet I.5.98); AdRN B, ch. 28 and many parallels; P.A. 2.8 (2.10f.); AdRN B, ch. 29, 58f.; P.A. 5.15 (5.18) ff; 5.12 (5.15). Cf. Plutarch, *Mor.* 78 E.

Judah Goldin has recently commented on the passage AdRN B, ch. 29, and several other passages referring to Johanan ben Zakkai's academy, *Traditio* 21, 1965, 1-21, "A Philosophical Session in a Tannaitic Academy"; similarly, *Harry Austryn Wolfson Jubilee Volume*, Heb. Section, Jerusalem 1965, 69-92, "*Mashehu 'al beth midrasho shel Rabban Yohanan ben Zakkai*." The atmosphere of Pharisaic-Tannaitic teaching becomes alive in these articles. The historical assertions, however, that, for example, an actual session on the particular subject took place and that the teachings are actually authored by the teachers mentioned, are, owing to the rhetorical-legendary nature of this material, highly improbable. Cf. n. 83.

[62] Cf. D.L.'s seven "Cynics." That there is an affinity to Hellenistic sources in similar structurings, for example in P.A. ch.1 (the sevenfold pattern as such has been described by L. Finkelstein in his *Mabo' le-masichtoth Aboth ve-AdRN*, New York 1950), has been effectively asserted by Élie (Elias J.) Bickerman, "La chaîne de la tradition pharisienne," *Revue Biblique* 59, 1952, 44-54 (a comparison with doxographic-diadochic patterns) and by Boas Cohen, "Peculium in Jewish and Roman Law," *op. cit.*, vol. I, 275ff. (comparison with the legal-historical Encheiridion of Pomponius, 129 A.D.). It is possible that both patterns may have merged in the consciousness of the rhetoricians when both jurisprudence and philosophy became aspects of the *sophos* concept.

[63] Cf. titles in n. 13, above.

[64] See "Cynicism" 11.16; related material in L.W. Daly and W. Suchier, "Altercatio Hadriani Augusti et Epicteti Philosophi," *Ill. Studies in Language and Literature*, 24, Nos. 1-2, Urbana, 1939, pp. 12, 17, 26.

[65] Although true for some of the Greek philosophers, the assertion of encyclopedic knowledge becomes a literary stereotype. Its Tannaitic equivalent, for example, the assertion that a Sage knew Halacha, Aggada, Mishna, Midrash, etc., down to the language of animals and plants, should therefore not be used as an unchecked

Almost all of these themes may occur as *chriae*, or brief dialogues (eristic form), or as factual statements.[66]

Similarly, another startling phenomenon is found in both cultures. The same gnome (aphorism, *sententia*, saying) may be quoted in the name of several different Sages, thus making for contradictory features in the overall portrait of a particular Sage. Further, and more important, the same gnome may occur:

(1) As the "punchline" of a *chria*,
(2) As an independent unit, without a story,
(3) Anonymously, often as a popular proverb,
(4) Occasionally as the moral of a fable.

It thus seems that the ascription of a *sententia* to a Sage might merely have been another means of stressing his importance and does not reflect an actual teaching of his. The Golden Rule, in a number of slightly different patterns, appears thus in connection with an impressive number of Greek and Roman rhetorical writers, put in the mouth of a Sage within a *chria*, or in a dialogue, or as an independent item in a gnomology.[67] It also appears in Hellenistic-Jewish rhetoric, in the Gospels and the Didache, and in chriic form attached to Hillel and Akiba. In all these cultures it is frequently accompanied by the same test case or by the assertion that the Golden Rule is a *kephalaion*, a basic and all-embracing rule, i.e., the "whole Torah" of the Midrash, and the "Law and the Prophets" of the Gospels, the Greek formulation preceding its Near Eastern parallels by centuries. To be sure, various forms of the Golden Rule had been current earlier in the Near East in general (Ahikar) and in Judaism in particular (Tobit, Sirah), as they were in other probably unrelated cultures (China, India).[68]

---

claim for the emergence of mysticism but can be regarded as an indication that "arcane" knowledge was important at the time of the creation of the legend.

The claim of having written fables is already doubtful for Socrates, Plutarch, *Mor.* 16 C after *Phaedo* 60 d. Fables recommended in Aristotle's *Rhetoric* II.xx.5-8, 1393 b-1394 a. Thus also for Solon, Antisthenes, Hillel, Meir and Akiba. Legendary fable tellers may become rhetorical (or "Cynic-Stoic") heroes: Odysseus, Aesopus. In detail in "Cynicism," 32.5.2.

[66] See "Cynicism" 11.16ff. for discussion and sources.

[67] For detailed references and discussion of the entire subject see "Cynicism" 19.16-20.

[68] Cf. L. Philippides, *Die Goldene Regel* (Diss.), Leipzig 1929; H.H. Rowley, "The Chinese Sages and the Golden Rule," *Bull. John Rylands Libr.* 1940, 321-352; A. Dihle, *Die Goldene Regel*, Goettingen 1962.

Story and history: observations on Greco-Roman Rhetoric and Pharisaism 73

The point here made is that Greco-Roman rhetoric reactivated and reformulated older original materials in the Near East.[69] A common historical fate, first under Alexander the Great, and then under the Roman Empire, must have favored this process.

However this may be, the genres used by both Greco-Roman rhetoric and Tannaitic literature must be recognized and evaluated. For Greco-Roman literature in general some of this task has been undertaken by classicists,[70] by New Testament scholars,[17] and more recently by folklorists.[72] The field is still wide open, however, for the same task in Tannaitic literature, in spite of the pleadings of the late Arthur Marmorstein[73] and recently of Jacob Neusner.[74] Apart from preliminary attempts, mostly in the form of prolegomena, some serious beginnings have been made,[75] especially in

---

[69] Lev. 19.18 may thus have been the original form of the Golden Rule in earlier Jewish culture, cf. Targum Lev. 19.18. Lev. and the rhetorical echoes together in the Akiba story.

[70] Among others, by Norden, *op. cit.*, Gerhard, *op. cit.*, Perry, *op. cit.*, R. Hirzel, *Der Dialog* I, Leipzig 1895; R. Reitzenstein, *Hellenistische Wundererzaehlungen²*, Leipzig, reprinted 1963; Eliz. Haight, *The Roman Use of Anecdotes In Cicero, Livy and the Satirists*, New York 1940; John Barns, "A New Gnomologium...," *Class. Quart.* 44 and 45, 1950 and 1951, 126-137 and 1-19. Scattered items in P.W. (cf. Index in vol. 23; 9 of 1959—which is exclusive of vol. 24;9A1 and Supplements IX-X) and v. Christ, Schmid, Staehlin, *op. cit.*, index.

[71] G. Rudberg's articles in *Symbolae Osloenses* 14 and 15, *Theol. Studien und Kritiken* C11; *Coniectanea Neotestamentica* II, etc., and the movement of Formgeschichte, especially the work of Rudolf Bultmann and Martin Dibelius.

[72] André Jolles, *Einfache Formen²*, Darmstadt 1930 (reprinted 1958); Trenkner, *op. cit.*; C.W.v. Sydow, "*Kategorien der Prosa-Volksdichtung,*" in *Selected Papers On Folklore*, Copenhagen 1948, 60-88; Kurt Ranke, "Einfache Formen," in *Suppl. Fabula*, Berlin 1961, 1-11.

[73] "The Background of the Haggadah," *Hebrew Union College Annual* 6, 1929, 184. He was aware of the relationship between "diatribe" and Midrash, but preferred a mixture of literary and theological analysis to a technical one. (His essays are reprinted in *Studies in Jewish Theology*, Memorial Vol., ed. J. Rabbinowitz and M.S. Lew, Oxford 1950).

[74] *A Life of Rabbi Yohanan ben Zakkai...*, Leiden 1962, p. 3.

[75] E.g., in Birger Gerhardsson's *Memory and Manuscript*, Uppsala 1961 (criticized in W.D. Davies, *The Setting of the Sermon on the Mount*, Cambridge 1964, Appendix XV); E. Stein, *op. cit.*; Dov Noy's extensive writings: Diss., an analysis of Hebrew material— yet unpublished—as an addition to Stith Thompson, *Motif Index of Folk Literature*, 6 vols., Bloomington, Ind., 1955-58; *ha-sippur ha-'amami...*, Jerusalem 1960 (mimeographed); *mabo' le-sifrut ha-aggada*, *ibid.*, 1961 (mimeographed.) Benjamin de Vries' "The Literary Nature of the Haggada," (Heb.), *Niger Jubilee Vol.*, ed. Arthur Biram *et. al.*, Soc. for Bibl. Research, Jeru-

the pioneering work of Siegfried Stein on symposia literature,[76] that branch of ancient literature which described a banquet as "a fellowship of seriousness and gaiety, and of discourse and activity," as Plutarch has it,[77] and finally began to include the treatment of food and eating habits as part of the conversation, culminating in Athenaeus' 15-"volume" *Deipnosophistae*. Sympotic literature of the Roman period leans heavily on rhetorical genres and devices, and rhetoric, in turn, has made heavy use of it.

Systematic treatment is overdue also for the smallest literary elements of rhetoric,[78] for motemes, as we called the minimal motif-like independent element, and for similemes, as one could call the minimal basis in literary comparison, such as in parable, metaphor, simile, and others. Such similemes are: the soul as a guest; life as a deposit; the choice of two ways at the crossroads;[79] the athlete; the craftsman; the statue; the theatre and the circus; all common in Hellenistic rhetoric as well as Tannaitic and Amoraic (200–500) Midrash.[80] Another such elementary unit is the numerical saying, i.e., items stating summarily the number of various phenomena, such as Anacharsis' three grapes of the vine—pleasure, drunkenness, disgust—and Thales' (or Socrates' or Plato's) three reasons for gratitude—to be a human, and not a beast; a man, and

---

salem 1959, 303-309, is a precarious attempt to prove that Gunkel's biblical categories are applicable to the Midrash. Cf. also Ben-Amos, *op. cit*. Mostly concerned with later periods is Bernard Heller, "Das hebraeische und arabische Maerchen," in J. Bolte, G. Polívka, *Anmerkungen zu den Kinder- und Hausmaerchen der Brueder Grimm*, 5 vols., Leipzig 1913-32, vol. IV, 315-418. For earlier articles on fable and *mashal* see Ben-Amos and Emanuel bin Gorion, *Shevile ha-aggada*, Jerusalem 1949.

[76] *Op. cit.*, n. 21.

[77] *Mor.* 708 D, *Quaestiones conviviales*.

[78] As distinct from genre research. The motemes of the *chria*, as far as they are pertinent for Tannaitic literature, have been treated in "Cynicism" IV, "The Atomistic Structure of the Chria."

[79] That is, the famous "Choice of Heracles," also called "Heracles at the Crossroads" or Prodicus' Fable, as in, for example, Xenophon's *Memorabilia* II.i.21ff. Its use and role in Greco-Roman literature, especially in Cynicism, are amply treated in Karl Joel's *Der echte und der xenophontische Sokrates*, 3 vols., Berlin 1893-1901.

[80] Parallels usually concern a single item but a sequence of similes attached to a *chria* on Hillel in *Lev.R.* 34.3, 776f., is paralleled by a similar sequence in Seneca, *Ep.* 64.9-10, see "Cynicism" 15.10f. This practically eliminates the possibility of coincidence.

Story and history: observations on Greco-Roman Rhetoric and Pharisaism 75

not a women; a Greek, and not a barbarian,[81] the latter being paralleled in the Tannaitic daily morning prayer[82]—Zeno's seven sophisms, D.L. VII.25, the seven treatments of a theme (among them hermeneutics) in *Auctor ad Herrenium* IV.iv. 57ff. (written c.85 B.C.), and Hillel's seven (occasionally three) hermeneutic rules, Tos. Sanhedrin 7 end. Proverbs; catalogues of vices and virtues;[83] and *thaumasta*, i.e., terse narratives expressing the

---

[81] D.L. I.103; I.33; Lactantius, *Div. Instit.* III.19 (Plato) cf. Plutarch, *Marius* 46.1 (third blessing: to be a contemporary of Socrates). On the parallels to the three (or four) stages of drunkenness of the Anacharsis item in midrashic and other cultures, see Max Gruenbaum, *Gesammelte Aufsaetze zur Sprach- und Sagenkunde*, ed. Felix Perles, Berlin 1901: "Die verschiedenen Stufen der Trunkenheit in der Sage dargestellt," pp. 435-441. Another example of the basic genre: Plato's three *archai*: God, matter, idea, as in (Pseudo-)Plutarch's (Aetius') *De placit. philos.* (quoted as Plutarch in Diels, *Doxographi*, p.1) and the three Tannaitic "things on which the world rests," i.e., *archai*, in P.A.1.2. and 1.18 (1.19): Torah, (Temple-)cult, active loving-kindness, etc.

[82] Initial blessings: "...not a barbarian; ...not a slave; ...not a woman," S. Baer, *Seder 'Avodath Yisra'el*, rev. ed., New York 1937. Cf. Tos. Berakhoth 7.18, p. 16, 1.22, BT Menahoth 43b; PT Ber. IX.2, 13b (Judah b. Ilai or R. Meir!); cf. Paul in Gal. 3.28. Cf. Ismar Elbogen, *Der juedische Gottesdienst*[3], Frankfurt 1931, p. 90.

[83] J. Goldin, *Traditio*, p. 12, failing to recognize the genre, considers (the five-fold catalogue of virtues and vices of) P.A. 2.9f. (2.12f.) as philosophical material once discussed at an actual session. Actually, it is closer to folklore, as are so many numerical sayings and "catalogues" in rhetoric, or, at best, popular-rhetorical ethics, and this is also the reason for the missing mention of Torah in the passage. Such catalogues are frequent, too, in early Christian non-philosophical works such as the Didache. To be sure, ethical propositions were prominently discussed in the Hellenistic philosophical schools but, as it seems, in a more technical and systematic manner. Johannes Straub, in his *Heidnische Geschichtsapologetik in der christlichen Spaetantike*, Bonn 1963, p. 113, represents a minority opinion in his assumption that for practical purposes the philosophical schools taught *Vulgaerethik* (under the term of *hypothētikos logos* and other terms) as a permissible popular summarization of the usual formal and technical (analytical, argumentative and decisory) ethics. Assertions that seem to confirm this opinion in Seneca's *Epistles* 94 and 95 are, however, already rhetorical rationalizations for the preponderance of popular ethics in rhetoric. On the other hand, Cynical ethics must have been of the popular variety to begin with (though perhaps not with Antisthenes), but then it was ethics of the street and not of the academy.

The pattern for Goldin's passage seems to have been a rhetorical catalogue of vice and virtue. The session is probably apocryphal, and the item glorifies the *sophos* and his world. Concerning these catalogues cf. Siegfried Wibbing, *Die Tugend- und Lasterkataloge im NT und ihre Traditionsgeschichte*, BZNT 25, Berlin 1959.

Sage's amazement at the contradictions inherent in any culture, are other such brief items.[84]

Sound method requires further the tracing of the dimensions of a literary phenomenon, i.e., its statistical properties. In the case of the cynizing *chria*, for example, there are 30-35 different examples in all of talmudic literature, whereas there are probably more than 1,000 in Hellenistic literature and the papyri, among them some 20 different items on the use of the Sage's stick alone.[85] There are probably over 5,000 different aphorisms in Hellenistic rhetorical and gnomological literature. There are hundreds of pseudo-rational explanations of "natural phenomena," such as answers to the question why Babylonians have elongated heads, which turns up in the widely distributed pseudo-Hippocratic collections as well as the first *chria* on Hillel of BT Shabbat 31a. Some of this material is contributed by Euhemerus and Euhemerism, e.g., the attempt to explain the origin of the gods by a historical-psychological theory, which made so profound an impression on the ancient world. The massiveness of these examples in Greco-Roman rhetoric puts a number of phenomena into proper perspective. It is, for example, of invaluable help in understanding the total literary pattern as well as the total content and value system of the genres. It becomes thus clear that in the *chria* all Sages were once slaves, all were abjectly poor, and almost all once did menial work. Only on these grounds can the interdependence of Cleanthes items and Hillel anecdotes be fully established and their probable non-historicity be suggested. To be sure, an entire profession may have occupied a certain rung on the economic scale—all monks are poor and in some countries all university professors—but, then, the *chria* speaks of the self-same Sage-Heroes as being wealthy,

---

[84] Examples of *thaumasta* below, p. 84.
The problem of rhetorical components of larger non-rhetorical genres, such as romance, aretalogy, martyrology, satire, mime, comedy, etc., is not mentioned here, since Tannaitic parallels to these genres are rare and mostly extra-rabbinical; e.g., the romance included in the Testament of Joseph (Phaedra and Hippolytus motif, cf. Martin Braun, *History and Romance in Graeco-Oriental Literature*, Oxford 1938). Theodore Burgess' *Epideictic Literature*, Chicago 1903, reconstructs a literary mood or aspect of much of rhetoric rather than a true genre.

[85] Cf. "Cynicism" 10.3. They are the pattern for Shammai's often misdiagnosed building ruler, *'ammath habinyan*, BT Shabbat 31a. This strange term seems to be merely a variant of this moteme, introduced owing to the use of the regular keyword "stick," *maqqel*, in the item immediately before, *ibid*.

so Diogenes, so Crates,[86] so Cleanthes, and so Hillel.[87] Attempts to harmonize such contradictions are as fruitful as the simple solution that was once offered when the "original" skull of a saint was shown at two different places: one skull was said to represent the saint in his younger years, the other in his ripe old age. Rather, the *chriae* are aimed at teaching incisive social ideals: *ataraxia*, self-knowledge,[88] the simple life, absolute freedom (*parrhesia*),[89] non-conformity, the acquisition of virtue through knowledge. Whereas the stress on these values does mirror a historical situation, the mention of the Sage may only indicate the esteem in which he was held as well as the esteem of the social value in question. "De personis indicatur, sed de rebus contenditur," says Quintilian rightly.

The concept of the great individual in later rhetorical culture is thus determined not by his actual achievement—which may have been merely the catalyst—and not by his actual teachings—which were frequently unknown—but by an *a priori* concept of the Sage, and it is this concept which seems to have determined the use of *chriae* and aphorisms in the description of his wisdom and career. In other words, the so-called problem of the "historical Socrates,"—as realistically recognized by Gigon and Chroust;[90]— of the "historical Thales" or Democritus, to whom cynicizing gnomic material was ascribed posthumously,—as rightly asserted by Classen, Snell and Stewart;[91]—the "historical Diogenes," —as critically analyzed by Gerhard, v. Fritz, Rudberg and

---

[86] Cf. D.L. VI.87 with Teles' item in Stobaeus III.1.98 (p. 44 W.H.). On Diogenes cf. Plutarch *Mor.* 499 D (*An vitiositas*); Suidas Δ 1143, ed. Adler, II, p. 101; Musonius, ed. Hense, 87 A, p. 43.

[87] D.L. VII.170; BT Ketuboth 67b cf. BT Sotah 21a. Fully documented in "Cynicism" 27.3 and 30.5ff. The motif that a *sophos* gives his entire fortune away, is another matter again.

[88] Even the Delphic "know thyself" occurs in the mouths of several Greek Sages.

[89] Preserved in the Hebrew-Aramaic cognate *parhesia*, which seems to occur occasionally in the original chriic sense.

[90] Olof A. Gigon, *Sokrates*, Bern 1947; Anton-Hermann Chroust, *Socrates, Man and Myth*, London 1957.

[91] C.J. Classen, in P.W. Suppl.X., 1965, *s.v.* "Thales," especially 931-935; Snell, *op. cit.*; Zeph Stewart, "Democritus and the Cynics," *Harv. Stud. in Class. Philol.* 63, 1958, 179-191.

Sayre;[92]—the "historical Jesus,"[93] as well as the "historical Hillel,"[94] reflects the general historical problem of all who were at one time or another considered *sophoi*.[95]

Among the statistical properties of a genre its distribution, i.e.,

---

[92] Gerhard, op. cit.; Rudberg, op. cit.; F. Sayre, *Diogenes of Synope*, Baltimore 1938; *The Greek Cynics*, Baltimore 1948. K.v. Fritz, *Quellenuntersuchungen zu Leben und Philosophie des Diogenes von Sinope*, Philologus Suppl. 18.II, Leipzig 1926.

[93] A huge field of endeavor, accessible through the Subject (Title) Index of Libraries, Introductions to the NT, surveys on recent NT research, or pertinent encyclopedias (Hastings, *Religion in Geschichte und Gegenwart*; etc.). Quite frequently the problem is seen in "reverse": apocalyptic, soteriological, proto-"gnostic," and Sonship portrayals are rejected as unhistorical, whereas the portrayal as *sophos* is taken at face value.

[94] In the light of the approach suggested here, the 19th century struggles between Abraham Geiger, Delitzsch and Renan as to the question of influences (Jesus/Hillel) are somewhat quixotic. If at least they had discussed the influences of the respective idealizations! Even recent biographies of Hillel use the talmudic material uncritically, except Kaminka, op. cit., and Hallewy, *Sha'are*. They, in turn, rely frequently on haphazard and unsystematic comparisons.

[95] Here the difficult problem arises as to what made a Sage important enough to deserve such posthumous recognition. As indicated before, this may be his creations and activities as a Founder. (The Founder and Inventor appears in myth as the Culture-Hero, e.g., Anacharsis as the inventor of the anchor and the potter's wheel, D.L. I.105.)

Intriguing is the further question whether the *sophos* features acquired in legendarization and rhetoric are in any intrinsic way related to the original contribution of the Sage. The answer, if any can be given with any certainty, will depend on the availability of other sources, especially genuine fragments, or on particular features within the rhetorical portrait that are not in line with the stereotype. It is thus certain from non-rhetorical sources that Thales is indeed the author of important mathematical insights, see Classen, op. cit., Diels, *Vorsokratiker*, and G.S. Kirk and J.E. Raven, *The Presocratic Philosophers*, Chicago 1964. Thales' mathematical pioneering apparently became the catalyst in the formation of his chriic and gnomic features as a Founder-Sage. These features, however, have little or nothing to do with mathematics. Similarly, Democritus' aphorisms (and his eternal smile) have little to do with his atomic philosophy or his equally important mathematics.

To be sure, many creative minds of the Western orbit have indeed excelled in science *and* philosophy. Thus Plato, Leibniz, Pascal and Bertrand Russell are known for both. If we would encounter, however, a popular-rhetorical report which would describe the philosophy of all these four as essentially one, as nontechnical, and, above all, as identical with the philosophy of the era of the report, a serious historical problem would present itself to the critic.

Hillel's main historical achievement (it may have been multiple) could have been a legal reform or measures of timely "emergency" halachah, probably historical if one compares similar emergency measures in the Rome of the Principate. For preliminary orientation see *Oxford Class. Dict.*, "Law and Procedure," 5.

the frequency of its use, its whereabouts and accessibility, are of significance. The Near East would hardly reproduce a *hapax legomenon* but would have a far better opportunity to get hold of an item that is quoted frequently. Once the "scope" of a genre has thus been established, its history has to be traced. The Greek *chria*, for example, is centuries older than the Pharisaic-Tannaitic examples, and developed from a static form, centering around the mere utterances of wisdom or bon mots, to the burlesque form of the Cynics Teles and Bion in the 3rd century.[96] Its great Roman revival slightly precedes Hillel's lifetime, as, for example, in the *Tusculan Disputations*, c. 45 B.C., or coincides with it, and is thus a *terminus a quo*. But one must not omit the fact that the Hillelite *chriae* occur for the first time in the codifications of c.200–250 A.D. This date coincides with the heavy *chria* users Aelianus, Athenaeus, Diogenes Laertius and the authors of the pseudo-Cynic letters,[97] as a *terminus ad quem* for the rise of the Tannaitic *chria*.

Another methodological desideratum is the determination of the social function of the genres. Undoubtedly rhetoric did not only provide a useful mode of expression and operation for the speaker, writer, jurist, and politician. It had become strongly ethicizing, propagating the way to virtue as ennobling or redemptory for a society in rapid change and under stress.[98] Rhetoric would thus also view the nature of man and the dimensions of the gods or even of God, using a fervent, pleading or sentimental tone, quite unlike the detached, objective, and systematic way of formal philosophy. And yet, a practical popular quasi-rational ethics that would weather the vicissitudes of life and encourage simplicity and ataraxy was central in rhetoric. It is perhaps owing to the usefulness of this rhetorical *sophos*-ethics that it could finally approximate an inter-cultural "currency" as much as Greek art or Greek burial custom; that the "pagan" and Christian versions

---

[96] See "Cynicism" ch.3.
[97] Ed. R. Hercher, *Epistolographi Graeci*, Paris 1873.
[98] The factors usually given for this historical situation are the "decline" of the polis and the rise of empire, the emergence of new social classes, the expansion of slavery, the continuous economic crisis (of Rome), earlier Greek particularism and later Roman civil wars, foreign invasions, the increasing number of competing cults and ways of life—all encouraging a flight into the self. Generalizations of this kind can be variously applied for the period of 400 B.C. (the proliferation of the Greek philosophical schools) to 400 A.D. (the establishment of Christianity). These are also the centuries of the domination of rhetorical culture.

of the *Sentences of Sextus* could largely overlap;[99] that "Pagan," Jew and Christian alike could view their lifelong struggle for virtue as an "athletic" and "ascetic" contest—i.e., as requiring continuous practice and strenuous effort;[100] and that Origen could claim that Christianity was a popular version of the same ethics of which Plato was a learned version.[101]

Rhetoric had also to provide the necessary legitimization and glorification of its own spokesmen, of the scholar-teacher-jurist-administrator class. To a certain extent, it is thus self-glorification. Chrysippus, according to D. L. VII.122, thus reformulated Plato's rule that the philosophers should be kings, quite realistically, when he recommended that the wise alone are fit to administrate, judge, and orate. Philodemus of Gadara, c.110–40/35 B.C., claimed that "rhetoric alone makes laws" and that the true rhetors were righteous.[102]

Since the belief in life after death had become quite common, we would expect that a class aspiring to *sophos*-status and propagating it as the true way of life would project this ideal into their concept of the Hereafter, most likely in the form of an academy or, at least, as a learning experience. This is, indeed, the case. Plutarch, c. 46–after 120, using ample Platonic precedents,[103] tells

---

[99] Cf. the recent edition of Henry Chadwick, *Texts and Studies*, Cambridge 1959, 2nd ser.

[100] W. Jaeger, *Early Christianity and Greek Paideia*, Cambridge, Mass. 1961, *passim*; F.C. Grant, *Roman Hellenism and the New Testament*, Edinburgh 1962, p. 164; Joh. Leipoldt, "Griechische Philosophie und fruehchristliche Askese," *Berichte ueber die Verhandlungen d. saechs. Akad. d. Wiss. z. Leipzig*, Philol.-Hist. Klasse, v.106, Heft 4, Berlin 1961, 1-67, *passim*; Y. F. Baer, *Yisra'el ba-'amim*, Jerusalem 1955, *passim*. The two latter fail to distinguish clearly between the rhetorical varieties of *askēsis* which are non-dualistic—i.e., not based on a dichotomy of body and spirit but practice-achievement directed and strongly Cynico-Stoic— and Pythagorean, Platonic, Neoplatonic and quasi-Gnostic varieties which presuppose the superiority of the "Spiritual" over the Physical; cp. especially the *non sequitur* in Leipoldt, *op. cit.*, p. 4. In most "pagan" and Jewish (-Palestinian) sources and in some (non-Pauline) Christian rhetoric the former type of *askēsis* prevails.

[101] *Contra Celsum* VI.1-2; VII.61.

[102] Cf. H.M. Hubbell, "The Rhetorics of Philodemus," *Transactions of the Conn. Acad. of A. and S.*, vol. 23, 242-382, p. 343 (*Fragm. inc.* Sudhaus II, 179, fr.III), cp. p. 360 (*Fragm. hypomn.* II, 275, fr. X) and *ibid.* (II, 279, fr. XXII). Some criticism of rhetoric, however, is proffered in Philodemus' treatise.

[103] Cp. *Timaeus* 30 B, 41-42, 90 A; *Phaedo* 81 B-C; *Phaedrus* 256 B, *Republic* 621 C-D; *Timaeus* 58 D, *Phaedo* 109 B, 111 B; *Phaedrus* 248 A-B; etc.

the tale of the gradual liberation and improvement of the mind-element after death of those who had made righteousness and reason dominant in their lives. Although this experience resembles more a mystical astral ascent and an initiation rite than an academic session, the developing "Spirits," nevertheless, see and learn a great deal.[104] Much clearer is Origen's case (c. 185-253). In Paradise God will organize a school for souls with angelic instructors, and syllabus, examinations and promotions to higher spheres are not missing.[105] In the Amoraic sources the concept of the Academy On High, *yeshivah shel maʿalah* (heb.) or *methibhta de reqiyʿa* (aram.) emerges in Palestine c. 250, in Babylonia c. 300. Details include talmudic discussion, God as teacher, the depth and esoteric character of the instruction—which is superior to angelic lore—and even a seating order.[106]

The intriguing question can now be asked whether the Tannaim and their Pharisaic predecessors, using rhetorical techniques and the ideology of the Sage in a similar fashion, represent in Judean culture the identical class, similarly entrusted with the practical tasks of law, administration and cult, similarly under the threat of a still more powerful ruler,[107] similarly concerned with the preservation of the ancient heritage by new techniques, and similarly clashing with the *hoi polloi*, i.e., the *ʿAm ha-ʾarets*. Indeed, its attractiveness as an ideology for an elite scholar-bureaucracy may have been among the reasons for the adoption of this rhetorical system in the first place.

---

[104] *Mor.* 943ff. (*de facie*). Cp. the use of the notions of joy (943 C), crowned victors, ray of light (D), and nourishment by exhalation (E) with the similar syndrome in BT Berakhot 17a (Rab, 160/175-247, Palestine and Babylonia) and AdRN, Version A, 3a, p.4 (anon.): "...the righteous sit (with) their crowns on their heads and are nourished by (Ber.: enjoy) the radiance of the Shekhinah..."

[105] *De principiis* (Rufinus), ed. P. Koetschau, II.2.4ff. (*Die Griech. Christl. Schriftsteller d. Ersten Drei Jahrh.*, Origenes Werke I), Leipzig 1913. Cf. E.R. Dodds, *Pagan and Christian in an Age of Anxiety*, Cambridge 1965, p. 129, who remarks that for Origen "Heaven is an endless university." The idea of the heavenly academy is here combined with concepts of purgation and sublimation that strongly resemble the situation in the Platonic item of Plutarch, above, whereas the details to be learned and their esoteric nature resemble the talmudic material quoted below.

[106] BT Pes. (Johanan, died 279, Palestinian); BT Baba Metsiʿa 85b (Pal.); 86a (Bab.); Pesikta de R. Kahana, ed. S. Buber, 107a; PT Shabbat VI, end, 8d (Krot.).

[107] A native tyrant or Rome. Exile or martyrdom was more often than not the fate of the major figures of both cultures.

While in this present study the existence of such a scholar-bureaucrat class in Palestine is proposed on the grounds of their *sophos*-ideology and their use of Greco-Roman rhetorical forms and stances, Prof. Urbach, in his aforementioned study and Prof. Neusner, in a recent essay[108] use historical and legal talmudic material to suggest the existence of such a judicial-administrative-instructional class. Prof. Neusner deals with the Babylonian Amoraim and is able to demonstrate that their influence on synagogue, piety and custom was only through their expository skill, while their official activities consisted of the adjudication of property transactions, family status and market supervision as well as other doings in the interest of the Exilarchate.[109]

The entire situation evokes further the suspicion that the Pharisees may have been the most Hellenized group in Judea and may have offered a desirable alternative to the creation of a foreign court bureaucracy, or native bureaucracy of their own, for the later Hasmoneans and the Herodians.[110] The strongly Israel-centered and devout makeup of the Pharisees and Tannaim does not preclude Hellenization. A revealing instance is the great Roman conservative and patriot Cato Major (M. Porcius, 234-149), who counts among the most brilliant Hellenists of the Romans.[111] Toynbee felt inclined to call his anti-Hellenism a pose, following herein Plutarch's evaluation.[112]

The inner dynamics of a bureaucracy of this type has recently been the subject of some special studies, such as those of Fred N. Riggs at Indiana, and Shmuel Noah Eisenstadt at Jerusalem.[113]

---

[108] Jacob Neusner, "The Rabbi and the Community in Talmudic Times," *C(entral) C(onference of) A(merican) R(abbis) Journal* 14, 1967, 65-76, cf. his *A History of the Jews in Babylonia* II, Leiden 1966.

[109] The essays by Urbach and Neusner were published after the conclusion of the present study and are otherwise not used in it. It is gratifying to observe that a cross-cultural and literary study as this one would arrive at a similar result. The Urbach and Neusner essays do not discuss literary genres nor the relation of talmudic materials to Greco-Roman situations.

[110] Cf. their periods of collaboration with the Pharisees. No clash between Hillel and the Judean court or Rome is reported.

[111] He was able to orate in vernacular Greek and to use the classics effectively. Plutarch, *Cato Major*, ch. 12; E.V. Marmorale, *Cato Major*², Bari 1949.

[112] A.J. Toynbee, *Hannibal's Legacy* II, London 1965, 414-428.

[113] Riggs: *Comparative Bureaucracy: The Politics of Officialdom*, Bloomington, Ind., 1962; *Administration in Developing Countries* (The Theory of Prismatic Society), Boston 1964. Eisenstadt: *Comparative Institutions*, New York 1964, Section III, "Bureaucracy and Bureaucratization."

Their observations, made on other bureacracies of this type, seem, at first glance, to throw a great deal of light also on Pharisaic moves, maneuverings, and attitudes. The Hellenist skills of Judean Pharisaism may quite well have developed with historical predecessors of theirs under the Ptolemaic regime, which was apparently a period of fruitful symbiosis.[114] Newly acquired political independence will sooner or later bring the most skillful class to the fore, unless their members have compromised themselves entirely through allegiance to their former oppressor.

An additional shortcoming of previous scholarship is the habit of juxtaposing in parallel columns talmudic materials with similar items of the New Testament. The largest attempt of this sort was Strack-Billerbeck's monumental commentary on the New Testament from Talmud and Midrash.[115] To be sure, this is in some respects a useful undertaking, but more often it leads to erroneous conclusions about relationships and sources. When passages seem to indicate rhetorical coloration, comparison should include the Greco-Roman parallels; i.e., a triple column is a must.[116] Thus, the Sermon on the Mount, Matt. V-VIII, Luke VI: 20-37, should be compared not only to a midrashic homily, or considered to be an echo of the Decalogue or a reaction to the Tannaitic legislation at Jabneh (Jamnia),[117] but also be explored in its relation to Greco-Roman rhetoric,[118] since it shows traces of rhetorical style and

---

[114] Cf. the Ptolemaic use of Jewish mercenaries and of Alexandrinian Jewish officials of many types, and Ptolemaic ties with the Tobiads. Cf. V.A. Tcherikover, *Hellenistic Civilization and the Jews*, Philadelphia 1959; and (with A. Fuks), *Corpus Papyrorum Judaicarum*, 3 vols., Cambridge, Mass. 1957-64. Cf. also the subsequent rapid Hellenization of the Hasmoneans. The latter must have fought for independence rather than for de-Hellenization.

[115] *Kommentar zum Neuen Testament aus Talmud und Midrasch*³, 7 vols., Munich 1926 (partial reprint 1961).

[116] Gerhard Kittel's (ed.) equally monumental *Theological Dictionary of the NT*, tr. G.W. Bromiley, 3 vols. (in progress), Grand Rapids 1964— is virtually a three column study (German: 6 vols., reprinted Stuttgart 1957. The usefulness of this work is lowered in many places by an artificial differentiation between Christian and non-Christian phenomena and an *a priori* devaluation of the latter). In a fourth "column" OT precedents are given. Still valuable is J.J. Wet(t)stein's *Hē Kainē Diathēkē*, 2 vols., Amsterdam 1751-52 (reprinted Graz 1962).

[117] So variously Asher Finkel, *The Pharisees and the Teacher of Nazareth*, Leiden 1964; W.D. Davies, *The Setting of the Sermon on the Mount*, Cambridge 1964.

[118] Illumination through Hellenistic materials: K.F.G. (also D.C.F.G.) Heinrici, *Die Bergpredigt*, BGENT III.1, Leipzig 1905 (biased). On early Christianity generally: Carl Schneider, *Geistesgeschichte des antiken Christentums*, 2 vols.,

sophos ideology. Public temple scenes in which Hillel or Jesus castigate popular piety must not be juxtaposed without relation to Diogenes' or Antisthenes' many similar actions.[119] When in Matthew's attempt at a *sophos* portrayal the central Sage attacks the hypocrisy of Pharisaism, no excess on the part of actual Pharisees living or dead may have been the cause, but rather the temptation to use the Greek cynicizing *thaumaston* in the style of Anacharsis, a Scythian Sage, who "uncovers" the hypocrisies of Greek culture: "He said he wondered (*thaumazein . . . elege*) how the Greeks should legislate concerning violence while they honor athletes for wounding each other," D.L. I.103, and a host of others. Only the representatives of Formgeschichte and Rudberg have moved in this direction, without committing themselves, however, in regard to questions of historicity.

The claim of such an adoption of rhetorical content by an otherwise apparently exclusive culture would be more plausible if parallels to it existed elsewhere. This is indeed the case. The early Church, for example, was so impressed with the rhetorical mold that, among others, Arrian-Epictetus' *Encheiridion* was more than once edited in the form of a Christian paraphrase, and Minutius Felix reworked Cicero's *De natura deorum* into his dialogue Octavius, all without mention of the original author.[120] Of course, in the Near East, the adoption of short rhetorical items was probably made "subconsciously," i.e., on the supposition that it was unthinkable that a true teacher would not have embodied in himself all known features of any positive ideal or happening. The Romans, hardly a spineless people, had made such adoptions from Greek rhetoric on a small scale. On a large scale, they preferred to

---

Munich 1954. Papyri: Adolf Deissmann, *Licht vom Osten*[4], Tuebingen 1923 (*Light From the East*, tr. L.R.M. Strachan, London 1911). Chas. Norris Cochrane, *Christianity and Classical Culture*, New York 1941, 1944 (reprinted 1957) and the writings of Henry Chadwick, Adolf Bonhoeffer, F. Pfister, W.L. Knox, C.H. Dodd, F.J. Doelger, F.C. and R.M. Grant and R. Bultmann.

[119] Derivation of these scenes from Greco-Roman rhetoric (and the suspicion of their non-historicity) does not preclude the possibility that these items counter the influence of another Teacher-Sage or movement, i.e., that Hillel items attempt to counter Jesus' portrayal, or vice-versa, or that Hillel's portrayal counters that of Nicolaus of Damascus (the latter idea briefly suggested by B. Wacholder, *Nicolaus of Damascus*, Berkeley 1962). For this reason, the attempts of Finkel and Davies (see n. 117, above) are of value.

[120] J. Stelzenberger, *Die Beziehungen der fruehchristlichen Sittenlehre zur Ethik der Stoa*, Munich 1937, ch. 14: *Paraphrasis Christiana* and Pseudo-Nilus.

identify themselves openly with the heroes of the Greeks and could thus leave the original names intact. This happened, too, in later patristic tradition, as, for example, with Maximus Confessor, c. 580-662, in his valuable collection *Loci communes*,[121] and in medieval Islam where scholarly habits were quite advanced.[122]

A final requirement of scholarship is a greater appreciation of what adoption actually means. Adoption is very rarely slavish. As a rule it signifies the recognition that a kindred spirit prevails in the other culture, or that an urgent common problem has been successfully solved there. When it comes to the means of survival, there is often little choice. But only vital and living cultures borrow; rigid and stationary societies do not. Moreover, the rhetorical world, in its stress on practical ethics and the ideal of the Sage, resembled ancient Oriental Wisdom Literature (c. 2500-700), which had been acceptable to the earlier Hebrew culture of the biblical period.[123] Indeed, philosophy, as Seneca understands it, is actually called "sapientia" in his 94th Epistle, 15f. and *passim*. Philosophy, rhetorically hypostasized, can "speak"—"inquit," 95.10—just as *hokhmah* in biblical and midrashic texts. Considerable sections of both Oriental Wisdom and Greco-Roman rhetoric were religiously neutral or inoffensive. Both seem to have been the product and tool of bureaucracies.[124] Rhetorical-Cynical nonconformism, especially the odd demonstrative act and the critique of the public by the Sages, resembled earlier Hebrew prophetic stances.

Adoption, furthermore, means adaptation. The latter was manifold and complex in early talmudic culture: the Greek *chria*, for example, was: (1) "naturalized," i.e., told of Pharisaic and Tannaitic heroes; (2) transcendentalized, i.e., used for the propagation of revealed Torah and the acquisition of immortality; (3) most often "legitimized" or "testimonialized" by the addition of a more or

---

[121] In *Opera Omnia*, J.P. Migne, *Patrologia Graeca*, vol. 91, Paris 1865.

[122] See Franz Rosenthal, *Das Fortleben der Antike im Islam*, Zurich 1965.

[123] All introductions to the OT. Further: J.C. Rylaarsdam, *Revelation in Jewish Wisdom Literature*, Chicago 1946 (he continues the work of Gressmann, Baumgartner and Fichtner); Robert Gordis, *The Book of God and Man*, Chicago 1965; James B. Pritchard, *Ancient Near Eastern Texts...*², Princeton 1955; ed. M. Noth, D. Winton Thomas, *Wisdom in Israel and in the Ancient Near East*, Leiden 1955. H. Schmoekel, *Kulturgeschichte des Alten Orient*, Stuttgart 1961.

[124] In the widest sense of the term. Robert Gordis speaks of a responsible middle class, "The Social Background of Wisdom Literature," *Hebrew Union College Annual* 18, 1943-44, 78-118.

less fitting confirmative biblical quotation, *a testimonium* or *martyrion* as it is sometimes called in Greco-Roman rhetoric where it is similarly used;[125] (4) "humanized," i.e., the Sages were made to be less mordant with the "victims" of their wit and, consequently, less witty. At a later stage, when the true chriic nature of the stories was perhaps no longer fully understood or no longer admissable, the *chria*, and with it the fictional debate and other genres, were (5) halachized, i.e., considered an actual event and legal precedent from which further law could be derived.[126] Adaptation of this sort, however, signifies a partial rejection of the original material, and its elevation from a popular level to serious legal use.[127] (6) Rhetorical material was, of course, only selectively adopted; and, finally, (7) its narrative technique was used creatively in the (still rhetorical) combination of chriic and other motemes into a new unit, as, for example, in the story of Hillel in the Snow, BT Yoma 35b, which is totally made up of chriic elements.

Many additional circumstances point to such an adoption of Greco-Roman rhetoric in early talmudic culture. The express distinction between oral and written lore and the consciousness of their problematic relationship is found in both cultures[128] and finally ended in a general wave of codifications of cultural materials of all types in both cultures from 150 to 250.[129] We find

---

[125] Definition in Cicero's *Topica* 73; see "Cynicism" 41.1.

[126] For example, the rather bawdy and witty report, totally composed of similar Greco-Roman elements, of Hillel's exhibiting a bull as a cow in the Temple, TB Betsah 20af. Chriae are also used to illustrate already existing law. Cf. "The Transformation of a Chria," *Erwin R. Goodenough Memorial Volume*, Suppl. Numen, XIV, *Religions in Antiquity*, Leiden 1968, 372-411, IV.2.

[127] The Hebrew *chria* is non-political; its Hellenistic counterpart is often aggressively political. In Judaic culture, however, opposition against Rome, empire and tyranny found expression in other literary media, such as the martyrology, the apocalypse, even the romance, halachah, and various midrashic forms. The political fable, however, exists in both cultures.

[128] Aristotle, *Rhet.* I.x.6, 1368 b; I.xiii.2, 1373b. Cf. Diogenes in D.L. VI.48 (oral transmission superior) with Hillel in Shabbat 31a (reliance on oral transmission necessary). Cf. Ben-Amos, *op. cit.*, pp. 19-29. Gerhardsson's work, throughout, is devoted to this subject: Rabbinic Judaism: 19-181; early Christianity: 182-335.

[129] West: grammar and criticism, curiosa, symposia, gnomes, philosophical *vitae* and, above all, law. Judea: earlier attempts and final Mishna, Tosefta, halachic Midrashim, AdRN, possibly Gen.R. and Lev. R., Megillath Ta'anith, earliest form of Seder Olam. Our contention is that some historical necessity (possibly a mere receding of creativity) in both cultures brought about practically simultaneous codifications of both Roman and Judean material by the representatives of similar bureaucracies.

the same singling out of Epicurus and Oenomaus as the *bêtes noires* of later rhetoric,[130] and the same diffusion and proportional distribution of echoes of popular Hellenistic philosophies, such as Pythagorean bits, some Platonic material, a fair amount of Stoicism (all twice if not thrice removed from their origin) and, above all, the all-pervading coloration of Cynicism, partly in the sense in which rhetors and even Stoics asserted "that the Sage cynicizes, Cynicism being a short-cut to virtue."[131]

If Pharisees and Tannaim—and similarly the Fathers of the Church—indeed have acquired and developed farther the literary tools of another bureaucracy, the possibility exists that Roman administrators may have borrowed from their Near Eastern counterparts. Indeed, the *Scriptores Historiae Augustae*, XLV. 6f., i.e., Lampridius, thus claims that the Emperor Alexander Severus recommended the ordination procedures used for Christian and Jewish "priests" (i.e., in the case of the latter: rabbis) to Roman officials for the installation of provincial governors, revenue officials and army officers! In LI. 5 Alexander Severus is shown to have made the Golden Rule, as received from Christians and Jews (thus expressly the text), an official imperial slogan, being used even in military law.[132]

A final example from the Christian hierarchy reflects the blurred borderlines between bureaucratic-rhetorical terminology, popular philosophy, and religious doctrine. Augustine calls the Golden Rule, as it appears in different formulations, "vulgare proverbium"

---

[130] Thus in *Orations* VI and VII of Emperor Julian. On a positive use of Epicurean materials in Rabbinic literature cf. *Encyclopaedia Judaica* (Engl.) Jerusalem-New York, 1969-70, *s.v.*, "Epicureans and Epicureanism."

[131] D.L. VII.121 (Apollodorus). Rhetorical nostalgia for Cynicism (often hand in hand with criticism of its abuses) with Philo, Seneca, Musonius Rufus, Epictetus, Dio, Favorinus, Lucian, Plutarch, Maximus of Tyre and Julian, also with a number of Church Fathers. Last but not least with Diogenes Laertius. On Philo's "Cynical source," reflected in a description of the festival cycle in Cynic-nostalgic terms, see Isaak Heinemann, *Philo's griechische und juedische Bildung*, Darmstadt 1929-32 (reprinted 1962), 142-145.

[132] The test cases supplied in this passage may have been older valid military law to which the Golden Rule became secondarily appended. On the other hand, similar test cases combined with the Golden Rule are already found in the Akiba passage, Philo, Luke, and some others, cf. n. 67.

Whether Lampridius' incidents are historically true or only express a certain tendentiousness of his work is not decisive for our argument. In either case, the existence of such a rhetorical-bureaucratic-ethicizing ideology is evident, either with the emperor or with his historian.

in *De ordine* II.8.25; he counts it among the "praecepta sapientium" and as part of Natural Law in *De quantitate animae* 73; he stresses its absolute validity in *De doctrina Christiana* III.14 but establishes closer ties with revelationary doctrine mainly in *Enarrationes in Psalmos*.[133]

A critical reflection on Greco-Roman rhetoric and its techniques and genres, as it was in fact undertaken in Greco-Roman antiquity in a highly sophisticated attempt, must be continued in modern scholarship and followed by an exploration of the Near Eastern genres. Only then can their significance for history, biography, and intercultural relations be determined. The historian, meanwhile, has to use this material only with the greatest of caution and the greatest of ingenuity.

---

[133] Migne, *Patrologia Latina* 32, p. 1006; 32, p. 1075; 34, p. 74. *Enarr.* Ps. 35 (sermo 1.34); Ps. 51 (sermo 10.23); Ps. 57 (sermo 1.8).

18

THE TALMUDIC-MIDRASHIC ADAM MYTH IN ITS RELATIONSHIP TO THE PERSIAN YIMA AND MESHIA[1] MYTH*

critically illuminated
by
Dr. Alexander Kohut

Translated by Eva Kiesele

In the rich mines of the Talmud and the midrashim, on the one hand, and the scriptures of the Parsees (*Parsen*), on the other, so much high-quality gold of what is worth knowing can be found, that it seems well worth the effort to extract it from its far-reaching mine shafts, fetch it up, and bring it into the light of day, so that we may critically sift it, separate it from its foreign constituents, and add it to the scholarly exchange. We wish to undertake just such a refining process in the present study, by gathering from the Talmud, *midrash*, and the Parsi scriptures those remarks and allusions, scattered far and wide, that pertain to the theme of the title, and we shall sift through the evidence and order the comparable material insofar as its abrupt nature allows us to combine it into a unified whole and bring it to a presentation that reproduces a closed system.

---

* This translation was completed by Eva Kiesele and reviewed by Prods Oktor Skjærvø. The translation retains some outdated terminology (e.g., Parsee and Parseeism for Zoroastrian and Zoroastrianism) and follows Kohut in using the personal name Yima when referring to both Avestan and Pahlavi texts (rather than Jamšēd). However, many terms have been standardized (e.g., *fragard* for Fargard) and an updated transliteration system for Avestan and Pahlavi sources has been employed. Translations of biblical and rabbinic texts have been supplied by Christine Hayes, but reflect the text cited in German by Kohut even when inaccurate, because Kohut's argument often relies on a particular rendering. Bibliographic details (often omitted by Kohut) have been supplied by the translator, Eva Kiesele, as well as by Prods Oktor Skjærvø. Travis Zadeh assisted with the Arabic citations. Comments and corrections are also set off by square brackets, and some appear as footnotes. In each case, the author of the comment or correction is identified by initials: EK = Eva Kiesele, POS = Prods Oktor Skjærvø, TZ = Travis Zadeh, and CH = Christine Hayes.

1 [Thus Kohut's original transcription. In the remainder of the translation, the standard transcription Mašīy will be used. (EK)]

The post-talmudic-midrashic Adam myth (*Sage*) presents a striking singularity with respect to its composition in the sense that, much in contrast to the other, sporadically distributed legends of the Talmud and Midrashim, it is not a motley accretion of miscellaneous motifs from foreign myth cycles (*Mythenkreise*), but fashioned from one casting, as it were. Although the canvas of the richly appareled Adam myth brims with color, an initiated expert's eye will easily distinguish the main colors; just as one readily spots the mythical fabric's warp and weft. But precisely these principal threads, which pervade the entire fabric, were in fact borrowed from the mythology of a foreign nation. This nation, in whose midst the Jews lived and with whom they found themselves in permanent rapport throughout so many centuries of vibrant intellectual activity and creative power, is the Persian. The Jewish mythologists drew from Parseeism with greater predilection all the more because the Persians were, not only at the height of ancient civilization, but primarily because they most strictly abhorred any form of iconolatry. The latter circumstance, in particular, seems to me to be the chief reason that a certain intellectual assimilation between Judaism and Parseeism could take place, despite the wall between them that the dualism of the latter presented *a priori*.[2] The possibility of assimilation was further conditioned by language. We should not underestimate this factor, as language constituted the only proper medium of mutual understanding. We see from tractate b. Sotah 49b, that the colloquial language of the Jews living in the Persian empire was Persian.

The Parsee literature has unfortunately come down to us only in a fragmentary and corrupted form, which means that the solution to a question of great cultural-historical relevance, namely how far the mutual dependence in the cultural give-and-take between Judaism and Parseeism reaches, will depend on whether we will be able to arrive at a secure understanding of them, free from hypotheses. If we speak of "giving" with regard to Judaism vis-à-vis Parseeism, we do so not just with reference to the known agreements (*Uebereinstimmungen*) between the Avesta and the book of Genesis, thoroughly discussed in particular by Spiegel (*Erān, das Land zwischen dem Indus und Tigris. Beiträge zur Kenntniss des Landes und seiner Geschichte*, 1863; p. 274f), but also with

---

2 Strictly speaking, the Parsee dualism can, despite its pronounced presence in the primary texts, nevertheless be reduced to a certain monotheism of *zrvâna akarana* [*zruuan akarana*] 'infinite time,' from which the twins (*yema* [*yəmā*, Yasna 30.3]) Ahura Mazdā and Angra Mainyu emerged, although it is true that this mediation of the former dualism under the unity of the *zruuana akarana* occurred only in the Sasanian period, which was replete with metaphysical speculation (cf. H. Brockhaus' instructive comment in his glossary; *Vendidad Sade. Die heiligen Schriften Zoroaster's. Yaçna, Vispered und Vendidad. Nach den litographirten Ausgaben von Paris und Bombay mit Index und Glossar hrsg. von Dr. H. Brockhaus*, Leipzig 1850, p. 361). The talmudic-midrashic borrowings of mythological, archeological and other points, however, draw also on earlier periods. [On the now outdated concept of 'Zurvanism,' see Albert de Jong, "Zurvanism," in *Encyclopædia Iranica* online version posted March 28, 2014 (http://www.iranicaonline.org/articles/zurvanism). (POS)]

respect to a certain point of agreement between Yima in the Zand[3] and the narration in Gen 2–12 that, to the best of our knowledge, has not yet been taken into account. Before we turn to the details of this demonstration, let us note only one general observation: similarly to the biblical Adam, Yima, too, as presented by the primary texts of the Zand is the sustainer of a happy, paradisiacal age, yet later loses his innocence through his fall (*Sündenfall*). If the entire myth about Yima contained no more than these two motifs, it would – as a reflex of the identical biblical idea concerning Adam – already be completely sufficient proof that the Yima myth served the sages of the *midrash* as a substrate for their own mythical embellishment of Adam, given the agreement of the two myths in the basic idea. But how much more likely is this when the Yima and Mašīy myths do in fact display *numerous* links with the story as told in the first few chapters of Genesis! The fact that the Yima and Mašīy myth now in turn serve the Jewish mythologists as a foil to develop the Adam legend in line with the stimuli obtained from the Zoroastrian sphere of ideas (*Ideenkreis*), and to surround it with the constructions of a vivid imagination; this fact is just one more proof for the alleged interchange between Parseeism and the aggadic portion of the Talmud. Here is now also the place to counter the potential objection as to why Talmud and Midrash would have borrowed their mythological lore specifically from the Yima and Mašīy myth. This can be explained by a psychological rationale, by which we mean a circumstance of supreme importance for our understanding of the Zoroastrian cosmogonic system and by far still insufficiently appreciated: that the Yima *and* Mašīy myths are unmistakably related. Beyond any doubt, both are mere subtle variations (*Nüancirungen*) of one and the same mythical material, while the conveyors of these myths must be distinguished *chronologically*. But in order not to dwell on conjectures (as they may seem until now, it is true) for too long, we shall let proof follow on the heels of the claims proposed so far. The remainder of our treatise is divided into the following enquiries:

1. The Yima myth of the Zand Avesta and demonstration of its sources deriving from Genesis.
2. Comparison of the Yima and Mašīy myths in their mutual relationship.
3. Demonstration of the aggadic borrowing of the Adam legend from the Yima myth.
4. Demonstration of the aggadic borrowing of the Adam legend from the Mašīy myth.

---

3 [In Kohut's time, Zand usually referred to the Avesta, also called Zand-Avesta, while, today, *zand* usually refers to the Pahlavi (Sasanian Middle Persian) rendering of Avestan texts with commentaries. (POS)]

1. The Yima myth of the Zand Avesta and demonstration of its sources from Genesis

All we need to do in order to bring conclusive evidence for this claim is to subject to analysis the second *fragard* of the *Videvdad*, which provides a continuous account of Yima's blessed period.

First, § 4 and 5 [V.2] relate that "with beautiful Yima, provided with good assembly, with him as the *first* among men did (Ahura Mazdā) converse"; then § 6-11 [V.2.2–4] disclose that Yima refused to become the announcer (*Verkünder*) and teacher of the Law; and then, finally, we read the following in §§ 12 and 13 [V. 2.4]:[4] *yezi mē yima nōiṯ vīuuīse marətō bərətaca daēnaiiāi. āaṯ mē gaēθå frāδaiia āaṯ mē gaēθå varəδaiia āaṯ mē vīsāi gaēθanąm θrātāca harətāca aiβiiāxštaca,* i.e., "if you, Yima, are not prepared to be the reciter and upholder of the Teaching [*daēnā*, (EK)] for me, then further my worlds, then make my worlds fertile, then be the nurturer, protector, and ruler (*Beherrscher*) of my earthly creatures."

Who does not, upon reading this citation, recall the words of Genesis: ויאמר להם פרו ורבו ומלאו את הארץ וכבשה ורדו וכ' (Gen 1:28)? [*And he said to them, "Be fruitful and multiply and fill the earth and master it,"* etc.]

After the remarkable blessing in § 20–30 [V. 2.8–17; note that Spiegel has rearranged the text (POS)], according to which the earth will abound in cattle, draft animals, birds, etc. (cp. Gen 1:22), § 31 [V.2.10=14=18] continues: *āaṯ yimō frašūsaṯ raocå ā upa rapiθβąm hū paiti aδβanəm.* Spiegel translates this difficult verse: "Thereupon Yima went forth to the stars, towards noon, to [probably 'along'] the path of the sun." The [Pahlavi] glosses do not know what to do with this paragraph, and interpret it: "It (the text) makes manifest that he who plans to travel on business in a dutiful manner must take three steps towards noon and recite a *Yaθā Ahū Vairiiō*; then the times are very good."[5] It is unclear, however,

---

4 I follow the edition of the *Vendidad Sade* by Prof. Brockhaus for the Persian text, under constant consideration of the variants. In my translation, however, I take an eclectic stance towards the translation by Windischmann (*Zoroastrische Studien. Abhandlungen zur Mythologie und Sagengeschichte des alten Iran, von Fr. Windischmann. Nach dem Tode des Verfassers herausgegeben von Fr. Spiegel*, Berlin 1863) and the one by Spiegel (*Avesta. Die heiligen Schriften der Parsen. Aus dem Grundtexte übersetzt, mit steter Rücksicht auf die Tradition, von Dr. F. Spiegel*, Leipzig 1852–63) – having carefully consulted with Spiegel's commentary on the Avesta, I felt compelled to prefer at times this, at times the other way of translation. (F. Spiegel, *Commentar über das Avesta*, Vienna and Leipzig 1864–1868.) [Today, references to the Avesta are usually according to K.F. Geldner, *Avesta. The Sacred Book of the Parsis* I–III, Stuttgart, 1896, supplemented by Niels Ludvig Westergaard, *Zendavesta or the Religious Books of the Parsis* I. Copenhagen, 1852–54 (repr. Wiesbaden, 1994). These will be added in square brackets, e.g., Videvdad "second *fragard* ... §4 and 5" are both Geldner's [V. 2.2]. For a more up-to-date translation of the texts quoted from *fragard* 2, see Skjærvø *The Spirit of Zoroastrianism*, New Haven and London, 2011, pp. 70–75. (POS)]

5 Cf. Spiegel's *Commentar*, p. 59, and his *Einleitung in die traditionellen Schriften der Parsen* II (Vienna 1860), p. 83. [The *Yaθā Ahū Vairiiō* (or *Ahunavairya*) is the introductory strophe to the Gāthās and the most important ritual formula in the Avesta; see transl. in Skjærvø *The Spirit of*

how this meaning is to fit into the wider context, but it becomes evident if we compare the paragraph with Gen 2:8. According to the biblical verse, the first human dwelled in Eden, planted מקדם ["*in the east*"]. Thus, when Yima directs his steps towards "the path of the sun," i.e., walks eastwards, we already *suspect* an agreement of this Zand passage with this verse from Genesis. But what can fully convince us is the addition of the subsequent four paragraphs [V.2.10=14=18 continued]: "*hō imąm ząm aiβišuuaṯ suβriia zaranaēniia. auui dim sifaṯ aštraiia uitiiaojanō friϑa spənta ārmaite fraca šuua vīca nəmaŋha barəϑre pasuuąmca staoranąmca mašiiānąmca*," i.e., "He split the earth with the golden lance. He pierced it with the goad, saying: with love, O Spənta Ārmaiti, [the Earth], go forth and spread out through prayer, you bearer of the cattle, the draft animals, and the men." There can be no doubt that these paragraphs are intended to convey that Yima cultivates the earth. This is what the Bible says about Adam (Gen 2:15): וינחהו בגן עדן לעבדה ולשמרה, ["*and he placed him in the garden of Eden, to till it and tend it*"] and cp. the end of verse 5.

The strongest proof that the interpretation of § 31–37 [V.2.10=14=18 and 11] developed here is not a bold one but rationally factual, and that, in particular, the expression "toward the path of the sun" (i.e. eastward) refers to the paradise in said manner, comes from §42 [V.2.20]. This paragraph continues the preceding lines as follows: *haṇjamanəm frabarata yō daδuuå ahurō mazdå haϑra mainiiaoibiiō yazataēibiiō srūtō airiiene vaējahi vaŋhuiiå dāitiiaiiå*, i.e., "Ahura Mazdā the Creator convoked a gathering with the heavenly *yazatas* ['deities'], in the famed Airiiana Vaējah of the good creation." If we now further consider that § 45 [V.2.21] explicitly states *ā taṯ haṇjamanəm paiti jasaṯ yō yimō xšaētō*, i.e., "into this gathering came radiant Yima" etc., then what we have here is but a more specific explanation of what was just noted in § 31. The Mēnōy ī Xrad indeed attests that Airiiana Vaējah is located in the far east of the Iranian plateau;[6] and the etymology of the root *vaējah* ('land of sources')[7] leads naturally to the

---

Zoroastrianism, pp. 219. (POS)] We cannot but cite the later tradition reproduced there, since it is identical to a corresponding talmudic passage: کار کنند چندان ایثا اهو ویریو خوانند وچون فلان جای شوند چندان بثا اهو ویریو گویند پس بروند که چون فلان, "when one does some business, one is to pray a number of *Yathā Ahuna Vairiia*; when one travels somewhere, one is to pray a number of *Yathā Ahuna Vairiias*, then one is to go. [Pahlavi V.2.10; the gloss is not in ms. L4 and its descendants, hence also not in Moazami 2014, pp. 50–51. It is in the descendants of K1, among them M3 (Bavarian State Library). (POS)] Cf. b. Berakhot 14a, where these two views are grouped together in the same way: אסור לו לאדם לעשות חפציו ["It is prohibited for a man to tend to his business before he says his prayers."]

6 Cf. F. Justi, Zendlexicon (= *Handbuch der Zendsprache von Ferdinand Justi. Altbactrisches Woerterbuch. Grammatik. Chrestomathie*, Leipzig 1864), p. 259, and the sources referenced there, as well as Spiegel's Avesta translation vol. I, p. 61n2. [MX. 27.29–31, see transl. in E.W. West in *Sacred Books of the East*, ed. F. Max Müller, vol. 24: *Pahlavi Texts*, part III, Oxford University Press, 1885, p. 60. (POS)]

7 [It is unclear what Kohut meant by 'Quellenland,' a land with sources or, more likely, a land that was the source = origin of the Iranians. (POS)]

parallel with the biblical גַן עֵדֶן [garden of Eden], the source of the four streams (Gen 2:10f).

From § 46 [V.2.22] onwards, the author of the second *fragard* touches on the historical account about Noah. Later Parsee interpreters relate §§ 47–61 [V.2.22–25] to the prophecy of the eschatological rain *malkošān* (מלקש).[8] More correctly, however, this passage must refer to the deluge (cp. Gen 6:13ff). Especially § 59 [V.2.24] does not really allow for any other sense than this one. *abdaca iδa yima aŋ^vhe astuuaite sadaiiāt̰* means in Spiegel's correct reading: "Clouds, O Yima, shall come to that bodily dwelling place (namely, of men)," which precisely matches the flood of water announced earlier.[9]

In §§ 61–129 [V.2.25–39], Yima is commanded to build a *vara*, a place confined and enclosed on all sides. The detailed description of his execution thereof recalls Noah's ark, not just in its general outline but even in the particulars. E.g., when § 61 states: *āat̰ təm varəm kərənauua carətu.drājō kəmcit̰ paiti caθrušanqm*, "therefore make the circumference the length of a race course toward *all four corners*," we are reminded of Gen 6:14, וכפרת אתה מבית ומחוץ ["*and cover it with pitch, inside and out*"]. Or § 62: *haθra taoxma upa.bara pasuuqmca staoranqmca mašiiānqmca*, i.e., "there you shall bring the seeds of the cattle, the draft animals, and the men," which again sounds strongly like Gen 6:19: מכל החי – מכל בשר – מכל תביא וכ' ["*Of all that lives, of all flesh, you shall bring, etc.*"].

In § 66 [V.2.26] the birds are especially emphasized, as in Gen 6:20.

In § 67 [V.2.26 cont.], Yima is further told to take food with him to the *vara*: *auui mat̰ zairi.gaonəm mat̰ x^vairiieite ajiiamnəm*, i.e., "(bring birds) and golden grain and inexhaustible food," as Windischmann correctly translates.[10] This compares to Gen 6:21, ואתה קח לך מכל מאכל אשר יאכל ["*As for you, take for yourself from every food that is eaten*"].

Likewise, §§ 68 and 69 [V.2.26 cont.]: *haθra nmānā̊ auuastaiia katəmca fraskəmbəmca frauuārəmca pairi.vārəmca*, i.e., "Install homes there, floors, columns, courtyards and fences" can be compared to the phrase תעשה תחתים שנים ושלשים (Gen 6:16) ["*make it with bottom, second and third decks*"].

Moreover, especially §§ 78 and 92 [V.2.28, 30] must be compared to the parallel expressions with the same wording in Genesis.

For the former paragraph says: *tē kərənauua miθβaire ajiiamnəm*, i.e., "all this make in pairs and imperishable" [§78 = V. 2.28][11] cp. Gen 6:20: שנים מכל יבאו אליך לחיות ["*two of each will come to you to stay alive*"]. Finally,

---

8 Cf. Spiegel, *Grammatik der Pārsisprache nebst Sprachproben* (Leipzig 1851), p. 167 § 20.

9 [Spiegel thought *abdaca ... sadaiiāt̰* meant "and clouds [*aβra*!] shall come"; *abda* usually means "wondrous, marvelous," hence *abdaca ... sadaiiāt̰* "it will seem marvelous." See also his doubts and different proposal in *Commentar*, pp. 68–69. (POS)]

10 Even more precisely § 76 [V.2.28]: *haθra vīspanqm xvarəθanqm taoxma upa.bara*, i.e., "there you shall bring the seeds of all foods." Similarly, in § 70 and 72 [V.2.27], the bringing of the seeds of men and all cattle species is repeated again, as happens in Gen 7:2.

11 [Kohut by mistake adds the beginning of §79 *vīspəm ā ahmāt̰*." (POS)]

in § 92 [V.2.30 cont.] Ahura Mazdā commands Yima: *apica təm varəm marəza duuarəm*[12] *raocanəm x*ᵛ*āraoxšnəm aṇtarə naēmāṯ*, i.e. "around this enclosure (make) a high door,[13] and a window, self-shining from the inside." In the exact same manner it says in Gen 6:16: תעשה לתבה – ופתח התבה בצדה תשים צהר ["*Make an opening for light in the ark...and put the door of the ark on the side*"].[14] The following paragraphs up to § 129 [V.2.39] describe the execution of the command given to Yima, with respect to the building of the *vara*.[15]

The paragraphs from § 130 [V.2.39] to the end engage in some general reflections on the inhabitants of the *vara*. In addition to all that has been said so far, the final comment in §§ 132–135 and 136 [V.2.40–41] seems to us to be important for our claim that the descriptions in the second *fragard* are formed after the narratives of Genesis.

For the first two paragraphs there have: *hakərəṯ zī irixtahe saδaiiaca vaēnaite starasca māscā huuarəca. taēca aiiarə mainiieṇte yaṯ yārə*, i.e., "Only once,[16] one sees the stars, the moon, and the sun. They think it is a day what is a year." Spiegel rightly explains (*Avesta*, p. 77n3): "The difference between day and night does not exist for the blessed ones in Yima's surrounding." Might not the author of the story in the second *fragard* have thought of Gen 1:5 ויהי ערב ויהי בקר יום אחד ["*and there was evening and there was morning, one day*"]? In light of the inner connection between these two paragraphs, indicating that the night coincided with the morning, and the immediately following remark that a year counted as *one* day, the above assumption does not seem too bold.

Yet another analogy with Genesis is proven by the statement in § 134 [V.2.41]:

---

12 [Kohut has *aipitâtem marezudvarem* for Spiegel's (*Avesta* I, p. 12) *aipica təm varəm marezudvarem*].
13 From this parallel, it becomes clear that the text's expression *marezudvarem*, which Windischmann simply translates as 'door', is not to be rendered 'wall,' as Spiegel, *Commentar* p. 76, suggests. In the Mēnōy ī Xrad [26/27.29–31; transl. West, p. 60] it says: "Then they will open the door of the *var* which Jamšid made. And humans and cattle and other creatures of the creator Ohrmazd will come from that *var*, and they will restore the world" (Spiegel, *Grammatik*, p. 167 §21f. [also Bundahišn 33.36, see Skjærvø, *The Spirit of Zoroastrianism*, 2011, p. 165. (POS)]) Following our explanation, this refers to the re-population of the world after the deluge.
14 Remarkably, the ancient versions translate צהר at times with "window," at times with "self-shining," just as the text of § 92 [V.2.30] places "window" next to the phrase "shining from the inside." The latter is also the opinion of the Midrash. Cf. Rashi ad loc.
15 The *Videvdad sāde*'s [=*Videvdad* mss. without Pahlavi translation] add [V.2.32]: *āaṯ yimō auuaθa kərənaoṯ yaθa dim išaṯ ahurō mazdā̊*, i.e. "Yima did as Ahura Mazdā had commanded." This recalls ויעש נח ככל אשר צוה ה' (Gen 7:5) ["*and Noah did according to all that the Lord commanded*"]. The following passage in the repetition (§ 123–124 [V.2.38]) is also important for our parallel: "*fratəməm daṅhōuš nauua pərəθβō kərənauua* [thus Spiegel, *Avesta* I, p. 12; Kohut: *kerenaoiṯ*] *maδəmō xšuuaš nitəmō tišrō*," i.e., "above in that region he made nine bridges, in the middle six, below three," which completely recalls תחתים שנים ושלשים ["*bottom, second and third decks*"].
16 [Kohut has 'Auf einmaligem [*sic*] Gang' for Spiegel's 'Auf einmalige Art und Gang': "in unique manner and only once" (?) (POS)]

caθβarəsatəm aiβi.gāmanąm duuaēibiia haca nərəbiia *duua nara us.zaiieiṇte miθβana strica nairiiasca*, i.e., "every forty years, two humans are born from the two humans, a pair, a male and a female child." The phrase incontrovertibly shows that paradise was imagined as inhabited by two humans alone, parallel to the perspective of Genesis. However, these abrupt, non-sequitur comments seem to stem from a later hand.[17] §§ 43, 63, 70, 79, 99, 125 [V.2.20, 25, 27, 28, 33, 38] clearly express the notion that many humans resided in the *vara* of Yima. Accordingly, the term *taēca narō* "these humans" in §136 [V.2.41 cont.] must, while its immediate reference is to §134, signify *all* humans living in Yima's *vara*, about whom it is now said that "they lead the most beautiful life."

Reviewing the parallels drawn between the second *fragard* and Genesis without prejudice, we can – many a discrepancy notwithstanding – no longer deny that the cited Zand passages have been borrowed from Genesis. The fact that these borrowings are to be taken with a grain of salt, as they pertain only to the basic idea, cannot diminish the results obtained. Neither does the objection hold that these borrowings bear the mark of Iranian thought. Conversely, we will be faced with the same impression from the talmudic and midrashic borrowings from the Yima legend: although the kernel of the mythical account has been taken from Parseeism, it has been dressed in a garb befitting the Jewish mind. This phenomenon rests simply on the individuality of the nation in question. Equipped with its own unique gift of repulsion, it first strips the material of its alien dress adopted from a foreign sphere, and discards anything irreconcilable with its own outlook and way of thought. This imitation of a mythical character like Yima from a biblical prototype was obvious enough to the author of the second *fragard* since Yima, just like Adam in Genesis, is meant to illustrate the incarnation of the paradisiacal age.

That said, we would still have to prove that also the Mašīy myth, contained in the Bundahišn and, as is well known, based on old traditions, rests on the account in Genesis. We can keep this point shorter, given that Windischmann's keen eye has already detected several related features between Mašīy and Mašyānīy of the Bundahišn, on the one hand, and the narratives of Genesis, on the other. So let us now try to place Windischmann's cautious allusions on firmer ground, and partly complete them. The texts we shall cite are from the fifteenth chapter of the [Indian] Bundahišn [= chap. 14 of the Iranian Bundahišn], "On the nature of man."[18] Before delving into this chapter, though, we cannot

---

17 Cf. R. Roth's excellent study: "Die Sage vom Dschemschid," *Zeitschrift der Deutschen Morgenländischen Gesellschaft* (*ZDMG*) 4 (1850), pp. 417–433.

18 [The Bundahišn is found in two recensions, one in Indian manuscripts, hence "Indian Bundahišn," and one in Iranian manuscripts, hence "Iranian Bundahišn," commonly also "Greater Bundahišn," since it contains more text than the Indian. Today, the Bundahišn is usually cited after B.T. Anklesaria, *Zand-ākāsīh. Iranian or Greater Bundahišn*, Bombay, 1956 (transliterated text and translation), whose numbering is given in square brackets. On Gayōmard and Mašīy and Mašyānīy, see also Skjærvø, *The Spirit of Zoroastrianism*, pp. 108–112.]

but recall the passage from the fourth chapter of the Bundahišn, according to which, when the primordial bull dies, Gayōmard (the first human) emerges on its right-hand side [Bd. 4a.1].[19] In line with this, Mojmal al-Tawārik states:[20] چون سی سال بر آمد بمرد ونطفه از صلب اندر زمین افتاد, "when thirty years had lapsed, he died; his seed fell from *his loins* onto the ground" etc.[21] The myth is evidently an imitation – *mutatis mutandis*, of course – of Genesis 2:21. When, moreover, the tenth chapter of the Bundahišn [Bd. 6e.3] says about the semen of the primordial bull that it was purified by the light of the moon and then "*breath* was instilled in the body," we have again just a reminiscence of Gen 2:7: ויפח באפיו נשמת חיים ["*he blew into his nostrils the breath of life*"]. The same is the case when the fifteenth chapter of the Bundahišn [Bd. 14.11] says in Ahura [Mazda]'s name about the first human couple (Mašīy and Mašyānīy):[22] "You are humans, *fathers* (beings [*Wesen*]) of the living you are," which is precisely the end of the sentence quoted: ויהי האדם לנפש חיה ["*and the human became a living being*"]. Just as, in Gen 1:30, Adam may eat only vegetables,[23] the Bundahišn too permits the primordial human couple to eat meat only after they defect from Ahura Mazdā [Bd. 14.21], just as the consumption of meat is authorized only after the deluge. Cf. Gen 9:3.

Another defection of the first humans from their creator consists in the fact that they "go hunting (nskr[24]) after thirty days" [Bd. 14.18]. Here the author might have imagined the characters of Nimrod, Yishmael, and Esau as hunters.

"Thereupon," the Bundahišn continues "they first wore garments of skin." Cf. Gen 3:21.

"Thereupon they dug a hole in the earth and hit iron, and they struck it against a rock and *sharpened* it into an *axe* (*tick* [*tēx*])"[25] [Bd. 14.24]. Cf. Gen 4:22 לטש כל חרש נחשת וברזל ["*he forged all instruments of copper and iron*"].

"Then they cut a tree and prepared wooden huts" [ibid.]. Cf. Gen 4:20 הוא היה אבי ישב אהל ["*he was the ancestor of those who live in tents*"].

"Thereafter, they revealed by themselves this evil (*abārōn*) envy against each other. *They set upon each other, and they brawled*" etc. [Bd. 14.25[26]]. This is an obvious imitation of the fratricide that originated with Cain's envy (Gen 4:5f.

The first humans having lost their innocence, "upon the completion of fifty years, a desire to procreate arose in them, *first* in Mašīy and then in Mašyānīy"

---

19 [Kohut's source for this tradition is unclear. Spiegel's translation, *Einleitung* II, p. 102, is correct: when the Bull died it fell on its right side, Gayōmard on his left side. (POS)]
20 Cf. Windischmann, *Zoroastrische Studien*, p. 212ff.
21 Cf. the more detailed citation, to which we will return below, in F. Spiegel, *Einleitung* II, p. 105n3.
22 [Bd. chap. 14 is translated in Skjærvø, *The Spirit of Zoroastrianism*, pp. 108–111.]
23 Cf. also Hesiod's identical view in Windischmann, *Zoroastrische Studien*, p. 212n1.
24 [*sic*. Kohut adopts this reading from Windischmann's *Zoroastrische Studien* p. 82, where, however, no transcription is provided. Modern philologists tend to read the word as *wiškar*, 'wilderness,' and accordingly, "they went into the wilderness." (EK)]
25 [The reading *tick* is from Windischmann, *Zoroastrische Studien*, p. 225, who compared Pers. *tiše* "axe." (POS)]

[Bd. 14.28a²⁹]. Cf. Gen 4:1 והאדם ידע את חוה אשתו, ("*and the man knew Eve his wife*") following the tale that the primordial couple had been banned from paradise.

"Thereupon seven pairs came from them:" the third pair is called Frawāk and Frawākain [Bd. 14.34]. As Windischmann notes (*Zoroastrische Studien*, p. 228), this word appears as a noun in the Zand texts [*frauuāka* 'utterance'], cp. Vispered 18.7, 13 [Vr. 21.0]; Yasna XIX.37, 57 [Y. 19.14, 20]; Dēn Yašt 3 [Yt. 16.3]; Yašt fragment II.38 [Yt.1.28]; Yašt fragment I.1 [Hādōxt nask 1.1]; Bahrām Yašt 28 [Yt. 14.28]. In all these passages, it refers to the enunciation of the sacred word. So it might almost seem as if this patriarch was conceived somewhat like Enoch, in whose time *"they began to invoke the name of God"* (Gen 4:26). Finally, just as Genesis (11:1) describes an incipient mass migration of tribes following the multiplication of mankind, so does the Bundahišn: the end of chap. 15 has the multiplied couples "from whom derives the entire advancement of the race of the living" [Bd. 14.35] (cp. Gen 10:25, 32) migrating into the diverse regions of the earth and populating them.

* * *

Given so much evidence, should we really still hesitate to proclaim that both the Yima and the Mašīy myth were, in their core idea, sketched and developed along the contours of Genesis' account of the first humans and their experiences? We are so very convinced of this that we would not think twice to make this assumption the basis of further deductions and conclusions. Its impact on the dating of the Zand's composition or, rather, redaction, can hardly be overrated. But we shall confine ourselves to what we have already said, lest we digress from the actual theme. That our assumption of the borrowing of the Zand Avesta from the narrative portion of Genesis is hardly arbitrary is also proven by the most curious agreement between the Zoroastrian and biblical chronologies. We cannot find a worthier conclusion for this chapter than to place here Windischmann's affirmative words which confirm our claim (*Zoroastrische Studien*, p. 162, a view with which Spiegel, *Erān*, p. 286f, completely concurs): "It is most remarkable that the teaching of the magi about Yima [Bd. 35.52] counts precisely 35 generations from Yima, the fallen first man, down to Zarathustra; just like biblical chronology counts 34 generations from Adam to David, i.e. 10 from Adam to Noah, 11 from Shem to Abraham, 13 from Isaac to David. And according to precisely this chronology, David, too, rises as a prophet and king at the end of the third millennium since the beginning of the world, while, at the inception of the Zoroastrian religion, these qualities are divided among Zarathustra and king Vištasp. We will have to parallel the ten generations from Yima down to Θraētaona to the 10 patriarchs from Adam down to Noah; the twelve from Θraētaona to Manuščihr to the eleven from Shem to Abraham (or the twelve down to Isaac, the promised seed); the thirteen from Manuščihr to Zarathustra to the thirteen from Isaac to David."

2. The comparison of the Yima and Mašīy myths in their mutual relationship

Yima and Mašīy share not only the fate of having been reworked in their mythical design [*Ausgestaltung*] from one and the same source – Genesis, but also have manifold points of contact and comparison. Far from being coincidental, this phenomenon is due to the close relationship between Yima, on the one hand, and the primordial humans Mašīy and Mašyānīy, on the other. As someone with a deep knowledge of Parseeism puts it, "Gayōmard with his further development, Mašīy and Mašyānīy, is the first human in the theosophical form of the *Zoroastrian system*; Yima is the first human of the *ancient Aryan myth* who, however, had to assume a different position in the system – although here, as well, the paradisiacal state shines through most clearly." (Windischmann, *Mithra. Ein Beitrag zur Mythengeschichte des Orients*, Leipzig 1857 = Abhandlungen für die Kunde des Morgenlandes (AKM) 1, 1959, p. 76 n. 1.)

The correctness of this view immediately stands to reason once we consider the kinship relations of these two mythical heroes. In what follows, are compiled, with extreme brevity, the main features shared by both.

1) In the primary texts (cp. *Videvdad* 2.20, 23, 31, 43, 45 [V. 2.20, 21];[26] *Videvdad* 19.132 [V. 19.39]; Yasna 9.13 [V. 9.40]; Yašt 5.25, 98 [Yt. 5.25, 72]; Yašt 15.15; Yašt 17.28; Yašt 19.31, 35; Yašt 23.3 [Āfrīn ī payɣambar Zardušt 3]), Yima bears the name *xšaēta* (whence the later [mod. Persian] contracted name Jamšid), that is: 'radiant Yima.' He moreover bears the honorific epithet *huuarə.darəsō mašiiānąm*, "who most gazes at the sun among men."[27] This is to be compared with the myth about the first human inasmuch as we also learn regarding Gayōmard that his seed, from which Mašīy and Mašyānīy came, was purified in the sunlight (Bundahišn[28] chap. 15, p. 28, line 14).[29] In our opinion, the meaning of this view, which can be verified in the primary texts, is only that the first human was endowed with heavenly splendor. Indeed, Bundahišn chap. 24 p. 57, l. 5 [Bd. 17.1] says: "as the first one of humankind Gayōmard was formed, *radiant*, white-eyed." This feature of the myth is also

---

26 [Kohut has *Videvdad* 2.20, 23, 31, 43: but 20, 23, 26 (not 31) [V.2.8, 12, 16] have *xšaθrāi* (Spiegel 'zum Reich'), not *xšaētāi*. (POS)]

27 [*sic*, following Spiegel's translation of the Avesta. The phrase is commonly understood as "like the sun to look at among men," and Kohut seems in fact to have interpreted it this way, given the conclusion of this paragraph. (EK)]

28 [These and subsequent Bundahišn references are to pages and lines of Niels Ludvig Westergaard's handwritten facsimile of the codex K20 in the Royal Library Copenhagen (*Bundehesh: liber Pehlvicus e vetustissimo codice Havniensi descripsit ...* Copenhagen, 1851) Only two of the three references here are correct, some later references are also incorrect. (POS)]

29 [Bundahišn chap. 15, p. 28, l. 14 [K20, fol. 101v, Bd. 13.4], cited by Kohut here, is about the semen of the bull being purified. The passage about Gayōmard's semen is on p. 33, lines 5–7 [K20, fol. 104r, Bd. 14.5–6]. (POS)]

explained by Bundahišn chap. 3, p. 10, 1. 1, 14;[30] we shall discuss this passage later.

2) In *Videvdad* 2.5 [V. 2.2], after Ahura Mazdā is asked to whom he taught the Zoroastrian law, he replies: *yimāi srīrāi huuq9βāi ašāum zara9uštra. ahmāi paoiriiō mašiiānqm apərəse azəm yō ahurō mazdā̊*, "with beautiful Yima, provided with good assembly,[31] O pure Zarathustra, with him I conversed as the first among men, I who am Ahura Mazdā." In the same vein, in Fravaši Yašt 87 [Yt. 13.87] it is said about Gayōmard: "we praise the *fravaši* of the pure Gayōmard, who *was the first to hear Ahura Mazdā's thought and his commands*."

3) On analogy with the Vedic Yama and Yamī, who are thought to be twins, it is also told about Yima "that a couple was given birth to by Jam and Jamag, who was his twin sister" (Bundahišn chap. 32, p. 81, 1. 7).[32] But it also says the same about the first human originating from Gayōmard "that he was created in the shape of a single-stemmed reïva plant[33] – and they resembled each other so much that it was not apparent who was man and who woman" (beginning of the fifteenth chapter of the Bundahišn[34] [Bd. 14.6–7]).

4) According to *fragard* 2.8 [V. 2.3], Yima is told: *vīsaŋ^vha mē yima srīra vīuuaŋhana mərətō bərətaca daēnaiiāi*, "obey me,[35] O beautiful Yima, son of Vīwanghwan, as the one who remembers and upholds the law." And according to Bundahišn chap. 15 p. 34 [K20, fol. 104v, Bd. 14.11], the first human couple is also exhorted to perform and propagate "the works of the precept with perfect mind."

---

30 [Bundahišn chap. 3, p. 10, lines 1, 14 (K20, fol. 92v, Bd. 4.10, 22) is about the attack of the Evil one on the creation and Ohrmazd's bringing sleep (*xwēy*) upon Gayōmard (See below, in chap. 4). The second passage where Gayōmard is described as *spēd-dōysr* is K20, fol. 104r, Bd. 14.1. (POS)]

31 [Spiegel rendered *huuq9βa-* as "mit guter Versammlung versehen"; the Pahlavi translation has *huramag* "with good herds," which is how the epithet is commonly understood today. (POS)]

32 [Bundahišn chap. 32, p. 81, line 7 (Bd. 36.5) is about how the *x^varənah* left Jamšid (cf. below, pt. 8). The passage about Jam and Jamag is on p. 77 line 6 [K20, 127r, Bd. 35.4]. (POS)]

33 [Spiegel gives correctly *reivâs* (also Windischmann, *Zoroastrische Studien*, p. 216), which Kohut, strangely, seems to have interpreted as plural, hence his *reïva*. The Pahlavi has *rēbās*, cf. Persian *ribās* "rheum ribes" (thus Windischmann), see also J.L. Schlimmer, *Terminologie médico-pharmaceutique et anthropologique française-persane, avec traductions anglaise et allemandes des termes français*, Teheran, 1874, p. 489: "rheum ribes, rhapontic rhubarb"; Pers. *rivās*, however, is "sorrel." (POS)]

34 Mojmal al-Tawārik̲ (in Spiegel, *Einleitung* II p. 105n3 [Mohl, "Extraits du Modjmel al-Tewarikh: Relatifs à l'histoire de la Perse," *Journal asiatique* 11 (1841), p. 151]) mentions *two* reïva plants, probably in order to emphasize the androgynity of the first human couple: i.e., پس دو نبات بر مثال ریواس از ان بر آمد وبعد مدتی باجنس مردم بودند بیک قامت ودیدار ونام شان مشی ومشیانه بود "then two plants grew up in the manner of reïva [*rivās*] plants; after some time, they obtained human genders. They were of identical stature and looks, their name was Mašī and Mašyāna."

35 [Spiegel rendered *vīsaŋvha* as "gehorche"; today, the verb is thought to mean approximately "declare oneself ready to be." – Pahl. *bowandag menišn* "perfect mind" renders Av. Ārmaiti, the Earth, and here refers to the fact that they were born from Spandarmad, Av. Spəntā Ārmaiti "the Life-giving Earth" (cf. V. 2=10=14=18, above). (POS)]

5) In Yasna 32.8 [Y. 32.8] it is told about Yima: *yō mašiiəṇg cixšnušō ahmākəṇg gāuš bagā x*[v]*arəmnō*,[36] "who has taught us men *to eat meat in pieces*." And with regard to Mašīy and Mašyānīy, the Bundahišn (loc. cit., p. 35 [K20, fol. 105r, Bd. 14.21b]) emphasizes that they cut the cattle (the first they found) into three parts.

6) About Yima it is said (*fragard* 2.17, 18 [V. 2.6]), *āaṯ hē zaiia frabarəm azəm yō ahurō mazdå. suβrąm zaranaēnīm aštrąmca zaraniiō paēsīm*, "then I brought forth *weapons* for him, I who am Ahura Mazdā; a golden *lance* and a goad made from gold." Also, according to Ferdowsī, Yima makes weapons for fifty years, and Ali Shir Newai's *History of the Kings* concurs with this, informing us that, with regard to Jamšid, "he is known for amazing inventions, among which is the invention of the tools of war" (cp. J. Berezin, "Beschreibung der türkisch-tatarischen Handschriften in den Petersburger Bibliotheken," *ZDMG* 2 1848, p. 255). I assume that the Mēnōy ī Xrad (Spiegel, *Grammatik*, p. 167 [MX. 26. 18, transl. West, p. 58]) is alluding to the same when he says about the first man "that the metals were created from his body," as Ferdowsī too says about Yima: "then he invents the precious metals and gemstones."[37]

7) According to Aši Yašt 30 [Yt. 17.30], just as the blessed period of Yima's reign lasted for a thousand years (although it is not too unlikely that 'year' here is to be understood as 'day;' cp. *Videvdad* 2.133 [V. 2.41]), so also one thousand days[38] and nights elapse until the first humans encounter the ram they kill (Bundahišn loc. cit.), and thus reveal their inclination towards earthly pleasures and their fall from Ohrmazd conditioned by it.

8) Like Yima, the first human couple forfeits paradise, both of them in the wake of identical transgressions. About the former, it is told in Zamyād Yašt 33f [Yt. 19.33–34]: "During his rule there was no cold, no heat, no old age, no death, no envy created by the *daēvas* – on account of the absence of the lie, (namely)

---

36 Haug (*Die fünf Gāthās, oder Sammlungen von Liedern und Sprüchen Zarathushtra's, seiner Jünger und Nachfolger I*, Leipzig 1858, p. 31) offers a different translation: "He who blessed men with his talents and filled our parts of the earth with his light." Haug takes *bagā*, comparing Yasna 19.3, 5, 7, to mean 'part' and *xvārəmnō* as homonymous with *x*[v]*arənah*, 'splendor,' cf. ibd. p. 170. However appealing this explanation might be, the first view will nevertheless merit greater attention, as it is supported by our parallel and, in addition, the account in the *Sad-dar* p. 94 (Spiegel, *Avesta* II, p. 100n2 [: *ito et et equos et boves et oves mactato et coquito et libere dato* "(the king of kings = Jamshid) said:) Go and kill horses, bulls, and sheep, cook them, and give liberally!"; checked against Meherji Rana Library ms. F64 fol. 62r, kindly supplied by Daniel J. Sheffield. The forms and meanings of the three last words in the Avestan are hotly disputed, and there is no agreed-upon translation. Note that Kohut has qaremnô from Spiegel's *xvarəmnō* (*Avesta* II, p. 143), but notes the reading of A (= K5) *xvārəmnō* in the list of variants (p. 270). (POS)]
37 [See Jules Mohl, *Le livre des rois par Abou'lkasim Firdousi*, 1838; repr. Paris, 1976, I, pp. 48–52, and Arthur George Warner and Edmond Warner, *The Sháhnáma of Firdausí done into English*, London, 1905, I, p. 133. (POS)]
38 [Windischmann's (*Zoroastrische Studien*, p. 82 §4) misreading of the numeral 30 as 1000 presumably from Westergaard 1851, p. 35 line 1 [K20, fol. 105r, Bd. 14.21]. (POS)]

before he began to love lying, untruthful speech. Then, once he began to love lying, untruthful speech, the majesty visibly fled from him."[39] The fall of the primordial human is motivated in a similar way (Bundahišn p. 34 [K20, fol. 104v, Bd.14.16]): "When the lying speech was spoken, it was spoken at the will of the *dēws*. By this ungodly speech, they both became ungodly (*druwand*), and their soul is in hell until the future body (i.e., until the resurrection)." It is also noted, by the way, that Yima will be thrown into hell, but will eventually be liberated through Zarathustra's prayer.[40]

9) The myth has apes, tailed creatures etc. descend from Yima as well as from the primordial human; cp. Bundahišn p. 56, line 13 [K20, fol. 115v, Bd. 14b.1] together with the end of its fifteenth chapter [Bd. 14.38], to which we shall return below [see end of article, pt. 15].

* * *

A few other, secondary points aside, these are by and large the conclusive passages and points of comparison on the basis of which we formulated the mythical relationship of Yima and Mašīy and put forth our claim. We claim that these two mythical stories, even if they did not draw from one and the same source and ran parallel like two rivers, nevertheless sprang from a *common* origin of cosmogonic outlook; that they still bear surface traces of this homogeneity which cannot be obliterated and might even have been much more pronounced before each dug its own particular riverbed. It is no less natural that the myths in question bore an intimate relationship in the collective consciousness of the people, not just as theosophical philosophemes, but as mythico-historical traditions, than it is certain that the legendary accounts contained in the Zand Avesta remained fluid within a body of tradition that grew continuously from generation to generation for a long time before they were committed to the rigid letters. Who will now be surprised to encounter the descriptions of the primordial age evoked by the Yima and Mašīy myth so frequently, nay almost at every turn, in the talmudic-midrashic mythical embellishment of the Adam legend? After all we have said above, it can hardly come as a surprise that these points, borrowed from the sphere of Persian cosmogonic cycle, link at times to the Yima, at times to the Mašīy myth. Nor does it appear strange that these concepts, borrowed from a *foreign* conceptual sphere and shifted into the region of *aggadah*, were either read into the letters of the sacred Scripture or deduced from the latter. That is, in fact, the usual way

---

39 [Here $x^v arənah$ is rendered as *'majesty,'* but elsewhere as *'splendor' (Glanz). (POS)*]

40 [Windischmann (*Zoroastrische Studien*, p. 28) cites the note in Anquetil-Duperron, *Zend-Avesta: Ouvrage de Zoroastre* ... vol. 1, part 2, Notices, p. xxviii. Cf. *Sad-dar Bondaheš* chap. 31 in B.N. Dhabhar, *The Persian Rivayats of Hormazyar Framarz and Others. Their Versions with Introduction and Notes*, Bombay, 1932, pp. 524–526. See also the translation of the *Pahlavi rivāyat* 31 in Alan V. Williams, *The Pahlavi Rivāyat Accompanying the Dādestān ī Dēnīg*, 2 vols, Copenhagen, 1990, II, pp. 57–59. (POS)]

that *aggadah* processes any borrowings from foreign territory – provided that this material possesses sufficient potential for acclimatization to accord with and fit snugly into the Jewish mind.

After these preliminary remarks, we may now justifiably commence to demonstrate the sources of the talmudic-midrashic Adam legend without having to fear coming up against a *terra incognita*.

3. Demonstration of the talmudic-midrashic borrowing of the Adam legend from the Yima myth[41]

Since we already presented the relevant original Zand passages in the preceding two sections, we will now have to confine ourselves to mere references to the latter. The comparanda between Yima and the Adam myth are grouped around the following main points.

1) Just as Yima, as we have seen above, bears the consistent ornamental epithet *xšaēta* 'the radiant,' further *x˅arənaŋ˅hastəmō* 'the sun-like,' and finally *srīrō* 'the beautiful,' and was called Jamšid on account of the splendor radiating from him, as the author of the Mojmal rightfully remarks,[42] so also does the *aggadah* indulge in an extensive description of Adam's beauty and radiant splendor. In b. Bava Metsiʻa 84a it is said that: "The beauty of our ancestor Jacob was of the same kind as the beauty (שופרא) of the first human,"[43] and b. Bava Batra 58a repeats the same, adding: "When R. Banaʼa reached the burial cave of the first human, a heavenly voice was heard saying thus: you may well have looked into the image of my countenance, yet into my countenance itself you cannot see."[44] The comparison is thus taken from the sun, here as with Yima, and in b. Bava Batra loc. cit., it even states explicitly: "R. Banaʼa said, I saw the two heels of Adam that resemble two orbs of the sun."[45] Perfectly in line with the naming of Jamšid given by the Mojmal and Hamza II, p.21, we read in b. Ḥagigah 12a: "With the light

---

41 Mr. [Joshua Heschel] Schorr has already made some efforts towards a possible parallelism of the Adam and Yima myths on a narrow *in quarto* page (32–33) in the seventh issue of *He-Ḥalutz* [Frankfurt-am-Main, 1865; see Secunda, *The Iranian Talmud: Reading the Bavli in its Sasanian Context*, Philadelphia, 2014, p. 149 (POS)]. This page is the only oasis amidst the wasteland of vague hypotheses and conjectures pervading the entire issue. But since Mr. Schorr is unable to drop his (already once criticized) unfortunate etymologizing, he connects even Jem with אדם (!), failing to consider that the former is a corrupted form of the Zand's Yima and does not have anything to do with the Semitic אדם.
42 Cf. "Extraits du Modjmel al-Tewarikh. Relatifs à l'histoire de la Perse, traduits par Jules Mohl," *Journal Asiatique* XI (1841), p. 154f. and p. 279.
43 שופרא דיעקב אבינו מעין שופרא דאדם הראשון. Rashi ad loc. correctly explains the first word as: זיהרורי תוארו וקירון עור פניו, "the splendor of his looks and the radiance of his facial skin."
44 כי מטא (ר' בנאה) למערתא דא"ה יצתה בת קול ואמרה נסתכלת בדמות דיוקני בדיוקני עצמה אל תסתכל
45 א"ר בנאה נסתכלתי בשני עקיביו ודומים לשני גלגלי חמה, cf. with Leviticus Rabbah 20. B. Bava Batra loc. cit. defines the beauty of Adam thus: the relation of Eve's beauty to that of Adam equals the relation of the beauty of a monkey to that of a human being.

that God created on the first day, Adam looked from one end of the world to the other."[46]

2) We have already seen that Yima was asked and assigned to become the announcer and upholder of the law (*fragard* 2.8 [V. 2.3]). The same is said about Adam: "R. Yehuda the son of Simon said: Adam would have been worthy for the Teaching [Torah] to have been revealed through him" (Midrash Genesis Rabbah chap. 24).[47] Only, just as Yima proved to be unusable (*fragard* 2.10 [V. 2.3 cont.]), so did Adam. For God said, "If you did not abide by even the six commandments that I gave to you, how should I give him [*sic*] 613 positive and negative commandments?" (Genesis Rabbah loc. cit.[48])

3) In *fragard* 2.13 [V. 2.4], we saw Yima being commissioned to expand the world and make it *fertile*. Adam is praised similarly: "Every strip of land that Adam settled on according to the divine plan was cultivated" (b. Berakhot 31a; b. Sotah 46b).[49]

Genesis Rabbah 19 moreover says, "God took Adam and let him make the round of the entire world, speaking to him: Here (there shall be) a planting, here a field for seed. This is what is written (Jer 2:6) 'a land that no one passes through, where no one lives,' i.e. where the first human did not settle."[50]

4) In the Parsee view, Yima was destined for immortality until he succumbed to sin. Many passages attest to this. In Yasna 9.15–18 [Y. 9.4–5] it is expressed thus: *yaṯ kərənaoṯ aiṅhe xšaϑrāδa amaršənta pasu vīra, aŋhaošəmne āpa uruuaire, xvairiiqn xvarəϑəm ajaiiamnəm. yimahe xšaϑre auruuahe nōiṯ aotəm åŋha nōiṯ garəməm, nōiṯ zauruua åŋha nōiṯ marəϑiiuš, nōiṯ araskō daēuuō dātō*, i.e. "because on account of his rule, humans and cattle were immortal, water and trees not drying out, edible food inexhaustible. In the wide dominion of Yima there was no cold, no heat, no old age, no death, no envy created by the *daēvas*." Other passages further attest that immortality, prosperity and bounty were present during Yima's rule, e.g.: Rām Yašt 16 [Yt. 15.16]; Aši Yašt 29–31 [Yt. 17.29–30]; Zamyād Yašt 32 [Yt. 19.32]; Goš Yašt 10 [Yt. 9.10] et. al.

The same is expressed in various formulations in the Jewish sources. Most clearly, it emerges from the beginning of chap. 38 of Midrash Exodus Rabbah that the first human had originally been created for eternal life and immortality: "'*You are from the beginning, O Lord, my God, my Holy one; we shall not die*' (Hab 1:12). This verse can be applied to Adam before he ate from the fruit of the tree. Had he not eaten from it, he would never have died; but since he transgressed

---

46 אור שברא הקב״ה ביום א׳ אדם צופה ומביט בו מסוף העולם עד סופו. – Genesis Rabbah 14. In y. Shabbat 2[:6, 5b], Adam is explicitly called נרו של עולם ["the light of the world"].

47 א״ר יהודה בר סימון ראוי היה א״ה שתנתנן תורה על ידו

48 [The original consistently speaks of Adam in the third person. (EK)]

49 כל ארץ שגזור עליה אדם הראשון לישב נתישבה

50 נטלו הקב״ה ותחזירו בכל העולם כלו א״ל כאן בית נטע כאן בית זרע הה״ד בארץ לא יגבר בה איש ולא ישב אדם שם לא ישוב א״ה שם

Your command, You brought death upon him."⁵¹ In a parallel passage in Midrash Leviticus Rabbah chap. 27, it is said: "If someone should ask you how Adam would have been able to live eternally if he had not sinned and had not eaten from the fruit of the tree, then reply that Elijah, who did not sin, enjoys eternal life."⁵² The passage in b. Shabbat 55b is similar: "Why was death imposed on Adam? A minor rule I assigned to him, and he transgressed it."⁵³

With reference to Job 14:20 and with the same firmness, Midrash Genesis Rabbah chap. 21 expresses the fact that Adam's creation was originally destined for immortality thus: "The power which the Holy one, blessed be His name, gave to Adam would have been forever and eternity; but since he left the design of God behind and complied with the will of the snake, he was chased away from there disfigured and damaged."⁵⁴

We even encounter the view (mentioned above) that bounty prevailed before the fall of Adam in Midrash Genesis Rabbah chap. 12: "Although the world was created for abundance, it decreased as soon as Adam sinned."⁵⁵

5) The repeatedly mentioned passage in Zamyād Yašt 34 [Yt. 19.34] tells us about the fall of Yima thus: "Then, when he began to love lying, untruthful speech, the Majesty visibly fled from him. When radiant Yima with good assembly, the supreme, no longer saw the Majesty, then *Yima, dissatisfied, staggered away* to evil thoughts; *frightened he fell down on the earth*."⁵⁶

All of the points mentioned here recur in the *midrash*.

First, also the point that Adam's fall was provoked by the lie is confirmed. Midrash Genesis Rabbah chap. 19, it is said with reference to Prov 30:6: "'*And do* [plur.] *not touch it*' (Gen 3:3). This can be compared with the verse (Prov 30:6) '*Do not add to his words, lest he rebuke you, and you be deemed a liar.*' R. Ḥiyya taught: Do not make the fence higher than what is actually essential (the garden), lest it fall down and destroy the plantings; similarly, God, blessed be His name, said: '*On the day on which you will* eat' etc. (Gen 2:17); however, she (Eve) did not report it thus, but that God spoke with falsity [by reporting his command as]: '*do* [plur.] *not eat from it and do not* touch *it* [*lest you die* (Gen 3:3)]'"⁵⁷ Likewise,

---

51 הלא אתה מקדם ד' אלהי קדושי ולא נמות עד שלא עמד הראשון ואכל את האילן כך היית אומר שלא יאכל מן האילן ולא ימות – אלא מפני שביטל צוויך הבאת עליו מיתה.

52 אם יאמר לך אדם שאלו לא חטא א"ה ואכל מאותו העץ היה חי וקים לעולם אמור לו אתה כבר היה אליהו שלא חטא וכ'.

53 מפני מה קנסה מיתה על א"ה מצוה קלה צויתיו ועבר; cf. further b. Avodah Zarah 8a, b. 'Eruvin 18b.

54 תוקף שנתן הקב"ה באדה"ר לנצח לעולם היה כיון שהניח דעתו של הקב"ה והלך אחר דעתו של נחש משנה פניו ותשלחהו. [literally, "The power which the Holy one, blessed be His name, gave to Adam would have been forever and eternal; but since he left the design of God behind and followed the design of the snake, "he changed his face and sent him away" (Job 14:20). (CEH) [The homily has a parallel in Genesis Rabbah 16. (EK)]

55 אע"פ שנבראו הדברים על מליאתן כיון שחטא אד"ה נתקלקלו.

56 The subsequent four paragraphs describe the gradual withdrawal of the divine Majesty, as in Numbers Rabbah 13.

57 ולא תגעו בו הה"ד אל תוסיף על דבריו פן יוכיח בך ונכזבת תני ר' חייה שלא תעשה את הגדר יותר מן העיקר שלא יפל ויקצץ הנטיעות כך אמר הקב"ה כי ביום אכלך והיא לא אמרה כן אלא אמר אלה' לא תאכלו ממנו ולא תגעו בו.

it says in the Talmud (b. Sanhedrin 38b): "Adam was a liar and an apostate."[58] Even the more distant point that God's Majesty departed from Adam has been preserved by the *midrash*. "When Adam sinned, the Majesty ascended to the first heaven; when Cain sinned, it ascended to the second heaven" etc. (Numbers Rabbah 13).[59] Genesis Rabbah 21 moreover provides the following analogy to Yima's "*dissatisfied* staggering away": "After He (God) had hurled him down, he began to lament him."[60] The Zand imagery "frightened, he fell down" has also left its traces in the *midrash*, inasmuch as the latter reports: "What are the words '*the first man and his wife hid themselves*' (Gen 3:8) meant to convey? That Adam's height was diminished after he had sinned."[61]

Analogous to the Zand's expression that the splendor went away, it says in Midrash Genesis Rabbah chap. 11: "He took away from him his splendor."

Elsewhere (Genesis Rabbah chap. 12; Numbers Rabbah chap. 13), the *midrash* specifies: "Six things were taken away from Adam as a result of his sin: his (serene) splendor, his vital power, his body height, the relish in the fruits of fields and trees, and the radiance of his facial splendor."[62] That even the relish in the fruits of fields and trees, i.e. their taste, was taken from the first human – we will return to this later – finds its analogy in Zamyād Yašt 32 [Yt. 19.32], where it says about the blessed period of Yima: "During whose reign were eaten foodstuffs inexhaustible for the body,[63] water and trees that never dried out" (cp. also Yašt 15.16 [Yt. 15.16] and the Zand passage already mentioned above, Yasna 9.14–18 [Y. 9.4–5]). The Mašīy myth also knows of a reduction of the enjoyment of food, as we shall see later.

6) Opinions diverge on the nature of Yima's lie, of which the primary texts speak. Some think it consisted in his haughtiness (*Hochmut*). Ferdowsī believes that Yima in his hubris (*Ueberhebung*) denied God the adoration he demanded for himself. We encounter both opinions in the aggadah with regard to the cause

---

58 רב אמר אד״ה מין היה – כופר בעיקר היה
59 Cf. also Genesis Rabbah 19: כיון שחטא אד״ה נסתלקה שכינה לרקיע הראשון חטא קין נסתלקה לרקיע השני.
60 כיון שטרדו התחיל מקונן עליו.
61 Numbers Rabbah 13: מהו ויתחבא האדם ואשתו א״ר איבו באותה שעה גרעה קומתו של אד״ה. However, in the interest of truth it must be admitted that the feature of Adam's body height, of which the Talmud says in b. Sanhedrin 38a-b, b. Ḥagigah 12a that it reached from one end of the world to the other (cf. also Genesis Rabbah 21) does not have a basis in Iranian; on the contrary, special mention is made of one of the blessings of the period of Yima (*frag. 2.121* [V. 2.37]) that *mā paēsō yō vītərətō tanuš*, i.e., that there was no bodily form that exceeded the normal measure of the body. [*mā paēsō yō vītərətō tanuš* (with an inexplicable) *mā* "let not" for Spiegel's (1853, p. 14) *nōiṯ* "not"] is in the context of people with defects who were not to be admitted into the *vara* and probably means "nor a leper whose body is sequestered ..." (POS)] On the other hand, the Muslim myth teaches that Adam was created in the length of 60 ells, cf. al-Suyūṭī's collection of traditions, *al-Jāmiʿ aṣ-ṣaghīr [min ḥadīth al-bashīr al-nadhīr]*, § 3689.
62 ו׳ דברים נטלו מא״ה ואלו הן זיוו חייו וקומתו ופרי הארץ ופרי האילן ומאורות זיוו; cf. further Yalqut on Ruth § 609.
63 [The quotation is incomplete, cf. pt. 4, above (EK).]

of Adam's fall. Midrash Numbers Rabbah chap. 13 combines the two views: "R. Tanḥuma the son of 'Abba said, '*A person's pride is his humiliation*' (Prov 29:23)" – this statement refers to Adam. For when Adam transgressed God's prohibition to eat from the tree, God still wanted him to do penitence. But Adam resisted this wish: no sooner had his verdict been rendered than he began to curse and blaspheme."[64] In Genesis Rabbah chap. 15 it says: "The trees called out to Adam: here is the thief who beguiled the will of God (who has betrayed God)! – One may now apply the following verse to this (Ps 36:12): 'Do not let the foot of pride tread on me,' i.e. the foot of one who acted with pride and behaved with hubris (*überhob sich*) against his creator."[65]

But also the second view, that man claimed divinity for himself, left its traces. Genesis Rabbah chap. 9 has, "Adam would have been worthy of not having been forced to taste the flavor of death. But death was imposed on him because God foresaw that Nebuchadnezzar and Hiram, king of Tyre, would make themselves into gods."[66] According to another opinion, the angels themselves wanted to offer divine worship to Adam. In Genesis Rabbah chap. 8 it says: "When God had created Adam, the angels erred and wanted to invoke Adam as 'Holy'!"[67] For the sake of illustration, the *midrash* relates a nice parable: "A king and an eparch (איפרכוס) were sitting in a cart (בקרונין, *currus*). The inhabitants of the land wanted to say *Domine* (דומינו) to the king, only they did not know which of the two was the king. The king pushed the eparch out of the cart, and everyone realized that this one was the eparch. In the same fashion, the angels erred regarding Adam until he lost consciousness [in sleep], and then they all realized that he was

---

64 א"ר תנחומא בר אבא גאות אדם תשפילנו זה אדם הראשון כיצד שעבר אדם על צוויו של הקב"ה ואכל מין האילן ביקש הקב"ה שיעשה תשובה – ואמר אדם אי אפשי – כיון שיצא אדם מן הדין התחיל מחרף ומגדף; cf. also Genesis Rabbah 21 and b. Sanhedrin 70b.

65 ומה היו אומרים (האילנות) הא גנב דגנב דעתיה דברייה (דבוראו) הה"ד אל תבואני רגל גאות רגל שנתגאה על בוראו.

66 ראוי היה אד"ה שלא לטעום טעם מיתה ולמה נקנסה בו מיתה אלא צפה הקב"ה שנבוכדנצר וחירם מלך צור עתידן לעשות עצמן אלהות.

67 בשעה שברא הקב"ה אד"ה טעו מלאכי השרת ובקשו לומר לפניו קדוש. In Avot de-Rabbi Nathan 1 it says similarly: וירדו מלאכי השרת לשרתו ונטלו הקב"ה ונתנו תחת כנפיו. Conversely in the Quran: as is well known, here the angels are *commanded* to prostrate themselves before Adam. All did so except for Iblis (διαβολος?), who had become haughty (*hochmütig*) and proved to be an infidel; cf. Sura II v. 34; likewise, Sura XV 30.31; XVII, 62; XVIII, 51; XX, 114. In the small anthology [*al-Jāmi'aṣ-ṣaghīr*] of Suyūṭī it says in agreement (§2082): the angels wished Adam good things and repeated four times "God is great." And in §3689, too, where God says to Adam: "'Go and greet these persons, namely the angels; hear the good things they wish you and your descendants.' Adam went and said, 'Greetings to you!' and they replied: 'Greetings to you, and to God's mercy!' They added God's mercy to their greeting." Of interest is a learned dispute among the church fathers on the question of whether the angels had also been created in God's likeness. Chrysostom answers this question in the negative, since otherwise (he said) one would have venerated them on account of their divinity, which was not the concern with man. Cf. R. Schröter, "Erster Brief Jakob's von Edessa an Johannes den Styliten." *ZDMG* 24 (1870), p. 284. If Chrysostom had known this *midrash*, he would surely have dismissed the claim that the angels erred also concerning man!

only a human." Cf. J. Levy (1867), *Chaldäisches Wörterbuch über die Targumim und einen grossen Theil des rabbinischen Schriftthums* I, *ad* איפרכוס.

7) On account of his disobedience, Yima falls victim to the terrible snake Dahāka (cp. Windischmann, *Zoroastrische Studien*, p. 29),[68] and a similar parable illustrating this basic idea is told about the first human (Genesis Rabbah chap. 19). "A man of bad character asked the wife of a well-reputed man: 'How does your husband treat you?' 'Very well,' she said, 'except that I have no power over this barrel here which, as he said, is supposed to be full of snakes.' That evil man replied, 'That must be where all his treasures and jewels are' (קוזמיקין; more correct is the reading קוזמין, κοσμος, 'jewel'). What did she do? She opened the barrel and was bitten by the snakes. When the husband came along he told her, 'This happens on account of your disobedience.'"

8) According to the Rivāyats reproduced in Spiegel, *Einleitung* II, p. 323f, Yima incurred a malign leprosy when he touched Angra Mainyu, while attempting to rescue his brother Tahmūraf from the former's belly.[69] According to Bundahišn chap. 15 [Bd. 14.15], the adversary also beguiled and *defiled* the thought of the first human couple. And similarly, it says in b. Yevamot 103b, b. Shabbat 146a, b. Avodah Zarah 22b that Eve "incurred a permanent stain (menstruation) through contact with the snake (Satan-Samael)."[70]

9) According to Bundahišn p. 77, line 8 [K20, fol. 127r, Bd. 35.5], it was Spitūr [Kohut has the Av. form Spitiiura (POS)] who sawed Yima apart,[71] to which the primary texts, too (cp. Zamyād Yašt 46 [Yt. 19.46]), allude. Something similar is also said about the first human couple, who were created androgynous: that they were sawn apart (Genesis Rabbah chap. 8 and Midrash Yalqut on Psalms § 887).

10) According to the later Parsee scriptures, Yima, in his misfortune, regretted his mistakes and converted.[72] Adam, too, fasted and performed acts of improvement after he learned about the punishment for his sin and that death had been imposed upon him.[73] "When Cain returned home from God after his remorseful confession (Gen 4:15), he met Adam. The latter asked him, 'What is the punishment for your sin?' 'I have done penitence,' he replied, 'and have served my sentence.' Thereupon Adam covered his face with his hands crying, 'So great is the power of repentance, and I did not know!' Immediately he stood and broke into

---

68 [Windischmann (*Zoroastrische Studien*, pp. 28–29) cites Bundahišn, p. 40 line 15 (K20, fol. 107v, Bd. 18.8). Further references in "Jamšīd," in *Encyclopædia Iranica* XIV/5, pp. 506–509. (POS)]
69 [See *EncIr*. XIV/5, p. 507 with further references. (POS)]
70 More about this in our study "Über die jüdische Angelologie und Dämonologie in ihrer Abhängigkeit vom Parsismus," *Abhandlungen für die Kunde des Morgenlandes* (*AKM*) 4 (1868), p. 66 and 66n3 [where he also refers to the origin of menstruation through the *Jahī*, the primordial evil woman (POS)].
71 In b. Yevamot 49b, we are told about Menasseh that he had the prophet Isaiah sawn apart.
72 Cf. the Mojmal (Mohl, "Extraits du Modjmel," p. 154f. [general material] and 279 [*il se répentit*]), and Roth, Dschemschid ["Die Sage vom Dschemschid"], p. 423.
73 b. ʿEruvin 18b. ר' מאיר אמר אד"ה חסיד גדול היה כיון שראה שנקנסה מיתה על ידו ישב בתענית מאה ושלשים שנה ופירש מן האשה מאה ושלשים שנה.

a thanksgiving prayer.'"[74] According to another account, "Adam sacrificed a bull for thanksgiving."[75]

11) The Parsee literature attributes to Yima the institution of the six annual holidays (the Gahanbārs, *gahanbār*), which are invoked in Visprad 1, 2–7 [Vr. 1.2] and are supposed to commemorate the creation.[76] The *Sad-dar*, p. 94 (quoted from Spiegel, *Avesta*, Introduction to vol. II, p. Cn2[77]) describes the institution as follows: "*scito haecce sex Gahanbâr instituta fuisse a Gjemschîd: horum inquam observationem Deus ostendit Gjemschîdo, qui habuit (pro viatoribus) mensam: ei enim mos fuit, ut quicunque peregrinus (hisce diebus) ab itinere adventaret, eum ad coquinam suam mitteret ut se cibo satiaret. Die quodam aliquis diabolus per ostium ingressus est sub forma viatoris: quem cum a Gjemschîdo festinanter cibum peteret, Gjemschîd illum ad culinam misit, coquo praecipiens ut huncce hominem cibo satiaret*" [= "Know that these six Gahanbārs were instituted by Jamšid: I say, god showed Jamšid how to observe them, who held table (for travelers): for it was his custom that he sent any stranger (on these specific days) who came from the road to his kitchen so he could satiate himself with food. One day, some devil entered by the front door in the form of a traveler. When he promptly asked Jamšid for food, Jamšid sent him to the kitchen, telling the cook to satiate this man with food."].[78] Then follows another description of this demon's insatiability and of how Jamšid sacrificed bulls and sheep at God's command. "*Ex eo tempore*," the account concludes, "τὰ *Gahanbâr instituta sunt et in hominum bonum patefacta*" [= "From that time, the Gahanbārs were instituted and revealed as a good thing for men"].

In perfect agreement, the Talmud relates in b. Avodah Zarah 8a that Adam instituted festivals in order to commemorate the creation occurrences following

---

74 Genesis Rabbah, end of 22: פגע בו (בקין) אד"ה א"ל מה נעשה בדינך א"ל עשיתי תשובה ונתפשרתי התחיל אד"ה מטפח על פניו אמר כך היא כחה של תשובה ואני לא ידעתי מיד עמד אד"ה ואמר מזמור שיר ליום השבת.

75 Cf. b. Avodah Zarah 8a, b. Shabbat 28b, b. Ḥullin 60a. In the basic texts, too, the first human is often mentioned together with the primordial bull; especially in invocations, cp cf. Yasna 13.7 *gə̄uščā hudåŋhō gaiieẋiiācā maraθnō ašaonō frauuašīm yazamaide*, "we invoke the genius of the well-knowing bull and of pure, mortal life" (i.e. Gayōmard). Yasna 26.13–14 [Y. 26.4–5] *gə̄uš huδåŋhō uruuānəm yazamaide; gaiiehe marəθnō ašaonō frauuašīm yazamaide*, "we invoke the soul of the well-knowing bull; we invoke the genius of pure, mortal life." Still more passages mention the first human together with the primordial bull. Now, in my view, the above talmudic passage, according to which the first man sacrifices a primordial and, as can be gleaned from the above citations, fabulous (קרניו קודמין לפרסותיו [= "his horns preceded his hooves"] bull, wishes, I suspect, to polemicize against the widespread belief of the Parsees that the human race derives its origins from the *bull* killed by *Ahriman* (cf. Bundahišn chaps. 4, 10, and 15). [This is a curious mistake by Kohut: the human race comes from Gayōmard's semen, while the Bull's semen gave rise to plants, healing herbs, and animals; only Bd. chap. 10 (Bd. 13.1–4) is relevant here. (POS)]

76 Cf. Spiegel, *Einleitung* II, p. 82.

77 [Spiegel quotes the Latin translation of the *Sad-dar* by Thomas Hyde. Cf. T. Hyde (1700), *Historia Religionis Veterum Persarum eorumque Magorum*, Oxford, 1700, p. 485f. (EK)])

78 We cite the passage at length as it exhibits a surprising similarity to what we have said in our aforementioned paper, p. 67n6.

the laws of nature. Given its agreement with the idea underlying the institution of the Gahanbārs, the passage deserves to be quoted in full.

The story goes as follows: "When Adam saw the days becoming increasingly shorter (because of autumn), he thought, 'Woe is me, on account of my sin the world is darkening all around and will return to the earlier chaos; perhaps this is the death which has been imposed upon me by heaven.' Adam fasted for eight days (cp. *Sad-dar*, ibid., *Gjemschîdo coram Deo ingemiscente* [= " when Jamšid complained before god"). But seeing that the days grew longer, he said, 'So, this is a law of nature!' He therefore spent eight days in solemn celebration. The following year he instituted these days as festivals; he also stood up and sacrificed a bull."[79]

A more remote agreement with Yima, whom Parsee tradition holds to have instituted the "*gāthā*" times, is told in Avot de-Rabbi Nathan chap. 1: Adam defined times and certain prayers to be recited at them. Thus, also Yima is commanded to recite a *mąθθa* (prayer) ([Avestan gloss in the Pahlavi commentary on V.2.6] cp. Spiegel, *Einleitung* II, p. 82).[80]

12) At this very point [Spiegel, ibid.], a gloss on *Videvdad* II.16 [Pahlavi V. 2.5] is cited, as follows: "As far as Yem is concerned, he possessed the dignity of a *hērbed* and disciple."[81] This accords with a note in Ferdowsī (chap. 4 v. 6) according to which he has Yima say:[82]

منم گفت با فرّهٔ ایزدی
همم شهریاری و هم موبدی

[*man-am goft bā farrah-e izadi
ham-am šahriyār-i o ham mowbed-i*

I am, he said, (endowed) with the divine *farrah* ('majesty').
I am both a king and a mowbed (POS)]

---

79 לפי שראה אד״ה יום שמתמעט והולך אמר אוי לי שמא בשביל שסרחתי עולם חשך בעדי וחוזר לתוהו ובוהו וזו היא מיתה שנקנסה עלי מן השמים עמד וישב ח' ימים בתענית ובתפלה כיון שראה תקופת טבת וראה יום שמאריך והולך אמר מנהגו של עולם הוא הלך ועשה שמונה ימים טובים לשנה האחרת עשאן לאלו ולאלו ימים טובים——עמד והקריב שור ...

80 [Kohut appears to regard *mąθθa* as a synonym of *mąθra*. Spiegel does not translate the gloss, but Justi (*Handbuch der Zendsprache*, p. 236) has *mąθθa* "thought, speech" (POS)].

81 [Kohut does not cite Spiegel's (ambiguous translation) quite correctly: "As far as Yem is concerned, he did *not* have this: he had the dignity of a *hērbed* and disciple; but because he was devoted to the good law, he was pure." Spiegel did not yet know the function of the conjunction *tā* "until," which he rendered as "*weil*, because." The text should probably be translated as: "Because Jam did not have the status of *hērbed* and disciple *until* he became a Weh-dēn [Zoroastrian] and 'righteous,' ..." (POS)].

82 [See Mohl, *Le livre des rois* I, pp. 48–52, and Warner and Warner, *The Sháhnáma of Firdausí*, I, p. 133 (POS)].

But Adam, too, is regarded as a priest. Thus, in y. Shabbat 2[:6, 5b] and Numbers Rabbah chap. 4, it says: "Adam was the firstborn of the world, and when he brought his sacrifice, he donned high-priestly garments." [Also,] "God created Adam in his image, i.e. after the likeness and in honor of his creator, so that he would be a high priest anointed to serve and officiate before God" (Tanḥuma, beginning of *Piqudei*).

13) According to Ferdowsī [ibid.], Yima made numerous inventions: he softens iron and makes weapons for fifty years; he takes another fifty years to invent the textiles: linen, silk, wool, beaver fur, etc. In brief, he is an expert in every craft (cp. Berezin, "Beschreibung der türkisch-tatarischen Handschriften," p. 255). Similarly regarding Adam: כל האומניות למד אד"ה, i.e. "Adam learned all crafts" (Genesis Rabbah chap. 24[83]; Yalqut on Genesis §40).

14) The final mythico-historical correspondence between Yima and the first human consists in the imputation of the origin of abnormalities and apes to each of them.

Concerning Yima, Bundahišn, p. 56, line 13 [K20, fol. 115v, Bd. 14b.0–2] states: "About the nature of apes and bears it is said: When the splendor withdrew from Jam, out of fear of the demons he took a demoness to wife and wedded his sister Jamag to a demon. Thereupon apes and tailed bears descended from them, and other *pernicious species*. This is what they say: under the rule of the snake, a young woman approached a *dēw* and a young man a *parīg*; and then they touched."[84] We may compare this to Genesis Rabbah chap. 20, b. Eruvin 18b, Yalqut on Genesis §42: In the period of about 130 years during which Adam lived separately from Eve, Eve was impregnated by male demons and Adam enticed to sexual intercourse by female ones. More on this in our treatise previously mentioned, p. 66f; we shall only add that according to *fragard* 18.101–102 [V. 18.46–47], also nightly pollution comes from impregnation by *daēvas*: "If anyone in his sleep emits his seed, he covers me as other men cover women during intercourse,"[85] so, too, does b. Eruvin 18b explain the existence of the *shedim*, spirits and specters of the night, from the involuntary pollutions of Adam: כי קאמרינן שבכבת זרע שיצא ממנו לאונסו ["as we have said, the nocturnal seminal emission that emerged from him involuntarily"].[86]

---

83 [*sic*. The correct text is כל האומניות אדם הראשון למד. (EK)]
84 [The end of the passage (not cited completely) means: "They also say this: Až ī Dahāg, during (his) reign let loose a demon upon a young woman and a witch upon a young man. And they had intercourse (K.'s 'touching') while he watched." The terminology is that of making farm animals copulate. (POS)]
85 [The passage is from a conversation between the divine Sraoša and the Druj (the cosmic Deception) about the three things that impregnate *her*; the man who emits his semen while asleep is the third of these. (POS)]
86 [*sic*. This phrase does not appear in b. Eruvin 18b; it appears in the Yalqut to Gen 5:3. (CH)]

4. Demonstration of the aggadic borrowing of the Adam legend from the Mašīy myth

As we saw in the preceding section, it is easy to assume, after the numerous proofs that the Adam myth was adorned by its borrowings from the Yima myth, that the Adam myth points to Persian conceptions at every turn. However, from careful comparison of the talmudic-midrashic sources with the Persian sources, to the extent that these concern accounts of the primordial creation, we learn that the elaborated Adam myth does not confine itself only to the points of borrowing demonstrated so far. In our search for Persian sources that treat the Mašīy myth, we will, lacking other accounts, unfortunately have to content ourselves with the fifteenth chapter of the Bundahišn (Bd. 14), which is dedicated to this myth. We may take comfort in the well-known fact that the Bundahišn drew from ancient traditions, as its frequent references to the Div [Dēn] attest.[87] At least this fact relieves us of the trouble of trying to first adduce evidence for the credibility and authenticity of the myths told. Indeed, these myths must be reckoned as a manifestation of prevalent popular belief if only for the reason that the Talmud and midrashim, too, reflect them faithfully, albeit through the broken prism of anti-Iranian presentation. We could no doubt capture even richer booty if the sources dealing with the Mašīy myth did not flow so sparsely. Yet the points of comparison that we can adduce have the power to convince us with a certainty that smashes every doubt of the use of Persian myths by the aggadists. For we can illustrate the narratives of the fifteenth chapter of the Bundahišn (Bd. 14) almost by point with identical midrashic or talmudic conceptions.

Already the etymology of the name of the first human: Gayô-meretan [*Gaiiō marətān*], i.e. "mortal life," and of the first human couple which came from him: (Mašīy and Mašyānīy, meaning "mortal,"[88]) reflect in their core meaning the frailty and infirmity of human nature, much in contrast to similar designations among other nations, like the Indians,[89] Greeks,[90] and Romans.[91] This fact presents

---

87 [I suspect that Div here is a typo for Dîn, as Windischmann has it. The *dēn* (of the Mazdayasnians), commonly rendered as 'religion,' is better viewed as the totality of the Zoroastrian oral tradition. (POS)]

88 Windischmann correctly explains (*Der Fortschritt der Sprachenkunde und ihre gegenwärtige Aufgabe. Festrede*, 1848, p. 23) '*mesha*' as the opposite of [Av.] '*amesha*' [*amaəša*] (immortal). On other etymological derivations cf. Justi, *Handbuch der Zendsprache*, p. 230. [In fact, '*mesha*,' Pahlavi *mašīy*, is most probably from Av. *mašiia* '(mortal) man.']

89 Where man is called *manu, manuja, mānuṣa*; from *man* 'to think' (cf. Latin *mens* = human). [Kohut appears to equate (etymologically) Latin *mens* and German *Mensch*, but this may be a misunderstanding of A.F. Pott, *Etymologische Forschungen auf dem Gebiete der Indo-Germanischen Sprachen ... Zweiter Teil*, Lemgo, 1836, p. 69, where Pott explains *Mann* as "der Mensch als denkendes Wesen." (POS)]

90 ἄνθρωπος i.e. 'of blossoming face'; cf. Pott, Etymologische Forschung I, p. 158 (but cf. the interpretation given in the second edition II, p. 924: "Mannesbild").

91 *homo*, i.e. 'calling one,' 'one endowed with the skill of language'; cf. C. Hofmann, "Ueber homo

in itself already an important point of contact with the Hebrew designation of man as אדם, i.e. "earthen one, dustborn."[92] This nomenclature reveals a characteristic conception of human destiny that is opposed to the pagan conception: by naming man not after a spiritual signification, but rather after an earthly-material, mortal essence, it expresses that his calling is to ascend from the humid earthly depths to the sun-bright height of purified knowledge and rationality. Man shall accordingly strive to ascend from his natural state, his earthiness, towards the highest level of development, to perfection. This idea evidently underlies the designation of אדם [Adam] as well as Gayōmard and Mašīy, even if Parsee cosmogony does not have the first human come from dust, or at least does not teach that he came from dust anywhere. This latter contrast can be seen most clearly by juxtaposing the respective sentences that contain this idea.

As for the Jewish sources, it is repeatedly said that all the various regions of the earth had to contribute their share to the creation of the first human – thus linking back to the etymon of the word "earth," and illustrating the cosmopolitan nature of man. Midrash Tanḥuma on *Piqudei* reasons about this in the following way. "God constructed," it says here, "the body of man from dust taken from all corners of the earth, in order that the earth could not make the claim, 'the dust of your body is not taken from me;' so that if someone, for example, was born in the East and were to die in the West, the earth in the West may not claim, 'Your body's dust has not been taken from me, I will not receive you.' For this reason, God assembled the body of the first human from dust hailing from all regions

---

und deus." ZDMG 1 (1847), p. 321ff. [He compares Skt. Hvā/hū "to call." (POS)]

92 We must understand this in analogy with αὐτόχθων, 'born from the earth' (Eusebius, I. Praepar. Evang. chap. 10, p. 36), and ἐπίγειον, 'earthen.' However, many exegetes derive אָדָם from אֲדָ, arab. أَدُمَ, أَدَمَ 'to be red,' s. W. Gesenius, *Thesaurus Philologicus Criticus Linguae Hebraeae et Chaldaeae Veteris Testamenti*. Leipzig 1839, p. 25. Josephus, *Antiquities* I, 1 §2, expresses the same view: σημαίνει δὲ Ἄδαμος κατὰ γλῶτταν τὴν Ἑβραίων πυρρός, ἐπειδήπερ ὑπὸ τῆς πυρρᾶς γῆς ἐγεγόνει, τοιαύτη γάρ ἐστιν ἡ παρθένος γῆ καὶ ἀληθινή ["This man was called Adam, which in the Hebrew tongue signifies one that is red, because he was formed out of red earth, compounded together; for of that kind is virgin and true earth"]. [The Arabic should be in the verbal form, following Gesenius, p. 24 col. 1 and, p. 25 col. 2: *aduma, adima*, 'to be brown or the color of clay.' Lane, *Arabic-English Lexicon*, pp. 36–37, renders this as 'having a tawny color'; The original Arabic should therefore be أَدِمَ, أَدُمَ. (TZ)] Of interest are the attempts at etymological derivation in the Arab writers. Thus Gawaliqi (*Gawaliqi's al-Mu'arrab*, ed. by E. Sachau, Leipzig 1867, p. 8) claims that the word آدم was good Arabic! For the names of all the prophets are, as he believes, loanwords, e.g. Ibrahim, Ismail, Ishaq, Iljas, Idris, etc. – with the exception of four, which are good Arabic: آدم صالح شُعَيْبٌ ومحمّد. Abu'l-Baqa's view (*al-Kulliyāt*, p. 341) complements this erudite note: "The names of all angels are loanwords, except for منكر ونكير ومالك ورضوان." The same writer provides us with some views about the etymology of the name Adam on p. 25. Some believe that the name means as much as من اديم الارض, because Adam meant 'dust' in Hebrew and he was created from dust. Others say that it was derived from Syriac, where אדם meant 'the resting one': الساكن (he probably thought of דום, דמם!). Mas'udi (*Murug ud-Dahab* I, p. 52) generally refers to the first opinion, but adds: وقيل غير ذلك. Baidawi I, p. 49, also assembles several opinions. See also the *Studien über Tanchum Jeruschalmi* by Dr. J. Goldziher (1870), p. 12n4, for examples of what fantastic etymologies even indigenous words have to suffer.

of the earth."⁹³ Even more poignantly, b. Sanhedrin 38b states: "The trunk (the lower part of the human body) God created from Babylonia (the lowland); the head (the seat of intelligence) from Palestine (the highland), and the other bodily members from the remaining countries."⁹⁴ Related to this conception is a cosmogony found in Islamic legends, to which the famous poet Jalāl-al-Din Rumi lends vivid expression in the myth he treats extensively in his Masnavi [Book V, vv. 1556–1606]:⁹⁵ When God wanted to form man from clay, he first commissioned the angel Gabriel, then Michael, then Israfil, to bring a handful of earth of seven different colors. But these archangels, weakened by the earth's plea to spare it, returned to their highest commissioner without having done what he asked them. Only when God dispatched the angel of death with the same assignment, did he return with a handful of seven-colored earth, and Adam was created. This seven-colored earth contained the material for the different races of man, all of which were contained implicitly in the first human. One can still recognize the white earth in white people, the black one in black people, the half-black one in the Nubians and Barabras, the yellow one in the Mongolians, the green one in the olive-colored Indians, the brown one in the Arabs, and the red one in the diverse tribes living in the wild.⁹⁶

Things are different, however, following another Persian cosmogony, according to which the substrate of the creation of man is not the earth in itself, but rather the σπέρμα of Gayōmard ("of mortal life," a clever expression for his short lifespan,⁹⁷ on the one hand, and of human frailty, on the other), who was created by Ahura Mazdā and killed by Angra Mainyu, and from whose seed the first human couple Mašīy and Mašyānīy came. It is nowhere stated from precisely which material the first human,⁹⁸ Gayōmard himself, was formed. Judging by an unfortunately very obscure passage in the Bundahišn, chap. 3, p. 10, line 14 [K20, fol. 92v, Bd. 4.23], Gayōmard rises from the *khei* [the Bundahišn has *xvəy* in Avestan characters] which can be compared either with New Persian *xayu* 'saliva' or *xʷei* 'sweat' and hence must mean either 'saliva' or 'sweat.'⁹⁹ It would be worth

93 והתחיל מקבץ את גופו של אד"ה מארבע רוחות העולם כדי שלא תאמר הארץ אין עפר גופך משלי אם לוקח ממזרח ויפטר במערב כדי שלא תאמר ארץ מערב אין עפר גופך משלי לא אקבלך ולפיכך נטלו מארבע רוחות העולם כדי שבכל ר' מאיר א' אד"ה מכל העולם כלו הוצבר עפרו שנ'. More simply b. Sanhedrin 38a: מקום שיפטר שיקבלו הארץ גלמי ראו עיניך וכתיב כי ד' עיניו משוטטות בכל הארץ. The last verse is omitted in the variant preserved in Yalqut on Psalms § 888; Avot de-Rabbi Nathan 1 has: אד"ה הוצבר עפרו.
94 אד"ה גופו מבבל וראשו מארץ ישראל ואבריו משאר ארצות.
95 [See R.A. Nicholson, ed., *The Mathnawí of Jalálu'ddín Rúmí*, London, 1925–40; vol. 5, pp. 101–102 (text), vol. 6, pp. 96–97 (transl.); reference kindly supplied by Justine Landau (POS)].
96 This myth appears to me as a mere imitation of the almost identical myth about Moses' preparations for his death (in the end of Deuteronomy Rabbah; cf. our study p. 70n3).
97 According to Bundahišn, chap. 3 p. 11 [K20, fol. 93r, Bd. 4.25], he lived only thirty years.
98 [Av.] *nâ ashava* [*nā ašauua*], as it says in the primary texts, or *gabrai âa ruban [mard ī ahlaw]*, as it says in Bundahišn chap. 3, p. 8, lines 7, 13 [K20, fol. 91v, Bd. 4.1, 4].
99 Cf. Windischmann, *Mithra* p. 75n1 and the publication by Haug cited there, "Über die Pehlevi-Sprache und den Bundeshesh," Göttingische Gelehrte Anzeigen (GGA) 3 (1854), p. 42, who

the effort to examine whether an early Gnostic influence may not be detected in the notion that the first human arose from the creative principle of the water;[100] but in order not to stray too far, we content ourselves with merely suggesting this assumption. Keeping our parallel before our eyes, we shall without further ado turn to the analysis of the fifteenth chapter of the Bundahišn.

For the sake of greater clarity, we wish to discuss this chapter phrase by phrase, based on the second revision of Windischmann's translation (cp. *Zoroastrische Studien*, p. 213f), and support it with talmudic-midrashic passages.

1) "About the constitution of man it is said in the law: Gayōmard emitted seed when he died. This seed was purified in the course of the sunlight; Nēryōsang received two parts to keep, and Spandarmad seized the other part. After forty years, they (Mašīy and Mašyānīy) grew up from the earth in the shape of a *rëiva* plant with a single stem; fifteen years old during the [festival of] Mihragān in the month of Mithra; in such manner that their hands were behind their ears, one joined to the other; both of like appearance, and their middle combined; they were so very similar in shape that one could not tell which of them was man and which woman."

Regardless of the extent to which these introductory words of the Bundahišn chapter bear the mark of authentic Iranian thought, the basic idea nevertheless entered the imagination of the *aggadah*, albeit in much more ethical and pleasing

---

explains *khei* as: "name of a legendary water, according to the tradition." [The Pahlavi forms are *xayūg* "saliva" and *xwēy* 'sweat,' but *xwēy* is also 'sleep' and a homonym of *xwāb* 'sleep.' Today, it is commonly thought that Gayōmard rose from his *sleep*." (POS)]

100 In particular, Valentinians and Ophites regarded water as a symbol of *hyle*, because of its transformative power, which they related to the biblical phrase: the spirit of God hovered over the surface of the waters. It is therefore possible that the Persian cosmogonic idea that Gayōmard emerged from the *khei* (the primordial water) was shaped with an eye to Gen 1:2. Proof that this claim is not overly bold comes from Midrash Tanḥuma § *Tazria*, which explains the cited verse Gen 1:2 as follows: ורוח אלהים מרחפת על פני המים זו נפשו של אדם הראשון ["*and the spirit of God swept over the surface of the water*" – this is the spirit of the first man"]; and cf. Yalqut on Genesis §4. However, in Palestine, farther away from Parsee influence, they were not ready to accept this notion. We find therefore the following polemic in y. Ḥagigah 2:1 מי שאמר מתחילה היה העולם מים במים הרי זה פוגם, i.e., "whosoever adheres to the idea that the primary substance of the creation was water, adheres to a misguided view," which is a reservation against the Persian cosmogonic belief. (H. Grätz, *Gnosticismus und Judenthum*, Krotoschin, 1846, p. 30 gives another explanation.) For this reason, the interpretation זה נפשו של א״ה ["this is the spirit of the first man"] found in Tanḥuma and Yalqut is absent from the *midrash* Genesis Rabbah redacted on Palestinian ground; in chap. 2, the biblical phrase מרחפת ע״פ המים ["*hovered over the surface of the water*"] is, in fact, interpreted as זה רוחו של מלך המשיח ["this is the spirit of the King Messiah"]. The popularity of the Persian notion of the creation of man from water is already obvious from the fact that this idea found expression even in amulets, e.g. in the Persian amulet of Lord Byron, where it says: "the one who created (man) after his likeness," s. J.V. Hammer-Purgstall, *Die Geisterlehre der Moslimen*. Vienna, 1852, p. 37. Highly noteworthy for our claim is furthermore the important point that *Apąm napå* (the genius of water) was seen and revered as the creative power of vitalization, fertilization, and reproduction in the same way as the etymologically and semantically cognate Vedic *Apām napāt* in the Indian tradition. For comprehensive evidence thereof see Windischmann, *Zoroastrische Studien*, p. 177f.

form. Here, too, the first human is conceived as a plant, as it were, growing up from the earth.[101] However, this "as it were" constitutes a rather large partition between the Indogermanic and Semitic worlds of thought: there, this cosmogonic image is taken for most vivid reality – here, in the picture of a *parable* and illustrated.

For this parable goes as follows (Genesis Rabbah chap. 8; Yalqut on Psalms §834 and elsewhere): "At the creation of man, Grace, Truth, Justice, and Peace started arguing. Grace spoke: 'May God create him, for he will practice acts of love.' 'Do not create him,' Truth called out, 'for he will commit acts of deception.' 'Form him,' Justice raised its voice, 'so that he may dispense justice.' But Peace objected, 'Do not create him, for he will only stir hatred and strife.' Then God seized *Truth* and threw it down on the earth so that it should *grow* up, as it says (Ps 85:12): 'Let truth spring up from the ground!'"[102] In this way, the creation of the first human is spoken of as growth, although with reference to the expression of the psalmist (Ps 85:12). It seems all the more remarkable that Truth was thrown down on the earth, of all things, and shall grow from there – to say nothing of the moral-ethical aspect of this parable – as the growth of the *rëiva* plant occurs just on Mihragān, the calendrical day of Mithra, who, as is well known, is the representative of truth *par excellence*.

Now, as for the myth mentioned in the Bundahišn of the *rëiva* having a single stem, which is meant to symbolize the *one* origin and undividedness of the human couple, the Adam legend too, knows this feature. Avot de-Rabbi Nathan chap. 1 says: "When God created the first human, he shaped him in front and in back (i.e. androgynous), as the psalmist says (Ps 139:5): "You shaped me before and behind."[103] With reference to this verse it says elsewhere:[104] "God created the first human דו פרצופין, (i.e. δύο πρόσωπα, with two faces), for it says, 'You shaped me behind and before.' Rav and Shmuel differ on this. According to one, his (the first human's) face was androgynous, according to the other, his genitalia." I find it likely that we must revindicate the latter opinion of Shmuel as we can glean from numerous references that he was well familiar with the Persian way of thought. Indeed, we have seen that the quoted passage from the Bundahišn emphasizes greatly and in various formulations that the first humans were conjoined into a

---

101 The Italic myth, too, has the first humans grow from trees; cf. Virgil, Aeneid VIII 131, and Juvenal Satires VI 11 [refs. from Windischmann, *Zoroastrische Studien*, p. 213].
102 In Rigveda II.35.8 it says about the deity *Apām napāt*: "Like branches, the other creatures grow forth from him; like plants with their shoots." [Kohut understands the *midrash* to say that Truth is cast to the ground so that humankind can grow forth from it; in fact, the *midrash* appears to say that Truth's objections to the creation of humankind are overcome when God casts it to the ground to silence it, enabling him to turn to the creation of humankind unimpeded. (CH)]
103 כשבראו הקב"ה לא"ה צר אותו פנים ואחור שנא' אחור וקדם צרתני.
104 b. Berakhot 61a, b. ʿEruvin 10b, b. Sanhedrin 38b: דו פרצופין היה לא"ה שנאמר אחור וקדם צרתני רב ושמואל חד אמר פרצוף וחד אמר זנב. The same appears in Genesis Rabbah 8 and Yalqut on Psalms § 834 with the added point that the first human couple was sawed apart; cf. above.

single being by their genitalia, such that one could not discern who was man and who was woman.

2) The Bundahišn continues: "When both had grown from plant shape into human shape, that splendor [xwarrah] which is the soul entered them spiritually. Still now, the tree grew forth in this way, bearing as its fruits *ten types of humans*."

The meaning of this obscure statement is, I assume, that the first man envisaged as a plant already contained the seed and basic conditions for the development of future generations, and bore in him the nature dwelling in *all* human beings. The following, frequently recurring, phrase is a counterpart to this image:[105] "When God created Adam, he chose him as the first material, and (the seed) for all successive generations was placed in him."

3) "Ahura[106] spoke to Mašīy and Mašyānīy: You are humans; you are fathers of the worlds." This last passage is meant to express the destiny of man to be a citizen of two worlds. Correspondingly, it says in Midrash Genesis Rabbah chap. 14: "Two creations are completed in man, since he contains within himself the nature of the earthly beings and of the heavenly ones."[107] And further: "Man possesses a drive towards good and towards evil";[108] "Behold, said God, I create him in the image and likeness of the heavenly creatures, and such that he shall multiply in the way of the earthly creatures. If I created him only after the image of the upper ones, he would live and never die; if I created him only in the way of the lower ones, he would die without ever living (spiritually), therefore he shall participate in the nature of these and those."[109] The human, it says in perfect analogy with the Bundahišn, belongs to two worlds, to this world and the beyond.[110]

4) "You have been created by me with perfect mind, and pure; you shall perform the works of the commandments with perfect mind, think good thoughts, speak good words, do good deeds, and do not sacrifice to the *dēws*" (Bundahišn).

The aggadic sources also treat the first human's perfection exhaustively. "Adam is the light of the world,"[111] by means of which he could see from one end of the world to the other.[112] "Adam was the last and yet the first of the world's creation. Created last on the sixth day, he was nevertheless the first creation of this day,

---

105 b. Bava Metsi'a 85b, b. Avodah Zarah 5a, Genesis Rabbah 8, Yalqut on Psalms 139 § 887:
בשעה שברה הקב״ה את אד״ה גולם בראו והיה מסוף העולם ועד סופו הה״ד גלמי ראו עיניך.
106 [Kohut uses Avestan Ahura [Mazdā] for Pahl. Ohrmazd throughout this section. (POS)]
107 ב׳ יצירות מן התחתונים ומן העליונים.
108 ב׳ יצירות יצר טוב ויצר הרע.
109 הרי אני בורא אותו בצלם וכדמות מן העליונים פרה ורבה מן התחתונים – אם אני בוראו מן העליונים הוא חי ואינו מת מן התחתונים הוא מת ואינו חי אלא הרי אני בוראו מאלו ואלו.
110 ב׳ יצירות אחד לעולם הזה ואחד לעולם הבא ["two creations – one in this world and one in the world to come"].
111 y. Shabbat 2:6, 5b: אד״ה נרו של עולם ["the first Adam was the light of the world"]; (like Yima, i.e., Jamšid, the Radiant One). [Kohut erroneously lists Genesis Rabbah 14 (גמר חלתו שלעולם), and Numbers Rabbah 4 (בכורו דל עולם) as parallels. The phrase does have parallels in Avot de-Rabbi Nathan (B 9 and B 42) and Tanḥuma (מצורע and בהעלותך). (EK)]
112 b. Ḥagigah 12.

because with him the creation of physical life was completed, as it says (Gen 1:24): '*Let the earth bring forth living creatures.*' Adam came into being last, after everything else had been created, yet he was the beginning of all creation."[113] And further,[114] "All things were created perfect with Adam; only through his fall they became defective."

"'*And God saw that everything he had made was good and perfect,*' (Gen 1:10 [*sic*; actually Gen 1:31 (CH)]) – this refers to Adam," it is said.[115] "Who is so wise?" (Qoh 2). "That is Adam."[116] "'*He was wiser than all men*' (1 Kings 5:11) – this again refers to Adam,"[117] whose "wisdom surpassed even that of the angels."[118]

Just like the Bundahišn, the *midrash* connects Adam's perfection to his new obligation to observe the divine commandments. Adam's calling is to be proven by keeping the seven Noahide commandments (b. Ḥagigah 12a, b. Bava Batra 75a, Genesis Rabbah chap. 24).

"*The Eternal God took Adam*" (Gen 2:15) is explained in Genesis Rabbah chap. 16 as: Adam shall take on his calling, for the word 'take' signifies the same as (in) the expression (Hos 14:3) "*Take with you* [plur.] *words and return to God.*" "*He placed him in the garden*" (Gen 2:15), it says further, i.e. he protected him and let him relish the delights of the trees, but also in order "*to work it and to care for it*" (Gen 2:15). This last statement refers to the observance of the divine precepts, for the work certainly did not consist in digging, ploughing, harrowing, etc., since, after all, the trees of Eden prospered all by themselves. Neither did it consist in watering them, since the streams of the garden provided this (Gen 2:10). The work thus consisted solely in fulfilling the prescribed commandments..."[119]

5) "They both thought this, delighted one in the other: this is a human being" (Bundahišn [Bd. 14.12]). So, only through the mutual completion of the two halves did they become aware of their joy and their own humanity. This should be compared to the analogous statement in the Talmud, b. Yevamot 63a: מי שאין לו אשה אינו אדם ["he who has no woman is not a man"];[120] cp. also Yalqut on Genesis §23, כל אדם שאין לו אשה אינו אדם שנ' זכר ונקבה בראם ["any man who does not have a woman is not a man for it is written, 'male and female he created them'"]. The latter [the Yalqut on Gen 2:18] also says on analogy with Bundahišn: כל אדם שאין לו אשה שרוי בלא טובה בלא שמחה בלא ברכה ["any man who does not have a woman is without goodness, without joy and without blessing"].

---

113 Genesis Rabbah 8; Tanḥuma § *Tazria*.
114 Genesis Rabbah 12; Exodus Rabbah 30. [Kohut paraphrases. (EK)]
115 Genesis Rabbah 9 והנה טוב מאד זו אדם הראשון
116 Numbers Rabbah 19 מי כחכם זו א״ה
117 Ibid., ויחכם מכל אדם זו אד״ה
118 Ibid., אדם שאני רוצה לבראת חכמתו מרובה משלכם
119 [No open quotes are provided for the closed quotes here. The motif of Adam studying Torah appears not in Genesis Rabbah (which describes Adam as observing only six, and on one view all seven, of the Noahide laws) but in Sifre Deuteronomy to Deut 11:13. (CH)].
120 [*sic*; the Vilna p.e. reads כל אדם שאין לו אשה אינו אדם. (EK)]

6) "And they did this as their first act: when they came together, they mingled"[121] (Bundahišn [Bd. 14.13]).

The *midrash* also reports that the mating took place already on the first day of the creation of the human couple (Genesis Rabbah 22): "Three miracles occurred on that day (when Adam was created): on that very day they were created, on that very day they practiced coitus, on that very day they produced offspring."[122] Avot de-Rabbi Nathan even gives an hour-by-hour account of their activities: "In the sixth hour the soul was given to him, in the seventh he stood on his feet, in the eighth he united with Eve."[123]

7) "Then they spoke this as their first speech: Ahura created water, earth, plants, animals, stars, moon and sun, and all those good things that are manifest through purity – all of them" (Bundahišn).

According to Numbers Rabbah chap. 19, Adam names the creatures created by God, and recognizes the greatness and justice of God.[124] The following passage from Tanḥuma *Piqudei* applies to them: "When they (the angels) saw Adam, they feared him, for they believed he had created them. Then they wanted to worship him, but he said to them, 'why do you want to bow down before me? Come, let us take a look at all the creatures whom He, blessed be His name, created.' When he beheld them, he marveled and pitched a hymn of praise, saying (Ps 31:20), 'How great is your goodness, that you have laid up for your pious ones!' And he further exclaimed, 'How great are your works, O God!'"[125]

8) "Then the adversary rushed into their mind and *defiled* (*āhōgēnīd*, in Spiegel's reading) their thought, and they lied: Ahriman created water, earth, plants, animals, and everything else. Because this lying speech was spoken, it was spoken at the will of the *dēws*" (Bundahišn).

Windischmann (*Zoroastrische Studien*, p. 218) locates the source for Ahriman's ability to manipulate the thought of the first human couple in the inverted order of action, namely in the fact that Mašīy and Mašyānīy pursued their cravings and sensual desires *before* they expressed their gratitude towards their creator. Similarly, it is said about Adam: "He did not pitch a hymn of praise immediately upon his creation,"[126] for which reason the verse (Lam 2:6) [ויחמס כגן שכו] "He has

---

121 [Actually "urinated." (POS)]
122 ג׳ פלאים נעשו באותו היום בו ביום נבראו בו ביום שמשו בו ביום הוציאו תולדות.
123 ששית נתנה בו נשמה שבעית עמד על רגליו שמינית נזדוגה לו חוה. Cf. also b. Sanhedrin 38b.
124 כיון שברא אדם העבירן לפניו א״ל מה שמותן של אלו אמר לזה נאה לקרות שור ולזה ארי ולזה סוס ולזה חמור ולזה גמל ולזה נשר – א״ל הקב״ה אני מה שמי א״ל יי״י למה שאתה אדון על כל הבריאות ["When he created Adam he passed them before him. He said to him, 'What are their names?' He said, 'It would be appropriate to call this one an ox, and this one a lion and this one a horse and this one a donkey and this one a camel and this one an eagle.' The Holy One, blessed be He, said to him, 'What is my name?' He answered him, 'The Lord, for you are the lord of all creation.'"]
125 וראוהו ונתיראו מלפניו היו סבורים שהוא בראם ובאו להשתחות לו אמר להן למה באתם להשתחות לי נבוא כלנו נראה כל הבריות שברא הקב״ה והיה תמה בלבו התחיל משבח ומפאר ליוצרו ואומר מה רב טובך אשר צפנת ליראיך ואמר מה רבו מעשיך יי״י.
126 Exodus Rabbah 23: ברא אד״ה ולא אמר שירה; cf. b. Avodah Zarah 8a, according to which Adam only brought a thanksgiving offering once he had gained insights into the eternal laws of nature.

stripped his tabernacle, like a garden"] is applied to Adam, who proved himself ungrateful for the grace dispensed to him. Cf. Midrash Lamentations Rabbah on the above verse.

On analogy with the expression in the Bundahišn [Bd. 14.15] that Ahriman polluted the senses of the first man (a variant of which appears in Bundahišn, p. 11, l. 12 [K20, fol. 93r, Bd. 4.27]), it also says about Satan, embellished after the model of Ahriman (Satan, too, is regarded as a snake, similarly to the Persian Aži Dahāka), that he poured filth over Eve.[127] See the references above; also the text passages already given, above, showing that Adam, too, was said to have been expelled from paradise on account of lies and deceit.

9) "Their souls will be in hell until the future body." Thus, the sin of the first human will not be atoned for until the resurrection, i.e., until the arrival of the "Healer Saošyans" in the view of the Parsees. At the resurrection itself, "the bones of Gayōmard will rise first, then those of Mašīy and Mašyānīy, and then those of the other humans."[128] And further below in the text it says [Bd. 34.8], "half of the light that is with the sun shines on (or: makes recognizable) Gayōmard, the other half on the rest of mankind."

From all these passages it is now sufficiently clear that the first human will nevertheless be the first to partake in the divine blessings at the time of resurrection, although he has forfeited the divine grace on account of his fall and is now called *druwand* (ungodly). The *midrash* makes a similar assessment about Adam.

In Midrash Genesis Rabbah chap. 21 it says: "'I shall behold your face in righteousness and when I awake, I shall delight in your likeness' (Ps 17:15); Only when the one will rise who has been created after your likeness, namely the messiah,[129] I, Adam, will behold your face."[130] Indeed, in line with the Parsee conception we have discussed extensively elsewhere,[131] Adam is mentioned among the fifteen personalities effecting the resurrection. Likewise, Adam as the first human is often connected with the messiah, who represents the final link in the chain of human generations;[132] thus, e.g., when it says, in Genesis Rabbah chap.

---

127 [The sentence is confused: Bd. 4.27 refers to the pollution of the fire; see above, p. 524 and n70. (POS)]

128 Cf. Bundahišn chap. 31, p. 72 line 11 [K20, fol. 124v, Bd. 34.6]: מְשִׁיאָנִי יְ מָשִׁיָא זַד אַחַר אַנְכֵּיגִית רָאֵרָא זַד אַחַר אַפָּאנִיךְ מַרְתּוּגְמָאן וּנַזְדָסְתָ אָסַת זַד יְ גִּיוֹמַרְת [probably after Spiegel, *Einleitung* II, p. 245 line 10.]. [*nazdist ast ān ī Gayōmard ul hangēzēd pas ān ī Mašīy Mašyānīy pas ān ī abārīg mardōmān.* (POS)]

129 As already mentioned earlier, Genesis Rabbah, Yalqut and Tanḥuma interpret the verse "*the spirit of God hovered over the surface of the water*" as meaning that this is the רוחו של משיח ["the spirit of the Messiah"] who carries the spirit of God within him.

130 אני בצדק אחזה פניך אשבעה בהקיץ תמונתיך לכשיקיץ אותו שנברא בדמותך באותה שעה אני אחזה פניך באותה שעה אני מצדיק מאותה גזרה.

131 See our study, "Was hat die talmudische Eschatologie aus dem Parsismus aufgenommen?," ZDMG 21 (1867), p. 574.

132 The Zand Avesta, too, frequently uses the phrase *haca gaiiāṯ marəθnaṯ ā saošiiantāṯ vərəθraynaṯ*, i.e., "from Gayōmard to the Saošyant, i.e., from creation to resurrection." Cf. Yasna 26.33

12: "The six things that were lost from the world on account of Adam's sin will return at the time of the messiah."[133] "The messiah will not appear until all the souls recorded in the book of Adam have been created."[134]

10) "They went about without food for thirty days, and wore black garments" (Bundahišn).

The thirty day period during which the primordial humans abstain from food – in response to their grief, as Windischmann correctly notes – corresponds to the thirty prayers for the dead prescribed in *fragard* 12. 3, 4 [V. 12.1] for the *dahmanqm* (pious). The donning of black garments[135] refers of course to this mourning. The Talmud states in agreement (b. Eruvin 18b; cp. Yalqut on Genesis § 42): "Adam fasted for 130 days and donned a belt of fig leaves as a sign of mourning."[136]

11) "The *dēws* came with force and deprived them of the taste of food, so that of a hundred parts only one remained" (Bundahišn).

If Mašīy and Mašyānīy already openly displayed their fall from Ahura Mazdā by turning away from the original nourishment, fruits (cp. Bundahišn, p. 70, l. 13 [K20, fol. 123v, Bd. 34.1]), and toward dairy consumption, i.e., by the transition to foods of animal origin,[137] then their transgression becomes only much graver as they *express their joy* about the new diet, saying: "Greater joy it is to me when I enjoy this." But, no sooner had they uttered this ungodly word than their punishment befell them: the *dēws* take away their delight in food, as the cited passage

---

[Y. 26.10], Yašt 13.145. [The phrase is only applied to the fravashis, implying that the first fravashi in this world belonged to Gayōmard and that the last fravashi in this world will belong to the Saošyant. (POS)]

133 Numbers Rabbah 13: אלו הן ו' דברים שנטלו מאד"ה – עתידין לחזור בימות המשיח.

134 Genesis Rabbah 24: אין המלך המשיח בא עד שיבראו כל הנשמות שעלו במחשבה להבראות ואלו הן הנשמות האמונות בספרו של אדם. In b. Avodah Zarah 5a, Yalqut on Isaiah §831 it says: אין בן דוד בא עד שיכלו כל הנשמות שבגוף ["The son of David will not come until all the souls in the body have been exhausted"; translation of Yishai Kiel]. The difficult word שבגוף has, to the best of my knowledge, not yet been explained. I derive it from the Zand term, *gup*, 'to conceal.' That is, the messiah will not come until all the souls that are still concealed will have come into being, i.e. be created. [Av. *gup* 'to conceal' is probably taken from Justi (*Handbuch der Zendsprache*, p. 105), who sees this (Indic) verb in Av. *gufra-* 'deep,' an etymology that is no longer accepted. (POS)]

135 See Diodor XI.57 [Diodorus Siculus, *Fragments* book XI, 57.3] on the Persian custom to put on πεντίμην ἐσθῆτα ['garment of mourning'] as a sign of mourning.

136 According to b. Avodah Zarah 8a, Adam fasted for only eight days, the common period of mourning in the stricter sense.

137 Adam was also barred from foods of animal origin, according to b. Sanhedrin 59b: אד"ה לא הותר לו בשר לאכילה ["The first man was not permitted to eat meat"]. We will cite a contrary opinion later. A Tibetan-Mongolian myth exhibits an undeniable similarity with the Persian one. According to this myth, the first inhabitants of the earth were similar to the gods in their perfection; however, they degenerated after they began eating from the white, sugar-like *schima* which sprouted forth on the surface of the earth. As soon as they had eaten from this food, a fermentation occurred in their intestines ... Their hunger disappeared, the splendor vanished from their faces (as we heard earlier about Adam and Yima), etc. Cf. E.F.K. Rosenmüller, *Das alte und neue Morgenland* I, Leipzig 1818, p. 13.

relates [Bd. 14.19–20].[138] Adam also lost his sweet-smelling and tasty food on account of his sin, as Genesis Rabbah 20 notes: "Had you not transgressed, you could have taken herbs from the garden of Eden and tasted in them all the delicacies in the world; but now that you sinned you have to eat the herbs of the field."[139] A related view recounts, "When Adam heard the penalty for his sin announced: 'Thorns and thistles it will bring forth for you' (Gen 3:18), his eyes overflowed with tears, and he exclaimed, 'Is there only one food for the cattle and me? Will I eat from the same trough as my ass?'"[140]

12) "After one thousand days and nights they came to a fat white ram. They killed it, and according to the instructions from the celestial *yazata*s, they let fire descend from the trees Kunār and Šimsār. For these two trees produce fire" (Bundahišn).

This myth about the *yazata*s teaching the first humans to eat meat, reminiscent of the Prometheus myth about the fire being brought down to earth, reappears in the Talmud. B. Sanhedrin 59b says: "Adam was sitting in the garden of Eden, and the angels were frying meat and cooling wine for him."[141]

13) "For fifty years they did not have any desire to mingle, and if they had mingled, no children would have been born. By the end of the fifty years, they experienced a desire to procreate, first Mašīy and then Mašyānīy" (Bundahišn). We noted already at the end of section III that b. Eruvin 18b, Genesis Rabbah 20, Yalqut on Genesis §§ 33 and 40, and many other passages report about Adam that he did not feel any sexual desire. So, let us here only add the motivation for this separation of Adam from Eve, as it is given in Yalqut §34: "After Adam saw that his descendants would one day be consigned to hell, he abstained from sexual pleasure. But when he learned that after 26 generations his descendants would be

---

138 In contrast to *Rāman xvāstra* (the genius of the air), whom the later tradition calls *Rāmišn xwālom* because he gives the food its taste [see Pahl. Y.1.3, etc.], the *dēws* deprive the foodstuffs of their taste (cf. Spiegel, *Avesta ... aus dem Grundtext übersetzt* II, p. 6, 37; III, p. xxxiv), which is why we hear above that the *food* was *inexhaustible* during Yima's rule, because the *dēws* had no power.

139 אילו זכית היית נוטל עשבים מתוך גן עדן וטועם בהם כל מעדנים שבעולם עכשיו שלא זכית ואכלת את עשב השדה.

140 b. Pesaḥim 118a; Avot de-Rabbi Nathan, end of 1.

141 א"ה מיסב בג"ע היה והיו מלאכי השרת צולין לו בשר ומסננין לו יין. Cf. also Avot de-Rabbi Nathan loc. cit., which has the correct reading מצננין. According to one view, the enjoyment of wine caused Adam's fall (cf. Genesis Rabbah 15). There is an interesting parallel in the poet Abu Nuwas who, describing his confidential acquaintance with Satan, relates among other things: "He (Satan) spoke: Do you have a small wine / stored at the time of Adam," etc. See Hammer-Purgstall loc. cit., p. 33. To return to the cited passage in b. Sanhedrin 59b and Avot de-Rabbi Nathan 1, let us mention its ending, which says: הציץ בו נחש וראה בכבודו ונתקנא בו ["The snake looked and saw the honor (paid to Adam) and became jealous of him"]. The envy caused by Adam would, accordingly, have been the reason for the fall. This corresponds to the following passage from the fifteenth chapter of the Bundahišn [Bd. 14.26]: "Thereupon they brought this evil envy (*abārōn*) upon each other. Thereupon the *dēws* raised their voices from the depths: 'You are humans – sacrifice to the *dēws*, until your devil of envy finds rest!'" That envy did not exist in the golden age we have seen above.

deemed worthy of the divine revelation, he became obliged to beget offspring."[142] From this passage we also learn that the impulse to unite came from Adam, just as in the Bundahišn. This is supported by the formulation והאדם ידע ["and the man knew"] in Genesis 4:1.

14) "Seven couples came from them, male and female, all brother and sister, husband and wife" (Bundahišn). The Midrash confirms the exact same idea and further emphasizes that all the children who came from the first human saw the light of day as twins, so that there were seven of them, Adam included.[143]

15) At the end of the fifteenth chapter it says in the Bundahišn [Bd. 14.38]: "Twenty-five species emerged from the seed of Gayōmard, namely: land humans, water humans, single-eared, single-eyed, single-legged ones, the winged ones such as the bats, the tailed ones, and those who have hairy bodies."[144]

We have already stated that such abnormalities and specters of the night are said to have come into being during the period when Adam lived separately from Eve (see above).

* * *

Looking back at the outcome of our comparison of the Adam myth with the Yima myth, on the one hand, and with the Mašīy myth, on the other, we find the thesis of the mutual relationship between the Persian and Jewish sources, which we posited at the beginning of this treatment, fully confirmed. Yet we can also derive another lesson from the example of the Adam myth developed here: that the compilation of the talmudic-midrashic passages, as meritorious as this micrological labor may be,[145] will remain merely mechanical as long as it is not supplemented and illuminated by the juxtaposition of the pertinent Persian sources.

---

142 וכיון שראה אדם שבניו עתידין ליאבד בגיהנם מעט עצמה מפריה ורביה וכיון שראה שאחר כ"ו דורות עתידין בניו לקבל התורה נזקק להעמיד תולדות והאדם ידע את חוה אשתו.

143 Cf. Genesis Rabbah 22: עלו למטה שנים וירדו שבעה קין ותאומתו והבל ושתי תאומותיו ["Two entered the bed and seven left it: Cain and his twin sister and Abel and his two twin sisters"]. Identically, Yalqut on Genesis §35. The fact that the *midrash* rather forcefully lets two twins be reborn in order to reach the number seven indicates that this assumption rests on said Persian notion.

144 b. Niddah 24b also mentions winged human abnormalities: המפלת דמות לילית אמו טמאה לידה ולד הוא אלא שיש לו כנפים ["An aborted fetus that has the likeness of Lilith, the mother is impure because she has given birth to a child except that it has wings"]. In our study "Über die jüdische Angelologie," p. 88, this passage is rendered incorrectly and needs to be corrected accordingly.

145 As, for instance, the article "Adam" in Dr. Hamburger's *Geist der Agada*, Leipzig 1876, p. 75 ff.

INDEX

Abba, R. 168, 175, 220, 223, 285
Abbahu, Rabbi 199n10, 199, 216, 352–3, 355–6, 356n36, 360–361, 361n74, 362, 383
Abel 6, 52–5, 72, 420, 539
abortion 83, 110
Abraham 33–4, 45, 306, 324–5, 333, 347, 391, 409, 438, 514
Abtalion *see Avtalyon*
academy 6, 77, 197, 216–17, 221–3, 225, 228–9, 250–251, 255, 423, 425, 496–7 *see also bet midrash* and *see also* house of study
Adam 277, 507, 509, 512–14, 519–27, 529–30, 533–9; beauty and radiant splendor 519; creation of 521; body height of 522; legend of 507, 518–19, 528, 532; myth of 505–6, 519, 528, 539; perfection of 534; sins of 537
administration 159, 191, 201, 206–8, 237–8, 242, 253, 497–8; central 205, 223, 226, 237; local 207–8, 232, 237, 377; religious 202
adultery 58, 75–7, 96, 99, 411
aggadah 6–7, 10, 12, 43–5, 47–50, 51, 53, 58, 60–61, 64–7, 71, 77, 275, 277–9, 305–6, 484, 489, 518–19, 522
aggadic composition 256, 275
Agrippa, Marcus 145–7, 151, 160, 442
Ahura Mazdā 508–9, 511, 513, 516–17, 530, 537
Akiva, R. 15, 32, 50, 62–3, 68–9, 140, 175–8, 192–3, 218–20, 270, 273, 286, 295–9, 307–14, 371–2, 375–7, 396, 488
Albeck, Ḥanoch. 216, 222, 224–5, 283, 285, 292, 295, 297, 299, 302
Albright, William F. 437
Alexander, Elizabeth Shanks 10, 44

Alexander the Great 147–8, 185, 419–23, 482, 489
Alexander, Philip 18
Alexander Yannai *see* Yannai, Alexander
Alexandria 4, 45, 48, 287, 289, 395, 411, 421–2, 439, 447
Alexandrians 85, 101, 102, 107, 398
Alon, Gedalyahu 8–9, 23, 442
alphabet 60, 81–2, 270, 275, 398
altars 97, 112, 147, 185, 293, 312, 379, 392, 405; erecting of special 380; external 143; heathen 185; idolatrous 185–6; inner 289
am ha'arets 8, 16, 20, 168, 193-4, 214, 439
Amoraim 208, 232–4, 239, 268, 283, 285–6, 303–5, 308, 451, 453–4
ancestors 38, 251, 253–4, 257, 390, 431, 444, 513
ancient Christianity 435, 443
ancient Jewish school systems 259, 263–4, 266–7, 270–271, 274–6, 278–80
angels 44–5, 76, 114, 439, 452, 454, 523, 529, 534–5, 538
animals 82, 86–7, 169, 173, 177, 296, 310–311, 460, 462, 535; draft 508–10; firstborn 221; pregnant 112; wild 75, 78, 407
Antigonus of Soko 424, 427
Antioch 48, 233, 365, 367, 421
Antiochus Epiphanes 261, 283, 293, 328, 368, 379, 381, 419
Antisthenes 428, 478, 488, 491, 500
Antonia 139, 141–3, 146, 157–9
Antonines 218, 235, 238
Antoninus 65, 110, 355
aphorisms 32, 39, 303, 432–3, 488, 492–3
apostates 244, 353, 440 *see also* heretics

INDEX

appointments 202, 204, 209–10, 212–13, 216–17, 220–223, 228–9, 236–7, 239–40, 242–3; of judges 243; local 213; making of 236, 241; permanent 224; of sages 229; secular 228; unworthy 236
Aptowitzer, Victor 6–7, 9, 139, 387
arbitration 9, 205, 215, 231, 243; and arbitrators 207, 230–234; courts of 231, 243; institution of 230; system of 9
Aristeas 146–7, 156, 477
aristocracy 213, 429, 440–441
Aristotle 320, 322, 400–401, 403–4, 406, 411, 413–14, 416, 425–6, 478; doctrine of 114; and Theophrastes 426
Asherah 179–80, 182
ashes of red heifer 139, 143–5, 161
Ashkelon 139, 156, 175, 191–2, 244
assembly 66, 153–4, 171, 208, 289, 291, 365, 376; collected 375–7; decisive 264; of the townspeople 208
asylum 96–7
atonement 7, 65, 71, 118, 121–2, 137, 143, 149, 200, 468
Auctor ad Herennium 401, 403, 406, 483, 487, 491
Augustus 421–2
authority 11, 21, 203–5, 217, 220–226, 231–2, 235–7, 240–241, 284–6, 379–80; administrative 202, 208; central 205, 219–20, 225, 235, 237, 241–2; civil 9, 323; communal 217; delegated 232; divine 375; early 34, 287, 389; Halakhic 202; judicial 208, 211, 232, 234–5, 237, 242–3, 442; juridical 216, 231; medieval 356; public 207, 227; supreme 208, 237; Tannaitic 283
Av Bet Din (Head of the Court) 199, 205–6, 218, 251
Avesta (or Zand-Avesta) 496, 505, 507, 506–8, 511, 515, 517, 525, 538
Avi-Yonah, Michael 462, 465, 470
Avtalyon 288, 292, 294, 395, 428–9, 432
Azzai, Rabbi Shimeon ben 39, 47, 77, 211, 226

Babylonia 13, 191, 200, 250, 252–4, 256, 318, 321, 323–6, 497–8; courts of 76; houses of study in 274; and Jewish culture of 23; and Jewish schools 48; literature of 342; and the Rabbis 357; traditions of 217, 224, 226, 228

Babylonian Talmud 5–6, 23–4, 65–8, 79, 82, 86–7, 99–100, 103, 109, 215–17, 219–20, 232–4, 304, 308–9, 378; and Pahlavi Literature 23 *see also* Talmud
Babylonians 7, 22, 77, 200, 208, 224, 249, 256, 323–4, 328
Bacher, Wilhelm 12, 66–7, 167, 192, 259–80, 352–4, 366–7, 384, 396–7, 429
Bakhos, Carol 14–15
Balberg, Mira 8, 11
Bar Kokhba rebellion 213, 219–20, 223, 230, 234–5, 238, 271
Baron, Salo 203, 240, 462, 468, 470, 479
Baskin, Judith 4–5
beasts 140, 407, 410, 449, 453, 456, 490; brute 99; wild 77, 372
Becker, Adam 5, 16, 38, 468
Berkowitz, Beth A. 6, 11
Bet (ha-)midrash 58, 60, 62, 78, 114, 197
Beth Alpha 456
Bible 14, 59–60, 94, 267–71, 273, 276, 304, 310, 313, 334–5, 372, 395, 399–400, 422–3; didactic content of 43; instruction in 270, 273, 275, 277; teachers 268, 275, 276; and tradition 276
Biblical law and literature 6, 8, 14, 18, 460, 462, 464, 466, 468, 470
Bickerman, Elias J. 19, 444, 461–2, 464–5, 467–70, 487
Bidez, Joseph 366, 427, 429
birth 66, 88–91, 94, 101, 109–10, 112–13, 250, 263, 354–5, 516, 539 *see also* embryo
blood 11, 54–6, 68, 78, 83, 110, 118, 123, 125–7, 356; circulation 53–4; congestion 52; loss of 54; shedder of 77, 83
body 58, 64–6, 68, 90–91, 104–5, 112–13, 368, 372, 522, 529; celestial 278; central 237; defilement of 163; human 530
Bonsirven, Joseph 420, 423–5, 428–9, 431
"book of decrees" 300
bouleute 238–40
Boyarin, Daniel 5, 10–11, 16
Braun, Martin 35, 492
bread 38, 67, 153, 155, 171–2, 275, 295–6, 311, 448, 451
Brockhaus, H. 506, 508
Büchler, Adolf 7–9, 72, 76, 77–8, 204–7, 213–14, 236, 252–3, 255–6, 291–2, 471
buildings 32, 46, 145–6, 158–60, 179, 187,

542

190–191, 201, 325, 327; of the Second Temple 148; and statues in Jerusalem 187
Bultmann, Rudolf 477, 489, 500
bureaucracies 22, 498–9, 501–3
Burgess, Theodore 492

Caesarea 5, 17, 159, 191–2, 351–65, 368, 371–2, 376, 379, 392; *apparitores* of 371, 373; bishop of 392; Christians of 352, 354; Jewish and Samaritan communities in 191, 351, 358; the judges of 205; officials in 361–2; pillars of 356; proconsul of 353, 372; Rabbinic academy in 352, 382; Talmud of 352, 364; in the third and fourth centuries 352
Cain 52–5, 513, 522, 524, 539
Calder, W.M. 360–361
Canaan 48, 184
canonization 318–20, 340
Capernaum 454, 456
capital punishment 54–8, 73, 78, 108, 110–111, 300, 451
Caplan, Harry 483
Cappadocia 439
ceremonies 39, 146, 204, 301, 336, 360–362, 377–8, 380, 467
Chadwick, Henry 467, 500
Chajes, Zvi Hirsch 9, 108–9, 161, 172, 203
cheese 153, 171–2, 177; Bithynian 172; Gentile's 172, 177
childbirth 125–8, 152
children 66–8, 71, 89–90, 95, 100–101, 264–9, 271–6, 318–19, 325, 346–7; beloved 345; in Bible and tradition 268; births 83; education of 268, 275–6; female 512; teachers of 264, 268, 272–4, 275; tender and weak 53; unborn 67, 84, 86–8, 107–8, 110; *see also* school children
chreia (Greek) 22, 482
chria (Latin) 22, 481–5, 488, 490, 492–3, 495, 501–2
Christ *see* Jesus
Christianity 3, 5, 7, 20–21, 345–6, 353, 363, 373, 460, 468, 495–6, 499, 500, 502,; and relationship with Judaism 5
Christians 339, 353–4, 356–7, 359–63, 373, 376–81, 387, 391–2, 438–9, 495–7; and governors 243; and Jews 47, 200, 373, 503; martyrs 362–3, 370–371;

373, 378–9, 381; scholars 16, 116, 357; symbols 462; and the theologians 315; and traditions 202, 439
Chrysippus 478, 496
Chrysostom 202, 476, 523
Church Fathers 4–5, 43–5, 47–8, 112, 201, 315, 485, 503, 523
Cicero 399–405, 407, 410–411, 413–15, 426, 429, 476–7, 483, 485, 487
circumcision 130, 150, 356, 374–6
cities 135, 185–92, 206, 210, 223–4, 228–30, 237–42, 268–9, 299–300, 364–5; besieged 294; of Eretz-Israel 200, 237, 242; Greek 204, 481; Hellenistic 185, 204, 208; holy 135; idolatrous 454; Palestinian 268; populous 364; of
citizens 96, 157, 206–9, 212, 242, 268, 358, 397, 441, 479
classes 11, 13, 19-20, 22, 208, 212-3, 235, 237–8, 240, 263-4, 267, 273, 275, 335, 496, 498
Cleanthes 478, 482, 485, 492–3
Clement of Alexandria 4, 18, 44–6, 467, 477
clothes 118, 121–2, 140, 156, 162, 165, 168, 238, 241; black 332; civilian 157; high priest's 122; white 140
Cohen, Boaz 22, 428, 452–4, 465
Cohen, Shaye J.D. 11, 19, 22
commoners 213, 230, 236–7, 240, 245
communities 96–8, 185, 206–8, 210, 227–9, 235–8, 240–242, 245, 268, 272; of Jews 48, 202, 436, 439; Judaean 327, 343; and leadership in the diaspora 239, 241–2; new 323–5, 327
compensation 73, 82, 104–6, 273, 297, 338
congregations 202–3, 207-8, 229, 260, 262, 277, 456, 467
controversy 14, 16, 68–9, 87, 104, 106, 131, 141, 243, 272, 301, 308, 337, 339, 357, 423
corporal punishment 274
corpses 68–9, 116, 119, 131–4, 138, 143–5, 161, 164, 178–80, 397
corruption 122, 198, 240, 381
courts 203–5, 214, 230–234, 236–7, 244–5, 283–6, 290–292, 299, 378, 476; of arbitration 231, 243; authorized local 100; cases in 432; civil 191, 237; communal 9; composite 205; institution of 265; Jewish 110, 204; pagan 75;

INDEX

permanent 203–4, 231, 234; procedures of 100; regular 230–231; rulings of 288; selection of 233; temporal 73, 83; three-judge 231; verdicts of 216
Cover, Robert 7
Cumont, Franz 422, 427, 429
Cureton, William 351–2, 363–4, 371–2
customs 98, 149, 285, 318–20, 322, 359, 402, 430
Cynico-Stoics 477, 488, 496
Cynics 478–9, 482–3, 486, 487

damages 82, 87, 105, 232, 338, 467
Danielou, Jean 461–2, 464–5, 468, 470
Daube, David 18, 22, 393–418, 480
David 61–2, 249, 251–7, 323–4, 326, 329, 341, 344–5, 398, 422, 514
Davidic ancestry 11, 249-50, 253, 255-6
Davies, Philip R. 18
Day of Atonement 65, 71, 118, 121–2, 143, 149
de Rossi, Azariah 33, 35, 107, 140, 198, 298, 301, 371, 424
Dead Sea Scrolls 14, 294
death 53–61, 69–73, 75–6, 78–81, 83–4, 91–6, 300, 354–8, 367–8, 377–9; by burning 300; by execution 300; for murder 71, 80; natural 58, 60, 70, 219; sacrificial 460; sentence 56, 96, 107; by stoning 300; by strangulation 55–7, 300; and torture 368; unnatural 58, 60
death penalty 51, 57–9, 68–9, 75–6, 78, 80; Torah commands 57; unqualified 57, 59, 78; *see also* death sentence
debtors and debts 204, 318, 417–18
decapitation 55, 75, 78–80
decrees 14, 129, 153–6, 161–2, 164–5, 265–6, 269, 283–4, 298, 300–301, 376, 379–80, 415; basic 98; of capital punishment 56; of death 100, 107; of Hadrian 376; imperial 200, 358; special 128, 377
defilement 7, 116, 119, 120–8, 130, 142–4, 147, 153, 155–6, 159–68, 176–9, 182, 189, 193–4; biblical 124; Gentile's 127, 128, 163, 166, 171
Derenbourg, Joseph 292
descendants 168, 249, 251–4, 256–7, 324–5, 327, 329, 333, 509, 538; authentic 257; of David 250; of Judah 253; spiritual 347
destruction 9–10, 14, 16–17, 160–162,

165–6, 191, 193, 206–7, 267, 292, 376–7, 379–80, 440; of Judaism 376
di Rossi, Azariah 33, 35, 301
dialogues 254, 316, 477, 488
diaspora 11, 191, 201, 234, 244, 435–6, 439, 445, 471
Dinaburg (= Dinur, Ben-Zion) 197–8, 209, 212–13, 218, 222, 227–8, 236, 243–4
Dinkier, Erich 461–2, 467
Dinur, Ben-Zion *see* Dinaburg
Diocletian 205, 222, 243–4, 354, 357–60, 368, 373, 384
Diogenes 428, 478, 482–5, 493–4, 500, 502
Dionysus 431, 454, 460, 463
disciples 201, 214, 217–19, 221–2, 226–7, 266, 272–3, 337–40, 370–371, 426, 428, 444, 526
disease 124, 192, 382
disputations 315–16, 400; frequent 321; polemical 47
disputes 123–6, 130, 207–9, 211, 231–5, 241, 285–7, 297–300, 307–9, 312–13; academic 134; authentic 301; halakhic 199; last 140; learned 523; legal 287; recording of 156
doctrines 32, 68, 87, 114, 327, 399, 402, 408, 411, 426
documents 3, 27, 243–5, 255, 294, 319, 353, 423–4, 436; historical 36, 256, 351; religious 279
Domitian 368, 440, 442, 476
droughts 382–3
drownings 54, 58, 61, 75
drunkenness 49–50, 174, 490–491

earth 44–5, 382, 438, 453, 508–9, 513–14, 516–17, 529–32, 535, 537–8; and heaven 44, 333, 363; and populating 514
eating 8, 170, 172–4, 177, 193, 436, 467, 537
Egyptians 72, 84, 95, 98, 365, 422
elders 147, 205, 207, 213, 221, 228–9, 239–40, 284–6, 288–9, 293–4; appointment of 216; of Bathyra 249, 254; and judges 207; rebellious 299
Eleazar, Rabbi Simeon ben 71, 130, 166–8, 183, 211, 216, 229, 329, 364, 391
Eliav, Yaron 23
embryo 64, 68–9, 81–2, 86, 87, 89–91, 95, 102, 104–6, 108–12, 113-4 *see also* birth

emperors 182, 201, 243, 355, 373, 375, 377, 379, 384, 440
Epstein, Yaakov Nahum 15, 57, 60, 77, 282, 287, 294–5
Eretz-Israel 200–201, 203–4, 206–8, 210, 232, 235, 237–9, 242, 244, 345 *see also* Palestine
Esau 66, 260, 262, 269, 513
Essenes 16, 137, 162, 208, 216, 316, 344, 438, 441–2, 445
eternal life 227, 381, 520–521
ethics 32, 95–6, 98, 260, 476, 479, 483, 491, 496, 501; Aristotelian 32; Cynical 491; Jewish 98; popular 491, 495; traditional 400
Eusebius 352, 354–7, 359, 361–3, 368, 370, 372, 376–7, 382–3, 387
evil 76, 129, 331, 338, 345, 513, 516, 524, 533, 538
exegesis 13-14, 18, 277, 279, 282–3, 288, 290, 291, 292–7, 299, 302, 304, 398–9, 435, 470, 481
exilarchate 11, 498
Ezra 184–5, 263–5, 281, 299, 326–7

fables 355, 419, 481–2, 487–8, 490
Feast of Tabernacles 136, 138, 146, 149
Feldman, Louis 23
festivals 121, 141–5, 147, 157, 165–6, 284, 292, 359–60, 526, 531; idolatrous 191; Jewish 439; national 378; of pilgrimage 121, 134–7, 139, 156; religious 136
Fine, Steven 19, 22
Finkelstein, Louis 15, 203, 209, 212, 217, 366, 369, 423–4, 429, 432
Fischel, Henry A. 22, 475
Fishbane, Michael 14
Flatto, David 7, 11
foetus *see* birth; *see* embryo
Fonrobert, Charlotte 10–11
food 87, 141, 153–4, 160, 165, 166–73, 510, 520, 522, 525, 537–8; of animal origin 537; enjoyment of 522; leavened 140–141; ordinary 169, 171; prohibited 169
forecourts 137, 146–7, 150–152, 160, 194
"Fourth Philosophy" 344–5
Fraade, Steven 6
Fraenkel, Yonah 14
Frankel, Zechariah 43, 81, 83, 91, 111–12, 281–2, 287, 289, 354, 364
Fredriksen, Paula 5

Friedmann, Meir 57, 62, 67, 73, 78, 80, 82, 309–11, 366, 371

Gafni, Isaiah 5, 12–13
Galilee 22, 67–9, 131, 136, 162–4, 166–7, 170–171, 222–3, 439–40, 444, 451, 454
Gamaliel, Rabban ('Berabbi') 198-9
Gamaliel II, Rabbi (of Yavneh) 66, 165–6, 174–5, 192–3, 198, 212, 217–18, 220, 226, 228, 237, 286, 296–7
Gamalielian Patriarchs 11
Gans, Edward 3
gardens 425, 509–10, 521, 534, 536, 538
Geiger, Abraham 3, 81, 83–4, 86–7, 91, 96, 108, 111, 118, 249–50; articles of 87; and the food laws 87
Gentile launderers 140–141, 165
Gentile traders 136, 138, 141
Gentile 8, 115–17, 127–41, 144–6, 150–172, 175–6, 191–4, 363–4, 378–81, 453–5; cheese 172, 177; corpses of the 132, 154; presence in Jerusalem 116, 129, 135; Levitical impurity of 144, 153, 157, 160–161, 166, 170, 194; male 160, 165; non-hallowed 135; pagan 244; pious 364; ritual impurity of 8; spittle 122, 154, 160, 162; uncircumcised 150; wine 171, 174–6; women 117, 119, 121, 123, 126–30, 152, 153, 154–6, 159–61, 163–5, 170 *see also* non-Jews
Gerhardsson, Birger 489
Ginzberg, Louis 80, 87, 91, 96, 198, 200, 228, 231, 240, 293–4, 389, 420–421
God 44–5, 60–61, 135–6, 259–60, 273–6, 324–6, 333–5, 343–7, 520–525, 529–37; children of 333; and fate 333; knowledge of 279; power of 333; spirit of 531, 536
Goodblatt, David 11–14
Goodenough, Erwin R. 21–2, 436, 438, 459, 461–72
Goodman, Martin 9, 11
Gordis, Robert 501
gospels 16, 291, 339–40, 344, 392, 439, 465–6, 488
government 197, 200, 205, 218–19, 241, 243, 291–2, 353, 357, 441; internal 292; municipal 208; officials 361; and upper-class 442; wicked 375–6, 378
governors 136, 138, 157, 188, 204, 206, 360–361, 363, 370–371, 373

INDEX

Graetz, Heinrich 2, 4, 43, 45, 47, 49, 122, 137, 358, 366
graves 130–133, 142, 151, 160, 163, 166, 180–181, 448–9, 453, 456; defilement of 130, 144; images in Jewish 454; symbols in Jewish 451
Great Synagogue 329, 396, 424, 429, 432
Greco-Roman 12–13, 17, 475, 477, 481, 484; antiquity 504; civilization 450, 456; culture 17, 259–60, 479; Jews 448; literature 485, 489–90; parallels 499; period 21, 23, 436, 447–57, 463, 468; society 443, 460; symbolism 463
Greek cities 204, 481
Greek philosophers 111, 260, 322, 435, 437, 487
Greeks 95, 97, 259–61, 363–4, 386–8, 413–14, 436–7, 444, 481–5, 500–501; contemporaneous 7; in Jewish Palestine 17, 352–3, 382, 386–8, 421, 437, 480; and Romans 260; and their philosophy 111, 398, 425, 444; vernacular of 498
Gross, Simcha 5, 24
Gruenbaum, Max 491
Guttman, Alexander 295, 298

haggadah see aggadah
halakhah 6, 9–10, 13, 43, 51, 63–8, 70–71, 82, 87–9, 91, 100, 107–8, 163, 171, 198-9, 203-4, 205, 208–10, 213–15, 217, 224, 226, 229, 231, 233–4, 277–8, 281–8, 294–300, 302, 304–7, 310, 313–14, 409, 429
Halakhic decisions 197–8, 206, 224–6, 239
Halakhic Midrashim 14–15, 303–5, 307
Halberstam, Chaya 6
Ḥanina, Rabbi 44n3, 71, 110, 211, 229, 370–371, 376n221, 378–9
Hasmonean dynasty 46
Hasmonean period 12, 284, 317–18, 322, 481
Hauptman, Judith 10
Hayes, Christine 7, 8, 22
heathens 191, 359–60, 362; altars of 185; temples of 178–80, 184
heave-offerings 70, 163, 166–9, 176
Heinemann, Isaac 288, 480, 503
Helios 436, 454, 466–7
hell 391, 518, 536, 538
Hellenism 17–18, 20, 289–90, 301, 436–7, 450, 465, 480–481
Hellenization 17, 19–22, 341, 435, 437, 444–5, 452, 469, 498; of Jews 21, 23, 436, 468-9; of Palestinian Judaism 20, 436
Hengel, Martin 20
heretics 327, 337, 423, 438 *see also* apostates
Hermann, Geoffrey 23
Herod 24, 136–8, 145–6, 152, 158–60, 187, 208, 250, 436, 442
Herod's Temple 137
Herr, Moshe David 23, 40
Heschel, Joshua 519
Hezser, Catherine 3, 9, 12–13, 22–3
Hezekiah 167
Hidary, Richard 19
high priests 118–22, 137, 139, 141–7, 202, 265, 291, 323–4, 326–7, 424; Alkimos 129; Joshua 266; Kaiaphas 144; Simeon 159; Simeon Kamithos 123, 128, 151
Hillelites 19, 116–17, 119, 125, 127–8, 130–131, 133–5, 139–41, 143–4, 153–5, 160–161
Hirsch, Isaac 314
Hirshman, Marc 5, 12
Hoenig, Sidney 290, 479
Hoffmann, David 14–15, 61, 74, 78, 82, 180, 240, 282, 298, 303–14
Holy Scripture *see* Bible
Horbury, William 18
house of study 13, 225, 239, 259–63, 267–9, 271, 276–8, 285, 375; of Hillel and Shammai 267; and the synagogue 261–2; of Tiberias 268; to Yavneh 267; of Yoḥanan 267 *see also* academy; *see also bet midrash*
House of Shammai 117, 119, 123, 125-132, 133–4, 139–40, 153, 155–6, 161, 287, 294, 342, 398, 400, 423–5, 427, 430, 432, 478
hypocrites 16, 71, 331–2, 339–40, 441, 500
Hyrcanus, John 46, 204, 272, 328–9, 442

idolatry 155, 168, 176, 178–9, 184–6, 189–91, 357, 359, 451, 456; and sacrifices 177, 185; and temples 179, 192–3, 260, 269; impurity of 189; practising of 357, 379; spirit of 185
idols 175–84, 186, 189–91, 359, 361, 363–4, 373, 379–80, 453-4; Jews worshipping of 358, 360, 379–80
images 184, 186–9, 191–2, 449, 452–5, 466–8, 470–471, 478, 527, 533;

annulling 455; carved 185; cosmogonic 532; emperor's 188; of idols 189; in Jewish graves and synagogues 454; pagan 464; religious 200
immersion 130, 138, 142–5
impurity 7-8, 119–20, 123–6, 134–6, 154–6, 165–6, 168–9, 189–90, 285, 287; concept of 117, 119–20, 127–8, 154, 156, 158, 179, 287, 295, 299; degrees of 155, 330; and laws of purity 315–16; menstrual 298; ritual 8, 298; of spittle and urine 126; *see also* Levitical impurity
inner forecourts 137, 147, 150–151, 160, 194; *see also* forecourts
inscriptions 203, 243–4, 360–361, 386–7, 389, 391, 432, 436–7, 451, 457
institutions 12–13, 231, 234–5, 259–63, 266, 280, 293, 335–6, 339, 525–6
interpretation of scripture *see* exegesis
interpreters 19, 290, 293–4, 316, 395, 401–2, 433, 440
Isaac, Benjamin 8, 37, 221, 275, 306, 325, 333, 347, 383, 514
Ishmael, Rabbi 56–7, 68–70, 80–81, 110–111, 172, 177, 297, 306–14, 390, 415
Israelites 119, 122–4, 128, 130–132, 147, 154, 184, 193, 209, 336, 345; defiled 127, 132

Jacobs, Martin 11
Jaffee, Martin 13
Jamšid 511, 517, 519, 526
Janneus, Alexander *see* Yannai, Alexander
Jehoshaphat 264
Jehudah, Rabbi *see* Judah ha-Nasi, Rabbi
Jerome 4, 44, 48, 202, 421, 485
Jerusalem 13, 119–20, 134–9, 144–9, 156–9, 185–92, 263–4, 266–8, 429–30, 439–42; life in 141; civil court in 191; destruction of 191, 267, 440; Gentiles in 116, 129, 135; religious authorities in 119; synagogues in 267; teachers in 190; Temple of 119, 152, 192
Jesus 33, 250, 315, 337–40, 363, 397, 399, 409–10, 424, 433, 438, 451, 467, 476, 489
Jewish academies 452; advisers 376; art 21, 451–3, 468; artisans 164; attitudes 19, 450, 452; authors 31, 36, 432; books 3, 38; courts 110, 204, 243, 447; doctors 33; graves 451, 454; history 2–4, 6, 10, 14, 17, 34, 268; interpretations 460; judges 205, 211, 243, 378; law 6, 32, 75, 81, 83–5, 96, 98, 187, 362, 394; life 377; literature 3, 28, 32, 460; nation 9, 41, 261, 373; nationalist fighters 391; and non-Jewish sources 374; prisoners 368; rebellion 374–7, 380; relations 442; religiosity 21; rites 374, 376–8, 380; scholars 82, 87, 110, 352–4, 356, 366, 393; sources 9–10, 46, 48–9, 379, 387, 436, 520, 529, 539; traditions 4, 48, 433, 440, 450; women 168
Jewish Palestine 9, 17–18, 201, 207, 238, 289, 352–3, 382, 386–8, 437
Jews 28, 31, 47, 279, 333, 346–7; of antiquity 12; of Babylonia 13; and Christians 47, 200, 359, 503; contemporary 346; in Eretz-Israel 201; female 119, 126–8, 170, 194; in Galilee 167; and Gentile Christians in Caesarea 353; and Gentiles 169; German 28, 262; Hellenization of 23, 436; and Jerome 5; of Jerusalem 144, 187; and Judaism 4, 14, 17, 20, 37; in Macedonia 452; menstruous 119, 123, 159–60, 163, 194 127; of Mesopotamia 440; and non-Jews 39, 139, 191; observant 139, 437; Orthodox 363, 393, 455; in Palestine 368, 442; of Palestine 117, 200, 250, 259–61, 277, 377, 380, 440, 443; in patristic literature 5; in Rabbinic circles 437; religious life of 7; and worship 334
Joel, Karl 135, 335, 479, 490
Johanan, Rabbi *see* Yohanan, Rabbi
John the Baptist 438
Josephus 82–5, 136–8, 142–4, 148–50, 206, 321, 326–7, 329, 431, 438–43
Joshua b. Gamla, Rabbi 264-6, 269
Joshua (b. Hananiah), Rabbi 177, 211, 218, 228, 250, 270, 295–8
Joshua b. Levi, Rabbi 200, 222–4, 240, 271, 365, 385, 387-8
Joshua b. Perahiah, Rabbi 265-6, 287
Josiah 189, 415
Judaeans 320–321, 325–6, 333, 335–7, 339–40, 343–5
Judah ha-Nasi, Rabbi 80, 98, 162, 162n139, 163–5, 172–6, 176n100, 177–8, 181–2, 192–3, 193n24, 193,197, 217–20, 235–6, 243–4, 252–7, 292, 327–30, 375–6

INDEX

Judah Nesi'a II, Rabbi 198, 198n3, 198n5, 199n8, 200n16, 201n18, 201, 221, 221n87, 221
Judaism 4–5, 16–17, 19–23, 278–80, 346–7, 435–6, 440, 443–4, 449–52, 464–8; anti-rabbinic 471; diasporic 435; historical monuments of 259, 280; interpretations of 450; and Jews 4, 14, 17, 20, 37; mystical 21, 448, 460, 465, 467, 470, 471; native 450; normative 337, 449, 469; orthodox 20, 444, 448, 462; Palestinian 9–10, 13, 19–20, 75, 117, 435–8, 442–5, 466, 480; and Parseeism 506; Rabbinic 6, 13, 21–2, 436, 447, 460, 469, 502; scientific study of 10, 23; Second Temple 13–14; study of ancient 2–3, 11, 16; traditional 450
judgements 203, 205, 208–12, 214–15, 227, 232, 241
judges 83, 197, 199, 203–17, 222, 224–5, 227–38, 242–3, 352–3, 378, 415–16; ignorant 197, 202, 214, 240–241; non-ordained 207, 224, 232, 234; ordained 205, 232–4; selection of 229; unqualified 213–15, 230, 233–4; unworthy 197; wicked 213

Kaiaphas, Joseph 145
Kalmin, Richard 7, 22, 24
Kaminka, Arnold 480, 484, 494
Kamithos, Simeon 122, 145, 159
Katz, Steven T. 5, 20, 204
Klawans, Jonathan 8, 16
Klein, Samuel 182–3, 197, 209, 230, 237
knowledge 17, 116, 118, 147, 197, 199, 225, 272, 278–80, 340–341; ancient 430; of Classical Greek language and literature 17, 481; hereditary 431; human 278; mathematical 278; and religious experts claiming ancestral 20; of rhetoric and philosophy 372; scriptural 12
Kohut, Alexander 23–4
Koltun-Fromm, Naomi 5
Krauss, Samuel 4, 17, 275, 277, 353–4, 360, 368–71, 384, 389, 391
Kugel, James 14

Labovitz, Gail 10
Lactantius 112, 359, 361, 363, 491
land 184–5, 210, 296, 345, 347; of Egypt 325, 346; of Judah 185; unclean 184

Landau, Justine 530
Latin 17, 22, 377, 413–14, 485, 528; literature 18; terms 413; translations 388, 525
Lauterbach, Jacob Z. 207, 282, 287, 291, 301, 432
laws 6–7, 122–4, 186–9, 225–7, 281–90, 292–6, 311–12, 315–21, 374–81, 398–405; early 286–7; ethical 97–8; Levitical 118, 157; Mosaic 32, 98; natural 402, 416, 504; new 299, 322, 344; non-Scriptural 395–6; old 84, 361; Pentateuch 323, 325, 335, 337, 341; political 97–8; of purity 315–17; Rabbinic 7, 9, 21, 160, 176, 376, 394; sacred 430; statutory 322, 341; tithing 16; unwritten 319–23, 342, 344, 402, 430; written 194, 301, 320–322, 341, 397–8, 402; *see also* lawsuits; *see also* ordinances
lawsuits 108, 213–14, 216–17, 225, 230, 233–4; Torah 214, 233, 241; tried by non-ordained Sages 224; *see also* laws; *see also* ordinances
Levine, Lee I. 10–11, 22
Levitical impurity 115–21, 122–35, 137–9, 141, 155–7, 159–61, 163–71, 177–9, 183–5, 193–5; degree of 116, 133, 151, 153; general 130; Gentile's 8, 144, 153, 157, 160–161, 166, 170, 194; grave 117, 134, 164, 168–9; sources of 7, 127; *see also* impurity
Levitical purity 115–17, 123, 127, 137–8, 160, 165–7, 194; of food 167; and impurity 115, 123; laws of 123; in Temple times 117
Levy, Israel 10, 14, 227, 249, 257, 407
libations 175–6, 358–9, 361–3, 380
Lieberman, Saul 9, 17–18, 23, 211–12, 289–90, 294, 297–8, 301, 437–8, 444
Lieberman, Stephen J. 18–19
life 81–2, 90–91, 113; eternal 227, 381, 520–521; human 91–2, 107, 269; mortal 525, 528, 530; public 117, 235–6, 238; religious 7, 117, 185, 188, 200, 336–7, 448; spiritual 68, 71
liturgy 31, 293, 346, 417
Luther, Martin 49, 261
Lydda 164, 180, 364–7

Magus, Simon 438
Manasseh 46–7

Mandel, Paul 14
Martyr, Justin 4, 44, 47
martyrdom 5, 219, 358, 362, 364–6, 368–9, 371, 381, 390, 497
martyrs 353, 356, 364–5, 367–70, 378–9, 381, 385, 388, 390–391
Marx, Alexander 283
meals 167–8, 292, 316, 339, 378; sacramental 463; sacrificial 116, 130, 134–5, 137–8, 149–50, 161, 193–4
Meir, Rabbi 66–70, 77, 156–8, 162–8, 172–4, 218–20, 230–231, 233–4, 251–3, 259–60
Menaea 356, 363–4
Mendelssohn, Moses 32, 114, 457
menstruous women 120, 125–6, 128–9, 152, 154–5, 158, 160, 163, 165, 194
Messiah 40, 202, 213, 253–4, 294, 340–341, 345, 366, 531, 536–7
Meyer, Rudolf 96, 359, 480
Midianites 132–3
midrash 12–14, 277–8, 282–3, 304–5, 307, 387–8, 417, 487–90, 507, 521–3
midrash halakhah 13–14, 281–2
midrashim 15, 44, 50, 200, 304–7, 310–314, 368–9, 377, 379, 505–6; early 351, 385; halachic 502
Mokhtarian, Jason 24
monetary cases 213, 215, 227, 230–231, 234
money 83, 197, 200, 202, 211, 213, 273, 336, 338, 409; disputes 232; offering of 291
Morgenstern, Julian 447
Moser, Moses 3
Moses 61, 228, 240, 286–7, 296, 298, 301, 412–13, 415, 423, 427–31, 448–50; throne of 468
mothers 64–71, 69, 81, 86, 90–91, 93–6, 101–6, 107–14, 121–2, 271, 390
murder 52, 55–6, 68, 71, 73, 78–81, 83–4, 88, 107–10, 114
murderers 54, 57, 71, 73, 78–9, 83, 93, 97, 178, 299–300
mystic Judaism 448, 460, 467, 470

Naeh, Shlomo 5
Nathan, Rabbi 423n20
Nehemiah, R. 48, 228, 255–6, 263, 265, 327, 419
Neusner, Jacob 22, 432, 465–6, 469–70, 489, 498

Niehoff, Maren 19
Noahides 55–6, 59, 68–9, 71, 109–11
non-Jews 39, 117, 139, 148, 162, 168, 170, 191, 244, 380; in cities 191; and Jews 39, 139, 191 *see also* Gentile
Norich, Anita 23

Oinomaos of Gadara 167
Old Testament 18, 32, 34, 372, 409, 430, 435 *see also* Bible; *see also* Pentateuch
Oral Law 318, 320, 322, 325, 337, 341, 347, 396, 429–30, 433
ordinances 82, 89, 149, 219–20, 239, 283–4, 290, 298, 301; *see also* laws; *see also* lawsuits
ordinations 202, 216–29, 232, 236–7, 375, 378; performing 378; in practice 229; procedures 225, 503; of sages 9, 216, 221, 224–7, 230, 232, 241
Orthodox Jews *see also* Jews 363, 393, 455

pagan symbols 460, 463–5, 471
paganism 260, 430, 448
pagans 17, 260, 262, 315, 326, 381, 447–9, 456–7, 465, 495–7
Pahlavi texts 23, 505, 507–9, 511, 516, 526, 528, 530
paintings 34, 453–6
palaces 157–8, 361; in Jerusalem 142, 188; royal 157–9
Palestine 7–9, 259–60, 263–8, 359, 362–5, 368–70, 382–3, 436–42, 451–2, 465–6; and Babylonia 497; first-century 20, 447; Gentiles in 8; late antique 15, 22; provincial 23 *see* Eretz Israel
Palestinian 85–6, 122, 129, 203, 342, 365, 382, 435, 440, 496–7; cities 268; Judaism 9–10, 13, 19–20, 75, 117, 435–8, 442–5, 466, 480; mosaics 470; preachers 260; Rabbinic literature 23, 385, 388; Rabbis 10, 358, 384, 411, 471; sages 202, 485; sources 100, 228, 304, 385, 411, 436; teachers 103, 107–9, 111; traditions 216, 354
Palestinian Talmud 68, 79, 305, 308–9, 311, 313 *see also* Talmud
Palingenesia 405, 408, 412
Pardo, David 176
Passover 138, 142, 144–5, 149–50, 374, 399, 405, 484; in Jerusalem 145; lamb 405; sacrifice 134, 137–8, 149; sacrificial meal 142, 144, 179

Patriarchate 11, 197–8, 200–202, 205, 218–25, 232, 236–43, 253–4, 257; enfeebled 235; of Rabbi 256; servants of the 200
Patriarchs 9, 11, 197–205, 217–18, 221–6, 229–30, 232, 236–45, 252–7, 451–2; Gamalielian 11; Hillelide 19; house of 200, 224, 240, 471; and power 222; and Sages 224, 451; schools 272; and sovereign authority 200
patriotism 181–2, 188
Pentateuch 120, 122, 124, 269, 276–8, 316–20, 323, 325, 333–6, 344–6; *see also* Bible; *see also* Pentateuch
Pentateuchal 277, 347; injunctions 332; laws 323, 325, 335, 337, 341; passages 332
people of the land *see am ha'arets*
persecutions 38, 190, 266, 282, 293, 354–5, 357, 360, 362–3, 368, 373, 376–80; of Antiochus Epiphanes 379, 381; of Diocletian 358, 360; Hadrianic 373, 376, 379–81
perushim 16, 294, 303, 315–17, 326–7, 329–31, 337; *see also* Pharisees
Peskowitz, Miriam 10
Pharisees 16, 19–20, 265–7, 300–301, 315–47, 397–8, 431–3, 438–44, 465–6, 469, 476, 479–80, 484, 498–9, 501; alliance of aristocrats and 440; and council of judges 107; and Essenes 16; and exercise-practice 481; literature of 341; and rabbis 8; rules 119–20, 160, 168; and sages 301, 484; the sayings of the 317; and schools 444; and scribes 291; and traditions 419–33; women 119
Philo 72–3, 81–3, 85, 98–100, 110–112, 267, 322, 430–431, 450, 460–461, 467
Philodemus of Gadara 496
philosophers 40, 262, 369–71, 426, 428, 443–4, 477, 482, 484, 496; ascetic 441; Cynic 486; Greek 111, 260, 322, 435, 437, 487; pre-Socratic 494
philosophic schools 20, 397, 399, 426, 443–4, 450, 478–9, 491
philosophy 39–40, 317, 426, 431–2, 443–4, 450, 476, 478, 494, 495, 501; ancestral 262; ancient 428; Arabic 40; Cyrenaic school of 478; Greek 111, 398, 425, 444; Hellenistic 402, 503; Jewish 40
Philostratus 421, 486

pilgrimages 121, 135, 138–9, 156, 270
Pineles, Solomon 87, 108, 288, 374–5
Plato 111–12, 402–4, 414, 416, 425–6, 429, 431–2, 490–491, 494, 496; dialogues of 429; and his successors 478; praise of "ancestral customs" 397
Platonic 425, 496; doctrine 86; elements 114; items of Plutarch 497; precedents 496; and Pythagorean elements in rhetoric 479
Plutarch 95, 111–12, 476, 482–3, 485, 487–8, 490–491, 493, 496–8, 503
power 225, 232–7, 241, 265–6, 377–8, 380, 441, 451, 521–2, 524; creative 506, 531; divine 438; juridical 235; official 243; political 441; ruling 218, 235; supernatural 345
pregnancy 65–6, 82–3, 90–93, 95, 98–9, 101–3, 105, 108, 112–13
priests 121, 139–42, 146–7, 166, 176–7, 193–4, 209, 289–92, 297, 319; defiled 155; high 144, 265; noble 142, 145; officiating 50, 147, 160; and scribes 291
prison 204, 333, 371–3, 486
Pritchard, James B. 501
prohibition 153, 155, 172–7, 181–2, 184, 186–9, 276, 293–4, 296, 374–6; of circumcision 229, 374; of images 466; of marriage 293; scriptural 259
prophetic books 321, 323–4, 340
prophets 59–60, 135–6, 148, 189–90, 260–261, 318–19, 325–6, 340–341, 423–4, 427; Amos 325; Elijah 260; Elisha 318; Ezekiel 279; false 47, 64, 423; Isaiah 46, 326, 524; the last 424; law and the 488; Zechariah 323
public life 117, 235–6, 238
punishments 58, 60–61, 75–6, 78–81, 83, 97, 322, 378, 380, 524; of death 78; of decapitation 78–9; of drowning 61; of killing 102; legal 83; of strangulation 61, 64; uniform 73
purification 126–8, 130, 132, 137–9, 143, 156, 161, 164, 190, 194; Levitical 134; monthly 119–20, 123, 137, 160, 168; woman's 119
purity 7–8, 70, 119, 138, 186, 188–9, 277, 315–17, 330, 535; of Jerusalem 188; laws of 315–17; practices 16; state of 8, 138
Pythagoras 428, 432, 478, 487

Quintilian 400–402, 406, 414, 422, 433, 483, 493

Rabbis 8–11, 16–22, 65–8, 218–30, 236–41, 250–257, 393–4, 412–16, 438, 449–57, 470–471; contemporary 177; Babylonian 357
religion 20, 29–31, 259–61, 335–7, 344, 346–7, 439–40, 443–4, 460–461, 468–9; foreign 377; Greco-Roman 20; Iranian 23; Israelite 445; Jewish 31, 325, 345–7, 374; Judaean 324; nominal 359, 362; pagan mystery 447
religious authorities 115, 119, 134, 149–50
religious life 7, 117, 185, 188, 200, 336–7, 448; of Jews in Palestine 7
ritual impurity *see* impurity
Roman administration 159, 191–3, 481, 503
Roman authorities 11, 142, 205, 207, 254, 380
Roman emperors 65, 181, 366, 421, 482
Roman empire 238, 242, 354, 381, 422, 463, 471, 489
Roman government 214, 218–19, 227, 230, 237, 243, 253, 368, 376, 441
Roman jurists 407, 410, 427
Roman law 18, 32, 86, 96, 205, 285, 290, 373, 480, 487
Roman officials 193, 372, 379, 503
Roman soldiers 138, 157–9, 355
Romans 110, 188–9, 219–20, 253–4, 259–61, 344–5, 379–81, 384, 414, 440–441; ancient 399; early 205; great 146, 495, 498; and Greeks 260
Rome 205, 207, 260, 262, 265, 354–5, 394–5, 439–40, 442, 476
Rubenstein, Jeffrey 6, 24
rulers 38, 187, 200, 205, 289, 437, 442, 482, 492, 497; Maccabean 148; secular 341; universal 440
rules 9, 116–19, 123–4, 133, 155, 163–4, 251–2, 305–10, 406–7, 413; autonomous 207; exegetical 306; general 231, 291, 300; hermeneutic 491; interpretive 306–8; Levitical 159; logical 306, 311; Midrashic 308; Pharisaic 20, 119–20, 160, 168; religious 148, 188; Tannaitic 273, 413

Sabbath 32, 92, 121, 140, 147, 197–8, 212–14, 268, 272, 274, 292, 294, 301–2, 307–10, 399, 405, 409, 520–521, 524–5, 527
Sabinus 403, 407
sacrifices 136–8, 143–4, 146–51, 177–9, 186–8, 193, 256, 271, 335–6, 361–4; daily 335–6, 405; and food 87; to God 146–7, 160; holy 143; sacramental 463; vain 437
Sadducees 14, 16, 72, 118–23, 126, 128, 160, 300–302, 316–17, 321-2, 328–9, 333, 337, 342–6, 397-8, 400, 466; impurity of the 120; and Pharisees 16, 329, 400
sages 13–16, 197–206, 210–237, 239–44, 259, 270–273, 284–7, 289–94, 296–301, 313, 352, 367, 370, 376, 481–8, 492–4; of Galilee 223; of Jabneh 236; of Jerusalem 230; non-ordained 224, 226, 230; ordination of 9, 216, 221, 224–7, 230, 232, 241; Palestinian 202, 234, 485; Pharisaic 301, 484; pre-rabbinic 452
salvation 40, 268, 345, 460, 463
Samaritans 119, 123, 128, 158, 160, 162, 168, 326–7, 356–62, 397; communities of in Caesarea 358; libations of 358; members of 360; officials of 361–2; and Sadducee women 160; teachers of 438; women 119, 126, 128, 160, 163
Sanballat 327
sanctification 135, 137, 260, 319, 358, 364, 368, 379
Sanhedrin 9, 14, 197, 203–5, 208–10, 213–24, 229–33, 235–7, 290–293, 298–9, 307–9, 311–13
Satlow, Michael 23
Schäfer, Peter 21, 23
Schechter, Solomon 14, 113, 191, 227, 270, 369, 390
school children 262, 272, 274, 276; *see also* children
schooling 266, 271, 275; mandatory 269; public 265
schools 15, 123–33, 140–141, 153–5, 262–8, 270–276, 307–11, 425–6, 428–9, 443–4; central 192; community 238; Greek philosophical 481, 495; in Jerusalem 263, 268, 271; philosophic 20, 397, 399, 426, 443–4, 450, 478–9, 491; public 269; systems of 264–7, 278-9; teachers in 264, 272–3
Schürer, Emil 8, 128, 134, 144, 146, 157, 315, 317, 371, 374, 480

Schwartz, Daniel R. 10–11, 14, 298, 352, 372, 425, 428
Schwartz, Joshua 10
Schwartz, Seth 9, 11, 17, 22
Schwarz, Adolf 81, 122, 131, 176, 393, 395
sciences 3, 27–30, 32, 35, 37–40, 65, 411, 419, 485, 494
scribes 13–14, 37, 210, 265, 281–2, 288–92, 294–6, 298–9, 302, 386, 395-6; and Pharisees 291; and priests 291
Scripture 13–15, 281–3, 288–90, 297–302, 304–8, 313–14, 394–5, 398–400, 405, 412–14; study and exegesis of 13, 18, 281-3, 288, 290, 294-5, 297, 302-3, 313; words of 307
sentences 57–8, 61, 63, 75, 96, 100, 204, 207, 209, 369–71, 376–7, 524
Sepphoris (city) 183, 190, 204–5, 209, 229, 255, 272, 286–7, 356, 364
Septuagint 43, 81–2, 84, 99, 110–111, 288, 334–5, 420, 436; for Aquila's Greek translation 435; and Josephus 84; and Philo 110–111
servants 70, 149, 159, 168, 318, 452
settlements 207, 213, 232, 235–40; heads of the 214; urban 206–7
Severan Dynasty 201, 238–9
Severus, Alexander 354, 503
sexuality 5, 10–11, 24
Shabbat see Sabbath
Shammai, Beth *see* House of Shammai
Shammaite School *see* House of Shammai
Shammaites *see* House of Shammai
Shapur 253
She'arim, Beth 455, 470
sheep 219, 407, 409, 484, 517, 525
Shefatyah ben Avital 254–5, 257
Simeon (ben Gamaliel), Rabban 56–7, 80–81, 104–6, 162–9, 173–5, 189–90, 197–8, 209, 218–19, 222, 226–7, 440–441
Simeon the Just 424
Simon, Marcel 46–7, 50–54, 56, 59, 250–254, 266, 269, 281, 286, 291–2
Simon-Shoshan, Moshe 6, 11
sin 7–8, 39, 193, 199, 291–2, 520–522, 524, 526, 536, 538; prevalent 129; sexual 300
Sinai 212, 286–7, 298, 307, 423–4
slaves 86–7, 104, 166–7, 313, 319, 394, 476, 491–2

Smith, Morton 20–22, 53, 82, 156, 239, 480
snakes 75, 453, 521, 524, 527, 536, 538
Socrates 428, 478–9, 484, 488, 490, 493
Sodom 45, 437
sodomy 154–5, 194
soldiers 95, 134, 157–8, 355, 378, 380
Solomon's Temple 137, 468
soul 58, 64–5, 68, 70, 94–6, 111–14, 267, 333, 381, 535–7; animal 113; and body 64; complete 113
Spiegel, Friedrich 506, 508, 510–511, 513–17, 522, 524–6, 535–6, 538
spitting *see* spittle
spittle 118, 120–128, 147, 151, 153–4, 156, 158, 162–3, 165–6, 193, 297
statutes 51, 86–7, 91–4, 96, 98-9, 268, 271, 401–2, 404, 406–7, 410, 415–16
Stein, Batya 5
Stoicism 478, 503
Stoics 111–13, 428, 479, 482, 503
stoning 75–8, 94, 107, 300
strangulation 54–8, 61–2, 64, 75, 77–9, 300
students 227, 263–4, 271, 274–5, 279, 282, 286–7, 289, 295
swords 56–9, 72, 78–80, 190, 367, 376–7, ymbol391–2, 453
symbols 21, 66, 332, 448-9, 450–452, 457, 460–465, 467–71, 531
synagogues 170, 259–62, 267, 271–2, 274, 436, 448–9, 451–2, 454–6, 466; ancient Jewish 456; building of 200; carving of 470; Galilean 451, 454; and houses of study 259, 261–2, 271; in Jerusalem 267; Jewish 438; symbols in 451

Talmud 277–9, 304–7, 505–7, 528; of Caesarea 352, 364 *see also* Babylonian Talmud; *see also* Palestinian Talmud
Tannaim 231, 233–6, 282–3, 303–5, 307, 309, 312–13, 451, 453–4, 479, 497–8
Tannaitic literature 15, 315–17, 321, 324, 337, 340–341, 483, 486, 489–90
Tcherikover, Saul 23, 499
teachers 62–3, 163–6, 171–5, 180–184, 187–91, 266, 268–75, 287, 289, 291–3
Temple 45–6, 116–19, 141–53, 160–162, 184–7, 191–4, 291–3, 327–8, 335–6, 366–7; services 146, 249
Temple Mount 119, 133–4, 138, 147, 150–152, 187–8, 194, 286, 299

Tertullian 47, 66, 90, 112, 345, 360, 373, 477
Thales 428, 478, 484–5, 490, 493–4
Third Temple 366–7; *see also* Temple
Tiberias 183, 190, 199, 201, 222–4, 268, 275, 353, 419
tithes 165, 292, 315–16, 374, 396
Tomson, Peter J. 10
Torah 263–5, 276, 281–2, 286–91, 295–301, 309–13, 346–7, 412–13; interpreters of 19, 293; knowledge 219, 235, 242; scholars 197–8, 236, 239, 241, 259, 264–7; scrolls 271, 468; shrines 448, 460, 468; status of 13; teaching of 197, 199, 239, 263; words of 270, 298; written 282, 286, 301, 304, 402, 412–13
torture 190, 365, 368–9, 371–3, 377, 379

universe 6, 38, 49, 328, 334–5, 346–7, 422–3
Urbach, Ephraim Elimelekh 5, 9, 13–14, 21, 23, 451, 454–5, 465–6, 498
urine 123–8, 153–5, 162

Weiss, Abraham 83, 95, 110, 139, 216, 249, 282, 290, 299
Wimpfheimer, Barry 6–7
wisdom 66, 74–5, 289, 292, 372, 432, 443, 493, 495, 501; practical 32; scholastic 39; scribe's 289
Wissenschaft des Judentums 1–3, 6, 9, 23
Wolfson, Harry 430, 436, 444, 450

women 10, 36, 83, 101, 125, 137, 152, 154, 159, 193; condemned 99; Gentile 117, 119, 121, 123, 126–30, 152, 154–6, 159–61, 163–5, 170; Jewish 168; menstruous 120, 123, 125–6, 128–9, 151–2, 154–5, 158, 160, 163, 165; Pharisee 119; pregnant 65–6, 71, 82, 91–3, 95, 98–9, 101–3; Sadducee 118–19, 123, 126, 128, 160; Samaritan 119, 126, 128, 160, 163; sterile 101
worship and worshippers 137, 158, 178, 180, 190, 333–4, 361, 363, 380, 453–6

Yannai, Alexander 46, 255, 266, 293, 441
Yerushalmi *see* Palestinian Talmud
Yima 507–8, 510–512, 514–22, 524–7, 533, 537; beautiful 508, 516; blessed period of 522; "radiant" 509, 515, 521
Yoḥanan, Rabbi 44, 48, 65, 87–8, 92–4, 113, 139, 169–70, 182–3, 222–3, 233–4, 267, 270, 272–4, 285, 292, 295–7, 299, 302, 359–60
Yoḥanan ben Zakkai, Rabban 139, 191–2, 218, 267, 270, 292, 295, 297, 299, 302
Yosi, Rabbi 198

Zand-Avesta 506–8, 511, 515, 517, 525, 538
Zechariah 148, 297, 323–4, 326, 423–4
Zeitlin, Solomon 16, 129, 153, 282, 295, 315–47
Zoroastrianism 23, 505, 508–9, 511–13
Zunz, Leopold 2–3, 9, 43, 78, 255